The Oxford History of the Biblical World

The Oxford History of the Biblical World

Edited by Michael D. Coogan

OXFORD
UNIVERSITY PRESS

Frontispiece

A thirteenth-century BCE stela from Ugarit (47 centimeters [18 inches] high) showing the god El seated on his throne, his hand lifted in blessing toward the worshiper (the king?) to the left. El was the king of the gods in Ugaritic mythology and is called "the kind, the compassionate" in the Ugaritic texts. El is also the name of the patron deity of Israel's ancestors according to the book of Genesis.
(Erich Lessing/Art Resource, NY)

OXFORD
UNIVERSITY PRESS

Oxford   New York
Athens   Auckland   Bangkok   Bogotá   Buenos Aires   Calcutta
Cape Town   Chennai   Dar es Salaam   Delhi   Florence   Hong Kong   Istanbul
Karachi   Kuala Lumpur   Madrid   Melbourne   Mexico City   Mumbai
Nairobi   Paris   São Paulo   Shanghai   Singapore   Taipei   Tokyo   Toronto   Warsaw

and associated companies in
Berlin   Ibadan

Copyright © 1998 by Oxford University Press
Issued as an Oxford University Press paperback in 2001.

Published by Oxford University Press, Inc.
198 Madison Avenue, New York, New York 10016-4314

Oxford is a registered trademark of Oxford University Press

Library of Congress Cataloging-in-Publication Data
The Oxford history of the biblical world /
edited by Michael D. Coogan.
p. cm.
Includes bibliographical references and index.
ISBN 978-0-19-513937-2
1. Bible—History of contemporary events.
2. Civilization, Ancient.
3. Bible—History of Biblical events.
I. Coogan, Michael David.
BS635.2.O94   2001
220.9'5—dc21   00-060612

The editor and publisher gratefully acknowledge permission to quote from the New Revised Standard Version Bible, copyright © 1989 by the Division of Christian Education of the National Council of Churches of Christ in the U.S.A. Used by permission. All rights reserved.

Contents

List of Maps

Preface

T he Bible is one of the foundational texts of our culture and of the three major monotheistic traditions, Judaism, Christianity, and Islam. It is a complex document—a set of anthologies, in fact. Thus, fully to understand the Bible requires a knowledge of the contexts in which it was produced, the many cultures of the ancient Near East and the ancient Mediterranean—the biblical world. For numerous reasons, presenting a history of the biblical world is an ambitious task. The scope of that history is vast, covering at the very least more than two thousand years and spanning three continents. Through archaeological research, new discoveries continue to be made, requiring modifications to earlier views and sometimes reconsideration of interpretive models based on less complete data. Moreover, the study of history itself is in flux. New approaches require, for example, broadening the focus of earlier scholars on the elite, their rulers, and their struggles for power to include the lives of the mostly anonymous ordinary people in the societies of which the elite were only the upper crust. These new data and new perspectives make it possible to take a fresh look at the well-traveled terrain of the biblical world.

The geographical focus of this history is the region variously known as the land of Canaan, Israel, Judea, and Palestine, with appropriate attention to the larger geophysical context and the geopolitical entities that over millennia were the matrix for biblical Israel and its successors, the Jewish, Christian, and Muslim communities. When to begin and end a history of the biblical world is more difficult to decide. The Bible itself begins with creation but dates it aeons later than modern scientific understanding of the origins of the universe allows. As the early chapters of this book will show, it is impossible to correlate with any certainty the events described in the first books of the Bible with known historical realities. Yet it is appropriate to set the core of our history into a larger context, as biblical tradition itself does, for there are demonstrable continuities between the earliest civilizations of the ancient Near East and ancient Israel, early Judaism, and early Christianity. The book thus begins with a sketch of the prehistory of the region.

When to end is also problematic. Surveys of the history of ancient Israel sometimes conclude with the revolt of the Maccabees in the mid-first century BCE, which corresponds to the dates for the latest books of the Hebrew Bible (the Jewish scriptures); or the Roman general Pompey's capture of Jerusalem in 63 BCE; or the destruction of the Second Temple in Jerusalem in 70 CE; or the end of the Second Jewish Revolt against the Romans in 135 CE. This last is also a frequent terminus for surveys of

Christian origins, since the scholarly consensus is that the latest books of the New Testament had been completed by then.

Our approach, however, emphasizes continuities and trajectories. The formation of a canon, a collection of writings defined as scripture, was in fact not a discrete event but part of a process that began before any part of the Bible was written and continued after religious authorities in Judaism and in different branches of Christianity limited the contents of their respective canons. The communities that shaped the Bible became, as they developed, communities shaped by the Bible—"People of the Book," as the Quran puts it. And because this connection to the Bible is not only Jewish and Christian but also Muslim, our history concludes by briefly considering developments in the first few centuries of Judaism and Christianity and the beginning of Islam.

Most earlier historical syntheses have focused largely on political history and monumental remains. While not neglecting such areas, this volume also includes within its scope themes that have emerged in recent scholarship. These include the roles of women in various periods and the tensions between urban and rural settings, royal and kinship social structures, and official and popular religion. In this volume, then, we intend not just to present the outlines of political history but to set the progress of archaeological ages and historical eras, of kings and emperors, of conquerors and conquests, into as broad a social context as possible—to provide, as it were, harmony for the melody of the chronological sequence followed in this book.

Within the last decade, some scholars have adopted what has come to be called a minimalist approach to ancient Israel. In its most extreme form, this approach discounts the Bible as a credible witness because of the ideological bias of its historical narratives and because they were written centuries after the times they purport to describe. In a minimalist view, without independent contemporaneous confirmation, the events and individuals described in biblical tradition are at best suspect and in many cases may be purely fictional. Thus, for example, for minimalists the narratives about the establishment of the Davidic dynasty have no historical core, being later constructions intended to legitimate political structures of another era. Such radical skepticism recalls the view, which no responsible scholar would now accept, that the absence of contemporaneous evidence for Jesus of Nazareth means that he did not exist. To be sure, there is fictional narrative in the Bible, and myth, and most certainly ideological bias. But that does not discount it as an indispensable historical witness. Rather, the Bible must be carefully and critically considered along with all other available data—including not just other ancient texts, but nonwritten artifacts as well. For, as much as any sherd or stratum uncovered by archaeologists, the Bible too is an artifact—a curated artifact, in William Dever's apt phrase—requiring interpretation in the light of its immediate and larger contexts and by comparison with parallels. The contributors to this volume share that methodological conviction as well as a commitment to the historical enterprise—the reconstruction of the past based on the critical assessment of all available evidence. They also share a tempered optimism that such a reconstruction is possible. As indicated above, this is of necessity an ongoing task, as new discoveries continue to be made and new paradigms are brought into play.

Each of the distinguished contributors to this book is a scholar of extraordinary breadth and depth. Cumulatively, they have mastered dozens of languages and spent many decades in the field excavating and interpreting material remains, and they have devoted their careers to the historical enterprise. They bring to their chapters different perspectives and differently nuanced interpretations of the complex and often incomplete data, and I have not attempted to reconcile their views into a superficial consistency. Given our incomplete knowledge, unanimity on a variety of issues would be misleading; some overlap at the margins between chapters is deliberate and may assist readers not entirely familiar with the details of the evidence.

The translation of the Bible normally used in the pages that follow is the New Revised Standard Version (NRSV), except when contributors have supplied their own translations to elucidate their arguments. Following the custom of most translations since antiquity, the NRSV substitutes "the Lord" for Yahweh, the proper name of the god of Israel; contributors have often returned to the original name both in quotation of biblical material and in discussion of Israelite beliefs and practices. In accord with growing practice by scholars and nonscholars alike, in this volume the designations BCE (for "Before the Common Era") and CE ("Common Era") are used for the chronological divisions respectively abbreviated as BC and AD.

Finally, a few words of gratitude. For assistance in tracking down photographs and illustrations. Alan Gottlieb has been of immeasurable assistance. I have been especially fortunate to have as collaborators not just the contributors themselves but also a number of talented editors in the Trade Reference Department at Oxford University Press. Among these I especially thank Linda Halvorson and Liza Ewell, for assistance in developing the book's concept; Liz Sonneborn, who helped transform the concept into coherent reality; James Miller, for his skillful editing of the first draft of the volume; and Ellen Satrom, who with patience and expertise guided the book through the complicated final stages from manuscript to publication. Their shared commitment to this project has been a model of professionalism and dedication, and I am grateful to them all.

Michael D. Coogan
Concord, Massachusetts
July 1998

The Oxford History
of the Biblical World

In the Beginning

The Earliest History

MICHAEL D. COOGAN

Ex oriente lux goes the Latin tag—"from the East, light." Civilization begins, from a European perspective, in the East. In its full form, the tag evinces a questionable Eurocentric bias: *ex oriente lux, ex occidente lex*—"from the East, light; from the West, law." According to this euphonious phrase, civilization only began in the East; it took the genius of Rome to order the undeniable but undisciplined creativity of the peoples east of the Mediterranean. Even the terminology for the region is culturally determined: east of Europe, of course, or where the sun rose—the Orient, the Levant. Later, as Europeans moved farther into the vast reaches of Asia, it became the Near East, or (in modern nomenclature) the Middle East. But despite its arrogant assertion of Western superiority, the tag has some merit: civilization did arise in what is, from a European perspective, the East.

Not that the Near East and northeast Africa produced the only early civilizations that the world has known—far from it. There was genius before Homer not only in the Near East, but also in other regions, many of which invented rather than borrowed their own forms of civilization. But the cultures of the ancient Near East are the direct ancestors of our own in many respects, especially as mediated though the Bible. To take just one example, nearly every genre found in biblical literature, from creation account and Flood story through proverb, parable, historical narrative, letter, law code, love poem, and prophecy, has an ancient Near Eastern antecedent or parallel. Hence, knowledge of the ancient Near East, and of the classical world as well, is essential for readers and interpreters of the Bible.

Since the early nineteenth century, the ancient Near East has been an object of Western curiosity, exploration, and scholarship. Napoleon's invasion of Egypt in 1798 inaugurated an age of discovery that is still going on. First the French, and then other

Europeans, began to unearth the tombs, temples, and palaces of Egypt's extraordinarily long-lasting civilization. Since then, throughout the Near East, scholars from the West, joined in the twentieth century by Israelis and Iraqis, Turks and Jordanians, Iranians, Syrians, Lebanese, Palestinians, Egyptians, and others, have unearthed dozens of languages and peoples, thousands of mounds and other sites, and countless texts and artifacts. With only brief interruptions caused by global and regional conflicts, this work continues today. It has given us an increasingly more complete reconstruction of the ancient Near East and the larger Mediterranean world, its history, its societies and institutions, its beliefs and practices, its people and their lives.

From the perspective of their contemporaries at least, ancient Israel and early Judaism and Christianity were only marginally important. But the books that these communities produced, a selection of which came to be called *The Book* (for that is what *Bible* means), became one of the foundational texts of Western culture. Hence the focus of this book: the world in which the Bible took shape, the biblical world.

The Setting

The explicit geography of the Bible extends from Spain in the west to India in the east, with sporadic references to parts of North Africa west of Egypt, to Ethiopia, and to Arabia. New Testament writings are also set in Greece and Asia Minor, as well as in Italy. This is the extent of the world mentioned by biblical writers, though they knew much of it only indirectly. The principal setting of the biblical narratives is Egypt and the Fertile Crescent, the band of arable land that extends northward from the Nile Valley along the eastern coast of the Mediterranean, curves around the great Syrian desert, and continues southward through Mesopotamia to the Persian Gulf.

The western part of this Fertile Crescent, encompassing modern Syria, Lebanon, Israel, Palestine, and Jordan, has the same environment as the rest of the Mediterranean basin: a limestone substratum beneath a thin terra rossa topsoil, best suited for olives and grapes and for sheep and goats. For the past ten thousand years or so, the climate has remained more or less constant: mild, wet winters and warm, dry summers, with abundant rainfall from late fall to early spring. Jerusalem, for example, has a mean temperature of 10°C (50°F) in the coldest month, January, and 25°C (77°F) in the hottest, August. Its rainfall averages 550 millimeters (22 inches) annually, about the same as London, but this precipitation occurs on an average of fifty days per year as compared with London's three hundred. Except in upper elevations, snow is rare.

This region along the east coast of the Mediterranean—the Levant—consists of several parallel zones. Moving with the prevailing winds from west to east, first comes a coastal plain. In antiquity it was wetter than now, even swampy in places, so that the main route to and from Egypt skirted it, occasionally hugging the foothills to the east (the biblical Shephelah, or "lowland"). Along this route lay several of the major cities of ancient Palestine. Broad in the south, the coastal plain narrows as one moves north up the coast from Egypt, and the Shephelah tapers off as well, ending at the promontory of Mount Carmel, which juts into the sea at modern Haifa. In parts of Lebanon the coastal plain virtually disappears.

East of the coastal plain and, in the south, of the Shephelah, runs a mountainous ridge, comprising what the Bible calls the "hill country of Judah," "the hill country of Ephraim," the hills of lower and upper Galilee, and "the Lebanon." This mountainous spine is extremely rugged, with the elevations increasing from south to north. The name *Lebanon* derives from the word for "white," because the frequent snow in its mountains lasts into early summer. The mountains of Lebanon were also densely forested with cypress and cedar. The rugged terrain of the mountains made travel though them difficult, except in the transverse valleys that lead through them from the coast to the Rift Valley.

Next comes the Rift Valley itself, a deep gouge in the earth's surface that extends over 6,500 kilometers (4,000 miles) from southern Turkey into East Africa. The Orontes River Valley in Syria, the Diqa in Lebanon, the Jordan Valley, the Arabah, and the Red Sea are all parts of this gash, which reaches its lowest point where the Jordan ends, at the Dead Sea—the lowest elevation on the entire surface of the earth. The descent from the hills to the Rift Valley is abrupt. Jerusalem, for example, has an elevation of about 762 meters (2,500 feet) above sea level, and lies about 55 kilometers (35 miles) east of the Mediterranean, but only 25 kilometers (15 miles) from the Dead Sea, which itself is nearly 400 meters (1,300 feet) below sea level. The Rift Valley is watered by major watercourses—the Orontes River in Syria and the Jordan River in Palestine—making those parts of the valley highly productive agricultural regions, despite the infrequent rainfall in the lower Jordan Valley, which lies in a rain shadow. At the northern end of the Jordan Valley is the setting of much of the Gospels, the Lake of Galilee. Another indication of the dramatic changes in the landscape in a small area is that from the Lake of Galilee, some 210 meters (700 feet) below sea level, can be seen the snow-covered peaks of Mount Hermon, which, with an elevation of more than 2,800 meters (9,200 feet), is the highest mountain in the region. South of the hill country is a marginal zone, the biblical Negeb, which merges with the Sinai Peninsula. The Sinai and the Arabian Peninsulas essentially constitute an extension of the North African desert, separated from it by the Red Sea.

West of the Rift Valley in Palestine, the ascent to the plateau of Jordan is equally abrupt. Mount Nebo, from which Moses with his extraordinary eyesight could view the entire Promised Land (Deut. 34.1–3), is some 50 kilometers (30 miles) due east of Jerusalem and has the same elevation. Between the two lies the northern tip of the Dead Sea, making a total change in altitude of nearly 2,000 meters (6,400 feet) as one moves from one location to the other. The Transjordanian plateau lies slightly higher than the hill country west of the Jordan, and receives somewhat less rainfall— sufficient, however, for agriculture and for sheep and goat herding. It is also cut by several rivers that flow westward into the Jordan and the Dead Sea. Along its entire length, from Damascus in the north and southward to the eastern arm of the Red Sea (the Gulf of Aqaba/Eilat) and beyond to Arabia, ran the "King's Highway" (Num. 20.17), the principal route for traders in incense and spices.

To the east of the relatively level Transjordanian plateau is a region largely uninhabited since prehistoric times, the Syrian desert. Separating the eastern and western parts of the Fertile Crescent, the desert extends northward to the Euphrates and southward into the Arabian Peninsula, where its easternmost extremity is called the "Empty Quarter." This desert, punctuated by only a few oases, was an effective barrier, forcing traders and armies to move either along the coastal plain or along the plateau to its west. The Levant thus constitutes a narrow corridor whose geographical

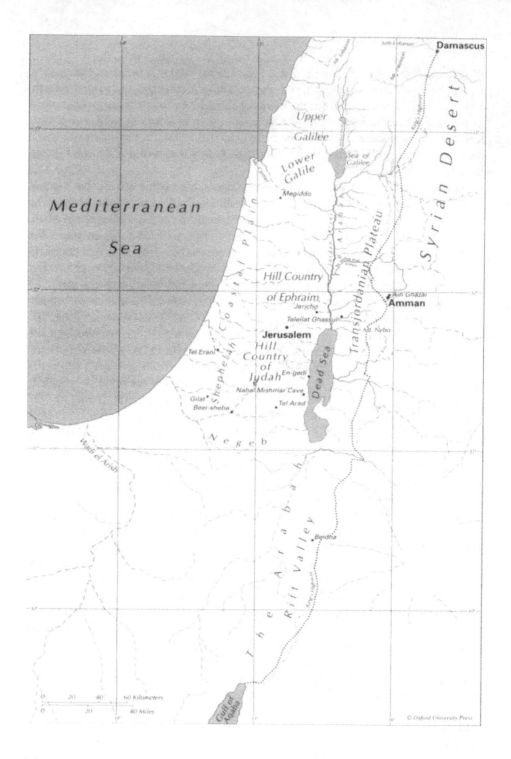

Palestine: Principal Geographic Divisions.

setting made it a constant arena of contention between more powerful entities in Egypt to the southwest and Mesopotamia to the northeast.

Egypt essentially forms part of the vast desert extending from the Atlantic Ocean across northern Africa and through the Arabian Peninsula to the Indian Ocean. But Egypt contrasts with the surrounding sands because of the river that defined it in antiquity and continues to do so today. In the famous phrase of the ancient Greek historian Herodotus, Egypt is the "gift of the Nile." Spring rains in the African highlands south of Egypt swelled the Nile's tributaries, causing an annual summer flooding of normally 7 to 8 meters (23 to 25 feet). The abundant water also carried silt in suspension, providing a regular overlay of fertile topsoil. The Nile was thus the lifeline of Egypt, providing water year-round and guaranteeing food production. More than any other factor it explains the extraordinary longevity, stability, and conservatism of Egyptian culture. A second-millennium BCE hymn to the Nile voices the blessings the river brought: "When he rises, then the land is in jubilation, then every belly is in joy, every backbone takes on laughter, and every tooth is exposed. The bringer of food, rich in provisions, creator of all good, lord of majesty, sweet of fragrance" (trans. John A. Wilson; p. 372 in James B. Pritchard, ed., *Ancient Near Eastern Texts Relating to the Old Testament*, Princeton, N.J.: Princeton University Press, 1969).

Harnessing this annual beneficence required effort; dikes and dams, irrigation ditches and canals, and pumps of various sizes extended the watered land and made possible irrigation after the summer flood. The result was a ribbonlike oasis dramatically visible from the air today, extending some 1,200 kilometers (750 miles) from the First Cataract at Aswan to the Mediterranean. For the ancient Egyptians, this was the "black land," a stark contrast to the "red land" of the virtually rainless desert.

The pyramid, the familiar element of Egyptian architecture, found not only in the tombs of the early dynasties but also as the top of every obelisk, is the stylized representation of the primeval mound of earth left behind by the receding Nile waters. Behind the tip of the pyramid are the rays of the sun, under various names the principal deity of the ancient Egyptians, responsible not only for agricultural production but also for the desert on both sides of the Nile.

This desert is relieved by only a few major oases. It effectively isolated Egypt from its neighbors, giving the ancient Egyptians an arrogant resistance to foreign influence and contributing to their cultural conservatism. But because neither the Nile Valley nor the desert could satisfy Egypt's needs and desires, throughout its history Egypt launched repeated imperialistic excursions, seeking to control access to raw materials such as cedar from Lebanon and copper from Sinai, as well as agricultural commodities that Egypt's mostly semitropical climate could not support, such as olive oil and wine.

Far to the northeast lay Mesopotamia, a region that was home to a succession of Egypt's rivals for control of the Levant. The term *Mesopotamia* is relatively late, first attested in Greek geographers of the Hellenistic period. But it is apt, for the region "between the rivers" forms a large geographic unit. The Euphrates to the west and the Tigris to the east united the lands through which they flowed; like Egypt's Nile, they provided water for irrigation and major avenues of transport. The Euphrates and the Tigris, roughly 2,800 kilometers (1,740 miles) and 1,850 kilometers (1,150 miles) long, respectively, both originate in the mountains of Armenia. From there they wend their separate, slowly converging ways in a generally south-southeasterly direction through the hilly terrain of northeastern Syria and northern Iraq into the great plain of southern Iraq, until they finally meet some 160 kilometers (100 miles) northeast of the Persian Gulf at Basra.

Southern Mesopotamia was essentially a floodplain. In distant geological prehistory the two rivers flowed separately into the Persian Gulf, but alluvial deposits gradually extended the floodplain, as the ancients themselves recognized. In the very beginning,

> When skies above were not yet named,
> Nor earth below pronounced by name,
> Apsu, the first one, their begetter
> And maker Tiamat, who bore them all,
> Had mixed their waters together.
> (Dalley, 233)

Thus the beginning of *Enuma Elish,* the "Babylonian Creation Epic," describes how the world began with the mingling of the waters of the rivers (the god Apsu) with those of the sea (the goddess Tiamat). From their union land emerged, and so the horizon and the sky itself, among the first of a series of births that in the epic culminates with the birth of the storm-god Marduk and his emergence as king of the gods and creator of human beings

The rivers of Mesopotamia were not, however, as benign as the Nile. They flooded unpredictably, sometimes even violently. The Euphrates especially seems to have shifted its bed repeatedly over the course of the millennia, one indication of recurrent severe flooding. Mesopotamia also had less than abundant rainfall, often insufficient for sustaining agriculture. Together these factors led to the development of irrigation by ditches and canals, which is attested before historic times.

For much of its history, Mesopotamia has been split by antagonism between the north, in later antiquity generally controlled by Assyria, and the south, or Babylonia. In the third millennium, the southern part itself was fragmented. The lower part, Sumer, gave its name to the culture of the Sumerians. The upper region of southern Mesopotamia was Akkad, originally the name of the city from which its Semitic rulers spread their control. (The general term *Akkadian* for the Semitic languages of Assyria and Babylonia derives from this name.) But despite sometimes intense rivalry, the differences between north and south were much less significant than their shared culture. Allowing for local variations, by 2000 BCE they had the same language, the same pantheon, the same views of themselves and their place in the world. Blocked on the east by the Zagros Mountains, on the south by the Persian Gulf, and on the west by the northern expanses of the Arabian Desert, and watered by the same two rivers, they formed a natural unity whose imperialistic impulse was northward and westward—to Asia Minor and the Levant, and even at times into Egypt itself.

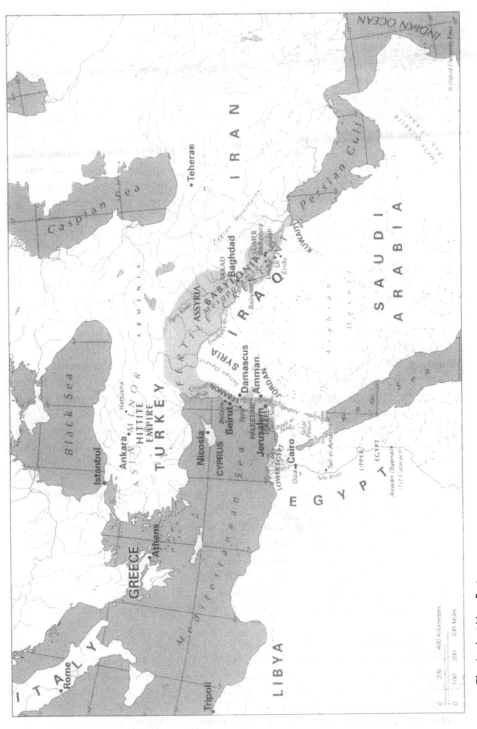

The Ancient Near East

The Rise of Civilization

The slow evolution of the human species and its gradual adaptation to and control of the environment is beyond the scope of this volume. The earliest vestiges of hominid activity in the Levant date to the early Paleolithic era well over a million years ago and, as elsewhere, consist principally of worked stone tools. Over the aeons technological sophistication very gradually increased, and sites where artifacts and occasionally human bones occur become more numerous, suggesting a growth in the number and size of the usually isolated small groups. Eventually the sites can be recognized as seasonal camps, characteristically with scatters of stone artifacts and occasionally faunal and floral remains, the tantalizingly sparse traces of small bands of hunters and gatherers. But as the climate warmed toward the end of the last Ice age, the archaeological record reveals an increasingly rapid rate of change and a concomitant increase in population. These developments seem to have occurred independently in several different regions, although even in the earliest stages there is evidence of contact, perhaps in the form of trade, between relatively widely separated groups. By the Upper Paleolithic (ca. 43,000–18,000 BCE) and Epipaleolithic (ca. 18,000–8500 BCE) eras, we find occasional semipermanent settlements, some with burials that have been interpreted as evidence for both social structure and religious beliefs.

Not long after 10,000 BCE, as the glaciers receded and the region became less wet, the changes in climate coincided in the Near East with significant developments in technology, settlement patterns, social organization, and the size of human populations. Sometimes termed the "Neolithic revolution," this process was gradual rather than sudden, and different regions (and different sites within those regions) exhibit considerable variation in the pattern and pace of change. Still, by the mid-ninth millennium (a date determined principally by radiocarbon dating), the aeons-old mode of subsistence based on hunting wild game and gathering wild fruits and vegetables was giving way to food production. The domestication of both animals and plants remains one of the most remarkable human accomplishments. Grains and legumes came under cultivation, and the breeding of sheep, goats, dogs, and, later, pigs and cattle began. The men and women engaged in these activities were of necessity settled, or, in the case of pastoralists, seminomadic. Their camps, villages, towns, and even cities are more and more in evidence as the four millennia (ca. 8500–4500 BCE) of the Neolithic Age unfold. Their populations grew, their technology advanced, they had frequent encounters with other groups, some quite distant. The Neolithic Age, then, set patterns for successive millennia of development. Down to the present, subsequent changes in many respects have been elaborations of those patterns.

One of the largest and most important sites of this period in the entire Near East has only recently been excavated. It is located just northeast of modern Amman, Jordan, at a spring called in modern Arabic Ain Ghazal ("the spring of the gazelle") that feeds the Zarqa River (the biblical Jabbok), and was continuously occupied for more than two millennia, beginning about 7200 BCE. At its greatest extent Ain Ghazal covered over 12 hectares (30 acres), making it three times as large as its contemporary, Neolithic Jericho. The earliest settlement was relatively small, covering 2 hectares

(5 acres), and half of the faunal remains recovered were of wild animals. Forty-five species are represented, reflecting the area's rich ecosystem, with gazelle the most frequently occurring.

The Neolithic revolution had already begun at Ain Ghazal in the village's earliest years. Domesticated goats constituted half of the entire faunal repertoire, showing that domestication was well under way. In addition to wild fruits and nuts, such grains as wheat and barley and such legumes as chickpeas, peas, and lentils were grown. The houses were permanent structures, usually with two or three rooms, some of which were as large as 5 meters (16 feet) square. The stone walls, and later the floors, were plastered, and some were decorated with a red paint in a variety of designs. Adults and children were buried under the floors of the houses or in their courtyards, perhaps an expression of the continuity of the family even after death. Some of the skulls had been removed from the rest of the skeleton and plastered over, perhaps in the likeness of the deceased. A number of figurines of humans and animals have also been found, and, most remarkably, a group of over thirty clay-plaster statues and busts of both adults and children, some nearly a meter (3 feet) long.

In the succeeding centuries, the settlement grew because of its ecologically advantageous location and the growing sophistication in agriculture and animal husbandry. By 6000 the village had become 10 hectares (25 acres) large. Domesticated pig and cattle made their appearance, as did dogs, and the villagers' dependence on hunting for animal protein had diminished. During the next five centuries (ca. 6000–5500 BCE, Pre-Pottery Neolithic C), the site reached its maximum size of more than 12 hectares (30 acres) and had a population of perhaps several thousand. Domesticated animals by now accounted for 90 percent of the animal bones. Not surprisingly, architectural styles had changed, and the typical house had become smaller, another sign of population expansion.

Like other Neolithic sites, Ain Ghazal gives evidence of trade with distant regions. There are seashells from both the Mediterranean and Red Seas, and copper and semiprecious stones from sources as distant as the Sinai Peninsula. Obsidian is also found. This volcanic glass was often favored in the Neolithic Age for use in knives and other tools and weapons, although stone continued to be the primary raw material for these artifacts. Analysis of the chemical composition of obsidian has traced it to two areas, in southeastern Turkey and central Armenia, with obsidian from both regions occurring in Neolithic sites in the Levant as far south as Beidha, hundreds of kilometers away. Whether the trade in obsidian was direct or indirect cannot be determined, but its existence shows the beginning of economic, cultural, and eventually political interrelationships among widely separated communities.

The final period of occupation at Ain Ghazal, from 5500 to 5000 BCE, brings with it yet another significant innovation, pottery. For the ancients the development of ceramics was probably less significant than it has proven for modern researchers. Although pottery made long-term storage more convenient, such storage was already possible in the form of baskets for dry goods and animal skins for liquids—both of which continued in use for millennia. The discovery that clay, when fired at high temperatures, would become hard and durable, was made independently at a number of sites in different regions and at different times in the Neolithic Age, and it occurs relatively late at Ain Ghazal. The new technology, however, became widespread, and by 5000, ubiquitous. Clay, the raw material for ceramics, was readily available, and most pottery was locally made, at first by hand, then on the wheel (although hand manufacture continued to be reserved for some types of vessels). Although ceramic bowls, cups, plates, jars, and other forms are easily broken, they were easily and inexpensively replaced, and the sherds simply discarded. But these sherds are indestructible, and they have become one of the most commonly found and most important tools for archaeologists.

From the end of the Neolithic Age on, pottery fragments, even on the surface of the ground, are a sure sign of human occupation. Over the millennia, pottery changed, but slowly and generally synchronously, so that the materials used, the forms, and the decorations became cultural and chronological markers. Over the past hundred years, archaeologists have accumulated a repertoire of these changes, so that pottery becomes an important tool for dating, especially in later periods when radiocarbon dates are less precise. Indeed, until coins become widely used beginning in the Persian period, pottery can be the most important chronological indicator for the Near Eastern sites and levels in which it is found, since datable written remains are often sparse or nonexistent. Within a narrow confine, different types of ceramics can be used to elucidate social stratification and political control. Moreover, as containers for goods traded and even as an object of trade itself, pottery is an indicator of commercial and hence cultural interchange.

Another important site for this period is Jericho, in the Jordan Valley just north of the Dead Sea; until the discovery of Ain Ghazal it was the type-site for the Levant. Like Ain Ghazal, Jericho (Tell es-Sultan) is endowed with an abundant water supply, in the form of a spring that produces as much as 4,000 liters (1,000 gallons) per minute. This spring produced a large oasis in a region of marginal rainfall and warm climate, enabling agriculture to be carried out with ease and virtually year-round. At Jericho, we find essentially the same chronological development as at Ain Ghazal, although the occupation at Jericho begins earlier and is not continuous. As at Ain Ghazal, the burials at Jericho are generally beneath the floors of houses and often have special treatment of the skulls.

In one respect Jericho is anomalous. In general, Neolithic sites are unfortified villages, as are settlements of the immediately following Chalcolithic period, but at the very beginning of the Neolithic era Jericho is a walled enclosure—perhaps even, anachronistically, a city. A stone rampart surrounds the site, at this time covering about 4 hectares (10 acres). This wall was successively rebuilt over the centuries, reaching a maximum width of 3.5 meters (11.5 feet) and a height of more than 6 meters (20 feet). A moat encircled the wall, and just inside the wall was at least one massive circular stone tower, more than 8 meters (26 feet) high, with a diameter of about 9 meters (30 feet) at the base and 7 meters (23 feet) at the top. Inside this tower was a twenty-two-step staircase leading from its base to its top. This complex enclosure system was in use for only a millennium or so, and its function is unclear, although defense is the most reasonable hypothesis. (An alternative explanation proposes a religious use, but archaeologists too often attribute religious functions to discoveries they do not fully understand.) In any case, the construction and maintenance of the system would have required considerable labor, presumably by spe-

cialists whose activity the larger community (probably numbering fewer t.
sand) would have had to compensate. At Jericho, then, and probabl
Neolithic sites as well, we should presume the existence of specialization ol
concomitant complexity in social organization that will in the Early Br(.gc
(around 3000 BCE) evolve into full urbanism.

Because of its ecologically advantageous setting, Tell es-Sultan in the Jericho oasis
was rebuilt in successive periods, although with some gaps in occupation. It thus
exemplifies one of the most familiar features of the ancient and modern Near Eastern
landscape, the mound known in Arabic as *tell*, in Hebrew as *tel*, in Turkish as *huyuk*,
and in Persian as *tepe*. A tell is the accumulated debris—generally trapezoidal in
silhouette—of successive human occupations. Originally, settlers would choose to
live on a natural hill, both for defensive purposes and because springs are often
found at the base of hills. Houses were built of stone and sun-dried mud-bricks,
and, from the Early Bronze Age on, fortifications as well. These settlements often
survived for centuries, but eventually they fell victim to natural catastrophes or war,
or were simply abandoned because of a change in rainfall patterns or the drying up
of the water supply. But other settlers returned to the same site, sometimes immediately and sometimes later, building their town atop the ruins of the previous
one. As this pattern was repeated, sometimes a dozen or more times, the site slowly
built up, with the earlier debris often held in place by the foundations of the fortifications. Thus were formed the mounds of many cities, to borrow a phrase from
Frederick Bliss, a late nineteenth-century excavator of Tell el-Hesi in southwestern
Palestine.

Understandably, these mounds were the primary focus of archaeological work in
the Levant in the first century or so of systematic excavation. They can often be
identified with cities mentioned in biblical and other texts, and thus their occupational history is illuminated by references to them in ancient sources. Moreover, their
stratigraphy, though invariably complex, provides a diachronic record of changes in
architecture, burial customs, technology, food sources, and the like—changes that
can be dated by ceramic chronology. Because of the preoccupation of many excavators with the relationship between excavated remains and the Bible, many of the
principal tells in Palestine have been partially excavated more than once, cumulatively
yielding a detailed record of the political history and material culture of the region
since prehistoric times. As one moves farther away from Palestine, the number of
excavated tells decreases, even though in such areas as northern Syria the mounds
are more numerous. In Jordan and Syria especially, countless sites have never been
excavated.

Since the last third of the twentieth century, more attention has focused on smaller
sites, often occupied for only one period, and these have been studied not only by
actual excavation but also often by surface survey. This type of investigation often
pays more attention to social history than to political history, which is essentially the
record of the elite. Many of the sites cannot be identified with ancient place-names,
and some are no more than small villages not mentioned in ancient sources. But the
investigation of these sites has illuminated the settlement patterns of various periods
and the complex relationships between large urban centers and smaller satellite towns
and villages, as well as the way of life of ordinary people.

The Chalcolithic Age

The periodization of history—its division into various eras, and the nomenclature given to those eras—is misleading. It implies sudden change, caused by migration, invasion, variations in climate, or other punctual events. But what is more apparent from the archaeological record is continuity, both through time and across a wide geographical area. Change occurs, of course, but it is almost always gradual and the process is observable.

In the mid-fifth millennium BCE there begins the so-called Chalcolithic Age, a name derived from the Greek words for copper and stone. This period (ca. 4500–3300 BCE) was so named because metallurgy becomes widespread, although stone tools also abound. The Chalcolithic is followed, in archaeological nomenclature, by the Bronze Age (subdivided into Early, Middle, and Late) and then by the Iron Age. But this terminology, based on technology, conveys the wrong impression. Stone artifacts continued to be used throughout the Bronze Age and beyond; some agricultural villages in the Middle East today still use stone blades in harvesting and threshing tools, and stone mortars and pestles have been commonplace in daily life up to modern times. Moreover, iron objects appeared before the beginning of the Iron Age, and well into it bronze remained the most widely used metal.

Once recorded history begins, periodization is based on political events in Egypt and elsewhere. This is the case with the subdivision of the Bronze Age and the beginning of the Iron Age. Subsequent periods are delineated by shifts in imperial control—the Persian, Hellenistic, and Roman periods, for example.

The culture of the Chalcolithic in many respects evolved from the preceding Neolithic Age. Ceramic forms developed in the earlier period continued to be used in the later, as did stone (usually flint) tools. The process of domestication continued, with olives, dates, and flax added to the repertoire of cultivated flora. Chalcolithic settlements, like those of the Neolithic, were unfortified. In Palestine the number of known sites is much larger for the Chalcolithic, and they are often found in previously unsettled regions. In part because of the expanding repertoire of food supplies, diet improved and population increased. Given the demonstrable continuities with the preceding period, earlier theories that posited migration as the source of innovations now seem unlikely.

Yet there were innovations in this period as well, some of short duration and others longer-lasting. New ceramic forms developed, often ornately painted or incised. Some are ossuaries, small receptacles for the secondary interment of bones after the flesh has decomposed. In the Neolithic, apparently only skulls were given this secondary treatment; now the entire skeletal remains of adults were gathered together, deposited in the ossuaries, and placed in burial caves. The ossuaries are usually large boxes, averaging 70 centimeters (2 feet 3 inches) long, 60 centimeters (2 feet) high, and 30 centimeters (1 foot) wide. Some are elaborately decorated, giving them the appearance of a house, with openings for doors and sometimes windows. Although not all Chalcolithic burials are of this type, secondary burial was at least widely practiced, and continued for millennia.

Since the Chalcolithic period is still prehistoric in the sense that we have no texts to help us interpret the material culture, we know nothing about the ideas underlying secondary burial in ossuaries. Is this an attempt to give the dead a home, if only on a reduced scale? Why are architectural details of the ossuaries inconsistent with ordinary houses of the period? Why are some ossuaries shaped like animals, and some elaborately decorated with disembodied eyes? Why are some interment sites distant from settlements, and why are some corpses not given secondary burial? Our inability to answer such questions reveals how little we know of ancient peoples in this and prior and even subsequent ages. What archaeologists excavate at a site of any size is only a small fraction of what was there when it was a vibrant, flourishing entity. Moreover, much excavated material from all periods is prehistoric in precisely this sense, coming from sites and individuals that will forever remain anonymous. Even after writing was developed, the overwhelming majority of texts were produced by and for a small elite. Their social attitudes and religious beliefs and practices can only partially, and even then with difficulty, be projected to nonelite, nonurban, ordinary folk, whose social history and thinking must largely be inferred from the fragmentary survivals of their material culture.

The same sort of questions arise about another type of artifact of the Chalcolithic Age, the zoomorphic and anthropomorphic figurines. Usually ceramic, but sometimes carved in ivory or stone, these figurines are carefully executed artistic expressions whose function and interpretation are unclear. The stone exemplars are carefully executed, portraying what seems to be a woman in an abstract violin-like shape. In the media of pottery and ivory, both males and females are portrayed more realistically, with their sexual organs rendered in explicit, sometimes exaggerated, detail. Plausibly this suggests some association with fertility ritual. The same theme is also apparent in two complete ceramic examples. One is a nude seated woman who holds on her head a large churn, a well-attested ceramic form from the period generally. The other is a ram, on whose back are three tapered cups, or cornets, another common Chalcolithic form. The torsos of both the woman and the ram are churnlike in shape. Human and animal reproduction and milk production thus seem to have been understandable preoccupations of Chalcolithic people, although the rituals in which these needs were expressed are unknowable.

Chalcolithic settlement is found throughout Palestine, from upper Galilee and the Golan Heights to the Negeb. The best-known large sites are a cluster of three in the Beer-sheba region, the source of most of the ivory figurines, and Teleilat Ghassul, just northeast of the Dead Sea. Approximately midway between them lie the sites of two major discoveries. During the systematic exploration of caves in the Judean wilderness to the west of the Dead Sea that followed the discovery of the Dead Sea Scrolls in 1947, a large cache of copper objects was recovered from a cave on the Nahal Mishmar. Dubbed the "Cave of the Treasure," it contained hundreds of ivory and copper objects, along with pottery, textiles, stone tools, basketry, and several burials. The large number of copper objects and their technical and artistic sophistication is unparalleled elsewhere in the same period and for centuries to come. The hoard included ten crowns, some intricately decorated with animal heads and horns, birds, and knobs. There were also more than 100 standards, many decorated with the same elements as the crowns. Copper jars and baskets, chisels and a hammer, and more than 240 mace heads were also found. Since the lost-wax process was used in casting the objects, there are no exact duplicates among the more than 400 in the cache.

The origin and function of this trove are a mystery. There was no nearby contemporary settlement of any size. Some 12 kilometers (7.5 miles) to the north-northeast, on a terrace overlooking the Dead Sea near the prolific spring at En-gedi, are the remains of a complex of structures that has plausibly been interpreted as a Chalcolithic shrine. A screening or temenos wall separated the shrine from its immediate environment, enclosing an area of about 375 square meters (4,000 square feet). Two gates in the wall gave access to an open courtyard, and projecting inward from the wall were two large rectangular buildings of what is known as the "broadroom" type, with their entrances on the long side. The larger of the two measures 5.5 meters (18 feet) by 20 meters (65 feet), and has opposite its entrance a raised platform, flanked, as was the doorway, by benches. The isolation of the complex, the finds found within it (for example, nearly 70 percent of the pottery was cornets), and parallels to its design at other sites suggest that this was a religious center, probably used by several communities. The trove from the Cave of the Treasure may have originally belonged to this sanctuary.

Together with burial practices and figurines, the complex at En-gedi is evidence for an organized system of communal practices based on the shared belief, or hope, of a reality greater than the human, perhaps even a life after life. There is a similar complex at the important site of Megiddo (Tell el-Mutesellim), also with a temenos wall and two broadroom structures, each with a platform, or altar, opposite its entrance. The date of the original construction of this complex is disputed, whether in the Chalcolithic or the immediately succeeding Early Bronze I Age, but the interpretation of its function as religious is supported by the presence of temples in the same area at Megiddo in uninterrupted succession for over two thousand years, until the beginning of the Iron Age.

The Chalcolithic Age, then, was a brief era of both relatively peaceful existence and extraordinary artistic expression. The construction and maintenance of the public architecture and the manufacture of the copper, ivory, and ceramic artifacts must have been the primary occupation of specialized groups. The movement toward complex social organization thus continued. This was apparently an internal development, rather than the result of massive invasions from outside the region. The Chalcolithic ended mysteriously, with some of its principal sites simply abandoned and never resettled. But many of the elements of its culture continued to be used in the succeeding Early Bronze Age, suggesting continuity rather than disruption.

The Rise of Cities and Nation-States

The phenomenon of urbanism in the Early Bronze Age throughout the Near East was not a sudden development. As populations grew, societies became more complex, resulting in ever more specialized occupations. Competition increased among villages and towns for natural resources, especially arable land and water, and one specialization that developed was military. Defensive and offensive weapons become increasingly lethal, and settlements began to be fortified with increasingly elaborate ramparts, towers, and gates.

During the apparently peaceful, artistic Chalcolithic Age in Palestine, urbanism was already developing in Mesopotamia, and shortly thereafter, in Egypt. By the beginning of the fourth millennium BCE, at Uruk and elsewhere in southern Mesopotamia, true cities had appeared. They are characterized by monumental public architecture that had both religious and administrative functions, by sophisticated technology in various media, and, eventually, by the use of writing. As populations increased, agriculture also became a specialized activity. No longer could each family or domestic unit supply its own food. Many of its members might pursue other occupations—soldiers, builders, priests, potters, metallurgists, administrators—and their needs would have been met by others—farmers, herders, traders.

The development of cities also brought greater cultural unity. This is evident, for example, in the homogeneity of ceramic traditions over a large region. Cities vied with each other for control of the region, with first one urban center and then another dominant. A text called the *Sumerian King List* illustrates these shifts in hegemony: "When kingship was lowered from heaven, kingship was [first] in Eridu. [In] Eridu, A-lulim [became] king and ruled 28,800 years. Alalgar ruled 36,000 years. Two kings [thus] ruled it for 64,800 years. I drop [the topic] Eridu [because] its kingship was brought to Bad-tibira. [In] Bad-tibira, En-men-lu-Ana ruled 43,200 years" (trans. A. Leo Oppenheim; p. 265 in James B. Pritchard, ed., *Ancient Near Eastern Texts Relating to the Old Testament*, Princeton, N.J.: Princeton University Press, 1969). This chronicle, composed late in the third millennium BCE, continues to list in detail five dynastic cities before "the Flood swept over [the earth]." There follows a list of postdiluvian cities and their rulers, concluding with the fall of Ur, by which time the lengths of the rulers' reigns have become plausible.

Although at least for the early periods the names and dates in the *King List* are clearly legendary, underlying it is perhaps an authentic historical memory of the prominence of various urban centers in the third millennium and even before. The first city mentioned, Eridu, is the oldest known Mesopotamian site where the beginning of urbanism is identified, as far back as the fifth millennium BCE, during the Chalcolithic Age in the Levant.

In these cities, by the early fourth millennium, centralized government was monarchic. The kings of ancient Sumer, the dominant region of southern Mesopotamia for several centuries, provided the necessary coordination of the specialized occupations. They directed the maintenance of the irrigation system, and presided over the complex exchange network that distributed goods from producers to consumers. In the process they acquired immense wealth. Some of this accumulated capital went for the construction of elaborate temple complexes, which, like the public works projects of later times, provided employment for segments of a growing population. At the same time, the temples visually testified to royal power, and became the stuff of legend. The biblical narrative of the Tower of Babel (Gen. 11.1–9) is on one level a description of the construction of a ziggurat, an enormous stepped pyramid that served as the base for a temple. Such structures are attested at cities throughout southern Mesopotamia from the third millennium into the first. The deity worshiped in the temple atop the ziggurat was the city's most important god, whose earthly representative was the reigning king. And although temple and crown sometimes competed for power and wealth, in general religion served the political ends of the state.

A similar development took place in Egypt during approximately the same period. About 3100 BCE the geographical unity provided by the Nile was translated into political unity, as northern and southern Egypt were united under one ruler. The third-century BCE Egyptian historian Manetho organized the history of his land into dynasties, a classification still followed today, and he calls the first king of the first dynasty Menes. This name does not, however, appear on ancient Egyptian monuments, and scholars generally identify Menes with Narmer, who is thus the first ruler of all Egypt. (The traditional designation *pharaoh* will not be used until centuries later.)

With unification came the beginning of Egyptian interest in the Levant as well. Narmer's name has been found incised on pottery fragments from two sites in southern Palestine, Tell Arad and Tel Erani, during the Early Bronze I period, and an abundance of imported Egyptian pottery and other artifacts begin to occur at many sites. These discoveries may be evidence only of trade, but within a few centuries— during the dynasties of the first major division of Egyptian history, the Old Kingdom—Egypt established political dominance over this region.

During the Old Kingdom internal control was also solidified. Egyptian society was organized in a pyramid-like fashion, with the pharaoh, the son of the sun-god, at its apex, presiding over a vast bureaucracy that controlled all aspects of Egyptian life. The most familiar evidence of the success of this system is the great pyramids at Giza, constructed with enormous labor as the final resting places of the rulers of the Old Kingdom.

The Invention of Writing

Up to this point we have been dealing largely with prehistory. Even subsequent eras are often prehistoric in the sense that we cannot set down any typical political history—for most of the Early and Middle Bronze Age in Palestine, for example, few names of cities or rulers are known, nor are even the language or languages that the inhabitants used. But first in Sumer, and then in Egypt, a technology is invented that will enable history in the more familiar sense to be reconstructed, that is, to be written. That technology, one of the most significant inventions of early Near Eastern civilizations, is writing itself.

Writing was invented to ease the administration of the various tasks, goods, and services exchanged by groups whose specialization made it inefficient or impossible to be self-subsistent. In increasingly complex societies, some form of record-keeping was essential. True writing appeared first in the Sumerian city-states of Mesopotamia toward the end of the fourth millennium BCE and slightly later in Egypt. Egyptian writing may have developed independently, or, as many scholars think, it was at least generically adapted from the Mesopotamian system.

Both systems originally used a pictographic system in which a picture or icon represented a single object, action, or concept. These pictures rapidly became stylized, and soon some were also used as phonograms, to represent a sound or syllable. Because of the necessity of learning hundreds of symbols in order to represent even a limited vocabulary, literacy was for the most part restricted to a specially trained class known as scribes.

In Sumer, as subsequently in its successors Babylonia and Assyria, the principal medium of writing was clay. Before the moistened clay had fully hardened, the symbols were inscribed on it with the sharpened point of a reed, resulting in wedge shapes; each wedge or combination of wedges represented a symbol or syllable. The tablets were then fired, like pottery, becoming essentially indestructible. The great majority of texts recovered that use this wedge-shaped, or cuneiform, writing are on clay tablets, but it was adapted for other media, such as stone and wood. Cuneiform continued to be the standard form of writing for millennia, not only in Mesopotamia but throughout the Levant, and was used for a variety of languages and even different writing systems, including a form of the alphabet. Thus, the Amarna letters, corre spondence from Canaanite rulers to their Egyptian suzerain in the mid-fourteenth century BCE, were written by Canaanite scribes in a form of the Babylonian language that employs much local idiom.

In Egypt, a locally available reed, papyrus, was processed to become a cheap and durable writing surface—what the ancient Greeks called *papyros*, from which the English word *paper* is derived. On papyrus Egyptian scribes wrote with the ancient equivalent of pen and ink, using a pictographic repertoire that would much later, and erroneously, be called *hieroglyphic*, or sacred writing, for many texts have no explicitly religious content. As in Mesopotamia, other media could also be used for writing.

In the dry Egyptian climate papyrus is not subject to the kind of decomposition that organic materials undergo in other regions. And because much writing in Mesopotamia was on baked clay tablets, they too survive. Consequently, countless texts of all types—political, literary, scientific, commercial, and religious—have come to light and continue to do so, enabling modern scholars to study the ancient Near East at all levels, from the mundane to the sublime.

With the development of writing we leave prehistory and enter historical periods. Texts enable historians to assemble a chronological record of local, regional, and international politics. Individuals mentioned in one source appear in others, and ancient sources themselves frequently provide synchronisms, correlating events and rulers of their own geopolitical entity to those of others. These ancient records have enabled modern historians to construct a detailed and virtually continuous chronology. Although specialists will often quibble about the details of the chronology, there is consensus as to its general accuracy.

Myth

Written texts also provide insight into belief systems, at least those of the elite. Often these take the form of what are traditionally called myths, narratives about the gods and the heroes of an apparently distant past. In the ancient Near East as a whole, and even within distinct cultures, these myths exhibit an often bewildering variety of perspectives and details. As attempts to explain the origins of the world and the nature of the human condition, ancient myths are neither consistent nor systematic. They are, however, an important body of data that, like tools, pottery, fortifications, and other artifacts, shed light on historical development.

The genesis of the natural and social order is usually expressed as the result of the activity of an individual deity, who presided over and coordinated the collective efforts of other gods and goddesses. The origins of this deity are sometimes expressed in a theogonic narrative describing how a series of divine generations led to the birth and ultimately the assumption of power of the creator-god.

Creation myths are usually etiological, explaining how the world as their writers and audiences perceived it came to be. They thus project that world, already agricultural and often urban, back into primeval times. In Mesopotamian tradition,

> At the very beginning, Plough married earth
> And they decided to establish a family and dominion.
> "We shall break up the virgin soil of the land into clods."
> In the clods of their virgin soil, they created Sea.
> The Furrows, of their own accord, begot the Cattle God.
> Together they build Dunnu forever as his refuge.
> (*Theogony of Dunnu;* trans. Dalley, 279)

This was the time before the creation of humans, when, according to another myth,

> The gods instead of man
> Did the work, bore the loads. . . .
> The gods had to dig out canals,
> Had to clear channels, the lifelines of the land . . .
> For 3,600 years they bore the excess,
> Hard work, night and day.
> (*Atrahasis,* tablet 1; trans. Dalley, 9–10)

Atrahasis goes on to describe the creation of humans out of a mixture of clay and the blood of a slain god, so that they would do the necessary work of construction and dredging canals, or, as *Enuma Elish* puts it, so that the gods might enjoy a life of leisure. Humans would not only maintain the essential irrigation channels, but also build the houses of the gods—their temples—and prepare their meals—the sacrifices.

The Bible itself begins, appropriately, with an account of the origins of the cosmos and of civilization that is largely mythological. Much of the material in Genesis 1–11 is clearly related to ancient Near Eastern accounts of origins, and mythological language is used throughout the Bible.

The ancient Israelites did not live in a cultural vacuum. From prehistoric times on Palestine was linked by trade with Egypt and Mesopotamia, and one or the other politically dominated it for much of the period from the mid-third millennium to the late first millennium BCE. Biblical traditions also relate how some of Israel's ancestors, and later some of Israel itself, spent considerable time in Egypt, Assyria, and Babylon. Thus, while Israelite literature and religion as preserved in the Bible and as uncovered by archaeologists have many distinctive features, in their lives and in their writings the Israelites inevitably shared perspectives with their ancient Near Eastern contemporaries. They were familiar with other cultural expressions and freely adopted and adapted them in articulating their own specific formulations.

The marvelous epic of *Gilgamesh* provides one example of the interrelationship of ancient Near Eastern cultures. The earliest forms of the epic are from Sumer, where it seems to have originated in the late third millennium BCE as an account of the adventures of an actual king of Uruk, who had lived a few centuries earlier. Subsequently, different writers and cultures freely expanded and revised the epic, much like the treatment of the Arthurian legend in European literature. Tablets containing all or at least parts of the epic have been found in ancient libraries throughout Mesopotamia, with the latest dated to the second century BCE, as well as in the Hittite capital of Hattusas in central Asia Minor and at Megiddo in Israel. Gilgamesh himself is mentioned by name in the Dead Sea Scrolls and by Claudius Aelianus, a Roman who wrote in Greek in the early second century CE. This chronological and geographical spread testifies to the myth's extraordinary popularity, and it is no surprise that scholars have detected themes from *Gilgamesh* in both the Bible and the Homeric poems. But the same spread also makes it impossible for us to determine precisely which version was being read at a given time.

Gilgamesh was not the only widely known ancient Near Eastern text. Similar examples of literary proliferation abound, and collectively they demonstrate a shared repertoire throughout the ancient Near East, including biblical Israel. It is rarely possible to establish a direct link between a specific nonbiblical source and a part of the Bible, both because of the random nature of discovery and because of the complicated processes of composition, editing, and collection that finally produced the Bible. Still, the cumulative evidence shows that most biblical genres, motifs, and even institutions have ancient Near Eastern parallels.

Like other accounts of origins, the early chapters of Genesis relate the beginnings of a world in which agriculture is practiced and urbanism soon develops. Yahweh God plants a garden in Eden from which flows a river with four branches (Gen. 2.10–14). Two are the Tigris and Euphrates, and another is Gihon, the name of the spring that was ancient Jerusalem's principal source of water. The symbolic imagery of Solomon's Temple in Jerusalem both informs and is informed by the description of the Garden of Eden. This garden is Yahweh's plantation, in which like a country gentleman he regularly strolls in the cool late afternoon (3.8). And the first human, formed by Yahweh from the soil as a potter shapes a vessel and infused with an element of the divine, is made to cultivate and tend the garden.

The first children of Adam and Eve are Cain and Abel, a farmer and a herder, and Cain's son Enoch is the first to build a city (Gen. 4.17). Cain's descendants go on to make musical instruments and bronze and iron tools. In a later generation, after the Flood, Noah will be the first to plant a vineyard (9.20).

As in the *Sumerian King List* and other Mesopotamian traditions, this primeval history was divided into antediluvian and postdiluvian epochs. Before the Flood came a distant past, when humans lived extraordinarily long life spans. The biblical narrative of the Flood provides the clearest example of direct dependence on other ancient myths. Many of its details are virtually identical to Mesopotamian accounts of the Flood, especially in *Gilgamesh* and *Atrahasis*. In both traditions, a god warns the hero of the impending deluge. Following divine instructions he constructs a boat, waterproofs it, and brings on board his family and all sorts of animals. They ride out the storm, and the boat comes to rest on a mountain. Then, to see whether it is safe to disembark, the hero releases three birds. Here is the way the hero Utnapishtim recounts this episode in *Gilgamesh*:

> When the seventh day arrived,
> I put out and released a dove.

> The dove went; it came back,
> For no perching place was visible to it, and it turned round.
> I put out and released a swallow.
> The swallow went; it came back,
> For no perching place was visible to it, and it turned round.
> I put out, and released a raven.
> The raven went, and saw the waters receding.
> And it ate, preened, lifted its tail, and did not turn round.
> Then I put (everything) out to the four winds, and I made a sacrifice. . . .
> The gods smelt the fragrance,
> The gods smelt the pleasant fragrance,
> The gods like flies gathered over the sacrifice.
>
> (trans. Dalley, 114)

Likewise, in Genesis, Noah releases three birds. The third brings him an olive leaf and when released again does not return. So Noah and his family and all the animals leave the ark.

> Then Noah built an altar to the LORD, and took of every clean animal and of every clean bird, and offered burnt offerings on the altar. And when the LORD smelled the pleasing odor, the LORD said in his heart, "I will never again curse the ground because of humankind." (Gen. 8.20–21)

As in the *Sumerian King List,* in Genesis lives are shorter after the Flood, society becomes more complex, and populations increase. The story of the Tower of Babel, set at the end of the primeval period, tells how the building of a "tower with its top in the heavens" and a city (Gen. 11.4) results in linguistic diversity.

Like their ancient Near Eastern colleagues, biblical writers used myth to explain the origins of their world. However, for them both, this was not just myth, but history too. The modern distinction between history and myth is perhaps too sharply drawn, since mythic conventions informed the interpretation of the past in ancient historiography, and to some extent do so in modern as well.

Like the rest of the Hebrew Bible, Genesis 1–11 received its final form well into the first millennium BCE, and was clearly intended as an overture to the narratives that follow. These chapters set the story of Israel's ancestors, its Exodus from Egypt, and its vicissitudes in the Promised Land in a larger, universal context, and consciously connect that later history with creation and primeval events. For the authors of Genesis 1–11, then, the accounts of creation, of the Garden of Eden, of the Flood, were historical as well, connected by genealogy with their own more immediate past. The "generations of the heavens and the earth" (Gen. 2.4), the creation of the world, became the first of a series of births, summarized periodically in the lists occurring throughout the book of Genesis of the descendants of Adam, Noah, Abraham, Ishmael, Esau, and finally Jacob, whose name is changed to Israel. These genealogies join as in a continuous history the birth of the world with the birth of Israel, first the family, then the nation, that will be the primary focus of the Bible's subsequent books.

*   *   *

This, then, is the beginning of history in the biblical world, the world in which prophets and sages, poets and historians, storytellers and apologists, produced their works, eventually to be edited and collected into two anthologies of early Jewish and early Christian traditions: the Hebrew Bible—the Torah, Prophets, and Writings—and the New Testament.

Select Bibliography

Albrektson, Bertil. *History and the Gods: An Essay on the Idea of Historical Events as Divine Manifestations in the Ancient Near East and in Israel.* Lund, Sweden: CWK Gleerup, 1967. An important monograph that shows significant similarities between ancient Israel and its neighbors in the interpretation of historical events as divine revelation.

Bar-Yosef, Ofer. "Prehistoric Palestine." In *The Oxford Encyclopedia of Archaeology in the Near East,* ed. Eric M. Meyers, 4.207–12. New York: Oxford University Press, 1997. An up-to-date synopsis of the Paleolithic and Neolithic periods.

Clifford, Richard J. *Creation Accounts in the Ancient Near East and in the Bible.* The Catholic Biblical Quarterly Monograph Series, 26. Washington, D.C.: Catholic Biblical Association, 1994. A valuable summary, with detailed comparisons.

Dalley, Stephanie. *Myths from Mesopotamia.* Oxford: Oxford University Press, 1989. A reliable translation of ten major Mesopotamian myths.

Ehrich, Robert W., ed. *Chronologies in Old World Archaeology.* 3d ed. Chicago: University of Chicago Press, 1992. A comprehensive survey of the archaeological data for prehistoric chronology.

Gonen, Rivka. "The Chalcolithic Period." In *The Archaeology of Ancient Israel,* ed. Amnon Ben-Tor, 40–80. A detailed interpretive summary of the evidence.

Grimal, Nicholas. *A History of Ancient Egypt.* Trans. Ian Shaw. Oxford: Blackwell, 1992. A current summary.

Orni, Ephraim, and E. Ephrat. *Geography of Israel.* 4th ed. Jerusalem: Israel Universities Press, 1980. A detailed treatment.

Postgate, J. N. *Early Mesopotamia: Society and Economy at the Dawn of History.* New York: Routledge, 1992. A synthesis of archaeological and textual data into a detailed social and economic history.

Potts, D. T. *Mesopotamian Civilization: The Material Foundations.* Ithaca, N.Y.: Cornell University Press, 1997. Provocative synthesis of archaeological data with historical, literary, and artistic evidence.

Rollefson, Gary O. "Invoking the Spirit: Prehistoric Religion at Ain Ghazal." *Archaeology Odyssey* 1.1 (1998): 54–63. An illustrated discussion by the excavator of Ain Ghazal. For further bibliography, see his "'Ain Ghazal," in *The Oxford Encyclopedia of Archaeology in the Near East,* ed. Eric M. Meyers, 1.36–38 (New York: Oxford University Press, 1997).

Saggs, H. W. F. *Civilization before Greece and Rome.* New Haven, Conn.: Yale University Press, 1989. A thematic overview.

Schmandt-Besserat, Denise. *Before Writing.* Vol. 1, *From Counting to Cuneiform;* vol. 2, *A*

Catalog of Near Eastern Tokens. Austin: University of Texas Press, 1992. An innovative investigation of the origins of writing.

Snell, Daniel C. *Life in the Ancient Near East, 3100–332* B.C.E. New Haven, Conn.: Yale University Press, 1997. A chronologically arranged social history.

Soden, Wolfram von. *The Ancient Orient: An Introduction to the Study of the Ancient Near East.* Trans. Donald G. Schley. Grand Rapids, Mich.: Eerdmans, 1994. A thematic survey by a distinguished Assyriologist.

Trigger, B. G., et al. *Ancient Egypt: A Social History.* Cambridge: Cambridge University Press, 1983. An innovative historical survey that focuses on social and economic aspects of Egyptian history, with extensive use of archaeological data.

CHAPTER ONE

Before Israel

Syria-Palestine in the Bronze Age

WAYNE T. PITARD

B y the time the nation of Israel emerged as a political entity in the late thirteenth century BCE, Near Eastern urban civilization had already grown ancient—more than two millennia old. In Mesopotamia, the Sumerian and Old
and Middle Babylonian cultures had long since risen and fallen. For Egypt,
the final days of imperial glory were at hand.

The Israelites felt their late-coming keenly, even emphasizing it in the narrative
traditions that told of their beginnings. In this they differed from other Near Eastern
peoples, whose stories of national origins tended to merge with their accounts of the
creation of the cosmos. For example, in the Babylonian creation epic, *Enuma Elish*,
Babylon's foundation culminates the creation of the world, thereby obscuring the
city's relatively late surge into political prominence in Mesopotamia. But Israelite
tradition set the nation's birth within a historical rather than a mythic framework.
Biblical stories of the Israelites' origins deal with their slavery in Egypt, their subsequent escape, and their eventual conquest of the land of Canaan, which would become their homeland. Biblical accounts of the creation of the world remained distinct
from those that related Israel's own origins. Indeed, between its accounts of creation
and its record of the rise of Israel, biblical tradition placed a series of tales about
several generations of ancestors; according to the tradition's own chronology, these
progenitors lived centuries before Israel came to be. Now preserved for the most part
in the book of Genesis, these narratives told the story of a pastoralist named Abraham—the nation's ultimate father—and his descendants. In the form in which we
know them, these tales tell the stories of four generations of Abraham's family, explaining how they migrated through the land of Canaan and eventually settled in the

Nile Delta in northern Egypt. There, the tradition goes on to narrate, Abraham's descendants lived for four hundred years, eventually growing into the nation of Israel.

In this chapter we look at the ancestral narratives in Genesis 12–50 and consider their relationship to the history of Israel. We then examine the wider history of Syria-Palestine from the late third millennium to 1200 BCE, exploring the historical and cultural milieu in which Israel was born. We conclude by examining aspects of second-millennium culture that illuminate some of the ancestral traditions that Genesis preserves.

The Narratives of Genesis 12–50

The ancestral tales of Genesis 12–50 depict four generations of pastoralists whose primary grazing lands lay in the land of Canaan. The story begins in Genesis 11.27–29 by introducing Abraham and his wife Sarah (who are called Abram and Sarai in the early chapters). Genesis 11.29 introduces a serious problem for the couple, whose solution forms a major theme of the Abraham/Sarah cycle: Sarah is infertile. The first action of the cycle, Genesis 12.1–7, presents the overarching theme, not only of the Abraham cycle, but also of the entire narrative that stretches from Genesis through the book of Joshua. In this passage, God calls Abraham to migrate to Canaan and makes two critical promises to him: that Abraham's descendants will become a great nation, and that God will give them the land of Canaan as their own. The fulfillment of these promises is the primary strand unifying the entire epic of Israel's origins.

Most of the narratives about Abraham and Sarah's adventures in Canaan (Gen. 12–25) are related to one or the other of God's promises. In several cases the characters' own actions place the fulfillment of the promises in jeopardy. For example, in one story (Gen. 12.10–20) Sarah, who is destined to be the mother of the child through whom Israel will arise, is taken into the harem of the Egyptian pharaoh, and Abraham nearly loses her. But God intervenes and returns Sarah to her husband. In Genesis 13, a threat to the promise of the land arises when Abraham and his nephew Lot come in conflict over where they are going to pasture their enormous flocks. Abraham allows Lot to choose which part of the land he wishes to take. Were Lot to select the area of Canaan that God had pledged to Abraham, the promise would be void. Lot, however, prefers the land east of the Jordan River to the region that will eventually become Israel.

The birth of the promised heir also falls into doubt. As Abraham and Sarah age and Sarah remains childless, she gives her husband her maidservant Hagar as a surrogate wife to bear a child. But this son, Ishmael, is not the child of the promise. Finally, Sarah, at the advanced age of ninety, conceives and gives birth to Isaac, the divinely designated heir.

Few traditions about Isaac are preserved in the narratives. Most of the stories of Isaac present him as a character secondary to the main protagonists, who are either his father, Abraham, or his sons, Jacob and Esau. The only narratives in which Isaac does play the primary role (Gen. 26) virtually duplicate stories told earlier about Abraham. For the most part these quasi-reruns reiterate themes found in the Abraham cycle.

Isaac and his wife Rebekah have twin sons, Jacob and Esau. The brothers are intense rivals. Jacob, the younger, usually gets the best of the dull-witted Esau, tricking him into selling his birthright (Gen. 25.29–34) and stealing his firstborn's blessing from their blind father (27.1–40). Eventually Jacob must flee to avoid the anger of Esau, and so he sets out for Haran in northern Syria. There he meets his extended family and marries his uncle's two daughters, Leah and Rachel (Gen. 29).

Although portraying Abraham as the ultimate father of Israel, the tradition reserves to Jacob the honor of giving the nation its name and its twelvefold tribal makeup. There are, in fact, two stories in which God changes Jacob's name to Israel (Gen. 32.22–32 and 35.9–15), and, in Genesis 29.31–30.24 and 35.16–18, Jacob sires twelve sons, who become the eponymous ancestors of the twelve tribes of Israel.

Beginning in Genesis 37, the focus of the story shifts to the sons of Jacob/Israel, and especially to Joseph, the beloved son by Rachel. But more than just the subject is changed; there is a noticeable difference in the literary and thematic style of the Joseph story compared to the preceding narratives. Whereas the stories of Abraham, Isaac, and Jacob are made up of loosely connected episodes, often independent of one another, the Joseph story is intricately plotted and complex. With the exception of the story of Judah and Tamar in Genesis 38 (clearly an intrusion), no episode between chapters 37 and 45 can be dropped easily without creating a hole in the plot. Here we have a finely crafted narrative with detailed plot and character development, the story of how Joseph was sold into Egyptian slavery by his jealous brothers, only to rise to high position in the government of the pharaoh. When a famine strikes Canaan, Joseph, after testing whether his brothers have matured over the twenty years since they sold him, brings his entire family to Egypt and settles them in the eastern Nile Delta.

All these ancestral narratives act as a prologue to the epic story of Israel's emergence as a nation that begins in the book of Exodus. God's two promises, that he would make the descendants of Abraham a great nation and that he would give them the land of Canaan, move toward fulfillment in the books of Exodus through Joshua.

There are many reasons to be skeptical of these narratives as historically accurate accounts of the lives of Israel's progenitors. Indications within the narratives suggest that they had a substantial prehistory as oral literature. Modern studies of oral transmission demonstrate that stories preserved in this manner do not primarily serve a historical or antiquarian purpose; rather, they are meant to present cultural values that must be passed on to younger generations. In modern parlance, their function is sociological rather than historical. Usually, historical facts quickly become garbled in an oral tradition, which adapts such information to make whatever point the story is intended to convey. Events and characters are often manufactured for the narrative purposes, and variant versions of a single story develop alongside one another.

Several of these characteristics appear in the book of Genesis. A number of stories occur in duplicate or variant versions. Thus there are two accounts of God changing Jacob's name to Israel (Gen. 32.28 and 35.10), two of the naming of the well called Beer-sheba (Gen. 21.31 and 26.33), and two of the naming of the town of Bethel (Gen. 28.19 and 35.15). In three different stories (Gen. 12.10–20; 20; 26.6–11) the patriarch (twice Abraham and once Isaac) tries to pass off his wife as his sister.

This repetition of stories, along with a recognition of more than one literary style, has suggested to most scholars that the current text of Genesis (and of Exodus through Numbers) has been spliced together from multiple literary sources. Three primary documents have been identified as the foundations of the final text of Genesis. Because they are anonymous, these sources are named according to notable characteristics. Scholars call the earliest the Yahwist source (abbreviated as J, following the German spelling of the divine name *Yahweh* [*Jahweh*]) because it characteristically uses the name *Yahweh* (traditionally rendered "The LORD") for God throughout the book of Genesis; in contrast, the two other sources avoid that name until it is revealed to Moses in the book of Exodus. Although most scholars would date this version of the origins of Israel to the tenth century BCE, others have recently argued for a date as late as the sixth century BCE. The second source is usually called the Elohist source (abbreviated E) because it regularly uses the Hebrew word *'elohim* ("God") as its title for Israel's deity. It is much more fragmentarily preserved in the biblical text, apparently edited into the J version only as a supplement, and is often dated to the ninth/eighth centuries BCE. The third source is called the Priestly document (abbreviated P) for its many priestly concerns. It is generally considered the latest of the sources (sixth century BCE), although it preserves considerable material that can be identified as much older.

Scholars have also observed a number of anachronisms in the stories, another characteristic of oral literature. For example, in Genesis 20 and 26, the king of Gerar is identified as a Philistine ruler. But the Philistines did not occupy the coast of Canaan until the twelfth century BCE, long after the events connected with him. Camel caravans are mentioned in Genesis 26 and 37, but camels were probably not used in this way before the beginning of the Iron Age (1200 BCE), when Israel was already emerging as a nation.

In addition, major elements of the stories can be shown to be artificial by comparing evidence drawn from other parts of the biblical text, as well as from archaeological discoveries. Take, for example, the idea that all of Israel descended from the twelve sons of Jacob. The book of Judges preserves an ancient poem from the late second millennium, usually called the Song of Deborah (Judg. 5.2–31), in a section of which the poet honors those tribes of Israel that joined in battle against a Canaanite coalition and castigates those that held back. Only ten tribes are named, and two of these are not tribes that occur in the canonical list of twelve. Apparently the twelve tribes did not unify as a political entity until the eleventh century, and when a tribe joined the confederation, the tribal name was personalized and the eponym placed in the list of the sons of Jacob/Israel. The other stories about the national origins of Israel's neighbors (that the Edomites descended from Esau, the Ammonites and Moabites from the offspring of Lot and his two daughters, and so forth) are likewise artificial, and were designed to indicate first-millennium political relationships rather than historical ancestry.

Accurate historical documentation was thus not a defining element in the development and transmission of these stories. Any attempt to make use of this material in reconstructing the prehistory of Israel requires great caution. There are, however, fascinating hints that suggest that genuine memories from the pre- and proto-Israelite periods survive in these stories. For example, the names of the characters in the ancestral narratives seem to be genuinely ancient. They are not names that were popular or characteristic in Israel during the Iron Age (1200–586 BCE), when the nation took shape and its oral tradition was first written down. Most of Israel's personal names incorporate some form of the divine name *Yahweh*, but not a single name in the ancestral stories does. This is particularly significant because two streams of the traditions, the Priestly source and the Elohist, insist that the name *Yahweh* was not known before the time of Moses, that is, before the emergence of Israel. The large number of non-Yahwistic names in the narratives suggests, then, that the ancestral names reflect a genuine pre-Israelite and pre-Yahwistic tradition.

Additionally, some of the stories seem to preserve descriptions of social and legal customs not characteristic of the later period of Israel's existence. For example, Abraham plants a sacred tamarisk tree at Beer-sheba (Gen. 21,33), and Jacob sets up a standing stone at Bethel (28.18–22); both practices would be prohibited in later Israel (see Exod. 34.13; Deut. 7.5; 12.2–4). Jacob marries both of Laban's daughters, Leah and Rachel (Gen. 29.16–30), without any issue being made of the situation, even though later Israel forbade marrying two sisters (Lev. 18.18).

One of the most significant elements from the protohistorical period found in these stories is their preservation of aspects of ancestral religion. Although the narratives presuppose that the religion of the ancestors and that of later Israel were the same, several aspects of proto-Israel's religion as recorded in Genesis differ significantly from Israel's religion as depicted in the rest of the Bible. We will return to this important subject at the end of this chapter.

But whatever the genuine memories that they preserve, the ancestral stories provide modern historians with few data to reconstruct the historical, cultural, and sociological developments from which eventually the Israelite nation arose. None of the names or events described in Genesis 12–50 appear in any other Near Eastern documents; none of the kings (several of whom are named) or pharaohs (who are never named) can be identified from outside sources. No specific date is provided for any of the characters in the narrative. And, not surprisingly, never do the stories attempt to see the actions of the ancestors from a wider political or cultural perspective. Because of this, a modern account of the history of this region during the second millennium BCE virtually never intersects with the stories of the ancestors in Genesis.

To understand the background of Israel's rise and the cultures that preceded it in the land, we must leave the Bible. Our primary sources instead must be the archaeologists' discoveries of material remains and inscriptions from sites across the Near East, especially those in Syria-Palestine. These finds have made it possible to reconstruct with some certainty the complicated but fascinating history of this region.

Syria-Palestine during the Late Third Millennium BCE

Before examining the history of this region, we should discuss nomenclature briefly. First, the term *Syria-Palestine* designates the area covered by the modern states of Syria, Lebanon, Israel, the recently formed Palestinian entity, and Jordan. Although the compound name may seem to suggest that this region existed as a single political and cultural continuum, like Mesopotamia or Egypt, such was not the case. Syria-Palestine was never culturally unified. Rather, it was the home of several distinct, but interrelated, contemporary cultures. The states of northern Syria, for example, developed differently from those on the Mediterranean coast, in southern Syria, and in Palestine. Northern Syria felt the strong influence of Mesopotamian culture and often looked in that direction for commercial opportunities and political models. This relationship owed largely to northern Syria's vital economic importance for southern Mesopotamia, which had to import many of its most basic needs, including stone and wood for construction. On the other hand, southern Syria and Palestine, along with the Mediterranean coastal cities, developed differently and in some aspects exhibit Egyptian influence. Each region of Syria-Palestine must be approached individually, so that its own distinctive cultural and political role in the history of the Near East can be delineated.

Second, what do the important geographical and ethnic terms *Canaan* and *Canaanite* mean? They have been used in a number of ways, by both ancient and modern writers, designating various areas and their inhabitants. During the second millennium BCE *Canaan* was often the name used for western Palestine (the area west of the Jordan River), whose northern boundary fluctuated between southern and central Lebanon. Modern scholars generally use the term in referring to the wider region in Syria-Palestine where a substantial cultural continuum defined as *Canaanite* can be discerned. Encompassing western Palestine, most of Lebanon, and coastal Syria as far north as Ugarit, this more extensive area was never considered a political or cultural unit by its ancient inhabitants. The close relationships among its cultures nevertheless often make this wider designation useful. In this chapter, the term *Canaan* will be used in its ancient sense when it designates a political territory, while *Canaanite* will refer to the culture of the larger region.

As described in the prologue, urban civilization arose in the Near East during the second half of the fourth millennium BCE. It appeared first in Mesopotamia and shortly thereafter in Egypt. Syria-Palestine, however, was only peripherally involved in this important development until early in the third millennium, when small fortified cities began to emerge throughout the region.

At present we know more about Palestine during the first half of the third millennium than about Syria, simply because many more southern than northern sites of the period have been excavated and more finds from them have been published. That evidence tells us that Palestine's population increased in the Early Bronze I period (3300–3100 BCE), but that not until about 3200 did walled fortifications first appear. During the Early Bronze Age II (3100–2700) and III (2700–2300), Palestine contained several fortified towns ranging in size from 8 to 22 hectares (20 to 55 acres), as well as many small villages scattered throughout the countryside. Early Bronze Age Palestinian civilization reached its climax during the period designated as Early Bronze III, when the population increased, more cities were founded, fortifications reached new levels of size and sophistication, temples and palaces (probably influenced by northern culture) were built, and a northern-oriented trade developed. While commercial links between Egypt and Palestine flourished during the Early Bronze I and II periods, Egypt apparently abandoned its overland route through Palestine early in the Early Bronze III period in favor of the sea route to Byblos in Lebanon, with which it formed a close relationship. The loss of the Egyptian trade may have forced the Palestinian cities to look toward Syria.

So far, no texts (besides a few small Egyptian examples from the Early Bronze I period) have surfaced in Early Bronze Age Palestine. Thus we know little about the political history of this era. Some general conclusions, however, can be drawn. The presence of substantial temples and palaces in the various towns suggests that Palestine was divided into a number of small city-states, each controlling its adjacent lands and unfortified villages. And although large-scale urbanism did not develop there (as it did in northern Syria), Palestine shared the cultural milieu of the age and was not isolated from it.

In northern Syria, more slender evidence suggests that life in the first half of the third millennium followed the same general pattern. Modest fortified towns developed shortly before 3000, but not major cities like those already flourishing in southern Mesopotamia. Sites that later expanded significantly remained small until 2500 BCE. For example, Tell Leilan, located on the Upper Habur River plain, during the first half of the third millennium was a town covering no more than 15 hectares (37 acres), a moderate size even by backwater Palestinian standards. Nor does Ebla, an important city located southwest of modern Aleppo, appear to have reached significant size before 2500.

About midway through the millennium, however, a striking change occurred in northern Syria. A number of very large cities suddenly sprang up, cities rivaling in size the major ones of southern Mesopotamia. Tell Leilan expanded from 15 hectares (37 acres) to nearly 100 hectares (247 acres); so did others in the vicinity, such as Tell Hamoukar, 48 kilometers (30 miles) east of Leilan, and Tell Mozan, 45 kilometers (28 miles) west of Leilan. The same expansion occurred toward the east (for example, Tell Taya, 101 hectares [250 acres]), to the west of the Habur (Tell Chuera, 100 hectares [250 acres], and Ebla, 61 hectares [150 acres]), and as far south as Qatna in central Syria (100 hectares [247 acres]). This extraordinary development must be related to the economic situation and suggests that the cities of northern Syria had taken charge of those natural and agricultural resources previously controlled by the cities of southern Mesopotamia and so vital to their interests. This new ascendancy altered the economic and political relationship between Syria and Mesopotamia, creating a new situation that the south apparently did not like—for in it the Syrian cities now were at least equal partners and no longer served as mere conduits through which commodities passed. The economic control that these large cities began to assert in Syria must have been perceived as a threat to Sumer's international trade. Shortly after 2500 BCE, there occurred the first known Mesopotamian military campaigns against Subir (the Habur region) and areas farther west, including Armanum and Ebla. In these clashes the rulers of Sumer and Akkad tried to consolidate the control over this area that southern Mesopotamia had once exercised with much greater ease. Rulers such as Eannatum of Lagash, Lugalzaggisi of Uruk, and Sargon and Naram-Sin of Akkad led their armies against the great cities of Syria. The repetitive nature of these invasions implies their lack of enduring success.

Our greatest insight into Syria during the last half of the third millennium BCE comes from the ancient city of Ebla, modern Tell Mardikh. Located some 56 kilometers (35 miles) southwest of Aleppo, Ebla is one of only three Syrian cities to have yielded written documents from this period (the others being Mari, discussed below, and Tell Beidar, where seventy tablets were found in 1993).

Tell Mardikh has been under excavation by an Italian team since 1964. During the 1960s and early 1970s, the excavators made a number of significant discoveries relating to Middle Bronze Age Ebla (2000 to 1600 BCE). But in 1973, Paolo Matthiae, the director, opened a field along the edge of the acropolis to examine the late-third-millennium stratum of the site, and came down on part of a royal palace. In 1974, 32 cuneiform tablets were found in a room of the palace, all of them economic documents and using the Sumerian script, although occasional words, written syllabically, belonged to a Semitic language. In 1975, a second room with texts (Room 2712) was excavated; it had about 200 tablets, along with some fragments. But it was eclipsed by the discovery of Room 2769, south of the main entry into the palace. Here thousands of tablets and fragments were unearthed in a main archive room. Many had been stored on shelves that had collapsed when the palace was destroyed by fire, so that the tablets lay in rows amid the rubble on the floor. By the end of 1975, there were 17,000 catalogued tablets and fragments, which when put together represented about 2,500 tablets, approximately 2,100 of which were found in the main archive. This number makes Ebla's one of the largest recovered archives of the third millennium BCE from the Near East.

The Ebla texts are difficult to decipher, and initial reports of direct links between them and the Bible have been proved wrong. What we now know is that approximately 80 percent of the tablets are economic and administrative documents, mostly recording royal dealings in a wide variety of goods—gold, silver, clothing, wood, olive oil, spices, and weapons, as well as livestock and their by-products. Textiles seem to have been particularly important commodities. The tablets give detailed information about the type of long-distance trade that was carried on by the great cities of Syria and Mesopotamia during this period. Scholarly suppositions about the importance of trade in the development of cities, as described above, seem borne out by the picture of Ebla's economic activity that these tablets give.

The administrative texts also show that Ebla controlled a large area of northern Syria, in part directly through appointed governors or local overseers and in part through client kings. They also reveal the highly developed bureaucracy of the city, which the king headed and which a wide range of subordinate officials administered.

Among the noneconomic tablets are a few literary texts (such as hymns); incantation texts; lists of animals, birds, professions, and the like; Sumerian vocabulary lists, some with Semitic equivalents; lists of geographical data; and a few mathematical texts. Unfortunately, most of these writings do not provide information about Eblaite culture because they are actually copies of Mesopotamian works used as part of scribal training at Ebla. A notable exception is a large vocabulary list that may give the Eblaite equivalents to hundreds of Sumerian words. This and other fragments of the local language show that the language of the city, called Eblaite, is closely related to Old Akkadian, a Mesopotamian Semitic dialect.

The tablets provide only the most superficial information about the religion of Ebla, but it is clear that many of the great West Semitic deities were worshiped there. Gods such as Ilu (El), Hadad, Athtar, Dagan, Rashap (biblical Resheph), Malik, and the sun-god (whose name is not spelled out) are all deities well known from later texts, including the Bible. The Ebla tablets also mention Sumerian and otherwise unknown deities.

Despite the wealth of information in the tablets, several basic facts about the Ebla archives remain unclear. For instance, the date of the archives is still in question. Matthiae, the archaeological director of the Ebla excavations, has argued that they should be dated to 2300–2250 BCE, based on the supposition that the palace in which they were found probably was destroyed by the Mesopotamian king Naram-Sin. But others, including the original epigraphist of the Ebla team, Giovanni Pettinato, have argued from the style of the script and other internal indications that the tablets were composed as much as two centuries earlier.

It is also not certain over what length of time the tablets were written. Originally they were thought to be the archives of at least five kings over a period of 100 to 150 years. But more recently scholars have tended to attribute the archive to the reigns of two or three kings at the most, covering a span closer to fifty years.

The Decline of the Early Bronze Age

The last quarter of the third millennium brought instability and decline throughout the ancient Near East. In Mesopotamia, the first great empire, that of the Akkad dynasty, collapsed in 2193 BCE, ushering in nearly a century of political fragmentation. In Egypt the Old Kingdom monarchy, which had produced the mighty pyramids, also dissolved after centuries of relative stability, leading to the chaos of the First Intermediate Period (2160–2010 BCE). In Syria-Palestine, no written documents survive to describe the events, but the archaeological record testifies to a serious economic and political decline there too.

In Palestine, evidence points to a nearly complete collapse of urban civilization at the end of the Early Bronze III period (2300 BCE), a situation that lasted about three hundred years. Habitation of the fortified cities ceased, with many destroyed violently and others simply abandoned. This period is now most commonly called Early Bronze IV, although some scholars designate it Middle Bronze I or Intermediate Early Bronze–Middle Bronze. At this time most of the population of Palestine, on both sides of the Jordan River, followed a pastoral existence, regularly migrating to various seasonal camps throughout the region. Such campsites provide few remains that archaeologists can locate. Only one town, Khirbet Iskander, occupying a 3-hectare (7.5-acre) site in Jordan, is known to have been surrounded by a wall during the Early Bronze IV period. Other villages existed in Transjordan at this time, but they were only pale reflections of the urban culture that had preceded them. Few settlements existed west of the Jordan River until about halfway through the period, when seasonal villages were constructed in the southern marginal lands.

Not until about 2000 did cities begin to revive in Palestine. Their reappearance marks the inauguration of the Middle Bronze Age (2000–1550 BCE), the period that saw the genesis of the Canaanite culture that would dominate Palestine throughout the second millennium. From this culture Israel would emerge around 1200 BCE.

In northern Syria, excavations have yet to give a clear picture of the Early Bronze IV period. Evidence from such sites as Ebla and Leilan bespeaks a significant decline during this time, and Leilan may have been abandoned for a while. Certainly this region avoided the complete urban collapse that befell Palestine. Thus, following its destruction, Ebla was rebuilt, although on a more modest scale. Despite the decline, however, the written sources of Sumer show that extensive trade continued to move through cities such as Ebla. Gudea of Lagash in southern Mesopotamia mentions trade dealings with several cities and regions in Syria, including Ebla and Ursu, during the twenty-second century. Cedars from the Lebanon Mountains, as well as wood, precious metals, and other goods from Anatolia (Asia Minor), continued to cross Syria as caravans brought them into Mesopotamia. This kind of trade also took place during the Ur III Dynasty (ca. 2112–2004 BCE). Except for these scraps of information from Sumer, we know little else from this time about northern Syria's social makeup or even the location of its primary political entities, although several city-states remained viable despite the chaos that erupted from time to time.

Northern Syria and Mesopotamia during the Middle Bronze Age

The opening of the second millennium BCE brings a much better documented period. An extraordinary number of archives have been discovered in cities of Syria and northern Mesopotamia that provide considerable insight into the political, social, economic, and religious situation in Syria and, to a lesser degree, Palestine. The incomparable texts from Mari on the middle Euphrates River have shed light on an important forty-year period of Syro-Mesopotamian history during the late nineteenth and early eighteenth centuries. The Mari tablets have been supplemented by smaller contemporary or near contemporary archives from other sites in the region, including Tell er-Rimah, Tell Asmar, Chagar Bazar, Tell Brak, Terqa, Tell Shemshara, and Tell Leilan. These sources show that Syria during the Middle Bronze Age formed a critical component of the political and cultural situation in the Near East, comparable in importance to the states of Mesopotamia during the same period. They also illuminate the two great empires of the Middle Bronze Age, that of Shamshi-Adad I, who controlled all of Upper Mesopotamia for twenty to thirty years, and that of Hammurapi (Hammurabi) of Babylon, who brought all of Mesopotamia under his sway.

The Middle Bronze Age in northern Syria and Mesopotamia has been called the age of the Amorite kingdoms. Most of the states in these regions were ruled during this era by kings whose names belong to a language called Amorite, a Northwest Semitic tongue that most likely originated in northeastern Syria.

The Amorites were a large and complex group of peoples, and their origins and spread across the Near East are only partially understood. Earlier studies of the Amorites tended to portray them as primarily nomadic tribespeople, sweeping in from the steppe land that borders the great Syrian desert, attacking the urban centers of Mesopotamia, and eventually bringing down Neo-Sumerian culture at the end of the third millennium. Following their triumph, so it was said, the crude Amorites found themselves overwhelmed by the advanced culture they had subdued, and they began to settle down and develop into city-dwellers. It is now clear that this portrait is distorted. Although there was a substantial pastoralist, seminomadic element among the Amorites, large portions of the tribes were sedentary folk, living both in agricultural villages and in the larger urban centers. By the mid-third millennium, in fact, considerable numbers of Amorites had migrated south into Mesopotamia, settling in the cities and becoming established yet distinct members of Mesopotamian society. The collapse of Neo-Sumerian culture cannot be attributed entirely, nor perhaps even largely, to invasions of nomadic Amorites; many other factors played a role in this decline. The Amorite clans who eventually gained dominance over various cities were those that had long since been fully urbanized and already had a substantial power base in the cities.

When written sources begin to appear toward the end of the nineteenth century BCE, most of the major cities of Mesopotamia and northern Syria were ruled by kings with Amorite names. Many of the cities that had played major roles in the Early Bronze Age were replaced by new cities that assumed political dominance.

The great archives of Mari supply the foundation for our understanding of Syria and Mesopotamia during the nineteenth and eighteenth centuries BCE. These archives were recovered from the ruins of the palace of Zimri-Lim, the last king of Mari before its destruction by Hammurapi of Babylon about 1760 BCE. The palace itself was an extraordinary building, sprawling over about 2.5 hectares (6 acres) and boasting more than 260 rooms, courtyards, and corridors on the ground level, as well as an undetermined number on the second floor. In this enormous building culminated centuries of construction that had begun in the late third millennium. Reports of its splendor spread widely in the Near East.

But more significant than the ruins of the palace for the study of Syro-Palestinian history and culture are the collections of tablets found within the city. Some twenty-five thousand tablets, dating between the twenty-fourth and eighteenth centuries, have come to light at Mari, most of them dating from its final decades during the late nineteenth and early eighteenth centuries, the period roughly contemporary with Shamshi-Adad I of Upper Mesopotamia and Hammurapi of Babylon. About two thousand of the tablets are letters, while most of the rest are economic, administrative, and juridical documents. Besides the tablets, a number of official royal inscriptions also provide much important information.

All of the documents are valuable in reconstructing the political, social, and economic history of the region, but the letters in particular give extraordinary insight into life at Mari and throughout Syro-Mesopotamia during one of the most interesting periods of its history. The letters come from a host of different people, including kings and administrators, Mari diplomats in other states, family members, priests, and prophets. Most were sent to the kings of Mari, who thus kept themselves abreast of what was going on in their kingdom and, at times, in the kingdoms round about. The letters provide inside information, not royal propaganda. Thus they give us a view, unmatched from any other archive, into the workings of an ancient royal city, as well as into individuals living through extraordinary times.

The tablets are particularly informative about the major political powers in Syria and Mesopotamia during this period. Farthest south was Larsa, an important city that during the reign of Rim-Sin (1822–1763) held sway over a significant part of southern Mesopotamia. About 200 kilometers (125 miles) to the northwest of Larsa lay Babylon, which first began to emerge as an important city in the late nineteenth century and rapidly reached its first period of political dominance during the 1760s, the latter years of Hammurapi's reign. Eshnunna (Tell Asmar), a city east of the Tigris, along the Diyala River, had made itself master of Assyria and the region west of the Tigris about the time the Mari archive begins, but later lost the area to Shamshi-Adad I. After Shamshi-Adad's death, Eshnunna's fortunes revived briefly, soon to be dashed with the rise of Hammurapi.

Along the middle Euphrates was Mari itself, whose fortunes waxed and waned during the period of the archives. It first appears as an independent state of consid-

erable strength under the rule of Yahdun-Lim. But not long after his death, the city
passed into the empire of Shamshi-Adad I. Mari later regained its independence and
prestige under Zimri-Lim, only to be overthrown forever by Babylon.

On the upper part of the Habur River was the city of Shekhna, in the land of
Apum. Shamshi-Adad I chose the town as the primary capital of his empire, renaming
it Shubat-Enlil. Recent discoveries at the site of Tell Leilan have shown decisively that
it should be identified as ancient Shekhna/Shubat-Enlil. Modern historians often call
Shamshi-Adad the first great king of Assyria, but this is misleading. He appears to
have belonged to an Amorite tribe whose homeland lay in northern Syria, which may
have been why he moved his capital to the Habur Plain. Assyria was the first part of
his empire, however; he had an enormous impact on the Assyrians' imperial ideology
and long survived in their memories as one of their greatest kings.

Farther west was Yamhad, a powerful state whose capital occupied the site of
modern Aleppo. Yamhad blocked both Shamshi-Adad I and Hammurapi of Babylon
from expanding into western Syria. During much of the Middle Bronze Age it was
the leading state of northern Syria. To the south of Yamhad, in central Syria, was the
major city-state of Qatna, closely linked with Mari by the trade route that connected
them across the desert via Tadmor/Palmyra. Moving south into northern Canaan, a
traveler would have reached the city of Hazor, which seems to be mentioned several
times in the Mari letters (although some of the references suggest that there was
another Hazor in central or northern Syria). The largest city in Canaan (72 hectares
[180 acres]), Hazor may have been the dominant Canaanite town of the Middle
Bronze Age, but it was on the periphery of Mari's economic horizon.

The Mari tablets, along with other sources, allow us to sketch the political history
of Syria and Mesopotamia in the early centuries of the second millennium BCE. The
written sources are particularly helpful in illuminating the rise of Shamshi-Adad and
the collapse of his empire following his death, in tracing developments at Mari before,
during, and after Shamshi-Adad's reign, and in chronicling Hammurapi's slow rise
to dominance over Mesopotamia.

The early years of Shamshi-Adad's long career as king are known only from a text
called the *Mari Eponym Chronicle*, first published in 1985. The *Chronicle* lists the
names of the years of Shamshi-Adad's reign, along with brief notes of important
events that occurred in each year. From it we know that he became king as a youth.
The original seat of his kingdom is not known, and his true rise to power took place
only after he had occupied his throne for approximately twenty years. In his twenty-
first regnal year, he conquered the city of Ekallatum, just north of Ashur. There he
ruled for three years before overthrowing Erishum, king of Assyria, and seizing his
victim's crown. From the capital city of Ashur, Shamshi-Adad began to expand his
empire westward, eastward, and southward, taking over the Habur region and the
Balikh River to the west, subduing Mari and other cities to the south, and expanding
eastward as far as Shusharra on the Little Zab River. Within a few years he had formed
a major empire and become the most powerful king of the region.

Having established his empire, Shamshi-Adad moved his own capital westward to
Shekhna, in the land of Apum, changing its name as we have seen to Shubat-Enlil.
Excavations since 1979 at Tell Leilan have begun to yield significant information
about this city. Several important public buildings from the time of Shamshi-Adad

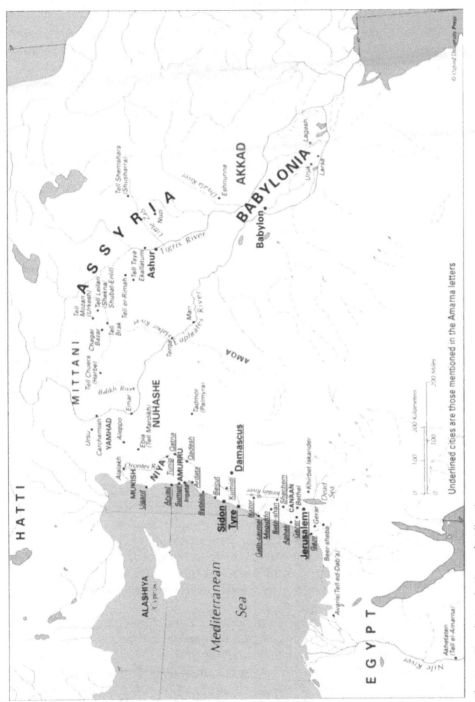

The Near East during the Second Millennium BCE

Underlined cities are those mentioned in the Amarna letters

have been excavated, including a large temple located on the acropolis and a palace in the lower city, which has produced about 600 tablets that date from the end of his reign (1781 BCE) until about 1725. While most of the tablets are administrative texts, approximately 120 are letters to two successors of Shamshi-Adad at Shekhna. In addition, fragments of 5 treaties between kings of Apum and their neighbors have been recovered. In 1991, archaeologists found another substantial administrative building, containing a group of 588 small receipt and disbursement tablets that date from the final years of Shamshi-Adad's reign. Still awaiting full study, these tablets promise to add much to our knowledge of Upper Mesopotamia during the eighteenth century BCE.

By the time he became the ruler of this empire, Shamshi-Adad had two grown sons, whom he appointed subrulers over parts of his realm. The elder son, Ishme-Dagan, resembled his father as an able soldier and administrator. The letters of Shamshi-Adad show the two men's close relationship and reveal the father's pride in his son. Ishme-Dagan was appointed ruler of Ekallatum in Assyria to keep control over the eastern part of the empire.

Much to his chagrin, the king's other son, Yasmah-Adad, proved incompetent and lazy. Shamshi-Adad placed him in charge of Mari, once he had captured that city, hoping that the young man would look after the southern part of the empire. But Shamshi-Adad found himself spending much of his time patching up Yasmah-Adad's poor handling of his job. The letters between father and son vividly show their strained relationship. "Are you a child and not a man? Have you no beard on your chin?" Shamshi-Adad wrote on one occasion. "While here your brother is victorious," he scolded another time, "down there you lie about among the women!" A letter survives in which Yasmah-Adad defended himself against one of his father's barbs, arguing that his subordinates must have been lying about him to his father.

The archives at Mari, as well as smaller ones from Tell Shemshara (Shusharra) and Tell er-Rimah, show Shamshi-Adad as an energetic administrator, constantly moving about his empire and involving himself in all the important—and many of the unimportant—decisions made in the cities that he ruled. It is a tribute to his personal abilities that he held his empire together so well.

Shamshi-Adad ruled for thirty-two years after his conquest of the city of Ashur. His empire, however, did not survive his death. Once he died, the city-states Eshnunna in the southeast and Yamhad to the west immediately began reestablishing their influence in the region. Ishme-Dagan maintained control of Assyria for a while, but he had to surrender the rest of the empire. Yasmah-Adad was overthrown in Mari within four years of Shamshi-Adad's death, and the previous dynasty returned, Zimri-Lim assuming the throne.

Most tablets from Mari come from the reign of Zimri-Lim. From them we not only learn many details about this king and his domain, but also gain important background information about his family, whom Shamshi-Adad had forced from the throne of Mari. This information explains much about Zimri-Lim's actions as king.

About the time of Shamshi-Adad's rise to power in Assyria, Mari was ruled by Yahdun-Lim, a member of the Simal (northern) branch of the Hanean tribal confederation. Inscriptions that survive from his reign depict him as a potent rival to Shamshi-Adad. But eventually Yahdun-Lim suffered a serious defeat in battle and was apparently assassinated by a member of Mari's royal court, Sumu-yamam, who may in fact have been Yahdun-Lim's son. Within two years Sumu-yamam himself fell victim to a palace coup. Shamshi-Adad thereupon saw his chance to expand southward and incorporate an important rival into his kingdom. Capturing Mari, he placed his son Yasmah-Adad on the throne.

The young Zimri-Lim, apparently either Yahdun-Lim's son or nephew, had fled Mari before Shamshi-Adad's conquest of the city and found asylum in Aleppo, the capital of Yamhad. Sumu-epuh, the king of Yamhad and Shamshi-Adad's most significant rival, presumably considered that offering support to Zimri-Lim as the legitimate heir to Mari's throne might give him valuable leverage against Shamshi-Adad.

After Shamshi-Adad's death, Zimri-Lim returned to Mari and regained his family's throne. In this he got substantial support from Yarim-Lim, Sumu-epuh's successor in Aleppo. Zimri-Lim not only came to dominate the land around Mari, but he also brought all of the middle Euphrates and the Habur River Valley under his sway and opened extensive trade relations throughout the Near East. He maintained good relations with Yamhad, marrying Yarim-Lim's daughter, Shiptu, early in his reign. But he also cultivated cordial relations with Babylon to the south and with Qatna to the west.

The correspondence of Zimri-Lim shows that he followed Shamshi-Adad's example in maintaining close contact with his governors, vassals, and officials. A wide variety of issues filled the letters dispatched to the palace at Mari. Messages from various governors kept him informed about the political situation throughout his realm. His ambassadors to other states sent regular reports. Numerous letters concerned relations between the government and the pastoral nomads who migrated through the middle Euphrates and the Habur region. Reports from members of his palace staff and his family also found their way into the archive, as did letters from religious personnel, often reporting omens, prophecies, or unusual dreams that seemed to affect the king.

Zimri-Lim's correspondence makes possible a partial account of his reign. Soon after assuming the throne he violently suppressed a rebellion among the Yaminite tribes, the southern members of the Hanean tribal confederation, who apparently saw no benefit in supporting a restoration of the Yahdun-Lim line at Mari, which belonged to a northern, Simalite clan. Of all the pastoral nomadic groups in Zimri-Lim's domains, the Yaminites remained the least cooperative. The tablets also indicate that Eshnunna tried to regain territory in the Habur region that it had controlled prior to Shamshi-Adad's reign, and they show that Zimri-Lim was deeply involved in opposing this attempt at expansion. We can also watch the slow rise to power of Hammurapi, king of Babylon, who for years remained a faithful ally of Zimri-Lim. But as he gained control of Lower Mesopotamia, Hammurapi suddenly turned on his old friend, overthrew him, and in 1760 BCE destroyed Mari. Thus abruptly ended its political power.

Following the overthrow of Mari, the middle Euphrates remained only briefly under Babylon's control. After Hammurapi died, the city of Terqa took Mari's place as the capital of the region. The land bore the name *Khana* during this time, but we have little information about its economy. Few material remains of the period have been excavated, and although recent digs at Terqa have produced some tablets, these come largely from private archives.

Western and Central Syria during the Middle Bronze Age

The most powerful kingdom to the west of the Euphrates was Yamhad, which thwarted the expansive plans not only of Shamshi-Adad but also of Hammurapi. It continued to dominate the north through the seventeenth century. Despite its importance, we know little about Yamhad during the Middle Bronze Age. Excavations at Aleppo, its capital, have uncovered no levels of this period and only one fragmentary inscription (as yet unpublished). We know Yamhad only from outside sources, such as the Mari tablets and a small but helpful archive from an important trade city along the Orontes River called Alalakh, over which ruled members of the royal family of Yamhad for about a century. The Alalakh archive dates to a few decades after the fall of Mari and provides information about the late eighteenth and part of the seventeenth centuries BCE.

The Mari letters illuminate the conflict between Shamshi-Adad and Yamhad. The two states were evenly matched, both militarily and politically. Thus Shamshi-Adad astutely formed an alliance with Qatna, the major power south of Yamhad, while the kings of Yamhad allied themselves with Hammurapi of Babylon, who opposed Shamshi-Adad from the southeast. After Shamshi-Adad's death, Yamhad played a major role in the sundering of his empire, as shown by Yarim-Lim's success in returning Zimri-Lim to the throne of Mari as a staunch ally of Yamhad.

Hammurapi of Babylon seems not to have attempted to conquer Yamhad, which continued to prosper into the seventeenth century. The Hittites, who rose to power in Anatolia in the seventeenth century, spoke of Yamhad as having a "great kingship," a term they used only in referring to the most powerful states. We do not know the full extent of Yamhad's domain, but the Alalakh tablets indicate that city to have been Yamhad's vassal, as Ugarit on the coast may also have been. To the south Yamhad controlled Ebla, and to the southeast it dominated Emar on the Euphrates. Yamhad maintained its leadership in northern Syria until the opening years of the sixteenth century. Then, during a burst of military energy, the Hittites of what is today central Turkey, led by King Mursilis I, attacked and destroyed Aleppo. Although the Hittites could not exploit their great victory, Yamhad never recovered from the disaster.

To the south of Yamhad the next major power was Qatna. Again, the site itself has provided no written sources, but the city is mentioned in the Mari tablets. It formed the western end of an important trade route that crossed the Syrian desert from Mari, running through Tadmor (Palmyra) to Qatna. This was a much shorter route from Mesopotamia to the southwestern Levant, cutting many miles off the road that looped north along the Euphrates, and it made Qatna one of the major trade hubs of the Near East. The kings of Qatna found it important to befriend whoever controlled Mari, the eastern terminus of the route. When Shamshi-Adad took control of Mari, Ishkhi-Adad of Qatna made an alliance with him, sealing it by marrying his daughter to Shamshi-Adad's younger son, Yasmah-Adad, now the king of Mari. Such an alliance also greatly benefited Shamshi-Adad, whose northern access to the Mediterranean Sea Yamhad blocked. But when Zimri-Lim returned to Mari, the new king of Qatna, Amut-pi-el, became his ally, and they too maintained cordial relations. The Mari letters also indicate that Amut-pi-el made peace during this period with Yamhad. Otherwise little is currently known of Qatna.

Even more obscurity shrouds the area south of Qatna. The Mari letters called it the land of Amurru ("the West"), which appears to have consisted of several small kingdoms. We know that the Damascus area was known as the land of Apum, the name also given to the land around Shubat-Enlil in northern Syria. This southerly Apum is mentioned in an Egyptian document, and also apparently in as-yet-unpublished Mari letters. It is here that Egyptian influence begins to outweigh that of Mesopotamia and northern Syria.

The Lands of Canaan and Egypt during the Middle Bronze Age

The land of Canaan stretched to the south of present-day Damascus. In the second millennium BCE, its culture bore some resemblance to that in Syria, but at the same time it had distinctive features. The Canaanite cultural sphere covered all of Palestine, as well as modern Lebanon and coastal Syria as far north as Ugarit. Only peripherally did Palestine enter into the affairs of northern Syria; the predominant outside influence was Egyptian. Complex relationships united the land of Canaan and Egypt during this period, with cultural influences flowing in both directions. Unfortunately, little documentation survives that might lift the veil on Canaan and its affairs. The paltry written sources include a few texts from Egypt and even fewer from Canaan itself. During the first part of the Middle Bronze Age (2000–1700 BCE, a period contemporary with the Middle Kingdom of Egypt), inscriptions point to a significant Egyptian role in the economic, and perhaps also the political, situation of Canaan. Beginning in the early eighteenth century, Semitic migrants from Canaan began drifting into the delta region of Egypt, and eventually they came to dominate it.

In the centuries between 2300 and 2000, Palestine was largely home to pastoral nomads, but during the twentieth century BCE, a revival of the region's urban life led to the reoccupation of most of the old Early Bronze Age cities and the founding of several new ones. Most cities were fortified with huge ramparts that required constant remodeling and reinforcement throughout the Middle Bronze Age. For the most part the cities did not approach the size of the large towns of northern Syria, with only one real exception—Hazor, which at 72 hectares (180 acres) was larger than Ebla. Most Middle Bronze Canaanite towns covered less than 20 hectares (50 acres). As in the Early Bronze Age, Palestine remained on the periphery of the predominant cultures of the Near East, but it was neither isolated nor unsophisticated.

The revival in Canaan coincides with a similar upsurge in Egypt. The end of the third millennium had constituted a period of political and economic disintegration for the ancient land of the Nile, but Egypt's disruption ended about 2000 BCE, when the country was reunited under the rule of the pharaohs of Dynasty 12. Archaeological evidence from various sites in Palestine indicates that the revival of Egypt brought a restoration of Egyptian trade into Canaan. Byblos, on the Lebanese coast, had been the primary trade port for Egypt during much of the third millennium, and it became such again. But unlike the situation during the Early Bronze III period (2700–2300

BCE), when the Egyptians' sea trade with Byblos had simply obviated their need to import goods overland through Canaan, during the Middle Bronze Age a considerable Egyptian economic influence spread all over the land.

Middle Bronze Age Canaan has yet to produce any significant literary remains. Accordingly, written historical sources are confined to documents from surrounding states, especially Egypt. We gain some sense of the political makeup of the region from the Execration Texts, Egyptian magical texts that name potential enemies of Egypt. The lists were written on bowls or figurines, which were then broken as part of a ceremony believed to render the enemies helpless. Among the foes named in these texts are numerous Canaanite princes, the rulers of small city-states, none of which compared in extent or power to those in Syria.

The close connections between Egypt and Canaan took a surprising turn as the Middle Bronze Age unfolded. Excavations in the Nile Delta have shown that as early as the nineteenth century, large numbers of Canaanite immigrants began to settle there, building towns similar to those in Canaan. Tell ed-Dab'a, ancient Avaris, is such a town. By the mid-seventeenth century, the Semitic population in the delta had managed to gain political control of much of northern Egypt, with Avaris as their capital. During the next century (1650–1550) their domination widened, encompassing most of Lower and Middle Egypt. Only partially did they assimilate Egyptian cultural characteristics. The Egyptians called these nonnative kings *heqaw khasut*, "rulers of foreign lands," a designation rendered into Greek during the first millennium as "Hyksos." This extraordinary period, when northern Egypt became virtually an extension of Canaan, finally ended when the native Egyptian rulers of Thebes (Dynasty 17) launched a revolt against the Hyksos and eventually reestablished native political authority over the north. Following the reunification of Egypt, the rulers of Dynasty 18 carried the attack into Canaan itself in a series of military campaigns. Egypt's emergence as a new imperial power was one of the major forces that brought the Middle Bronze Age to a close in Canaan.

We cannot leave our discussion of Middle Bronze Age Canaan without noting that this region produced one of the most important innovations in the history of civilization. About 1700 BCE, someone in Canaan, needing a notational system to keep records but lacking time or opportunity to master either of the complex writing systems available at the time, Akkadian or Egyptian, created the alphabet. This brilliant achievement would revolutionize the development of writing and literacy throughout the Western world. The new script used drawings of common objects, but they designated only the first sound of the name of each object. Since Canaanite, like most languages, had only about thirty sounds, a compact, easy-to-learn system of writing had been invented. This is the beginning of what is popularly known as the Phoenician alphabet (*Phoenician* is the Greek word for *Canaanite*), the ancestor of every Western alphabet, including the one you are reading now.

The Late Bronze Age

During the Late Bronze Age (1550–1200 BCE), new imperial powers emerged in the Near East. Each sought to dominate Syria-Palestine, motivated partly by that region's strategic location in the trade network. One of these newcomers, Mitanni, took shape in northeastern Syria itself and came to control all of northern Syria for nearly two centuries. The second primary power was the revived Egypt, which under the pharaohs of the New Kingdom (1550–1069) ruled an empire that encompassed all of Palestine and southern Syria and contended for control of central Syria, a goal that naturally brought it in conflict with Mitanni. The third state, Hatti in central Turkey, did not emerge as an interregional power until the rise of King Suppiluliumas in the mid-fourteenth century. Once on the scene, however, Hatti replaced Mitanni as the master of northern Syria and as Egypt's primary rival. Syria-Palestine thus served as both arena and object of conflict between the northern states and Egypt.

Aleppo, the old capital of Yamhad, sank to lesser status after its destruction by the Hittites in the early sixteenth century. It managed, however, to retain some importance during the Late Bronze Age. To the northeast of Aleppo was Carchemish, a well-fortified city located at a strategic crossing of the Euphrates River, which came to play an important part in the political drama of the period.

Northwest Syria was divided into several states, including Mukish, with its capital at Alalakh, Ugarit on the coast, and Niya and Nuhashe in the interior. Farther south, three important cities lay on or near the Orontes River—Tunip, Qatna, and Qadesh/Kinza. These cities formed the buffer zone between the spheres of influence of the northern and southern powers; each had to play dangerous political games, striving either to maintain its independence or to choose one imperial power as its protector. To their west lay the area known as Amurru, another bone of contention between the great powers. Several important coastal cities, including Arvad, Sumur, Gubla (Byblos), Beruta (Beirut), Sidon, and Tyre, played an active commercial role during this period. Between the Lebanon and the Anti-Lebanon mountain ranges were the states of Tahshi in the north and Amqa in the south. The area around Damascus—at an earlier date called Apum—was now known as Upi. Amqa and Upi marked the northernmost bounds of the area regularly controlled by Egypt throughout the Late Bronze Age. In Canaan proper the land was divided into more than a dozen small, weak city-states, none of which had any political clout, with Hazor, Shechem, Megiddo, Gezer, and Jerusalem as the most prominent.

The end of the Middle Bronze and beginning of the Late Bronze Age saw the expansion of an important population group known as the Hurrians in northern Syria and, later, as far south as Canaan. Mitanni, in northeast Syria, dominated by Hurrians, became the most significant Hurrian power of the period, controlling the northern half of the Near East by the early fifteenth century. Despite its great importance, however, we know little about Mitanni. Its capital city, Washukani, is one of the few major capitals that remain as yet unidentified, and only a few Mitannian documents have been found in the archives of other cities. It is clear, however, that after 1470, Mitanni, under King Saushtatar, extended its sway over all of northern Syria to the Mediterranean, as well as eastward through Assyria. The states of central Syria as far south as Qadesh, on the southern end of the Orontes, may also have become Mitannian vassals.

While Mitanni was becoming established in northern Syria, Egypt was beginning its expansion from the south. Having expelled the Semitic-speaking Hyksos from the delta, the Egyptians apparently began to see both the economic and the political value of controlling an empire. The first three kings of Dynasty 18—Ahmose, Amenhotep I, and Thutmose I—moved quickly to seize control of the Canaanite city-states in

Palestine. Thutmose I (1504–1492) marched his troops all the way to the Euphrates River in the second year of his reign.

Thutmose III (1479–1425) brought Egypt to its greatest power during the New Kingdom. In a series of campaigns he managed to impose Egyptian control over Canaan, as well as most of southern and central Syria. His first campaign brought Thutmose up against a large coalition of Canaanite and Syrian city-states led by the central Syrian city of Qadesh. The enemies clashed in a famous battle in the Jezreel Valley in northern Canaan. After a brief skirmish, the coalition members hastily retreated into the fortified town of Megiddo, which Thutmose besieged. After seven months the trapped rulers surrendered, all then being forced to pay a heavy tribute and to take an oath of loyalty. Thutmose's inscriptions claim that the coalition was composed of 330 princes, but this is an exaggeration. A more realistic number is found in the temple of Amun at Karnak, containing a list of 119 towns whose rulers are said to have been captured in the siege of Megiddo. More likely, this list enumerates all the towns and villages that came under Thutmose's control as a result of the campaign, whether or not their rulers had capitulated at Megiddo. Canaan was now firmly in Egyptian hands.

His appetite whetted, Thutmose began his efforts to secure control of Syria as well. He built a fleet of ships that allowed him to sail his army to the Syrian coast, thus saving the men a grueling march through Canaan. Three campaigns against the powerful city-states of Tunip and Qadesh/Kinza succeeded only partially, but they prepared the way for Thutmose's greatest military achievement in his thirty-third year, when he and his army marched to the vicinity of Carchemish in northern Syria and crossed the Euphrates, meeting only minor resistance from Mitanni.

But control of the kingdoms of Syria was always tenuous for the Egyptians, and Thutmose found himself fighting in northwest Syria during several subsequent years. At his death the Syrian states quickly rebelled, obliging his successor Amenhotep II (1427–1400) to lead three campaigns into Syria to enforce Egyptian control. But these came early in his reign; during his latter years Amenhotep appears to have given up. Under Thutmose IV a peace treaty between Egypt and Artatama of Mitanni presumably delineated each empire's sphere of influence in Syria. Evidently both sides realized that an equilibrium had been achieved, for the treaty was renewed by the successors of the two kings, Amenhotep III of Egypt and Shuttarna II of Mitanni. The boundaries between the two states probably coincided with those that were in force later during the mid-fourteenth century. Coastal Syria as far north as Ugarit came under Egyptian control, along with southern Syria—the Damascus region, the Biqa Valley of Lebanon (Amqa), and the lands of Qadesh and Amurru. Qatna and the northern states, including Niya and Nuhashe, fell within the Mitannian orbit.

Shuttarna of Mitanni probably saw good reason to keep the peace with Egypt because he was threatened on two sides by growing powers. In the late fifteenth century Assyria, which had been under Mitannian control for about a century, became increasingly independent. And in Anatolia, the Hittites briefly repeated their earlier attempt to extend their influence into northern Syria; they were not successful, and by the end of the fifteenth century they were fighting for their lives against enemies in Anatolia itself. Still, they could not be counted out, and Shuttarna did not need any complications in his dealings with the Egyptians.

The final king of independent Mitanni was Tushratta, a younger son of Shuttarna. Despite coming to his throne in an irregular way, he maintained his authority securely for several years. He continued cordial relations with Egypt, sending his daughter Tadu-Hepa to marry Amenhotep III in a gesture reaffirming the close ties between the two countries. But relations with Amenhotep IV (Akhenaten) deteriorated after Akhenaten sent Tushratta wooden statues covered with gold foil, not the solid gold statues that Amenhotep III had promised.

Mitanni's downfall was, however, at hand. Tushratta was not prepared to face the extraordinary recovery of Hatti shortly after the great king Suppiluliumas came to its throne. Suppiluliumas was a remarkably able soldier and an astute politician. He saw Mitanni as his primary rival for control of Syria and set about forming alliances to weaken Tushratta's position. Eventually he marched his army directly into Mitanni and attacked its capital, Washukani. Tushratta apparently had no means to resist the Hittite advance and fled his capital before Suppiluliumas arrived. Meeting no Mitannian opposition, the Hittite king turned westward and promptly conquered all of northern Syria except for Carchemish.

Suppiluliumas was apparently prepared to stop with the conquest of the states in the Mitannian sphere of influence, but the king of Qadesh/Kinza, a vassal of the Egyptians, attacked the Hittite army. Suppiluliumas easily defeated the Qadeshite army and then marched southward, taking over Qadesh and perhaps also Amurru. By the end of Suppiluliumas's reign, then, all of central Syria, as well as the coast, lay under Hittite control, including the former Egyptian vassals of Ugarit, Amurru, and Qadesh. Such a violation of Egyptian territory would not go unchallenged for long.

Tushratta, the king of Mitanni, meanwhile, met his end, creating further instability. One of his own sons murdered him. With Assyrian help a puppet ruler, Shuttarna III, took control of what was left of Mitanni. Outraged, the Hittite king Suppiluliumas within a short time sent an army under his own son to place Shattiwaza, another son of Tushratta, on the throne as a Hittite vassal.

Mitanni had by now become a mere bone of contention. After the death of Suppiluliumas, the Assyrians began a long struggle to wrest for themselves the control of Mitanni, and from the late fourteenth to the end of the thirteenth centuries, its allegiance swerved back and forth. But it never played an independent role again. Northern Syria to the west of the Euphrates, however, continued to be part of the Hittite empire. In the seventh year of the reign of Mursilis II, the son and second successor of Suppiluliumas, Nuhashe and Qadesh/Kinza, rebelled with the support of Egyptian troops dispatched by Pharaoh Horemhab. This revolt was suppressed, but the Egyptians were not ready to relinquish their claims to Qadesh and Amurru.

With the ascent to the throne of Seti I in the early thirteenth century, a final period of hostilities began between the Egyptians and the Hittites. Central Syria was the battleground and the prize. After suppressing revolts in Palestine, Seti marched north and reconquered both Qadesh and Amurru. The Hittite archives record the official withdrawal of Benteshina, ruler of Amurru, from his alliance with Hatti. This brought the Egyptian sphere of influence to its greatest extent since the rise of Hittite power several decades earlier.

Rameses II ascended the throne of Egypt in 1279 BCE and in his fifth year met

Muwatallis of Hatti at one of the most famous battles of the ancient Near East, the battle of Qadesh. Here Rameses found himself caught by surprise by the Hittite forces, barely escaping with his life. Although his inscriptions portray the outcome as a great victory, it was in fact a disaster for the Egyptians. Rameses and his troops retreated southward, followed by the Hittite army, which temporarily occupied most of southern Syria and regained more permanent possession of Amurru. Over the next sixteen years other battles raged in Syria. Although Egyptian sources claim several victories, these were at best substantial exaggerations, for the Hittites remained lords of central Syria for as long as Hatti existed.

Eventually, in Rameses' twenty-first year, he and Hattusili III negotiated a peace treaty that ended the warfare between the two countries. Although boundaries are not mentioned in the treaty, they must have coincided substantially with those at the end of Suppiluliumas's reign, with Hatti in control of Amurru and Qadesh, and Egypt retaining southern Syria, including Upi and Amqa.

From the mid-thirteenth century on, the political situation in Syria-Palestine remains obscure. The end of the thirteenth century, however, saw the beginning of the extraordinary collapse of Late Bronze Age culture. The collapse would lead to the disappearance of Hatti, the fall of the New Kingdom in Egypt, and the decline— temporary, to be sure—of Assyria and Babylonia. Numerous major cities throughout northern Syria would be destroyed, and the classical Canaanite civilization in Palestine and coastal Syria would be eclipsed.

Exactly how all these cataclysmic changes happened is unclear. But the results are indisputable. We know that the entire complex network of trade that bound together the Near East and its neighbors, including Cyprus and Greece, simply collapsed. Many populations appear to have migrated, their movements sometimes accompanied by great violence. Hatti apparently fell to such hordes. Egypt was attacked by groups called "Sea Peoples." They were repelled from Egypt, but the Egyptians could not stop them from taking over the Canaanite coast. The Philistines, who conquered the southern coast of Canaan and came to play an important role in the history of Israel, were among these Sea Peoples. Another group, called the Tjeker, appropriated land farther north on the Canaanite coast.

Recent environmental studies have suggested that two severe droughts at the end of the thirteenth and the beginning of the twelfth centuries extended all across Europe and the Near East. These droughts would have caused food shortages that may be the key to the collapse of economic systems throughout the area and the concomitant migrations. It was amid this collapse that Israel emerged.

The Amarna Letters

Written remains from two sites stand out for the insights they provide into the social and cultural milieu during the late second millennium BCE. These are the famous Amarna letters and the tablets from the city of Ugarit. Part of the archives of Pharaoh Amenhotep IV (Akhenaten; 1352–1336), the Amarna letters were found in the ruins of his capital city, Akhetaten (modern el-Amarna). Most were discovered by peasants in 1886–87, sold to antiquities dealers, and eventually bought by museums in Europe and Cairo. Currently 382 tablets are known to scholars, of which 350 are letters, most from the reign of Akhenaten. Forty-four of these letters were written by rulers of foreign states not under Egyptian control—Mitanni, Assyria, Babylonia, Arzawa, Alashiya (Cyprus), and Hatti. Most of the others are from Palestine and southern or central Syria, mainly sent by vassal kings.

Almost all of the letters are in Akkadian, the Mesopotamian tongue that was the international language of the day. Even when the king of Hatti wrote to the king of Egypt, the language used was Akkadian, not Hittite or Egyptian. The quality of the Akkadian varies widely in the letters. The international correspondence is generally well written, although it and also many of the letters from northern Syria contains a number of Hurrianisms, as one might expect from the Hurrian influence in that area.

The letters from southern Syria and Canaan proper for the most part are written in terrible Akkadian, loaded with mistakes and filled with Canaanisms. Some of the texts may be described as written virtually in Canaanite using Akkadian script. Actually, scholars are happy that the scribes did such a poor job, because the Canaanisms in the texts have become a primary source of information about the Canaanite language during the Late Bronze Age. Several detailed studies of the grammars of the various letters have shed light on the prehistory of biblical Hebrew, itself a Canaanite dialect that developed directly out of the language reflected in many of these texts.

Out of the Amarna letters emerges important insight into the structure of the city-states that made up Late Bronze Age Canaan. These small states were ruled by "kings" who seem to have spent much of their time contending with their neighbors. A surprising number of the vassals' letters to the pharaoh plead for Egyptian military assistance against another vassal who, the writer claims, has rebelled against the pharaoh and is now threatening the writer's city. Indeed, say many of the writers, the whole land has rebelled against the king, except of course his majesty's faithful servant. This rebellion often takes the form of the enemy kings turning their lands over to people called the Apiru. Although there is considerable controversy as to the exact definition of the term, the Apiru appear to have been a class of persons in Canaan who had withdrawn their allegiance from any of the states in the region and fled into the countryside, often living by banditry. It is a decidedly pejorative term in the Amarna letters. Writers from both sides of the hostilities take every opportunity to accuse their enemy of becoming an Apiru, while proclaiming their own loyalty to the pharaoh.

Let us, for example, hear Abdi-Hepa, king of Jerusalem:

> To the king my lord say: Message of Abdi-Hepa your servant. At the feet of the king my lord I have fallen seven and seven times. Here is the deed that Milkilu and Shuwardatu have done against the land—they have led the troops of Gezer, the troops of Gimtu, and the troops of Qiltu against the land of the king my lord. They have taken Rubutu. The land of the king has gone over to the Apiru. And now, in addition to this, a town belonging to Jerusalem, Bit-Ninurta by name, a town belonging to the king, has gone over to the men of Qiltu. May the king listen to Abdi-Hepa, your servant, and send archers to restore the land of the king to the king. If there are no archers, the land of the king will go over to the Apiru! The act against the land was done at the orders of Milkilu and Shuwardatu, along with Gintu. So let the king take care of his land! (El Amarna, 290; my translation)

Simultaneously, however, Milkilu, king of Gezer and enemy to Abdi-Hepa, thus appeals to the pharaoh:

> To the king, my lord, my god, my sun-god say: Message of Milkilu, your servant, the dust under your feet. I have fallen at the feet of the king my lord seven and seven times. Let the king my lord know that the war against me and against Shuwardatu is powerful. Thus may the king my lord save his land from the power of the Apiru. If not, may the king my lord send chariots to get us, lest our servants kill us! Further, let the king my lord ask Yanhamu, his servant, about what is going on in the land. (El Amarna, 271; my translation)

And also Shuwardatu, whose royal city is not known, made sure that the pharaoh heard his side:

> To the king my lord, my god, my sun-god say: Message of Shuwardatu, your servant, the dust under your feet. I have fallen at the feet of the king my lord, my god, my sun-god, seven and seven times. The king my lord allowed me to make war against Qiltu. I made war, and it is now at peace with me. My town has been restored to me. Why has Abdi-Hepa written to the men of Qiltu saying, "Accept some silver and follow me"? May the king know that Abdi-Hepa has seized my town! Further, may the king conduct an investigation. If I have taken a man or a single piece of cattle or a donkey from him, then he is within his rights! Further, Labayu, who had previously taken our towns, is dead, but now, Abdi-Hepa is another Labayu, and he is the one who is conquering our towns. Thus may the king pay attention to his servant because of this act, but I will not do anything until the king responds by a word to his servant. (El Amarna, 280; my translation)

Who is the aggressor here, and who is the victim? Perhaps the pharaoh and his court were as uncertain as we.

The wars described in these letters were not large-scale events. When the vassal rulers specify the number of troops they need, they rarely seek more than a hundred, and sometimes only fifty. Nor should we imagine that the battles were major assaults on heavily fortified cities. In fact, few of the major cities in Late Bronze Age Palestine had any walls surrounding them. Heavy fortifications appear to have been discouraged by the Egyptian administration, perhaps even forbidden.

The texts indicate that the Egyptians divided their Syro-Palestinian empire into three large provinces, each administered by an official located in a city under Egyptian control. The area of Palestine and the coast up to Beruta (Beirut) was controlled from Gaza on the southern coast. The coastal region to the north of Beirut and the area covered by the kingdom of Amurru fell within the sphere of the coastal town of Sumur, probably Tell Kazel in Syria. The lands to the east of the Lebanon Mountains, northward toward Qadesh and southward to Hazor, answered to the commissioner at Kumidi, located in the Biqa Valley of Lebanon. In addition, the Egyptians established towns in which small numbers of Egyptian troops were stationed; some of these towns have been excavated, including Beth-shan, Jaffa, and Aphek.

The conflicts between vassals evident in the letters have led some scholars to conclude that during the Amarna period Egyptian authority in Asia had largely collapsed and that Akhenaten took no interest in foreign affairs, being too busy with his reforms at home. Others, however, have argued that the letters indicate that

Egyptian administration in the provinces was intact. Egyptian policy allowed the rulers of the city-states considerable freedom in running their domains as long as they paid the required tribute and fostered trade, and the Egyptians kept out of the internal conflicts unless their own interests were jeopardized. But when a ruler began to expand his control over an extensive area, the Egyptians did intervene. Thus at the end of the reign of Akhenaten, when the northern kingdom of Amurru defected to the Hittite camp, arrangements were made to send a major Egyptian force to oppose the Hittite encroachment. This campaign had to be postponed when Akhenaten died, but the evidence does not sustain the notion that Egyptian administration of the provinces had collapsed.

One Canaanite town—Shechem—did manage to expand its territory significantly. Under its ruler Labayu and his sons, the town came briefly to control much of central Canaan. Labayu had already begun his expansion before the letters that we possess were written, and he had taken control of part of the coastal plain. He apparently made treaties with the rulers of Gezer and Gath-carmel that allowed him to turn his attention toward the Judean hills, notably Jerusalem. However, the Egyptians eventually sent troops to bring Labayu to Egypt so that he might account personally to the king for his deeds. On the journey he was murdered by his enemies, and his small empire collapsed. Some time later, Labayu's sons tried to regain control over the coastal regions west of Shechem and also made conquests to the east of the Jordan River. This second attempt at expansion by Shechem does not seem to have been successful.

The situation in Syria was much more problematic for Egypt, particularly given the rise of the new Hittite empire under Suppiluliumas. The complexities can be seen in the activities surrounding the state of Amurru during the Amarna period. Amurru became a significant power in central and southern Syria under the rule of Abdi-ashirta and his son Aziru. Abdi-ashirta's origins are obscure, but from humble beginnings he appears to have risen to a position of great power by organizing the numerous malcontents, or Apiru, in the mountainous regions of Lebanon. Using this army, he then attacked and captured several important coastal cities, including Ardata and Irqata. His imperial dreams climaxed with his seizure of the city of Sumur, the capital of one of the Egyptian provinces.

We can follow Abdi-ashirta's progress primarily through the letters of Abdi-ashirta's greatest—or at least most vocal—enemy, Rib-Addi, the king of Byblos on the Lebanese coast. Rib-Addi wrote or received sixty-seven of the letters preserved from the Amarna archive, many times more than any other ruler. In his letters Rib-Addi begs repeatedly for the pharoah's help to oppose Abdi-ashirta. He accuses Abdi-ashirta of rebellion against the pharaoh, whose last faithful vassal on the coast he claims to be. The pharaoh's consistent policy of ignoring Rib-Addi frustrated the latter to no end, and several of the petty king's letters take on a startlingly bitter tone. At one point the pharaoh sent Rib-Addi a reply asking why he wrote so many letters, a not-so-subtle way of telling him to stop (El Amarna, 106).

The Egyptians were in fact keeping a close eye on Abdi-ashirta, and as long as they thought he would stay within the Egyptian orbit, they did not interfere with his expansion. Eventually, however, they became alarmed at his increasing power, and he was killed. The exact circumstances remain cloudy.

This was not the end of Amurru or of Abdi-ashirta's family, however. Eventually his sons, led by Aziru, recaptured the area that had been controlled by their father. Again capturing Sumur was the climactic victory, and again Rib-Addi of Byblos fired off letter after letter warning the pharaoh of treachery. Like his father, Aziru carefully cultivated the Egyptian court, assuring them of his faithfulness. The tactic worked, for Aziru was accepted as a vassal and even made a trip to Egypt without problems. He returned to Sumur just when the Hittites were making important advances into the area, perhaps during Suppiluliumas's first Syrian war. Despite being a newly confirmed Egyptian vassal, Aziru almost immediately switched sides and pledged himself a vassal to Hatti. Expanding his area of influence to Tunip, all the while he sent letters to Egypt expressing his great loyalty to the pharaoh! Eventually the Egyptians realized what was happening (too late to save their loyal nuisance Rib-Addi) and understood that they had lost much of the northern part of their empire.

The Amarna letters offer a remarkable picture of the kaleidoscopic politics of Canaan during the century prior to the emergence of Israel. Filled with a welter of tiny, contentious city-states, the land revealed in this Egyptian archive corresponds well to the land of Canaan as described in the ancestral narratives of Genesis, as well as in Numbers, Joshua, and Judges.

Ugarit

The textual discoveries at Ugarit (modern Ras Shamra) rival the great Mesopotamian tablet finds in their impact on the study of the Bible and ancient Israelite religion. Ugarit lies on the coast of northern Syria, just north of the modern city of Latakia, and the site has undergone regular excavation from 1929 to the present, except for a hiatus in the 1940s. The original excavator, Claude Schaeffer, decided almost at the outset to concentrate largely on the remains of the final major phase of occupation, and thus about half of the Late Bronze Age city has been uncovered. No other Syro-Palestinian city from this period is so well known. The royal palace and several other major public administrative buildings have been uncovered, as have some temples and extensive residential areas of both the upper class and of the more modest folk.

The archaeological remains of Ugarit are spectacular. The palace, an enormous edifice built and expanded between the fifteenth and thirteenth centuries BCE, covered nearly a hectare (over 2 acres), boasting some ninety rooms and six large courtyards on the ground floor, as well as a considerable second story. On the highest part of the site were found the remains of two impressive temples. One was the temple of Baal, Ugarit's patron deity, and the other may have been dedicated either to the head of the Ugaritic pantheon, El, or to Dagan, Baal's father according to the mythology.

Although the material finds are significant, they pale beside the tablet discoveries. In the first excavation season Schaeffer opened a field on the highest area within Ugarit and immediately came upon a well-built house with clay tablets strewn across its floors. To his great surprise the tablets were not in Akkadian cuneiform, or in any other script known at the time. The script was cuneiform, but it had only thirty different characters, none of which were immediately identifiable. With such a limited number of signs it was assumed that the script must be alphabetic, and scholars deciphered it quickly, showing as well that the texts were written in a West Semitic language, related to Canaanite. It was immediately dubbed Ugaritic.

The house was apparently the dwelling of the high priest of Baal, whose temple stood nearby. The tablets found in the house over the first four seasons of excavation were the priest's library. The most important component of this library was a collection of myths and epic poems, the only such collection preserved from Canaan. These provide us with considerable insight into the nature of the Canaanite pantheon: El, the father of the gods and their king; Baal, the storm and fertility deity and the active ruler of the gods, though not without dissension; Asherah, the wife of El and mother of the gods; and Anat, the volatile sister of Baal and goddess of war.

The most significant mythic texts are a series of tablets that feature Baal as their main character. Several of the tablets are fragmentary, but three major stories about Baal are substantially recoverable. The first, the story of Baal's conflict with the god Yamm (literally, "sea" or "ocean"), climaxes with a battle between the two in which Baal is victorious. A number of thematic parallels link this episode to the famous Babylonian creation story, *Enuma Elish*. The latter tells the story of the battle between the storm-god Marduk, patron deity of Babylon, and the goddess Tiamat ("ocean"), which ended in Marduk's victory and the creation of the world out of Tiamat's corpse. Several biblical passages indicate that Israel's traditions included a similar story about a conflict between Yahweh and the Sea (for example, Ps. 74.12–17), which was also connected with the creation of the world. The Ugaritic story as preserved, however, does not conclude with the creation.

A second story tells of the building of Baal's palace by the gods, and the third details Baal's conflict with the god of sterility and death, named Mot ("death"). Baal is killed by Mot, but returns to life after his sister Anat finds and slays Mot. Many interpretational problems beset these texts, and the relationship between the various stories is not clear. But the myths are helpful in understanding Baal as he is portrayed in the Bible, since in the first millennium BCE he was the chief rival of Yahweh in Israel.

In addition to the myths, parts of two epic poems with human heroes as protagonists were found in the library, the Kirta and the Aqhat epics. The former traces the tribulations of Kirta, king of Bit-Hubur, who, after losing his entire family in a series of disasters, is shown by El, the king of the gods, how to win Hurraya, the beautiful daughter of King Pabil of Udm, as his new wife. He succeeds in marrying her, but then angers the goddess Asherah by failing to fulfill a vow he made on his way to Udm; as a result he is stricken with a deadly illness. El eventually intervenes and saves Kirta's life, but then the king has to stave off a rebellion by one of his own sons. The end of the epic has not been preserved.

The Aqhat epic is of great interest because of its close thematic similarities to the ancestral narratives of Genesis, in particular the story of Abraham and Sarah. In the Aqhat epic, the elderly king Daniel has no son and prays fervently to his patron deity, Baal, for an heir. Baal brings the request before El, who grants Daniel and his wife a child, named Aqhat. The boy is given a marvelous bow by the craftsman of the gods, Kothar-wa-Hasis, and goes into the forests hunting. The goddess Anat covets the bow, and when Aqhat refuses to give it to her, she has one of her devotees, named Yatpan, kill Aqhat. Aqhat's sister, Pughat, goes in search of her brother's killer. She comes to Yatpan's dwelling, gets him drunk, and then . . . the text breaks off and the end is lost!

The library of the priest of Baal was far from being the only collection of tablets found at Ugarit. In the royal palace, excavated largely in the 1950s, five separate archives were found. Some contained tablets written in the Ugaritic script, but others had mostly tablets in Akkadian cuneiform. The latter included international correspondence from the mid-fourteenth century to the end of the thirteenth, when the city was destroyed. These texts allow us to reconstruct the general outlines of political developments during the reigns of seven kings of Ugarit. They indicate that Ugarit was able to steer itself well through the political turmoil of the period of competition between Egypt and Hatti. Ugarit had kept close ties with Egypt during much of the second millennium. Even when they found it necessary to submit to Hittite dominance the kings of Ugarit were able to maintain economic relations with Egypt, apparently with Hittite acquiescence. The texts reflect a number of problems that arose between Ugarit and its neighbors, including Amurru, which entered into alliances with Ugarit sealed by royal marriages. Relations with Amurru went sour, however, during the reign of Ammistamru II, who divorced his Amorite wife and sent her back to her native land. The texts, along with the economic documents and the archaeological remains, also show that Ugarit was a cosmopolitan, prosperous trade port that flourished until its violent destruction at the end of the thirteenth century.

In addition to the royal archives, other libraries have been recovered. Private houses have produced archives belonging to high government officials, priests, lawyers, and professional scribes. Discoveries continue to be made: excavations in 1994 and 1996 found a large library of more than four hundred tablets in the house of an important administrator.

Ugarit and Amarna are not the only two Late Bronze Age sites to produce archives relevant to the study of the ancestral narratives. At Nuzi, located east of the Tigris River in Mesopotamia, several thousand tablets dating between 1550 and 1400 BCE, largely of an economic and legal nature, have been found in both official and private contexts. Scholars have often pointed to legal situations referred to in the Nuzi texts as parallels to events described in the Bible's ancestral narratives and have argued for a close cultural and chronological relationship between the narratives and the Hurrian culture exemplified by the Nuzi tablets. Activities such as the adoption of a slave as an heir (Gen. 15.2–3) and the provision of a surrogate by a barren wife (Gen. 16.1–4) were thought to be attested in the legal documents of Nuzi. Most of these proposed parallels have been shown to be mistaken, but the ones that are valid provide a sense of the legal milieu out of which the ancestral stories emerged. For example, marriages arranged by a woman's brother normally required the assent of the woman, while those arranged by a woman's father did not. Compare to this the biblical negotiations concerning Rebekah's marriage (Gen. 24.50–61) and those of Leah and Rachel (29.15–30), and note also the importance of household gods within the family (Gen. 31.33–35). The appearance of Late Bronze Age parallels to certain marriage, inheritance, and family religious customs in Genesis cannot be used as evidence that such stories preserve ancient traditions of the second millennium, since most of these customs continued into the first millennium BCE when the Genesis narratives were written down. So the Nuzi texts have a limited, largely illustrative function.

The tablets from Emar, located along the west bank of the Euphrates southeast of Aleppo, were discovered in the mid-1970s and published in the mid-1980s. Over a thousand thirteenth-century tablets, written in Akkadian, were found by excavators (and several hundred others by illegal diggers, which have shown up on the antiquities market). The primary collection came from the ruins of a temple and included nearly two hundred tablets and fragments describing religious rituals performed at Emar. Several texts refer to a number of cultic officials called *nabu*, a word parallel to the Hebrew word for "prophet," *nabi*. Others describe the practice of anointing a priestess at her installation into office, a custom attested in Israel for priests of Yahweh, but largely unattested elsewhere.

The Ancestral Narratives in the Light of

Second-Millennium Discoveries

It is no exaggeration to say that the Ugaritic tablets have revolutionized the study of the Bible. Until their discovery, we had almost no direct information about Canaanite religion. The discoveries at Ugarit opened up for the first time a major part of the Canaanite religio-mythological background, out of which Israelite religion developed, and have allowed us to see the enormous number of Canaanite reflexes in the Bible. They have provided insight into the earliest period of biblical religion by illuminating aspects of the ancestral narratives of Genesis that preserve authentic ancient memories. In addition, the epic tales have thematic parallels to biblical texts and thus have helped develop new understanding about the literary nature of the Genesis narratives. Ugaritic poetry is closely related to the style of Hebrew poetry and has shed light on a number of their common characteristics. Ugaritic vocabulary, being closely related to Hebrew, can often clarify obscure passages in the biblical text. At the same time, there is a danger in drawing too many parallels between Ugarit and biblical Israel. Scholars have sometimes assumed that the Canaanite culture of Palestine was identical to that of Ugarit, and they have reached conclusions about Israel's relationship to Canaanite culture that go beyond the evidence. Although a cultural connection existed between Ugarit, Palestinian Canaan, and Israel, each was in many ways distinctive. Caution is always necessary when using Ugaritic culture as a point of comparison to Israel.

Perhaps the most significant pre-Israelite element in the ancestral narratives is the name of the deity whom Israel's progenitors worshiped. The biblical narratives themselves indicate that Israel recognized a discontinuity between the ancestral religion and its own. To understand this, we must look briefly at some of the names of Israel's God found in the biblical texts.

The most common name by which the God of Israel is identified in the Bible is *Yahweh*. But he is also referred to as *'elohim*, "God," and *'el*, the latter related to, but distinct from, the former. While the name *'el* is sometimes used as a title (meaning "the god"), it most often occurs in the Bible as a proper name, thus El. All three of these names appear in the ancestral narratives, but *Yahweh* is used primarily by the source J, and sparingly by the other two. Both E and P declare that the name *Yahweh* was revealed first to Moses, and therefore had been unknown to the ancestors. This is most clearly indicated in the Priestly account of God's revelation of the name *Yahweh* to Moses in Exodus 6.2–3: "I am Yahweh; I appeared to Abraham, Isaac, and Jacob as El Shadday, but by my name Yahweh I did not make myself known to them." El Shadday is often translated "God Almighty," but it apparently means "El (proper name), the Mountain One." This passage preserves a tradition that the ancestors worshiped God under the name *El*. This tradition is further sustained by a number of passages in the ancestral narratives in which the name *El* appears, usually with a descriptive epithet. For example, in Genesis 14.18–20 Melchizedek, the king of Jerusalem, is described as a priest of El Elyon, "El, the Exalted One," creator of heaven and earth. Verse 22 identifies El Elyon with Yahweh. In 21.33, Abraham calls on Yahweh El Olam, "El, the Eternal One." In 33.20, Jacob builds an altar on the land he purchases from the people of Shechem and names the altar El-elohe-Yisrael, which means, "El is the God of Israel." And finally, the name *Israel* (*Yisra'el*) itself contains the name *El*—"El contends."

The significance of this tradition is that while the name *Yahweh* relates virtually exclusively to Israel, the god El was well known—across the Near East and in the Canaanite myths from Ugarit—as the king of the gods. In fact, as he is portrayed in the Ugaritic texts, El closely resembles the patron deity of the ancestors as described in Genesis. Although Baal and Anat are the primary subjects of the mythological tablets, El plays a critical role. He is the creator of the universe, and although Baal is sometimes portrayed as the de facto ruler, the status of El as the king is never actually questioned. The creator of creatures, the father of humanity, the father of gods and humans, the father of years, the kind, the compassionate—such are El's attributes. He lives on a mountain, from the foot of which come forth the sources of all the fresh water of the world. He lives in a tent rather than in a temple. In the Kirta and Aqhat epics, El is the deity who alone can provide offspring to the childless.

The patron deity of the Bible's ancestral narratives is portrayed in strikingly similar ways. The fundamental theme of El providing an heir for the heroes of the narrative is paralleled in both of the Canaanite epics found at Ugarit, those of Aqhat and Kirta. It is also striking that the characterization of Yahweh beginning in Exodus differs from the portrayal of the deity in the ancestral narratives. The biblical texts from Exodus on portray God primarily with storm-god imagery, the kind of imagery that was commonly used for Canaanite Baal rather than El. It is this transformation that the E and P sources recognized and explained in their accounts of the revelation of the name *Yahweh* to Moses. They perceived the disjunction between the religion of the ancestors and that of their contemporary culture, but wanted to emphasize continuity as well. Thus P, in the passage quoted above, explicitly insists that El and Yahweh are the same God. E emphasizes the same point in Exodus 3.13–16. It is reasonable to conclude, then, that the traditions preserved, if only vaguely, the memory that the ancestors of Israel worshiped the god El as their patron deity, and that the beginnings of the worship of Yahweh in early Israel were perceived as a break from the older tradition, a change that at least some parts of Israel could not ignore, but indeed felt called upon to explain.

Another area in which research on the second millennium BCE has illuminated the ancestral stories has been the understanding of the pastoralist way of life described in the narratives. The ancestors of Israel appear in Genesis as pastoral nomads living along the edge of settled society in the land of Canaan, having occasional dealings with city-dwellers, sometimes even briefly moving into a town. For much of the nineteenth and early twentieth centuries, modern biblical scholars tended to illustrate the life of the ancestors by reference to the modern nomads of the Near East, the bedouin. They were often portrayed as fully nomadic wanderers, isolated from settled life and generally hostile toward the sedentary population. Scholars usually saw an evolutionary pattern at work in nomadic societies, in which the nomads would come out of the desert, clash with the sedentary population, but eventually give up the nomadic way of life and become town-dwellers themselves. This pattern was used to reconstruct the beginnings of the nation of Israel as it emerged from its nomadic origins. There was some skepticism about the accuracy of the depiction of the pastoral life in Genesis, since the stories have the families moving back and forth between nomadic and town dwelling with relative ease.

The past three decades have seen considerable anthropologically based research on the ancient pastoral way of life. This research has shown that pastoralism during the second millennium BCE differed considerably from that of the modern bedouin, and that the earlier evolutionary view of nomadism is incorrect. Of particular help have been the Mari tablets, which provide much information about the pastoralists who inhabited the middle Euphrates during the nineteenth and eighteenth centuries BCE.

The Mari tablets and other texts have shown that there was not a simple process of peoples moving from nomadism to sedentary life. Rather, members of tribal groups fluctuated between pastoralism and sedentary life, depending on their circumstances. In the ancient texts that have recently come to light, tribal groups largely characterized as pastoralists also had large elements within their tribes who were sedentary—some living in villages, and some found even in the large metropolises of the Near East. Nor is there evidence that the pastoralists were generally antagonistic toward sedentary life, regularly raiding and pillaging the towns. Rather, the texts point to a strong symbiotic relationship between the pastoralists and the inhabitants of the small towns, each providing goods that were necessary to the other. Pastoralists and small-town-dwellers alike resisted the large cities' attempts to impose political control over them.

This understanding of the pastoralist life seems reflected in the narrative of Genesis. The biblical ancestors camp near the towns, as one would expect (see Gen. 12.6–9; 13.12–18; 33.18–20), and at times even become sufficiently sedentary to carry out cultivation (26.12). They are portrayed as having close and cordial relations with townspeople (21.25–34), and in times of trouble they even come for a while to live in major towns as resident aliens (12.10–20; 20.1–18; 26.6–11). This mode of life was not restricted to the second millennium BCE and therefore cannot be used to argue for the authenticity of the ancestral narratives as historical documents. But information from other Near Eastern sources has given us a clearer understanding of the lifestyle described in these narratives.

Conclusion

The ancestral narratives provide few data about the background to Israel's emergence as a nation. Their function is theological rather than historical, and while they performed that function well, caution must be used in extracting archaic memories that would illuminate historical matters. These tales provide the overture to the overarching themes of the Pentateuch: God's creation of Israel and his grant of the land to the nation. They also emphasize the unity of Israel, portraying the nation as the collected descendants of a single couple, Abraham and Sarah. From a historical point of view, such a notion can be shown as inaccurate, and later chapters in this book will examine the great complexity of the ethnic groups that eventually become Israel. But from the perspective of ancient Israel, such an emphasis was vital, and these stories made an important contribution toward defining the soul of the nation.

Our sources for understanding the background of Israel's emergence come from archaeological excavations and the study of second-millennium epigraphic remains from the Near East. These provide considerable insight into the complex political, social, and cultural situation in Syria-Palestine during the Middle and Late Bronze Ages, as Canaanite civilization, out of which Israel emerged, grew and matured. The decline and collapse of Late Bronze Age culture led to the conditions that would allow the formation of the Israelite nation in the thirteenth and twelfth centuries BCE.

Select Bibliography

Biblical Archaeologist 47 (1984): 65–120. A collection of four articles on Mari by Marie-Henriette Gates, Dennis Pardee and Jonathan Glass, André Lemaire, and Jack Sasson, which, although now dated, provides an excellent discussion of this important site.

Chavalas, Mark W., ed. *Emar: The History, Religion, and Culture of a Syrian Town in the Late Bronze Age.* Bethesda, Md.: CDL, 1996. The first substantial introduction in English to this important site and its archives.

Coogan, Michael David, ed. and trans. *Stories from Ancient Canaan.* Philadelphia: Westminster, 1978. Accessible translations of the major Ugaritic myths.

Cross, Frank Moore. *Canaanite Myth and Hebrew Epic: Essays in the History of the Religion of Israel.* Cambridge, Mass.: Harvard University Press, 1973. The classic discussion of the relationship between Canaanite and Israelite religion.

Eichler, Barry L. "Nuzi and the Bible: A Retrospective." In *Dumu-e₂-dub-ba-a: Studies in Honor of Åke W. Sjöberg,* ed. Hermann Behrens, Darlene Loding, and Martha T. Roth, 107–19. Philadelphia: University Museum, 1989. A fine discussion of Nuzi's place in biblical studies.

Gurney, O. R. *The Hittites.* Rev. ed. New York: Penguin, 1990. Excellent introduction to Hittite history and culture.

Klengel, Horst. *Syria: 3000 to 300 B.C.: A Handbook of Political History.* Berlin: Akademie, 1992. The best description in English of Syrian history for this period.

Mazar, Amihai. *Archaeology of the Land of the Bible 10,000–586 B.C.E.* New York: Doubleday, 1990. Chapters 6 and 7 provide an excellent summary of archaeological material from the Middle and Late Bronze Ages in Palestine.

Moran, William L., ed. and trans. *The Amarna Letters.* Baltimore: Johns Hopkins University Press, 1992. Superb translation of these important documents.

Parker, Simon B., ed. *Ugaritic Narrative Poetry.* Atlanta: Scholars Press, 1997. Solid translations of the major Ugaritic texts.

Pettinato, Giovanni. *Ebla: A New Look at History.* Trans. C. Faith Richardson. Baltimore: Johns Hopkins University Press, 1991. The most recent general study of Ebla in English, with many controversial interpretations.

Singer, Itamar. "A Concise History of Amurru." Appendix in Shlomo Izre'el, *Amurru Akka-dian: A Linguistic Study*, 2.135–94. Harvard Semitic Studies, 41. Atlanta: Scholars Press, 1991. Although included in a technical book, this very readable synthesis provides an excellent over-view of a major region dealt with in the Amarna letters.

Vaux, Roland de. *The Early History of Israel*. Trans. David Smith. Philadelphia: Westminster, 1978. After a quarter century, still a valuable discussion of the ancestral traditions in Genesis.

Wilhelm, Gernot. *The Hurrians*. Trans. Jennifer Barnes. Warminster, England: Aris & Phillips, 1989. Important introduction to the Hurrians, especially the state of Mitanni during the Late Bronze Age.

CHAPTER TWO

Bitter Lives

Israel in and out of Egypt

CAROL A. REDMOUNT

E*xodus*, a Greek word, means departure or going out. The Exodus is the Israelite departure from Egypt under the leadership of Moses, and the subsequent eventful journey through the Sinai wilderness. This Exodus is a defining, pivotal episode in the Bible, a cornerstone of Israelite faith and historical understanding. According to biblical traditions, through the Exodus events Israel first takes form as a nation. During the wilderness wanderings between Egypt and the Promised Land of Canaan, the major tenets of Israelite belief and ritual are handed down by God to Moses, whose name becomes synonymous ever after with religious law. Throughout the Bible and its long developmental history, the Exodus saga operates as the national epic of ancient Israel. Critical to Israel's understanding of itself and its relationship to God, the Exodus account constitutes Israel's confession of faith; and its unfailing invocation, sometimes in no more than capsule form ("the LORD who brought your ancestors up out of the land of Egypt"; "the law of Moses"), provides a perpetual affirmation of that faith. In the Exodus narrative, we find the core doctrine at the heart of one of the world's great religions.

The biblical Exodus account has been understood on a number of different levels. Literally, and apparently historically, the Exodus tells of the Israelites' slavery under a harsh Egyptian pharaoh, followed by their freedom flight from Egypt to Canaan, led by Moses. During this flight, God intensifies his special relationship with Israel and sets forth a comprehensive set of regulations and religious precepts for the community. Theologically, the Exodus embodies the themes of God acting through history, of divine promise and fulfillment, of eternal covenant, and of human suffering and redemption. Finally, paradigmatically, the Exodus is a powerful image of what Northrop Frye called "the definitive deliverance"; as the archetype for all subsequent redemption and liberation experiences, it has become a powerful symbol in Western political thought.

Two issues dominate contemporary scholarly discussion of the Exodus: the extent to which the narrative is historical in the usual sense of the word, and the placement of the various events in an ancient Egyptian and Near Eastern historical and geographical framework. Who was the pharaoh who did not know Joseph? What was the route of the Exodus? When did the Exodus occur? Are there any independent witnesses to the Exodus events? To answer such questions, it is first necessary to consider the character of the Exodus account itself, because its theological nature affected its recollection, literary formation, and interpretation, and because the ancient conception of history differed from our own. Only then can we evaluate historical issues as they relate to the biblical narrative, and place that narrative within a broader context.

The Biblical Narrative

The Exodus saga in the Bible incorporates events in Egypt after the death of Joseph through the Israelite departure, the wilderness wanderings, and the Sinai revelations, up to but not including the conquest of Canaan. The account, largely in narrative form, spreads over four books of the Pentateuch, the first five books of the Bible.

As the book of Exodus begins, Joseph and all of his generation have died, and Joseph's descendants "multiplied and grew exceedingly strong, so that the land was filled with them" (Exod. 1.7). There is now a new pharaoh ruling Egypt, "who did not know Joseph" (Exod. 1.8). This new king fears the Israelites as a large and potentially dangerous fifth column in his land. So he enslaves the Israelites, forcing them to build the supply cities of Pithom and Rameses, and making "their lives bitter with hard service in mortar and brick and in every kind of field labor" (Exod. 1.14). But harsh treatment only makes the Israelites grow more numerous and strong, so the pharaoh orders all male Hebrew babies thrown into the Nile. In this context we read Moses' birth narrative; to avoid the slaughter, the baby's mother places him in a reed basket along the bank of the river, where he is found by Pharaoh's daughter and, ironically, raised in the Egyptian royal court.

After reaching adulthood, Moses one day impetuously kills an Egyptian abusing a Hebrew. He flees Egypt, settles in nomadic Midian, and marries. Meanwhile the Israelites in Egypt groan under their harsh bondage. The old Pharaoh dies, only to be replaced by a new, equally pitiless ruler. Eventually God calls to Moses from a bush burning in the wilderness and commands him to return to Egypt to deliver his people from their oppression and lead them forth "to a good and broad land, a land flowing with milk and honey" (Exod. 3.8). Reluctantly accepting his commission, Moses goes back to Egypt, and initiates a series of patterned confrontations with Pharaoh. In each, Moses pleads with Pharaoh to "let my people go," Pharaoh is obdurate, Moses dramatically performs a miracle that devastates the Egyptians, Pharaoh first relents and then recants. In this way, nine spectacular plagues descend on the Egyptians: bloodwater, frogs, gnats, flies, pestilence, boils, hail, locusts, and darkness. The series culminates with the tenth and deadliest plague, in which all firstborn Egyptians, human and animal, die; this both leads into and explains the origin of the Passover ritual. At long last Pharaoh permits the Israelites to leave, only to change his mind one last time and send his army after Moses. But his Egyptian soldiers meet their death in the Red (or Reed) Sea, whose waters miraculously part for the fleeing Israelites and then close over Pharaoh's doomed army.

Delivered from their oppressor, the Israelites continue their journey into Sinai and camp at the base of the mountain of God. There, in one of the most momentous theophanies of the Bible, God appears to Moses and the Israelites. With Moses as mediator, God makes a covenant with Israel, whose stipulations include the Decalogue, or Ten Commandments, and the series of laws known as the Covenant Code or the Book of the Covenant (Exod. 20–23; 24.7). In addition, God reveals to Moses the specifications for building, furnishing, and staffing the tabernacle, where God will dwell in the midst of the congregation (Exod. 25–31). Almost as soon as it is made, the covenant is broken as the Israelites disgrace themselves in the golden calf incident (Exod. 32). The covenant is immediately reestablished, however, revealing God's mercy, and the tabernacle is constructed so that the glory of God may descend upon it.

The books of Leviticus, Numbers, and Deuteronomy continue the Exodus epic. More laws and ritual regulations are given, and the Israelites travel through the Sinai wilderness by stages, their itinerary provided in detail. The people are a tiresome and faithless lot during their long and arduous journey. They murmur, whine, and rebel constantly, blind to God's favors and signs. God's anger is kindled almost continuously, but he invariably forgives the Israelites, despite their unfailing intransigence, through the intercession of Moses, who continues to act as covenant mediator and interpreter of God's redemptive work. Finally, after an abortive attack on Canaan during which the people transgress yet again, God has had enough; he informs the Israelites that those whom he brought out of Egypt will not be permitted to enter the Promised Land. Rather, they will remain in the wilderness, and after forty years (that is, after the death of their entire generation) their children will be the ones to fulfill the covenant promise and occupy Canaan.

The Israelites remain at Kadesh-barnea for much of these forty years, but eventually move into Transjordan. There they encounter the kings of Moab and Edom and conquer the kings of the Amorites and Bashan. Anticipating the conquest of Canaan, the Israelites divide the land among their tribes by lot, delineate the borders of Israelite dominion, and designate the Levitical cities. In the book of Deuteronomy Moses gives a series of farewell addresses to his people: he reviews the mighty acts of God, stresses the Israelites' escape from Egypt with its associated miracles, reiterates the Decalogue, proclaims a second extensive corpus of laws and regulations, warns solemnly of coming temptations in the land of Canaan, and adjures the people to love and to remain loyal to God in the Promised Land. At long last, at the end of the book of Deuteronomy, Moses climbs to the summit of Mount Nebo and gazes across the Jordan River to the Promised Land. God shows Moses all the land and then tells him, "This is the land of which I swore to Abraham, to Isaac, and to Jacob, 'I will give it to your descendants'; I have let you see it with your eyes, but you shall not cross over there" (Deut. 34.4). And Moses, the servant of the Lord, dies, while below him on the fields of Moab his people ready themselves to conquer Canaan.

The Literary and Historical Character of the Exodus Narrative

This seemingly straightforward, historical account of Israel's escape from Egypt and sojourn in the Sinai wilderness is in fact a multilayered document, the culmination of a complicated, centuries-long process of composition, compilation, and transmission. A variety of sophisticated analytical methods have been brought to bear on the Exodus narrative since the advent of modern biblical scholarship in the nineteenth century CE. Initially, and until recently, critical methodologies concentrated on tracing the origins and historical development of the biblical narrative and stressed the predominantly historical character of the Bible. *Textual criticism* has sought to establish an original biblical text by comparing and contrasting all relevant documents surviving into the modern world. Thus, based on a gloss in the ancient Greek translation of the Bible (the Septuagint), one scholar equates the place called Pithom in Exodus 1.11 with Heliopolis, an ancient city whose remains are now covered by a modern suburb of Cairo, rather than with a site in the eastern Egyptian delta.

Literary or *source criticism* has pursued underlying sources, arranged these in historical order, and identified points where different sources were redacted, or edited together, to form larger units. This method of analysis produced the "Documentary Hypothesis" that, with variations, remains widely followed today. The Documentary Hypothesis posits for the Pentateuch four primary literary sources (J, E, P, and D), dated to different periods in the first half of the first millennium BCE, which were woven together by a series of mid-first-millennium redactors. Among those who accept this approach, however, major areas of dispute persist, including disagreements over the Exodus account. Scholars have differed about which passages belong to which hypothesized source, about whether the Exodus and Sinai traditions were originally separate, and, if so, to which, if either, the Moses story belonged. But there are also areas of substantial agreement, such as the dating of the D (Deuteronomic) source to the seventh century BCE and the placement of the Deuteronomic History (the books of Deuteronomy through 2 Kings) at the end of the present Exodus narrative, where it preempted an earlier conclusion to the saga. Thematically, the Exodus chronicle culminates with the conquest of Canaan, but in the canon we now possess this climactic event is postponed until Joshua, a book not part of the Pentateuch.

In recent years, challenges to the Documentary Hypothesis have increased steadily. The content, the date, and even the existence of some of the sources have been questioned, and the validity of the approach itself impugned. A few authorities have concluded that the core events of the Exodus saga are entirely literary fabrications. But most biblical scholars still subscribe to some variation of the Documentary Hypothesis, and support the basic historicity of the biblical narrative.

Form criticism endeavors to recover older stages of biblical traditions by identifying primary literary or oral genres, or "forms," and by establishing, as far as possible, the *Sitz-im-Leben,* or life setting, of these forms in order to understand how they functioned within their social contexts. There is general agreement that the Exodus account synthesizes a variety of primary forms, including narrative, folk tradition, etiological legend, myth, ritual instruction, covenant formulary, and hymn. Many of these forms are not, and should not be considered, historically based; Moses' birth narrative, for example, is built on folkloric motifs found throughout the ancient world.

Tradition or *redaction criticism* concentrates on later levels of textual development, where editorial activity becomes apparent. The redactors often functioned not merely as editors who integrated various preexisting materials into a smoothly flowing whole, but also as creative theologians who stamped their own beliefs on what they considered to be a definitive interpretation of the biblical text. Thus considerable literary effort has been expended to link, at one end, the Egyptian portion of the Exodus account with the prior ancestral narratives of Genesis and, at the other end, to join the wilderness sojourn of the Exodus narrative with the subsequent conquest of Canaan. Even more broadly, the biblical books of Genesis through 2 Kings have been placed purposely in sequence to create a continuous history running from creation to exile.

More recently, partly as a result of diminishing returns from and perceived limitations of the more traditional, historically based techniques, some scholars have taken a broader, holistic approach to the biblical texts. *Canonical criticism*, born in the 1960s, has aimed at comprehending the Bible as an integral part of a holy scripture that belongs to a believing and worshiping community. The final version of this canon of scripture has its own validity, meaning, and artistry, independent of the development of the parts. It is this overall unity that provides access to theological truth and religious experience, not the analysis of origins, sources, and layers of tradition, even though these may exist.

Finally, especially since the 1970s, some scholars have focused on the Bible predominantly as literature. In this newest form of inquiry, called *synchronic* or *final form interpretation*, the biblical text is treated as an organic whole with its own intrinsic artistic integrity. As with canonical criticism, the interpretive focus falls not on the historical background or development of the document, but on the completed text itself as a literary creation. In general, those espousing canonical or final form interpretations are less interested in historical approaches and less concerned with issues of historicity. Adherents of both these methods stress that the present canonical text of Exodus comprises a carefully organized document with a deliberately calculated literary structure and a compelling theological message.

Except for those conservatives who insist on Mosaic authorship of the Pentateuch (thereby giving Moses the unique privilege of recording his own death in Deut. 34.5–8), scholars of all critical schools agree that the Exodus account as it stands today is a composite, a literary construct, carefully composed and edited to achieve historical and theological coherence, and that this composite is made up of smaller units that have been transmitted and redacted over centuries. Ironically, despite—or possibly because of—our expanded analytical base and broader understanding, there is less agreement than ever as to the history, development, and character of the Exodus account, and biblical scholarship in general is in ferment.

Innumerable analyses, undertaken from many perspectives during the past century and a half, underscore that the original Exodus account, whatever its content and its time and place of composition, was something vastly different from the complex Exodus saga we know today. But this original version lies beyond our reach. The growing dissonance of scholarly opinion underscores the impossibility of tracing the details of the Exodus narrative's intricate evolution. Occasionally, however, partial outlines of the saga's long development can be sketched.

Most of the Exodus material was composed or collected long after the events narrated. In some cases additions were retrojected in time for placement within the legitimizing framework of Mosaic law—especially later ritual, legal, and regulatory matters. In other cases alterations or augmentations were introduced to bring events closer to an audience increasingly separated by time and circumstance from the original experiences. Such procedures introduced historical material into the narrative—but material that dated from long after the original happenings. Where detected, such later accretions or substitutions can be identified as anachronistic. Recent research indicates that even more of the extant Exodus account than previously thought comes from periods during or after the Israelite monarchy or even the exile. Presumably an original Exodus story lies hidden somewhere inside all the later revisions and alterations, but centuries of transmission have long since obscured its presence, and its substance, accuracy, and date are now difficult to determine.

The historicity of the Exodus narrative is thus a complex issue. Clearly, significant portions are not and were never intended to be historiographic. Yet the overall intent of the narrative was historical, despite nonhistorical elements in its compilation. In this context it is important to remember that the biblical writers' conception of history, particularly within what was primarily a theological document, differed from our own. The dominant historical concern of the Exodus account is to demonstrate that God acts in history: that Israelite bondage and salvation took place in history; that God's covenant with Moses and the Israelites was made in history; and that the fulfillment of that covenant also took place in history. All other historical concerns are secondary, but this underlying, elemental historicity suffices to make the account historical, and this dominating concern made it permissible to shift historical particulars in order to make the Exodus chronicle more accessible to successive generations. A similar process can be seen at work in European Renaissance art, where biblical figures are anachronistically dressed in contemporary clothing and biblical locations transformed into contemporary surroundings so that the material might speak more directly to its intended audience. Mythic events, too, were incorporated into the Exodus epic to enhance, rather than detract from, the basic historical foundation of the account. It was the enduring reality—expressed in the core historicity of the central events of the Exodus—not transient specific historical detail, which was important and eternal. Ultimately it is this compelling historical grounding of the narrative that sustains most scholars' belief in an actual historical origin for the Exodus events.

The biblical Exodus account was never intended to function or to be understood as history in the present-day sense of the word. Traditional history, with its stress on objectivity and verifiable, detailed facts as the building blocks of historical understanding, is a modern obsession. Not that the ancients were incapable of bald, factual rendering if they deemed it appropriate—they, too, had accurate tax records. But for most occasions, and especially for documents that expressed deeper truths and fundamental values, facts as such were not always valued, consistency was not always a virtue, and specific historical particulars were often irrelevant and therefore variable.

In the end, it was necessary that the theologically informed events of the Exodus epic relate to history, in the sense that a true historical heart to the narrative exist, but not that these events be bound by history. Particular, individual historical details were superfluous.

Thus, there is an inherent tension between an ancient and a modern understanding of the historicity of the Exodus. Mythical and historical categories of thought were not mutually exclusive in antiquity; on the contrary, the very miracles that make modern readers uncomfortable intensified the drama and significance of the historical base for the ancient. We do the Exodus narrative a profound disservice by uncritically seeking natural interpretations for the clearly miraculous, and it is misguided to supply scientific explanations for such nonhistorical events as the ten plagues of Egypt, the burning bush that spoke to Moses, or the pillars of cloud and fire that accompanied the Israelites in the wilderness.

In the end, the Exodus saga is neither pure history nor pure literature, but an inseparable amalgam of both, closest in form to what we would call a docudrama. For the Israelites, the Exodus events were anchored in history, but at the same time rose above it. The Exodus saga incorporated and reflected an original historical reality, and this reflection was all that was necessary to make the account historical in ancient eyes. The Egyptian captivity and deliverance were seen through a lens of communal faith, in which history provided the skeletal framework for structuring the actions of God. This skeleton was fleshed out by a variety of predominantly literary and religious forms.

Israel in Egypt

Attempts to anchor the Exodus events in broader historical currents typically begin with the biblical account, taking the text of the Bible at least initially as a primary source document. Superficially, the Bible does appear to provide historical data that might locate the Exodus account in history. As we have seen, however, serious problems arise when the biblical text is used for modern historical interpretations, and critical historiography casts doubt on the usefulness of the biblical narrative as a historical source for the Exodus. Potential factual information contained in the account falls into three categories: events within the borders of Egypt; the geography of the Exodus; and biblical reckonings—the figures given for establishing the date of the Exodus and for the number of participants in the flight from Egypt and the wilderness wanderings.

What is immediately striking about the earlier portions of the Exodus saga is the lack of distinctively Egyptian content and flavor, despite the Egyptian setting. The only description that contributes a slight Egyptian cast to the locale is that of Exodus 7.19 (echoed in 8.5), which refers to "the waters of Egypt . . . its rivers, its canals, and its ponds, and all its pools of water." None of the Egyptian pharaohs in the entire narrative—not those who presumably dealt with Joseph, Jacob, or the "sons of Israel," nor the pharaoh who did not know Joseph, and certainly not the pharaoh of the ten plagues and the Exodus who sent his army after Moses—are identified by name. Nor is there a hint of individual or historical idiosyncrasy by which to distinguish one pharaoh from another. There is, moreover, no characteristically Egyptian phraseology, no allusion, brief or otherwise, to distinctively Egyptian literary or historical material, and no invocation of local color (apart from the description cited above) that would help authenticate an Egyptian location or suggest an Egyptian origin for any part of the account. Instead, except for a few references and an occasional name (for example, Pharaoh, Nile, Moses, Rameses, Pithom), the purportedly Egyptian setting is so generic that the action could have taken place almost anywhere.

Given this curious absence of Egypt from the Exodus narrative, scholars have focused on the few clearly Egyptian terms that do occur, but with disappointing results. The supply cities of Pithom and Rameses bear indisputably Egyptian names, but neither can be situated with certainty. Pithom is derived from Egyptian *Pr-'Itm* (Per Atum), the temple domain or estate of the god Atum, a relatively common designation beginning with the mid-second millennium BCE. In Egyptian usage, *Pr-'Itm* would not stand alone but would be followed by a specific location designator, identifying the Per Atum of a specific place. In effect, the biblical rendering of Pithom strips the reference of its specificity and thus identifiability, and transforms it into a collective allusion equivalent to the generic references to "Pharaoh." Biblical Pithom's most plausible association to date is with Tell Retabah in the Wadi Tumilat, although it has also been identified with Heliopolis. The supply city of Rameses is most often equated with Per-Rameses, the delta capital founded by Rameses II (ca. 1279–1213; Dynasty 19) and occupied throughout the Ramesside period (Dynasties 19 and 20, ca. 1295–1069). This city is now identified with Qantir, an eastern delta site currently under excavation by a German archaeological team. At least one prominent Egyptologist, however, challenges the equation of Rameses and Per-Rameses. Moreover, in typically Egyptian fashion, the memory and name of Rameses II continued to live on and function in Egypt long after the king's death, and the name *Rameses* was used in a variety of place-names down to Greco-Roman times. Thus the name *Rameses* functions only as a *terminus post quem*: that is, any appearance of the name must date no earlier than the time the name first occurs. The place-name *Rameses* may even have been inserted into the biblical narrative at a later date, and some scholars have suggested that the reference to Rameses (and also to Pithom) is an anachronism reflecting the geography of a much later period, from somewhere within the sixth to the fourth centuries BCE.

The land of Goshen, identified as the area inhabited by the Israelites in Egypt (Exod. 8.22; 9.26), has never been localized with certainty. Most scholars assume that Goshen lay in the eastern Nile Delta, but the word *Goshen* does not occur in any Egyptian texts, and efforts to derive it from the Egyptian language are unconvincing.

The name *Moses* is most likely Egyptian, although other etymologies have been proposed. If so, the name comes from the Egyptian verbal root *msy*, meaning "born." In Egyptian usage this is generally linked with the name of a god. Thus *Ramose* means "the god Re is born," *Ptahmose* means "the god Ptah is born," and so forth. Such compounds are particularly common in the New Kingdom and later. In the biblical narrative, however, the divine element is missing, producing the abbreviated name *Moses*, a shortened form not common in Egyptian. The lack of the divine element in the biblical name is not surprising, however; if it existed, it could have been removed to avoid an affiliation between a central figure in the development of Israelite religion and a foreign god. Moreover, Aaron and his son Phinehas also have names of Egyptian origin.

And what of the harsh tasks inflicted on the Israelites during their servitude? Numerous Egyptian texts dating throughout the second millennium BCE tell us that "Asiatics" (*'amw*, the most common appellation employed by Egyptians for people coming from the general region of ancient Syria-Palestine), like all prisoners of war or foreigners in service to the Egyptian crown or temples, were forced to perform a variety of tasks, including agricultural labor and heavy construction work. But the oppressive task that the biblical narrative complains about most (Exod. 5.7–19) is brickmaking, not the most common of the responsibilities assigned to Asiatics in Egypt. Clearly, Asiatics were in no position to choose their work assignments, and brickmaking was an ever-present need in Egypt, particularly in the alluvial delta, where stone was at a premium. On the other hand, sun-dried bricks made without straw are found at sites in the delta from a variety of periods, and it is difficult to see how the making of such bricks imposed a significant hardship on the Israelites.

Do any of the Egyptian references in the Exodus narrative provide possibly useful historical clues? The name *Rameses*, as noted above, provides a *terminus post quem* for the Exodus events of Rameses I, the first ruler to bear the name. A similar beginning point is implied by the outfitting of Pharaoh's army with chariots and horses: both horse and chariot are unknown or rare in Egypt prior to Dynasty 18. The Egyptian term *Pharaoh* (*prʿ3*, meaning "great house") originally referred to the palace, and not until the reign of Thutmose III (ca. 1479–1425 BCE) in Dynasty 18 was it also used for the person of the king. In general, the limited linguistic evidence found in the narrative seems to date to the New Kingdom or later. Finally, the prominence in Pharaoh's entourage of magicians, who initially match Moses miracle for miracle, may reflect a first-millennium BCE setting.

The Route of the Exodus

The geography of the Exodus offers another potentially promising area for the Bible to function as a primary historical source. The biblical text provides detailed itineraries for the Exodus trek, most completely in Numbers 33.1–49, fragments in Numbers 21.10–20 and Deuteronomy 10.6–7, and further parallels elsewhere. These itineraries list, by name, all of the stopping points or stages on the Exodus journey. Theoretically, it should be possible to reconstruct the route the Israelites took out of Egypt. Unfortunately, it is not.

The wilderness itineraries form a distinct genre within the Pentateuch and belong to a literary form widely attested in the ancient world. The primary function of this genre, which survives mostly in official documents, is to describe routes. Nonbiblical examples confirm that these ancient itineraries customarily provided a complete and reasonably reliable record of the routes described. The geographical itineraries associated with the Exodus saga thus probably preserve details of one or more ancient routes.

As a structured literary genre, however, the itineraries most likely were incorporated into the biblical narrative during the process of literary composition and redaction that resulted in the final biblical text. We cannot date precisely this secondary merging of wilderness itineraries with the Exodus account, except to say that it occurred long after the original events. Moreover, the literary itineraries preserved within the Exodus saga derive from more than one source. As a consequence, some scholars have challenged the integrity of these geographical lists. On the other hand, the itineraries might reflect geographical sources much earlier than the time of their redaction into the biblical narrative. Recent efforts to relate the Exodus itineraries to Egyptian prototypes found in Ramesside geographical lists are intriguing, although far from decisive, and the large number of Asiatic sites in the Egyptian lists that cannot be identified convincingly is instructive.

Already in ancient times the locations of many of the places in the Exodus itineraries appear to have been lost. Of the approximately three dozen or more localities mentioned, few can be pinpointed on the ground, and none of the places listed in Egypt or the Sinai Peninsula can be situated with confidence. Thus, as we have seen, Rameses, the starting point of the Exodus, is customarily identified with the Ramesside delta capital of Per-Rameses. Succoth is taken by some as a Hebraization of Egyptian *Tjeku,* a district designation employed for the Wadi Tumilat that first occurs in the New Kingdom. Kadesh-barnea is now generally placed at Ain el-Qudeirat, the most fertile oasis in northern Sinai, located at the junction of two major routes across the peninsula. Tell el-Qudeirat, the ancient mound associated with the oasis, has recently been renamed Tel Kadesh-barnea by its excavators, despite a tenth-century BCE date for the earliest finds from the tell. But beyond these and a very few other tentative identifications, most sites in Egypt and Sinai listed in the Exodus itineraries remain unknown.

The sacred "mountain of God" also cannot be placed on a map. The biblical narrative refers to the mountain, when it is given a name, by two different appellations, Mount Horeb and Mount Sinai. Scholars do not agree whether the traditions refer to one or two mountains (although the weight of current opinion favors one mountain), let alone where one or the other mountain might be located. Suggestions for locating the mountain of God range from the southern Sinai Peninsula, to the Negeb, and even to the Arabian peninsula.

The crossing of the Red Sea has also touched off much discussion. Hebrew *yam suf* has been translated both as Red Sea and as Reed Sea; cogent grounds exist in support of both translations. There are biblical passages where *yam suf* is clearly unrelated to the Exodus and unquestionably refers to the Red Sea (such as 1 Kings 9.26). Moreover, both the Greek Septuagint and Latin Vulgate versions of the Bible render *yam suf* as "Red Sea," reflecting traditions current at the time these two translations were made (third century BCE and fourth century CE, respectively). But there are also philological grounds for translating *yam suf* as "Reed Sea," and in light of this interpretation scholars have sought to localize the destruction of Pharaoh's army in reed beds located in the northeastern Nile Delta. Such reed beds have in fact existed at various points along the northeastern Egyptian border in locations ranging from the Bitter Lakes in the south to Sabkhat el-Bardawil (classical Lake Sirbonis) adjacent to the Mediterranean coast in the north. A plausible case, for which there is no real support other than its plausibility, can be made for Bardawil as the location of the crossing of the Red Sea. The lake is separated from the Mediterranean Sea by only a thin strip of land, and violent storms have been known to lash the sea and cause sudden and intense flooding of the region. There are even historical parallels where ancient troops were trapped and partially destroyed by just such a storm.

Traditionally, two routes have been proposed for the Exodus: a southern route

The Sinai Peninsula

through southern Sinai and a northern one along the Mediterranean coast (although Exod. 13.17–18 expressly states that the latter, anachronistically called "the way of the land of the Philistines," was not taken by the Israelites). Recent studies emphasizing both the modern and the past ecology and ethnography of the Sinai Peninsula suggest, however, that four major east-west routes ran through Sinai in antiquity. The northernmost hugs the Mediterranean coast; the other three follow desert wadis, the main channels for water and communication through the huge, barren peninsula. Apart from the north coastal strip, the remainder of the approximately 36,000 square kilometers (23,000 square miles) that make up the Sinai Peninsula has few economic resources and little water, and its population has always been minimal. The largest concentration of ancient settlements occurs in mountainous and geographically isolated south-central Sinai. Here are found both an adequate water supply and a comfortable climate. The difficult terrain, the physical isolation, and the relatively hospitable living conditions all combine to make this area a prime candidate for the location of the Israelite sojourn in the wilderness. Equally important, the region was apparently never of any interest to Egypt: none of the ancient settlements in the area appear to be Egyptian, and there are no indications of ancient Egyptian suzerainty. At the same time, however, none of the ancient settlements in the area date to a period that might relate to an Israelite Exodus from Egypt: they are too early (Early Bronze Age) or too late (Iron Age). The localization of the wilderness sojourn in south-central Sinai therefore is an attractive but unproven hypothesis.

Research into the monastic settlements in south-central Sinai suggests that it was the establishment of the monastic population in this area during the Byzantine period (fourth to seventh centuries CE) that resulted in the identification of southern Sinai sites with various biblical locations. Most likely, the monks themselves generated the traditions of the southern Exodus route; the traditions arose along with the monasteries. At the same time as the monastic movement established itself in southern Sinai, Christian pilgrimages also were becoming popular. These pilgrimages further stimulated the development of monastic traditions both by encouraging the local placement of Exodus sites and, once made, by reinforcing those localizations. Pilgrimage practice thus helped preserve and perpetuate the very geographical identifications that it had helped create. As time passed the site correlations moved into popular lore and became sanctified tradition. Such a process is not unparalleled. Helena, mother of the Roman emperor Constantine, traveled throughout the Near East dreaming of the locations of various events in the life of Jesus. Over the years her identifications, some no doubt based on prior popular belief, became accepted as indigenous local traditions. This mechanism for creating and reinforcing popular tradition is not confined to antiquity: the renaming of Tell el-Qudeirat as Tel Kadeshbarnea is a modern example.

Thus, despite decades of research, we cannot reconstruct a reliable Exodus route based on information in the biblical account. Nor, despite intensive survey and exploration by archaeologists, are there remains on the Sinai Peninsula or in Egypt that can be linked specifically to the Israelite Exodus. Barring some future momentous discovery, we shall never be able to establish exactly the route of the Exodus.

Biblical Dates and Numbers

The biblical narrative also informs us about the length of the Israelite sojourn in Egypt and the date of the Exodus. The data are not, however, consistent. Thus, 1 Kings 6.1 dates the Exodus to "the four hundred eightieth year after the Israelites came out of the land of Egypt, in the fourth year of Solomon's reign over Israel." Although we do not know the exact year of Solomon's accession to the throne, we know its approximate date, the mid-tenth century BCE. This would date the Israelite departure from Egypt in the mid-fifteenth century. Exodus 12.40 tells us that the Israelites lived in Egypt for 430 years prior to the Exodus; this gives the early nineteenth century for the coming of Jacob and his sons into Egypt. In Genesis 15.13, however, the length of the sojourn in Egypt is given as four hundred years; and in Genesis 15.16, the time shrinks to three generations. Moreover, the figure of 480 years is suspiciously schematic: the Bible assigns twelve (a favorite and symbolic biblical number) generations between the Exodus and Solomon, and the standard biblical length of a generation is forty years.

The numbers given for the participants in the Exodus events are impressive, and improbable. Exodus 12.37–38 states: "The Israelites journeyed from Rameses to Succoth, about six hundred thousand men on foot, besides children. A mixed crowd also went up with them, and livestock in great number"; the report of the census in Numbers 1.46 reiterates this figure. By the time one adds women and children—and anyone else subsumed under the rubric of "mixed crowd"—it is a mass of people, at least 2.5 million, that is moving out of Egypt. Such a number, particularly when combined with "livestock in great number," would have constituted a logistical nightmare and is impossible; if all 2.5 million people marched ten abreast, the resulting line of more than 150 miles would need eight or nine days to march past any single fixed point. Taken at face value, such a host could not have crossed any ordinary stretch of water by any ordinary road or path in one night; nor could these numbers, or anything remotely approaching them, have been sustained in the inhospitable Sinai desert. Modern census figures suggest a current total of approximately forty thousand bedouin for the entire Sinai Peninsula; in the late nineteenth century CE the figure was under five thousand. The entire population of Egypt in the mid-thirteenth century BCE has been estimated at 2.8 million.

One hint of a more feasible figure for participants in the flight from Egypt is the reference in Exodus 1.15 to two Hebrew midwives; unusually, the midwives are even named. Together, the two met the needs of the entire Hebrew community sojourning in Egypt: in this case certainly not the hundreds of thousands or even thousands of women implied in a census of over half a million men. Perhaps, then, the two midwives reflect a superseded and now lost tradition of a much smaller group dwelling within and presumably departing from Egypt.

Biblical dates and numbers are thus indifferent to concerns of strict historical accuracy. As with other details, the biblical reckonings are subservient to theological images and themes. The improbabilities of the data can be rationalized in different ways: but once rationalized, they lose their claim to ancient authority, historical or otherwise.

The Bible and Primary Historical Sources

The biblical account makes an exceptionally poor primary historical source for the Exodus events. Possible historical data are mostly inconsistent, ambiguous, or vague. No Egyptian pharaoh associated with the Exodus events is named. When the king of Arad fights the Israelites in Numbers 21.1, he is merely called "the Canaanite, the king of Arad." In those few places where the Exodus narrative is meticulous about detail, the particulars are either unhelpful—such as the stages in the trek out of Egypt, or the names of the three Transjordanian rulers (King Sihon of the Amorites in Num. 21.21; King Og of Bashan in Num. 21.33; Balak, son of Zippor, king of Moab, in Num. 22.4) who are completely unknown outside the Bible—or inappropriate. In the latter case, biblical precision generally stems from concerns other than historical: standardized generation formulas grounded in symbolic numbers are applied backward to calculate the year of the Exodus; or historically impossible numbers are given for participants in the departure from Egypt to stress the event's significance.

The surviving biblical account of the Exodus has thus been shaped by later creative hands responding to overarching theological agendas and differing historical and cultural circumstances. Many of the preserved details are anachronistic, reflecting conditions during the first millennium BCE when the narrative was written down and repeatedly revised. As a consequence the final Exodus account should not be accepted at face value, nor can it function as an independent historical variable against which other sources of historical information are judged. Rather, it is a dependent variable whose historical value is judged by and against other, more reliable sources of historical information.

Over the past two centuries, scholars have learned an enormous amount about the ancient world. Vast quantities of raw data, both textual and archaeological, have been collected and processed; innumerable synthetic works have been produced; and anthologies of primary and secondary sources have proliferated. Granted, our knowledge is not perfect; a number of variously sized holes in our understanding remain to be filled, and individual historical sources can be problematic. Collectively, however, the weight of accumulated historical knowledge is both impressive and indisputable—and almost without exception decisive for larger issues of historical understanding.

Synchronisms among the ancient Mediterranean, Egyptian, and Near Eastern cultures have been worked out slowly and carefully by scholars in a variety of related fields. There is some quibbling in the decorative details of this structure, particularly for more poorly known eras, but the framework as a whole is solid. Absolute dates are disputed within a limited chronological range, but this does not mean that separate parts of the whole can be treated individually without regard to the broader implications for the entire structure. All parts are interrelated, and shifting one or more segments of the framework requires a concomitant movement of all other associated elements. Any substantive modification must be warranted on cogent historical grounds. The biblical narrative in particular, with its inherent inconsistencies, contradictions, and clearly problematic historical base, is not an appropriate venue for arbitrarily challenging fastidiously constructed and well-established chronologies and cross-cultural synchronisms.

Any search for a historical core to the Exodus saga must thus work within the network of established and interdependent chronologies for Egypt and the ancient Near East. The first step is to seek mention of Exodus events in nonbiblical ancient sources. Unfortunately, there are none: no texts from Egypt or anywhere else in the ancient Near East provide such an independent witness. Years of the most intensive scrutiny have failed to produce a single unequivocal, or even generally accepted, nonbiblical historical reference to any event or person involved in the Exodus saga. The first reasonably secure date in all of biblical history is Solomon's death around 928 BCE; and with one exception, no extrabiblical reference to Israel or Israelites by name occurs in historical sources earlier than the ninth century.

The exception occurs on the "Merneptah Stela," also known as the "Israel Stela." This black granite stela, over 3 meters (10 feet) high, was found in the ruins of Merneptah's funerary temple in western Thebes. A fragmentary copy also turned up at Karnak, the powerful state temple of the New Kingdom pharaohs (Dynasties 18–20; ca. 1550–1069 BCE) located in eastern Thebes. The stela tells us that it was carved in the fifth year of Merneptah (whose name is also rendered Merenptah), a pharaoh of Dynasty 19 who ruled approximately 1213–1203. The long text of the stela primarily glorifies Merneptah's military victory over Libyans and their Sea People allies, but its last two lines refer to a prior military campaign into Canaan, in which Merneptah says that he defeated, among others, Ashkelon, Gezer, Yanoam, and Israel. The hieroglyphs employed for Ashkelon, Gezer, and Yanoam include the determinative sign regularly used to refer to city-states: a throw stick plus three mountains designating a foreign country. The hieroglyphs with which Israel was written include instead the determinative sign usually reserved for foreign peoples: a throw stick plus a man and a woman over the three vertical plural lines. This sign is typically used by the Egyptians to signify nomadic groups or peoples without a fixed city-state home, thus implying a seminomadic or rural status for "Israel" at that time.

Recently some scholars have suggested that reliefs in the Karnak temple once attributed to Rameses II were carved during Merneptah's reign and provide a parallel account to the Canaanite campaign referred to on the Israel Stela, specifically illustrating the battles in which Ashkelon, Gezer, Yanoam, and Israel were defeated. If so, these reliefs would be the first known depictions of Israelites. Only Ashkelon, however, is named specifically; the identification of Gezer, Yanoam, and Israel must be inferred. This interpretation, as well as the dating of the reliefs, remains controversial. Ironically, the encounter with Egypt immortalized in the Merneptah Stela, the only indisputable extrabiblical mention of Israel prior to the ninth century BCE, is not recorded in the Bible, at least not in recognizable form.

Earlier in this century, a great deal of excitement arose with the discovery in Egypt of the Amarna tablets. These texts, dating to the fourteenth century BCE, mention a troublesome group of people found in ancient Syria-Palestine called the ʿApiru/ ʿAbiru, or Hapiru/Habiru. Scholars eagerly equated these Apiru with biblical ʿibrî, or "Hebrew," and at first thought they had found confirming, independent evidence of the invading Hebrews under Joshua. As more texts were uncovered throughout the Near East, however, it became clear that these Apiru were found throughout most of the Fertile Crescent (that well-watered arc of urban civilizations extending from the Tigris-Euphrates river basins over to the Mediterranean littoral and down through the Nile Valley) during the second millennium. They had no common ethnic or national affiliations; they spoke no common language; and they normally led a marginal and sometimes lawless existence on the fringes of settled society. The Apiru constituted, in effect, a loosely defined, inferior social class composed of shifting and shifty population elements without secure ties to settled communities. Apiru are frequently encountered in texts as outlaws, mercenaries, and slaves. Scholarly opinion remains divided as to whether there is an etymological relationship between Apiru and ʿibrî, though many scholars think that the Apiru were a component of proto-Israel.

Historical Analogues to the Exodus Events

Given the lack of extrabiblical witness to any part of the Exodus account, a second step toward placing the Exodus events in history has been to seek general historical parallels to the biblical data. Such analogues are most commonly invoked in three discrete categories reflecting the major components of the biblical narrative: "descent into Egypt," "sojourn in Egypt," and "Exodus from Egypt."

Virtually any movement into Egypt by Asiatics prior to the time of Merneptah can be considered a potential parallel for the biblical descent into Egypt by Joseph and Jacob and his entourage. Contacts between Egypt and Canaan can be charted at least intermittently throughout the late fourth and third millennia BCE and fairly regularly during the first half of the second millennium. These contacts become continuous during the second half of the second millennium, when Egypt ruled an empire that included most of ancient Syria-Palestine.

A variety of sources—tomb and temple paintings and reliefs, inscriptions, and papyri—indicate that during the second millennium BCE, large numbers of Asiatics found their way into Egypt. Many came as slaves: spoils of conquest from Egypt's numerous sorties into Syria-Palestine; tribute imposed on the vanquished by a victorious Egyptian state; or victims of the ancient slave trade. Demand for slaves in Egypt was considerable, from individual Egyptians as well as palace and temple estates. Slave ownership was not confined to the wealthiest elite; we know of one Syrian girl who was peddled door-to-door by a private trader in a village in western Thebes.

Trade was another reason for Asiatics to enter Egypt. A nineteenth-century BCE (Dynasty 12) tomb painting at Beni Hasan in Middle Egypt depicts an Asiatic donkey caravan. New Kingdom Theban tombs portray Syrian merchants. Major ports maintained foreign quarters that housed traders and trade missions. It is also suggested that the expression "to speak Syrian" became synonymous with "to bargain" in late New Kingdom times.

We know from later biblical sources that Egypt provided refuge for those fleeing political strife or persecution in ancient Syria-Palestine. In 1 Kings 11.16–18, Hadad and a small group of Edomites evaded David and Joab by escaping to Egypt, where the pharaoh gave them asylum. Similarly, in 1 Kings 11.40, Jeroboam fled to Egypt after his abortive revolt against Solomon and wisely remained there until Solomon's death. In 2 Kings 25.26, a remnant of those left behind after Nebuchadrezzar's capture and sack of Jerusalem fled to Egypt. Finally, in Matthew 2.13–15, an angel told Joseph to descend into Egypt with Jesus and Mary in order to avoid Herod's deadly search for the infant Jesus; there they remained until Herod's death.

Egypt also seems to have served as a haven for the less fortunate, particularly during times of famine or other hardship. Certainly the fertile, well-watered delta would have been an attractive destination, permanent or temporary, for a variety of groups from Syria-Palestine. There was probably a more or less constant flow of Asiatic and bedouin elements through Egypt's permeable northeastern border, as people sought pasturage, sanctuary, or a better life in Egypt's wealthier and more sophisticated civilization. At times of strong central government and strict border control this infiltration was probably a trickle; when the government was weak, foreign movement into the delta might become a flood. Unfortunately, there is a paucity of hard data for reconstructing delta history in detail, particularly for periods prior to the first millennium BCE.

Physical proximity to Asia made the delta, especially the northeastern delta, the main overland entry into Egypt for Asiatics. Goshen, the territory of the Israelite sojourn in Egypt according to the Bible, is traditionally located in precisely this area. The delta was also home to the two major routes connecting Egypt and Syria-

Palestine: the principal northern artery—the Ways of Horus and the Way of the
Sea—along the Mediterranean coast; and the peripheral southern route through the
Wadi Tumilat to the middle of the Sinai Peninsula.

Occasional written sources also provide glimpses into delta affairs. The "Instructions for Merikare," a literary work dating to the First Intermediate Period (ca. 2160–
1963 BCE), speaks briefly and generally of Asiatic infiltration into the eastern delta.
A late Dynasty 19 (ca. 1295–1186 BCE) papyrus contains a short scribal report concerning a group of Shasu bedouin whom the Egyptian government allowed to pass
the Fortress of Merneptah-Content-with-Truth, located in Tjeku (probably the Wadi
Tumilat). These Shasu wanted to water their flocks at the pools of Per Atum of
Merneptah-Content-with-Truth in Tjeku. The Shasu, a seminomadic group known
only from New Kingdom Egyptian documents and reliefs, apparently occupied southern Palestine east of the Jordan River and frequented much if not all of Canaan.
Egyptian texts refer to a "land of the Shasu," and reliefs depict the Shasu in a distinctive garb clearly differentiated from that worn by Canaanites. Like the Apiru, the
Shasu are often invoked in discussions of Israelite origins, and a number of scholars
think that elements of the Shasu were among the proto-Israelites who formed the
core of the settlers of the hill country of Canaan during the late thirteenth and early
twelfth centuries.

Historical sources identify only one group of Asiatics that migrated into and occupied the delta: the Hyksos. The Hyksos were a succession of foreign kings, based
in the eastern delta, which comprised Egypt's Dynasty 15 (ca. 1648–1540 BCE) during
the confused Second Intermediate Period. They were booted out of the country at
the beginning of the New Kingdom by a line of native Egyptian rulers from Thebes.
The Canaanite origin of the Hyksos has been established by archaeological
connections.

Potential counterparts thus exist for a "descent into Egypt" like that recorded in
the Bible. Such an event in principle would be far from unique. These analogues,
however, are only possibilities, and cannot be construed as hard evidence for a particular movement of Israelites into Egypt under specific circumstances. At most, they
tell us that a movement by Israelites into Egypt sometime during the second millennium BCE was neither impossible nor unlikely, and would have been compatible with
the tenor of the times.

Similar parallels exist for an Israelite "sojourn in Egypt." Diverse second-
millennium BCE Egyptian records attest to Asiatics, particularly individual Asiatics,
living in Egypt and functioning in a wide variety of capacities ranging from the most
menial of slaves to the highest of officials. From the Middle Kingdom (Dynasty 12)
comes a papyrus mentioning an "officer in charge of the Asiatics." Foreigners,
whether captives or mercenaries, were common in the Egyptian military from Old
Kingdom times on. The New Kingdom army, larger, more permanent, and more
professional than any before, utilized correspondingly larger numbers of mercenaries.
A Dynasty 13 papyrus lists, individually, seventy-nine slaves belonging to a private
household in Upper Egypt; of these, forty-eight had foreign names, mostly Semitic.
Middle Kingdom stelas in general often mention Semitic domestic slaves who apparently functioned as trusted family retainers. Indeed, so many household slaves in

Egypt were of Asiatic origin that the generic word for "Asiatic," 'amw, became synonymous in some contexts with "slave."

Information about Asiatics becomes particularly copious and varied during the
New Kingdom, reflecting both a larger number of preserved texts and depictions and
increased contact resulting from Egypt's conquest of southern Syria-Palestine. Children or other close relatives of local potentates in areas conquered by Egypt were
commonly sent to Egypt as hostages to guarantee the good behavior of the conquered
potentates. While in Egypt, these hostages were well treated and carefully acculturated
into Egyptian thought modes and lifestyles. Children were raised with the children
of the Egyptian elite; males often served in the Egyptian army. This policy was a
shrewd component of Egypt's colonial regime, forging a powerful bond between
Egypt and hostage, and enhancing vassal loyalty if and when the hostages returned
home to positions of power. Hostages who did not return home often rose to positions of importance within Egypt.

At or near the bottom of the Egyptian social ladder were the many slaves tied to
state and temple endowments. They were forced to toil on agricultural, industrial,
and construction projects, engaging in such tasks as weaving, cultivation, wine making, quarrying, and public works. Thutmose III (Dynasty 18, ca. 1479–1425) put
Syrian captives to work as "clothmakers" for the state temple of Amun at Karnak;
the same king also gave 150 Asiatic weavers to one of his favored officials. Generally
more fortunate were domestic slaves, particularly in the royal household, where they
might become trusted servants. Some Canaanite slaves held the royal sunshades; other
Asiatics served among the king's personal entourage, rising even to the high position
of chamberlain.

Within the Egyptian bureaucracy, some Asiatics attained positions of prominence
as priests and officials. Some achieved the lowest grade of the priesthood; a few rose
to higher ranks. A Canaanite named Pas-Baal became chief draftsman in the temple
of Amun; six generations later his descendants held the same office. Syrian scribes
were numerous, especially in the treasury; Canaanite butlers were commonplace
among palace officials, especially in Ramesside times. One Asiatic became superintendent of all the king's construction work; another, named Ben-Anath, became a
chief physician. A Canaanite from Bashan, Ben-Ozen, took the Egyptian name
Ramses-em-Per-Re and served as chief royal herald, fan bearer on the right of the
king, and first royal butler under Rameses II. Successful Asiatics in Egypt assimilated
totally. They adopted Egyptian names and portrayed themselves in Egyptian style and
dress. Often the only hint of their foreign origin was their Semitic name.

Most powerful of all were two Asiatics who rose to unprecedented heights in
Egyptian society. One, named Bay, has been known for many years. At the end of
Dynasty 19, a period of dynastic struggle ended in the brief rule of a queen, Tewosret
(ca. 1188–1186). During this time of strife, Bay, a high official probably of Syrian
extraction, apparently held the reins of power in Egypt. Bay seems to have been not
only Egypt's chancellor, but also the power behind the throne. A second high-ranking
Asiatic has only recently come to light. At Saqqarah, a major burial ground associated
with the Egyptian capital and administrative center of Memphis, a French mission
has excavated the family tomb of an otherwise unknown man named Aper-El. From

the inscriptions found in his tomb, our only source of information about this individual, it appears that Aper-El was a vizier, the most powerful secular official in the
bureaucracy, under both Amenhotep III and Amenhotep IV/Akhenaten of Dynasty
18 (ca. 1390–1336 BCE).

On occasion, captured foreigners might be settled as a group in Egypt because
they originated from the same place or because of some shared skill or ability. A
military unit might be kept together, for example. Thutmose IV relocated captives
from Gezer as a group; enclaves of foreigners were settled in both the delta and Middle
Egypt in Ramesside times. The Egyptians especially welcomed individuals or groups
of foreigners with specialized skills useful to the Egyptian crown and temples, particularly in crafts. Asiatic goldsmiths, coppersmiths, and shipwrights all appear in
Egyptian records.

We can thus cite numerous parallels for Asiatics dwelling in Egypt and assimilating
into Egyptian society. We know the names of a number of them, and we know that
a few rose to positions of power. Only occasional analogues exist, however, for the
settling of Asiatics as groups in particular locations in Egypt.

Counterparts, general or specific, to the Israelite "Exodus from Egypt" are more
difficult to establish. Rarely do we hear of Asiatics fleeing from Egypt. The Tale of
Sinuhe, sometimes cited in this context, is inappropriate because the fleeing protag-
onist is Egyptian, not Asiatic, although the first person Sinuhe encounters in Asia is
a local sheikh who had been in Egypt. A papyrus from late Dynasty 19 describes a
Tjeku troop commander's pursuit of two escaped slaves. The commander, sent by
the palace, failed to recapture the slaves, who may have escaped into Asia. The closest
historical parallel to the Israelite departure from Egypt, and the only known comparatively large-scale exodus of Asiatics from Egypt, is the expulsion of the Hyksos
that marked the end of the Second Intermediate Period and the beginning of the
New Kingdom. In fact, the Hyksos provide the only historical parallel that incorporates all three major elements of the biblical Exodus narrative—descent, sojourn,
and departure—a parallel to which we will turn shortly.

In general, surprisingly numerous analogues exist for the Hebrew descent into
and sojourn in Egypt. In the latter case we even have examples of individual Asiatics
rising to Joseph-like positions of power. What is most striking about these parallels
is the ease with which they can be established over a comparatively long time range.
Asiatics were common in Egypt, and wide-ranging contacts between Egypt and Syria-
Palestine were the norm, throughout the second millennium BCE, especially during
the New Kingdom, when a cosmopolitan Egypt ruled its Asiatic empire.

Such counterparts to elements of the Exodus narrative, unfortunately, provide no
hard evidence for a biblical movement of Hebrews into Egypt, nor do they prove
that a particular group of Hebrews ever resided in or exited from Egypt. No direct
connection can be established between the Exodus events and any of the historically
attested Asiatics in Egypt. Analogues provide only general evidence of Asiatics moving
into and living within Egyptian society; at most, they suggest that movement by
biblical Hebrews into and out of Egypt sometime during the second millennium BCE
was entirely possible. On its own, analogous evidence can neither confirm nor deny
the historicity of the Exodus saga, nor can it definitively place the Exodus in time.

The Date of the Exodus and Archaeology

In the end, efforts to place the Exodus events on a time line have had to resort to less-than-ideal inferences based on problematic biblical references and possibly analogous historical data. Archaeological discoveries are often invoked as an accompaniment to these inferences, either to support or to refute particular positions, but by their very nature archaeological finds are generally unsuitable for establishing detailed historical interpretations. A destruction layer, for example, typically provides graphic visual evidence in the form of black ash, charred material, and red-baked soil and brick, but it rarely supplies indisputable evidence of exactly how, why, or by whom the havoc was wreaked.

The archaeological data relating to the Exodus are subject to differing interpretations. But at no point in the known archaeological sequence for Egypt, Sinai, and Palestine does the extant archaeological record accord with that expected from the Exodus (or, for that matter, conquest) account in the Bible. No archaeological evidence from Egypt can be construed as representing a resident group of Israelites in the delta or elsewhere, unless one accepts a general equation of the Exodus group with the Hyksos. Nor is there any evidence of an early Israelite presence anywhere in Sinai. The Mediterranean littoral was heavily used by the Egyptian army during the New Kingdom, and the remainder of Sinai shows little evidence of occupation for virtually the entire second millennium BCE, from the beginning of the Middle Bronze Age to the beginning of the Iron Age or even later. Even the site currently identified with Kadesh-barnea provides no evidence of habitation prior to the establishment of the Israelite monarchy.

Compromise and selectivity are thus the keys to all hypotheses that have been advanced to date the Exodus events. Most often these hypotheses correlate aspects of the biblical narrative with particular historical settings and events and selected archaeological evidence. All assume that the "conquest" events, whether defined as actual conquest or the establishment of Israelite settlement or both, immediately followed the Exodus. None is entirely satisfactory from the point of view of critical historiography, archaeological evidence, or biblical testimony.

Dates proposed for the Exodus range from the third millennium to the eleventh centuries BCE. Dates at the earlier end of this chronological range do violence to our most basic understanding of the historical and cultural sequences and synchronisms for the ancient Near Eastern and Mediterranean worlds. Dates at the later end of the timescale conflict with our understanding of biblical Israel at the point where it is emerging onto the historical stage as well as with current interpretations of archaeological evidence. Few scholars hold to either extreme, and a broad consensus places the Exodus somewhere in the middle or toward the end of the second millennium, just before or during the Late Bronze Age, the Egyptian New Kingdom. Within this broad consensus, three alternative hypotheses have gained general credence. The earliest places the Exodus in the sixteenth century, the next in the fifteenth century, and the last in the thirteenth century.

The hypothesis dating the Exodus to the mid-sixteenth century BCE puts paramount importance on historical data and relies the least on biblical narrative. Since the expulsion of the Hyksos from Egypt is the only recorded historical occurrence of a collective movement of Asiatics out of Egypt prior to the first millennium, it is also the only occurrence that could be equated with the Exodus. A date at the beginning of the New Kingdom is only about a century earlier than that mandated by strict biblical chronology. Moreover, the ousting of the Hyksos follows an equally historical Asiatic descent into and sojourn in Egypt. Accordingly, as Josephus suggested nearly two thousand years ago (*Against Apion* 1.16), the Exodus should be equated with the Hyksos' expulsion from Egypt. Destruction levels in Palestinian sites dating to the transition between the Middle and Late Bronze Ages, often attributed to Egyptian military campaigns, could, according to this view, have resulted from an Israelite conquest and settlement of Canaan.

There are, however, a number of problems with this date for the Exodus. If the conquest/settlement occurred at the end of the sixteenth or beginning of the fifteenth century BCE, almost four hundred years must elapse before the Israelite state takes form under the monarchies of Saul and David at the end of the eleventh and beginning of the tenth centuries. Besides being too long a time span for the period of the judges, the putative four hundred years between conquest and kingship would occur during a period of known Egyptian hegemony over Syria-Palestine. Yet not a hint of Egyptian imperial might appears anywhere in the relevant biblical narrative. Moreover, in the last stages of the wilderness wanderings, just prior to the conquest, the Israelites are reported to interact with the kingdoms of Ammon, Moab, and Edom. Archaeological evidence, however, indicates little settled occupation in southern Transjordan throughout most of the second millennium, until the thirteenth century at the earliest.

The second hypothesis dates the Exodus to the fifteenth century BCE and stems from a literal reading of the biblical narrative. This view stresses the primacy of the Bible for historical interpretation and follows the biblical chronology, which dates the Exodus 480 years prior to Solomon's fourth year (1 Kings 6.1). By this reckoning, the Exodus began in the mid-fifteenth century, with the conquest coming forty years later. This Exodus chronology is generally part of a broader, biblically derived chronological and historical reconstruction that places the descent of Jacob in the mid-nineteenth century and the migration of Abraham in the mid-twenty-first century. In this scenario, historical and archaeological data play a secondary and supportive role and are invoked to bolster the primarily biblically derived chronology. A fifteenth-century Exodus date mandates a late fifteenth- or early fourteenth-century Israelite conquest. But the destruction layers required by a literal reading of the conquest narrative do not occur at the appropriate sites in Palestine. As a result, some scholars have tried to lower the date for the transition between the Middle and Late Bronze Ages in order to correlate site destructions of this date with the arrival of rampaging Israelites. Methodologically and historically, this attempt is unacceptable. The criticisms of the sixteenth-century Exodus date also apply here: the period of the judges becomes much too long; the Egyptians had firm control of Palestine; and settled life in southern Transjordan was minimal at best.

The third and most widely accepted hypothesis places the Exodus in the thirteenth century BCE. In this approach, the biblical narrative is judged and interpreted against the known historical and archaeological framework of the second millennium. Instead of working forward in time from the Exodus, this theory works backward from the Israelite conquest and settlement. Intensive archaeological research in the past twenty-five years has demonstrated a gradual proliferation of small rural settlements concentrated in the hill country of southern Canaan from around 1200, the beginning of Iron Age I. Accompanying these villages, many newly founded, was a material culture simpler than that of the large and cosmopolitan Canaanite cities of the plains. We know from contemporary texts and epigraphic material that by Iron Age II (ca. 1025) the hill country territories and their villages were inhabited by Israelites; it is but a short step to infer that it was the Israelites who established and occupied the settlements at the beginning of the Iron Age.

If the Israelite conquest and settlement occurred at the beginning of the twelfth century BCE, a time when the Egyptian empire was unraveling, then the Exodus and wilderness wanderings would have occurred slightly earlier, in the thirteenth century. This date accords better with the archaeological evidence for increased settlement east of the Jordan River in the regions of Ammon, Moab, and Edom. A thirteenth-century Exodus also fits well with the evidence of the Merneptah Stela, which would then reflect the situation in southern Palestine shortly after the Israelite settlement but prior to the development of the Israelite state. In addition, a number of sites west of the Jordan River were destroyed at the end of the thirteenth century; at least some of the destructions could be attributed to the Israelites.

If the Exodus and wilderness sojourn immediately preceded the Israelite settlement of Canaan, and if the most likely date for the settlement is the transitional thirteenth to twelfth centuries BCE, then any historical core to the Exodus events must have taken place toward the end of the Late Bronze Age, most likely during the thirteenth century.

The Late Bronze Age

The Late Bronze Age (ca. 1550–1200 BCE) was a brilliant, sophisticated, cosmopolitan era, in which great wealth accumulated and unprecedented international contacts and exchange occurred throughout the eastern Mediterranean. People, goods, and ideas flowed freely, by sea and by land, to an extent unparalleled in earlier times. The Late Bronze Age was also an age of empire, marked by complex political, economic, social, and cultural interactions, superpower politics, and an international way of life. Over the course of its three and a half centuries, the Late Bronze Age in the eastern Mediterranean saw the rise and fall of six major kingdoms or empires—those of Egypt, Mitanni (northern Syria), Kassite Babylon, Assyria, Hatti (ruled by the Hittites; Anatolia), and Mycenae. Of all these, Egypt's empire was the greatest, controlling the largest amount of territory, commanding the most prodigious wealth, and lasting the longest.

The era begins with the accession of Ahmose to the Egyptian throne in the mid-sixteenth century BCE and the final expulsion of the Hyksos from Egypt. Its end is generally dated to approximately 1200 BCE, when international trade connections ceased, anarchy spread throughout the eastern Mediterranean basin, empires splintered, and destruction or crisis struck the Canaanite city-states. In Egypt, the Late Bronze Age coincides with Dynasties 18, 19, and the beginning of Dynasty 20—the greatest part, literally and figuratively, of the New Kingdom.

The New Kingdom period was unsurpassed in Egyptian history for its wealth, power, and cosmopolitanism. An enormously rich, militaristic Egypt dominated much of Syria-Palestine throughout the Late Bronze Age. Palestine in particular remained yoked to Egyptian imperial might for the entire period and was controlled and exploited by Egyptian administrators mostly resident in the region. Since it is in Egypt and Palestine (including Sinai) that the Exodus narrative is set, we will concentrate on these areas, invoking broader international events and trends as appropriate.

A loosely organized patchwork of local city-states, each ruled by a "prince," dominated the political landscape of Syria-Palestine in the Late Bronze Age. The heart of the city-state system was a polity centered on one autonomous urban settlement; around this core lay hinterlands of varying sizes and compositions, contributing additional human and natural resources. The heavily fortified main city was usually located along at least one important trade and communication route. The city-states vied continually with each other for political, economic, and military dominance. Rarely were they completely independent: Syria-Palestine's position as corridor between Africa and Asia and outlet to the Mediterranean Sea attracted larger imperial powers like a magnet, one or more of whom invariably controlled the region. Alliances and allegiances, local and international, constantly shifted, as the military might of empires ebbed and flowed. The independent-minded city-states remained jealous of their lost autonomy, and scheming local rulers never missed an opportunity to rebel.

When Ahmose's victorious army ended its war of liberation against the Hyksos in the mid-sixteenth century BCE, a new era began in Egypt. Ahmose's ascension to the throne signaled more than just the beginning of Dynasty 18; it marked a break with past policies and attitudes. The rulers of Middle Kingdom Egypt (Dynasties 11–13; ca. 2106–1633) had intervened in Asia with only occasional military incursions to protect or secure their commercial interests. Middle Kingdom Egypt seems to have had few political and no territorial ambitions in Asia.

An increasing number of Asiatics nevertheless appeared in Egypt during the Middle Kingdom. Many undoubtedly came as slaves or mercenaries. Others seem to have percolated slowly but freely into the eastern delta, probably beginning sometime early in the second millennium BCE. As the Middle Kingdom gradually weakened and central control deteriorated over the course of Dynasty 13, the Asiatic influx into the delta increased and the power of the delta Asiatics grew proportionately. Eventually, sometime in the mid- to late seventeenth century, they became strong enough to seize control first of the eastern delta, then of the capital Memphis, and finally of the entire country, forming Dynasty 15. The Egyptians called these Asiatics "*heqaw khasut,*" "rulers of foreign lands," a term rendered in Greek as "Hyksos." Archaeological excavation in the eastern delta over the past thirty years, especially at the Hyksos capital of Avaris (Tell ed-Dabʿa) and the Hyksos enclave at Tell el-Maskhuta, have confirmed the Canaanite origin of the Hyksos.

Foreign subjugation, previously unknown, sent shock waves through the Egyptian psyche, which would reverberate throughout the New Kingdom state. After about a century of foreign rule, the native Egyptians from their base at Thebes finally broke Hyksos power. In a series of campaigns, the pharaohs of Dynasty 17 and early Dynasty

18 drove the Hyksos out of Egypt and into southern Palestine. The era inaugurated by Dynasty 18 is notable not only for renewed national unity but also for a militaristic spirit and an approach to foreign affairs fundamentally different from any before. New Kingdom Egypt maintained the country's first standing army and soon valued horse and chariot for warfare. Imperialism became a foreign policy, and official iconography emphasized the divine king as an indomitable warrior and universal conqueror.

The Egyptians rapidly recovered from the humiliation and indignity of Hyksos domination: fired by a "never again" attitude, in less than a century they carved out an extensive empire in Africa and Asia. Initially, for what remained of the sixteenth and the first half of the fifteenth centuries BCE, Egyptian kings from Ahmose to Thutmose III concentrated on securing Nubia. Canaan they kept pacified by sporadic military forays. Incursions into Syria-Palestine could be deep, however; Thutmose I (ca. 1504–1492) led an expedition to the Euphrates River in Syria.

Thutmose III (ca. 1479–1425 BCE), a brilliant general, directed Egyptian military might into Syria-Palestine. The catalyst was partly the death of Hatshepsut, his stepmother, aunt, and co-regent, and partly the revolt of a league of 330 Canaanite princes led by the prince of Qadesh (Tell Nebi Mend) in Syria. This Canaanite confederacy had gathered at Megiddo in a blatant challenge to Egyptian authority; provoked, Thutmose III marched rapidly northward at the head of a large army. The Canaanites were crushed and fled into the walled city of Megiddo, which fell after a seven-month siege. Even given the hyperbole of the time, the booty captured by Thutmose III's army was staggering in quantity and variety.

The battle of Megiddo inaugurated a new phase of Egyptian imperialism, with Egypt now aggressively pursuing territorial expansion into Asia. With Palestine under firm control, Thutmose III moved to subdue Syria, taking the coast as far north as modern Tripoli and capturing Qadesh on the Orontes. Instead of slaughtering his opponents, Thutmose III bound them to Egypt by loyalty oaths and then carted assorted Canaanite royal family members off to Egypt as insurance policies for princely good behavior. He also created a network of Egyptian garrison cities and headquarters to carry out Egyptian imperial policies and ambitions and to ensure the steady flow of tribute. Coastal and lowland plain cities, including Megiddo and Beth-shan, predominated in the network, but strategic considerations also dictated the establishment of key inland garrison cities to monitor trade routes and control the more sparsely occupied hill country. Syria-Palestine was partitioned into three large provinces, each controlled by an Egyptian official. Native rulers were generally left in place and the Egyptians remained mostly uninterested in local affairs—as long as the city-states respected Egyptian officialdom and delivered on time all required tribute, taxes, requisitioned goods and personnel, corvée labor, and military provisions.

But Egypt was not the only international power with imperial ambitions in western Asia in the fifteenth century BCE. Thutmose III's northern campaigns propelled him onto a collision course with Mitanni, the foremost northern power of the time. The kingdom of Mitanni, a coalition of Indo-Aryan and Hurrian elements, reached the peak of its power in the mid-fifteenth century. Mitannian territory extended from the upper reaches of the Tigris River (and possibly Armenia) across northern Syria to the Mediterranean. In his thirty-third year, Thutmose III launched a direct attack on Mitanni. He sacked towns along the Euphrates River as far as the great western bend, where he erected a stela on the riverbank next to an earlier one raised by his grandfather, Thutmose I; these stelae mark the farthest point ever reached by an Egyptian king in western Asia.

In the end, the confrontation between Egypt and Mitanni cost Mitanni most of its suzerainty west of the Euphrates and made Egypt the preeminent military and economic power of the Near East. At the height of his conquests, Thutmose III ruled an empire some 3,200 kilometers (2,000 miles) long, stretching from the Euphrates and Orontes Rivers in the north to the fourth cataract of the Nile in the south.

Thutmose III's imperious and ferocious son and successor, Amenhotep II (ca. 1427–1400 BCE), continued his father's campaigns in Asia, ruthlessly deporting masses of people and brutalizing prisoners in order to terrorize the local population and discourage dissension. Thutmose III's reign had produced a keen appreciation of the wealth available for the taking in Syria-Palestine; under Amenhotep II, Syria-Palestine was viewed as a conquered land ripe for constant plunder and exploitation. Egypt and Mitanni eventually made peace, probably sometime in Amenhotep II's reign. Their alliance was sealed by a marriage between a Mitannian princess and Thutmose IV (ca. 1400–1390), Amenhotep II's son and successor, who mounted at least one Asiatic campaign early in his reign, proceeding as far as the Orontes, and apparently taking captives from Gezer. By the close of the fifteenth century, Egypt's extensive empire in Asia was secure.

A *pax Aegyptica* settled over the Near East for the first half of the fourteenth century BCE, which coincided with the reign of Amenhotep III (ca. 1390–1352). Egypt reaped the fruits of empire. The frontiers were quiet, the land routes were secure, and the Egyptian garrisons functioned effectively. Sea trade around the eastern Mediterranean flourished. Amenhotep III cannily maintained the international balance of power through masterful diplomacy rather than military campaigns, marrying daughters of Babylonian and Mitannian kings to strengthen Egyptian alliances. Enormous wealth flowed into Egyptian coffers. Egypt stood at the height of its imperial power and glory.

Amenhotep III's death, however, inaugurated a troubled era in Egypt, known as the Amarna period. The throne passed to Amenhotep IV (ca. 1352–1336 BCE), who soon changed his name to Akhenaten ("One Effective on Behalf of Aten" or "Illuminated Manifestation of Aten") and moved his family and his court to the newly created city of Akhetaten ("Horizon of Aten"), located on the Amarna plain approximately halfway between Memphis and Thebes. From his isolated capital, Akhenaten launched an austere religious revolution. In short order, he overthrew the ancient gods, closed their temples, and forbade their worship. In their place, he ordered the worship of the Aten, the solar disk with its life-giving rays. According to Atenist theology, the Aten was the source of all creation, and the king and his beautiful wife Nefertiti were the Aten's earthly divine children and terrestrial co-regents. The Aten was to be worshiped through and alongside the royal couple, and the Aten and the king and queen formed a "divine family," which was supposed to be the only focus of religion for all of Egypt.

No figure of ancient Egypt is more controversial than Akhenaten. He has been judged lunatic, saint, and genius; monotheist, atheist, and henotheist; ruthless politician, mad revolutionary, and brilliant philosopher. Akhenaten's uncomfortable and largely sterile religious revolution barely survived his death, however, and the alacrity with which it was abandoned demonstrates its unpopularity among the Egyptian people. The artistic revolution that accompanied the religious upheaval lasted longer, and "Amarna art," despite the early excesses including grotesque depictions of the king with an ambiguous sexuality, promoted a naturalism that had a more lasting impact on Egyptian culture.

Neither did the new capital long survive the death of its founder, and the royal court returned to Thebes under Tutankhamon (1336–1327 BCE), born Tutankhaten. But ironically, the rubble of Akhetaten at Amarna, a site of fleeting importance and negative associations for the ancient Egyptians, has produced one of our most valuable resources for illuminating New Kingdom foreign policy and foreign relations. The Amarna letters, baked clay tablets with cuneiform inscriptions, were part of the official Egyptian court archive. Approximately 350 letters have been recovered, mostly dating to the reigns of Amenhotep III and Akhenaten. The exact chronology of the Amarna letters remains problematic, but scholars generally agree that the preserved archive covers fifteen to thirty years, beginning around year 30 of Amenhotep III and extending no later than Tutankhamon's year 3, when Akhetaten was abandoned.

The Amarna correspondence provides a rare and detailed glimpse into the intricate game of international power politics as practiced in the mid- to late fourteenth century BCE. The archive includes two groups of letters, the first consisting of correspondence between Egypt and independent foreign powers, and the second of missives between the Egyptian crown and its Asiatic vassals. The majority of the letters originated outside Egypt, although occasional material of Egyptian origin was also preserved.

A number of sovereign powers dealt with Egypt as equals, including Babylonia, Assyria, Mitanni, Arzawa (in western Anatolia), Alashiya (Cyprus), and Hatti (the Hittite empire). Following diplomatic convention of the time, the rulers of these independent kingdoms addressed each other as "brother." Correspondence between the Egyptian king and his royal rivals centers largely on the exchange of "gifts" and brides. The pharaoh sought foreign royal brides to forge or strengthen political alliances and to enhance his position as the foremost potentate in the ancient Near East. Egypt never returned the favor, however, and no Egyptian women were sent abroad as royal mates. What foreign rulers demanded most from Egypt was gold, which Egypt reputedly possessed in limitless quantities. Much ceremony accompanied the exchange of consorts and gifts, the latter including raw materials, manufactured commodities, and human and animal resources.

The majority of the Amarna letters deal with the administration of Egypt's empire in Syria-Palestine. The pharaoh wrote to his vassals to procure goods and personnel, to introduce Egyptian officials and certify their authority, and to exact needed logistical support for Egyptian activities. The vassals seem to have written to the Egyptian court neither regularly nor by choice, communicating only in response to some request of the king. Unfortunately, vassals were not permitted to address a king by name, which makes it difficult for us to correlate letters and monarchs. As a whole, the vassals' letters are a litany of bitter grievances against compatriots, charges and countercharges of sedition, assertions of innocence and fawning protestations of loyalty, and urgent requests for Egyptian military aid. An unappetizing picture emerges of petty dynasts jockeying for position vis-à-vis each other and their overlord.

In the north, the Amarna letters reflect increasing political and military pressure from a revitalized Hittite state in Anatolia. Some of the Syrian vassals soon acceded to the more immediate demands of this close and growing power. Others, also far from Egypt, embarked on their own glorification and expansion; the most successful was Amurru, which transformed itself into an important kingdom. In the south, vassal politics remained more insular, and the Amarna letters reflect shifting local coalitions and internecine rivalry and conflict. In the thick of this strife were the Apiru, the outcasts and troublemakers first documented in the area under Amenhotep II, who generally allied themselves with the less loyal of Egypt's vassals. Abdi-Hepa, ruler of Jerusalem, complained of the havoc wreaked by the Apiru in the central hills as he pleaded for Egyptian military support.

We have few corroborating sources for the Amarna letters. It is therefore difficult to assess the validity of the vassals' complaints. Had Egypt really abandoned its empire? Originally, scholars assumed that the correspondence reflected a disintegrating Egyptian empire neglected by a religious fanatic. Today it is believed that the documents reflect only business as usual in the quarrelsome Asiatic provinces, with the vassals attempting to exploit each other and to extort Egyptian support. Leaving the vassals to their own divisive devices is seen as a laissez-faire technique of implementing a divide-and-conquer policy. Egypt was not so paralyzed by religious turmoil that it ignored its interests in Asia. In fact, territorial loss in Asia during the Amarna period resulted less from internal dissension than from an unfortunate combination of revived Hittite potency and increasingly virulent disruptive elements such as the Apiru and the Shasu.

The resurrection of the Hittite state under Suppiluliumas I in the mid-fourteenth century BCE heralded the dawn of a new international balance of power. As "great king" of the Hatti, Suppiluliumas I first annihilated Egypt's ally Mitanni and absorbed the city-states of Syria formerly under Mitannian suzerainty. He then expanded southward, making his new frontier in southern Syria and appropriating Egypt's northern vassals. This Hittite expansion triggered a superpower rivalry that dominated politics in Syria-Palestine for much of the next century.

Egypt's Dynasty 19 ushered in both a new century and a new spirit. The Dynasty 19 kings started the thirteenth century BCE by returning to the ideals and practices of the great pre-Amarna pharaohs of Dynasty 18. Rameses I, the founder of Dynasty 19 (1295–1186), came from an eastern delta military family and ruled only briefly. He was succeeded by his son, Seti I (ca. 1294–1279), who set out to recapture the glory days of the empire. Invoking the optimism of the new age, Seti termed his first year of rule "the renaissance," and marched forth to consolidate Egypt's power over the Asiatic provinces. Control had grown so lax that Seti had to begin his campaign in Sinai battling Shasu bedouin who menaced traffic along the Ways of Horus, which connected Egypt and Gaza. In his vigorous reign, Seti I skirmished with the Apiru, defeated a local Canaanite alliance at Beth-shan, brought the northern coastal cities to heel, and even briefly returned Qadesh to the Egyptian fold.

Rameses II (1279–1213 BCE) succeeded Seti I and ruled for one of the longest reigns in Egyptian history. He created a new eastern delta capital at Pi-Ramesse,

"Domain of Rameses," identified with Qantir, a site adjacent to the Hyksos capital of Avaris/Tell ed-Dabᶜa. After consolidating his position at home, the young king marched into Syria, penetrating as far as the Dog River (Nahr el-Kalb) near Beirut and subduing the kingdom of Amurru. The return of Amurru to Egyptian control infuriated the Hittites, who recognized Egyptian aggression for what it was: an attempt to reclaim lost Syrian territories and resurrect Thutmose III's empire. Major conflict between the two superpowers was inevitable.

In his fifth year, Rameses II again marched into Syria. This time, however, an enormous Hittite army lay in wait just east of the city of Qadesh. Cleverly, the Hittites permitted the capture of two of their spies, who led the Egyptians into a trap sprung by an estimated seventeen thousand Hittite soldiers. Only the pharaoh's personal bravery prevented total annihilation of the Egyptians. Both Hittite and Egyptian accounts of the battle are preserved, and both sides declared victory. In reality, the battle was a draw that led to political and military stalemate. Rameses II continued to campaign throughout Asia in succeeding years, but never regained Qadesh. Eventually a changing world forced the two parties to the peace table. The growing power of Assyria pressured the Hittites from the south, and Libyans and their allies menaced Egypt from the west. In the twenty-first year of Rameses II's reign, a full peace treaty was signed and hostilities between Hatti and Egypt ended. Copies of the treaty have been found in both Anatolia and Egypt. Essentially it enshrined the status quo: the Hittites retained Qadesh and northern Syria; Egypt kept southern Syria and Palestine. Thirteen years after its signing, the treaty was commemorated by the marriage of Rameses II to a Hittite princess.

Merneptah (ca. 1213–1203 BCE), Rameses II's thirteenth son, became king as a mature man of over fifty. During his reign, Egyptian territorial integrity in the western delta was threatened by a large Libyan army aided by an ominous assortment of Sea Peoples. Merneptah's defeat of this Libyan coalition is immortalized on the "Israel Stela." Unfortunately, Merneptah soon died, leaving the crown in dispute and Egypt teetering on the brink of anarchy. The murky remainder of Dynasty 19 left little obvious mark on western Asia beyond an occasional inscribed object. The last nominal ruler of the dynasty was a queen, Tewosret; the power behind her throne, as already noted, was apparently the foreigner Bay, a man of Syrian origin.

Eventually Setnakht restored order and inaugurated Dynasty 20 (ca. 1186–1069 BCE). He ruled only briefly, leaving a temporarily renewed kingdom to his son Rameses III (ca. 1184–1153), the last great New Kingdom pharaoh. Rameses III successfully faced an immediate threat in the western delta from another Libyan coalition. A far greater menace, however, loomed just over the horizon. The Sea Peoples—who were neither a people nor, strictly speaking, entirely from the sea—were moving inexorably toward Egypt, spreading havoc throughout the eastern Mediterranean basin.

The enigmatic Sea Peoples seem to have been a shifting coalition of diverse population elements, probably originating in Anatolia and the Aegean. Egyptian records give us the names of their component groups—a total of fourteen are known—and occasional depictions. They first appear in the Amarna letters, and again in Rameses II's accounts of the battle of Qadesh and Merneptah's commemorations of his victory over the Libyans. They seem initially to have allied themselves with various Near

Eastern powers, alliances that probably kept them under temporary control. By the time of Rameses III, however, a new confederation of Sea Peoples was on the move independently. In the closing years of the thirteenth century BCE and the opening years of the twelfth, these Sea Peoples, their families in tow, left a trail of carnage throughout the eastern Mediterranean. What precipitated this mass movement of population is unknown, but its consequences are clear.

By the time the Sea Peoples menaced the borders of Egypt, they had sacked the Hittite capital and territories and plundered Cyprus and Syria. Vivid testimony of the passage of the Sea Peoples and the destruction in their wake comes from Ugarit, where a kiln full of clay tablets was abandoned during the fall of the city. These tablets report famine in the Hittite empire and Cyprus, and the urgent transfer to the north of Ugarit's army and navy. The city-state was left defenseless to face the Sea Peoples' fury; one tablet even records the sack of the city.

Rameses III was compelled to mount a massive defense of Egypt. He deflected the Sea Peoples in major land and sea battles in his eighth year. Although these Sea Peoples, identified as the Peleset (Philistines), Tjeker, Shekelesh, Denyen, and Wesh-esh, did not breach Egypt's borders, it was a pyrrhic victory. Egypt entered a period of decline that would last for centuries. Initially, it sought to retain its hold on Palestine, and sporadic Egyptian control continued briefly until the middle of the twelfth century BCE. After this, however, Egyptian authority collapsed completely.

Archaeological data are our primary source for the history and culture of Syria-Palestine in the Late Bronze Age. Supplemented by some textual material, they inform us that population and settlement density declined in the area, a number of important cities were abandoned or shrank in size, and marginal areas were deserted. Southern Transjordan, Galilee, and the central hill country became sparsely populated; the few major cities in these areas, such as Shechem and Jerusalem, lay much farther apart than did lowland cities. The population that did exist was highly heterogeneous, and along with the settled occupants of the city-states it included such disruptive stateless elements as the Apiru and Shasu. Substantial destructions and the partial abandonment of major sites dominate the archaeological record of the second half of the sixteenth and the first half of the fifteenth centuries BCE. The remainder of the fifteenth century gives evidence of severe population disruptions, likely triggered by mass deportations carried out by Thutmose III and his successors. Then, in the fourteenth and thirteenth centuries BCE, archaeology in Syria-Palestine reveals a heightened Mediterranean trade; evidently superpower confrontations were not permitted to disrupt international commerce. From the Amarna period in the fourteenth century to the end of the thirteenth, archaeological evidence of Egyptian presence in Palestine grows much stronger. Fortified Egyptian citadels have been found in northern Sinai and Palestine; so-called Egyptian residencies are known in a number of cities; and Egyptian or Egyptian-inspired temples appear in several sites, notably Beth-shan.

The Late Bronze Age ended with the death or exhaustion of all the major participants in its power struggles. International trade and cosmopolitanism declined sharply, as did the standard of living throughout the eastern Mediterranean. Many of the fortified cities, the centers of urban Canaanite culture, were destroyed. Out of the wreckage of the Late Bronze Age empires arose a changed world marked by a new political pattern. In the early Iron Age, new settlements were smaller, and located in areas only sparsely populated during the Late Bronze Age. A series of small nation-states grounded in ethnic affiliations developed; in southern Canaan, these included Philistia, Israel, Ammon, Moab, and Edom.

Given the omnipresence of the powerful Egyptian empire in Late Bronze Age Palestine, even during the Amarna period, it is difficult to understand Egypt's minimal role in the biblical account of the Exodus. After the Israelites leave Egypt, the Egyptians disappear from the narrative. If the Exodus occurred in the sixteenth or fifteenth centuries BCE, events prior to the establishment of the Israelite monarchy would have played out in the middle of Egyptian imperial might. Yet not a trace of Egyptian hegemony appears in the Bible. If, on the other hand, the Exodus occurred in the thirteenth century BCE, just prior to the dissolution of Egyptian power, the absence of Egypt from the Exodus account is understandable.

Conclusion

A study of the Exodus narrative raises many questions about the historicity and historical setting of the Exodus events, but provides few definitive answers. The biblical text has its own inner logic and consistency, largely divorced from the concerns of secular history. Over time, various hands shaped and edited the biblical narrative, combining and blending different sources and literary categories according to theological truths rather than historical imperatives. Historiographic methods alone can never do full justice to the spiritually informed biblical material; conversely, the Bible, never intended to function primarily as a historical document, cannot meet modern canons of historical accuracy and reliability. There is, in fact, remarkably little of proven or provable historical worth or reliability in the biblical Exodus narrative, and no reliable independent witnesses attest to the historicity or date of the Exodus events.

To some, the lack of a secure historical grounding for the biblical Exodus narrative merely reflects its nonhistorical nature. According to this view, there was no historical Exodus and the story is to be interpreted as a legend or myth of origins. To others, still in the majority among scholars, the ultimate historicity of the Exodus narrative is indisputable. The details of the story may have become clouded or obscured through the transmission process, but a historical core is mandated by that major tenet of faith that permeates the Bible: God acts in history.

It is most likely that the Israelite settlement of Palestine occurred in the period beginning about 1200 BCE. Archaeologically, socially, politically, economically, and militarily, the twelfth century makes the most sense as the context of the conquest/settlement and of the judges, even if the historical and archaeological records do not match the biblical exactly. Granting the essential historicity of the Exodus and the wilderness wanderings, and assuming that the conquest/settlement followed directly, then the Exodus itself must have occurred in the thirteenth century BCE, a date that accords with our knowledge of contemporary sociopolitical and settlement patterns in the broader region.

Another alternative may be suggested tentatively, since it involves dislocation of the biblical text. If one posits initially separate Exodus and conquest/settlement traditions, then no longer must the Exodus events occur immediately prior to the conquest/settlement. By this scenario, the descent, sojourn, and Exodus in the biblical narrative could reflect Hyksos occupation and rule over Egypt, the Exodus would date to the sixteenth century BCE, and the Exodus account would have a clear historical core. A fifteenth-century date is also possible, although one must discard adherence to the biblical narrative as the major criterion for evaluation, since separating the Exodus and conquest does violence to the narrative's theological design. If one assumes more generally that the Exodus reflects an encapsulation and telescoping of Egyptian imperial power, then the events could be dated at any time in the Late Bronze Age.

Some future historical or archaeological discovery may provide concrete, indisputable evidence for the historicity of the biblical Exodus. Until then, however, the details of the biblical Exodus narrative and even its ultimate historicity will continue to be debated. Admittedly, we cannot prove that the Exodus took place; but we also cannot prove that it did not. As with so much else in the Bible, belief or disbelief in the historicity of the Exodus narrative becomes a matter of faith.

Select Bibliography

Baines, John, and Jaromír Málek. *Cultural Atlas of Ancient Egypt*. Rev. ed. New York: Facts on File, 2000. A lavishly illustrated, invaluable introduction, with detailed discussions of geography, history, sites, and daily life.

Dothan, Trude, and Moshe Dothan. *People of the Sea: The Search for the Philistines*. New York: Macmillan, 1992. A personal, popular account by two Israeli archaeologists of their decades of research into the Philistines and related archaeological discoveries at a number of important sites.

Frerichs, Ernest S., and Leonard H. Lesko, eds. *Exodus: The Egyptian Evidence*. Winona Lake, Ind.: Eisenbrauns, 1997. Six papers by well-known scholars provide a useful overview of recent thinking on the Exodus and Israelite settlement, with extensive bibliographies.

Friedman, Richard Elliot. *Who Wrote the Bible?* New York: Summit, 1987. A readable and thorough account of the history and development of the Documentary Hypothesis intended for a general audience.

Hoffmeier, James K. *Israel in Egypt: The Evidence for the Authenticity of the Exodus Tradition*. New York: Oxford University Press, 1997. A detailed examination of the biblical account of the Exodus incorporating recent textual, historical, and archaeological scholarship, which concludes that the main points of the narratives are plausible.

Johnstone, William. *Exodus*. Sheffield, England: JSOT, 1990. An excellent, concise introduction to the book of Exodus outlining major thematic, historical, literary, and religious concerns.

Leonard, Albert, Jr. "Archaeological Sources for the History of Palestine: The Late Bronze Age." *Biblical Archaeologist* 52 (1989): 4–39. A useful summary of Late Bronze Age archaeological finds in the southern Levant correlated with New Kingdom Egyptian history.

Merrillees, Robert S. "Political Conditions in the Eastern Mediterranean during the Late Bronze Age." *Biblical Archaeologist* 40 (1986): 42–50. A general summary of historical events, with particular emphasis on the fourteenth and thirteenth centuries BCE.

Metzger, Bruce M., and Michael D. Coogan, eds. *The Oxford Companion to the Bible*. New

York: Oxford University Press, 1993. An invaluable one-volume reference resource. See especially the articles by Michael D. Coogan on "Exodus, The" and by John I Durham on "Exodus, The Book of."

Perevolotsky, Aviram, and Israel Finkelstein. "The Southern Sinai Exodus Route in Ecological Perspective." *Biblical Archaeology Review* 11, no. 4 (July–August 1985): 27–41. An illuminating discussion of the relationship between Exodus traditions and the rise of monasticism in Sinai, as well as of the ecology of the region.

Redford, Donald B. *Egypt, Canaan, and Israel in Ancient Times.* Princeton, N.J.: Princeton University Press, 1992. An impressive overview of interrelationships between Egypt and the Levant from prehistory to the early sixth century BCE. The general reader must be cautious, however, as some of the author's views are disputed.

Sandars, N. K. *The Sea Peoples: Warriors of the Ancient Mediterranean 1250–1150 B.C.* Rev. ed. New York: Thames and Hudson, 1985. A classic review of the major issues concerning the Sea Peoples and the evidence for understanding their origins and actions.

Stiebing, William H. *Out of the Desert? Archaeology and the Exodus/Conquest Narratives.* Buffalo, N.Y.: Prometheus, 1989. A general overview and evaluation of the archaeological and textual evidence for and the main historical theories about the Exodus and conquest.

Time-Life Books. *Ramses II: Magnificence on the Nile.* Alexandria, Va.: Time-Life Books, 1993. A nicely done, well-illustrated popular overview of the life and times of Rameses II, with an excellent bibliography.

CHAPTER THREE

Forging an Identity

The Emergence of Ancient Israel

LAWRENCE E. STAGER

hortly after 1200 BCE the once great Hittite empire in Anatolia and the Mycenaean empire in mainland Greece—the Trojans and the Achaeans, to use the language of Homeric epic—collapsed, releasing different centrifugal forces. Within the Mycenaean and Hittite worlds an internal process of fragmentation and ruralization began, leading to what archaeologists often call a "dark age." This in turn triggered mass migrations by sea to the already crowded coastlands of the Levant and Cyprus, sending repercussions into the interior of Canaan as well. The Philistines were one group taking part in these migrations. Not long before, another group had appeared in the land of Canaan, although by a process that is much more disputed. This group called itself Israel, and according to the biblical story it also had arrived from a foreign land—escaping slavery in Egypt, crossing a body of water, and eventually entering Canaan from the east. This chapter focuses on reconstructing the early history of these two new groups, the Philistines and the Israelites, in the land of Canaan, insofar as the textual and archaeological evidence permits such a synthesis.

The Egyptians maintained some control over parts of Canaan until just after the death of Rameses III in 1153 BCE. By the first half of the twelfth century, Canaan had become a virtual mosaic of cultures, including Canaanites, Egyptians, Israelites, and the mysterious "Sea Peoples," of whom the Philistines are the best known. The settlement process in highland Israel began a generation or two before the Sea Peoples arrived on the coast. An event of such magnitude must have had powerful repercussions on the indigenous Canaanite population as it was being squeezed out of the plains. Some of these displaced inhabitants probably entered the frontier communities located in the highlands east and west of the Rift Valley—the polities of early

Israel, Moab, Ammon, and perhaps Edom. The displacement and migration of the tribe of Dan from the central coast to the far north is symptomatic of the ripple effects of this event.

Early Written and Iconographic Sources

The Egyptian pharaoh Merneptah (1213–1203 BCE) provides the earliest nonbiblical reference to ancient Israel, in a short poem appended to a much longer prose account of his self-proclaimed victory over the Libyans and their allies, the Sea Peoples. The victory stela (now usually known as the "Israel Stela") was erected in 1209 in Merneptah's funerary temple at Thebes. The relevant part of the victory ode reads:

> The princes are prostrate, saying "Shalom" [Peace]!
> Not one is raising his head among the Nine Bows.
> Now that Libya [Tehenu] has come to ruin,
> Hatti is pacified.
> The Canaan has been plundered into every sort of woe;
>   Ashkelon has been overcome;
>   Gezer has been captured;
>   Yanoam is made nonexistent;
> Israel is laid waste and his seed is not;
> Hurru is become a widow because of Egypt.

The leading adversaries of the Egyptians—three city-states, or kingdoms, designated by their capitals (Ashkelon, Gezer, and Yanoam), and a people known as Israel—lie within the larger geographical framework of Canaan and Hurru. The latter, bereft of her spouse, has become a "widow" because of Egypt. Ironically, Merneptah's premature proclamation of the demise of Israel is the first reference in history to this polity, which survived for another six hundred years as a "nation," first as a confederation of tribes and later as a monarchy (1025–586 BCE).

Within the larger territorial framework of Canaan, the Egyptians use the determinative for a fortified city-state to designate the smaller kingdoms of Ashkelon, Gezer, and Yanoam; Israel is correctly distinguished as a rural or tribal entity by the determinative for "people." In Egyptian the names of foreign countries, provinces, and cities are treated syntactically as feminine. But Israel, with the "people" determinative, is a masculine collective, probably indicating its identity with an eponymous patriarchal ancestor. Clearly the Egyptians regarded Israel as a different kind of polity from the other three, although all were apparently equal adversaries, if not part of an organized anti-Egyptian Canaanite coalition. The campaign against Canaan proceeds from the southwest to the northeast, Ashkelon to Gezer, and then farther north to Yanoam, somewhere near the Sea of Galilee.

Where was this early Israel located, and what was its settlement pattern and social structure? The people determinative can be used of tribally organized pastoralist or agriculturalist groups, with or without territorial boundaries. The Egyptian designation could apply equally well to an unsettled or to a settled group or confederation organized along tribal lines. This early entity must have had sufficient military strength to stand on par with the three other city-states, or kingdoms.

When the rebellion of Canaanites and Israelites against Egypt is placed in broader perspective, it appears that this was just one of many trouble spots that threatened Egyptian control and order in the late thirteenth and early twelfth centuries BCE. The first wave of Sea Peoples (which did not include the Philistines), allied with the Libyans, lapped right up to the shores of Egypt itself during Merneptah's reign. Three decades later a second wave of Sea Peoples (including the Philistines) threatened the Nile Delta and carved out coastal kingdoms in Canaan at the expense of the Egyptian empire under Rameses III.

In this larger context of disorder in the eastern Mediterranean it is abundantly clear from the Merneptah Stela that Israel was a political-ethnic entity of sufficient importance to the Egyptians to warrant mention alongside the three Canaanite city-states. Indeed, this event of about 1200 BCE was the nearest thing to a real revolution in Canaan—and it was against the Egyptians.

An elegant and precise pictorial complement to the victory hymn of Merneptah has recently been identified in four battle reliefs at Karnak. Formerly attributed to Rameses II but now assigned with confidence to Merneptah, these reliefs depict the three city-states (Ashkelon is mentioned by name in the reliefs) and the "people" Israel.

In the Merneptah reliefs, the Israelites are not depicted as Shasu, but wear the same clothing and have the same hairstyles as the Canaanites, who are defending the fortified cities of Ashkelon, Gezer, and Yanoam. This new evidence does not, of course, settle the perennial question concerning the "origins" of Late Bronze Age Israel, that is, whether it consisted predominantly of pastoralists, peasants, new immigrants, or all three. But it does undermine the older notion that the Israelites were only the Shasu known by a new name, who settled down in agricultural villages about 1200 BCE.

Another victory ode, this time from the early Israelites themselves, is preserved in Judges 5 and is known as the Song of Deborah. George Foot Moore considered the poem the "only contemporaneous monument of Hebrew history" before the United Monarchy. It probably dates from the twelfth century BCE. As a celebration of victory over the Canaanite coalition at the battle of Kishon, the poem is a masterpiece of Semitic literature. As a historical document, it is important for the self-portrayal and self-understanding of early Israel that the poet provides.

The poem portrays Israel as a confederation of ten (not twelve) tribes, a theopolity known as the "people [kindred] of Yahweh" (Judg. 5.13). Marching forth from the southeast, from Seir and Edom, Yahweh leads his people to victory over the Canaanites "at Taanach, by the waters of Megiddo." Through divine succor from the heavenly host and a flash flood in the Wadi Kishon, the Israelites rout the better-armed Canaanites, who are equipped with chariots. The final blow of the battle is struck by Jael, a woman of the Kenite clan (a subgroup of the Midianites), who drives a tent peg through the head of Sisera, leader of the Canaanite coalition.

Early in the twelfth century BCE the confederation of ten tribes was occupying a variety of ecological niches on both sides of the Jordan, and carrying on a variety of professions, such as highland farming (Ephraim, Machir, Benjamin, Naphtali), sheep and goat herding (Reuben), and seafaring (Dan and Asher). Such a wide-ranging confederation of disparate groups committed to the kindred of Yahweh did not always act in concert, as the Song of Deborah indicates. Sometimes individual tribal interests and economic entanglements prevailed: Reuben, Gilead, Dan, and Asher declined to answer the call to arms. The positive response to the muster came from the highland village militia of the six other members of the confederation.

The Israelite understanding of themselves as a kindred of Yahweh in Judges 5 is compatible with the Egyptian designation of Israel as a "people," although the constituency of that polity probably changed from the late thirteenth into the early twelfth centuries. When considered together with the archaeology of the region, both documents provide an invaluable resource for reconstructing aspects of the social, political, and religious life of nascent Israel.

The Conquest Narratives

The literary sources for the biblical account of the conquest of Canaan by twelve tribes under the command of Joshua are embedded in the great work of the Deuteronomic Historian(s) (DH), writing some six hundred years after the event he purports to describe. From the perspective of DH, the conquest of Canaan was a unified, lightning-fast event that swept from east to west—from Ammon and Moab, across the Jordan River to the hill country of central Canaan, and then north to Galilee. It was a conquest of the indigenous "Canaanites" by "outsiders," namely, the "Israelites," under the protection and guidance of their deity Yahweh. Although DH's theological perspective is incompatible with modern historiographic methods, he can by ancient standards be considered among the "first historians," as Baruch Halpern has phrased it, every much a historian of ancient Israel as Herodotus was of ancient Greece.

DH tells a coherent story from entry into the Promised Land to the end of the monarchy. He creates dialogue for his leading characters. At the same time, however, DH makes use of the limited sources available to him. These include a variety of earlier oral traditions and written documents, the only survivals of which are now in the Bible. They range in date and genre from early poetry of the twelfth century, such as Judges 5, to boundary lists of the seventh century, such as Joshua 15.

DH sometimes weaves multiple accounts of the same event into his narrative, even when they are at variance or are contradictory. The most obvious example is the prose account of the battle of Kishon (Judg. 4), in which two tribes battle the Canaanites. This is followed in the next chapter by the poetic account, the Song of Deborah, in which at least six tribes fight. All scholars agree that the prose account is later and dependent on the poetic version. Nevertheless, perhaps wishing to preserve a variety of traditions, DH chose to present both versions of the same event.

This same concern for sources leads to the tension between the monolithic conquest of Canaan as presented in the book of Joshua and the partial takeover that introduces the book of Judges. In his use of sources DH differs radically from another ancient Israelite historian, the Chronicler, writing more than a century later. The Chronicler has winnowed his sources and constructed a narrative into a unified whole that does not allow for variant or multiple accounts of a single event.

Nevertheless, for all the care that DH lavished on his sources, most of them derive from the period of the monarchy, several centuries later than the purported era of Joshua and the conquest of Canaan. As Nadav Na'aman has observed, many of the conquest narratives were modeled on later battles, such as those of David against the

Philistines or the Arameans, or Sennacherib's campaign against Judah. Thus it is extremely difficult for the modern historian to disentangle the many strands of DH's braided narrative, composed as it is from a very particular historiographic perspective, and including invented dialogue and limited sources presumed to be contemporary with the era of conquest but mostly dating much later.

The Conquest Hypothesis

Of the three regnant scholarly hypotheses formulated to account for the emergence of Israel in Canaan, the "conquest" hypothesis conforms most closely to the biblical presentation of DH. W. F. Albright developed a powerful formulation of the conquest hypothesis, which many American and Israeli archaeologists later espoused, G. Ernest Wright and Yigael Yadin being two of its most notable proponents. They were confident that the essential historicity of the conquest narratives could be vindicated by the use of external evidence provided by archaeology. Until relatively recently, many archaeologists believed that excavations at sites thought to be identified with biblical Heshbon, Jericho, Bethel, Ai, Lachish, Eglon, Debir, and Hazor actually supported the notion of a unified conquest of Canaan by outsiders in the latter part of the thirteenth century BCE. This interpretation relies heavily on the conquest narratives in the book of Joshua (chapters 6–12) and, to a lesser extent, in Judges 1. For this group of scholars the archaeology of widespread and synchronous destruction at many of these key cities as well as the cultural change that followed about 1200 BCE buttress the validity of the biblical accounts preserved in the Deuteronomic History, many of which are based, according to this view, on much older oral and written sources. In this view, Israel swept into Canaan from the eastern desert and swiftly conquered city after city.

Archaeologists agree that dramatic cultural change affected not only parts of Canaan but also much of the eastern Mediterranean at the end of the Late Bronze Age (ca. 1200 BCE). How much of that change was brought about by the migrations and/ or invasions of newcomers to Canaan, and specifically by invading Israelites, is still an open question. To make a persuasive archaeological case for the mass migration of peoples from one homeland to another, certain criteria must be met:

1. The implanted culture must be distinguishable from the indigenous cultures in the new zones of settlement. If the intrusive group launches an invasion (as proponents of the Israelite "conquest" postulate), then there should be synchronous discontinuities, such as destruction layers, separating the previous "Canaanite" cultures from the newly established "Israelite" cultures in the zone of contention.

2. The homeland of the migrating/invading groups should be located, its material culture depicted, and temporal precedence established in its place of origin. In the case of invading Israel, this should be in Transjordan or in Egypt.

3. The route of migration/invasion should be traceable and examined for its archaeological, historical, and geographical plausibility. If the new immigrants took an overland route, the spatial and temporal distribution of the material culture should indicate the path and direction of large-scale migrations.

As the Israelites advanced from Egypt toward Canaan, the conquest narratives have them taking Heshbon (modern Hesban), the city of Sihon, and Medeba in

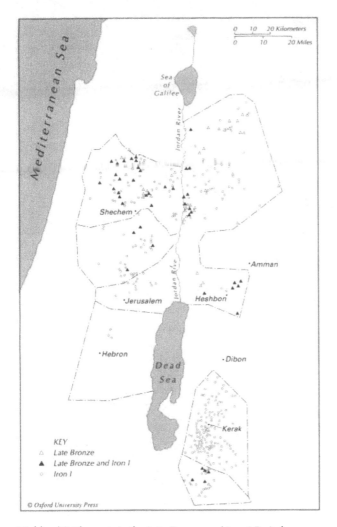

Highland Settlements in the Late Bronze and Iron I Periods

Ammon, as well as Dibon (modern Dhiban) in Moab (Num. 21.21–31). At Heshbon and Dibon, extensive excavations have uncovered no Late Bronze Age occupation, and only meager remains from Iron Age I. The situation at Medeba is being investigated. As the settlement map indicates (see above), most of Transjordan was unoccupied when the Israelite invaders are said to have moved through these territories in the late thirteenth century BCE.

After crossing the Jordan River, Joshua and his troops conquered Jericho (Josh. 6). They blew the rams' horns and shouted in unison until the walls of Jericho collapsed. This miracle has no archaeological reflex; in fact, there is little or no occupation at Jericho in the thirteenth century. Kathleen Kenyon, the British archaeologist who pioneered stratigraphic excavations at the site, thought that erosion had deprived history of the Late Bronze Age city that Joshua captured. But the

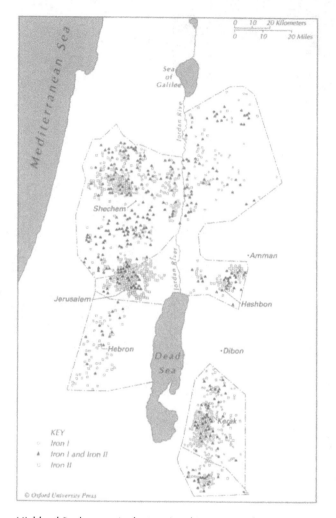

Highland Settlements in the Iron I and Iron II Periods

absence of tombs and even potsherds from this period makes Kenyon's view highly unlikely.

When Joshua and his troops moved farther west, up the wadi to Ai (Josh. 7.2–8.29), they ultimately scored a great victory over the king of Ai and the inhabitants of the city. But here again archaeology demonstrates that a tall tale is being told. Ai, whose name means the "ruin," had not been occupied during the second millennium. Its "ruins" dated from the latter part of the third millennium, among which an Iron Age I village was planted in the twelfth century. As German scholars have long maintained, Ai is a showcase example of how etiological explanations were used to enhance the conquest narratives by explaining extensive ruins as the result of early Israelite victories. Nearby Bethel was put to the sword (Judg. 1), and archaeology has confirmed its destruction in the thirteenth century.

The next major conquest occurs in the north at Hazor, the former "head of all those kingdoms." All of the dependencies of Hazor were taken, but only Hazor itself was burned to the ground (Josh. 11.10–13). This was the largest city of Canaan, its inhabitants numbering twenty thousand or more. The only agents who claim responsibility for destroying this Canaanite city are the Israelites. There is no reason to deny them their claim.

Finally, there is a summary of Joshua's victories west of the Jordan (Josh. 12.9–24). Following this list, the identifications of the ancient sites and the archaeological evidence are summed up in table 3.1 (see pp. 98–99).

Of the thirty-one cities said to be taken by Joshua and the Israelites, twenty have been plausibly identified with excavation sites. Of these, only Bethel and Hazor meet criterion 1, and even there, it is debated whether the destruction of Hazor XIII was as late as that of Late Bronze Age Bethel. The conquest of Laish/Dan, recounted in Judges 18, may be reflected in the destruction of Tel Dan, Stratum VIIA (ca. 1175–1150 BCE)—too late to be synchronized with the demise of Late Bronze Age Bethel and Hazor. The Late Bronze Age city of Lachish VII was destroyed in the latter half of the thirteenth century BCE. This destruction could have resulted from the purported Israelite invasion, but recent excavations have shown that the rebuilt city (Lachish VI) was an Egypto-Canaanite settlement, occupied as a buffer against Philistia during the reign of Rameses III, until about 1150. None of the Transjordanian settlements mentioned in the conquest of Sihon's "Amorite" kingdom by the Israelites (Num. 21) has Late Bronze Age occupation. The three cities of Philistia—Gaza, Ashkelon, and Ekron—listed as captured by Judah in Judges 1.18, according to the Masoretic Text, are said not to have been, according to the Greek version.

Thus by the most generous interpretation of the archaeological data, the "unified conquest" hypothesis fails to meet the minimal standards of criterion 1. Nevertheless, the insistence of the Deuteronomic Historian that Israel was an "outside" force, rather lately "conquering" Canaan and wresting control from the autochthonous population, is not so easily explained. This is especially highlighted by later Near Eastern historiography represented by Manetho's *Aegyptiaca*, Berossus's *Babyloniaca*, and Josephus's *Jewish Antiquities*. All three historians go to great length to establish the antiquity and priority of their respective peoples.

Perhaps, then, there is something to be said for a migration, if not an actual invasion, of Israelites into Canaan toward the end of the Bronze Age. For this more general explanation of culture change, variants of criteria 1 through 3 are still valid. They pertain to the other hypotheses concerning the emergence of early Israel as well. But before those are explicated, it is necessary to summarize new data in the archaeology of the Late Bronze Age and Iron Age I, which have come from excavations and, especially, systematic surface surveys of sites on both sides of the Rift Valley. (For a summary, see tables 3.2 and 3.3 and the settlement maps.)

The Archaeological Evidence of Early Israel

and Neighboring Polities

In the nine areas surveyed, eighty-eight Late Bronze Age sites occupy a built-up area of more than 200 hectares (500 acres), for an estimated total population of about

Table 3.1   Cities in Joshua 12.9–24

ANCIENT PLACE-NAME	BIBLICAL REFERENCES	ARCHAEOLOGICAL EVIDENCE
1. Jericho	Joshua 12.9; 6; 24.11	Meager LB II occupation
2. Ai	Joshua 12.9; 7.2–8.29	No occupation from 2250 to 1200
3. Jerusalem	Joshua 12.10; Judges 1.21	No destruction at the end of LB II
4. Hebron	Joshua 12.10; 10.36–37; 14.13–15; 15.13–14; Judges 1.10	No evidence
5. Jarmuth	Joshua 12.11; 10.5	LB II to Iron I occupation
6. Lachish	Joshua 12.11; 10.31–32	City VII destroyed in late thirteenth century; City VI destroyed ca. 1150
7. Eglon	Joshua 12.12; 10.34–35	Tell 'Aitun; LB occupation unclear
8. Gezer	Joshua 12.12; contra Judges 1.29	LB destruction, probably Merneptah or Philistines
9. Debir	Joshua 12.13; 10.38–39; 15.15–17; Judges 1.11–13	Tell er-Rabud, no destruction at end of LB
10. Geder	Joshua 12.13	Khirbet Jedur; LB II and Iron I pottery; not excavated
11. Hormah	Joshua 12.14	Identification unknown
12. Arad	Joshua 12.14	No LB occupation
13. Libnah	Joshua 12.15; 10.29–31	Identification unknown
14. Adullam	Joshua 12.15	Khirbet 'Adullam; not excavated
15. Makkedah	Joshua 12.16; 10.28	Identification unknown
16. Bethel	Joshua 12.16; 8.17; Judges 1.22–26	Destruction in the late thirteenth century
17. Tappuah	Joshua 12.17	Tell Sheikh Abu Zarad; not excavated
18. Hepher	Joshua 12.17	Tell el-Muhaffer; not excavated

Table 3.1 (*continued*)

ANCIENT PLACE-NAME	BIBLICAL REFERENCES	ARCHAEOLOGICAL EVIDENCE
19. Aphek	Joshua 12.18	LB destruction followed by Iron I "Sea Peoples" occupation
20. Lasharon	Joshua 12.18	Identification unknown
21. Madon	Joshua 12.19	Identification unknown
22. Hazor	Joshua 12.19; 11.10–13; Judges 4.2	LB city, Stratum XIII, destroyed in thirteenth century
23. Shimron-meron	Joshua 12.20	Identification unknown
24. Achsaph	Joshua 12.20	Khirbet el-Harbaj: LB II and Iron I pottery
25. Taanach	Joshua 12.21; contra Judges 1.27	Meager LB II remains; Iron I village destroyed in latter half of twelfth century
26. Megiddo	Joshua 12.21; contra Judges 1.27	LB II/Iron I city, Stratum VIIA, destroyed in latter half of twelfth century
27. Kedesh	Joshua 12.22	Tell Abu Qudeis; Iron I settlement, Stratum VIII, destroyed in latter half of twelfth century
28. Jokneam	Joshua 12.22	LB II settlement, Stratum XIX, destroyed in late thirteenth or twelfth century; gap follows
29. Dor	Joshua 12.23; contra Judges 1.27	"Sea Peoples" known as Sikils occupy city in twelfth century; transition from LB to Iron I not yet determined
30. Goiim	Joshua 12.23	Identification unknown
31. Tirzah	Joshua 12.24	Tell el-Farah (N); LB II and Iron I occupation; no evidence of destruction

Table 3.2   Survey of Sites by Region and Period Appearing on Settlement Maps

	LATE BRONZE	IRON I	IRON II
Judah	0	18	68
Benjamin	0	52	180
Ephraim	4	102	89
Manasseh	32	147	220
Gilead	19	77	53
Jordan Valley	20	40	41
Hesban (in Ammon)	6	32	61
Moab*	0	170	98
Wadi el-Hasa (in Edom)	7	40	42
Total	88	678	852

*In the absence of Mycenaean or Cypriot imported pottery and lack of local pottery with exclusively LB II characteristics, all of the LB sites in the Kerak Plateau Survey have been reassigned to the Iron I period.

50,000. In the same areas there are 678 Iron Age I settlements, each site being a hectare or less, for a total of about 600 hectares (nearly 1,500 acres), with an estimated 150,000 inhabitants (see table 3.2 and settlement maps). Six hundred and thirty-three, or 93 percent, of these Iron Age I sites are new foundations, usually small, unwalled villages. Most of these new settlements are located in the highlands or plateaus on both sides of the Jordan River. Settlement is especially dense in the territories of Manasseh and Ephraim in the west and in Gilead and Moab in the east, both "frontiers" having been sparsely settled in the Late Bronze Age. This extraordinary increase in occupation during Iron Age I cannot be explained only by natural population growth of the few Late Bronze Age city-states in the region: there must have been a major influx of people into the highlands in the twelfth and eleventh centuries BCE.

Recent attempts to distinguish movements from east of the Jordan into the west, or vice versa, lack sufficiently precise chronological control to be convincing. What can be said is that Iron Age I settlements throughout the highlands display a similar material culture, which is best identified with rural communities based on mixed economies of agriculture and sheep-goat herding. That many of these villages belonged to premonarchic Israel (as known from Judg. 5 and perhaps from the Merneptah Stela) is beyond doubt. This is especially clear from the continuity of settle-

Table 3.3   Continuity of Settlement Patterns from Late Bronze Age II to Iron Age I and from Iron Age I to Iron Age II

	LATE BRONZE	IRON I		IRON II
Judah	→	0%	→	22%
Benjamin	→	0%	→	19%
Ephraim	→	4%	→	84%
Manasseh	→	14%	→	38%
Gilead	→	0%	→	68%
Jordan Valley	→	23%	→	61%
Hesban	→	19%	→	39%
Moab	→	0%	→	47%
Wadi el-Hasa	→	13%	→	45%
Total	→	7%	→	42%

ment patterns from Iron Age I into Iron Age II (see table 3.3) in the survey zones of Ephraim, Manasseh, and Gilead, the heartland of monarchic Israel.

Biblical sources indicate that premonarchic Israel was structured according to tribal principles of social organization. Archaeology is providing support for understanding the social organization of premonarchic Israel and other Transjordanian polities (for example, Moab, Midian, Ammon) as kin-based, "tribal" societies. In the Iron Age I highland villages, the heartland of early Israel, it is possible to distinguish multiple family compounds, such as those at Khirbet Raddana. These family compounds, comprised of two or three houses set off from their village surroundings by an enclosure wall, formed the basic socioeconomic units of the community, usually with a population of no more than one hundred to two hundred persons per village. In such villages, the extended or multiple family unit was the ideal type. Such a household may have constituted a minimal "house of the father" (Hebrew *bêt 'āb*), or a small patrilineage.

Further clues to the composition of early Israelite villages can be deciphered from compound place-names. The first element of the place-name reveals the settlement type, such as "hill," "enclosure," "diadem"; the second element, the name of the founding families or leading lineages. Examples are Gibeah ("hill") of Saul (1 Sam. 11.4), Hazar ("enclosure of")-addar (Num. 34.4), Ataroth ("diadem of")-addar (Josh. 16.5), and Ataroth-beth-joab ("diadem of the house of Joab"; 1 Chron. 2.54). Likewise, on the regional level territories could take their names from the dominant large families, either lineages or clans, who lived there. Samuel, a Zuphite, lived at his ancestral home at Ramah, or Ramath(aim)-zophim, named after his Ephraimite ancestor (1 Sam. 1.1), in the land of Zuph, through which Saul passed in search of his father's lost asses (1 Sam. 9.5). District or clan territories remained important subdivisions of tribal society even during the monarchical period, as the Samaria ostraca attest.

Without clear indications from texts, it is doubtful that archaeologists can distinguish one highland group from another. The cluster of material culture, which includes collared-rim store jars, pillared houses, storage pits, faunal assemblages of sheep, goat, and cattle (but little or no pig), may well indicate an Israelite settlement, but this assemblage is not exclusively theirs. Giloh and Tell el-Ful (Saul's Gibeah) are generally considered to be "Israelite" villages, but they have many things in common (for example, collared-rim store jars) with neighboring "Jebusite" Jerusalem and "Hivite" Gibeon. "Taanach by the waters of Megiddo" seems to be Canaanite in the Song of Deborah, yet its material culture is hardly distinguishable from that of the highland villages. There is a greater contrast between the twelfth-century city of Canaanite Megiddo (Stratum VIIA) and the contemporary Canaanite village of Taanach than between putative Israelite and Canaanite rural settlements. The differences derive more from socioeconomic than from ethnic factors.

The evidence from language, costume, coiffure, and material remains suggest that the early Israelites were a rural subset of Canaanite culture and largely indistinguishable from Transjordanian rural cultures as well.

The Pastoral Nomad Hypothesis

In 1925 the German scholar Albrecht Alt articulated the second regnant hypothesis to explain the appearance of early Israel. Alt used texts to compare the "territorial divisions" of Canaan with those of the Iron Age. From this brilliant analysis, made without the aid of archaeology, Alt concluded that early Israel evolved from pastoral nomadism to agricultural sedentarism.

This interpretation, which has held sway especially among German scholars, accepts the biblical notion that the Israelites were outsiders migrating into Canaan from the eastern desert steppes as pastoral nomads, specialists in sheep and goat husbandry. These clan and tribal groups established more or less peaceful relations with the indigenous Canaanites, moving into more sparsely populated zones, such as the wooded highlands of Palestine or the marginal steppes—areas outside the domain of most Canaanite kingdoms and beyond the effective control of their overlords, the Egyptians. These pastoralists have sometimes been identified specifically with a wide-ranging group called the Shasu in Egyptian texts dating from 1500 to 1150 BCE. They appear as mercenaries in the Egyptian army, but more often they are regarded as tent-dwelling nomads who raise flocks of sheep and goats. Their primary range seems to be in southern Edom or northern Arabia (known as "Midian" in the Bible). In Merneptah's time, Egyptians recognized the "Shasu of Edom." A Dynasty 18 list mentions among their tribal territories the "Shasu-land of Yahweh," perhaps an early reference to the deity first revealed to Moses at Horeb/Sinai in the land of Midian (see below).

Recent anthropological research has rendered obsolete the concept of the pastoral nomads who subsist on the meat and dairy products they produce and live in blissful solitude from the rest of the world. Equally outworn is the concept of seminomadism (still embraced by too many scholars of the ancient Near East) as a rigid ontological status, marking some cultural (pseudo-)evolutionary stage on the path to civilization, from desert tribesman to village farmer to urban dweller: in archaeological parlance, the "from tent-to-hut-to-house" evolution.

Scholars of the ancient Near East are only recently rediscovering what the great fourteenth-century CE Arab historian Ibn Khaldun knew well. In his classic *Muqaddimah: An Introduction to History,* he observed:

> Desert civilization is inferior to urban civilization, because not all the necessities of civilization are to be found among the people of the desert. They do have some agriculture at home but do not possess the materials that belong to it, most of which [depend on] crafts. They have ... milk, wool, [camel's] hair, and hides, which the urban population needs and pays Bedouins money for. However, while [the Bedouins] need the cities for their necessities of life, the urban population needs [the Bedouins] for conveniences and luxuries. (p. 122; trans. Franz Rosenthal, abr. and ed. by N. J. Dawood, Princeton, N.J.: Princeton University Press, 1967)

The Israeli archaeologist Israel Finkelstein has adapted and updated Alt's nomadic hypothesis to explain the hundreds of new settlements that have been recorded in archaeological surveys. But it is difficult to believe that all of these new-founded, early Iron Age I settlements emanated from a single source, namely sheep-goat pastoralism. In symbiotic relations the pastoral component rarely exceeds 10 to 15 percent of the total population. Given the decline of sedentarists in Canaan throughout the Late Bronze Age, it seems unlikely that most of the Iron Age settlers came from indigenous pastoralist backgrounds.

The Peasants' Revolt Hypothesis

The third leading hypothesis to account for the emergence of ancient Israel was posed by George E. Mendenhall and elaborated further by Norman Gottwald. For them, the Israelites consisted mainly of oppressed Canaanite peasants who revolted against their masters and withdrew from the urban enclaves of the lowlands and valleys to seek their freedom elsewhere, beyond the effective control of the urban elite. In this sense, they represent a parasocial element known as the Apiru in second-millennium BCE texts from many parts of the Near East. Moshe Greenberg has characterized them as "uprooted, propertyless persons who found a means of subsistence for themselves and their families by entering a state of dependence in various forms. A contributory factor in their helplessness appears to have been their lack of rights as foreigners in the places where they lived. In large numbers they were organized into state-supported bodies to serve the military needs of their localities. Others exchanged their services for maintenance with individual masters" (*The Hab/piru,* New Haven, Conn.: American Oriental Society, 1955, p. 88). These were propertyless persons in a state of dependency on a superior. They might be servants in a household or hired laborers. In hard economic times and periods of social disintegration, they became gangs of freebooters and bandits under the leadership of a warlord, such as Jephthah (Judg. 11) or David before he became king. Whether this was a revolution from the bottom up, which resulted in the new Yahwistic faith (according to Gottwald), or whether the new faith served as the catalyst for revolutionary change (according to Mendenhall), both variants of the "peasants' revolt" hypothesis consider the participants to be insiders, not outsiders—an underclass of former Canaanites who took on a new identity as they joined the newly constituted community "Israel."

The "peasants' revolt" model and concomitant "Yahwistic revolution" have only partial explanatory power. If these farming villages were the product of this Yahwistic revolution, then how does one account for an almost equal number of "egalitarian" villages outside the confines of premonarchic Israel? They appear over a much wider landscape than even the most maximalist views of early Israel could include, ranging from Ammon to Moab and even into Edom, not to speak of those settlements within Canaan itself, where the ethnic identity of their inhabitants is in question.

It is unlikely that all these newly founded early Iron I settlements derived from a single source—whether of Late Bronze Age sheep-goat pastoralists settling down, or from disintegrating city-state systems no longer able to control peasants bent on taking over lowland agricultural regimes for themselves or pioneering new, "free" lands in the highlands. When one considers the widespread phenomenon of small agricultural communities in Iron Age I, it becomes even more difficult to explain it all by any hypothesis that would limit it to "Israelites" alone, as all three hypotheses do.

To draw the boundaries of premonarchic Israel so broadly as to include every settlement that displays the most common attributes of that culture (pillared farmhouses, collared-rim store jars, terraced fields, and cisterns), or to claim that all of these villages and hamlets on both sides of the Jordan are "Israelite" just because they share a common material culture, is to commit a fallacy against which the great French medieval historian Marc Bloch warned, namely, of ascribing a widespread phenomenon to a "pseudo-local cause." A general phenomenon must have an equally general cause. Comparison with a similar but widespread phenomenon often undermines purely local explanations. Now that archaeologists have collected the kinds of settlement data that provide a more comprehensive pattern, the focus must be widened to include a more comprehensive explanation than the regnant hypotheses allow—whether they relate to an Israelite "conquest," a "peasants' revolution," or "nomads settling down."

It would be overly simplistic to draw the boundaries of premonarchic Israel so broadly as to ascribe the change in the settlement landscape to this historical force alone. This, of course, does not preclude the use of particularistic, historical studies to elucidate aspects of the larger process. Once the results of highland archaeology need not be accounted for by an exclusively "Israelite" explanation, one can then look at this well-documented polity as a case study within the larger framework.

A Ruralization Hypothesis

From the changing settlement patterns in the Levant and elsewhere in the eastern Mediterranean, it seems that the pattern of deep, structural change had more to do with the process of ruralization than revolution. In the Late Bronze Age there must have been acute shortages of labor in the city-states, where attracting and retaining agricultural workers was a constant problem. Evsey Domar (*Capitalism, Socialism, and Serfdom*, New York: Cambridge University Press, 1989) has isolated a set of interrelated variables that may help explain the proliferation of agricultural villages in frontier areas, where such entities as Israel, Moab, and Edom are already found in thirteenth-century BCE Egyptian sources. According to this formulation, only two of the three following variables can coexist within the same agricultural regime: free land, free peasants, and nonworking landowners. In the Late Bronze Age city-states, free land (in the highlands and marginal regions), nonworking landowners, and "serfs" existed. With the decline of some city-state systems, there would have been a centrifugal tendency for peasant farmers to settle beyond areas of state control, especially in the less accessible mountain redoubts.

So long as the Late Bronze Age markets and exchange networks were still operating, the sheep-goat pastoralists would have found specialization in animal husbandry a worthwhile occupation. However, with the decline of these economic systems in many parts of Canaan in the late thirteenth to early twelfth centuries BCE—when "caravans ceased and travelers kept to the byways" (Judg. 5.6)—the pastoralist sector, engaged in herding and huckstering, may also have found it advantageous to shift toward different subsistence strategies, such as farming with some stock-raising. This group undoubtedly formed part of the village population that emerged quite visibly in the highlands about 1200.

Especially in marginal "frontier" zones, the trend was toward decentralization and ruralization, brought about by the decline of the Late Bronze Age city-state and, in certain areas, of Egyptian imperial control. It is in this broader framework that we must try to locate the more specific causes that led to the emergence of early Israel.

Israel developed its self-consciousness or ethnic identity in large measure through its religious foundation—a breakthrough that led a subset of Canaanite culture, coming from a variety of places, backgrounds, prior affiliations, and livelihoods, to join a supertribe united under the authority of and devotion to a supreme deity, revealed to Moses as Yahweh. From a small group that formed around the founder Moses in Midian, other groups were added. Among the first to join was the Transjordanian tribe of Reuben, firstborn of the "sons of Jacob/Israel." Later, this once powerful tribe was threatened with extinction (Deut. 33.6). But by then many others had joined the Mosaic movement scholars call Yahwism.

Midianites, Moses, and Monotheism

Nearly a century ago the historian Eduard Meyer traced the origin of Yahwism to the Midianites and to one of their subgroups, the Kenites. Recent archaeological discoveries in northern Arabia and elsewhere have revived and revised the "Midianite/Kenite" hypothesis, most elegantly expressed in the writings of the biblical scholar Frank M. Cross. A biography of Moses, the founder of Yahwism, cannot be written from the biblical legends that surround him. But several details in his saga, especially concerning the Midianites, seem to be early and authentic.

According to the epic source called J (Yahwist), Moses, after killing an Egyptian, fled from an unnamed pharaoh (perhaps Seti I) to the land of Midian. The heartland of Midian lay in the desert of rose-red mountains and plateaus above the great Rift Valley, east of the Gulf of Aqaba in northwestern Arabia. Medieval Arab geographers still referred to this region as the land of Midian; today it is known as the Hijaz. There Moses married the daughter of the Midianite priest Jethro (called Reuel or

Egypt, Sinai, Arabia, and the Land of Midian

Hobab in other sources). During this initial episode in Midian, Moses experienced the theophany of Yahweh in the thornbush, which was blazing but was not consumed (Exod. 3.1–4.17).

After the Exodus from Egypt (probably during the reign of Rameses II), Moses returned with his followers to the same "mountain of God [*'elohim*]" in Midian, where he experienced a second theophany. In this episode Moses received the Ten Commandments and sealed the covenant between God (*'elohim*) and his people. Moses' father-in-law, the priest of Midian, counseled him about implementing an effective judicial system among the Israelites, apparently based on one already in use among the Midianites (Exod. 18.13–27).

Jethro expressed his commitment to God (*'elohim*) through burnt offerings and sacrifices, and his solidarity with Moses and his followers through a shared meal "in the presence of God [*'elohim*]" (Exod. 18.12). Later Moses' father-in-law helped guide this group through the wilderness as far as Canaan, but he declined to enter the

Promised Land, averring that he must return to his own land and to his kindred (Num. 10.29–32).

The traditions of benign relations between the Midianites and the Moses group reflect the period prior to 1100 BCE, that is, before the era of Gideon and Abimelech, when the camel-riding and -raiding Midianites had become the archenemies of the Israelites (Judg. 6). The Midianites, like the Kenites, the Amalekites, and the Ishmaelites, disappear from biblical history by the tenth century BCE. It strains credulity to think that traditions about Moses, the great lawgiver and hero who married the daughter of the priest of Midian, were created during or after these hostilities.

Early Hebrew poetry suggests that the "mountain of God," known as Horeb (in the E and D sources) and as Sinai (in the J and P sources), was located in the Arabian, not the Sinai, Peninsula. When Yahweh leads the Israelites into battle against the Canaanites in the twelfth-century Song of Deborah, the poet declares:

> When you, Yahweh, went forth from Seir,
> When you marched forth from the plateaus of Edom,
> Earth shook,
> Heaven poured,
> Clouds poured water;
> Mountains quaked;
> Before Yahweh, Lord of Sinai,
> Before Yahweh, God of Israel.
> (Judg. 5.4–5; my translation)

Likewise in the archaic "Blessing of Moses":

> Yahweh came from Sinai,
> He beamed forth from Seir upon us,
> He shone forth from Mount Paran.
> (Deut. 33.2; my translation)

And the same locale is given for Yahweh's mountain home in Habakkuk 3:

> God came from Teman,
> The Holy One from Mount Paran. . . .
> He stood and he shook earth,
> He looked and made nations tremble.
> Everlasting mountains were shattered,
> Ancient hills collapsed,
> Ancient pathways were destroyed. . . .
> The tents of Cushan shook,
> Tent curtains of the land of Midian.
> (Hab. 3.3–7; my translation)

The tribesmen of Cushan were already encamped on the southeast border of Palestine in the early second millennium BCE, according to Middle Kingdom texts from Egypt. Later they were absorbed into the confederation of Midianites.

The epic traditions concerning Moses and the Midianites occur in story time between the Exodus from Egypt and the conquest of Canaan. The setting for these encounters on or near the "mountain of God" is connected with Edom, Seir, Paran,

Teman, Cushan, and Midian. There, in the Arabian, not the Sinai, Peninsula, Yahweh is first revealed to Moses, and it is from there that the deity marches forth to lead the nascent Israelites into battle, according to the earliest Hebrew poetry.

In historical time the benign relations between Midianites and Israelites should be set before 1100 BCE, a period that also coincides with the floruit of "Midianite ware" (see below) and the presence of pastoralists in the region. The Egyptians of the New Kingdom included those tent-dwellers under the general rubric *Shasu*. Among their territories southeast of Canaan mentioned in the lists of Amenhotep III, one is designated the "land of the Shasu: *S'rr*," probably to be identified with Seir; another is known as the "land of the Shasu: *Yhw3*," or Yahweh.

Until the enmity between Israelites and Midianites, exemplified in the wars of Gideon, dominated their relations, the two groups were considered kin, offspring of the patriarch Abraham: Israelites through Isaac, son of the primary wife, Sarah, and Midianites through Midian, son of the secondary wife or concubine, Keturah, whose name means "incense." From Moses on, Midianites were also linked to Israelites by marriage to the founder of Yahwism.

All of this changed dramatically during the period of the judges. The about-face in attitude and policy toward the once-friendly Midianites is nowhere more vividly portrayed than in the polemic against the worship of Baal of Peor in Moab. In the J summary of the event (Num. 25.1–5), the Israelites are depicted as fornicators, whoring after the "daughters of Moab" and their deity Baal of Peor. Apparently a plague interrupted the festivities, and to ward it off the leaders of the Israelites "who yoked [themselves] to Baal of Peor" were executed. In the P account (Num. 25.6–18), Phinehas, who represents the later priestly household of Aaron, calls into question the genealogical charter of the priestly household of Moses and challenges the legitimacy of this dynasty of priests. When Phinehas finds a notable scion of the Israelites copulating with a notable daughter of the Midianites within the sacred precincts of the tent-shrine or tabernacle, the Aaronide priest skewers them both with a single thrust of his lance.

In the lineage of Abraham in Genesis, Keturah's "sons" represent tribes and peoples trafficking in goods from Arabia (Gen. 25.1–4). Midianites and Ishmaelites settle in the land of Havilah (25.18), through which one of four rivers of Eden flows, a land rich in gold, bdellium, and carnelian (Gen. 2.11–12). Another river of paradise flows around the land of Cush (2.13), or Cushan, whose descendants include not only Havilah but also Seba/Saba/Sheba (Gen. 10.7; 1 Chron. 1.9).

When the queen of Sheba (modern Yemen, in south Arabia) visited King Solomon, she brought camel caravans loaded with aromatics, gold, and gemstones (1 Kings 10.2). Her "gifts" to the Israelite potentate of the tenth century BCE differ little from the tribute exacted from Sheba by the Assyrian emperor Esarhaddon three centuries later. Yautha, king of a confederation of North Arabian tribes known as the Kedarites, delivered to the Assyrian monarch 10 minas of gold, 1,000 choice gems, 50 camels, and 1,000 leather bags of aromatics of all kinds.

In the sixth century BCE the great Phoenician seaport of Tyre was exporting the wealth of Arabia to other parts of the Mediterranean: the Kedarites brought young bull-camels, rams, and he-goats; the Dedanites, from an oasis north of Yathrib (Medina), traded in saddle cloths for riding; and Sheba exported gold, incense, and all kinds of gemstones (Ezek. 27.20–22).

Even later the book of Isaiah (60.6–7) anticipated that Arabia's riches would be brought to a restored Jerusalem:

> A multitude of camels shall cover you,
>   the young bull-camels of Midian and Ephah [a son of Midian in Gen. 25.4];
>   all those from Sheba shall come.
> They shall bring gold and frankincense. . . .
> All the flocks of Kedar shall be gathered to you.

Thus whether the great caravaneers of Arabia were known as Midianites (Gen. 37.28, 36; Judg. 5.10), or later as Arabs and Kedarites, or later still as Nabateans, the merchandise and produce they exported to the rest of the ancient Near East and to the Mediterranean remained basically the same.

Linkage between remote desert oases in Arabia required the camel. It was the only pack animal that could survive the long distances between watering holes in the desert oases, the vital links between the resources of southern Arabia and the wider world. W. F. Albright's assessment, based on contemporary texts and limited faunal remains, that dromedary camels became important to the caravan trade only toward the final centuries of the second millennium BCE, is still valid.

In Sheba grew the best aromatics in the world. Frankincense is a white resin obtained from trees that grow in abundance on the mountainous south coast of the Arabian Peninsula, in the Hadhramaut and Dhofar. It was burned as a pungent aromatic incense or as a compound in other fragrant offerings to the gods. Myrrh, harvested from bushes growing in the steppes of Punt (modern Somalia) and Sheba, was another aromatic in great demand for its use in cosmetics, perfumes, and medicines.

By the Late Bronze Age, the aromatics trade had become the most lucrative business in the ancient Near East thanks to the dromedary camel. Not only did the merchants become rich; so did the camel breeders, the escorts who provided protection for caravans through hostile territory, and the rulers who exacted tolls from caravaneers passing through their kingdoms (see 1 Kings 10.15).

As J. David Schloen has recognized, it was the disruption of this lucrative caravan trade under the aegis of the Midianites and the protection of the Israelites that sparked the battle between Canaanites and Israelites, celebrated in the Song of Deborah, when:

> In the days of Shamgar ben Anat,
> In the days of Jael,
> Caravans and trailblazers held back,
> Caravans traveled by circuitous routes,
> Village tribesmen in Israel held back.
> They held back until you arose, Deborah,
> Until you arose, a mother in Israel.
>   (Judg. 5.6–7; my translation)

The heroine of the victory was Jael, the wife of Heber the Kenite, who drove a tent peg into the temple of the Canaanite commander Sisera (Judg. 5.24–27). In one tradition Moses' father-in-law is identified with the Kenites (Judg. 1.16), whose descendants dwell among the Amalekites in the northern Negeb near Arad (1 Sam. 15.5–6). Moshe Kochavi has plausibly suggested that the main Amalekite center was located at Tel Masos. Apparently the Kenites and the Amalekites were part of the large confederation of Midianites, who in the twelfth century BCE were still on friendly terms with the Israelites. Genealogical traditions identified Kenites with Cain (*qayyan* means "metalsmith" in Aramaic) and Tubal-cain "who made all kinds of bronze and iron tools" (Gen. 4.22).

The date and distribution of "Midianite painted pottery," also called "Hijaz painted pottery," corroborates and clarifies some of the Midianite traditions adumbrated above. The key site is a large urban oasis known today as Qurayyah in northwestern Arabia, in the heartland of ancient Midian. The site awaits systematic excavation, but using intensive surface surveys Peter Parr has been able to provide many details about it. The citadel of this center is extremely large, encompassing about 35 hectares (86 acres), below which lies a fortified settlement of another 15 hectares (37 acres). As many as ten to twelve thousand inhabitants lived in this caravan city. Some local subsistence for the large community was provided by an elaborate system of irrigation farming utilizing seasonal floodwaters.

The most striking artifact from the survey is a beautiful painted pottery, found at Qurayyah in abundance. It is decorated with painted geometric designs (probably imitating textiles) and zoomorphic motifs, such as the desert ostrich. Pottery kilns at the site and petrographic analysis of this "Midianite painted pottery" leave no doubt that Qurayyah was a major production center for it, exporting it southeast as far as the great oasis at Tema and north as far as Amman and Hebron. Small amounts of this ware have also been found in the northern Negeb at Tel Masos and at Tell el-Farah (S), and in the foothills of Canaan at Lachish; another sherd has been found at Tawilan in Edom.

The date of this pottery and its association with copper metallurgy has been confirmed by excavations at Timna in the Wadi Arabah, 200 kilometers (125 miles) north of Qurayyah. There, in an Egyptian sanctuary nestled beneath a cliff, Midianite painted pottery made up about 25 percent of the pottery assemblage. Associated objects inscribed in Egyptian dated to the thirteenth to twelfth centuries BCE. In its final stages the sanctuary was appropriated and rededicated by iconoclastic Midianites. Three hundred kilometers (186 miles) north of its production center Qurayyah, Midianite painted pottery has been found in quantity in the greatest copper mining district of the Bronze and Iron Ages—at Khirbet Feinan, known in the Bible as Punon (Num. 33.42), one of the stopping points of the Israelites during their desert wanderings.

Thus the distribution of Midianite painted pottery, from its production center(s) in northern Arabia (Midian) to a wide range of settlements in the Negeb, the Arabah, and beyond, fits rather nicely the locale and routes of a people known for their metalsmithing and caravaneering. The floruit of this distinctive pottery is precisely the era in which most biblical historians (quite independently of this ceramic evidence, which has only recently come to light) would date the Israelite Exodus from

Egypt, their sojourn through Midian and Transjordan, and their settlement in Canaan in the late thirteenth and twelfth centuries BCE.

Circumstantial evidence of time and place suggests Midianite antecedents and contributions to Yahwism. Such formal elements as the proper name *Yahweh,* his sacred mountain in Midian as the locus of Moses' theophanies, and the prominent roles of Moses' father-in-law (priest and sheikh of the Midianites) and his wife Zipporah provide tantalizing hints about the relationship. But until more is known about Midianite religion, these connections will remain tentative at best.

What is known, however, is that only a century before the "Mosaic era" and the advent of Yahwism, Egypt experienced a brief episode of radical monotheism during the so-called Amarna Revolution. The pharaoh Akhenaten (1352–1336 BCE; formerly Amenhotep IV) proclaimed Aten—the luminous, numinous power of the sun disk—the sole and universal god of Egypt and its empire (including Canaan). Atenism was suppressed by succeeding pharaohs, who reinstated the traditional pantheon; nevertheless, the memory of this radical monotheism survived in some circles, and centuries later the Israelite poet who composed Psalm 104 borrowed directly from the sublime Egyptian "Hymn to the Aten." Thus, by the latter part of the second millennium BCE, the Egyptians had had a brief experiment with monotheism that may have had repercussions beyond Egypt and affected other Near Eastern cultures.

In more complex societies like Egypt and Mesopotamia, whether there were one or many intracosmic deities, rulers were either the incarnated or the designated "sons" of the deity, intermediaries between heaven and earth, between the divine ruler and the ruled. The populace identified with its geographical territory and its rulers, who interceded on its behalf with the patron deities.

There is a sense in which Yahwism represents a radical break with the past and a breakthrough in the history of religions and in human consciousness. The philosopher and political scientist Eric Voegelin has analyzed this change in the following terms: the pragmatic escape of the Hebrews from Egypt becomes, at the same time, a "spiritual exodus from the cosmological form of imperial rule. The sonship of god is transferred from the pharaoh to the people of Israel in immediate existence under Yahweh" (*The Ecumenic Age,* 26). It is the constitution of a "people" or "kindred" directly under the patrimonial authority of Yahweh that forges a new relationship between deity and community and a new identity for those who participate directly in this new order.

Tribes and Tribalism in Early Israel

The tribes of premonarchic Israel continued to exist in various forms and permutations throughout the monarchy and even thereafter. One reason for this is that by the early Iron Age I, they were territorial entities with boundaries and rights established in part by the nature of their tribalism.

Some scholars see an egalitarian, kin-based tribal confederation being supplanted by a hierarchical state in which class displaces kin, and patronage dominates relationships. G. Ernest Wright ("The Provinces of Solomon," *Eretz-Israel* 8 [1967], 58*–68*) suggested that Solomon's provincial system led to crosscutting kin groups by gerrymandering tribal territories in the interest of breaking up old sodalities forged through common descent (whether real or fictive) and a radical realignment based on production and service to the king and his royal household. According to Wright, this reorganization of the countryside by Solomon (1 Kings 4.7–19) had the beneficial effect not only of replacing old kin loyalties with royal ones but also of distributing the tax burden to each provincial unit according to its proportion of the gross national product, so that each of the twelve units ("tribes" become "provinces") was required to provide for one month's living expenses at the king's quarters in Jerusalem.

That such a rational system never existed in ancient Israel and that the premonarchic clan and tribal allocations remained intact are partially demonstrated by the Samaria ostraca, receipts found in the capital of the northern kingdom and dated to the eighth century BCE. They refer to the collection of taxes in kind of olive oil and vintage wine, which were presented to the king by the notables or clan leaders—the local elite—who commanded enough loyalty and honor to represent various clan districts from that territory still intact more than two and a half centuries after the establishment of the monarchy. This could not have occurred if the reorganization of Solomon's kingdom had been as radical as suggested by those who believe that tribes and states cannot coexist.

Tribalism could wax and wane, sometimes depending on external circumstances and threats either from other tribes or, more often in the case of tribal Israelites, from neighboring states or alien tribal polities. At that time the symbolic systems could be reactivated and the contrast with those outside the group highlighted. Vis-à-vis the Philistines, this took the form of various contrastive rituals given the force of religious injunctions, such as circumcision and the pig taboo in food. They might assert their myth of common ancestry as a son of Jacob/Israel through genealogies. At the tribal level these function as social charters expressing allegiance through fictive kinship and the obligations that issue therefrom.

But to describe tribes as kin-based or kin-ordered groups is insufficient, especially since there are many other ties that bind these larger entities together. Notions of descent, of course, and implied kinship can be operative at the village and clan level in nontribal societies. At these lower levels, descent functions to secure property rights (in the case of Israel, landed ones) and to organize food production. On the higher and broader levels, descent as expressed in genealogies locates these smaller social units within the broader polity through the language of common ancestry. Genealogies, it must be emphasized, are charters of sociopolitical organization, not necessarily actual family trees that detail blood relations. Tribalism then becomes a political statement of group allegiance and identity. In Israel kinship expressed through common descent provided a unifying principle at the tribal level, but it was not sufficient to account for larger polities.

Commitment to the people, or kindred (Hebrew 'am), of Yahweh ranked above individual tribal affiliation. This also required a more inclusive system of beliefs, which transcended tribal boundaries, local polities, and intermeshing economic networks. Through the revelation of Yahwism to Moses came a newly constituted people or kindred. Sanctuaries sprang up during the period of the judges at central locations in the highlands, such as Shechem and Shiloh. Through these central sanctuaries, where covenant ceremonies were celebrated (Josh. 24.1–28), religious unification was reinforced. Thus, as in early Islam, both the confederation and the monarchy of Israel were established on religious foundations, which helped centralize authority. The political, social, and economic systems were based on beliefs informed by revelation, whether to Moses or Muhammad. During the twelfth and eleventh centuries that new entity was the tribal league; in the tenth century and later, it was the monarchy.

The Israelite 'am resembles the Islamic 'umma in that religious allegiance to a single deity, whether Yahweh or Allah, required commitment to the larger "family," or supertribe. In the case of the early Israelites, they understood themselves to be the "children" of an eponymous ancestor Jacob (who retrospectively became "Israel") and, at the same time, to be the "people" or "kindred" of Yahweh. It was a religious federation with allegiance to a single, sovereign patriarch or paterfamilias—Yahweh. He was the ultimate patrimonial authority, in Max Weber's formulation, for those bound to him through covenant as kindred or kindred-in-law.

The Israelite terminology of self-understanding was probably no different from that used by neighboring tribesmen and kinsmen, living east of the Jordan River, who became the kingdoms of Ammon and Moab. The J strand of the Israelite epic preserves an odd tale (Gen. 19.30–38) that could go back to the formative stages of these polities in Transjordan, when various tribal groups were trying to sort out their respective relations and alliances. According to this social etiology, Lot, while drunk, impregnated his two daughters, who then gave birth to Moab (the firstborn) and Ammon, thus making these two "brothers" fraternal "cousins" of Jacob. In the Bible the Ammonites are generally called the "sons of Ammon" (for example, Gen. 19.38; 2 Sam. 10.1) and in the Assyrian annals the "House of Ammon." In the epic sources (J and E, Num. 21.29; also Jer. 48.46) the Moabites are referred to as the "kindred" of Chemosh, after their sovereign deity.

Through these familial metaphors one sees a series of nested households, which determined position in society and in the hierarchy of being. At ground level was the ancestral house(hold) (bêt 'āb). This could be small, if newly established, or extensive, if it had existed for several generations. From the Decalogue it is known that the neighbor's household included more than the biological members of the family: an Israelite was not to covet his neighbor's wife, male or female slave, ox or donkey, or anything else that came under the authority of the master of the household (Exod. 20.17; Deut. 5.21). At the state level in ancient Israel and in neighboring polities, the king presided over his house (bayit), the families and households of the whole kingdom. Thus, after the division of the monarchy the southern kingdom of Judah is referred to as "house of David" (byt dwd) in the recently excavated stela from Dan, and probably also in the Mesha Stela, just as the northern kingdom of Israel is known as the "house of Omri" (bīt Ḫumri) in Assyrian texts.

The Arrival and Expansion of the Philistines

The Philistines were one contingent of a larger confederation known collectively as the Sea Peoples. Beginning about 1185 BCE and continuing a generation or two, they left their homeland and resettled on the southeast coast of the Mediterranean, in a region that had been occupied by Canaanites for a millennium or more. This movement is documented by a variety of written sources in Akkadian, Ugaritic, Egyptian, and Hebrew, by Egyptian wall reliefs, and by archaeology.

According to the biblical prophets Amos (9.7) and Jeremiah (47.4), the Philistines

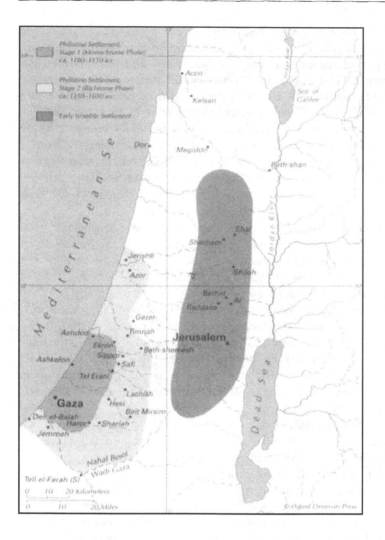

The Expansion of Philistine Settlement, ca. 1180–1050 BCE

came from Caphtor, the Hebrew name for Crete; as we shall see, archaeological evidence suggests that this later tradition may preserve an accurate historical memory. Biblical and Assyrian sources indicate that Philistine culture emanated from a core of five major cities—the Philistine pentapolis—located in the coastal plain of southern Canaan (Josh. 13.2–3). For nearly six centuries, during most of the Iron Age, these five cities—Ashdod, Ashkelon, Ekron (Tel Miqne), Gaza, and Gath—formed the heartland of Philistia, the biblical "land of the Philistines." Each city and its territory were ruled by a "lord" called *seren* in Hebrew (Josh. 13.3), perhaps a cognate of the Greek word *tyrannos* (compare English "tyrant"). Four of the five cities have been convincingly located. Ashdod, Ashkelon, and Ekron have been extensively excavated; Gaza, which lies under the modern city of the same name, has not. Gath is usually located at Tell es-Safi, but its proximity to Ekron makes this unlikely.

The archaeology of the Philistines can be divided into three stages:

Stage 1 (ca. 1180–1150 BCE). The Philistines arrive en masse on the coast of southwest Canaan. The path of destruction along coastal Cilicia, Cyprus, and the Levant suggests that these newcomers came by ship in a massive migration that continues throughout most of Stage 1, and perhaps into Stage 2. They destroy many of the Late Bronze Age cities and supplant them with their own at the four corners of their newly conquered territory, which extends over some 1,000 square kilometers (386 square miles). During Stage 1 the Philistines control a vital stretch of the coastal route, or "Way of the Sea," which had usually been dominated by the Egyptians and their Canaanite dependencies.

During this stage the Philistines have much the same material culture as other Sea Peoples. The process of acculturation has not yet begun, which will lead to regional differences among the various groups of Sea Peoples. In their new settlements along the eastern Mediterranean coast and along the coast of Cyprus, the new immigrants share a common pottery tradition, brought or borrowed from Aegean Late Bronze Age culture. It is a style of Mycenaean pottery, locally made, which is usually classified as Mycenaean IIIC:1b (hereafter Myc IIIC).

Along with this shared potting tradition, the Philistines bring other new cultural traditions to Canaan: domestic and public architecture focusing on the hearth; weaving with unperforated loom weights; swine herding and culinary preference for pork; drinking preference for wine mixed with water; and religious rituals featuring female figurines of the mother-goddess type. Most of these cultural elements are found in the earlier Mycenaean civilization, which flourished during the Late Bronze Age on the Greek mainland, in the islands, especially Crete (Caphtor), and at some coastal enclaves of Anatolia. Around the Philistine heartland, Egypto-Canaanite cultural patterns persist well into the twelfth century as Egyptians garrisoned in predominately Canaanite population centers try to contain the Philistines.

Stage 2 (ca. 1150–1050 BCE). With the breakdown of Egyptian hegemony in Canaan after the death of Rameses III (1153 BCE), the Philistines begin to expand in all directions beyond their original territory, north to the Tel Aviv area, east into the foothills (Shephelah), and southeast into the Wadi Gaza and Beer-sheba basin. Their characteristic pottery is known as Philistine bichrome ware, which, like other items, shows signs of contact and acculturation with Canaanite traditions.

Early in this stage, the Israelite tribe of Dan seems to have been forced to migrate from the coastal plain and interior to the far north, though remnants of that tribal group remained in the foothills. The Samson saga (Judg. 13–16) illustrates limited Philistine and Israelite interaction along the boundaries shared by two distinctive cultures, Semitic and early Greek.

Stage 3 (ca. 1050–950 BCE). Through acculturation, Philistine painted pottery loses more and more of its distinctive Aegean characteristics. The forms become debased, but they are still recognizable. The once-complex geometrical compositions and graceful motifs of water birds and fishes of stage 2 bichrome ware are reduced to simple spiral decorations (if any at all) painted over red slip, which is frequently burnished.

This process of acculturation in the material repertoire does not, however, signal assimilation or loss of ethnic identity among the Philistines. As a polity they are never stronger. During the latter half of the eleventh century BCE their expansion into the highlands triggers numerous conflicts and outright war with the tribes of Israel. Philistine military advances into the Israelite highlands are so successful, and the crisis among the Israelites so great, that the latter demand the new institution of kingship.

After the investiture of the successful warlord David as king over a fragile yet united kingdom, the tide of battle eventually turned against the Philistines. By 975 BCE David and his armies have pushed the Philistines back into the coastal territory controlled by the pentapolis, finally completing the Israelite "conquest" of Canaan.

Philistine Pottery

The most ubiquitous and most distinctive element of Philistine culture, and a key in delineating the stages summarized above, is their pottery. The Myc IIIB pottery of the Late Bronze Age was imported into the Levant, whereas all the Myc IIIC wares found in the pentapolis in the early Iron Age were made locally. When Myc IIIC (stage 1) pottery from Ashdod and Ekron in Philistia or from Kition, Enkomi, and Palaeopaphos in Cyprus is tested by neutron activation, the results are the same: it was made from the local clays. This locally manufactured pottery was not the product of a few Mycenaean potters or their workshops, brought from abroad to meet indigenous demands for Mycenaean domestic and decorated wares, as the large quantities found at coastal sites from Tarsus to Ashkelon demonstrate. At Ras Ibn Hani in Syria and at Ekron, locally made Mycenaean pottery constitutes at least half of the repertoire, at Ashdod about 30 percent. Local Canaanite pottery, principally in the forms of store jars, juglets, bowls, lamps, and cooking pots, makes up the rest of the assemblage in the pentapolis.

The appearance in quantity of Myc IIIC in Cyprus and the Levant heralds the arrival of the Sea Peoples. At Ashdod, Ashkelon, and Ekron new settlements characterized by Myc IIIC pottery were built on the charred ruins of the previous Late Bronze Age II Canaanite, or Egypto-Canaanite, cities. These Philistine cities were much larger than those they replaced. This new urban concept and its impact on the landscape will be discussed further below.

Stage 2 Philistine pottery is a distinctive bichrome ware, painted with red and black decoration, a regional style that developed after the Philistines had lived for a generation or two in Canaan. To the basic Mycenaean forms in their repertoire they added others from Canaan and Cyprus, and they adapted decorative motifs from Egypt and a centuries-old bichrome technique from Canaan.

This bichrome ware was once thought the hallmark of the first Philistines to reach the Levant, early in the reign of Rameses III. An earlier contingent of Sea Peoples had fought with the Libyans against the Egyptian pharaoh Merneptah, but the Philistines were not among them. This pre-Philistine or first wave of Sea Peoples supposedly brought the Myc IIIC potting traditions to the shores of Canaan, where they founded the first cities on exactly the same sites later identified with the Philistine pentapolis.

But the battle reliefs of Merneptah make it clear that Ashkelon, the seaport of the pentapolis, was inhabited by Canaanites, not Sea Peoples, during that pharaoh's reign. The simplest explanation is that the confederation of Sea Peoples, including the Philistines, mentioned in texts and depicted in reliefs of Rameses III were the bearers of Myc IIIC pottery traditions, which they continued to make when they settled in Canaan. The stylistic development from simple monochrome to more elaborate bichrome was an indigenous change two or three generations after the Philistines' arrival in southern Canaan. The eclectic style of bichrome pottery resulted not from a period of peregrinations around the Mediterranean during the decades between Merneptah and Rameses III, but from a process of Philistine acculturation, involving the adaptation and absorption of many traditions to be found among the various peoples living in Canaan. This acculturation process continued among the Philistines throughout their nearly six-hundred-year history in Palestine.

As one moves from core to periphery in the decades following stage 1, the material culture of the Philistines shows evidence of spatial and temporal distancing from the original templates and concepts. Failure to understand the acculturation process has led to the inclusion of questionable items in the Philistine corpus of material culture remains, such as the anthropoid coffins (or worse, to a denial of a distinct core of Philistine cultural remains) just two or three generations after their arrival in Canaan at the beginning of stage 2 (ca. 1150 BCE).

Shortly before the final destruction of Ugarit, a Syrian named Bay or Baya, "chief of the bodyguard of pharaoh of Egypt," sent a letter in Akkadian to Ammurapi, the last king of Ugarit. Bay served under both Siptah (1194–1188) and Tewosret (1188–1186). His letter arrived at Ugarit while Myc IIIB pottery was still in use. At nearby Ibn Hani, however, the Sea Peoples built over the charred ruins of the king's seaside palace, which contained Myc IIIB ware. More than half of the ceramic yield from their new settlement was Myc IIIC pottery, a proportion comparable to that of stage 1 settlements in Philistia. The final destruction of Ugarit, as well as of many other coastal cities in the eastern Mediterranean, occurred only a decade or so before the events recorded by Rameses III (1184–1153) in his eighth year:

> The foreign countries [Sea Peoples] made a conspiracy in their islands. All at once the lands were removed and scattered in the fray. No land could stand before their arms, from Hatti, Kode [Cilicia], Carchemish, Arzawa, and Alashiya [Cyprus] on, being cut off at [one time]. A camp [was set up] in one place in Amor [Amurru]. They desolated its people, and its land was like that which has never come into being. They were coming forward toward Egypt, while the flame was prepared before them. Their confederation [of Sea Peoples] was the Philistines, Tjeker [Sikils], Shekelesh, Denye(n) and Weshesh, lands united. (Trans. John Wilson; p. 262 in James B. Pritchard, ed., *Ancient Near Eastern Texts Relating to the Old Testament*, Princeton, N.J.: Princeton University Press, 1969)

Seaborne Migration

The Sea Peoples established beachheads along the entire coast of the eastern Mediterranean. Their route can be traced by the synchronous destructions of Late Bronze Age coastal cities from Tarsus to Ashkelon. The same pattern of devastation is found in several cities of Cyprus, which the raiders could have reached only by ship.

The renaming of whole territories after various groups of Sea Peoples provides another measure of their impact. After the Sea Peoples' invasion of Cyprus, its name was changed from Alashiya to Yadanana, "the isle of the Danunians/Danaoi/Denyen." The Philistines bequeathed their own name to Philistia (and later to all of Palestine). The Sikils, who settled at Dor, also sailed west and gave their name to Sicily, and the Sherden, who probably established a beachhead in Acco, gave theirs to Sardinia.

On Cyprus the sequence of beachheads followed by stage 1 settlements is remarkably similar to those in the Levant. New cities, with Myc IIIC pottery, were built over the ruins of Late Bronze Age cities, many of which had received the last of the Greek imported pottery known as Myc IIIB. On the coastal promentories the newcomers built fortified strongholds, such as Maa and Pyla. Farther inland, the Sea Peoples founded new settlements, such as Sinda and Athienou.

Cypriot archaeologists invoke the Achaeans or Danaoi of Homeric epic as the agents of culture change in Cyprus; in the Levant, the same change is ascribed to the Sea Peoples. Both agents participated in the event recorded by Rameses III and should be related to the same confederacy of Sea Peoples, or Mycenaean Greeks, who invaded the coastlands and the island of Alashiya (Cyprus) around 1185–1175.

Correspondence between the king of Cyprus and the king of Ugarit can be correlated with the archaeology of destruction to provide vivid details of the Sea Peoples' onslaught. The capital of a Syrian coastal kingdom under the suzerainty of the Hittites, Ugarit had over 150 villages in its hinterland and a population of 25,000, nearly the same as that of Philistia during stage 1. Its king also controlled a nearby port and had a seaside palace at Ras Ibn Hani.

During the final days of Ugarit, letters (in Akkadian cuneiform) exchanged between its king, Ammurapi, and the king of Cyprus show how desperate the situation was, as well as the source of the trouble. The Cypriot king writes to Ammurapi:

> What have you written to me "enemy shipping has been sighted at sea"? Well, now, even if it is true that enemy ships have been sighted, be firm. Indeed then, what of your troops, your chariots, where are they stationed? Are they stationed close at hand or are they not? Fortify your towns, bring the troops and the chariots into them, and wait for the enemy with firm feet. (Sandars, 142–43)

Ammurapi replies:

> My father, the enemy ships are already here, they have set fire to my towns and have done very great damage in the country. My father, did you not know that all my troops were stationed in the Hittite country, and that all my ships are still stationed in Lycia and have not yet returned? So that the country is abandoned to itself. . . . Consider this my father, there are seven enemy ships that have come and done very great damage. (Sandars, 143)

An earlier text explains to whom the marauding ships belong. The Hittite king writes (also in Akkadian) to a veteran official of Ammurapi about hostage taking:

> From the sun, the great king, to the prefect: Now, with you, the king, your master, is young. He does not know anything. I gave orders to him regarding Lanadusu, who was taken captive by the Shikalayu, who live on ships. Now, I have sent to you Nisahili, he is an administrative official with me, with instructions. Now, you (are to) send Lanadusu, whom the Shikalayu captured, here to me. I will ask him about

the matter of the Shikila and, afterwards, he can return to Ugarit. (trans. Gregory Mobley)

The Sikils, "who live on ships," were sea traders who were terrorizing Ugarit before it fell to them about 1185 BCE, not long before events recorded by Rameses III, who also mentions the Sikils (Tjeker) as part of the Sea Peoples' confederation.

In the Egyptian reliefs of the naval battle, the Sea Peoples' ships are oared galleys with single sails and with finials in the shape of water birds at prow and stern. These resemble the "bird-boat" painted on a krater from Tiryns, another clue to their Aegean origin.

The Sikils then sailed down the coast and landed at Dor, identified as a city of the Sikils in the eleventh-century Egyptian tale of Wen-Amun. They destroyed the Late Bronze Age Canaanite city and constructed a much larger one over its ruins. During stage 1 the Sikils fortified Dor with ramparts and glacis, and created an excellent port facility for their ships.

All of this evidence—their beachheads, the coastal pattern of destruction (followed in many cases by new cities with Myc IIIC pottery), references to living on ships, and illustrations of their craft—leave no doubt that the Sea Peoples, including the Philistines, had the necessary maritime technology and transport capacity to effect a major migration and invasion by sea.

Philistines and Egyptians

From Egyptian texts and wall reliefs at Medinet Habu, a reconstruction of the battle between Rameses III and the Sea Peoples and its aftermath has been developed that has attained nearly canonical status. According to this reconstruction, the Sea Peoples came to the Levant by land and by sea. The reliefs show whole families trekking overland in ox-drawn carts, and warriors in horse-drawn chariots fighting with the Egyptians in a land battle on the northern borders of Canaan. A flotilla of their ships even penetrated the Nile Delta before Rameses III repelled them. After his victory, Rameses III engaged troops of the defeated Sea Peoples as mercenaries for his garrisons in Canaan and Nubia, and reasserted Egyptian sovereignty over southern Canaan. Egypt once again controlled the vital military and commercial highway successively known as the Ways of Horus, the Way of the Land of the Philistines (Exod. 13.17), and the Way of the Sea (Isa. 9.1).

Some Egyptologists have rightly challenged this reconstruction. The wall reliefs of Rameses III show only one scene of departure before the land battle and only one scene of victory celebration after the sea battle. The Sea Peoples threatened the Egyptians at the mouth of the Nile, not in far-off northern Canaan. If the Philistines had settled in southern Canaan before 1175 BCE, when the battle for the Nile Delta took place, both the chariotry and the oxcarts could have come from their settlements there; they would not need to be interpreted as transport for a long overland trek of Sea Peoples through Anatolia into the Levant. As we have seen, they migrated by sea.

The hypothesis that Rameses III reestablished Egyptian control over Canaan and used Philistine mercenaries in his garrisons there was apparently bolstered by the evidence of the clay anthropoid coffins found at such Egyptian strongholds as Bethshan, Tell el-Farah (S), and Lachish. At Tell el-Farah (S), the discovery of large bench tombs with anthropoid clay sarcophagi, Egyptian artifacts, and Philistine bichrome pottery led the excavator, Sir Flinders Petrie, to conclude that these were the sepulchers of the "five lords of the Philistines." Other scholars proposed Cypriot and Aegean prototypes for the style of the bench tombs themselves. One of the anthropoid clay coffins from Beth-shan had a feathered headdress, which was compared with the headgear of the Philistines, Denyen, and Sikils shown on the Medinet Habu reliefs. But in the 1970s excavations at the cemetery of Deir el-Balah, southwest of Gaza, uncovered dozens more of these clay coffins dating to the Late Bronze Age, a century or two before the Sea Peoples arrived in Canaan.

The ideal for Egyptians living abroad was to be buried back in Egypt. However, with the expansion of the New Kingdom empire, more Egyptian troops were stationed abroad, in both Canaan and Nubia, and it became impractical to return every Egyptian corpse to the homeland. But Egyptians who died outside Egypt could at least be buried abroad in suitable containers, such as anthropoid clay coffins.

Further support for interpreting the anthropoid clay coffins as Egyptian comes from a sarcophagus excavated at Lachish, in a tomb dating to the time of Rameses III. On this coffin is a depiction of the Egyptian deities Isis and Nephthys, along with an inscription that some have labeled Egyptian pseudohieroglyphs or Philistine gibberish. But some Egyptologists have interpreted the text as a perfectly good Egyptian funerary inscription: "Thou givest water [a traditional mortuary offering] (of the) West [the region of the dead] to the majesty (of) thy [. . .]."

Thus the most parsimonious hypothesis is that the anthropoid sarcophagi found in Canaan in the Late Bronze and the Iron I periods belonged to Egyptians stationed there, and should not be connected with the Sea Peoples and their burial customs. When so interpreted, these coffins are important evidence for delineating cultural (and hence political) boundaries between Canaanite territory still under Egyptian control and Philistia.

During stage 1 the Philistines occupied a large region in southern Canaan, taking it from the Canaanites and their overlords, the Egyptians. The boundaries of this territory can be plotted by using settlements whose ceramic repertoire has more than 25 percent Myc IIIC pottery. This rectangular coastal strip was about 20 kilometers (12 miles) wide and 50 kilometers (31 miles) long and had an area of 1,000 square kilometers (386 square miles), and the Philistines located their five major cities at key positions along its perimeter. Unlike the Egyptians, the Philistines did not govern their territory by installing military garrisons within Canaanite population centers. Rather, they completely destroyed those centers, and then built their own new cities on the ruins of the old. This wholesale takeover must have resulted in the death or displacement of much of the Late Bronze Age population.

Along the northern coast of their territory, the Philistines destroyed by fire the large Egyptian fortress at Tel Mor and the neighboring city of Ashdod. Over the ruins of Ashdod they built a new city, while the Egyptians rebuilt the fortress at Tel Mor, although on a smaller scale. Farther inland, some 20 kilometers (12 miles) to the east, was the small Canaanite city of Ekron (Tel Miqne), about 4 hectares (10 acres) in area. The Philistines burned it too, and over its ruins raised a city five times larger than its predecessor, with massive mud-brick fortifications and organized on a grand scale. In the layer of occupation were found large quantities of Myc IIIC pottery.

Northeast of Ekron was Gezer, a major Canaanite city from which some of the Amarna letters had been sent. At the end of the Late Bronze Age it too was destroyed by fire, either by the Philistines or by Pharaoh Merneptah in his campaign of 1209. In any case, Gezer, with no evidence of Myc IIIC, was rebuilt as an Egypto-Canaanite counterforce to Ekron during the reign of Rameses III. A faience vase bearing cartouches with that pharaoh's name is associated with this level of occupation, but there is no Myc IIIC pottery. A small percentage of Philistine bichrome pottery appears later, during stage 2.

The Late Bronze Age city of Ashkelon, on the Mediterranean coast between Ashdod and Gaza, was also destroyed, either by Merneptah or (more probably) by the Philistines. Egyptian policy was to garrison and control, not eradicate, the Canaanite population. There the Philistines built their main seaport, which during stage 1 must have extended along the coast for almost a kilometer (over half a mile) and occupied an area of 50 to 60 hectares (125–150 acres). Later, in the early Iron II period, the preexisting arc of earthen ramparts was fortified at the northern crest by two large mud-brick towers linked by a mud-brick curtain wall. Opposite this Philistine stronghold, about 30 kilometers (18 miles) to the east, Rameses III established another Egyptian control center at Lachish. Hardly a trace of Philistine bichrome pottery has been found there, but archaeologists have uncovered an Egyptian-inspired temple, hieratic bowl inscriptions recording taxes paid to the Egyptians, a large bronze gate-fitting inscribed with the name of Rameses III, and two anthropoid coffins, all attesting to the presence of an Egyptian garrison.

Philistia's eastern boundary during stage 1 was a 50-kilometer (31-mile) line from Ekron in the north to Tel Haror in the south, some 20 kilometers (12 miles) inland from Gaza. At Haror, the Philistines devastated the Late Bronze Age city, and both Egyptian and Myc IIIB pottery were found in the destruction debris. Above the ruins rose a new Philistine settlement, with Myc IIIC pottery as at the pentapolis sites.

Just across the border from Haror was another Egyptian center, Tell esh-Shariah. A large Egyptian administrative building or governor's residency, several hieratic bowl inscriptions, and Egyptian pottery all attest to Rameses III's containment policy. During stage 2, the Egyptians abandoned Shariah and it became a Philistine city, probably to be identified with biblical Ziklag. According to 1 Samuel 27.1–7, Ziklag was subject to Achish, the ruler of Gath, who gave this country town to his loyal retainer David and his personal army of six hundred men. Gath itself, Achish's capital and Goliath's hometown, is usually located at Tell es-Safi. But this site's proximity to Ekron, its distance from Ziklag, and the paucity of Myc IIIC pottery there make this an unlikely identification. Gath should be strategically located in the southeast corner of Philistia during stage 1, not far from its dependency Ziklag during stage 2; if so, the most plausible candidate for Gath is Tel Haror, which has both Philistine monochrome and bichrome pottery. Regardless of the identifications, it seems clear that Haror was inside and Shariah outside Philistine territory during stage 1, but both were within the Philistine domain during stage 2.

In the southwest corner of Philistia lay Gaza, a major outpost and caravan city of the Egyptians, presumably taken over by the Philistines during stage 1. Excavations at Gaza have been limited, and they have revealed little or nothing of the character of the Egyptian and Philistine cities. During stage 1 Philistia probably did not extend south of the Wadi Gaza (Nahal Besor). To protect his northern frontier, Rameses III built a formidable fortress and residency at Tell el-Farah (S), which remained under Egyptian control throughout much of the Ramesside era, well into stage 2, as the sequence of tombs with anthropoid clay coffins, Egyptian artifacts, and Philistine bichrome pottery attests.

The contrast is thus sharply delineated between the territory controlled by the Egyptians under Rameses III and that of the Philistine pentapolis, the latter characterized by the presence of Myc IIIC pottery and by the absence of Egyptian monuments, buildings, and artifacts. A new and formidable foreign power, the Philistines had carved out an independent territory right up to the Egyptian frontier. All Rameses could do was to attempt to contain them, a policy that continued until his death in 1153.

Philistine Economy

The total occupied area of the pentapolis was at least 100 hectares (250 acres), with a total population of about twenty-five thousand. To attain such size so soon after their arrival, boatload after boatload of Philistines, along with their families, livestock, and belongings, must have arrived in southern Canaan during stage 1. By the beginning of stage 2, natural growth had more than doubled the Philistine population, enabling their expansion in all directions. By the second half of the eleventh century BCE, in stage 3, they were a menace even to the Israelites living in the highlands to the east.

Their new home provided the Philistines with the natural and cultural resources to become both a maritime and an agrarian power. The sea offered fishing and shipping, and to its east lay rich agricultural lands suitable for growing grains, olives, and grapes. This region lacked timber and mineral resources, but even early in stage 1 the Philistines were importing both.

Philistia constituted a vital stretch of the coastal road. As the eleventh-century Egyptian tale of Wen-Amun makes clear, the Philistines, along with other Sea Peoples and the Phoenicians, soon controlled the maritime lanes as well. After some stability had returned to the eastern Mediterranean, the Sea Peoples once again became traders rather than raiders. Shortly after landing, the Sikils constructed the harbor at Dor. By the eleventh century, trade with Cyprus was bustling, and Ashkelon was a busy port again, exporting grain, wine, and oil from Philistia to other parts of the Mediterranean.

From Ashdod to Gaza, the coast of Philistia was ideal for the cultivation of grapes. The sandy soil and warm, sunny climate produced many good wines, from Ashkelon's light and palatable varieties to Gaza's heavier ones. At Ashkelon a royal winery, with pressing rooms alternating with storerooms within a large ashlar building, occupied the same central area in the seventh century where a major public building had stood in Iron Age I. Similar Iron II wine production facilities have recently been found near Ashdod.

In modern idiom, the term *Philistine* means an uncouth person, interested in material comfort rather than art and ideas. Archaeologists may inadvertently have assimilated this notion in their terminology: one of the most common Philistine ceramic forms is a jug with a strainer spout, usually called a "beer-jug." But the ecology of Philistia is better suited for grape-growing than for cultivating barley, the grain generally used for beer. Moreover, the repertoire of Philistine decorated pottery, both Myc IIIC and bichrome, indicates that wine rather than beer was the beverage of choice. The large bowl, called after its Greek name, *krater*, was used for mixing water with wine, apparently a Greek rather than a Canaanite custom. Such kraters were popular among the Mycenaeans, and in the Iron I period the relatively large proportion of kraters in Philistia compared with non-Philistine territory suggests that the Philistines continued to mix their wine with water. Large bell-shaped bowls for serving wine and small bell-shaped bowls or cups for drinking it are two popular forms of decorated Philistine pottery. The jug with the strainer spout completes the wine service; it was used as a carafe, and its built-in sieve strained out the lees and other impurities as the wine was poured. All these forms testify to the importance of viticulture and wine production during that era.

The inner coastal zone of Philistia, with its wide, undulating plains and deep, fertile soils, was ideal for growing wheat and olives. Oil produced here supplied not only Philistia but also other parts of the Levant, especially the perennial and enormous Egyptian market. In the seventh century BCE Ekron was the undisputed oil capital of the country: just inside the city's fortifications were more than a hundred olive oil processing facilities.

The Philistines also brought changes to the region's animal husbandry. Like their Canaanite and Israelite neighbors, the Philistines kept flocks of sheep and goats as well as cattle. To these they added a specialization in hogs. In the highland villages of the Iron I period, the bones of pigs are rare or completely absent, but in Philistia they constitute a significant proportion of excavated faunal remains: at Ashkelon 23 percent (but the sample is small), at Ekron 18 percent, and at Timnah (Tel Batash) 8 percent. These differences in pig production and consumption were due more to culture than to ecology. The Mycenaeans and later Greeks valued swine and preferred pork in their diet, a preference brought by the Philistines to Canaan in the twelfth century. It is probably then, the biblical period of "the judges," that the Israelites developed their taboo against pork consumption, in part to differentiate themselves from their Philistine neighbors; circumcision was another such distinctive cultural marker.

Urban Imposition

As we have seen, soon after the arrival of the first generation of new immigrants, the Philistines successfully sited their five major cities, taking maximum advantage of their military, economic, and political potential. The urban tradition embodied in their cities differed from the Canaanite patterns they replaced, and the details of their urban planning provide additional reasons for concluding that the Philistines were not a small military elite who garrisoned the indigenous population but a large and heterogeneous group of settlers who brought many aspects of their old way of life and culture into their new landscape. Behind the archaeological residues of the pentapolis one can detect, however faintly, the activities of a diverse community of warriors, farmers, sailors, merchants, rulers, shamans, priests, artisans, and architects.

Weaving industries were often found in major centers. At Ashkelon more than 150 cylinders of unfired clay, slightly pinched in the middle, were found lying on the superimposed floors of two successive public buildings, some still aligned along the walls as if they had been dropped from vertical weaving looms. The floors themselves had concentrations of textile fibers. Common Levantine pyramidal loom weights have perforated tops, but these were unpierced and were probably spools around which thread was wound and hung from the loom. Similar clay cylinders have been found at Ekron and Ashdod, on Cyprus in temple precincts at Enkomi and Kition (the Sea Peoples' emporia there), on the Mycenaean mainland, on Thera (in the Cyclades), and in Crete. At Ashkelon, Ekron, and Ashdod these spool weights are found in abundance in stages 1 and 2. They were made from the local clays, but the Aegean parallels further indicate the origin of the new immigrants.

The best example of urban planning comes from another pentapolis city, Ekron. Over the ashes of the Late Bronze Age city was built a much larger Philistine one, about 20 hectares (50 acres) in size, with perhaps five thousand inhabitants. Even during stage 1 at Ekron there are signs of urban planning: industry was located along the perimeter of the city, just inside its fortification walls. Next were houses for ordinary citizens, and in the center of the site were public buildings, including a palace-temple complex, which was rebuilt several times in the more than two centuries of its use.

In the long, pillared main hall of this complex was a large circular sunken hearth. Such a hearth was characteristic of Mycenaean palaces, and the same feature is found at several sites in Cyprus during stage 1, as well as at Tell Qasile, a Philistine settlement north of the pentapolis founded in the mid-twelfth century.

Three rooms of the stage 2 public building at Ekron opened onto its central hall. In the northernmost room dozens of spool weights were found, suggesting that it was for weaving, perhaps by religious functionaries who were making vestments for the statue of the great Mycenaean mother-goddess. (An analogy, perhaps, is the notice in 2 Kings 23.7 of women weaving garments for Asherah in the precincts of the Jerusalem Temple.)

A plastered platform, perhaps an altar, stood in the middle room, identifying it as the primary place of worship. Nearby was an ivory handle of a knife for sacrifice, identical to the complete example in the southernmost room. There were also three bronze spoked wheels, part of a mobile cult stand with parallels in Cyprus and in the Jerusalem Temple. In the third room, next to another small platform or altar, archaeologists found a complete bimetallic knife. Knives with iron blades and bronze rivets are also a rarity in the Levant, occurring more frequently at Aegean and Cypriot sites.

Thus, at the beginning of the twelfth century, some groups within Aegean society transplanted their urban life and values to the similar ecological setting of the eastern Mediterranean coast and Cyprus. This event, sketched above as a mass migration of Sea Peoples during the period 1185–1150 BCE, may have been precipitated by the dissolution of the highly articulated, finely tuned, hierarchical polities and economies of the Aegean and Anatolia, sometimes called the "palace economy."

Philistines and Israelites: Interaction and Conflict

The settlement process for highland Israel had begun a generation or two before the arrival of the Sea Peoples on the coast. That event would necessarily have swelled the highland polity of early Israel as the indigenous Canaanite population found itself squeezed out of the plains. The displacement and migration of the tribe of Dan from the coast to the north is a specific example of such a ripple effect. In biblical tradition there are important differences between Dan and the other tribes of Israel. The Danites never controlled the territory they were allotted, which extended to the Mediterranean coast as far as Joppa (Josh. 19.40–48). Moreover, unlike the other tribes, Dan has no extended genealogy (see Gen. 46.23; Num. 26.42). And in the Song of Deborah, Dan is characterized as serving as a client on ships (Judg. 5.17), although seafaring was not a characteristic Israelite activity. Because of these differences, some scholars have suggested that originally the Danites were not a part of Israel, but rather a member of the Sea Peoples' confederation, to be identified with the Danaans of Homer and the Denyen in Rameses III's inscription. Thus the Denyen should have been among those who settled along the coast during stage 1. But the Philistines did not settle in the Joppa region before 1150 BCE (stage 2), and the Sea Peoples do not figure in the twelfth-century Song of Deborah, so the identification of the biblical Danites with either Danaans or Denyen is dubious.

It is much more likely that the expansion of the Philistines into the Joppa region, marked by the founding of Philistine Tell Qasile, forced the Danites out of that area and sent most of the tribe to the far north, to the Canaanite city of Laish. There, according to Judges 18.27, "The Danites . . . came to Laish, to a people quiet and unsuspecting, put them to the sword, and burned down the city."

Evidence for this destruction has recently been discovered by Avraham Biran in his excavations at Tel Dan. Over the ruins of a prosperous Late Bronze Age city, a rather impoverished and rustic settlement was discovered. It had storage pits and a variety of collared-rim storage jars, but little or no Philistine painted pottery. The biblical traditions and the archaeological evidence converge so well that there can be no doubt that the Danites belonged to the Israelite, not the Sea Peoples', confederation.

Either before the move of the Danites to the north or after, with remnants of the tribe still remaining in the south, interaction between a Danite family and the Philistines is preserved in the legends of Samson (Judg. 13–16). Samson is portrayed as an Israelite "judge" from the tribe of Dan. But he is unlike other judges, typically tribal leaders of the Israelite militia of Yahweh. After the beginning of the account of Samson's birth (Judg. 13.2), the Danites are not even mentioned in the saga because most of the tribe had already migrated north. Philistine control over Judah is the larger issue in the stories.

Samson fights his battles alone and performs feats of strength more in the mold of the Greek Heracles than of the Israelite Gideon. Samson tells riddles, has seven magical locks of hair, and cavorts with Philistine women. His adventures take place on the border between the Israelites and the Philistines. Samson chooses a Philistine bride from the Philistine town of Timnah, where Philistine bichrome ware is abundant. This intermediate zone in the foothills between the highlands and the coastal plain was the first point of contact between the two cultures in the late twelfth century BCE and became a zone of contention and conflict thereafter.

Philistine expansion during stage 2 can be traced by the comparatively high yield of Philistine bichrome ware in the Gaza and Beer-sheba basins in the northern Negeb. The narrative in Genesis 26 concerning Isaac and King Abimelech of the Philistines reflects this era. The Cherethites, who served as mercenaries under King David, are probably to be identified with Cretans, a contingent of the Philistines ("Pelethites") who had settled in the semiarid Negeb (1 Sam. 30.14; 2 Sam. 8.18; 15.18; 1 Kings 1.38).

By the mid-eleventh century BCE (the beginning of stage 3), the Philistines had expanded into the Shephelah well beyond their earlier boundaries. From there they launched a military effort to conquer the highland home of the Israelites. One need only compare the large, cosmopolitan cities of the plain and their rich, fertile countryside to the impoverished villages of the hills and their tiny tracts of arable land to appreciate the advantages in wealth and power that the Philistines had over the Israelites.

A supposed Philistine monopoly on iron and steel is a modern myth, based on a misreading of 1 Samuel 13.19–22. But there is no mistaking their superiority in military organization and hardware. The Philistines were known as "chariot-warriors" in Egyptian inscriptions at Medinet Habu. They fielded expert bowmen (1 Sam. 31.3) and crack infantrymen. Bronze linchpins for war chariots have been found at Ashkelon and Ekron, but nowhere else. The top half of the Ashkelon linchpin is in the form of a Philistine goddess in the Aegean tradition. She leads and protects the elite corps of charioteers as they enter battle. These finds give substance to the biblical historiographer's lament that "Judah could not [following the ancient Greek rather than the Hebrew tradition] take Gaza with its territory, Ashkelon with its territory, and Ekron with its territory. Yahweh was with Judah, and he took possession of the hill country, but could not drive out the inhabitants of the plain, because they had chariots of iron" (Judg. 1.18–19). Of course the war chariot was not completely made of iron, but a most essential part of it was—the axle, which stood for the whole vehicle. Homer describes the splendid chariot of the gods as having bronze wheels on either side of an iron axle (*Iliad* 5.723).

The disparity in infantry is highlighted in the duel between David and Goliath. The latter is armed like the Mycenaean warriors depicted on the famous "Warrior Vase" (Myc IIIC, twelfth century BCE) found at Mycenae. These soldiers wear tunics with long sleeves, over which fit corselets; they hold semicircular shields in their left hand and in their right carry throwing spears with leaf-shaped heads. They wear greaves that reach just above the knee, and protective helmets: on one file of warriors, with two horns and a crest; on another, with a row of spikes reminiscent of the Philistine "feathers."

The champion Goliath "had a helmet of bronze on his head, and he was armed with a coat of mail; the weight of the coat was five thousand shekels of bronze. He had greaves of bronze on his legs and a javelin of bronze slung between his shoulders" (1 Sam. 17.5–6). He also carried a sword. His Israelite opponent, so the story goes, was armed with only a sling and a stone.

Had the Philistines accomplished their military goal, it would have been the first time in recorded history that a lowland polity had succeeded in bringing the highlands under its control. The once mighty Egyptian army of the New Kingdom had brought only nominal hegemony over this hilly, wooded frontier, where chariotry was of little or no use in battle. More often it was the highland kingdoms, such as that of Shechem under Labayu during the Amarna age, that consolidated their power over the lowlanders. Ignorant of historical precedents, the Philistines made valiant attempts to turn these natural, long-term odds in their favor.

In the battle of Ebenezer (ca. 1050 BCE), a site within a day's journey of Shiloh, the Philistines took a major step toward realizing their goal. Not only did they capture the ark of the covenant—the most sacred Israelite symbol, over which Yahweh, the divine warrior, was enthroned (the equivalent of capturing the statue of the warrior god in iconic cultures) (1 Sam. 4.1–11)—but they also advanced even farther upland, destroying the sanctuary of Yahweh at Shiloh and wiping out the Elide dynasty of priests serving there (see Jer. 7.12).

Recent excavations at Shiloh by Israel Finkelstein have confirmed the results of the earlier Danish expedition, as interpreted by W. F. Albright. Shiloh (Stratum V) flourished as a major Ephraimite center in the first half of the eleventh century BCE. Its temple served as a major annual pilgrimage site for the Israelite tribes in the autumn, during the wine (and New Year's?) festival. The destruction of this sanctuary by the Philistines around 1050 BCE reverberated in the memory of the Israelites for centuries (Ps. 78.60–64; Jer. 7.12).

After their decisive victory at Ebenezer, the Philistines continued to press their offensive against the Israelites. During the second half of the eleventh century, the Philistines reached the height of their power. This is the era of Samuel, too, and it is paradoxical that he is portrayed so positively by the biblical historiographers when actually he did so little to thwart the Philistine onslaught. In fact, military encroachment by the Philistines precipitated a crisis of leadership during Samuel's judgeship of such proportions that the people demanded a ruler capable of dealing with it. Popular pressure led to the anointing of Israel's first legitimate king, Saul of the tribe of Benjamin. By that time the Philistines had established garrisons in the hill country at Bethlehem, Geba, and Gibeath-elohim, and they were fighting the Israelites on their home turf at Michmash and near Jerusalem (1 Sam. 10.5; 13.3, 11; 2 Sam. 23.13–14).

It took the military genius of the outlaw and later king David to reverse the fortunes of war with the Philistines. The destruction of such predominately Canaanite cities as Megiddo, Beth-shan, and Tell Abu Hawam can be synchronized with that of predominately Philistine cities, such as Ekron, Tell Qasile, Timnah, and Dor—all in the first quarter of the tenth century BCE. The likely agent of this devastation is the Israelites under the leadership of King David. By the time Solomon set up his administrative provinces (1 Kings 4.7–19), Israel was in control of Megiddo, Taanach, and Beth-shan, formerly Canaanite city-states, and Dor, formerly a Sea Peoples' city-state.

The Philistines were driven back to the initial territory of stage 1, that of the pentapolis. Even there the coastal cities show signs of expansion at the expense of those in the inner plain. Ekron is reduced to one-fifth its former size, from a city of 20 hectares (50 acres) during stages 1 and 2 to one of 5 hectares (12 acres) at the end of stage 3. At the same time (after ca. 980/975 BCE), Ashkelon becomes a well-fortified seaport, covering more than 60 hectares (150 acres). Ashdod expands five times its former size to a large metropolis of about 40 hectares (100 acres). Thus as Israel expands from its highland heartland, Philistia retreats to well within its earliest boundaries.

By consolidating his base of support in the highlands and by uniting a loose-knit tribal confederation, King David was able to conquer and hold vast amounts of lowland territory, formerly under the control of the Canaanites and Sea Peoples. From his conquered capital of Jerusalem he was able to overcome the political fragmentation endemic to tribal confederations (as well as to the more cosmopolitan city-states of the enemy), creating a large territorial state under one patrimonial ruler. From the modern historian's perspective it is only after the reign of King David that the "conquest" of Canaan was complete.

Conclusion

The biblical historiographers attributed the rise of kingship in ancient Israel to external stimuli. Foremost of those military threats were the Philistines from the coast, who were occupying key settlements leading up to the highlands and planting garrisons in the heartland of Israel. Recent biblical scholarship, following anthropological models, has emphasized internal dynamics within the social system which led to kingship in Israel, minimizing the external threats. There was nothing in the social structure of premonarchic Israel that prevented the rise of a more permanent warlord, or ruler, later known as a king; in fact, just such permanence of leadership had been attempted in the cases of Gideon (Judg. 8.22–23) and Abimelech (Judg. 9). Structurally there was always a place under the deity and above the tribal leaders for a patrimonial ruler, known as *melek*, or "king." Monarchy was not a foreign or urban institution grafted onto a patrimonial order; it could have occurred in nascent or fully developed form at any time during the period of the tribal confederation. When kingship finally was established and acknowledged by the tribal polity, it was the external military threats that served as the catalyst for kingship.

Like others in the Israelite community, kings were to be subject to customary law and tradition (Deut. 17.14–20), and there were condemnations of royal excess (1 Sam. 8.11–18), but kingship could easily fit into the structure between the divine authority and the nested tribal authorities already established in premonarchic Israel. This seems clear from the language of house and household (*bayit*) used by the biblical writers to refer to the deity (*bêt Yahweh*), to the king, his household, and his dwelling (*bêt ham-melek*), and to the notables or heads of household (*bêt 'ab*). Each patriarch was sovereign over overarching domains, from joint families and their lineages, to clans, to tribes, to the king whose family and household included the whole kingdom. Because the landed patrimony was handed down from father to son(s), great importance was attached to orderly succession—the usufructuary right, whether to ancestral estate or to royal estate (the kingdom). And the patriarchal deity held ultimate sovereignty and proprietorship over the human estate and state(s), as well as over all creation. Thus the king and the state were the household and family estate writ large, and the national deity was the paterfamilias writ larger still. Domains of authority and dominance were not structurally incompatible, and kingship in Israel, "like other nations" (1 Sam. 8.5), was patrimonial. The real problems with kingship were not of principle or structure but of function. How could power and dominance be pragmatically exercised without infringement on the various overarching domains? Answers to that question led to various assessments of each king as he held office.

The tensions and balance of power among divine, royal, and familial forces provide much of the stuff of Israelite history.

Note

Sources for table 3.2 and the settlement maps: **Judah:** Ofer, Avi. *The Highland of Judah during the Biblical Period.* Unpublished doctoral dissertation. Tel Aviv University, n.d. **Benjamin:** Finkelstein, Israel. *The Archaeology of the Israelite Settlement.* Jerusalem: Israel Exploration Society, 1988. Finkelstein, Israel, and Magen, Yizhak, eds. *Archaeological Survey of the Hill Country of Benjamin.* Jerusalem: Israel Antiquities Authority, 1993. **Ephraim:** Finkelstein, Israel. *The Archaeology of the Israelite Settlement.* Jerusalem: Israel Exploration Society, 1988. **Manasseh:** Zertal, Adam. *The Israelite Settlement in the Hill Country of Manasseh.* Unpublished doctoral dissertation. Tel Aviv University, 1986. **Gilead:** Mittman, Siegfried. *Beiträge zur Siedlungs- und Territorialgesichte des nordlichen Ostjordanlandes.* Wiesbaden: Otto Harrassowitz, 1970. **Jordan Valley:** Ibrahim, M., Sauer, J. A., and Yassine, K. "The East Jordan Survey, 1975." *Bulletin of the American Schools of Oriental Research* 222 (1976): 41–66. Yassine, Khair. "The East Jordan Valley Survey, 1976 (Part 2)." In Khair Yassine, ed., *Archaeology of Jordan: Essays and Reports.* Amman: University of Jordan, 1988. **Hesban:** Ibach, Robert D. *Archaeological Survey of the Hesban Region: Catalogue of Sites and Characterization of Periods.* Berrien Springs, Mich.: Andrews University Press, 1987. **Moab:** Miller, J. Maxwell, ed. *Archaeological Survey of the Kerak Plateau Conducted during 1978–1982 under the Direction of J. Maxwell Miller and Jack M. Pinkerton.* Atlanta, Ga.: Scholars Press, 1991. **Wadi el-Hasa:** MacDonald, Burton. *The Wadi el Hasa Archaeological Survey 1979–1983: West-Central Jordan.* Waterloo, Ont.: Wilfrid Laurier University Press, 1988.

Select Bibliography

Albright, William F. "The Israelite Conquest in the Light of Archaeology." *Bulletin of the American Schools of Oriental Research* 74 (1939): 11–22. Dated but useful survey of archaeological evidence in support of the "conquest" hypothesis of Israelite origins.

Alt, Albrecht. "The Settlement of the Israelites in Palestine." In *Essays on Old Testament History and Religion,* 172–221. Trans. R. W. Wilson. Garden City, N.Y.: Doubleday, 1968. Originally published in German in 1925, a pioneering study of "territorial history" in support of the "pastoral nomad" hypothesis of Israelite origins.

Bietak, Manfred. "The Sea Peoples and the End of the Egyptian Administration in Canaan." In *Biblical Archaeology Today,* eds. Avraham Biran and Joseph Aviram, 292–306. Jerusalem: Israel Exploration Society, 1990. Superb study of the Sea Peoples, emphasizing their large-scale seaborne migrations to and early bridgeheads in Canaan, and delineating material cultural boundaries between Philistine and Egypto-Canaanite territories.

Biran, Avraham, and Joseph Naveh. "An Aramaic Stele Fragment from Dan." *Israel Exploration Journal* 43 (1993): 81–98. The stele has the earliest nonbiblical reference to the "house of David."

Cross, Frank Moore. *Canaanite Myth and Hebrew Epic: Essays in the History of the Religion of Israel.* Cambridge, Mass.: Harvard University Press, 1973. A masterpiece. For a more recent perspective, see the popularized account in *Frank Moore Cross: Conversations with a Bible Scholar,* ed. Hershel Shanks (Washington, D.C.: Biblical Archaeology Society, 1994).

————. "Reuben, First-Born of Jacob." *Zeitschrift für die alttestamentliche Wissenschaft* 100, Supplement (1988): 46–65. Chapter 3 in *From Epic to Canon: Essays in the History and Literature of Ancient Israel.* Baltimore: Johns Hopkins University Press, 1998. A brilliant synthesis of textual and archaeological data relating to Midianites and early Israelites.

Dever, William G. "Archaeology and the Israelite 'Conquest.' " In *Anchor Bible Dictionary,* ed. David Noel Freedman, 3.545–58. New York: Doubleday, 1992. Up-to-date, authoritative assessment of the archaeological evidence relating to the early Israelite settlement.

Finkelstein, Israel. *The Archaeology of the Israelite Settlement.* Jerusalem: Israel Exploration Society, 1988. The most comprehensive presentation and analysis of archaeological survey data relating to the Israelite settlement.

Gottwald, Norman K. "Israel, Social and Economic Development of." In *The Interpreter's Dictionary of the Bible: Supplementary Volume,* ed. Keith Crim, 465–68. Nashville: Abingdon, 1976. Condensed account of the author's "peasants' revolt" hypothesis. For the complete version, see his *The Tribes of Yahweh: A Sociology of the Religion of Liberated Israel, 1250–1050* B.C.E. (Maryknoll, N.Y.: Orbis, 1979).

Khoury, Philip S., and Joseph Kostiner, eds. *Tribes and State Formation in the Middle East.* Berkeley: University of California Press, 1990. A splendid collection of essays dealing with the relationship between tribe and state.

Machinist, Peter. "Outsiders or Insiders: The Biblical View of Emergent Israel and Its Contexts." In *The Other in Jewish Thought and History: Constructions of Jewish Culture and Identity,* eds. Laurence J. Silberstein and Robert L. Cohn, 35–60. New York: New York University Press, 1994. An illuminating study of Israelite historiography with focus on the relationship of the community to the land.

Mendenhall, George. "The Hebrew Conquest of Palestine." *Biblical Archaeologist* 25 (1962): 66–87. The original account of the "peasants' revolt" hypothesis, which stimulated a generation of creative biblical and theological research.

Na'aman, Nadav. "The 'Conquest of Canaan' in the Book of Joshua and in History." In *From Nomadism to Monarchy: Archaeological and Historical Aspects of Early Israel,* ed. Israel Finkelstein and Nadav Na'aman, 218–81. Washington, D.C.: Biblical Archaeology Society, 1994. Detailed analysis of the sources used by the Deuteronomic Historian to construct his account of the Israelite "conquest."

Parr, Peter. "Qurayya." In *Anchor Bible Dictionary,* ed. David Noel Freedman, 5.594–96. New York: Doubleday, 1992. Brief, authoritative overview of the archaeology of Midian, with an essential bibliography. Parr's archaeological survey of that region has contributed to the revival and revision of the Midianite hypothesis.

Sandars, N. K. *The Sea Peoples: Warriors of the Ancient Mediterranean 1250–1150* B.C. Rev. ed. New York: Thames and Hudson, 1985. An engaging account of the Sea Peoples for scholars and nonspecialists alike.

Schloen, J. David. "Caravans, Kenites, and *Casus Belli:* Enmity and Alliance in the Song of Deborah." *Catholic Biblical Quarterly* 55 (1993): 18–38. An imaginative and convincing interpretation of Judges 5, according to which disruption of the Midianite trade in aromatics leads to war.

Stager, Lawrence E. "The Archaeology of the Family in Ancient Israel." *Bulletin of the American Schools of Oriental Research* 260 (1985): 1–35. Influential synthesis that combines archaeological and textual data to reconstruct early Israelite society.

————. "Israelite Settlement in Canaan." In *Biblical Archaeology Today*, ed. Janet Amitai, 83–87. Jerusalem: Israel Exploration Society, 1985. First formulation of the "ruralization" hypothesis and an attempt to separate the process of Iron Age I settlement from the problem of Israelite origins.

————. "Archaeology, Ecology, and Social History: Background Themes to the Song of Deborah." *Supplements to Vetus Testamentum* 40 (1988): 221–34. A study that highlights the intersection of event (the battle of Kishon) and *la longue durée* (tribal economy and ecology).

————. "The Impact of the Sea Peoples (1185–1050 BCE)." In *The Archaeology of Society in the Holy Land*, ed. Thomas E. Levy, 332–48. New York: Facts on File, 1995. Up-to-date synthesis of texts and archaeology relating to the Sea Peoples, especially the Philistines, and their interaction with other groups in the Levant.

Voegelin, Eric. *The Ecumenic Age*. Vol. 4 of *Order and History*. Baton Rouge: Louisiana State University Press, 1974. The most profound study ever written of the symbols of order in the biblical and classical worlds. See also vol. 1, *Israel and Revelation* (1956).

Weber, Max. *Economy and Society*. Vol. 2. Ed. Guenther Roth and Claus Wittich. Berkeley: University of California Press, 1978. Classic exposition of the theory of patrimonial authority.

Yurco, Frank J. "3,200-Year-Old Picture of Israelites Found in Egypt." *Biblical Archaeology Review* 16, no. 5 (September–October 1990): 20–38. Popularized version of the author's extraordinary discovery linking the victory hymn of the Israel Stela to Merneptah's wall reliefs at Karnak.

CHAPTER FOUR

"There Was No King in Israel"

The Era of the Judges

JO ANN HACKETT

The period in Israel's history that extends for most of the twelfth and eleventh centuries BCE is the era of the judges, which archaeologists call Iron Age I. As the era begins, the group called Israel emerges in the central highlands west of the Jordan River. Over the course of the period, that early group expands to encompass the boundaries of later Israel and Judah, the familiar territories of the twelve tribes—an expansion that brings tension as early Israel conquers territory from the Canaanites in the valleys. Eventually, Israel's expansion is stopped by similar Philistine expansion eastward from the southern coast. These are the centuries before the establishment of a monarchy, a time when "there was no king in Israel" (Judg. 17.6; 18.1; 19.1; 21.25).

What do we know of this formative period in Israel's history, and how do we know it? The first question will concern us throughout this chapter; there are several answers to the second. Our most familiar sources of information for the time of the judges are the biblical books of Judges and 1 Samuel, and the book of Ruth may supply additional information. Furthermore, several poems in the Bible dated early in the Iron Age depict Israel's self-conception and beliefs during that era. Another, and fast-growing, source for the period is archaeology. Archaeologists and those who compare excavated remains with tribal societies the world over have expanded our understanding of Iron Age I society in Israel, and with each season of fieldwork they continue to provide new data to think about and integrate. A few written records from the era of the judges have also been recovered, which set in context also provide information. Finally, ancient sources and, again, archaeology inform us about the neighbors of ancient Israel during the early Iron Age, especially the Philistines, the

Transjordanian peoples (the Ammonites, Moabites, and Edomites), and some of the Phoenician cities.

We know only the rough chronology of the period. As we shall see, the ordering of stories in the book of Judges is artificial, and the kind of information archaeology offers can give only a broad outline of the times. Consequently, the discussion that follows is arranged topically rather than chronologically, with consideration of the sources as its organizing principle.

Biblical Narrative: Judges, 1 Samuel, and Ruth

Let us turn first to the biblical book of Judges and especially to the deliverer stories in chapters 1–16. The book is named for the heroes whose stories dominate its literature, but their title is misleading. Few of the "judges" of this period seem to have any judicial function, so that the modern idea of a judge cannot fully define them. Rather, the biblical judges were generally military heroes; they could be administrative or governing leaders as well, but they need not have operated in any strictly judicial capacity. As we will see, there is ample evidence both from the Bible and from other ancient Near Eastern sources to show that "judging" was more than simply judicial.

The judges' stories themselves are not uniformly presented. Those whose exploits are told in some detail are often called the "major" judges, while the five who are simply listed along with their region and term in office (and sometimes another item or two of information) are called "minor" judges. The minor judges' names occur in two lists: Tola and Jair in Judges 10.2–5, and Ibzan, Elon, and Abdon in 12.8–15.

Much of the book of Judges, as well as the early chapters of 1 Samuel, seems to originate in the premonarchical period, even though there is an obvious layer (or layers) of editing. Some editing extends throughout the Former Prophets (from the books of Joshua and Judges through 1 and 2 Samuel and 1 and 2 Kings) and is usually attributed to a Deuteronomic Historian(s) (DH), who selected and edited older materials according to a theological understanding of Israel's history. DH also composed some new material, especially speeches for central characters and a judgmental explanatory narrative that gives a theological framework to much of the work. DH's understanding of Israel's history was based on the covenant between Yahweh and Israel laid out in the core of the book of Deuteronomy (hence the title *Deuteronomic*), and in particular that Israel's national prosperity depends on its strict adherence to that covenant. For example, Judges 2.11–23, a Deuteronomic composition, tells in summary fashion a theme that will be repeated over and over in the stories of the judges: the people of Israel sin and fall away from worship of Yahweh; Yahweh sells them into the hand of oppressors; the people cry out, and Yahweh sends a deliverer, a "judge," to rescue them; there is peace in the days of the deliverer; the deliverer dies, and the people sin again; and so forth. The first judge's story in 3.7–11 is a good illustration of the pattern, with the whole process starting over again in verse 12:

> The Israelites did what was evil in the sight of the LORD, forgetting the LORD their God, and worshiping the Baals and the Asherahs. Therefore the anger of the LORD was kindled against Israel, and he sold them into the hand of King Cushan-rishathaim of Aram-naharaim; and the Israelites served Cushan-rishathaim eight years. But

when the Israelites cried out to the LORD, the LORD raised up a deliverer for the Israelites, who delivered them, Othniel son of Kenaz, Caleb's younger brother. The spirit of the LORD came upon him, and he judged Israel; he went out to war, and the LORD gave King Cushan-rishathaim of Aram into his hand; and his hand prevailed over Cushan-rishathaim. So the land had rest forty years. Then Othniel son of Kenaz died.

The Israelites again did what was evil in the sight of the LORD; and the LORD strengthened King Eglon of Moab against Israel, because they had done what was evil in the sight of the LORD.

The systematic way the judges' stories are laid out in the book of Judges suggests that this later editor took stories from the premonarchic era in Israel's history, mostly stories of war heroes, and superimposed upon them a formulaic beginning and ending. This is history as a series of champions' lives and actions, which as we will see is typical of tribal societies. The all-Israel context is also part of the secondary, editorial structure: the core stories themselves concern the exploits of one person within the context of his or her own tribe or region, and do not usually involve a larger association of tribes pledged to defend each other. By way of exception, the old poem in Judges 5, one of the earliest witnesses to this era in Israel, congratulates the tribes that came to the battle and castigates those that did not, as if at least by the time of Deborah in the twelfth century BCE such an understanding existed among a number of the components of the people Israel. The notion that Israel's political health depended on its adherence to its covenant with Yahweh, and especially on the exclusive worship of Yahweh, pervades the Deuteronomic History, and this means that in its final form the book of Judges has been shaped by the Deuteronomist(s).

The description of this era in the book of Judges includes features that are probably authentic to premonarchic Israel: the lack of centralization in the society in religious, political, and military matters and the concomitant lack of a permanent administration, including a standing army. These features clarify one of the most interesting aspects of the period of the judges as presented in the biblical text: the heroes themselves are often unlikely. Such unpredictable leaders more commonly emerge in a society and a time with little or no central organization, when no one is waiting to take the reins. In these contexts, women and outcast men can seize power that would be beyond their reach in a society ruled by a hereditary elite. The theological interpretation of this lack of predictable organization and of the noticeable inappropriateness of many of the era's leaders was that Israel's only true leader was Yahweh, and that a battle that Yahweh approved of and therefore fought in on Israel's side was of course won—but won by Yahweh, not by Israel's leaders and warriors.

The first leader we meet in this era, after Joshua and the elders of his generation have died (Judg. 2.6–10), is Othniel, a nephew of Caleb, a hero of the preceding era. Othniel's claims to fame are that he wins a wealthy wife (his cousin) in battle, and he wins the first battle described in the book of Judges as a true judge's battle, a battle sparked by a "charismatic" leader: the "spirit of Yahweh" came upon Othniel, and he "judged" Israel (Judg. 3.10). In other words, Othniel became Israel's leader not because he was the next-in-line of some hereditary or administrative hierarchy; rather, he led Israel by exhibiting identifiable and unambiguous signs of being the person who could succeed. The text identifies those signs as the spirit of Yahweh, although no detail is given. This is what the sociologist Max Weber meant by charismatic leadership—leadership that is not predictable according to any arbitrary scheme, but stems from the force of the leader's personality alone. The description of Othniel and his battle, however, is so brief, and the language of the description so close to DH's generic description of the era, that the narrative of Othniel's career gives little information about the judges' functions or position, or about the era itself.

The next leader mentioned, Ehud (Judg. 3.12–30), is remembered for his craftiness in killing the enemy king, and for his left-handedness. The quintessential man of the hour, he is the one who can get the job done, and that alone qualifies him for leadership. His most effective battle strategy is to kill by deceit the king of the enemy Moabites, and then he is able to convince Israelite fighting men from the hill country of Ephraim to follow him in cutting off and killing the Moabites fleeing back over the Jordan River. Shamgar (Judg. 3.31) is simply remembered for slaughtering many Philistines, practically bare-handed.

These first three judges were leaders not because they inherited or trained for the position, but because they proved themselves up to the task. Although we are often given their fathers' names and their home territories, they were not part of an ongoing chain of centralized command. Only their success counted.

Deborah's story, told twice in Judges 4 and 5, is paradigmatic. She is a woman who wields her power from, we assume, her home territory (4.5), in a local position. We are given her husband's name, but no other information about him. She seems to hold her power because of her abilities as a prophet. In a later era in Israel, she would not have had the power to call out the army—to be the person with supreme authority in a time of crisis—because by then a hereditary, all-male monarchy ruled. (Athaliah's brief reign in ninth-century BCE Judah is considered an aberration by the biblical authors; see 2 Kings 11; 2 Chron. 22.10–23.21.) But in the era of the judges, Deborah is described as the person with a link with the divine world, and so it is she who calls up the troops when Yahweh approves of the battle (Judg. 4.6–9). And she is not the only female deliverer in this story: another woman finishes off the enemy general. When Deborah predicts to Barak that he will not win the glory of this particular battle because Yahweh will give Sisera over to a woman, we assume she is talking about herself; but we later find that it is Jael, a different woman and at that one only marginally connected with Israel, who will be remembered as the "warrior" who took down Sisera.

The same story is told in Judges 5, in one of the oldest pieces of literature in the Bible. In this poem it is the stars and the Wadi Kishon who actually fight the battle on behalf of the Israelites (5.19–21), further indication that charismatic leadership in Israel was tied to the belief that it was not the human Israelites who determined the outcome of their military engagements, but, on a different plane, Yahweh and his "host" (natural and celestial elements) who fought and won the battles.

The next deliverer, Gideon, confesses himself to be a far-from-impressive character when Yahweh (represented by a messenger) comes to call him to lead Israel to victory against Midian. In Judges 6.15 Gideon protests that his clan is the poorest in Manasseh and that he is the least significant member of his extended family (Hebrew *bêt 'āb*, meaning literally "father's house"). The theological meaning of this motif is clearest here in Gideon's story, for Yahweh's answer is "but I will be with you" (6.16;

compare Exod. 3.12). Later, we are told that Gideon must pare down the size of his army before going to battle (7.2–8), so that Israel will know that it is Yahweh who wins their battles and not their own prowess. Toward the end of Gideon's story we see the beginnings of a longing for a more stable ruling system, when the people ask him to set up a dynasty. Although Gideon refuses, his son Abimelech takes advantage of this sentiment to have himself declared king in Shechem. His reign is short-lived, and we return for a while to an era of judges instead of kings.

The next judge about whom we have a narrative is Jephthah. As an illegitimate son and an outlaw, he too is in an inferior position until he proves to be the one to whom the Gileadites can turn for military help in a crisis (Judg. 10.18). Judges 11.8–9 makes clear that the basis of Jephthah's leadership position in Gilead is his military success over the Ammonites, not any office he has inherited or been trained for. There is no such permanent office; the elders of Gilead have no one else to help them in the emergency, and so they agree to appoint the outlaw Jephthah as their head if he is successful.

The accounts of the five minor judges in 10.2–5 and 12.8–15 all contain the phrase "after him" (or "after Abimelech" in the case of the first one, Tola), but this does not mean they were part of a line of rulers or had been trained according to any administrative process. For three of them no patronymic is given—another sign of inferior status. We have the father's name for Tola and Abdon, but neither father is said to have ruled or judged before his son. Rather, "after him" implies precisely the opposite: that the rule went from competent ruler to competent ruler, regardless of family or place of origin.

Since they are so different from the stories of the other judges, the Samson narratives (Judg. 13–16) should be viewed as a separate piece within Judges 1–16. Samson's battles are personal, not on behalf of a larger group, and he does not deliver Israel as a whole (despite the promise in 13.5), except by his killing or being a nuisance to large numbers of Philistines. His stories are probably inserted where they are in the book of Judges because they involve the friction between the Philistines and tribe of Dan that arose during this period; this also sets the stage for the conflict between the Philistines and all Israel that is the focus of much of 1 Samuel. However folkloric the narratives about Samson are, they also describe a time of no central authority—a time, instead, of a dependence on individual strength or charisma to overcome Dan's Philistine enemies. Samson's shortcomings are obvious: he is impetuous and none too intelligent, another unlikely leader in this era of opportunity. The ancient Israelite audience, and we as readers, have no trouble understanding that Samson's heroic acts would be utterly impossible without the support of Yahweh. The more unlikely the hero, the more understandable the message that it is Yahweh who rules.

Following the deliverer stories in Judges 1–16, chapters 17–21 also portray a time with no central authority. There are not even local leaders—no individual is described as a "judge" or a deliverer (see 18.28). Rather, it is a chaotic period, in which the conflicts are among Israelites: the Danites versus Micah in chapter 18, the men of Gibeah versus the Levite and his host in chapter 19, the rest of Israel versus the tribe of Benjamin in chapter 20, the Israelite army versus Jabesh-gilead in 21.8–12, and

Benjamin versus the women of Shiloh in 21.1–23. The one individual who musters the militia for battle is the nameless Levite of chapters 19–20, and ironically this is the only occasion in the entire book that all Israel unites for war—but against one of their own rather than an external enemy.

Outside the book of Judges, the first few chapters of 1 Samuel reveal the beginning of attempts to establish lineages of power within this premonarchic society. It is assumed that the sons of the priest Eli will succeed him in the priesthood, that he is part of a priestly family that transmits the priestly offices from father to son. Such a process is consistent with passages in Exodus through Numbers (such as Exod. 28.1, 41; Lev. 8; Num. 3.3) that establish a hereditary priesthood, but there is no evidence of such an organization in the book of Judges, and it may not have existed in that decentralized era. (The passages just mentioned come from the Priestly source of the Pentateuch, and although they purport to be about premonarchic times, their date is late in the monarchy at the earliest.) Eli is said in 1 Samuel 4.18 to have "judged Israel" for forty years, and so his sons could also have been considered judges. Along with their hereditary priestly roles, then, they might have filled what had become hereditary administrative or ruling offices.

Samuel's sons, too, were expected to follow in his footsteps, and in his case what they would have done was to rule or "judge" Israel. In 1 Samuel 8.1–2, Samuel appoints his sons judges "over Israel" in Beer-sheba. The people ask Samuel to bypass his sons because they are corrupt. The very request, however, assumes that judging had become a hereditary occupation by this time. The request for a king to rule over them formalizes the actual situation: the judge was no longer a charismatic, ad hoc leader, but a member of a family line, predictable by birth rather than talent. Calling such a person a king is the next step.

The book of Ruth seems to provide evidence about the premonarchic period. The story is set "in the days when the judges judged" (Ruth 1.1), and there is neither king nor central organization in the story. But much suggests that the book comes from a later period: several features of its language, the explanation in 4.7 of the custom of the redemption around which the end of the story revolves, and the denouement that traces the roots of the Davidic monarchy. So the book of Ruth may tell us nothing about the era of the judges beyond what an Israelite storyteller of a later period knew of it, but even that is worthwhile information. No competent storyteller would place a king in the era of the judges, so a decentralized society is no surprise; but we also learn that that storyteller saw the premonarchic era as a time when life revolved around the village and the family, and when decisions about property and caring for the poor were made on the basis of kin relationships. Naomi and her family, who are Israelites, move freely between Judah and Moab during the famine, and no army or national government interferes. Intermarriage between Israelites and foreigners is presented as an unremarkable experience, but religion does seem to be a "national" matter or a matter of ethnicity. In the famous passage in Ruth 1.16, the Moabite Ruth ties Naomi's god to her place and her people, and Ruth's impending trip from Moab to Israel apparently prompted her conversion. So even though the book of Ruth must be used cautiously, its picture of the premonarchic era conforms to modern expectations of a segmentary tribal society.

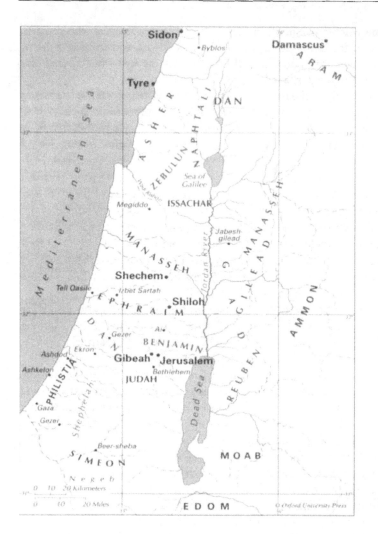

Palestine and Transjordan in the early Iron Age, showing the territory assigned to the twelve tribes of Israel.

The Shaping of the Narratives

A closer look at several aspects of the biblical narrative will help us better understand the era of the judges. The chronological scheme, particularly in Judges 3–16, might enable the dating of some of the events. Unfortunately, however, this chronology is artificial and formulaic. The framework of the deliverers' stories presents the judges as succeeding one another, although the order of the stories is more likely based on a south-to-north (and then east) geographical model, at least to a point, and so the chronological indications may be secondary. The second list of minor judges (Judg. 12.8–15) spoils the geographical scheme, but as we will see, these two lists (the first is in 10.1–5) probably had a separate transmission history from the narratives around them and were inserted secondarily into the text after the other stories had been gathered together in geographical order.

The geographical movement of the stories is apparent. The first judge, Othniel (Judg. 3.7–11), is from Judah (for Othniel, see also Josh. 15.15–19; Judg. 1.11–15). His story is so formulaic, so lacking in detail, that it is more a model than an authentic historical memory, but he is at any rate placed in the scheme at the beginning of the list of judges, in the far south. The second judge, Ehud (Judg. 3.12–30), is from Benjamin, north of Judah. The third is Shamgar ben-Anat (3.31), who is simply said to have killed six hundred Philistines, with no geographical location indicated. It is tempting to set the Samson-like Shamgar, who kills with an ox goad, in the southern holding of Dan, where Samson also clashed with the Philistines (compare Samson's killing a thousand Philistines with the jawbone of a donkey in 15.14–17; see also 14.5–6; 15.4–5); Dan is also north of Judah and west of Benjamin. Deborah, the fourth judge (Judg. 4–5), is said to be from Ephraim, north of Benjamin and Dan, even though her military activity takes place farther north at the Wadi Kishon and, according to the poetry in chapter 5, involves the northern tribes of Machir (which was part of or had replaced Manasseh), Issachar, Zebulun, and Naphtali, as well as Benjamin and her own Ephraim. The fifth judge, Gideon (Judg. 6–8), is from Ophrah in Manasseh, and he is followed by Abimelech (8.33–9.57), not really a judge at all; his story revolves around Gideon's Ophrah and Shechem. So the first five judges are identified according to their home regions in approximate south-north order: Judah, Benjamin, Dan (possibly), Ephraim, and Manasseh.

Next come the minor judges. The first of them is Tola (10.1–2), and he was from Issachar, just north of Manasseh (although he is said to have lived in Ephraim, 10.1). With the seventh judge, Jair, also a minor judge, we move east of the Jordan River (10.3–5); he hails from Gilead (in the eastern tribal allotment of Manasseh), the northernmost Israelite region in Transjordan. Even though they are minor judges, the stories of Tola and Jair do not interrupt the scheme, because like Jair, Jephthah, the eighth judge, also comes from Gilead (11.1–12.7). The minor judges' listings were probably introduced into the narrative secondarily, but geographical patterning may have determined the exact point of insertion for Tola and Jair. Thus, with or without the mention of Tola and Jair, there is a south-to-north and then eastward progression of the judges, from Othniel to Jephthah.

With the last of the minor judges, the approximate south-north scheme breaks down. The last three judges before Samson move us back west of the Jordan River, and do not follow any geographical scheme, unless we are to see a reverse, north-south, element in the last four judges listed. Ibzan comes from Bethlehem (Judg. 12.8–10), which may be either the well-known Bethlehem in Judah or the less familiar Bethlehem in Zebulun (Josh. 19.15). He is followed by Elon of Zebulun (Judg. 12.11–12) and Abdon of Ephraim (12.13–15). Samson, the twelfth judge, belonged to the tribe of Dan while it still held territory in the southern part of Canaan, near the land settled by the Philistines.

The geographical basis for the ordering of the stories in the book of Judges suggests that the sequential chronology implied by that placement is not historical. Furthermore, the number of years given in the book for the period of the judges is over four hundred, much too long a span considering the dating of the Exodus accepted by the majority of scholars, including the authors of this book. Another chronological contrivance supports this conclusion: the numbers of years of peace brought about by each of the major judges, or the number of years of their ruling, is a multiple of 20. Thus, after Othniel's defeat of Cushan-rishathaim, Israel had 40 years of peace (3.11); after Ehud, it remained free of strife for 80 years (3.30); after Deborah, for 40 years (5.31); after Gideon, for 40 years (8.28). Samson is said to have judged Israel for 20 years (15.20; 16.31). Even the final word on Eli the priest reports that he judged Israel for 40 years (1 Sam. 4.18). Only one judge about whom we have a sizable narrative had a tenure not a multiple of 20: Jephthah is said to have ruled Israel for only 6 years (12.7). In this way he bridges the major and minor judges. So we have what was originally a south-north list of heroes presented as if they followed one another chronologically, with many of the numbers of years given for them unlikely since they are multiples of 20. In contrast to this formula are the unusual numbers in the lists of minor judges: Tola, 23 years (10.2); Jair, 22 years (10.3); Ibzan, 7 years (12.9); Elon, 10 years (12.11); and Abdon, 8 years (12.14). No time period is mentioned in the brief notice about Shamgar ben-Anat (3.31).

Several factors thus indicate secondary reworking: the framework of Judges 1–16, the arrangement of the hero stories, and the chronology for at least the major judges. The lists of minor judges, on the other hand, may preserve memories of people and durations that were not shaped by those overarching patterns. Although their placement in the overall narrative may be secondary, they are brief, nonrepetitive notices stating that an individual judged Israel (after a previous judge); something memorable about him (not related to any heroic activity); and a time period that is not an arbitrary multiple of 20, but usually such a specific number (22, 8, and so on) that there is no reason to suppose that a later editor invented it. The two features of the minor judges' lists, then, that argue most convincingly for a separate transmission history are their style (list as opposed to narrative) and the realistic numbers of years of tenure that the lists report. Moreover, the lists, especially the second (Judg. 12.8–15), disrupt the geographical ordering of the narratives in Judges 3–16.

But this does not necessarily mean that the major and minor judges were two completely distinct groups of officials. The language used about the major judges differs from that used about minor judges, but the two are not entirely dissimilar, and the two lists of minor judges do not follow the same pattern. All five of the minor judges in the book of Judges (Tola, Jair, Ibzan, Elon, and Abdon) are said to "judge Israel," and only Tola is also said to "deliver Israel." In the early chapters of 1 Samuel, similarly Eli, Samuel, and Samuel's sons are all chosen to "judge Israel," and none is designated a "deliverer." Among the major judges in the book of Judges, Deborah is never called a deliverer, but all the other major judges are described as deliverer or delivering Israel. Both terms are used of Othniel and Samson, and both occur in the generic description of the era in Judges 2.16–19. Furthermore, although the minor judges Tola and Elon have only short notices, we know a little something, at least, about Jair, Ibzan, and Abdon. We know virtually nothing about the first major judge, Othniel. Among the minor judges, Tola and Jair in the first list "arise" and judge Israel, while of Ibzan, Elon, and Abdon in the second list the texts say merely that they judged Israel, after the previous judge. Shamgar (3.31) is difficult to fit into either category: his notice is shorter than any other, but he is said to "deliver

Israel" ("even he," as the text says), and he is mentioned in the oldest and best source for the period, the Song of Deborah (Judg. 5.6). The difference between the two groups, then, may be less substantial than at first appears.

All of this evidence suggests that the principal difference between the major and minor judges was how they were remembered: the major judges through a narrative telling and retelling of their exploits, even Shamgar's single-handed killing of six hundred Philistines; and the minor judges through some sort of annals that listed leaders' names, regions, and tenure in office. Separate processes for remembering do not mean, however, that one group of judges is less historical than the other. That we have more authentic-sounding numbers for the tenure of the minor judges may mean that the narratives of the heroes who were the major judges were not originally transmitted as the stories of successive leaders of Israel, and so did not include the notice that the person had "judged Israel" for a period of time. They were hero stories, narratives of exploits from this premonarchic era. When they were edited into a series of stories that were to be related chronologically, approximate figures for their time as leaders were added. Jephthah is the exception because he was remembered in both ways: as a name in a list that included years in office and as a hero whose exploits were narrated at length.

Who Should Rule? The Office of Judge

The stories of the judges preserved in biblical literature thus stem from varied sources, with both the framework of the book of Judges and the chronology of the era "when the judges judged" provided secondarily. But what of the office of judge itself? Is there anything authentic in the ascription of such an office to leaders in the period before the monarchy? What precisely was meant by the title *judge* in ancient Israel? The root in Hebrew that is used for the heroes in the book of Judges is *sh-p-t*, and a judge is a *shōphēt*. This root describes judicial activity first and foremost, hence the title *judge* for the deliverers in our texts; but it has other uses in the Bible as well. Moreover, this same root, or its related forms in cognate languages, is used in other ancient texts, and these clarify the biblical usages. A survey of this evidence will enhance our picture of the biblical judges and their likely position in Iron I society, confirming our inductive impression of the variety of functions Israel's judges performed.

The vast majority of the occurrences of the root *sh-p-t* in the Bible have a decision-making context: to judge, to decide between. This meaning is extended to the carrying out of the verdict, either in punishment or in vindication. For example, in Genesis 16.5 Sarah asks that Yahweh judge between her and her husband Abraham, whom she believes has wronged her. In Exodus 18.13–26, Moses sets up a dispute-resolution system for Israel, on his father-in-law's advice, and the decision-making activity is described using the root *sh-p-t*. In the resolution of dispute legislation in Deuteronomy 25.2, the "judge" (*shōphēt*) is also commissioned to carry out the punishment.

In the Bible *sh-p-t* can also mean "to defend the rights of the powerless." In Isaiah 11.1–4 we read that a shoot from Jesse will judge the poor with righteousness, and in Psalm 72.1–4 the root is used along with other verbs to describe what the king asks of God: to make it possible for him to judge (here the root is *d-y-n*) with righteousness, defend the cause (*sh-p-t*) of the poor among the people, and deliver the needy. In Psalm 10.18 Yahweh is asked to judge the fatherless and oppressed, that is, to defend their rights. A famous example of this nuance occurs in Psalm 82.3, where Yahweh sits in judgment over other gods in a divine council and chastises them for not defending the rights (*sh-p-t*) of the powerless.

In 2 Kings 15.5 (2 Chron. 26.21), in the context of the annalistic notice about King Uzziah's leprosy, we are told that Uzziah lived in a house apart, leprous until the day he died, and that his son Jotham was in charge of the palace, judging (*sh-p-t*) the people of the land. Presumably Jotham exercised all the governing functions of a king because of his father's illness, functions described using the root *sh-p-t*.

In 1 Samuel 8 the people ask Samuel to give them a king to judge them (v. 5); the same phrase is used in verse 6. In this context, "judging" is what a king does. Other words can be used to describe a king's function; *sh-p-t* may have been chosen here because Samuel himself was a *shōphēt*. The people want someone to replace Samuel because he is old and his sons are corrupt, but they decide to ask for a king like all the other nations to perform for them the governing functions that Samuel (and others) had performed as their "judge." The people are asking for Samuel's functions to be perpetuated and stabilized, especially to meet the Philistine threat at that time, and the kingly office is a comparable substitute.

There is also evidence about the term from nonbiblical sources. Much comes from Mesopotamia, and several texts from the eighteenth-century BCE city of Mari on the Euphrates, for instance, illustrate the broad usage of the title. One case concerns a man named Bahdi-Lim, who was the prefect of the palace at Mari and the administrator of the capital during the absence of the king, Zimri-Lim. (This regency is comparable to that of King Uzziah's son Jotham, mentioned above, who officiated during the king's illness.) Bahdi-Lim's title was *shāpit(um)*, a cognate to biblical *shōphēt*. His duties are described as maintenance of the canals and dams, care of religious and judicial matters and diverse administrative questions, supervision of royal property, intervention in military affairs, and keeping the king informed of the happenings in the city. These are governing duties, but Bahdi-Lim is not ruling as a dynast. Rather, his title refers to his governing functions while the dynast is away.

From ancient Ugarit (modern Ras Shamra) on the Syrian coast, we also have texts that use a cognate term for judging (*th-p-t* at Ugarit, related to Hebrew *sh-p-t*). In parallel lines of poetry, the sea-god Yamm is called Prince Yamm and *th-p-t* River, that is, Prince Sea and Judge River. Since *sea* and *river* are synonyms, the epithets that go with them must be synonymous as well, so that *prince* and *judge* are similar descriptions of authority. Elsewhere in Ugaritic literature, *throne of kingship* is used in parallel with "staff of *th-p-t*-hood"; here too the root describes a ruling or governing function rather than simply a judicial one. Moreover, as in the Bible, the term can also mean "to defend the rights of the powerless." In Psalm 82, the gods' failure to carry out this particular responsibility is grounds for replacing them; in the Kirta epic from Ugarit, King Kirta's similar failure was proposed as a reason to depose Kirta as king and substitute his son.

The inscription on the sepulcher of King Ahiram of the Phoenician city Byblos, dated to the early tenth century BCE, includes the phrase, "let the staff of his *sh-p-t*-hood be broken, let his royal throne be upset!" The "his" refers to individuals mentioned in the lines preceding this curse: any king, governor, or army commander who would open Ahiram's sarcophagus. Again, the meaning of the root concerns governing in a broad sense.

The first-century CE historian Josephus relates that the Phoenician city of Tyre was ruled in the sixth century BCE both by kings and by a series of appointed "judges." Josephus wrote in Greek, so the exact Phoenician term is not known, but other evidence we have examined suggests something from the root *sh-p-t*. There is a distinction between this office and that of king, but its function was similar to that of a king's, and there is no indication that the office was only judicial. Furthermore, there is evidence in inscriptions from the Punic colony at Carthage of administrators called *suffetes*, a word easily related to the root *sh-p-t* and to the Hebrew term for judge, *shōphēt*. (*Punic* is the term used for the colonies the Phoenicians established around the Mediterranean, such as Carthage, and subsequently for the colonies established by Carthage itself and for the language they used, a form of Phoenician.) The Roman historian Livy notes that these *suffetes* convened the Carthaginian senate and were comparable to Roman consuls.

So the term *judge* denotes one who not only was responsible for the administration of justice but also could perform duties that include some sort of governing. While there are in the Bible many examples of judges who hold a purely judicial office, that does not limit our understanding of the judges in the book of Judges: they were administrators and leaders in peacetime and in war. And in this premonarchic time period, it is important to stress the difference between this title and that of king or dynast. The Israelite leaders in the period of the judges were not called *king* even though their duties may have been similar, for this was an era of ad hoc charismatic leadership.

In fact, biblical writers have different views about which type of rule was appropriate for Israel. Some stories and editorial asides stem from a promonarchic stance, such as the stories in the latter part of the book of Judges, where social and political anarchy are summed up with "in those days there was no king in Israel" (Judg. 17.6; 18.1; 19.1; 21.25), twice followed by the remark that "everyone did as he wished" (17.6; 21.25). But other passages see the era of charismatic leadership as the ideal and denigrate the office of king. For instance, the end of Gideon's story is antimonarchic. Because of his success against Midian, the Israelites ask Gideon to establish a hereditary ruling line in Israel. Despite his near-royal lifestyle at the end of his life (he takes tribute from the people, falls into religious pluralism, possesses a harem), Gideon's answer is instructive: "I will not rule over you, and my son will not rule over you; the LORD will rule over you" (Judg. 8.23). Israel can have leaders in moments of crisis, and those leaders may even maintain power and prestige during the remainder of their lifetimes, but Israel is to have no king but Yahweh. The antimonarchic passages, then, proceed from the assumption that Israel is not a nation like others, with rule concentrated in one human line, but that only Yahweh truly rules Israel and raises up deliverers when Israel needs them. This is reflected in the language used earlier in the Gideon story, that Yahweh will deliver Israel through Gideon (6.36, 37; 7.2–7). The ultimate judge and deliverer, and only king, who rules Israel is Yahweh. (Yahweh is called the *shōphēt* in 11.27.) This is the importance of the phrases: Yahweh "raised up" deliverers or judges to deliver Israel (Judg. 2.16, 18; 3.9, 15); Yahweh was "with" the judge (Judg. 2.18; 6.12, 16); "the spirit of Yahweh came upon him and he judged Israel" (and the like; Judg. 3.10; 6.34; 11.29; 13.25; 14.6, 19; 15.14; 1 Sam. 11.6); and the many instances where Israel's victory in battle is claimed as Yahweh's victory, Yahweh's delivering the enemy into Israel's hand, Yahweh's confusing the camp of the enemy, and Yahweh's host in the heavens fighting Israel's battles.

A similar sentiment is voiced in 1 Samuel 8, a lengthy antimonarchic passage, which reports Samuel's and Yahweh's anger that the people have asked for a king to rule them. When Samuel prays about the situation, Yahweh responds that it is actually Yahweh that the people have rejected. At Yahweh's command, Samuel agrees to find a king, but describes for the people all the abuses they can expect under a monarchy.

Women's Lives

For biblical writers, then, whether they approved or disapproved, the period of the judges was a time without centralized or permanent religious, political, and military administration, a time in which there was considerable disruption from external powers. This stands out when we consider the descriptions of women in this period, because in many societies such features are characteristically major determinants of women's access to public power and authority.

The biblical books of Judges and 1 Samuel provide much provocative information about women's lives in premonarchic Israel. The society they describe is not a stable, centralized, hierarchical society, and we would not expect it to be, given the material remains so far discovered. Rather, it is a segmentary tribal society, in which concentric circles of kin relationships determine responsibility toward others; only at a higher level of organization, beyond the level where most members of the society are likely to know precise details of kin relationships, is kinship a convenient and elastic metaphor for group definitions and exclusions. In such a society, one's first allegiance is to the closest circle of kin, perhaps the extended family, but local at any rate. Many important decisions are made on this local level, and studies of women's history have shown that women have greater participation in decision making when it is localized rather than centralized over a large area.

Such studies also demonstrate that women and marginalized members of society are more likely to wield public power in times of disruption than in times of peace and stability. This clarifies the series of unlikely rulers who are the heroes of the era of the judges. Thus, rather than a stable and hereditary monarchy, within which one's next leader is known while the old leader is still alive (his eldest son will take his place), we are shown a society that operates locally rather than globally, and in which leadership positions are filled by whoever can get the job done. We see women in power, as well as sons who are neither from the top of the primogeniture ladder nor from the wealthiest families or tribes (Deborah, Jael, Abimelech, Jephthah, Saul, David): people who prove themselves by their abilities to be the person of the hour, whatever the hour may demand. Such power is charismatic rather than regularized.

Our sources provide additional insights into the lives of women in this period in Israel and among the Canaanites. Jephthah's daughter comes out to meet him—to her misfortune—"with timbrels and with dancing," and we know from other texts that it was the women in Israel who sang the victory songs for the returning warriors (see Exod. 15.20–21; 1 Sam. 18.7; and among the Philistines, 2 Sam. 1.20). The old poem about the battle at the Wadi Kishon in Judges 5 is literature with a decidedly female focus. As in the case of Jephthah's daughter, we are not surprised to have an Israelite woman singing a victory song, but Judges 5 is mostly about women, from the women who participated in the battle, Deborah and Jael, to the women who wait for news of the Canaanites' troops (Sisera's mother and her ladies, 5.28–29), to the women who are the inevitable victims of war, as assumed and imagined by Sisera's mother (5.30). Judges 5 is one of the few passages in biblical literature in which we do not have to ask: "But what did the women do?" In this poem, we are left wondering where the men are.

First Samuel 2.22 gives a tantalizing hint of a religious role for some women. Here (and in Exod. 38.8) we hear about "women who served at the entrance to the tent of meeting," although we know little else about their function. In 1 Samuel they are connected to the sexual misconduct of the priest Eli's sons, and in Exodus they are said to have mirrors. That Eli's sons were abusing their priestly offices by having intercourse with these women does not necessarily mean that the women's function was sexual; they may instead have been minor religious functionaries.

Archaeology and Early Iron Age Settlement

In 1930, the German scholar Martin Noth proposed an explanation for the organization of Israel during the period of the judges that dominated thinking about the period for several decades. He hypothesized that premonarchical Israel was organized as an "amphictyony," a confederation or league of twelve tribes centered around a central sanctuary. His theory was based on Greek examples of a later date, and helped explain why the number of the tribes of Israel in Israel's collective memory was set at twelve: in most of the lists of judges-era tribes the number was kept at the ideal twelve, even though the names and order of the tribes were not the same in each list. Noth posited that each cared for the central sanctuary one month of the year. So while tribes could die out, or could grow larger and split into two (like Joseph into Ephraim and Manasseh), there always had to be twelve. Noth's proposal was based not only on the Bible's insistence that there were always twelve tribes in this period of a tribal league, but also on the evidence of other twelve-tribe leagues mentioned in the Bible (such as the sons of Ishmael in Gen. 25.13–16 and the offspring of Edom in Gen. 36.10–14) as well as on six- and twelve-tribe leagues of later Greece and Rome. (In the six-tribe leagues, each tribe would care for the sanctuary for two months of each year.)

Noth's amphictyonic theory of early Israel, though ingenious, depended on Greek sources that date much later than early Israel, and no archaeological evidence for a central shrine in the era of the judges has been uncovered. Nor was there much biblical evidence to support the theory: no scenes of one tribe at a time taking care of a central sanctuary to which all the other tribes, during this period, are seen to travel during festivals. Despite its heuristic power, then, the amphictyonic model has largely been abandoned. More recently the premonarchic era has been compared not to religious leagues but to tribal societies, and especially segmentary tribal societies, that is, ones composed of descent groups that are, at least ideally, more or less equal, autonomous units, without central organization.

Archaeologists now describe a gradual shift from urban Late Bronze ("Canaanite") settlement to "Israelite" settlement in the early Iron Age. Study of settlement patterns and population estimates show the early Iron Age as an era of vastly increased settlement in the northern hill country (around Shechem and Shiloh), with an increase also in the southern hills (in the vicinity of Hebron) and in the area west of the Sea of Galilee. These settlements were mostly small, usually unfortified agricultural-pastoral villages. The regions of intensive settlement expanded throughout the pre-monarchic era, presumably because the settlements were thriving and population was growing. The western ridge of the central hill country became a center of population, while the settled area in Galilee grew northward and westward; in the south settlement intensified beyond Hebron and eventually even to the Beer-sheba area. These Judahite hills were settled late in the period, probably because they were more densely wooded and hence unsuitable for agriculture. Finally, at the end of this period, Israelite expansion extended to the previously Canaanite areas in the Jezreel Valley and, with David, to some Philistine settlements in the Shephelah and on the coast. It has been estimated that the population grew from about twenty thousand in the first Iron I highland settlements to about fifty thousand by the beginning of the monarchy in the late eleventh century BCE.

Assigning ethnic labels to settlements without any ancient written identification is risky. The coastal regions where distinctive types of pottery are found (Mycenaean IIIC and Philistine bichrome ware) were settled mostly by Philistines, because Egyptian texts place Philistines there at this time and because of the cultural connections, such as the pottery, with the Aegean world that we expect from the Philistines. The ascription of all the highland villages to an ethnic entity "Israel" is not so easy. It is noteworthy in this regard that remains of pigs are found in the coastal settlements and not in the highland villages, but the taboo against eating pork could have been shared by Israel and other emerging groups. An inscription on a stela of Pharaoh Merneptah, dated to the late thirteenth century BCE, plus a new interpretation of four battle scenes on a temple wall at Karnak, give a bit more information about early Israel.

The Merneptah Stela records his victory over several enemies in Syria-Palestine: the cities Ashkelon, Gezer, and Yanoam; the lands Hatti, Canaan, and Hurru; and the people Israel. All of these entities are denoted in Egyptian with markers that indicate they are place-names, except Israel, which is designated a people rather than a land. What precisely does this mean "Israel" was in the year 1209 BCE? A group that is a people but not a land suggests that early Israel was nomadic, an interpretation that corresponds to other theories of early Israel's origin as nomads. Some assistance has appeared recently from a different Egyptological quarter. Four scenes of victorious battles, traditionally dated to the time of Rameses II (1279–1213 BCE), have recently been reassigned to his son Merneptah. The setting of one of the four is identified in an accompanying inscription as Ashkelon. Three of the four are pictured as fortified cities on mounds. The fourth takes place in open country, with no sign of a fortified city. Since we know that one of the four pictures is Ashkelon, it is possible that the four scenes on the temple wall correspond to four enemies in Palestine mentioned in the Merneptah Stela, the cities Ashkelon, Gezer, and Yanoam, and the people Israel. Moreover, the enemy in the open countryside are pictured the same way as the people in Ashkelon and the other two fortified cities, that is, as

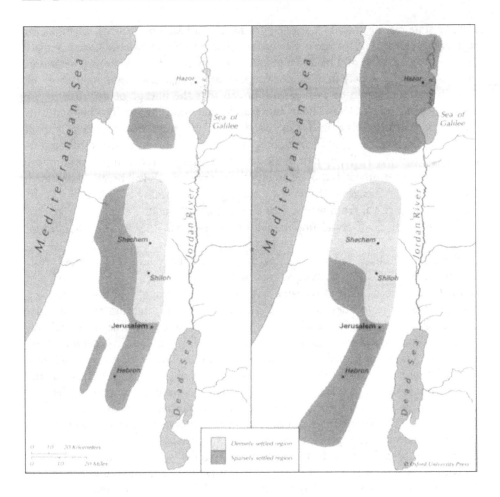

Israelite Settlement: The Early Stages and the Eleventh Century BCE

Canaanites and not as nomads. If the battle scenes and the Merneptah Stela record the same four victories, it is possible that "Israel" was a formidable enough group to be included in Merneptah's boasts; that the Egyptians saw them as Canaanites like the people in the three other scenes, and not as nomads; but that the Egyptians did not consider them a people with definite geographical boundaries that could be called the land of Israel. This leads to the conclusion that at the beginning of this period Israel was a group of Canaanite people, self-identified as "Israel" but not occupying any territory called "Israel," and therefore not a stable political entity. It also implies that on one occasion at least this Israel was allied with Canaanites against Egypt.

This picture resembles the impression that we derive from much of the book of Judges, and is also what we might expect from a segmentary tribal society lacking a central administration and a standing army. Segmentary tribal societies are well known from comparative social-scientific writing, and Israel's development over the course of this era from a segmentary society into a chiefdom and eventually a centralized state can be traced. A segmentary society is based on kinship relations, on segmentary lineages. A lineage is a record of relationships: a *unilineal* lineage is made up of a man (usually) and his male ancestors, for three or four or more generations, depending on the society in question; a *segmentary* lineage takes into account all the (usually male) children of each generation, so that the lineage of any man in the society reports not just his father and grandfather, but also his brothers and his father's brothers and his grandfather's brothers, in a "family tree" genealogy with all the branches. Over time, of course, some branches will die out; others will be productive and grow. Ideally, no part of a segmentary lineage is more important or more powerful than the others, but often an especially large branch will break off and form its own separate lineage, with members tracing their genealogies only as far as the nearest male ancestor from whom they all can claim descent. The new lineage thus establishes itself as of equal importance to the original lineage, and equilibrium returns.

The responsibilities and rewards of such a segmentary system are complex. While a man relates to his brothers as equals and would fight to defend them, brothers also compete for inheritance and recognition from the preceding generation. Moreover, a younger generation does not just gain inheritance and attention from an older generation, but also competes with it for power, waiting for the time when their age group will make the important decisions and monitoring the older generation's use of resources that will someday be theirs. Despite the competition, however, all trace their descent from some male ancestor, and so have obligations to each other that they do not have to outsiders. This is the "nested" nature of segmentary societies.

Segmentary societies tend not to be centrally organized over large numbers of people; rather, people in such societies often live in extended family compounds that comprise three or more generations, typically a husband and wife, their sons and their wives and children. In Israel we can identify these various groups to whom the individual owes some allegiance: the nuclear family, the extended family (Hebrew *bêt 'āb*), the clan (Hebrew *mishpāhâ*), and the tribe (Hebrew *shēbet* or *matteh*). Israel in the era of the judges is not organized centrally; people are described as living in an agricultural society, within the nuclear family or the *bêt 'āb*. Gideon in Judges 6 apparently lives in his *bêt 'āb* (vv. 15, 27), and Abimelech appeals to his mother's *bêt 'āb* and to its entire clan when he is looking for a power base (9.1); his own *bêt 'āb* is traced through his father, of course (v. 5). Jephthah in 11.2 is described as living in his *bêt 'āb* with his half brothers, and in his case we can see the politics of the extended family when the sons of the more prestigious wife kick him out; a similar dynamic is part of Abimelech's story. In spite of their behavior toward Jephthah, they feel they can call on his proven fighting ability in a crisis, presumably because of their kinship ties. Sometimes it is difficult to know whether *bêt 'āb* means a kin group or a place, as in the cases of Samson and his wife (Judg. 14.15, 19) and the Levite's concubine (19.2–3), but 16.31 refers to Samson's family: it is the *bêt 'āb* that is responsible for burying him. The *bêt 'āb* is mentioned in later texts as well, but not as often as in Judges, and only rarely meaning residency within the extended family.

Archaeological remains confirm that most Iron Age village dwellings probably housed only a nuclear family. These dwellings are pillared houses (also called four-room houses) with two to four rooms on the first floor and pillars set in rows to support an upper story. Part of the first floor space would have been used as stables, and low walls have been found in the remains of these houses with built-in feeding troughs. These pillared houses were not big enough to provide space for more than a nuclear family—mother, father, and children. But there are what appear to be clusters of dwellings at some sites that are made up of several individual houses built off a common courtyard, and this may be what the residential bêt 'ab or extended family dwelling looked like.

In times of crisis, segmentary societies tend to rely on charismatic leaders. In the book of Judges these are nonpermanent, ad hoc leaders who command by virtue of their personalities rather than with the authority of an office, and who ordinarily did not inherit their leadership and could not bequeath it. Despite the chronological note that a given person judged Israel for a period of time, their stories show them arising in response to an emergency, often invested with the spirit of Yahweh. These individuals lead in times of crisis not because they hold the office of "judge," but because something about them—described by the text as "the spirit of Yahweh" (see Judg. 3.10; 6.34; 11.29; 14.19; 15.14; 1 Sam. 11.6)—convinces others to follow them.

The fluidity that anthropologists describe for segmentary groups can be seen in the variety of names the Bible gives for the tribes of early Israel. The oldest passage with a list of tribes is the Song of Deborah in Judges 5, generally dated to the late twelfth or early eleventh century BCE. The Song lists only ten tribes (disregarding the otherwise unknown Meroz): Ephraim, Benjamin, Machir, Zebulun, Issachar, and Naphtali, who joined the fight; and Reuben, Gilead, Dan, and Asher, who did not. (Machir turns up in genealogies as Manasseh's son; see Gen. 50.23; 1 Chron. 7.14. Gilead is often associated with Gad in the Bible.) Two poems generally thought to be from the eleventh–tenth centuries take us closer to the canonical lists of twelve we get in the birth narratives in Genesis and elsewhere. Deuteronomy 33 lists eleven tribes: Reuben, Judah, Levi, Benjamin, Joseph (with both Ephraim and Manasseh named), Zebulun, Issachar, Gad, Dan, Naphtali, and Asher; and Genesis 49 lists twelve: Reuben, Simeon, Levi, Judah, Zebulun, Issachar, Dan, Gad, Asher, Naphtali, Joseph, Benjamin (see Gen. 29.31–30.24 and 35.16–18, 22–26).

Clearly, throughout the period of the judges the tribal "system" was undergoing change. Where the tribes lived (the migration of Dan, for instance, recorded in Judg. 17–18), what the tribes were called, how many tribes owed allegiance to each other, and how serious that allegiance was—all these were in flux. So, too, were the ties that bound them together. Although we can see a sort of confederation of ten tribes in the Song of Deborah, where all ten are expected on some level to respond to a crisis, the four tribes who failed to respond to the call to arms in Judges 5 are merely castigated—not cursed, as covenant ritual seems to have required. Perhaps the narrator understood that their position on the margins of the intensive settlement area of the central highlands would have made it difficult for those four tribes to participate in a purely "Israelite" battle; the Song of Deborah describes a battle involving "Israelite" tribes living in unwalled villages fighting against more urbanized "Canaanites." Reuben and Gilead/Gad were herders, and would have been dependent on urban areas for many necessities. In the Song the Reubenites "tarry among sheepfolds" and listen to the "piping for the flocks." Gilead "stayed beyond the Jordan." Asher and Dan were on the coast and again depended for their livelihoods on urban areas and their trading enterprises—Dan needed ships, while Asher "sat still at the coast of the sea." So this settlement-era tribal league, if it can be so called, apparently functioned under an arrangement for mutual defense, but did not have power to punish any members who failed to honor the arrangement.

Although ideally each segment within a tribal segmentary society like early Israel is equal and autonomous, some forces tend to push members of one segment or another into leadership positions. If people thrive under a leader, they can come to depend on that leadership and will look for ways of continuing it into the next generation. At the same time, leaders have privileges that they are often loath to relinquish at the end of a crisis. Handled well, an extended crisis allows both leaders and the led to wish to continue the pattern of leadership and can result eventually in hereditary, permanent offices, as well as a standing army if the extended crisis is military. And sheer wealth can command the same kind of dependence if the riches are shared with a society's more marginal members.

We can see signs of increasing centralization and of the amassing of wealth within the books of Judges and 1 Samuel. The story of Gideon/Jerubbaal is a good example of dependence on an outstanding leader. After Gideon defeats the Midianites, the people want to make him king and his family a dynasty (Judg. 8.22). Gideon's answer is the correct one for the time, that only Yahweh is king over Israel, but Gideon does ask for a reward of gold from the people, accepting wealth rather than a permanent position. He prospered through his life since he had seventy sons and many wives, a sign of wealth. Gideon's son Abimelech seems to assume that hereditary rulership had indeed been conferred on Gideon's family. His question, addressed to the citizens of Shechem—"Which is better for you, that all seventy of the sons of Jerubbaal rule over you, or that one rule over you?" (Judg. 9.2)—assumes that some configuration of Gideon/Jerubbaal's male descendants will continue to rule over Shechem. Despite Gideon's refusal of a crown, his family and apparently the people of Shechem had come to be comfortable with professional and efficient leadership. Perhaps they preferred peace in which to grow their crops to the kind of chaos the text describes at the beginning of Gideon's story (in 6.11 Gideon is beating out wheat in secret in a winepress so the Midianites will not steal it), even at the price of installing a hereditary office that will be both permanent and outside their control. The Shechem experiment fails, but it is noteworthy that some of the minor judges also are leaders who have amassed wealth and power: the mentions of Jair the Gileadite (10.3–5), Ibzan of Bethlehem (12.8–10), and Abdon son of Hillel (12.13–15) all contain descriptions of large families and, in the first case, landed holdings.

At the beginning of 1 Samuel, both Eli the priest (see 2.11–17) and Samuel as judge (see 8.4–5) seem to be in positions that will be passed down to their sons. While the people complain about each set of sons, they do not question the understanding that the sons will follow the father as religious or political leaders of all Israel. The concentration of political power follows in part from the pressure that a decentralized system feels from constant warfare against a strong enemy with a trained, well-equipped standing army: in this case, the Philistines. We also surmise from settlement patterns, specifically the expansion of highlands and Galilean settlements, that the population of Israelites had more than doubled in the two hundred years since the beginning of the twelfth century. Centralized economies with the possibility of specialization are often superior for feeding large numbers of people, another reason people voluntarily relinquish some amount of local control in favor of a centralized government.

Traditional societies, however, often do not move directly from a segmentary tribal organization to a hereditary, permanent, centralized monarchy. Many pass through an intermediate stage known as "chiefdom," and it is possible to designate Saul's reign and much of David's as more like a chiefdom, with Saul and David as the chiefs, than a full-fledged monarchy. The differences between a segmentary society and a chiefdom are easy to see; those between a chiefdom and a monarchy are more a matter of degree. In a chiefdom, the kinship ideal of equality between lineages and between members of the same lineage is given up, and those most closely related to the leader/chief take on increased status. A chief redistributes goods (such as spoils of war and agricultural produce) that have come to him, and those who benefit from the redistribution wish to maintain the power of the chief so that they may continue to benefit. Chiefdoms tend to encompass more population, to be settled more densely, and to have better-defined geographical borders than segmentary tribal organizations. There is no real legal system, however, to enforce the decisions of the chief, so he is still a type of charismatic leader who must prove himself in warfare, in diplomacy, and by redistributing goods to command allegiance. Chiefdoms gradually become dynastic, because people hope that whatever was extraordinary about the father will be passed on to the son, specifically the first son. Until that time, there is predictable competition for the chiefship, with bloodshed not unusual.

Saul's years of leadership did little to centralize power in one place or in one family. While Saul's family continued to have claims to the throne after David became a contender, it was still conceivable that someone outside his family (albeit a son-in-law) could rule instead of a male in the direct line from Saul (Ishbosheth, for instance, as in 2 Sam. 2.8–11). David's personal retinue is not only kin-based, but includes people who are loyal to David as an individual; they are also dependent on his leadership and the redistribution of booty that he provides (1 Sam. 22.1–2; 30). Again, a competition for David's throne breaks out among his sons, as though the principle was now established for the crown to pass to a son—but not yet any tradition backed by the rule of law that would designate precisely which son, so that the centralization and permanence of the position would be accomplished. This step is not completed until Solomon is appointed (1 Kings 1–2). Already during David's reign, or chiefship, a professional bureaucracy had grown up (2 Sam. 8.15–18; 20.23–26), a sign of a centralized monarchy. By Solomon's reign, the government is established in Jerusalem; a palace and a central temple are to be built; and the chief's occupations have become more specialized than in the time of Saul and David, both of whom performed religious functions as well as assuming political and military leadership.

Israel's Neighbors in the Early Iron Age

Iron Age Israel did not take shape in a vacuum. The Philistines and Phoenicians on the coast and the Transjordanian peoples to the east frequently appear in biblical sources, and so an understanding of these cultures contributes to a more complete

Major Philistine and Phoenician Cities in the Early Iron Age

picture of the period of the judges. The Philistines, Israel's southern coastal neighbors, have received particularly intense scholarly scrutiny, and recent excavations at ancient Philistine cities have greatly increased our knowledge of them.

Uprooted by the fall of the Mycenaean civilization in the Aegean at the end of the Late Bronze Age, the Philistines are one part of the group called "Sea Peoples" by the Egyptians. An earlier contingent of Sea Peoples fought the Egyptians under Pharaoh Merneptah in the late thirteenth century BCE, but Egyptian records do not list the Philistines among them. In inscriptions from the time of Rameses III (1184–1153 BCE), however, describing his victory over groups of Sea Peoples, the Philistines are listed, along with the Tjeker (or Sikils—compare "Sicily"), the Denyen, the Sherden ("Sardinia"), the Shekelesh, and the Weshesh. Other Egyptian sources inform us that the Sikils eventually settled in and around the coastal town of Dor, and the Sherden probably north of them, around Acco, while the Philistines occupied the southern coast about 1190. Philistine settlement is determined by the appearance of Mycenaean IIIC (monochrome) ware, in levels immediately above the earlier Mycenaean IIIB (imported) pottery and immediately below the later, locally made "Philistine" bichrome ware. Both the monochrome and the bichrome pottery (so named because they are decorated with one or two colors of paint, respectively) were made locally in Canaan, as we know from tests on the clays used, but they have Aegean antecedents in motifs and design.

The Sea Peoples destroyed many sites in their migrations—on Cyprus, in Anatolia, and along the Levantine coast, including the Syrian city of Ugarit and its port at Ras Ibn Hani—but they were defeated by Rameses III's troops about 1175 BCE in a land and sea battle. The Philistines remained in the area of southern Canaan where they had already established themselves, centered on a pentapolis (Ashdod, Ashkelon, Ekron, Gath, and Gaza) headed by five what the Bible calls serānîm, "lords" (a word perhaps related to Greek tyrannos). From there they prospered and grew, until by the second half of the eleventh century they had become a threat to their eastern neighbors, the Israelites.

The only Philistine temples so far excavated have been three phases found at Tell Qasile, on the outskirts of modern Tel Aviv. There is evidence of sacrifices, and in one phase a small, auxiliary temple accompanied the main temple (presumably for a consort or a secondary god), a feature typical of Aegean but not Canaanite temples. Many Philistine religious objects have been found, including a seated goddess with elongated neck, a piece with Mycenaean precedents; several zoomorphic vessels; and fragments of zoomorphic and anthropomorphic masks, presumably worn in rituals. A few Philistine seals from this period have also been found, with animal and human figures, such as the lyre-player from Ashdod, and some with writing that resembles the undeciphered Cypro-Minoan Late Bronze Age script.

Although we know less about the Transjordanian peoples in the early Iron Age than we do about the Philistines, we can still sketch the outlines of settlement there. The material culture of Iron Age I in the areas of Edom, Moab, Ammon, and the southern Jordan Valley was like that on the west side of the Jordan River: small settlements growing in number throughout the period. Despite biblical references to kingdoms in Edom, Moab, and Ammon, archaeological evidence suggests that these descriptions are anachronistic. These areas were settled during Israel's early emergence, but we do not find any sophisticated level of social and political organization in the early Iron Age in Transjordan. The northern Jordan Valley even shows evidence, in the later part of the period, of Philistine or Sea People incursion, probably through the Jezreel Valley.

Later inscriptions show that Ammonite, Moabite, and Edomite are all Canaanite languages, related to Hebrew and Phoenician. The evidence of material culture and of inscriptions, then, ties together the peoples east and west of the Jordan River in the period of the judges and later. Even in the immediately preceding Late Bronze Age, the archaeological evidence for northern Transjordan is much the same as that for Palestine to the west. The Late Bronze period saw a series of major cities on both sides of the Jordan River, with evidence of international trade. Southern Transjordan, however, presents a different picture, with sparse settlement. The question arises, as it does to the west of the Jordan, just where the people came from who make up the Iron Age Transjordanian entities. Were they part of the same movement that saw the highlands of Israel settled? Or did they move in from the north and the south to settle what later became Ammon, Moab, and Edom? Their languages and material culture suggest that at least some portions of the later kingdoms were closely related to their western neighbors, but beyond that we cannot go.

While Genesis 19.30–38 pairs Moabites and Ammonites as the descendants of the incestuous union of Lot and his two daughters (see also Deut. 23.3–6), the Bible elsewhere makes a distinction between the Ammonites on the one hand and the Moabites, Edomites, and other Transjordanian peoples on the other. According to the narrative in the book of Numbers, the Edomites, Moabites, and several Amorite groups had already established kingships by the time the Israelites come into contact with them. While the Israelites are wandering in Transjordan, before their entry into the land, they are confronted with a king of Edom who refuses them passage through his territory (Num. 20.14–21; see also Deut. 2.4–8) and with Balak, king of Moab, in the Balaam stories (Num. 22–24), plus the Amorite kings Sihon and Og (Num. 21.21–26, 33–35; Deut. 2.26–3.7) and an even earlier unnamed Moabite king mentioned in the Sihon story (Num. 21.26). The Ammonites, however, while said to have a strong boundary (Num. 21.25), are not described as a kingdom until Judges 11.12, in a passage that reprises the stories of Israel's way around Edom and Moab on their way to the land (see Num. 33.37–49). The narrative of the negotiation between Jephthah and the Ammonite king (Judg. 11.12–28) is confused, however, since it mentions Chemosh as the god of the people Jephthah was negotiating with, and Chemosh is the god of the Moabites, not the Ammonites. So even this mention of an Ammonite king may be a mistake or a confusion in the text.

The biblical narrative in Numbers and Judges, then, suggests that the Ammonites were not organized into a kingdom as early as the Moabites, Edomites, and Amorites of Transjordan. But archaeological evidence shows that the portions of these narratives seeming to indicate early political sophistication among the Transjordanian peoples are actually anachronistic and cannot be relied on to describe early Iron Age Transjordan. One of the oldest passages in the Bible also implies that that region was not organized into kingdoms. In Exodus 15.15 the tribal chiefs of Edom and the leaders of Moab are distressed when they hear about the approach of the Israelites. In this older description of Israel's meeting with Edom and Moab during their wanderings, we find not kings of Edom and Moab, but instead leaders with less sophisticated titles.

We know even less about the Phoenician cities in this period. Tyre, Sidon, Arvad, and Byblos are all mentioned in the fourteenth-century BCE Amarna letters found in Egypt, and none is completely independent of the great powers, especially Egypt, at that time. For the early Iron Age we have few written sources and none from the Phoenician cities themselves. Around 1100 the Assyrian king Tiglath-pileser I, on an expedition to procure cedar wood, claims to have exacted tribute from Sidon, Byblos, and Arvad. The eleventh-century Egyptian tale of Wen-Amun shows their independence from Egypt, since it involves an Egyptian envoy who was treated badly in Byblos while he too was on a journey to obtain cedar. The cities appear to have operated independently of each other, as well. There was no "Phoenicia," if by that we mean a unified state of any kind; there were only Phoenician cities and their spheres of influence.

That both the Homeric epics and the Bible refer to Phoenicians as "Sidonians" indicates that Sidon was the major city during the period of the judges. Sidon itself, as well as Arvad and possibly Tyre, was destroyed by the Sea Peoples in the early twelfth century BCE, but all were rebuilt. By the end of the Iron I period, Tyre was competing with Sidon for ascendancy as the most important of the Phoenician cities, and had an established monarchy. Epigraphic finds in Crete and Sardinia place Phoenicians there by the eleventh century, probably as merchant sailors. There is still no evidence of formal Phoenician colonization in the Mediterranean, however, before the ninth century.

More is known about Byblos and Tyre starting around 1000 BCE. From Byblos a series of tenth-century royal inscriptions gives us at least the names of the kings and shows us that the Byblian language and script are slightly different from those from other Phoenician sites. What we know of Tyre's rulers comes from the Tyrian annals reported by the first-century CE historian Josephus, supported in part by the ninth-century Nora inscription from Sardinia mentioning the Tyrian king Pummay (=Pu'myatan=Pygmalion).

Ancient Inscriptions

Among the most exciting archaeological finds are ancient inscriptions. For some eras, writings uncovered by excavation have filled out an otherwise sketchy political and social picture of the ancient world. Unfortunately, the era of the judges has not yet produced such abundant information. But while no inscriptions of any appreciable length have yet been recovered from the Iron I period in Syria-Palestine, several short inscriptions have appeared, giving the names of many ancient individuals and the occupations of some, and shedding light on the impact of a simple writing system on the lives of all sorts of people. The inscriptions from this period are incised or inked in one form or another of the linear alphabet, the forerunner to our own alphabet. This alphabet had been invented around 1500 BCE and by the early Iron Age was in widespread use. The largest number of inscriptions from this period are a group of bronze arrowheads from Lebanon and Israel inscribed with personal names, identifying the arrow's owner and often his father or master. We do not know why people inscribed their names on arrowheads—whether to make them easier to retrieve, or for divination, or simply for decoration of an arrowhead or javelin head that would never actually be used.

Most of the rest of the early Iron Age inscriptions are a mixed lot of potsherds, usually with only two or three letters inscribed, but sometimes with personal names; and seals, usually including a personal name. One exception is a twelfth-century BCE ostracon that includes an abecedary, found at Izbet Sartah east of Tel Aviv. An abecedary is an ordered listing of the letters of the alphabet, and several such inscriptions have been found in the Levant, including some from ancient Ugarit (modern Ras Shamra) on the coast of Syria, where the writing system was alphabetic cuneiform. The Izbet Sartah ostracon is crudely written, and the abecedary includes a number of mistakes; the first four lines of the ostracon seem to be a nonsense stream of letters, and the ostracon may be an exercise done by someone still learning to write.

Religion in Earliest Israel

Little is known of Israel's religious beliefs in this era. It is thus ironic that with the steady erosion in the reliability of other traditional markers of Israel's ethnicity (such as the finding of a pillared house at a given site or the discovery of collared-rim jars, now both found in non-Israelite Iron I sites as well) some contemporary scholars propose that what distinguished "Israel" from other emerging Canaanite Iron I societies was religion—the belief in Yahweh as one's god rather than Chemosh (of the Moabites), for example, or Milcom (of the Ammonites). Indeed, the early Iron Age marked the rise of national religion in the Near East, tying belief in the national god to ethnic identity. Thus the Israelites are the people of Yahweh, just as Moabites are the people of Chemosh; Ammonites, worshipers of Milcom; Edomites, of Qaus. And farther east, the Assyrians follow Ashur into battle. (The terms *national religion* and *national god*, though commonly used, are admittedly misleading; the particulars of modern nation-states should not be read back into these ancient societies.)

There is some evidence that ancestor cults were a part of Israel's belief system, in this period and later. It is important to note that "ancestor cults" are not synonymous with "ancestor worship." Rather, ancestor cults are associated with patrilineal societies (like Israel) and are a means for (living) males in the society to bond with each other, while at the same time defining themselves as part of their lineages, through the practice of blood sacrifice. Blessings from the dead to the living are expected for those who observe the cult conscientiously, and disaster might befall those who ignore its customs; but the ancestors are not necessarily worshiped as deities. Excavated burials indicate that throughout this period the dead were buried as if their continued existence were dependent on the care of their families. They are buried with food and drink, lamps, amulets, and tools. The many biblical injunctions against the cult of the dead (see, for instance, Deut. 26.14; Ps. 106.28; Jer. 16.5–9) imply that it flourished in Israel, and the archaeological evidence supports this conclusion.

The major religious symbol of the premonarchic era is a box or chest known as the ark of the covenant. (The Hebrew word for ark in this context is different from the word used for Noah's ark.) The story of the war against the Benjaminites in Judges 20 includes a reference to inquiring of Yahweh by means of "the ark of the covenant of God," with the help of the priest Phinehas. The ark in this narrative is a conduit to Yahweh and in some way represents his invisible presence among the Israelites. The ark is so much a representative of Yahweh that its arrival in the Israelite camp prompts their Philistine enemies to say that a god has come into the camp (1 Sam. 4.7), and its capture and deportation by the Philistines sets the stage for a "battle" between Yahweh and the Philistine god Dagon, which assumes that Yahweh or his power resides in or around the ark (1 Sam. 4–5). This same ark so represents traditional religion in Israel that David uses it to legitimate his new capital in Jerusalem (2 Sam. 6).

What was this "ark," and what can we know about it from other biblical passages and from nonbiblical sources? Numbers 10.35–36 is an early passage that reflects the same warfare usage of the ark. Here, "the ark of the covenant of Yahweh" was serving as a scout for the assembled Israelites in their trek through the wilderness. It would set out ahead of them and find a place for them to stop at the end of each day's march. This passage is set in the context of the wilderness wanderings, but it has a military flavor: each day, as the ark was setting out early in the day, Moses would say, "Arise, O Yahweh; may your enemies be scattered and may those who hate you flee before you." Again, the ark is a representation of Yahweh, and it is Yahweh and not an inanimate box who is serving as scout for the Israelite people. Psalm 68.1 uses virtually the same words without mentioning the ark: "May God arise; may his enemies be scattered; may those who hate him flee before him." At the end of the day, when the ark came to rest, Moses would say, "Return, O Yahweh, to the ten thousand thousands of Israel" (my translations here and below).

Two other early passages give a similar picture of the function of the ark. Psalm 132.8 says, "Arise, O Yahweh; to your resting-place, you and the ark of your might." Numbers 14.44 reports that the Israelites tried to invade Canaan from the south, even though Yahweh had not sanctioned such an invasion: "neither the ark of the covenant of Yahweh nor Moses had departed from the midst of the camp"—that is, an invasion without Yahweh leading, in the form of the ark, was doomed to fail, and it did.

A Priestly passage from a later period, Numbers 7.89, describes Moses conferring with Yahweh within the tent of meeting, and here too the ark is involved, this time not as Yahweh's representative but as his footstool. Moses would hear the voice speaking to him "from upon the mercy seat that was on the ark of the covenant, from between the two cherubim." The ark is specifically called Yahweh's footstool in 1 Chronicles 28.2: David tells the people that he had planned to build "a house as a resting-place for the ark of the covenant of Yahweh, for the footstool of our God." And Psalms 99.5 and 132.7 both mention worshiping at Yahweh's footstool, the first in a passage that refers to the cherubim throne and the second just before the ark is mentioned. Numbers 7.89, in turn, depends on Exodus 25.10–22, another Priestly passage that concerns the building of the ark and the cherubim throne. Here we learn that the ark was a box made of acacia wood overlaid with gold, with rings on two sides into which gold-covered acacia wood carrying-poles could be inserted. The tablets of the covenant, which Moses had brought down from the mountain, were to be stored in the ark, yet another of its functions; depositing a treaty in a box that served as the footstool of a deity has precedents in other ancient Near Eastern cultures. The golden "mercy seat," some sort of covering, was to be placed above the ark, with golden cherubim at each end of the mercy seat. Yahweh tells Moses that he will speak to Moses from above the mercy seat.

The description of the seat with flanking cherubim resembles the cherubim or sphinx thrones that have been found in art from other ancient Near Eastern cultures. Such a representation appears, for example, on an ivory panel from Megiddo and on the sarcophagus of King Ahiram of Byblos, both with boxlike footstools. If Yahweh speaks from above the "seat," then he is to be understood to be enthroned invisibly upon the seat, with the magical figures of the cherubim on each side of him. The ark above which the mercy seat is placed, then, is a footstool. The cherubim throne was also Yahweh's chariot, as 2 Samuel 22.11 (= Ps. 18.10) shows: "He mounted a cherub and flew; he soared on the wings of the wind." The chariot of Yahweh in Ezekiel 1 and 10, with four composite animals pulling it, is a permutation of the same mobile throne.

The ark could, like divine images in Mesopotamia, be one of the spoils of war. The Mesopotamian equivalents make clear that narratives like 1 Samuel 2.1–7.2, in which the captured deity manifests his or her power in a foreign land, are prompted by the humiliation of lost battles, especially since such losses can be interpreted as the defeat of one's own god by the enemy's god. (Hence the removal of the image to the victorious god's temple.) These stories of captured gods triumphing even in captivity serve to cheer the people in the face of loss and to maintain their belief in their own ability to triumph. Such narratives tend to be written in the immediacy of loss. The ark narrative in 1 Samuel 4–6 may thus preserve premonarchic views, both of the function of the ark as Yahweh's representative (because Yahweh was thought to be enthroned invisibly above this footstool) and of the role Yahweh played in Israel's life in this early period.

The ark is more than once called "the ark of the covenant" or "the ark of the covenant of Yahweh," and in 1 Samuel 4.4, "the ark of the covenant of Yahweh of hosts, who is enthroned on the cherubim." The Hebrew word for covenant used here, *berît*, means a mutual agreement or contract. In the strictest sense, the ark is the ark of the covenant because the tablets of the covenant are kept in the ark. But the covenant with Yahweh includes more than the Ten Commandments. For the era of the judges, the evidence points to the covenant with Yahweh as one of the defining elements of Israel's culture, and one that distinguished it from its neighbors: the covenant metaphor is not found in other ancient Near Eastern texts. According to the covenant, while other gods may exist for other cultures, Yahweh is Israel's god and they, in turn, are his people. Yahweh will protect them, give them space to live, and provide fertility for their animals and crops; and they in return will not worship other gods but will observe the form of Yahweh's worship that existed at that time. Israel's understanding of its relationship with Yahweh in this period is clearest in several of the oldest parts of the Bible.

Early Poetry

Israel's earliest literature comes from the era of the judges. Scattered within several narrative contexts are old poems that are the most archaic parts of the Bible, dated by their style and language. For instance, one can compare the structure and figures of Israel's poetry to those of the fourteenth-century BCE Ugaritic epics from Ras Shamra, or its language to Canaanite known from the Amarna letters of the same period found in Egypt. Among poems dated to this archaic category are the oracles of Balaam in Numbers 23–24; Deuteronomy 32; 1 Samuel 2.1–10; 2 Samuel 1.19–27; 22 (= Ps. 18); 23.1–7; Psalms 29; 68; 72; 78; and Habakkuk 3. But four poems are most likely from the twelfth–eleventh centuries: Exodus 15; Judges 5; Deuteronomy 33; and Genesis 49. We will focus especially on these four, using other archaic passages for corroboration, to determine what they can tell us about Israel's earliest beliefs about its relationship with Yahweh.

Exodus 15.1b–18, the Song of the Sea, while ostensibly about the Israelite escape from pursuing Egyptians, actually describes a battle between Yahweh and the Egyptians in which Yahweh wins by manifesting his control over nature, especially Sea. (The definite article is missing before the word *sea* in the Hebrew of this poem, except in vv. 1 and 4.) We see Yahweh described as a storm-god, an aspect of deity well known in the ancient Near East, especially when the deity is depicted as a warrior. These features can be found in abundance in Exodus 15:

> I will sing to Yahweh, for he has triumphed gloriously;
> horse and rider he has thrown into the sea. (v. 1)

> Yahweh is a warrior;
> Yahweh is his name. (v. 3)

> Your right hand, O Yahweh, glorious in power—
> your right hand, O Yahweh, shattered the enemy. (v. 6)

> At the blast of your nostrils the waters piled up,
> the floods stood up in a heap. (v. 8)

> You blew with your wind, [Sea] covered them. (v. 10)

Storm-god imagery also dominates Judges 5, the Song of Deborah, which is the poetic rendition of the battle between Deborah and Barak's Israelite forces and the Canaanite army led by Sisera; but here, as in Exodus 15, we see the power of nature harnessed to win the battle on the side of the Israelites, with Yahweh in his storm-god aspect as their warrior-champion. This "divine warrior" is typical of ancient Near Eastern myths, and in Israel's early poetry he often begins his battles by marching out to war, usually from the region to the south or southeast of biblical Israel, with a tumultuous effect on nature and the heavens (see, besides Judg. 5.4–5 and Deut. 33.2–3 treated here, Hab. 3.1–6; Ps. 68.7–18; and from a later era, Isa. 63.1–6). Judges 5.4–5 reads:

> Yahweh, when you went out from Seir,
> when you marched from the region of Edom,
> the earth trembled,
> and the heavens poured,
> and the clouds poured water.
> The mountains quaked before Yahweh, the One of Sinai,
> before Yahweh, the God of Israel.

Similar wording is found in Deuteronomy 33.2–3:

> Yahweh came from Sinai,
> and dawned from Seir upon us;
> he shone forth from Mount Paran.
> With him were myriads of holy ones;
> at his right, a host of his own.
> Indeed, O favorite among peoples,
> all his holy ones were in your charge;
> they marched at your heels,
> accepted direction from you.

Yahweh's "holy ones" are his heavenly host, the planets and stars that make up his army, understood as inferior deities (see Deut. 32.8–9; Ps. 82; Job 1–2). It is this heavenly host, along with the forces of nature, that wins the battle against the Canaanites in Judges 5.19–21:

The kings came, they fought;
  then fought the kings of Canaan,
at Taanach, by the waters of Megiddo;
  they got no spoils of silver.
The stars fought from heaven,
  from their courses they fought against Sisera.
The torrent Kishon swept them away,
  the onrushing torrent, the torrent Kishon.

The divine warrior's battles are sometimes won by eliciting terror and confusion in the enemy camp, as in Exodus 15.16:

Terror and dread fell upon them;
  by the might of your arm, they became still as a stone
until your people, O Yahweh, passed by,
  until the people whom you acquired passed by.

The Israelite army attended the battle, but in this period Israel's battles are seen as Yahweh's battles, Israel's triumphs are Yahweh's triumphs, underscoring seemingly impossible victories by an outnumbered, poorly organized, and unsophisticated fighting contingent. As Judges 5.11 says:

To the sound of musicians at the watering places,
  there they repeat the triumphs of Yahweh,
  the triumphs of his peasantry in Israel.

Another recurring theme in this archaic poetry is the bond between Israel and Yahweh. Other peoples have other gods, but Yahweh is Israel's god, as in Deuteronomy 32.8–9; they must recognize and proclaim this, and he will protect them and fight for them, and secure for them a fertile resting place:

There is none like God, O Jeshurun [a name for Israel],
  who rides through the heavens to your help,
  majestic through the skies.
He subdues the ancient gods,
  shatters the forces of old;
he drove out the enemy before you,
  and said, "Destroy!"
So Israel lives in safety,
  untroubled is Jacob's abode
in a land of grain and wine,
  where the heavens drop down dew.
Happy are you, O Israel! Who is like you,
  a people saved by Yahweh,
the shield of your help,
  and the sword of your triumph!
Your enemies shall come fawning to you,
  and you shall tread on their backs.
                    (Deut. 33.26–29; see also Exod. 15.2,
                          11, 13, 17; Judg. 5.3)

The makeup and structure of Israel in the premonarchic era are also treated in the oldest poetry, and for the purpose of tracing these early pictures of Israel we will add some of the prose of the books of Joshua and Judges. Three of our four earliest poems count off names of tribes and have something to say about each. The number and names of tribes included are different in each case, and only Genesis 49 uses the canonical list known from the birth stories in Genesis 29–35.

In Judges 5.14–18, each tribe mentioned is judged according to whether it came to the battle or preferred to sit it out. Only ten tribes are named. This earliest list of Israel's constituent tribes includes Ephraim and Machir (for Manasseh) rather than Joseph; Simeon and Levi are nowhere mentioned (see Gen. 34; Levi is rarely mentioned as a landed tribe, outside idealized pictures in Genesis, the conquest and settlement narratives in Joshua and Judges, and later in Ezekiel and Chronicles); and the southern tribe of Judah does not yet seem to be a part of Israel. The blessings in Deuteronomy 33 and Genesis 49 have still different lists of tribes. Deuteronomy 33 is missing only Simeon from the canonical twelve, and only Genesis 49 includes them all.

The allotments of tribal land in Joshua 13–19 reflect the earliest listing we have that gives territories either settled in or claimed by twelve landed tribes, that is, by the canonical twelve with the exception of Levi and with the split of Joseph into Ephraim and Manasseh. This enumeration reflects the tribal territories or claims at a time when Judah has joined the confederation.

The Deuteronomic introduction to the period in Judges 1 exhibits still another roster: Simeon is something of an afterthought, almost absorbed into Judah (see already Josh. 19.1, 9); Issachar has disappeared, its territory taken up by Manasseh; Benjamin is not doing well finding territory for itself, nor is Dan, who will later remove to the far north of the land. The Transjordanian tribes are not mentioned, but Judges 1 is about the "conquest" of the area west of the Jordan River, and in this scheme the Transjordanian tribes had already been settled during Joshua's time.

Reuben disappears from other fairly early sources, like David's census in 2 Samuel 24 and the ninth-century Mesha Stela from Moab, and that same stela places Gadites in what was once Reubenite territory. Reuben's stature as firstborn in the Genesis sources and in Deuteronomy 33 must reflect an early preeminence, preceding a subsequent rapid decline and disappearance. That preeminence might have depended on an early shrine: Joshua 22 implies such a shrine in Transjordan, and the Mesha Stela mentions a religious center at Nebo, in what was once Reubenite territory. We have also seen in our sketch of the religious beliefs exhibited in the early poetry (and supported by Exod. 3) the tradition that Yahweh himself originated in, or at any rate marched from, the land to the southeast of Israel; Reuben's territory would have been the closest early Israelite soil that such a march would have encountered.

Conclusion

The nature of the evidence makes it impossible to determine with certainty the makeup of Israel at any point in the period of the judges, but a few elements are dependable, from both literary and archaeological evidence. Archaeology suggests that the central hill country of Ephraim, Manasseh, and Benjamin was the core of early settlement, with occupation of parts of Naphtali, Zebulun, and Asher coming either contemporaneously or soon after. These results accord with the picture presented in Judges 4–6, although it is not yet clear what the status of Issachar was in the earliest settlement. Moreover, the book of Judges reports various assortments of northern tribes capable of concerted effort—Zebulun and Naphtali in Judges 4; Ephraim, Benjamin, Manasseh, Zebulun, Naphtali, and Issachar in Judges 5; Manasseh, Asher, Zebulun, and Naphtali in Judges 6, with Ephraim also volunteering. These are precisely the areas at the center of Israel's earliest existence. With the exception of the Deuteronomic frame and the model story of Othniel in Judges 3.7–11, Judah (and its subgroup Simeon) is largely missing from the stories of the early judges, and this, too, is not surprising since Judah was apparently settled late in the premonarchic era. Judah is prominent in the stories set at the end of the period: the Samson stories; several times in Judges 17–21; 1 Samuel 11.8 and 15.4, where Judah is listed separately from Israel; and in the stories of David. There is as yet no way to tie the settlement west of the Jordan River to that in Transjordan, and at the same time to observe ethnic differences between later Israelite Transjordan and later Moabite or Ammonite Transjordan. Whether any of these assortments of tribes argues for smaller, pre-Israel confederations is impossible to say, except to exclude the far southern tribes (Judah and Simeon) from the earliest conception of Israel and to note that Dan was never securely enough situated in the south to be of much help to its Israelite neighbors.

What then was the earliest confederation that was called "Israel"? Perhaps it comprised Benjamin, Ephraim, Manasseh, Naphtali, Zebulun, and Asher (and possibly Issachar); and perhaps it also encompassed the southern Transjordanian area north of the Arnon (thus Gad, and Reuben as long as it existed). Such an answer, however, begs several questions: whether a tribal Israel existed prior to the Iron I settlement of the central highlands and similar areas in Transjordan; whether the people in what became Israel can be separated from the other Iron I tribal societies that sprang up at the same time and in the same way, such as Moab and Edom; whether those who settled the eastern side of the Jordan were tied to Israel in Iron I, or to Moab, or to neither. In other words, did the people who moved into these marginal areas in Iron I already conceive of themselves as tribal confederations, with names and languages that tied some of the tribal groups together into larger entities (say, Israel or Moab, speaking Hebrew and Moabite) and at the same time separating those larger groups from each other? Or were they agriculturalists and pastoralists looking for free land in which to make their living—the withdrawal of Egyptian power at the end of the Late Bronze Age having opened up such possibilities, with structure at the tribal and larger levels coming only after they had settled in their new niches?

The southern Transjordanian area shares its material culture with the settlements west of the Jordan, but it also does with Moab, for instance. So there is no archaeological way to tie the southern Transjordanian areas exclusively with the area west of the Jordan in Iron I. By the ninth century BCE, the Mesha Stela assigns the area in question to the Gadites, but we cannot prove that a tribe Gad (much less Reuben) held this territory in Iron I, or that whoever held the territory was related by covenant to contemporaneous settlements west of the Jordan. The languages and dialects of the entire area in question were close enough to each other to have been mutually understandable.

The idea of a covenant or a confederation of tribes bound to each other and to a particular deity by treaty/covenant is not something archaeology can test, whether the question be about "Israelites" east and west of the Jordan River or about the hill country and Galilean settlements. We do know, however, that settlement of the central hill country west of the Jordan and the southern valley east of the Jordan began to flourish at about the same time at the beginning of the Iron Age, that they were part of later Israel, and that they were remembered as forming coalitions for defense based on their common adherence to the religion of Yahweh.

Select Bibliography

Bloch-Smith, Elizabeth. *Judahite Burial Practices and Beliefs about the Dead.* JSOT/ASOR Monograph Series, 7; JSOT Supplement, 123. Sheffield, England: JSOT, 1992. Archaeological survey covering 1200–586 BCE, describing types of burials and grave goods, as well as a discussion of the biblical material.

Boling, Robert G. *Judges.* Anchor Bible, vol. 6A. Garden City, N.Y.: Doubleday, 1969. A standard commentary, with archaeological information.

Callaway, Joseph A. "The Settlement in Canaan: The Period of the Judges." In *Ancient Israel: A Short History from Abraham to the Roman Destruction of the Temple,* ed. Hershel Shanks, 53–84. Englewood Cliffs, N.J.: Prentice-Hall, 1988. An accessible summary of archaeological evidence of conquest and settlement and of scholarly controversy about the evidence.

Campbell, Edward F., Jr. *Ruth.* Anchor Bible, vol. 7. Garden City, N.Y.: Doubleday, 1975. A commentary stressing literary issues, with much archaeological and ecological detail.

Cross, Frank Moore. *Conversations with a Biblical Scholar.* Ed. Hershel Shanks. Englewood Cliffs, N.J.: Prentice-Hall, 1994. An informal exposition of wide-ranging views from the dean of American biblical scholars.

Dothan, Trude, and Moshe Dothan. *People of the Sea.* New York: Macmillan, 1992. A popular and well-illustrated summary of Philistine history and culture.

Finkelstein, Israel. *The Archaeology of the Israelite Settlement.* Jerusalem: Israel Exploration Society, 1988. A technical exposition of the results of recent archaeological surveys in the central hill country, with conclusions drawn about Israel's earliest settlement.

Freedman, David Noel. *Pottery, Poetry, and Prophecy: Collected Essays on Hebrew Poetry.* Winona Lake, Ind.: Eisenbrauns, 1980. Several of the essays in this collection focus on what the earliest biblical poetry tells us about Israel's history and religion in the early Iron Age.

Frick, Frank S. *The Formation of the State in Ancient Israel.* The Social World of Biblical Antiquity Series, no. 4. Sheffield, England: Almond, 1985. A comparative social-scientific discussion of the stages in moving from a segmentary society to a centralized state.

Hackett, Jo Ann. "1 and 2 Samuel." In *The Women's Bible Commentary,* ed. Carol A. Newsom and Sharon Ringe, 85–95. Louisville, Ky.: Westminster/John Knox, 1992. A consideration and explanation of the various women's roles and gender issues in the books of Samuel, including a discussion of method.

McCarter, P. Kyle, Jr. *I Samuel.* Anchor Bible, vol. 8. Garden City, N.Y.: Doubleday, 1980. A sound and readable commentary stressing historical and text-critical issues.

Naveh, Joseph. *Early History of the Alphabet.* Jerusalem: Magnes, 1987. A survey of the earliest alphabetic inscriptions and of the later evolution of the script traditions.

Seow, Choon-Leong. "Ark of the Covenant." In *Anchor Bible Dictionary,* ed. David Noel Freedman, 1.386–93. New York: Doubleday, 1992. A concise and complete discussion of the history and literary uses of the ark.

Stager, Lawrence E. "The Song of Deborah: Why Some Tribes Answered the Call and Others Did Not." *Biblical Archaeology Review* 15, no. 1 (January–February 1989): 51–64. A study of Judges 5 utilizing linguistic and archaeological evidence, especially settlement patterns.

Wilson, Robert R. *Sociological Approaches to the Old Testament.* Philadelphia: Fortress, 1984. A short, informative introduction, including test cases.

Ivory figurines from the Beer-sheba region dating to the late Chalcolithic period (early fourth millennium BCE). The male figure on the right is about 33 centimeters (13 inches high); the perforations on his head were probably for attaching hair. Figurines like these may have been used in domestic or communal fertility rituals. (© The Israel Museum, Jerusalem)

TOP: A Canaanite caravan arrives in Egypt in this drawing of a nineteenth-century BCE tomb painting from Beni Hasan in central Egypt. Such depictions provide information about Canaanite culture, including dress, weaponry, hairstyles, and types of trade. Some of the items depicted are paralleled in archaeological discoveries from the Middle Bronze Age in Palestine. (Erich Lessing/ Art Resource, NY)

BOTTOM: Faience tiles from Medinet Habu, idealized but detailed depictions of Egypt's enemies that served as decoration for the temple and place of Rameses III (1184–1153 BCE). Shown here are, from the left, a Libyan, a Nubian, a Syrian, a Shasu bedouin, and a Hittite; each figure is about 2.5 centimeters (9.75 inches) high. (© Jürgen Liepe, Berlin)

TOP: Some of the more than forty anthropoid coffins from the fourteenth to twelfth centuries discovered by archaeologists and grave robbers at Deir el-Balah, near the Mediterranean coast about 13 kilometers (8 miles) southwest of Gaza. Once attributed to the Philistines and other Sea Peoples, such coffins were probably used by Egyptians stationed abroad during the latter part of the Late Bronze Age and the early Iron Age. (© The Israel Museum, Jerusalem/ Nahum Slapak)

BOTTOM: A typical Israelite pillared house. On the ground floor, food was prepared and the family's animals were stabled. On the second story, warmed in winter by the cooking fire and the heat of the animals, dining, sleeping, and other activities took place. (Courtesy Lawrence E. Stager)

TOP: Bronze bull figurine from the Iron I period (late first millennium BCE) in the central hill country of Palestine, 18 centimeters (7 inches) long. The bull may be either a symbol of a deity or a pedestal for a statue. The Canaanite gods El and Baal and the Israelite god Yahweh all have bull imagery associated with them. (© Zev Radovan, Jerusalem)

BOTTOM: Detail of relief on the sarcophagus of Ahiram, king of Byblos in Phoenicia in the late eleventh century BCE. Holding a lotus blossom in one hand and a cup in the other, the king is seated on a winged-sphinx throne, facing a table on which offerings have been set. His feet rest on a footstool, reminiscent of descriptions of the biblical ark of the covenant. (Erich Lessing/ Art Resource, NY)

TOP: Three joined fragments of the stela found at Dan, memorializing the victories of an Aramean king (probably Hazael) over, among others, the kings of Israel and Judah in the mid-ninth century BCE. (© Zev Radovan, Jerusalem)

MIDDLE: A seal impression on clay, or bulla. After a papyrus document had been rolled and tied, it was sealed with one or more lumps of clay on which individuals would impress their seals. Dozens of bullae like this were excavated in debris resulting from the Babylonian destruction of Jerusalem in the early sixth century BCE. This bulla, purchased privately, was made by a seal belonging to "Berechyahu, the son of the scribe," the longer form of the name of Baruch the son of Neriah, the scribe who wrote down the words of the prophet Jeremiah (Jer. 36.4). (© Zev Radovan, Jerusalem)

BOTTOM: Bronze cast of a Hebrew seal. The original, now lost, was found at Megiddo in 1904. It was made of jasper and was 2.7 centimeters (1 inch) high. Above the exquisite image of a roaring lion is the owner's name, Shemaand below is his title, "the servant of Jeroboam II." The date of the script makes it likely that the Jeroboam in question was Jeroboam II, king of Israel from 788 to 747 BCE. (© Zev Radovan, Jerusalem)

Detail from the reliefs from the palace of the Assyrian king Sennacherib showing his capture of the Judean city of Lachish in 701 BCE. In this scene, an Assyrian soldier is escorting two Judean captives, perhaps royal officials, before the king (not shown); their hands are raised in a plea for mercy. (Erich Lessing/ Art Resource, NY)

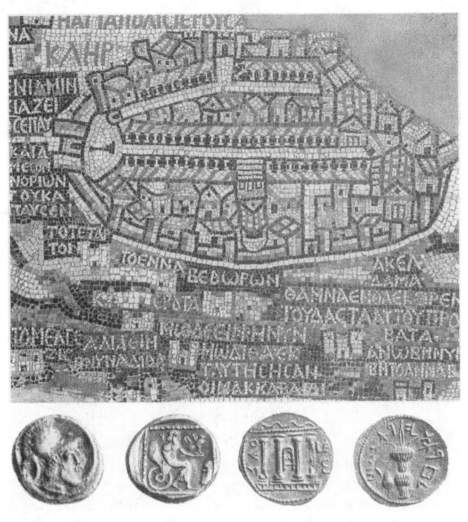

TOP: Detail from the sixth-century CE mosaic map of the Holy Land in the Church of St. George in Madaba, Jordan. This part of the map is its central portion, and depicts the Byzantine city of Jerusalem. A colonnaded main street (*cardo maximus*) traverses the city from north (left) to south (right), with the Church of the Holy Sepulcher represented on its west side. Excavations in Jerusalem have uncovered details corresponding to those shown on the map. (Erich Lessing/ Art Resource, NY)

BOTTOM, LEFT: Silver quarter-shekel of Judah. Inscribed *Yehud* in Aramaic script and dated to the early fourth century BCE, this is the single most discussed Jewish coin of any era. The obverse shows the head of a bearded, helmeted Greek warrior. On the reverse, on a winged wheel, sits a bearded male divinity, variously identified as the Jewish god Yahweh, the Greek god Zeus, or some other Greco-Phoenician deity. (© Zev Radovan, Jerusalem)

BOTTOM, RIGHT: A silver tetradrachm minted during the second Jewish revolt against Rome (132–35 CE). The obverse shows the façade of the Temple of Jerusalem, with the ark of the Torah between the central pillars; the inscription, in Hebrew reads "Simeon," the given name of the leader of the revolt (Bar Kokhba). On the reverse are Jewish symbols and the legend "for the freedom of Jerusalem." (© British Museum)

Detail from the Arch of Titus, in the Forum in Rome. Erected after his death in 81 CE, the monumental arch commemorated Titus's victory in the First Jewish Revolt a decade earlier. In this scene Roman soldiers are carrying the seven-branched menorah from the Jerusalem Temple in a victory procession. (Alinari/Art Resource, NY)

CHAPTER FIVE

Kinship and Kingship

The Early Monarchy

CAROL MEYERS

For nearly a century at the beginning of the Iron II period (ca. 1025–586 BCE), most of Palestine was organized as a national state with a dynastic figure—a king—at its head. During the preceding two centuries, coinciding with the emergence of loosely connected Israelite tribal groups, people had lived mainly in small settlements scattered throughout the central highland areas and in a sprinkling of small cities in the lowlands and valleys. Then, with startling rapidity, a centralized state was formed late in the eleventh century. By the middle of the tenth century, according to the biblical narrative, this state reached near-imperial proportions, complete with a capital city, complex regional centers, a royal court, luxury goods, and other social, economic, and political features associated with the concentration of power in a monarchy. The changes it wrought in the structure of society and the accompanying cultural expressions rank among the most important in ancient Israel's history.

The formation of a state in Iron Age Palestine, however its benefits and liabilities might be evaluated, was an extraordinary event. Never before in the millennia of sedentary life in the eastern Mediterranean had a territorial state existed in that land. And following the dissolution that would occur fairly soon, never again until the mid-twentieth century would this narrow stretch of the ancient Fertile Crescent be home to an autonomous cultural entity under local leadership. Brief as would be the lifespan of early Israelite kingship, its ideology would profoundly affect Western religious and political traditions. The very idea of the messiah in Judaism and Christianity is explicitly rooted in the dynasty of the "house of David." The notion that the eschatological resolution of the world's social tensions and inequities will be manifest in a "kingdom" of God flows directly from the impact of the tenth-century

BCE polity on its political and spiritual heirs. And the medieval concept of the divine right of kings would be based on biblical precedents associated with the Davidic dynasty.

Accounting for the origins of such a phenomenon requires us to consider the processes at work in state formation. We must identify the increasingly complex organizational structures that mark the development of a territorial state; and we must situate the emerging Israelite state within those trajectories of social, political, and economic development that across many different cultures constitute recognizable features of early, agriculturally based nation-states.

Yet addressing these crucial descriptive and analytical tasks is not enough. Profound moral issues hover in the background of the investigation of the Israelite monarchy, or of any such sociopolitical form. The monarchic state is an exceptionally powerful organizational construct. No matter how benign its rulers, it characteristically exists by dint of greater inequity in the distribution of resources than in virtually any other form of human collective. The pooling of resources can allow a state to make enormous changes, for better or worse, in the material and demographic shape of its territory. Furthermore, in giving up substantial amounts of individual or regional autonomy to state control, people may find themselves subject to despotic rule. Concentrating power in a single ruler and his or her support bureaucracies may often be beneficial, even essential, for the initial establishment of a state. Yet the famous dictum that power corrupts is everywhere evident in the often harsh and unjust policies that states impose on their populaces. Thus the empirical questions that we must ask in assessing the rise of the Israelite state, or any state, can never be separated from difficult philosophical problems of justice and equity in human affairs, of the sanction of violence, of the nature of political power and its abuses. Linking the Israelite state with the concept of divine favor makes the issue of morality all the more difficult, overshadowing all critical assessments. Yet the profound moral questions about the consolidation of power in the hands of a few should remain in the larger field of vision on which the specific shapes of Israelite monarchic rule will be sketched.

Let us begin with some conceptual and chronological definitions. Defining *state* is as difficult as defining the word *tribe*. Indeed, the comparison of state systems of sociopolitical organization with nonstate or pre-state systems often reveals no clear distinctions between them. Nonetheless, some salient features of a state, found consistently in many different geographical and temporal settings, provide useful components of a working definition. The organization of power and leadership along lineage systems or kinship units (whether real or constructed) characterizes segmentary societies, as in premonarchic Israel. In contrast, a state system involves the formal concentration of power on a basis other than kinship. States typically have a more or less stable hierarchy that can control resources and activities across the previously autonomous units that comprised its pre-state segments. Unlike other sociopolitical units—hunting bands, autonomous agrarian communities, perhaps even chieftaincies—states can overcome the tendency of such groups to split or subdivide as the result of local hostilities, competition for land and resources, and leadership struggles. Kinship ties within local communities remain integral to the activities of daily life; but as authority and status become detached from family or clan relationships and

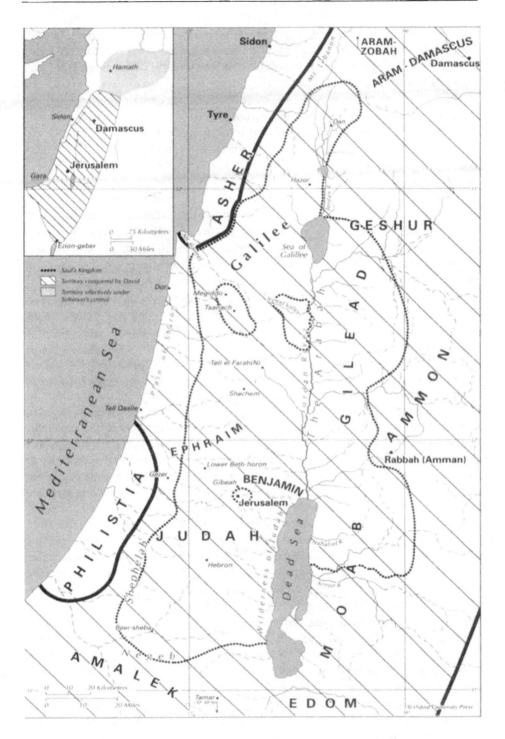

The Kingdoms of Saul, David, and Solomon

come to reside in national structures transcending local or traditional ones, kinship ceases to be the only determining factor in organizing community life. Kinship yields some functions to the power of kingship while maintaining others integral to daily activities and family life.

These comments describe early or archaic states, not modern or industrial nations. Early states such as ancient Israel were without exception agrarian, with largely sedentary populations and mixed agricultural economies. Such states can be described as either pristine or secondary. Pristine or original states emerged from a less complex system without knowledge of or contact with existing states. Such states are known only through archaeology. Their formation was not conscious or intentional but probably resulted from endogenous stimuli that slowly moved a society to increasingly complex, centralized, and hierarchical structures. Examples of pristine states, of which there were no more than a few dozen, are Teotihuacán in central Mexico in the early centuries CE, ancient Sumer, Shang China, and perhaps early dynastic Egypt. Secondary states share many of the same characteristics as pristine ones, but their emergence and shape are affected by contact with or pressures from existing state systems. They often take the organization and actions of existing states as models. Perhaps the simplest case of secondary-state formation occurs when one state arises out of a preexisting one in much the same territory, like the division of the early Israelite monarchy into two discrete kingdoms in the late tenth century BCE. A much more varied and complex dynamic is at work, however, when states existing elsewhere serve as a model or stimulus to the creating of structures of political control in an emergent state. Such were the processes at work in the early or United Monarchy in ancient Israel.

Closely linked to the concentration of power across kinship lines is the personality of the individual who wields power over the population comprising the state. The term *king* or its equivalent in other languages is the most obvious and frequently found term for the (male) sovereign whose authority extends over a region and its inhabitants. The king not only stands at the apex of centralized power of a state but also becomes its chief symbol; his personal and political successes and failures are intimately and inextricably linked to the fortunes of the kingdom.

To this point, we have not named the kings at the apex of the early Israelite state. Our resort to abstraction in this and other respects is deliberate. It is important that we think of ancient Israel as a monarchy apart from the individuals who first occupied the throne. Particularistic historical writing, of which the Bible is a prime example, often ascribes social change to the talent, luck, or whim of a few highly visible leaders. Although the role of individuals in bringing about a royal state and in heading its organizational structures is significant, that role is not necessarily primary. We must set aside the "great man" notion of the emergence of the Israelite monarchy, as resulting from the charisma of a person and/or the supernatural direction of a deity, in order to examine the social dynamics and environmental features of state formation and organization. The rise of a state system in Israel is best comprehended by identifying the social pressures and patterns hidden beneath the layers of traditional theological and political explanations.

The rapidity with which states become established and the length of time they endure differ enormously. Variables that coalesce at the moment a state system becomes visible may have been present, latently, long before any semblance of a state appears. The duration of an existing state is easier to estimate, and for the early Israelite state a reasonable chronology can be established. Here, the biblical record of the reigns of three men and the archaeological traces of centralization and territorial integration together specify the individuals and dates associated with Israel's United Monarchy.

The three men are Saul, David, and Solomon. All provided leadership above the kinship level, although whether all unequivocally qualify as kings of a national state is debated. Scholars have established the chronology of their reigns by calculating backward from the death of Solomon, the last of the three. Not until the late sixth century BCE can a date in Israelite history be securely established by comparing biblical and nonbiblical sources. But the books of Kings' chronologies for the Israelite and Judean kings do permit us to calculate, with an error factor of about ten years, the regnal spans of all the monarchs in question. These calculations place the death of Solomon at about 928 BCE. Working back from that date, it would seem simple to use the biblical information about the reigns of David and Solomon, were it not that these two kings are each said to have ruled for forty years (1 Kings 2.11; 11.42), a suspiciously round and symbolic figure. In the absence of other data, and because both kings apparently had long and eventful reigns, the date of David's ascension to kingship is generally placed at about 1005 BCE.

Estimating the duration of the reign of the preceding king, Saul, presents a different kind of problem—textual corruption. The relevant biblical passage states that he was "a year old when he began to reign; and he reigned two years" (1 Sam. 13.1; my translation). That flawed information is usually adjusted upward. If there is any validity to the multitude of events that the Bible narrates for Saul's reign, he ruled for at least ten years but not much more than twenty-five. Add to that the brief two-year reign of Saul's son Ishbaal (or Ish-bosheth), which may have overlapped with the early part of David's reign, and the beginnings of the monarchy in Israel can be dated toward the end of the third quarter of the eleventh century BCE. From beginning to end, then, the combined reigns of Saul, David, and Solomon lasted about a century, at the beginning of the Iron II period (Iron IIA).

This correlation between the United Monarchy and the Iron IIA period is not universally accepted. Some archaeologists hold that the material culture of Iron I does not change substantially enough until the end of the tenth century to warrant a change in period designation until that time; and others claim that features of the tenth-century Iron IIA culture continue well into the next century. The division followed here links historical-political events with material culture. The archaeological evidence contains differentiations that can be related to processes of state formation and consolidation. With allowances for a time lag between complex events and their traces in the archaeological record, the designation of the late eleventh and most of the tenth centuries as a distinct period seems justified.

Biblical Sources for Reconstructing the Early Monarchy

The task of understanding how and why Israel's monarchy emerged, and the changes it brought about in the lives of many Israelites, involves the use of a variety of materials and methods. Foremost among them is the Bible. Indeed, an earlier generation of historians of ancient Israel, confronting problems of the historicity of biblical texts and of large gaps in the record, were often frustrated in their attempts to reconstruct the ancestral history of Israel and to delineate the premonarchic period. They came to the monarchic era with a sense of relief. Here at last, they felt, was extensive textual documentation replete with specific places, times, and events—the stuff from which history can be written. The whole of 1 and 2 Samuel, along with the first eleven chapters of 1 Kings, were deemed exceptionally full and of great historical value. Although not actual historical records themselves, the biblical texts seemed to draw on eyewitness accounts and to provide a fuller picture of monarchic beginnings than of any other period in Israel's long history.

This optimistic perception meant that scholars holding divergent views about the ancestral and premonarchic periods often produced remarkably similar reconstructions of the beginning of the monarchy. That sequence began with the disastrous collapse of the tribal confederation in the face of severe military pressure from neighboring peoples, continued with the heroic deeds of Saul and David in rescuing the beleaguered people from the Philistine menace, and culminated in the development by David and then Solomon of a dynastic monarchy with a brilliant royal court and a glorious temple in Jerusalem. Opposition to these developments recorded in the biblical narratives was read as conservative resistance to change.

More recently, the traditional assessment of 1 and 2 Samuel and 1 Kings 1–11 as reliable sources for understanding monarchic history has been turned on its head. Literary studies have cast new light on the narratives about the first three kings, and also on those about Samuel, the charismatic figure whom the texts present as kingmaker in relation to both Saul and David.

Well before the advent of these newer literary analyses, scholars recognized that the dramatic tales of Samuel and Saul, and of David and Solomon, are embedded in the so-called Deuteronomic History (DH). A "school" or group of traditionists, probably originating in the northern kingdom of Israel after the division of the monarchy when Solomon died and shifting to Jerusalem after the collapse of that kingdom in 722 BCE, collected and told stories about Israel's emergence and history, beginning with the "conquest" of Joshua and extending to the demise of the southern kingdom of Judah in the sixth century BCE. An early version of this narrative formed part of the propaganda associated with Josiah's expansionist policies and economic and religious centralization in the seventh century. A final edition must have been shaped in the sixth century, after the destruction of Jerusalem and the exile of many Judeans. These two formative epochs in later monarchic history are the interpretive lenses through which the DH views all previous episodes of national life.

The biblical materials dealing with the rise and duration of the United Monarchy thus bear the mark of a distinctive DH style and perspective. As in Joshua-Judges, the Samuel-Kings narrative contains speeches and prayers, anticipatory leads and evaluative summaries, all of which put an unmistakable spin on the events recounted: the deeds of the people and their leaders are measured against the standards of the Torah of Moses. The DH knows how the story will end: the monarchy will divide, and each kingdom in turn will collapse. The DH's editorial framework and its inserted theological interpretations anticipate and explain the horror of those events. The last edition even gives a hint of repentance and restoration.

Table 5.1   Relative Lengths of the Narratives about Saul, David, and Solomon

	SAUL	DAVID	SOLOMON
Percentage of materials[a] in 1–2 Samuel, 1 Kings	12½[b]	67½	20
Number of chapters in 1–2 Samuel, 1 Kings	7[c]	40	9
Number of chapters in Chronicles	1	19	9

[a]Calculated on the basis of the total space of the component chapters and verses (not the total number of chapters, which vary in size).
[b]Increases to 21 percent if overlapping David-Saul materials are included.
[c]Does not include the overlap with David.

One of the best examples of the DH perspective comes in Solomon's long address in 1 Kings 8 at the dedication of the Temple. While he invokes the idea that God had covenanted with David to establish an eternal dynasty, Solomon also warns that the people will repeatedly disobey God and will have to be carried away into exile. But, he goes on, if they repent they will earn God's forgiveness and presumably will be restored to their homeland (vv. 22–26, 46–53). Other major instances of the DH worldview in the account of the early monarchy are Samuel's speech in 1 Samuel 12 about choosing to have a monarchic government, and the speech of the prophet Nathan with the accompanying prayer of David in 2 Samuel 7 about the divine promise of a "house" (that is, a temple) for God and of an eternal "house" (a dynasty) for David.

So effectively did the DH combine authentic sources with interpretive additions that it is difficult to read the narratives in 1 and 2 Samuel and 1 Kings 1–11 without being caught up in the ideological concerns of the ancient editors. The legitimization of the Davidic dynasty, the sacralization of its capital in Jerusalem, and the attribution of an active role to Yahweh (symbolically present in the ark and then in the Temple), have been inextricably interwoven into the shape, sequence, and content of materials selected for inclusion in the DH's dramatic portrayal of this epoch.

David—the epitome of the royal figure and the embodiment of the later hope for restoration—is the DH's central figure in its account of the early monarchy. A statistical glance (see table 5.1) at the balance, or rather imbalance, of materials about the first three kings reveals David's centrality.

In highlighting David and his deeds, the DH captures the sympathy of the audience. It is difficult to follow David's story without being caught up in his heroic rise from shepherd boy to dynastic paragon. That he perpetrates violence and brutality along the way, the DH takes for granted. What other recourse has he against his enemies, who are cast as God's enemies as well? One of the best examples of the aggrandizement of David is the Goliath story; the accomplishment of Elhanan in slaying the Philistine warrior (2 Sam. 21.19) becomes part of the David legend (1 Sam. 17).

The larger narrative context of the biblical account of the early monarchy—the entire history of Israel in the land, from Joshua to the exile—has also shaped the ancient editors' choice and arrangement of materials. Samuel's prominence as a "judge," for example, links him to the sequence of stories about charismatic leaders in the preceding block of DH materials. Remarkably, the etymology given for Samuel's name in 1 Samuel 1.20, the announcement in verse 28 that Samuel is to be dedicated to God, and the various references in 1 Samuel 1 to "requests" from God all contain wordplays on Saul's name rather than Samuel's. A narrative of Saul's birth has apparently been appropriated for Samuel, to give him thematic prominence as the connector between the rule of judges and of kings, and also because of the text's generally negative portrayal of Saul.

Within the interpretive setting provided by the DH, several major thematic segments can be discerned in the narratives of 1–2 Samuel and 1 Kings 1–11:

- A set of Saul stories, including an old cycle in which Samuel probably played no part, and later materials in which Samuel's role as kingmaker is prominent, are found in 1 Samuel 8–15, though Saul's story continues in subsequent chapters because his career overlaps with that of David until his tragic battlefield death.

- The account of David's rise to power, and of Saul's diminishing effectiveness, is given in 1 Samuel 16 to 2 Samuel 5.

- The Court History of David, part of which is sometimes called the Succession Narrative, appears in 2 Samuel 9–20 and climaxes with the final days and death of David in 1 Kings 1–2.

- The reign of Solomon is set forth in 1 Kings 3–11.

In addition to these substantial blocks of material, several smaller but thematically important sections appear in the two books of Samuel:

- The birth and call narrative of Samuel in 1 Samuel 1–3, with its supplement in 1 Samuel 7, connects the rule of kings with the preceding rule of judges. It also accounts for the legitimacy of the Zadokite priesthood, which prevailed in Israel from David's time until the exile and beyond, thereby replacing the priesthood of Eli and his family, which played a central role in premonarchic religious affairs.

- The story of the ark of the covenant, a central icon of early Israel, appears in 1 Samuel 4–7.2, and has links to 2 Samuel 6 and 7.

- A miscellaneous appendix in 2 Samuel 21–24 of psalms, lists, and narratives connected with David.

This bare listing does not, however, reveal what literary analysis makes clear: the historiographic framework embraces segments that are highly legendary and folkloristic, if not novelistic. The account of the early monarchy is replete with traditional literary materials, including stylized motifs such as the sending of messengers or the hiding of spies; repeated type-scenes such as battle accounts and news of defeat; private dialogues in settings that preclude eyewitness records; strong interest in the private life and character of a few individuals at the expense of details about their public works and worlds. These artful literary constructions depict tensions and conflicts in the personal lives of the first kings, and in so doing they convey, more subtly and successfully than explicit history writing could, the moral questions inherent in the concentration of power in the hands of a few.

Recognizing the complexity and diversity of the biblical sources for the early monarchy and acknowledging their biases does not, however, mean discarding them as lacking in historical value. On the contrary, some passages exhibit features of archaic language going back nearly to the time of the events that they narrate. Others contain details about procedures and propositions that reflect aspects of the sociopolitical dynamics of state formation. Such details are probably not later inventions; rather, they derive from the authentic reports of persons who experienced the transition from pre-state to state society.

The information about the material world of the early monarchy, especially in the passages describing Solomon's construction of a temple and palace in Jerusalem (1 Kings 5–7) and the wealth of his kingdom (1 Kings 10), is sometimes viewed as hopelessly exaggerated if not outright fictive. Yet as we shall see, the accounts of conspicuous wealth and grandeur, even if royal hyperbole, contain details of architectural and artifactual style that are rooted in the visual vocabulary of royal courts in the early Iron II period.

Mentioning the Bible's reports of the early kings' building projects brings us to a second major source of information, archaeology, that we shall consider more fully below. Recent archaeological surveys, for example, do confirm the historical value of topographical details and place-names in the narratives of 1 and 2 Samuel, and they indicate that sites newly founded in the late eleventh and early tenth centuries correspond with places mentioned in the Samuel narratives, particularly in connection with David.

Such external validation, while relatively rare, should not go unheeded. Nor should one ignore the Bible's own self-conscious claim to use ancient but no longer extant sources, at least for the presentation of Solomon (1 Kings 11.41; note also 2 Sam. 1.19). Indeed, the variety of styles and materials—from lists to legends, from poems to polemics—as well as the presence of conflicting items, imply that a rich array of traditional materials has gone into the canonical story of the early monarchy. The very inclusion of disparate materials suggests that the DH's ancient editors recognized their value. Authentic and ancient documentation of aspects of Israelite state formation is embedded in the final literary production, although it is difficult to separate the legendary embellishment from the record of historical experience. Yet the extent of the historical core of 1 and 2 Samuel and 1 Kings 1–11 is roughly indicated by the amount of material that is annalistic rather than literary. One can tabulate the extent of explicitly annalistic coverage—of economic activities, administrative decisions, military operations, and international affairs—as opposed to the space that the texts devote to legendary, folkloristic, and poetic materials. For Solomon, 45 percent of the coverage is annalistic, but for David it is only 8 percent and for Saul less than 5 percent. In short, although the bare outlines of the history of the early kings are found in these three biblical books, the preponderance of nondocumentary passages makes them less useful to the historian than their historiographic cast and vivid prose suggest.

First and 2 Samuel and 1 Kings 1–11 are not the only relevant biblical materials for the early monarchy. Additional information appears in 1 and 2 Chronicles, products (along with Ezra and Nehemiah) of early postexilic chronicle writing. These works have clear biases, especially in their glorification of Jerusalem and idealization of the two kings, David and Solomon, who were founders of the capital and its Temple, the sacred center of Israel. Because of these preoccupations, the authors of Chronicles include virtually nothing about Saul, who had no connection with the establishment of Jerusalem as a capital and center of worship.

First Chronicles begins with nine chapters of genealogy, and the rest of the book (nineteen chapters) presents the kingship of David. Solomon's reign is set forth in 2 Chronicles 1–9. For the most part Chronicles repeats, often word for word, large blocks of material from Samuel and Kings; but Chronicles also omits some Samuel-Kings traditions, especially when they cast David or Solomon in unfavorable light. In addition, Chronicles occasionally includes information, often little more than expositional expansion, not found in Samuel-Kings. Yet in a few instances the Chronicler drew on authentic ancient sources other than a protocanonical version of Samuel-Kings, preserving supplemental details or perspectives that cannot be dismissed as part of the Chronicler's bias. Furthermore, the topographical information in some of the genealogies and lists in Chronicles most closely approximates the settlement pattern that modern research has reconstructed (using archaeological excavation and survey) for the Iron IIA period or, more narrowly, the period of David.

With varying degrees of reliability, several other biblical works may also be related to the early monarchic period. Classical historical-critical study of the Bible postulates that the Pentateuch in its present form weaves together four major literary strands, assembled in the first five biblical books to tell the story of preterritorial and prenational Israel from the creation of the world to the moment of entry into the Promised Land. One, perhaps the corporate work of many talented storytellers, is called the Yahwist because of the prominence of the name *Yahweh* for God in the book of Genesis. This source, or its author(s), is also known as J, from the German spelling of God's name, "Jahweh." The existence, nature, and dates of four sources of the Pentateuch are continually debated by biblical scholars. Thus, in considering J as a creation of the early monarchy, which is the dominant historical-critical judgment, the larger issue of the formation of the Pentateuch must be kept in mind.

Scholars favor placing J in the mid-tenth century BCE primarily because of the way it favors Judah, the eponymous progenitor of the tribe from which the Davidic dynasty is said to have come, as well as the territory that became the monarchy's geographical core. In this interpretation, the successes of the first Israelite kings kindled nationalistic fervor and led to the composition of an epic that recounted the period before the monarchy, culminating in the glorious establishment of a territorial state whose dynastic ancestor was Judah. Thus, the promise to Abraham (in Gen. 15.18–21), for example, provides an etiology for later Davidic conquests of the peoples surrounding Israel's tribal core. Whatever its origin, J represents a powerful and artful presentation of the proto-Israelite story, and it is plausible that the royal court of tenth-century Jerusalem, which probably produced monumental architecture of world-class quality, also gave birth to a superb work of literature.

Both David and Solomon are also traditionally associated with significant blocks of material in the Ketubim, or Writings, section of the Bible, a product of the postexilic period. David's musical abilities are highlighted in several legendary vignettes in Samuel, so it is no surprise that the superscriptions of seventy-three psalms name the king himself as their author; thirteen of them even report the situation under which the psalm was composed. Similarly, Solomon's legendary wisdom links him with the authorship of the wisdom books of Proverbs and Ecclesiastes, and the report of his extensive marital liaisons similarly connect him with the Song of Solomon. Such claims for Davidic and Solomonic authorship of significant portions of the Writings are clearly late and unreliable. Yet some of the materials in the putative Davidic and Solomonic compositions may have tenth-century features. Davidic charisma and Solomonic diplomacy, characteristics integrally connected to the sociopolitical roles these men played, make it reasonable to trace the beginnings of Israelite psalmodic and sapiential traditions back to the early court in Jerusalem.

Other Sources for Reconstructing the Early Monarchy

Given the extent and grandeur of the early monarchy as depicted in biblical writings, it is striking that absolutely no references to Saul, David, Solomon, or the new Israelite kingdom appear in any ancient Near Eastern documents of the late eleventh or tenth century BCE. The first nonbiblical text that mentions a political entity in Iron Age Palestine comes from just after the split of the monarchy into two kingdoms at Solomon's death. Around 925 BCE, Pharaoh Shishak (Shoshenq I) marched into Palestine and, according to inscriptions on the wall of the Amun temple at Karnak, devastated a series of Palestinian towns or cities. At one of these, Megiddo, a fragment of a monumental stele bearing Shishak's name has been uncovered, thus supporting the inscriptions' claims about conquest. Unfortunately, the list of fallen sites does not name their national setting, nor is the configuration of the named sites particularly helpful in drawing the borders of late tenth-century Israel.

Two ninth-century inscriptions may attest to an Israelite monarchy in Palestine. One, an Aramaic inscription recently found at Tel Dan in northern Israel, was probably part of a basalt victory monument erected by a conqueror of Dan. It refers to the "king of Israel" and the "[king of] the house of David," the two monarchies that existed in Palestine by the ninth century, and in so doing names "David." The second inscription, discovered in 1868 in Moab, is known as the Mesha Stela because it was written to commemorate a victory by the Moabite king Mesha over Israel. A recent reevaluation of its lengthy text, which refers explicitly to Omri as the "king of Israel," suggests that this monument also mentions the "house of David."

But these finds are the exceptions. The biblical sources contain authentic political, economic, administrative, and topographic details of a tenth-century nation-state in much of Palestine and adjacent parts of Transjordan. Why then do other Near Eastern polities not acknowledge its existence? The answer probably resides in the circumstances of Israel's emergence. During precisely these years a power vacuum existed in the eastern Mediterranean. Until the end of the Late Bronze Age, Egypt had maintained some degree of hegemony over Palestinian city-states. But after the collapse of Egypt's Dynasty 20 around 1069 BCE, the Tanite kings of Dynasty 21 presided over a protracted economic and political decline. This period of Egyptian weakness, lasting over a century (1069–945 BCE), meant a relative paucity of monumental inscriptions. The kings had nothing to boast about in the usual fashion of royal texts; none would have reported Egypt's loss of its long-standing control over parts of the Palestinian corridor to Asia.

Similarly, the uncharacteristic silence of Assyrian sources of the late eleventh to early ninth centuries about the western territories it had long dominated can only mean that Assyrian control of the northern Levant had lapsed. Assyria, we know, suffered from the death of Tiglath-pileser I (ca. 1076 BCE) until its revival as the Neo-Assyrian empire under Ashur-dan II (934–912 BCE). Whether Assyria tried and failed to gain ascendancy over Syria-Palestine in the intervening years, or whether internal difficulties precluded foreign expeditions, is not clear. Babylonia likewise did not venture far beyond its borders for centuries after a raid on Assyria in 1081 BCE, and thus its records would hardly have mentioned a new dynastic state to the west. The emergence of a national state in Palestine is thus related to the weaknesses in the traditional centers of power in the Near East at the end of the second millennium BCE.

Important information about the early Israelite monarchy does, however, appear in nonwritten material remains. Since the beginnings of archaeological research in Palestine in the nineteenth century, sites and regions mentioned in the vivid biblical stories of Samuel, Saul, David, and Solomon have figured prominently in field projects. Yet this activity has not yielded a commensurate amount of information about the relatively short period of time represented by the early monarchy. Indeed, pinpointing that era in the archaeological record has proved to be fraught with controversy. Walls, artifacts, and buildings that some archaeologists assign to the time of David or Solomon are dated by others to earlier or later periods. In the absence of artifacts such as coins or inscriptions that allow for absolute chronology, the precise date of materials from the early Iron II period has been difficult to establish. Nonetheless, a tentative consensus now exists, and various structures and material objects of the late eleventh and early tenth centuries that throw light on the early monarchy will be discussed below.

What can the material remains tell us about the sociopolitical changes related to state formation? What environmental and technological features either determine or reflect a transition to a more complex sociopolitical organization? What sort of unity in the material culture suggests the advent of a centralized government with controls over an extensive territory? Not all of the reports of the older excavations contain the details needed to answer these questions. Thus the promise of archaeology to help us understand and reconstruct any period of biblical antiquity rests on more recent excavation projects—some that reexcavate the famous sites to which earlier archaeologists had been attracted, and others that investigate smaller sites that rarely can be identified with biblical place-names but that are representative of the village settlements inhabited by the majority of the population. Ultimately, establishing a fuller picture of the distribution and size of Iron IIA sites and their subsistence bases will contribute as much if not more to our knowledge of the early monarchy than all the past investigations of the major urban sites.

In answering the questions we have posed, techniques other than excavation are clearly valuable. One is archaeological survey, by which a region is systematically explored in order to locate and record its archaeological sites, their features, and relative sizes. By carefully sampling the surface finds of each site, the periods in which they were occupied can be determined with reasonable confidence. The formation of a monarchy is inextricably related to fluctuations in population and also to the arrangement of population on the landscape. Because surveys allow us to estimate population size and density, they provide information that can be related to what we know about population patterns in emergent states generally. Furthermore, settlements of varying sizes in particular configurations—such as a town site surrounded by smaller "satellite" villages—provide evidence of the centralization of economic and social functions that correlate with political centralization.

Surveys also investigate environmental factors that have a bearing on ancient historical changes. The study of the landscape and ecology of a region is necessary to understand human exploitation of the environment. Geological, hydrological, climatic, and topographic variables all help determine the subsistence base of a given site. Did environmental conditions allow local populations in the past to produce enough food to supply the needs of the number of people who are estimated to have lived at a site in a given period? Or did the ecosystem impose limitations that required the populations there to augment their food supply by trade? Is the environment especially suited for the production of one kind of commodity, thus making it possible to accumulate surpluses that can be exchanged for goods produced at other sites? The answers to such questions have great potential for identifying the economic patterns that figure in the state systems' mechanisms of control and exchange of goods.

Whether we can answer such questions depends not only on the presence and reliability of the data but also on the strategies we use to interpret them. Interpretive strategies drawn from ethnoarchaeology can help here. Ethnoarchaeology assumes that, in traditional societies, human beings today within a given environment relate to their material culture and their structures in ways similar to the manner in which the people of past societies in similar niches acted. With this assumption archaeologists can suggest how an ancient society may have functioned given the particular configuration of artifacts that they left behind. Much of the value of the social-science models and theories to which we shall next turn rests on the results of ethnographic research, which has amassed a considerable body of cross-cultural information about state formation and its relationship to the material world.

Interpretive Theories and Models

Especially since the 1960s, as a rich array of new data has become known about precolonial African sociopolitical systems, anthropologists' ethnographically based models have become highly relevant to the question of Israelite monarchic beginnings. Although there are pitfalls in the anthropological discussions of state formation, such as the way ideas about the early state are colored by the familiarity of theorists with precapitalist, occidental (European) nation-states, the heuristic value of models that generalize behaviors and structures across cultures is considerable. These models authenticate the biblical presentation of an emergent monarchy, and they correct the traditional historical-critical tendency to see the monarchy as both a foreign institution and yet one that became uniquely Israelite. The anthropological work that has most influenced assessments of the early monarchy sees an evolutionary development of societies: from simple bands and/or tribes, to chiefdoms, and ultimately to states. In this scheme, Saul's rise to power and David's early reign constitute the chiefdom stage. Thus, the fact that the texts designate both Saul and David with the Hebrew term *nāgîd* (1 Sam. 9.16; 10.1; 13.14; 25.30; 2 Sam. 5.2; 6.21; 7.8), translated "prince" or "ruler," may characterize each man as a charismatic premonarchic or protomonarchic military leader, that is, as the head of a chiefdom—rather than as a dynastic *melek*, or "king," as head of a state.

We may not, however, be entirely justified in associating Saul, and to some extent David, with chiefly office. Part of the problem lies in the difficulty of precisely dating the archaeological evidence for a chiefdom. Similarly, material evidence suggestive of Solomon and a full-fledged state may well originate in Davidic planning. Correlating different terminology—*nāgîd* and *melek*—with different kinds of sociopolitical leadership is also problematic, coming as it does from the much reworked Deuteronomic History of 1 and 2 Samuel. Furthermore, the critical aspect in identifying a chiefdom seems to be the number of levels of bureaucratic or administrative organization—in other words, how far the chief is structurally removed from the common folk. No means have yet been discovered to assess those levels in either the archaeological or the textual record. Finally, anthropologists themselves, in critiquing the evolutionary model, suggest that a chiefdom may be an alternative to a state system rather than precursor of it. Hence the question remains open whether we are justified in seeing the first two Israelite kings as chiefs. Fortunately, the answer does not seem to have serious consequences in assessing ancient Israel's path to statehood.

Perhaps the most important aspect of anthropological discussions of state systems is captured in the second of those two terms, *systems*. The state emerges as both an adaptive response to changes in a society and its environment and a formalization of those changes. Once formalized, the centralized control of human and economic resources itself creates demands and accommodations. The initial shift to a state structure in effect sets off a chain reaction of other changes that mark the ongoing development of the system.

The systemic nature of the state, or for that matter any political community, poses a problem for the examination of an ancient state, particularly one such as Israel, for which archaeological evidence is an essential source of information. States by nature have more complex, hierarchical organizational structures than do nonstate systems. Yet it is not clear how or where in the transition from pre-state to state the visible correlates of differentiated social, economic, and political groups emerge. For example, the concentration of wealth in the hands of a few may cause the appearance of new and more differentiated sociopolitical structures—or it may result from such forms. Or again, such concentration may be both cause and effect. To take another example, an increase in population can signal a change in sociopolitical structure with a concomitant ability to support more people, or it can reflect a need for adaptive change in order to accommodate a larger community. If archaeological remains of the late Iron I and the Iron IIA periods could be dated with more precision, some of these issues might be resolved.

Factors Relating to State Formation in Ancient Israel

Reading the biblical account of the emergence of the monarchy while simultaneously considering social-science models of state formation has led recent investigators to reassess the role of the Philistines. The accounts of both Saul and David in 1 and 2 Samuel are replete with war stories, and most scholars followed the lead of the biblical texts in linking the establishment of a kingdom with the Philistine menace. But is this an accurate portrayal of what happened in Iron IIA Palestine?

The Philistines were a group of people from the Aegean who arrived on the southern Palestinian coast at about the same time that the Israelite tribal groups were forming in the highlands. Portrayed in the Bible as aggressors, the Philistines are the quintessential "bad guys" in the narratives of the early monarchy. Hence their name has entered modern languages as a derogatory designation for someone lacking in culture, or whose interests are conventional and materialistic. The biblical texts describe them as commanded by warlords, as terrorists raiding Israelite settlements, as ruthless conquerors of tribal centers, as the villainous destroyers of the important religious shrine at Shiloh, and as the captors of the sacred ark, a symbol of Yahweh's divine presence among the people. According to the biblical narrative, the pressure of Philistine expansionism became so great that the people of Israel approached Samuel, the priestly prophet and judge whose leadership extended beyond his territorial home in Ramah, requesting that he appoint a king as his replacement. According to the biblical text, the Israelites perceived that he was aging and had no worthy successor. Passages such as 1 Samuel 9.16 explicitly connect the establishment of kingship with the Philistine threat. God, this passage reads, promises to provide the beleaguered Israelites with "a man from the land of Benjamin [Saul]. . . . He shall save my people from the hand of the Philistines; for I have seen the suffering of my people, because their outcry has come to me."

Such language, although widely understood as part of a later tradition of dubious historical value, has deeply influenced modern histories of ancient Israel. The Philistines have achieved the status of prime mover in the story of Israelite transition to statehood. Standard histories thus do little more than restate the biblical tales. Even scholars who pioneered social-science approaches to pre-state Israel tend to contrast an egalitarian tribal period with an exploitative monarchic one. This glaring contrast is attributed to the external threat of Philistine domination: if only the Philistines hadn't been around, tribal Israel would have survived in an idealized egalitarian form.

But the process of state formation is more complex than the biblical text and its traditional interpreters have led us to believe. Military pressure is only one of a constellation of internal and external stimuli, stemming from both environmental and sociopolitical conditions, that produced a new political form—the state. The territorial state in Israel was a system that could effect changes in technology and in the organization and behavior of people in order to meet the pressures not only of external aggressors such as the Philistines but also of internal crises in resource management. True, the early Israelite state is linked to the need for military forces that could deal with Philistine incursions. It also had to repel the raids of such groups as the Ammonites (1 Sam. 10.27) and Amalekites (1 Sam. 30.1), and perhaps meet threats from neighboring Moab, Edom, and Syria (1 Sam. 14.47; 2 Sam. 8.1–14). But conflict was not the only factor involved in the rise of the Israelite state.

Understanding state formation in early Israel thus means recognizing the convergence of complex variables, in addition to conflict, that required new organizational structures. Identifying those variables begins by considering the physical environment of the premonarchic settlements generally identified as Israelite.

Before the Iron Age, settlements in Palestine had for millennia been concentrated along the coast and in the major intermontane valleys. The beginning of Israel in the Iron I period (ca. 1200–1025 BCE) is associated with the establishment of new sites, mostly tiny agricultural villages, in the highland core of Palestine. Those sites occupied a marginal ecological zone. Uneven landforms, irregular stretches of fertile soils, and the lack of stable year-round water supplies made the establishment of viable farm communities a challenging enterprise. The cropping cycle in most of the better econiches of the highlands dictated that some months required labor-intensive efforts. At such times, having an adequate labor pool was the key to survival. The self-sufficient individual household was the primary economic unit of these highland villages; and an ethos encouraging a high birthrate and thus enough children to ensure a satisfactory labor supply for each household unit emerged as an important adaptive element.

Enlarging family size, as several biblical texts exhort, met with some success: Israel's population grew. At the same time, the early Iron Age villages found relief from Late Bronze Age plagues, one of the waves of epidemic disease that periodically decimated premodern peoples. Furthermore, the agrarian settlers of the highland sites were probably joined by a small element of pastoralists who were taking up a sedentary lifestyle. Although a few human societies maintain a demographic equilibrium that keeps them at or below the ability of the environment of a settlement to yield enough foodstuffs to sustain the population, more often populations move inexorably toward overpopulation. The highland villages of pre-state Israel were no exception.

The most obvious solution to the problem of overpopulation is birth control (or infanticide), for which there is no evidence in early Israel. Alternatively, kinship-based societies can increase their agricultural productivity by developing new technologies or by putting existing ones to more extensive use. Highland villagers both expanded their acreage and raised their productivity by increasing use of agricultural terracing and cisterns. This agricultural intensification, however, required more labor, which in turn reinforced cultural sanctions for increasing family size. Thus there arose a self-perpetuating spiral of growth that eventually required other adjustments.

The unpredictable rainfall patterns of the region complicated this cycle. Agricultural intensification alone could not always provide a growing population with a secure food supply in the face of periodic water deficiencies. The highlands of Palestine as a whole are a medium-risk environment with respect to rainfall variability; periodically there occur years with subnormal amounts of rainfall, defined as more than 30 percent below average. Typically three successive subnormal years will occur twice in a forty-year span, with such three-year droughts bringing an average farming household to the brink of disaster (see 2 Sam. 21.1). Even a delay in rains in a normal year can reduce the productivity of the soil as much as does an actual drought. Clearly the average highland farm family lived insecurely.

Increased family size and/or diminished rainfall, even with measures of intensification, characteristically require changes in the way resources are made available. Such changes appear in the organization of society above the village and kinship level. In precolonial African chiefdoms, redistribution of agricultural products was one of the ways in which a more complex sociopolitical structure could respond to increases in population density and periodic shortfalls of food supplies. Such redistribution, however, implies an altruism that may not be easily institutionalized in a centralized power structure. Other kinds of redistributive mechanisms that were part of the emergence of centralized governance may have dealt with such problems in other ways.

Another remedy by which agrarian societies have tried to deal with the rise of population above the land's carrying capacity is out-migration. Usually the emigrants are second and third sons who cannot inherit a large enough plot to support a new household. Such sons move to unsettled lands, usually as near as possible to their own family's village but sometimes in a neighboring lineage's territory. This solution is viable, of course, only while new lands are available and allow for a proper balance of cropping. Constraints in either or both of these solutions create pressures for other, larger-scale adaptive measures.

The thorough archaeological survey of the highland territory forming part of the area occupied by the traditional tribe of Judah—in the area east of but not including Jerusalem—provides data about settlement patterns that seem to reflect out-migration. As a whole this region has a marginal character, although some areas are more hospitable to balanced agricultural productivity than others. In the Iron IIA period, from the late eleventh century well into the tenth century, settlement in the Judean hill country almost doubled compared to any earlier period. The thirty-four Iron IIA sites represent an increase of about 90 percent over the Iron I period; and the total amount of settled area increased about 80 percent, from 19.5 hectares (47.7 acres) to 33.5 hectares (83 acres).

Equally important to this radical demographic change is the distribution of sites by size. Several prominent sites (ca. 3 hectares or 7.5 acres each) lie in the most favorable environments, and five second-level sites (1.5–2 hectares [3.75–5 acres]) are distributed throughout the region. These in turn are surrounded by even smaller settlements. The range in site size and their configuration suggests "central places," larger sites that interact with smaller ones in the exchange of goods and services. The necessity for differential site size in relation to the expanding population of this region arises in part from the location of new settlements in less fertile areas of the Judean hills. The environmental niches most conducive to cultivation had been settled in the Iron I period. But out-migration by the expanding population of those sites, which had reached the limit of what their usable lands could support even with technological innovations, led to the settlement of less productive areas. So too did an influx of people from nearby areas just to the north. The biblical and archaeological record of the destruction of Shiloh at about this time shows how the Philistine conquests caused the displacement of segments of the hill country population.

Whatever caused the population explosion in the Judean hills, clearly many of the new settlements occupied ecological niches that did not allow for balanced cropping. Such balance is essential for the characteristic Mediterranean pattern of "grain, wine, and oil," supplemented by occasional animal protein provided by small herd animals. If a given econiche cannot provide a sufficiently varied set of food crops, its settlers must trade for them. For example, a subregion more suited by terrain, soil types, and water supply to the growing of grain would intensify its cereal production so that its surpluses could be exchanged for the surpluses of other communities in nearby eco-niches with different cropping potentials. Such exchanges, in the absence of a true market economy, probably took place through religious activity. Regional ritual events, which we know involved the collection of offerings, allowed for priestly re-distribution of commodities.

The groupings of Iron IIA sites in the Judean highlands suggest intraregional commodity exchange. Intensive surveys elsewhere in the central highlands, especially in Ephraim, the hill country north of Jerusalem, reveal the same pattern of sharp increases in the number of settlements as in the Judean hills, and also their expansion into subregions not suitable for the regular self-sufficiency of producing households. An increase in population density was clearly not a localized Judean phenomenon in the Iron IIA period; throughout the tribal lands there arose a need for adaptive mechanisms that transcended the activities of local, related kinship groups.

Agricultural intensification, local exchanges or redistributions, and the introduc-tion of technological changes are all features of emergent states that are responsive to internal pressures ("integrative features," social scientists call them). Centralized political systems not only can offer their subjects protection from military threats; they also can coordinate and organize large numbers of people cutting across tribal or geographic divisions to provide access to resources.

In addition, states can establish the social stability that local leaders lack the power to provide. As a population expands in a finite territory with limited agrarian poten-tial, internal conflicts over matters such as land and water usage become increasingly difficult for village or even tribal leaders to resolve. A centralized judicial system, enforceable by the greater authority of a royal official, becomes necessary to deal with incidents that disrupt community life. In just such terms did the DH evaluate pre-monarchic conditions: "In those days there was no king in Israel; all the people did what was right in their own eyes" (Judg. 21.25). And note also the prominence in the David traditions of the king's role as the font and purveyor of justice: "So David reigned over all Israel; and David administered justice and equity to all his people" (2 Sam. 8.15; see also 2 Sam. 15.5; 23.5).

A need for centralized organization grew out of another feature of the technoen-vironmental setting of the emerging monarchy, particular to the eastern Mediterra-nean in the early Iron Age. The very name *Iron Age* points to the issue. Although archaeologists and historians have long dated the inception of the Iron Age in Pal-estine to around 1200 BCE, that date does not mark a significant transition from bronze to iron as the dominant metal used for tools and weapons. For reasons that historians of technology do not yet fully understand, the copper and tin needed for the production of bronze implements were disrupted at the end of the Late Bronze Age. International trade, essential to the distribution of the raw materials and finished products of bronze-producing metallurgy, was severely limited during the early cen-turies of the Iron Age. Iron ore was likewise scarce. New procedures for smelting iron, in which carbon was introduced to produce a metal stronger and more durable than bronze, did emerge with the advent of the Iron Age. Yet these techniques were not widely used for everyday purposes until the tenth century, partly because of a lag in the diffusion of the new technology and partly because trade disruptions precluded the wide availability of ores.

The population expansion in Iron IIA in the Palestinian highlands increased the demand for agricultural implements. Iron by then was preferred, especially for plow tips: its greater durability made it better suited to the rockier soils of the marginal lands settled in the out-migrations and population shifts of the late eleventh and tenth centuries. Although Palestine has iron ore deposits, most are of poor quality and were never mined in antiquity. Only the organizational and distributional potential of centralized government could ensure security to the trade networks through which raw materials flowed and the population centers where the specialists who produced agricultural tools lived.

Population increase, shifting areas of settlement, and new technologies thus became intersecting variables creating the need for international trade and occupational specialization, features widely associated with state systems. Along with integrative and military functions, the emergent Israelite state provided necessary access to technologies and raw materials critical for the growing population in diverse highland environments.

Material Features of the Early State in Israel

A chief characteristic of a monarchic system is a territorial base that transcends traditional, older, and prior territorial segments or regions. The biblical texts' recounting of the military exploits and political actions of the first three kings, however stylized or legendary the accounts, reveals the core area in which Saul rose to power. The nucleus of Saul's territory, whether a chiefdom or an inchoate state, was his own tribe of Benjamin. His son Ishbaal, whose brief reign overlaps with David's, appoints Benjaminites as his servants (see 2 Sam. 2.15, 25, 31). It is noteworthy that Ishbaal claims to rule not only over Benjamin but also over other areas: Ephraim, Gilead, the Jezreel, and perhaps Asher (2 Sam. 2.9). The biblical assertion that Saul ruled "over all Israel" may be an editorial exaggeration, but Saul's early military success would have gradually rallied an expanding group of followers and created an area of control beyond Benjamin. Saul is portrayed as a charismatic military leader in the tradition of the preceding judges, and his continued feats on the battlefield were of just the sort to lead to an expanded sphere of control.

David's political and military achievements apparently created a still larger territorial entity. Clearly his own tribal base in Judah, indicated by the Judean origins of the folk traditions attached to him, figured prominently in David's rise to power. In the early years of his reign he had sovereignty over Judah alone (see 2 Sam. 5.5). David made his capital for over seven years at Hebron, a well-situated site in the Judean hills. From there he expanded his influence over all of the southern hill country and adjacent Shephelah, the northern Negeb, and the eastern Judean wilderness. (This territory, larger than the tribe of Judah itself, ultimately encompassed the ideal or maximum boundaries of the southern kingdom of Judah after the later dissolution of the United Monarchy.) Expanding to the north and east, David incorporated into his realm the Benjaminite, Ephraimite, and other areas of Saul's territory, as well as Galilee and parts of Transjordan.

One other expansion of the Judean core of tenth-century Israel is significant. At the southern periphery of Judah and of the kingdom lay the northern Negeb or Beer-sheba basin, where settlements had existed prior to early Israel and the United Mon-

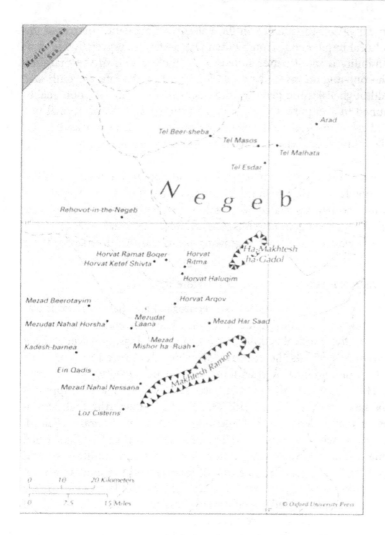

Negeb Settlements of the Tenth Century BCE

archy and continued afterward. In the early monarchy, however, numerous settlements penetrated into the Negeb highlands to the southwest: most are stone fortresses or towers with domestic structures and animal pens scattered in the vicinity. The pottery at these sites indicates that they were occupied for a limited period, from the end of the eleventh century at the earliest to their destruction or abandonment at about the time of Shishak's march through the Negeb in 925 BCE. These sites, in other words, are chronologically congruent with the reigns of David and especially Solomon.

These Negeb settlements have other interesting features. The dwelling types, and even some of the towers themselves, resemble the domestic structures of tenth-century sites in Israelite territory. Similarly, a large percentage of the pottery forms are the same as those found in villages to the north. Finally, the settlements typically are in areas of limited water sources and without soils suitable for subsistence farming. Taken together, these factors indicate that the western Negeb settlements were outposts of the early kingdom, initiated and supported by the state, and populated by groups sent southward by state authorities to represent state interests. Although agricultural and pastoral activities are evident in the archaeological remains of these sites, their inhabitants could not have survived without external support.

Just what were the interests of the state in populating this barren region? Because about 80 percent of the fortresses and dwellings were built on high ridges commanding panoramic views, they obviously helped protect the southern borders of the monarchy. The Philistines at that time had extended their settlements southward along the farthest western area of the Negeb highlands. Egypt's gradually increasing interest in regaining control of Palestine, culminating in the Shishak invasion, likewise points to the Israelite need for military protection at the southwestern limits of its territory. In addition, by the Solomonic period, Israel had developed an international trade with an important southern component so that the Negeb outposts also served as way stations along a route to the Red Sea and thence to East Africa and South Arabia. These frontier settlements thus supported several geopolitical and economic interests of the early monarchy.

Aside from archaeological data, researchers usually reconstruct the full extent of the Davidic domain with such sources as the census list of 2 Samuel 24 and the list of Levitical cites in Judges 21. Important as these lists may be, however, they are incomplete and resist exact dating. Nonetheless, the strong tradition of direct Davidic rule over all the tribal groups means that biblical information about tribal boundaries can be used to determine the extent of the Davidic kingdom as well as that of Solomon, the heir to an established and extensive territorial base. Traditional premonarchic tribal regions are generally equated with the territory of the Davidic-Solomonic state.

The supranational boundaries of the early monarchy are less clear. Biblical sources claim conquests of Moab, Edom, and Ammon (including the land of Geshur) across the Jordan; and David is said to have extended Israelite dominion over parts of the Aramean territories as far as Damascus. Parts of Philistia were reportedly captured or reclaimed, and Negeb peoples such as the Amalekites were subdued. Israelite domination over these extra-Israelite lands has often been considered part of the nationalist exaggeration of the biblical sources, which tend to aggrandize David and Solomon. Still, the idea of a quasi-imperial sprawl by the early monarchy cannot easily be rejected. The political weakness of the power centers surrounding Palestine at this time makes such a scenario possible, as do other economic and diplomatic features of the early kingship.

Leaving aside for a moment the matter of imperial control, one can see within the traditional territorial borders of the new state aspects of material culture that reflect political unity. Tenth-century ceramic vessels exhibit considerable homogeneity throughout the land. In contrast to the preceding period, with its distinct local pottery traditions, and also to the succeeding period, in which pottery forms and wares diverge into northern and southern groups, the ceramic assemblages of the early monarchic period show many similar features. Sites of varying sizes—urban centers and more remote villages—seem to share a common ceramic idiom, at least by the mid-tenth century. The variety of new ceramic forms and features is impressive, particularly in comparison to the previous period. Despite the general difficulty of closely dating Bronze and Iron Age archaeological materials, archaeologists have been able to identify the pottery of the early monarchic era because of the ubiquitous appearance of a characteristic ware—red slip with a rough burnish applied by hand—on a variety of vessels. Careful statistical and stratigraphic analysis of these red burnished sherds has given them unusually precise chronological parameters. Emerging about 950 BCE, this pottery can justifiably be called "Solomonic ware." Furthermore, the unburnished red-slip wares that precede them can perhaps be assigned to the Davidic period.

The relative uniformity of the ceramic repertoires of the Iron IIA period can best be explained by increase of intersite contacts effected by a centralized government. To foster exchanges, to shift labor forces, to monitor revenues, and to establish communication with local clients and leaders, a state system needs to maintain roadways and contacts with all parts of its domain. We can see this by carefully examining the distribution of pottery types in a small region of southern Palestine bordering on Philistia. A group of sites with similar ceramic horizons lies along a reconstructible Israelite trading loop; but the nearby site of Ashdod, which remained a Philistine outpost in this period, clearly lay beyond the borders of an emerging distinctively Israelite material culture.

Secure exchange routes within a territorial state are an important determinative factor in the diffusion of common pottery types within its borders. Ethnographic evidence suggests that under such conditions common wares can easily be transported, usually by itinerant traders using pack animals, to markets 250 kilometers (155 miles) or more from the production site. Such a radius corresponds strikingly with the distance between the traditional northern and southern borders of Israel— 245 kilometers (152 miles) from Dan in the north to Beer-sheba in the south (see 1 Sam. 3.20; 2 Sam. 3.10; 24.2; etc.). Ceramic similarity clearly requires favorable conditions for interregional travel and trade; it also can be affected by the relocation of village potters. The increases in Iron IIA population already mentioned induced outmigration from existing villages and the establishment of new ones. Village pottery traditions thus migrated to new locations along with the shifting population.

Burial practices reveal another trend toward homogeneity. The preceding Iron I period yields relatively little evidence, partly reflecting low population density and partly because making more permanent burial sites requires expenditures of time and resources perhaps unavailable to the premonarchic highlanders. Those few known examples tend to be the single interment cist graves known from Late Bronze coastal or Canaanite sites, although a few cave tombs also appear. Cave tombs are natural caves, sometimes enlarged or enhanced by hewing out receptacles for bodies. Such tombs tend to be used over long periods of time, the desiccated skeletal remains being heaped in a central repository to make room for fresh burials. The bench tomb, found in the highlands throughout the Iron Age beginning in the tenth century BCE, is an artificially constructed version of the cave tomb. A cavity is hewn out of rock outcroppings or cliffs, benches are carved along its sides to receive corpses, and a pit is dug in the center to receive bones from old burials. The grave goods also show a uniformity that mirrors the pattern of ceramics at that time. In contrast to the limited pottery repertoire of Iron I burials, Iron IIA tombs show a marked increase in the number of pottery forms and also of imported wares. Not surprisingly the latter are Cypro-Phoenician vessels, the major forms of foreign ceramics in habitation sites.

These bench tombs and their cave tomb antecedents were family burial sites, reused over generations by the members of a single family group or of related ones. The tombs contain the remains of males and females of all ages, with no differentiation by gender or age in the treatment of skeletons. The tomb group as a whole, however, represents families that had amassed some wealth. Carving out a bench tomb and depositing grave goods required resources above the subsistence level. In addition, the known tombs, even assuming that many are as yet undiscovered, could not account for the burials of the entire population. Poorer folk were laid to rest in simple pit graves with few or no grave goods, and no traces now survive.

Architectural remains of the early monarchic era show a similar trend toward innovation and uniformity. Important new building techniques and structures can be dated to the Iron IIA period, especially in its latter stages during Solomon's reign. According to 1 Kings 9.15–20, Solomon amassed labor forces "to build the house of the LORD and his own house, the Millo and the wall of Jerusalem, Hazor, Megiddo, Gezer . . . , Lower Beth-horon, Baalath, Tamar in the wilderness, within the land, as well as all of Solomon's storage cities, the cities for his chariots, the cities for his cavalry, and whatever Solomon desired to build, in Jerusalem, in Lebanon, and in all the land of his dominion." Besides the capital, Jerusalem, this text mentions six cities as the focus of Solomonic regional urbanization, of which only the first three have been located with certainty. Excavations at those sites—Gezer, Megiddo, and Hazor—have provided a wealth of information about the public architecture of the early monarchy.

Anthropological assessments of the material features of monarchic rule stress that the erection of structures serving regional and national needs, rather than simply domestic or local ones, are part of emerging state systems. Fortifications and other large public buildings require expenditures of capital and labor beyond the resources of smaller-scale societies. Such projects have important economic and political functions, as well as less tangible symbolic and psychological ones. They contribute to the royal administration of national territory, while also signifying the power of the king. Urban development at Gezer, Megiddo, and Hazor thus constitutes archaeological data reflecting royal administration.

A striking uniformity in public architecture appears at Gezer, Megiddo, and Hazor in the early monarchy. The dating and interpretation of the public structures at these three sites are still debated among archaeologists, but attributing them to the period of Solomon enjoys wide support. Fortification walls in the Iron Age were of two types: the solid wall, usually 2.5 to 4.5 meters (8–15 feet) thick, and the casemate wall. The latter consisted of two parallel walls, the inner usually less substantial than the outer, which averaged 1 to 1.5 meters (3–4.5 feet) wide, and the distance between the two walls varying between 1.5 and 4 meters (4.5–13 feet). The two walls are linked by cross-walls; the rooms thus formed in the wall could be used for storage. Sometimes casemates form part of the adjacent houses, suggesting that this type arose when the outer walls of a series of houses were packed tightly around the perimeter of a site, forming a defensive structure. Whatever their origin, casemate walls became rare after the tenth century. Their nearly simultaneous appearance at Gezer, Hazor, and probably Megiddo can be linked to Solomonic building activity, as can their presence at other urban sites newly emerging or reemerging on the Palestinian landscape in the tenth century.

The similarity in casemate wall construction of the second half of the tenth century is also evident in the gateways associated with those walls. The typical city gate consisted of four to six chambers, two or three on each side of the opening and projecting inward from the line of the wall. Gezer, Megiddo, and Hazor all feature six-chambered gates that are close enough in size and proportion to indicate a common architectural plan, with variations for local conditions. The façades of all three gates included projecting towers, and the width of the central passage was exactly the same—4.20 meters (13 feet 10 inches)—at each site. The gates of the major urban sites of the tenth century were constructed with evenly dressed stone blocks known as ashlars. More costly than the roughly trimmed field stones used for most buildings of the period, these blocks occur in formal buildings—palaces and shrines—at sites that, by virtue of their strategic locations, also served as regional royal cities. The formal architectural style of these buildings often included the earliest use of a particular kind of capital, called proto-Ionic (or proto-Aeolic) because it seems to be the prototype of the double volute Ionic capital of classical Greek architecture. Its curved volutes have their origin in the palm tree motif ubiquitous in ancient Near Eastern art. More than thirty-five such capitals have been discovered in Palestine, all at six or seven urban centers. The earliest two come from tenth-century Megiddo.

The high quality and uniformity of these features of the monumental architecture of the tenth century represent a building style that may have been designed in the United Monarchy by an unknown royal architect. It became popular thereafter in both kingdoms of the divided monarchy, as well as at neighboring Phoenician and Philistine sites. Some architectural historians suggest an Israelite origin for these fine Iron Age construction techniques and embellishments; others point to precursors in eastern Mediterranean culture at the end of the Late Bronze Age. Whatever their origin, their presence in the fortifications and palaces of regional centers is evidence of how the centralized government housed and protected the officials who carried out state policies.

Another kind of large building at several urban centers provides further evidence of state economic and political policies. These large rectangular structures, as big as 11 × 22 meters (35 feet 9 inches × 71 feet 6 inches), are subdivided into three internal longitudinal sections by two rows of internal columns running the length of the building. The prominence of the columns led archaeologists to call them "pillared buildings," a fortunate designation in light of a controversy over their function: were they barracks, stables, or storehouses? Whatever their function, their origin in tenth-century royal cities can be related to political centralization—to the stationing of cavalry units in strategic cities (see 1 Kings 9.19), to the provisioning of officials loyal to the crown, or to the storage of materials being exchanged on the trade routes of the early state.

The urban architecture of Iron IIA was distinctive, as were the cities themselves. The preceding Iron I period saw deurbanization throughout Palestine. The rise of a state system in the tenth century BCE coincided with an urban revival within the boundaries of the Israelite national territory. Most of the new urban centers were built on the sites of the old Bronze Age cities, although a few represent the continuation of Iron I village sites. The Iron II cities in some ways continue the Bronze Age urban traditions in their layout and location. But differences in size and in internal building types are indicative of a nation-state, rather than of the autonomous city-states of the Bronze Age.

As a whole, the Iron IIA cities—even major royal centers such as Gezer, Hazor, and Megiddo—are smaller than their Bronze Age precursors. Other cities were even smaller, with differing layouts and building types, and often they lacked fortifications or other prominent public buildings. With their dwellings crowded together in irregular fashion, many were villages grown large. Thus they differ in character from most Bronze Age urban sites, which were relatively independent political units, each featuring buildings that served the economic, military, royal, religious, and residential functions of a self-governing entity. Iron IIA cities, smaller and less complex, were part of a centralized state, with many governing functions reserved to the capital city or regional centers. The presence of a national state effected a new mode of urban existence.

One other feature of the royal cities mentioned in 1 Kings 9 is salient. The three cities that have been only tentatively identified seem to be located at strategic locations: Beth-horon, commanding the major access to Jerusalem from the north; and Baalath and Tamar, probably situated at the southern and southeastern borders of the kingdom. The three known sites mentioned in 1 Kings 9 are especially well placed. Gezer occupied one of the most important crossroads in ancient Palestine, guarding the place where the ascent to Jerusalem and other highland sites branches off from the major north-south coastal route, the "Way of the Sea." Thus it protected southern trade routes and was also critical to the defense of Israel's southwestern border, on the edge of lands still controlled by Philistines or sought by Egypt. Megiddo had a similar strategic importance because of its location near the intersection of the "Way of the Sea" with routes through the Jezreel Valley toward the east. Finally, Hazor commanded a strategic position at the junction of the main north-south highland route, connecting northern Palestine with the Phoenician coast and with the east-west highway extending toward Damascus.

It is no coincidence that these three cities occupied the three main intersections of the historic trading routes of the eastern Mediterranean. In addition to serving as regional centers, they were fortified and equipped with the administrative machinery and appropriate large-scale buildings to secure international trade in the Solomonic period. Whether this trade had already begun in Davidic times is difficult to ascertain. Most likely, foreign conquests and tribute provided the luxury items and other materials not available locally for the newly formed state and its bureaucrats from the beginning of the monarchy. Still, the cessation of warfare during Solomonic rule meant an increase in international trade connections during the middle to late tenth century. The brief flowering of central Negeb highland settlements in that period belongs to the same picture of commercial internationalism.

Other material remains also give evidence of a flourishing foreign trade. Imported wares, absent from the limited ceramic assemblages of the Iron I period, begin to appear in large quantities in the tenth century. Most prominent of these is the so-called Cypro-Phoenician ware, a designation for fine or luxury vessels usually covered with a red slip and decorated with black concentric circles. Cypro-Phoenician ceramic vessels from abroad fed into an internal distribution network comprehensive enough to ensure their wide availability. The prosperous trading cities of the Phoenician coast, the source of these wares, also provided materials and technological expertise for building projects associated with Solomonic if not Davidic rule (see 2 Sam. 5.11; 1 Kings 5.1–12; see also 1 Chron. 22.3–4).

Iron objects, also indicative of international trade, appear in significant numbers for the first time in the tenth century. Indeed, twice as many iron artifacts have been recovered from Iron IIA contexts as from Iron I sites. Only in the tenth century did iron begin to play a significant role in political, economic, and military aspects of Israelite life. Its greatly increased use in weaponry, in tools for expanded agricultural activity, and in prestige items met various needs of the early monarchy.

The availability of iron, Phoenician pottery, and other imported goods depended for the most part on overland trade routes secured by the regional royal cities and the southern Negeb outposts. But maritime activity played its role in early monarchic international trade. The Philistine coastal city at Tell Qasile, probably destroyed by Davidic forces, became an Israelite port city, as did other contemporary sites on the Mediterranean. One of them, Tel Dor at the foot of Mount Carmel, was a Phoenician colony in the eleventh century. By the late eleventh century and then in the tenth, it became Israel's leading harbor town, facilitating trade with Phoenicia and Cyprus. Other sea trade toward the south is known only from texts, notably the claim that Solomon built a fleet of ships to sail south from Ezion-geber at the Red Sea to acquire precious items, such as the highly valued incense, spices, rare woods, and gemstones of South Arabia and East Africa (see 1 Kings 9.26–28; 10.11–13). Archival records of Assyrian trade and its commodities from periods both earlier and later than the tenth century attest to the long history of trade in these items. Monarchic Israel had every reason to participate in that trade by southern sea routes connecting with overland caravans.

A major impetus for seeking secure routes and a lucrative international trade stemmed from the special needs and strategies of the state system's urban nerve center, its capital. Saul is said to have ruled from Gibeah in Benjamin, although the biblical texts associating him with that site (probably Tell el-Ful just north of Jerusalem) are beset with difficulties. David first established his power base at Hebron but ultimately moved it to the city forever associated with his name: Jerusalem, the core of which was known as "the city of David" (2 Sam. 5.7). Whether David acquired Jerusalem by conquering its Jebusite inhabitants or through negotiation with them is uncertain. But the strategic brilliance in establishing a capital city outside the traditional areas of any existing tribal groups is clear: Jerusalem and its public buildings were a unifying factor in the early monarchy.

Archaeological evidence for the royal and administrative capital of the new monarchy is disconcertingly poor, especially in comparison with the recovery of so much from the regional centers of Solomon's day. After more than a century and a half of archaeological excavation of the city of David, virtually no structural remains of the tenth century can be identified securely. Even the monumental "stepped stone structure," for decades thought to be part of Davidic construction activity, has recently

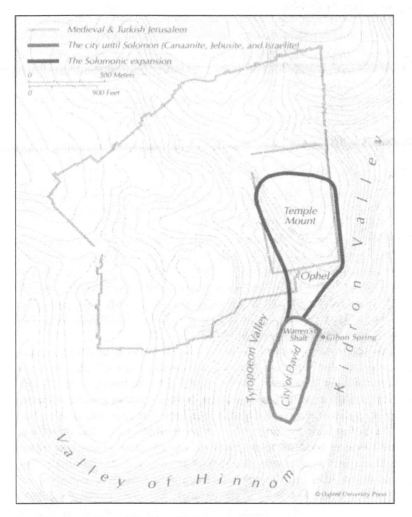

Jerusalem in the Time of David and Solomon

been dated to the end of the Late Bronze Age (although it is likely to have been reused during the Iron IIA period as a retaining wall for the royal precincts built then). The same is true for "Warren's Shaft," a subterranean water channel at first identified with the "water shaft" mentioned in 2 Samuel 5.8 in connection with the Davidic capture of Jerusalem; some archaeologists now date it later than Iron IIA. Only fragmentary walls and scattered artifacts, none of which elicit images of the monumentality and grandeur of what David and Solomon are said to have constructed in Jerusalem (2 Sam. 5.9; 2 Kings 5–7), incontrovertibly belong to the period of the early monarchy.

Yet the biblical record of monumental architecture in Jerusalem is not fictitious, and the discrepancy between textual records and material remains should not be used to discredit the former. The very importance of the city and its public buildings led to the obliteration of the earliest Israelite structures. For thousands of years successive rebuildings, many of which sank foundations down to bedrock, have disturbed earlier remains. The sanctity of the temple-palace precinct especially attracted continual construction activity. Indigenous kings as well as the foreign imperial powers that controlled the city often tore down and built anew its most important buildings. That three postbiblical religious traditions—Judaism, Christianity, and Islam—have vied for position at sacred locales, putting many sites off-limits for excavation, has further contributed to the archaeological nightmare.

Jerusalem's ancient conquerors, moreover, routinely destroyed the public structures of the enemy and carried off as spoils its wealth (see 2 Kings 25.8–17). Because public buildings symbolized the state, demolishing or taking possession of them invariably followed a conquest. Even if one could excavate under the present-day shrines and holy places, some right over the sites of ancient ones, few if any coherent traces of the monumental architecture of the tenth century would turn up.

A different kind of archaeological data, however, underscores Jerusalem's pivotal role. Surveys in the eastern Judean hill country, in addition to showing the increased settlement density of the Iron IIA period, also indicate that these settlements belonged to a more extensive territorial unit. The arrangement of sites on the tenth-century landscape points to a center—Jerusalem—outside the region. This recent interpretation of settlement patterns provides some assurance that the biblical texts' depiction of Jerusalem as national center is rooted in reality.

Finally, we can test details recorded in the biblical description of the two major buildings in the capital—the Temple and the adjacent palace—against what we know of construction technology, architectural styles, and artistic motifs of the tenth century BCE. All have parallels in structures and artifacts discovered at ancient Egyptian, Phoenician, Syrian, Assyrian, Canaanite, and Hittite sites. The royal palace described in 1 Kings 7.1–11 had at least five units, the largest of which was called the House of the Forest of Lebanon because of its extensive use of cedar beams and pillars imported from Lebanon. Another unit, the Hall of Pillars, with its colonnaded entryway and its access to other units of the palace complex, may have resembled the Near Eastern *bit-hilani* structures. Most of the parallels, however, postdate the tenth century, a "dark age" in art and architecture because of the decline of the historic centers of political power in that period. This leaves Israel, with its reported construction of an extraordinary temple-palace complex in Jerusalem, as a trendsetter in the material world of its day. Ancient Israel is best known in postbiblical religious tradition for its spiritual and literary contributions, for its wisdom documents and prophetic calls for justice. But for one brief period in the millennium or so of its history it may have taken the lead in artistic creativity.

Sociopolitical Features of the Early Monarchy

The military, techno-environmental, and demographic factors leading to state formation in early monarchic Israel, along with the spread of new settlements and the proliferation of public works, inevitably meant changes in the patterns of local leadership and in the relatively equal access to resources characteristic of the preceding Iron I period. Village, clan, or tribal elders lacked the supratribal power necessary to establish and equip a successful army, to move goods and people, and to embark on the monumental construction projects necessary for the administrative structures of the emergent state's extended territory. The archaeological record leaves no direct trace of the different levels of human activity and status connected with new socio-political arrangements. Thus scattered clues in the biblical narrative are important, as are social-science models, if used cautiously.

Most of the scarce biblical information about the earliest decades of the monarchy concerns military operations. We learn that Saul created a standing army (1 Sam. 13.2) under his direct command, but presumably with high-ranking officers in addition to his own son Jonathan and his cousin Abner (1 Sam. 14.50). He also seems to have appointed a priestly officer (1 Sam. 14.3, 18), a supervisor for his staff (1 Sam. 22.9), and someone to be in charge of his pasturages (1 Sam. 21.7). These textual references to administrative positions indicate a small nucleus of state officials. With a relatively tiny capital at Gibeah and a focus on warfare, there would have been little time, need, or resources for complex organizational development. But Saul's military successes, and then David's, ultimately did necessitate organizational complexity. At the same time, victory in warfare, with spoils and tribute, provided an economic base for specialists and workers in the overlapping domains of judicial, religious, commercial, diplomatic, and constructional activities.

As might be expected for a king who ruled longer than Saul and whose reign eventually saw the cessation of conflict, David expanded and systematized his predecessor's rudimentary administrative structures. The most direct evidence for the organization of the new state under David and then Solomon comes from three lists of high officials given in 2 Samuel and 1 Kings. (See table 5.2 for the positions listed, in the order given in the texts.) The second of the two listings for David, presumably dating later in his reign than the first, indicates the adjustments he made as he gained experience in royal office. The most significant are a doubling of military officials; a shift from David's sons to Ira of the post of a palace or Jerusalem priestly officer, the second priestly official in both lists; and the addition of an overseer for the labor forces.

The double set of military officers—one commanding the army, presumably an Israelite muster, and the other in charge of the Cherethites and Pelethites, two foreign mercenary units—reflects the importance of the fundamental source of royal power: the coercive strength of the military. The two types of military forces can be related to the king's efforts to maintain his troops' allegiance. The mercenaries, sustained and supported away from home by the crown, served the king directly and were inherently well controlled by their commander. A standing army is another story. The books of Samuel mention the king distributing spoils of war (1 Sam. 22.7; 30.21–25; see also 1 Sam. 17.25), an act meant to help secure the army's loyalty. Another important aspect of the army and its faithfulness is that its leadership core consisted, for Saul, of fellow Benjaminites (1 Sam. 13.2; 22.7), and for David, fellow Judeans (1 Sam. 22.1–2). Likewise, Judeans in general, and not just those who served as soldiers, benefited materially from the successes of their kinsman David (1 Sam. 30.26–30; see also 2 Sam. 19.42; 20.2). Although David was commander in chief, he appointed "cabinet-level" chiefs of staff to maintain tight control of his military power base.

The double set of priestly administrators reflects another crucial aspect of royal

Table 5.2   Officials under David and Solomon

2 SAMUEL 8.16–18	2 SAMUEL 20.23–26	1 KINGS 4.1–6
(David)	(David)	(Solomon)
Over the army	Over the army of Israel	Priest
Recorder	Over the Cherethites and Pelethites	Secretaries
Priests	Over the forced labor	Recorder
Secretary	Recorder	Over the army
Over the Cherethites and Pelethites	Secretary	Priests
Priests (David's sons)	Priests	Over the officials
	David's priest (Ira)	Priest and king's friend
		Over the palace
		Over the forced labor

control. Royal rule depended in part on priestly groups stationed at shrines through-out the kingdom. Their appointment, perhaps accompanied by personal land grants, was from the crown and thus ensured loyalty to the throne. With the royal and ritual governments inextricably linked, priestly officials had more to do than simply per-form ritual acts. Their business also included communications, adjudications, and the collection of revenues (in the form of offerings), although these functions may have overlapped with traditional procedures under the control of village and tribal elders. The network of priestly officials was closely linked to the redistribution of goods and thus deserved high-level government supervision.

Finally, the second Davidic list of officials contains an officer not found on the first list: a labor supervisor. Military success brought spoils of war, which filled the royal and priestly coffers (see especially 2 Sam. 8.7–12 and 12.30, and also 1 Sam. 15.9 and 27.9) and secured the loyalty of the army and key officials; and it also brought war captives into the kingdom. According to the narratives, foreign servitors came from Ammon, Moab, and Edom, as well as from the various Aramean cities that David encountered in his campaigns to the northeast (2 Sam. 8.2–14; 12.31). These captives constituted a workforce, with their own chief administrator, for the building projects initiated by David (2 Sam. 5.9, 11; 12.31; see also 1 Chron. 22.2).

The massive public works of the early monarchy are attributed to Solomon and were certainly completed during his reign. Yet some biblical texts suggest that Davidic military operations brought two important resources: capital, from spoils and tribute; and labor, from war captives. The local economy alone could not have supported such projects without severe deprivations to the indigenous subsistence farmers, nor would local residents endure the hardship of construction-gang work with much enthusiasm. Thus the wealth and labor acquired through war provided the human and fiscal resources for erecting the nation-state's material structures. It would be a stretch to claim imperial control in the tenth century for the Jerusalem-based monarchy. Yet the small states or city-states between Palestine and Assyria, which normally paid tribute to one or another of the Mesopotamian states or to Egypt, could well have directed such payments to Jerusalem during the ascendancy of Davidic rule and the weakness of the traditional powers.

The monumental building projects of the early monarchy were crucial to the new regime. Such projects enhanced the image and status of the ruler and his bureaucracy. They won support from the newly appointed officials, or clients, whose loyalty depended on getting their share in the riches and on their access to the lifestyle of the royal court. Finally, monumental structures functioned as visual propaganda, announcing to neighbors that Israel had the military might to secure the resources to build them—and thus to demand the continued flow of tribute to the new capital. In such ways, monumental building projects, by integrating resources and labor, signified the emergence of a state system. At the same time they signaled the state's coercive potential.

Other than the lists of David's cabinet in 2 Samuel 8 and 20, little can be gleaned from available sources about the administrative structure of the kingdom. The governing class—courtiers, officials, generals, wealthy merchants and landowners, priestly leaders—constituted only a tiny fraction of the total population. The biblical texts concerning the monarchy contain a strong tradition of the elders and "all the people" having a voice in governance, suggesting that the Israelite monarchy was not a strongly authoritarian regime—not an "oriental despotism" such as some social scientists have modeled. Rather, it was more a participatory monarchy, with many royal decisions presumably both limited and directed by consultation with wider popular interests.

The advent of Solomonic rule, not surprisingly, brought in its wake a more elaborate set of bureaucratic functions. The passages in 1 Kings 4.7–19 and 27–28 describing the twelve officials "who provided food for the king and his household" (each for one month of the year) indicate new administrative hierarchies. This list of officers and their regions partly approximates existing tribal units but in other places diverges from them. Indeed, the list is full of places and names that resist conclusive identification. The known places also are irregularly scattered, and there are overlaps. Thus it is unlikely that, in establishing this set of officials, Solomon was setting up new administrative districts in order to break down existing tribal boundaries and thus tribal loyalties. It is more useful to focus on the functions of the officials in the list.

The twelve officials provisioned the royal establishment, and they supplied fodder for the royal horses. These officers may have served as a rudimentary tax-collecting organization, each charged with collecting in his district sufficient foodstuffs for the court and its steeds. But at least some taxation was channeled through the priestly hierarchies. Another possibility for these officials and the strange topography of their bailiwicks is that they managed crown properties or plantations—lands confiscated or captured by David from pockets of non-Israelite settlements. This explanation accounts for the striking absence of an official in Judah. The New Revised Standard Version, with several Greek manuscripts, supplies "of Judah" at the end of 1 Kings 4.19; but the Hebrew omits reference to Judah. Presumably, no royal estates in Judah were meant to supply provisions for the court. This fits David's policy of favoring his own tribe with the fruits—lands as well as goods—of his military accomplishments.

The Solomonic "cabinet" list in 1 Kings 4.1–6 for the most part retains the officers established by David. The few modifications reflect the changing organization of the early state. To begin with, there are now two "secretaries"—officials perhaps charged with record keeping and/or diplomatic correspondence, which increased significantly in Solomon's reign. The role of the military is reduced: the chief army officer no longer comes first, and an officer over mercenary forces has been dropped. Apparently Solomon, while holding a considerable supply of arms and chariots along with a standing army, did not wage wars. Rather, he maintained control through diplomacy over the territories conquered or forced to pay tribute by David's war efforts. His legendary coterie of wives and concubines, criticized by the DH (which records their presence in Jerusalem), represents liaisons with tributary states secured through marriage or concubinage (1 Kings 11.1–8).

That such "foreign affairs," which maintained a flow of goods to the capital (1 Kings 4.21), resulted from his diplomatic skill is suggested by Solomon's association with wisdom and wisdom literature. The narrative of his legendary relationship with the queen of Sheba (1 Kings 10.1–10) builds on his fame as a wisdom figure. In addition, the DH reports a special source, the Book of the Acts of Solomon, for the Solomonic segment of the Samuel-Kings account of the monarchy. This is the only such source cited for a single king; such a work is not even mentioned for David. The use of a special source is indicated by the way 1 Kings 3–11 constitutes a highly structured and self-contained work, unified by the themes of wealth, honor, and wisdom. That source provided information about "the acts of Solomon, all that he did as well as his wisdom" (1 Kings 11.41). Solomon's reputation for wisdom is an aspect of the internationalism of his reign. He succeeded in maintaining Davidic holdings not by battle but by persuasive speech, backed by a well-stocked arsenal and the reputation of his father's brilliant military leadership.

Other changes in the list of Solomon's cabinet indicate a growing bureaucracy. An added official "in charge of the palace" was perhaps the majordomo overseeing the elaborate palace complex, now visited by many foreign emissaries as well as by local officials. The person designated to serve "over the officials" was another new cabinet officer, appointed to coordinate the twelve officials charged with supplying provisions for the court on a monthly basis. Finally, the priestly representation on the cabinet expands, as one might expect in a state erecting a major temple building; there is now a third priestly officer, the "king's friend," who perhaps integrated the sacral and secular functions of the Temple institution with those of the royal administration.

An officer in charge of the labor forces remains on the list, as the need to oversee the workers in building projects, begun by David, continued and expanded during Solomon's rule. The question is, who were the laborers? Davidic claims to have secured prisoners of war for laborers appear likely. A similar claim is made for Solomon—he conscripted a levy of "forced labor out of all Israel" (1 Kings 5.13), a workforce that, according to 1 Kings 9.20–22, consisted only of non-Israelites still remaining within national territories. This claim seems dubious because of counterclaims in 1 Kings 11.28 and 12.10–11 about Solomonic conscription of Israelites for work gangs. Those texts, however, form part of DH's rationale for the breakup of the United Monarchy, so that Solomon's maintenance of a foreign rather than a domestic labor force remains likely. Even the famous protest (1 Sam. 8.11–17) against a state system attributed to Samuel stops short of warning the people that they would be conscripted into labor gangs; they would serve in the military and in service professions but their servants (presumably nonnatives) would work on state projects.

Sacral-Royal Ideologies of the Monarchic State

The ability of a national ruler to exercise power over a large group of people—over kinship groups with which he has little or no connection—was facilitated by military successes, by favorable redistribution policies (2 Sam. 6.18–19), and by securing loyal subjects and staff through both those means. All these processes are related to or contingent upon an ideological component of royal rule. A king's power ultimately rested on and was legitimized by a series of symbolic acts, attitudes, icons, and structures connecting the king with the deity and human kingship with divine rule. Ancient Israel clearly shared in this fundamental aspect of the construction of kingship, both in its general features and in its specifically Near Eastern manifestations. The king in Israel was accepted because he was perceived as appointed by Yahweh; and Yahweh's character in turn was increasingly and richly expressed by the metaphor of divine kingship.

The conceptualization of the right of a king to rule over his subjects appears, for example, in the use of anointing as part of the ritual of accession to the throne. Anointing a king to office is a religious rather than a secular act throughout the ancient Near East, as elsewhere. Samuel pours oil on Saul's head, but Yahweh is attributed with anointing him ruler over Israel (1 Sam. 10.1). The elders make David king at Hebron by anointing him because Yahweh instructed that he thus be made ruler over Israel (2 Sam. 5.2–3; see also Ps. 89.20). And the priest Zadok anoints Solomon, with the prayer that Yahweh ordain his rule (1 Kings 1.35–39). Royal as well as priestly recipients of unction are designated "Yahweh's anointed" (for example, 1 Sam. 16.6), never "Israel's anointed." The ceremony of anointing was a sign of divine election and legitimated the king's right to rule.

Another aspect of Near Eastern kingship ideology that finds its counterpart in ancient Israel also emphasizes the divine-human connection: the king is said to be the "son of Yahweh." This appears in the adoption formula of 2 Samuel 7.14, where God says of Solomon: "I will be a father to him, and he shall be a son to me." In several psalms (Pss. 2.7; 89.26–27; and perhaps 110.3) the Israelite king, probably David, is presented as God's (firstborn) son. These texts are all difficult to date and may not come from the period of the early monarchy. Yet the wide occurrence of "son of god/goddess" as a royal title in the ancient Near East makes it likely that this familiar way of expressing divine sanction for a human ruler was part of the ideology accompanying the establishment of kingship in Israel. The use of son-of-god terminology, however, does not necessarily mean that the king himself was considered divine. Near Eastern sources vary in this respect, with Egyptian rulers claiming actual divinity but Semitic ones, Israel included, using the concept metaphorically to connote divine sanction for dynastic power.

These aspects of royal ideology are recovered mainly from Near Eastern and biblical texts. Yet the most important representations of royal-sacral ideology were communicated visually, through crowns (2 Sam. 1.10; 2 Kings 11.12; see also Ps. 132.17–18), scepters, garments, and thrones (2 Sam. 14.9; 1 Kings 2.12). These symbols of royal power are also accoutrements of divine rule in Near Eastern iconography; indeed, deities are signified in art by their distinctive headgear, clothing, and insignia of office. In Israel, with its aniconographic stance precluding images of God, the throne especially served as a visible sign of Yahweh. The many enthronement and other royal psalms conveyed the idea of Yahweh's royal power (Pss. 47.8; 89.14; 93.1; etc.), as did the references to God enthroned on cherubim (Pss. 80.1; 99.1; Isa. 37.16). The ark of Yahweh (or of the covenant, or of God) with the attached cherubim was conceptualized as Yahweh's throne (1 Sam. 4.4; 2 Sam. 6.2). Just as God ruled from a throne in a heavenly abode, so divine presence and power emanated from an earthly structure—a temple. The ark was placed within the Temple as the locus of Yahweh's unseen reality. The Temple building itself served many of the integrative functions of an emerging nation-state, and it was also the primary visual representation of the divine election and sanction of the king who built it and of his dynastic successors. Royal authority compelling people to act against individual or kinship group interests was powerfully legitimized as God's will as represented by God's earthly dwelling in the capital city.

The idea of constructing the Temple in Jerusalem probably originated with David. The various stages of temple building are well known from other ancient Near Eastern states, and David seems to have carried out most of them. The explanation of the DH about David's failure to complete the project—1 Kings 5.3 attributes it to his preoccupation with military operations—probably has validity. At the same time, the census attempted by David (2 Sam. 24), perhaps related to the need to secure revenues for construction projects, coincided with one of the era's periodic and deadly outbreaks of pestilential disease. Such a trauma, understood as a sign of divine disfavor, would have sufficed to keep David from temple building. Instead, he is said to have brought the major icon of the premonarchic era—the ark of Yahweh—to Jerusalem (2 Sam. 6.17) and to have constructed the future Temple's altar on the very site where the Temple would stand (2 Sam. 24.25; 1 Chron. 22.1). Whatever David's role in initiating the process of building and dedicating a temple, it was Solomon who completed it.

If the ark was a national or Israelite symbol of divine presence, effective in communicating to the people of the realm that God favored the king and his bureaucracy, the Temple was essential for projecting that message internationally. Israelite forces achieved military dominance over neighboring states or areas; the legitimization of that political dominion was then made known through the Temple to the tribute-bearing envoys and other representatives of non-Israelite polities who came to Jerusalem. The newly established capital in Jerusalem could not effectively serve its diplomatic, imperialistic, and national functions without the visual sign of Yahweh's sanction of the monarchy.

The artistic and architectural features of the Solomonic Temple are known principally from 1 Kings 5–7. According to that detailed description, the resplendent tripartite building and its accoutrements contained elements recognizable in the Phoenician, Egyptian, Canaanite, Aramean, and Neo-Hittite artistic vernacular of the Iron II period. Representatives of all the foreign peoples either dominated by the early monarchy or with which it had established at least parity, as well as Israelite pilgrims and tribal officials visiting Jerusalem, would see the Temple as a symbol of the Israelite god's presence and power. The Temple's architectural and artistic conventions thus formed a visual idiom meaningful to the widest audience.

Two gigantic pillars stood at the entrance to the Temple, each 23 or more cubits (over 10 meters [33 feet]) high and bearing the enigmatic names *Jachin* and *Boaz*. As freestanding columns, they flanked the building's forecourt (NRSV "vestibule"), just as pillars marked the monumental gateways of sacred precincts throughout the ancient Near East. Carved reliefs of such gateways show that the completion of a temple was marked by a grand procession and celebration, which brought the statue of the realm's chief god into the temple. The 1 Kings 8 account of bringing the ark into the Jerusalem Temple depicts just such a significant religio-political act: installing a deity into a new abode. The highly visible pillars—the only elaborately decorated elements in the otherwise stark and plain exterior of the Temple—thereafter communicated the legitimizing presence of Yahweh to all onlookers.

The interior of the Temple in Jerusalem, like most other such buildings in the ancient Near East, was not a place of public worship. Rather it was the dwelling place of God's unseen presence, entered regularly by just a few senior priestly officials. The size of the Temple building, considerably smaller than the adjacent palace in the royal-sacral precinct of Jerusalem, thus does not mean that it was simply a royal chapel nor that God's house was less important than the king's house. The palace complex was inhabited by scores of people and was the major government building; its interior space needs were considerably greater than that of a temple that was home to a single deity. Yet the Temple had important exterior space—courtyards for sacrificing and where pilgrims could gather. In addition, the Temple interior was flanked by an extensive, three-storied series of side chambers, all contained within the exterior walls of the building, that served as storage rooms for the valuable items of tribute acquired by David and Solomon (see 1 Kings 7.51), as well as for items received as offerings. Befitting its role as a national treasury, the building itself in architectural plan was fortresslike in its exterior appearance—looming high above its platform and surrounding courts. While its interior space was smaller than that of the palace complex, its main hall, lacking interior columns, was as large as such a space could be; and the building as a whole was larger than any other known sacral structure of its time in the Levant. Jerusalem thus became the core of a royal Zion theology heralding

Yahweh's choice of the city as the seat of dynastic rule and concomitant divine presence.

Change and Continuity in the Period of State Formation

The monumentality and grandeur of the Jerusalem Temple did not mean that it replaced local shrines. The diverse expressions of religious life in villages and cities distant from the capital continued, and local priestly families remained important in various aspects of community life. Regional centers of worship from the tenth century have been located, for example, at Megiddo and at Taanach, each with its own repertoire of vessels and ritual objects, not all compatible with Jerusalem ideology; later Deuteronomic and prophetic tirades against such local shrines provide further evidence. The continuing existence of these religious centers is just one dimension of the complex dynamics of the transition to statehood in ancient Israel. The emergence of the state did not obliterate other existing features of Israelite culture, and not everyone was caught up in the political, religious, and economic culture of a dynastic state.

The persistence of strong kinship-based culture in monarchic Israel is apparent in the Bible's continued attention to tribal identities and territories. Indeed, tribal ideology colors the stories and narratives of Israel's premonarchic period, materials that apparently took shape under the monarchy. While tribal structures and values may be at odds with those of a state, they can also be complementary and supportive of the state's stability, as ethnographic evidence shows. This is particularly true when tribal solidarity, manifest in grassroots support for local lineage heads, is transferred to the crown, as in the Judean segment of the premonarchic tribal units. Supratribal administrative organs diminish aspects of tribal influence and power; but in smaller villages and settlements, and among those distant from the central or regional authorities, group identity and loyalty normally abides in the kinship and clan units that constitute the tribe.

Legal cases, for example, tend to be decided at the lowest available authority level. Family households resolve the simplest disputes. As societies become larger and more complex, the family locus of managing conflict is complemented by the formation of lineage judicial authorities—the elders. When disputes cross lineage lines, clan or tribal leaders conduct legal proceedings. The problems of premonarchic Israel that led to state formation included those requiring supratribal authority to deal with disputes. In biblical texts associating the king with justice, David holds a paradigmatic role. The connection of monarch with judicial authority represents general social stability under a state system. In terms of everyday adjudication, the king acts as a kind of highest court of appeals—the court of last resort. The incident in 2 Samuel 15.1–6 seems to represent a rival's distortion of David's success in settling claims (see also 1 Kings 3.16–28, where Solomon's adjudication is linked to his wisdom). Yet royal or national-level adjudication was the exception rather than the rule; the absence of a cabinet-level judicial officer from the Davidic and Solomonic lists is significant in this regard.

The sociopolitical shift involved in Israelite state formation did not mean organizational discontinuity. Many elements of pre-state society were surely left intact for a long time after the emergence of a new political structure and its accompanying ideologies. Nor did the new administrative apparatus entail the dissolution of prior ones; the state added layers of sociopolitical organization to existing ones. The successful functioning of the state system thus depended on the continued operation of kinship structures, and state and tribe were not in constant and inevitable tension.

Yet the Bible does express reservations about centralized monarchic government. Most noteworthy are the antimonarchic passages of 1 Samuel (8.4–28 and 10.17–19; see also 1 Kings 12.1–4 and the "law of the king" in Deut. 17.18–22), in which Samuel warns the people about negative aspects of a state system. The dating of these texts is unresolved, although the weight of the evidence seems to preclude an authentic eleventh-century speech of Samuel. State systems are usually not contested by a groundswell of public complaint against monarchic hierarchies, policies, conscription, or even taxes. Rather, they break down as the result of jealousies among leadership factions over the perquisites of being at the top of a distribution system that clearly advantages the king and his courtiers. In this regard, the legendary accounts of usurpers and of succession struggles in the books of Samuel and also in Kings reveal the true nature of the opposition: to the privileges of individual kings and their followers, not to kingship itself. From the outset the monarchy was meant to be dynastic. David was in fact a wildly successful usurper, however the later pro-Davidic narrative of the DH justifies his replacement of Saul's line. Having established a loyal patronage among Judeans, the army, and a priestly faction, David was well situated to move into the position of God's chosen once Saul had died. Yet his sons struggled against each other to achieve their father's vaunted power, and Solomon's heir was opposed and ultimately rejected by a northerner.

Those who claimed the throne often argued that they simply represented a constituency from among the people. In fact, they hoped to win for themselves the benefits of life in the palace. Judeans, favored by the crown, had no problems with royal power. But northern leaders grumbled that the wealth of the capital did not sufficiently extend to them. During David's reign and for much of Solomon's, the flow of spoil and tribute meant that the tax burden for the royal building projects was minimal or perhaps even nonexistent, if David's failure to complete a census is any indication. Similarly, the use of Israelites in forced labor crews was never an issue, at least while the supply of prisoners of war and their offspring was maintained (1 Kings 9.20–22).

Another dichotomy in Israelite society was in some respects more important than the tribe-state or kinship-kingship one. Near Eastern kingship was overwhelmingly an urban phenomenon. The urbanization reflected in David's development of Jerusalem and in the Solomonic program of establishing regional centers, and perhaps storage and chariot cities (1 Kings 9.19), was epitomized by the lifestyle in the capital. However exaggerated it may be in the biblical account, the ruling urban elite of Jerusalem enjoyed the material benefits accruing to the leaders of a state system.

That lifestyle, and the visible differentials of wealth, had little effect on the rural villages under the early monarchy. The ideology of the Bible claims a national unity that was unlikely as yet to have existed, socially or economically. In this sense, modern occidental ideas of a nation-state prevent us from understanding that the early state in Israel had more in common with the Bronze Age traditions of city-states, writ large, than with a state composed of a citizenry all directly affected by and identifying with the state. At least during the period of the United Monarchy, when state expenses were met from extranational sources, the royal house did not reshape existing economic patterns nor fund its projects with surpluses extracted from the farmers. Indeed, Solomon's budgetary excesses were resolved by ceding property to the Phoenicians rather than by securing funds internally (1 Kings 9.11–14; see also 1 Kings 5.11). Conversely, the flow of goods and imports to the capital had little impact outside the temple-palace complex; they reinforced and legitimized royal rule but hardly percolated into the countryside.

The tenth century saw the recovery of tribal lands lost to Philistines, the capture or incorporation of nontribal enclaves still surviving in tribal territories, the development of regional centers, and the establishment of trade routes. The different ecological niches of the country could thus be exploited more advantageously, with less risk to the individual farm family, to support the burgeoning population spread out in new settlements across the land. Most of that population lived in agrarian villages, not in cities. Even Jerusalem in this period was a relatively tiny city with a small population, consisting mostly of government officials and servitors with their families. With exceptions such as crown lands serving as royal plantations, the tenth-century economy was based in the family. Each household remained a discrete production unit, functioning in and around residences identified as the typical pillared (three- or four-room) house of Israelite settlements throughout the Iron Age. Each household was relatively self-sufficient, producing and processing its own food and clothing except for some agricultural products acquired in exchange for what specialists such as metallurgists provided. The royal hierarchies of Jerusalem, and later those of the other developing urban sites, had no counterparts in village life. Even in the larger villages, household buildings were strikingly uniform in size. There may well have been wealth differentials, expressed in greater access to luxury goods rather than in increased house size, but differences in wealth are not the same as a class system. Whatever status accrued to lineage or clan leaders in the segmentary society that preceded the monarchy continued, and such status was distinct from class hierarchies.

The continuation of agrarian village life, relatively untouched in any negative ways by the tenth-century monarchy, had implications for gender relations. In the pre-state period senior males and females in the family households stood in relative parity with respect to subsistence specialization, control of family resources, and authority over the younger generation and other household dependents. This parity continued into the tenth century. In the kinship-based configurations that characterized village settlements, females enjoyed a status that was related more to the prestige of their household than to their gender. Only to the extent that traditional kinship patterns were disrupted by the new state would female household authority have been reduced—especially in urban settings, where emerging hierarchies inevitably meant the increasing subordination of women. The relative authority of women tends to decline with the rise of state institutions, although some women (such as queens) exercise social power through their class position.

Although the relatively distinct urban and rural spheres meant that women in agrarian households continued to have authoritative roles, the emergence of a state system set in motion other dynamics that ultimately lowered female status. With a male dynastic figure in place, and with permanent male-headed government offices established, public office and accomplishment were represented almost exclusively by men. Great symbolic value rests in this formal association between males and political power, an association that inevitably disadvantages women. Furthermore, Yahweh became the ultimate symbol of Israelite national identity; and Yahweh's royal image was built on metaphors drawn from the male domains of military and political power. The accompanying emphasis on the kingship of God eventually obscured in the state ideology female aspects of divine power, although village communities as well as some portions of the urban population retained more diverse divine imagery, including goddess worship, until the demise of the monarchy.

Conclusion

The early Iron Age village communities would not have survived without the protective and integrative function afforded by the emergent state. At least in the tenth century BCE, villagers do not seem to have suffered from the changes wrought by the superimposition of an urban-based state system over the existing territorial lineages. The flow of goods and servitors into the capital as the result of the military genius of David and the diplomatic sagacity of Solomon precluded the exploitation of the agrarian population. It is no wonder, then, that these first two members of the Davidic dynasty achieve great elaboration and respect in the legendary accounts of the early monarchy in the Bible. The Israelite people as a whole were well served by the establishment of a monarchy in its early stages, for it brought widespread social, economic, and political stability.

The need for historical myths and heroes is characteristic of every national culture; and such myths and heroes invariably arise from the uncertainties and insecurities of its beginning stages. The exceptional actions of individuals, in this case the first three biblical kings, were expanded as symbols of the processes that successfully resolved the difficulties surrounding the emergence of the new culture, Israel's early monarchy.

Select Bibliography

The list below contains works in biblical studies relevant to the early monarchy. This chapter, however, draws extensively on the works of social and political anthropologists, including Robert L. Carniero, Henri J. M. Claessen, Ronald Cohen, Timothy K. Earle, Morton H. Fried, Susan M. Kus, Herbert S. Lewis, Christopher S. Peebles, Barbara J. Price, Elman R. Service, and Henry T. Wright. References to many of their publications as well as to those of other social scientists appear in several of the bibliographies of the works in this list.

Finkelstein, Israel. "The Emergence of the Monarchy in Israel and the Environmental and Socio-Economic Aspects." *Journal for the Study of the Old Testament* 44 (1989): 43–74. A concise reconstruction, integrating recent archaeological survey data with sociopolitical analysis, of the dynamics of state formation in Israel.

Flanagan, James W. *David's Social Drama: A Hologram of Israel's Early Iron Age.* The Social World of Biblical Antiquity Series, 7; and The Journal for the Study of the Old Testament

Supplement Series, 73. Sheffield, England: Almond, 1988. A provocative study focusing on David's reign, drawing on archaeological, biblical, and sociological information, and using holography as a model for such interdisciplinary work.

Frick, Frank S. *The Formation of the State in Ancient Israel.* The Social World of Biblical Antiquity Series, 4. Sheffield, England: Almond, 1985. A comprehensive proposal for the emergence of the monarchy, focusing on the need for agricultural intensification.

Fritz, Volkmar, and Philip R. Davies, eds. *The Origin of the Ancient Israelite States.* The Journal for the Study of the Old Testament Supplement Series, 228. Sheffield, England: Sheffield Academic Press, 1996. A collection of essays with differing and controversial perspectives on state formation in early Israel.

Gottwald, Norman K. "Monarchy: Israel's Counter-revolutionary Establishment." In *The Hebrew Bible: A Socio-Literary Introduction,* 293–404. Philadelphia: Fortress, 1986. An excellent analysis of the literary sources for the monarchy.

———, ed. *Social Scientific Criticism of the Hebrew Bible and Its Social World. Semeia* 37 (1986). Seminal essays by F. Frick, M. Chaney, N. Gottwald, and R. Coote and R. Whitelam on the social world of the monarchy.

Halpern, Baruch. *The Constitution of the Monarchy in Israel.* Harvard Semitic Monographs, 25. Chico, Calif.: Scholars Press, 1981. An erudite analysis, based on biblical sources, of the sacral and political aspects of the monarchy.

Holladay, John S., Jr. "The Kingdoms of Israel and Judah: Political and Economic Centralization in the Iron IIA–B (ca. 1000–750 BCE)." In *The Archaeology of Society in the Holy Land,* ed. Thomas E. Levy, 368–98. New York: Facts on File, 1995. A masterful look at social, political, and economic aspects of the monarchy, using archaeological data and social-science models in groundbreaking ways.

Ishida, Tomoo, ed. *Studies in the Period of David and Solomon and Other Essays.* Tokyo: Yamakawa-Shuppansha, 1982. A useful collection of essays by leading biblical scholars and archaeologists on various features of the United Monarchy.

Knight, Douglas A. "Political Rights and Power in Monarchic Israel." In *Ethics and Politics in the Hebrew Bible, Semeia* 66, ed. Douglas A. Knight and Carol Meyers, 93–118. Atlanta: Scholars Press, 1995. A thoughtful look at political rights and privileges at both local and national levels during the monarchy.

Malamat, Abraham, ed. *The Age of the Monarchies.* World History of the Jewish People, no. 4. Jerusalem: Massada, 1979. A somewhat dated but handy anthology of articles by leading scholars about the monarchy, in two volumes: 1, Political History; 2, Culture and Society.

Mazar, Amihai. "The United Monarchy" and "General Aspects of Israelite Material Culture." In *Archaeology of the Land of the Bible 10,000–586 B.C.E.,* chaps. 9 and 11. New York: Doubleday, 1990. A balanced presentation of the archaeological evidence for the early monarchy.

Meyers, Carol. "David as Temple Builder." In *Ancient Israelite Religion: Essays in Honor of Frank Moore Cross,* ed. Patrick D. Miller Jr., Paul D. Hanson, S. Dean McBride, 357–76. Philadelphia: Fortress, 1987. An examination of David's building activities, including the beginning of temple construction, as part of imperial domination.

———. "The Israelite Empire: In Defense of King Solomon." In *Backgrounds for the Bible,* ed. David Noel Freedman and Michael Patrick O'Connor, 181–98. Winona Lake, Ind.: Eisenbrauns, 1987. An analysis of Solomon's policies as necessary for maintaining his father's regime rather than as exploitative royal materialism.

———. "Temple, Jerusalem." In *Anchor Bible Dictionary*, ed. David Noel Freedman, 6.350–69. New York: Doubleday, 1992. A full treatment of the architectural and artistic features as well as the symbolic, religious, economic, and sociopolitical aspects of the Temple built by Solomon and its successors.

CHAPTER SIX

A Land Divided

Judah and Israel from the Death of Solomon to the Fall of Samaria

EDWARD F. CAMPBELL JR.

Solomon died in 928 BCE, amid severe strains in Israel's body politic and on the international scene. Almost immediately, his state was split into two unequal parts, to be centered on Samaria in the north and Jerusalem in the south. Two hundred years later, Assyria would put an end to the era that had started with Solomon's death, destroying Samaria's society and infrastructure and so threatening Jerusalem that its life could never again be the same. This troubled era is the focus of this chapter.

The two political entities, self-designated as "Israel" and "Judah," rubbed against one another at a boundary in the tribal territory of Benjamin, only 15 kilometers (10 miles) north of Jerusalem. Beginning there, the boundary curved south and east, encompassing within Israel all the fertile Jordan Valley. To the west the line ran to the Mediterranean, meeting the boundary of Philistia as it neared the coast. Israel held the coast from the Mount Carmel peninsula past Dor to Joppa, between Phoenicia and Philistia. At times the Israel-Judah borderline was contested, but mostly it just existed and was probably quite permeable. To judge from the earlier history of the land and from settlement patterns, the boundary followed a line of social and cultural fracture of long duration. In the fourteenth-century Amarna period, two city-states had flanked it, Shechem in the central hill country and Jerusalem. Ancient settlements known from archaeological surveys are more numerous from Bethel to Jerusalem and around Shechem; a strip of land from Ramallah to the Valley of Lubban between these two clusters had few ancient sites. When they were strong, the two kingdoms together controlled the same territory as had the Davidic-Solomonic empire, but in times of weakness they both contracted drastically.

Even when strong, Israel was separated from the Mediterranean by the extended strip of the Phoenician coast, though generally relations between Israel and the Phoenicians were established by treaty and remained stable. To the north and east of Israel lay the Aramean states of modern Syria, notably the kingdoms centered on Hamath and Damascus. Israel's conflicts were mostly with Damascus, which almost constantly contested its control of northern Transjordan. Much of the time, Israelite rule extended from the regions of Gilead and Bashan southward to Moab—as far as the Arnon River, which reaches the Dead Sea halfway down its eastern shoreline. Whenever Moab submitted to Israel, Israel's influence reached farther south and encountered Edom near the south end of the Dead Sea. Ammon, lying between Israelite land and the desert to the east, played a minor role during the period of the Divided Monarchy.

Judah, by contrast, was effectively landlocked. To its south in the forbidding territory of the northern Negeb, reaching down to the tip of the Red Sea at Elath, it vied with Edom. When strong, Judah held the copper and iron resources of the Arabah, and it exported and imported through Elath. Its core territory, though, was a rough rectangle lying between the boundary with Israel in the north and Beer-sheba and Arad to the south—about 80 kilometers (50 miles) north-south and, from Philistia to the Dead Sea, hardly 60 kilometers (38 miles) east-west.

When rulers of the north and south could cooperate and were strong in relation to their neighbors, they controlled the trade routes through the region, both north-south and east-west. Israel had better rainfall and contained the fertile valleys of Jezreel and the Jordan, but Judah held the key to the mineral resources in the south and to the port that gave access to Africa and the Arabian Peninsula. Controlling as they did the land bridge between Eurasia and Africa, both constituted crucial interests for Egypt and Mesopotamia.

The character of the land had an important role in determining the internal well-being of the people and in shaping their relations with neighboring nations. From the boundary south to Jerusalem and past it to the Bethlehem-Hebron region, Judah's land was hilly and cut by extended valleys. Average rainfall diminishes significantly from north to south, and agricultural potential diminishes with it. South of Bethlehem and Hebron stretches even more arid territory, extending to a line from Gaza on the Mediterranean southeast to Beer-sheba and east to Arad, thence to the Dead Sea at a point opposite the south point of the Lisan peninsula, some three-quarters of the way down the Dead Sea coast. With Beer-sheba begins the Negeb, unsuitable for permanent settlement except around oases (Kadesh-barnea, for example), unless specific measures were taken to provision outposts and fortresses.

In Israel, the territory of Ephraim and Manasseh constituted the central highlands, limestone hills with thin soil cover surrounding upland valleys of quite fertile soil. The hills receive enough rain to sustain grain crops and fruit trees, although rainfall amounts vary from year to year and water was (and is) always a matter of concern. Springs, some of them very abundant, flow from the tilted limestone layering of the hills and provide sufficient water for settlements. This central highland region extends to the Jezreel Valley, which angles from the northeast slopes of Mount Carmel southeast to Beth-shan near the Jordan. The valleys were kept free of settlement and covered with agricultural parcels; the villages and towns lay on the low flanks of the hills, while agricultural terracing extended on the adjacent slopes around and above the

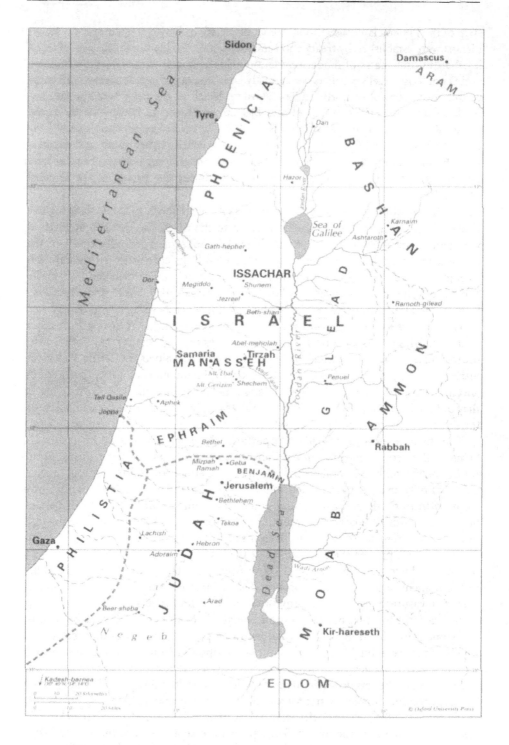

The Divided Monarchy: Judah and Israel from 928 to 722 BCE

villages. Terraces represented in some sense discretionary land—expandable, capable of supporting grain crops, olive and fig trees, and vineyards. Creating terraces, however, was slow work and required patience for the soil to become viable; terraces were no answer to emergencies, such as drought.

The ancient historians of Israel reflect, mostly indirectly, a good deal about these enduring conditions. Their focus, however, is on the course of political history. One of them, the author of the Deuteronomic History (designated "DH" by modern scholars), recounted the story in the books of Kings. The DH was probably first compiled in the eighth century BCE, given definitive form under Josiah in the late seventh century, and augmented in the exile. The other ancient historian, now known as the "Chronicler," composed an edition of the books of Chronicles in the late sixth century that was greatly augmented in subsequent periods.

Both histories saw the division of the monarchy in 928 as a critically important event. The DH used the north's experience as an object lesson for king and people in the southern capital, Jerusalem, during the time of Assyrian control—indeed, turning his history into a manifesto for reform under Judah's kings Hezekiah and Josiah. The Chronicler, however, barely noticed events in the north except where they impinged upon Judah, instead selecting mostly Judean vignettes and shaping them into a picture of how Judah should govern itself after the return from exile in Babylon.

Both historians had sources. The DH made reference to "the Book of the Annals of the Kings of Israel" or "Annals of the Kings of Judah." The Chronicler used the DH and in addition cited "records" of prophets, such as Nathan, Shemaiah, and Iddo. These "records" consisted of traditional lore and stories, notably about the interaction of kings and prophets. Both historians selected radically, citing their sources as though anyone interested could readily consult them.

The historians composed their accounts late in the course of the story of ancient Israel, and they made the perspective of their own times plain for all to see. Prior to their particular outlooks, though, lies another perspective question: What were the social and political commitments that sustained earliest Israel's sense of the meaning of life? Few matters are more deeply contested in biblical interpretation.

This chapter's fundamental assumption is that a widely shared ideology lay deep within the ethos of the people called Israel—one that honored a national deity named Yahweh, who offered and guided the destiny and vocation of his people and who willed an essentially egalitarian social community. If not explicitly articulated in terms of "covenant," this ideology was effectively covenantal. Based in divine gift, human gratitude, and mutual trust, the covenant demanded exclusive loyalty to the deity and human responsibility in communal relations. In such a perspective, government and the practice of community life mattered deeply. So did the conduct of relations with other nations. There could be differences over how leadership should be passed down and over what constituted appropriate loyalty and obedience to the state, but norms of justice and responsibility prevailed. Nor were these norms the exclusive possession of an elite and imposed on the populace. This was a shared ideology, exercising wide influence in the land, in both the north and the south. One carrier was the prophet, institutionalized in those circles of followers who arose to spread his message; another carrier was the amorphous entity called the "people of the land" and the elders of the towns and villages.

Dealing with Sources

As noted earlier, both the DH and Chronicler depended on source material. A few examples may help give a sense both of the character of these sources and of the way historians worked to highlight the ideologies they wished to convey.

Example 1. First Kings 12.1–16 (see also 2 Chron. 10.1–16) tells of an assembly at Shechem at which Rehoboam, Solomon's son, was to be made king by "all Israel." Jeroboam had heard about the assembly and thereupon returned from Egypt, where he had fled when Solomon tried to kill him for rebellion (1 Kings 11.26–28, 40). Jeroboam and the assembly challenged Rehoboam to reduce Solomon's burden of service; after consultation, Rehoboam chose instead to add to it. That was the breaking point, and "all Israel" ended the parley with the poetically structured proclamation:

> What share do we have in David?
>   We have no inheritance in the son of Jesse.
> To your tents, O Israel!
>   Look now to your own house, O David.
>   (1 Kings 12.16)

The cry appeals to the theme of resistance to monarchy expressed in many passages in 1 Samuel, and recalls the ancient ideal of autonomy and freedom from exploitation expressed in Israel's early self-definitions.

This conflict of perceptions about proper royal conduct must lie at the base of the disruption of the United Monarchy. But 1 Kings 12 is not a report; it is a well-told story. Ten of its twenty verses tell of Rehoboam's advisors, the older ones from Solomon's entourage who counsel reducing the burden, and Rehoboam's young cronies who urge turning up the heat. This ironically comic diversion recalls a frequent motif in the DH: watch out whose advice you follow (note Ahithophel and Hushai in 2 Sam. 17, and 1 Kings 12.28). The drama is protracted by the use of a retarding device: having Rehoboam take three days to decide.

Second, the DH editor in verse 15 connects Rehoboam's unwise decision to the prophet Ahijah's divine designation of Jeroboam to receive ten tribes as a kingdom (1 Kings 11.29–39). Thus God fulfills the punishment promised in response to Solomon's idolatry. This prophetic theme of injustice and its consequences is a strong DH concern.

Third, there is a question about Jeroboam's participation in the assembly. The traditional Hebrew text of verse 2 says "Jeroboam stayed in Egypt," not that he returned; this is inconsistent with verses 3 and 12, where Jeroboam is included in the assembly's encounter with Rehoboam, and verse 20 indicates that Jeroboam was summoned to the assembly only after Rehoboam's folly. The Chronicler's parallel in 2 Chronicles 10.2 has "Jeroboam returned" and omits the note about Jeroboam's being summoned and crowned, thus resolving the problem.

Moreover, another stream of tradition, the ancient translation of the Hebrew scriptures into Greek known as the Septuagint, has a twenty-six-verse elaboration after 1 Kings 12.25. This addition provides details about Jeroboam: he had begun an insurrection against Solomon; he returned at Solomon's death and fortified his hometown; he had already received the ill omen of his own failure (found in the traditional Hebrew text in chap. 14); it was he who initiated the assembly at Shechem.

Thus we see in these passages a number of elements. There is a story based on a historical event; there has been editorial work on this material emphasizing that a prophetic promise must be fulfilled; and there is a mix of competing textual traditions about Jeroboam's part in the assembly. Out of such confusing material the modern historian coaxes data.

Example 2. First Kings 20 and 22 tell of three conflicts between Israelite kings (with a Judean cohort in 22) and Ben-hadad of Damascus. In the traditional Hebrew text of 1 Kings 20 the Israelite king is named "Ahab" in verses 2, 13, and 14, but eleven other places in the chapter speak only of "the king of Israel"; other ancient manuscript traditions give Ahab's name at other places as well. First Kings 22.1–38 names the Israelite king Ahab only in verse 20, going on to tell of his death in battle. Verses 39–40 are not part of the narrative; they contain the DH editor's concluding formula, "Now the rest of the acts of Ahab . . ." and speak of Ahab "sleeping with his ancestors," an expression used to signify a natural death.

The circumstances portrayed in the biblical text do not fit Ahab at all well. Israel's military strength seems puny compared to what a text from Shalmaneser III reports Ahab as having contributed at the battle of Qarqar in 853 BCE: a force of two thousand chariots and ten thousand infantry. The Syrians' explanation in 20.23–25 of why they lost the first battle but will win the second—that they will engage Israel not in the hills but in the plains—implies that their advantage lies with chariotry whereas Israel's does not.

A number of historians advocate relocating the three battles in these two chapters into the time of Jehoash or Joash a half century later, after Jehu had ended the Omri-Ahab dynasty and when Israel was less able to cope with the Arameans of Damascus.

These two chapters are narratives about prophets. They address the question of what it means to be a prophet who brings a message to a capable and self-confident court inattentive to God's directives. The emphasis in both chapters is on the conduct proper for any and all kings. Again, a modern historian must assess their historical value in the light of such considerations.

Example 3. In the summers of 1993 and 1994, three chunks of a basalt stela bearing portions of thirteen lines of Aramaic text came to light, incorporated into the ninth/eighth-century BCE fortification wall at the city of Dan. The arrangement of the fragments is nearly certain. The text's content, as well as the ways in which the letters are formed, date it to the ninth century (recently published claims that it is a forgery are untenable). It celebrates victories of an Aramean king over many opponents, among them a king of Israel and a king of the "house of David." The two smaller fragments contain the end of Jehoram's name as king of Israel and the beginning of Ahaziah's name as king of Judah. That points to 842 BCE, when Ahaziah (who reigned only that single year) overlapped with Jehoram (Joram; 851–842). Clear indications in the early part of the text suggest the Aramean king's identity: Hazael (a usurper, even though he refers to his predecessor as his "father") gained the throne of Damascus in 842. Thus the stela recounts Hazael's side of the battle mentioned in 2

Kings 8.25–29 and 2 Chronicles 22.5–9; it also makes plain that later in his reign Hazael could take Dan and there erect a celebrative stela. This is only implied by 2 Kings 13.3–5, 22.

The year 842 coincides with Jehu's purge of the Omri-Ahab dynasty (see below). According to the stela, the Aramean king killed Ahaziah of Judah and apparently also Jehoram of Israel. This conflicts with the account in 2 Kings 9, where Jehu is reported to have killed both kings: Jehoram, recovering from wounds suffered in conflict with Hazael in 9.15, goes out to meet Jehu, who dispatches him, and Ahaziah, visiting Jehoram, flees but is shot down (see also 2 Chron. 22.5–9). The inscription shows that Syria held Dan at least briefly in the ninth century. But the stela's shattered condition and its reuse as building stone attests to the Israelites' recovery of Dan, unceremoniously nullifying an Aramean monument.

Example 4. Excavations at Samaria produced over a hundred ostraca (inked notes on sherds) dating probably from the first part of Jeroboam II's reign (roughly 770 BCE). The notations on each contain all or part of a range of information: a date referring to the king's reign, a place of origin, one or more personal names associated with a product, and the nature of the product (wine or oil). They probably record shipments to be credited to the account of persons resident at the capital. These are not receipts, but notes for a catalogue of incoming supplies.

These notations serve as the raw material for reconstructing life at the capital. Fine commodities are coming in charged to the credit of people who now live in the capital but obtain their produce from their country holdings—they are absentee landlords, or at least offspring of families holding property elsewhere. The commodities are luxury items, not basic provisions. The occupants of the capital complex are, then, functionaries who have come to live there at the behest of the king. It may be that they are provisioned from their own estates. Or, alternatively, the provisions may be imported from the towns and country districts, forming a semicircle with a radius of 15 kilometers (9 miles) to the south of Samaria, which had been laid out as royal lands by the king. From these records scholars have reconstructed a roster of the names of Samaria residents. These names furnish significant historical evidence. A large minority of them are compounded from the divine name *Baal*, but the majority are Yahweh-compound names. Thus the population was religiously cosmopolitan, confirming biblical indications of the kind of court the Israelite kings assembled in Samaria.

The Samaria ostraca give us a snapshot of social history. Since they date only a generation or so before Amos and Hosea, they tell us something about these prophets' audience.

Having looked at these instances of the kind of sources historians must interpret, we can return to the sequence of events.

Division and Conflict

The Shechem assembly marked the collapse of the United Monarchy. According to 1 Kings 12.17–20, Rehoboam sent his supervisor of forced labor, Adoram, on a mission to enforce royal control over the north, but Adoram was stoned to death and Israel's unrest turned into open rebellion. Rehoboam retained control over the tribal territories of Judah and Benjamin, the latter being a narrow strip stretching hardly 15 kilometers (9 miles) north to south and 40 kilometers (25 miles) east to west, just north of Jerusalem. Jeroboam, meanwhile, asserted his rule in the north from points that had defined the Late Bronze Age city-state of Shechem, straddling the boundary between the tribal territories of Ephraim and Manasseh; he "built" (that is, fortified) first the city of Shechem and then Penuel, across the Jordan from the opening of the Wadi el-Farah, which leads down from the Shechem region to the river.

Jeroboam's control north of the central hill country, extending into the Galilean hills, receives virtually no attention in the biblical record. Only one detail stands out: he established as sanctuary centers Dan at the northernmost limit of the land and Bethel on the border between Ephraim and Benjamin. Dan lies about 135 kilometers (85 miles) from Bethel, but it is only 29 kilometers (18 miles—a day's trek) from Bethel to Shechem.

It is plausible that, as 1 Kings 12.28 has it, Jeroboam needed to provide alternatives to worship in Jerusalem. The iconography of the sanctuaries at Bethel and Dan consisted of a gilded bull calf forming a throne or pedestal for God. The biblical account relates that Jeroboam established a priesthood for these sanctuaries, choosing his priests from among the people rather than from Levites (who alone, according to the DH, would have been legitimate). Moreover, Jeroboam is said to have appointed an autumn feast day "on the fifteenth day of the eighth month," a month out of synchronism with the festal schedule in Jerusalem (1 Kings 8.2). Jeroboam also established "high places," a term that for the DH symbolizes apostasy on the part of Israelite as well as Judean kings, and rejection of which is the ultimate criterion of remaining faithful.

These details were supplied by the DH but omitted by the Chronicler, who presumed at least some of them in 2 Chronicles 11.13–17 and 13.8–10. Both streams of historical interpretation denigrate the northern religious establishment for introducing idolatry and violating the appropriate priesthood.

From a more neutral point of view, Jeroboam probably intended to employ earlier iconography of Yahweh drawn from that of El; El as a designation for the god of Israel was doubtless current in the north—hence the validity of using the name Isra-El for the northern political entity. Jeroboam's move, then, was not idolatrous or even newly syncretistic, but probably invoked ancient Israelite traditions, including a legitimate enlistment of priests from among the people. Frank Cross has proposed that Bethel and Dan served a compromise agenda. Jeroboam, he surmises, reestablished the Bethel sanctuary as the locus of Aaronite priestly family hegemony, and Dan (Judg. 18.30) for priests of the Moses line—the two families whom David had placed in Jerusalem (2 Sam. 8.15). In short, Jeroboam's moves were calculated but (from a non-Jerusalem perspective) legitimate. Only from the perspectives of the DH and Chronicles were they idolatrous.

At Bethel, archaeology has provided no information on the Jeroboam sanctuary. At Dan, however, Avraham Biran's excavations have recovered an elevated platform showing at least two phases of development. The core of the platform, some 19 meters (62 feet) long by about 9 meters (29 feet 6 inches) wide and constructed in ashlar masonry, belonged to the Jeroboam era, and was destroyed in the early ninth century BCE. With it went a 5 meters × 6 meters (16 feet 6 inches × 19 feet 9 inches) altar, a plastered pool, and an oil press—an appropriate feature of a sanctuary, since fine oil was needed for religious observance. It is unclear whether a masonry superstructure rose above this platform, or a structure of less permanent material; conceivably what sat on the platform conformed to the tabernacle, not the Solomonic Temple, in contrast to the Jerusalem religious establishment but in accord with "Moses" standards.

From 928 to roughly 882, a conflict raged between the two divisions of the land, both of which also faced an external threat. Rehoboam had returned to Judah: and although the DH had him assemble a vast army (1 Kings 12.21–24) which was deflected from its purpose on orders from Yahweh, the DH offers no detail of battles between north and south. The Chronicler presents one theologically rationalized battle account in 2 Chronicles 13.13–21 involving Jeroboam and Rehoboam's son and successor, Abijah (Abijam), emphasizing the religiously valid south over the invalid north and claiming that Bethel was taken. Such an assertion is hard to credit as historical.

What is reported by both historians is the campaign of Pharaoh Shishak (Shoshenq I) of the Egyptian Dynasty 22 (1 Kings 14.25–28; 2 Chron. 12.2–12). The campaign took the form of a lightning raid that ranged through both north and south. The degree of devastation is hard to assess, either from biblical indications or Shishak's own depiction at Karnak; he claimed to have taken over 150 locales, though whether by destroying them or receiving their capitulation is not clear. The Chronicler reports Rehoboam's capitulation of Jerusalem. Archaeology shows that a number of sites in the central Negeb highlands, which Solomon had established as fortresses, were put out of commission. Towns all along the coastal route show signs of having been attacked, and Megiddo, in the pass through the Carmel range, suffered extensive damage; Shishak left a victory stela there. An Egyptian foray into the central hills attacked Shechem and other upland locales, though the Bible says nothing of how this affected Jeroboam. It would seem that Shishak raided the north as a show of strength but let it go at that, or at least could not follow up any advantage he had gained.

The Egyptian raid came in the fifth year of the Divided Monarchy, according to the Bible. What relation the raid bore to the loss of Solomon's empire holdings cannot be said, but apparently the division of Israel from Judah cost the divided monarchies any grip on the entities surrounding them. Philistia (1 Kings 15.27), Ammon (by inference), Moab (to judge from the Mesha inscription, see below), and perhaps Edom all seem to have broken loose from Israel and Judah. One indicator of the loss of control is the report in 2 Chronicles 11.5–12 of the fifteen towns Rehoboam fortified in an arc around Jerusalem, none farther from the capital than Lachish (about 43 kilometers [27 miles]) or Adoraim (about 35 kilometers [22 miles]). Israel and Judah had become minor players within the larger international scene.

The DH and the Chronicler agree in assigning twenty-two years of reign to Jeroboam and seventeen to Rehoboam. But with that begins a problem of keeping clear the chronology. Two systems are available: either numbers of years for each king's reign, such as could be derived from annals; or synchronisms between kings, for which parallels are harder to find. Data of both types are distributed throughout 1 Kings 14–22 and 2 Chronicles 12–18, which carry events down to the death of Ahab.

The difficulty is that although the synchronisms work out, the years from the division to Ahab's death, synchronized with Jehoshaphat's third year (1 Kings 22.12, though Ahab is not named), add up to eighty-three or eighty-four years. That would put Ahab's death in 844 BCE—more than a decade after the date suggested in Assyrian records. By the Assyrian reckoning, Jehu took the throne in 842, and there remain still two Israelite kings, Ahaziah and Jehoram, with nine years assigned to them, to fit in between Ahab's death and Jehu's rise. Even if an earlier starting date is chosen, usually 931 BCE, the regnal years do not add up. Students of chronology have tried to resolve the difficulty by assuming co-regencies and varying dating systems, but no completely satisfactory solution has ever been worked out. Apparently neither the DH nor the Chronicler thought it necessary to clear up the problem.

The period from Jeroboam through Elah in the north (some forty-six years, 928–882) and from Rehoboam to the end of Asa's reign in Judah (about sixty-one years, 928–867) receives little attention from the DH and only a little more from the Chronicler. Jeroboam's son Nadab reigned for something under two years and was assassinated by Baasha, from the territory of Issachar, just north of the central hills on the other side of the Jezreel Valley. This was the first of three violent upheavals within a quarter century in the north, and it signals the region's characteristic attitude toward the crown. In the south, which followed the dynastic principle of succession and where violent usurpation usually occurred within the Davidic family, Rehoboam was succeeded by Abijah for three years and then by Asa, Abijah's son, for a forty-one-year reign. The DH and the Chronicler part company on the events they narrate, DH focusing on the north and the Chronicler on the south.

Baasha's reign occurred within the span of Asa's much longer one. Both sources report a struggle over the boundary between the two nations, and both introduce King Ben-hadad of Damascus (1 Kings 15.16–22; 2 Chron. 16.1–6). Baasha pushed down to Ramah in Benjamin first, but Asa persuaded Ben-hadad to break a previous alliance with Baasha and press his rival on the north; this diversion worked, so that Asa could move the boundary a few kilometers north of Ramah, to Mizpah and Geba, where it apparently remained for as long as the two kingdoms survived. The appearance on the scene of Ben-hadad meant the temporary loss of much of the far north of Israel, including Dan. The latter's destruction appears to have terminated the first phase of the Dan sanctuary. The date would have been in the decade prior to 882, although on this matter the Chronicler (2 Chron. 16.1) and the DH (1 Kings 16.5–8) flatly disagree. Syria has now become a part of the story for the northern kingdom.

Asa receives high marks from the DH, but in very general terms (1 Kings 15.9–15). The Chronicler fills out the story with a description of his religious reforms and of the peace over which he reigned, combined with narratives about prophets (Azariah ben-Oded in 2 Chron. 15.1–7; Hanani "the seer" in 16.7–10) and an account of an otherwise unattested combat with "Zerah the Ethiopian," which has fabulous elements to it but certainly enhances Asa's stature. It is noteworthy that archaeological work in Judah has found little to distinguish ninth-century remains from those of the eighth, and thus to illumine events told by the Chronicler for this stretch of time.

The first phase of the lives of the two divided nations ends with the assassination of Baasha's son Elah, who reigned less than two years, and the concluding years of

Asa. While short on political detail, the brief portrayals in the biblical histories display the ideologies at work as the two kingdoms go their separate ways.

The first pointer to the distinction in ideologies between Israel and Judah is the role of Shechem in the story of the division. This city, which in the seventeenth and sixteenth centuries BCE contained the largest Canaanite temple structure preserved from ancient Palestine, played a powerful role in Israel's memory. Successive phases of the old sanctuary lasted down to about 1150 BCE. Traditions about crucial events from the days of the tribal confederation cluster about Shechem: the covenant ceremony in Joshua 24; the story in Judges 9 of Abimelech's attempt to reestablish a Canaanite city-state entity there, with oath taking at the temple of El/Baal of the Covenant; the directive to Moses in Deuteronomy 27.4 to place the stones with the terms of the covenant at an altar on Mount Ebal, just above Shechem, and the fulfillment of this directive by Joshua (Josh. 8.30–35); and the cursing and blessing ritual of Deuteronomy 11.26–32 (see also 27.11–26). In the traditions of Israel's forebears, Abraham, Jacob, and Joseph all find their way to Shechem. Narratives about Abraham (Gen. 12.6–7) and Jacob (Gen. 33.18–20 with 35.1–4) both involve sacred sites there.

So deeply does the theme of covenant at Shechem pervade the book of Deuteronomy and the work of the DH that a modern historian must offer a judgment about the heritage of the Deuteronomic tradition and its part in shaping the royal ideologies of Israel and Judah, as well as in forming the prophets' perspective and in creating the expectations of the people who called themselves Israel.

Virtually all scholars agree that the book of Deuteronomy—or at least a good part of it (chapters 5–26 and 28 are often nominated)—was the scroll found in the Temple when Josiah was carrying out his reforms in the last quarter of the seventh century BCE. Its concerns, however, do not suggest that it was a Jerusalem-oriented document. It focuses primarily on the Levites from the countryside. It is full of attention to the Mosaic covenant at Horeb, and it speaks of a prophet like Moses. Its theological perspective emphasizes worship at a central location where Yahweh has placed the "name" that gives people access to the divine. But Deuteronomy never designates that central location as Jerusalem. On the matter of how Israel is to be governed, it carries an ideology at odds with that of Jerusalem. In only one passage does it discuss kingship (Deut. 17.14–20), and there its tone evinces opposition to the way Solomon conducted his reign.

All these indicators suggest that Deuteronomy originated outside Jerusalem—among Levites of the "Moses" rather than the "Aaron" leaning, steeped in the ancient Exodus-Sinai covenantal tradition, suspicious of many of the accommodations that monarchy entailed. Levites were distributed throughout the land. Joshua 21 lists the Levitical cities, a list that antedates the United Monarchy, although it was augmented and schematized under David and probably subsequently revised. The geographical listing implies differences in perspective among Levitical groups, related to their family connection.

Shechem stands out both as a Levitical city and as a "city of refuge" (Josh. 21.20–21; 20.9), with a family connection to the Kohathites among the Levites. It is quite plausible that Levites at Shechem leaned toward the Moses perspective, which had been nurtured at an ancient sanctuary with covenantal ties. Such is the perspective reflected in 1 Kings 12—dubious of monarchy at least in its Davidic-Solomonic manifestation, and egalitarian in social perspective. At Shechem Jeroboam began his reign. But here Jeroboam finally did not stay, probably because of the accommodations he felt he needed to make in maintaining his style of monarchy. He moved his capital to Tirzah (1 Kings 14.17; 15.21, 33), and placed his sanctuaries at Bethel and Dan.

Shechem emerges, then, as a candidate for the place of origin and maintenance of early Deuteronomic thought. A modern historian must resort to indirect reasoning to reach this conclusion: both the DH and the Chronicler display a powerful Jerusalem bias, and they obviously adapt ancient traditions in validating Jerusalem and the Davidic line. Fortunately, the DH especially chose the path of adaptation, not fabrication, and so left the footprints of Shechemite/Levitical perspective to be discerned in his finished product.

The pathway of "proto-Deuteronomy," northern and Levitical in perspective, moves on through the ninth and eighth centuries BCE (Hos. 6.9). It is carried south to Jerusalem by Levite refugees fleeing from the fall of Samaria in 722. What was by then a "book" went underground after the time of Hezekiah, reemerging with Josiah's reform and thereafter guiding and disciplining the work of the historian who composed the DH.

A second pointer to ideological distinctions between north and south, related to the Shechem covenantal one, is the attitude toward kingship characteristic of the north. In 1951, the historian Albrecht Alt contrasted a "dynastic" style in the south and a "charismatic" style in the north, at least until the Omri dynasty came to the throne. We now must give nuance to this contrast. In the northern kingdom Jeroboam's son Nadab succeeded his father to the throne, and although a number of disruptions occurred (beginning with Baasha), the expectation of dynastic succession applied. The story of the north is filled with indications of God's displeasure with various kings' actions, often expressed by prophetic figures; sometimes these prophets help stimulate the removal of kings—note Ahijah's interventions with both Jeroboam and Baasha. But it is not the case that each king is installed solely on the basis of popular acclamation and divine approbation, with no expectation of dynastic succession; sons can and do succeed fathers. Furthermore, repeated indications of accommodation to pragmatic considerations filter through the DH's account. Jeroboam emerges as both a good leader and a failed one; so will Omri and Ahab. No northern king will receive the DH's blanket approval, but there are indications that many in the north considered dynastic kingship valid. Standards had to do with religious compromise and with whether the king cared for the poor and the needy, the widow and the orphan.

There was, then, a continuum of ideology about kingship. The Deuteronomy tradition sketched above was one articulation, dubious about kingship, with the passage about kings in 17.14–20 as a grudging concession (unless it is a late addition tailored to the reign of Josiah, which would leave "original" Deuteronomy silent on the issue of monarchy). Others in the north emphasized the validity of a kingship that practiced righteousness, placing beside the king the equally potent institution of the prophet as an established office in the ideology of governance. Theologically, this view was wedded to the claim that God, who desired a righteous realm, would intervene to promote peace and justice.

An expression of this assertion of God's freedom, only slightly different from that of the Deuteronomic stream, may be the northern stream of tradition about Israel's origin. This strain is known in literary analysis as E, the work of the "Elohist." Although it is difficult to isolate E in Genesis and Exodus, and it may not be present at all in Leviticus and Numbers, it emphasizes the themes of righteousness and accountability. The Elohist history strives to protect God's transcendence and freedom to act; it features prophetic persons and prophetic action; it emphasizes the fear of God (Hebrew *'elohim*) as motive for vocation and living; and it can condone rebellion if a leader's behavior demands it. It presents stories of the north, enhancing the portrayal of Jacob and featuring Joseph and his sons Ephraim and Manasseh, and it gives particular attention to the founding of religious centers of the north, notably Shechem and Bethel.

As with proto-Deuteronomy, E's origins and agenda glimmer dimly through the dominant Jerusalem perspective. Was the Elohist work a stream of tradition independent of J, the Yahwist stream, which supported the Solomonic monarchy? Most scholars have seen it that way. But recently Robert Coote has proposed instead that E is a statement of Jeroboam's political ideology, composed under the aegis of his court and consisting of an augmentation of J, turning it toward support for the northern style of monarchy. Coote's view has the virtue of accounting for E's qualified approval of a certain governance style, and it gives E a time, a place, and a purpose. But the more widely held alternative view—that E came from prophetic circles in the north and dates from the ninth century after some experience of monarchy—can still be defended.

From Omri to Jehu

The shortest "dynasty" to sit on a biblical throne was Zimri's: "In the twenty-seventh year of King Asa of Judah [ca. 882], Zimri reigned seven days in Tirzah" (1 Kings 16.15). Commander of half of Elah's chariot corps, Zimri struck down Elah, who is pictured as drunk and incompetent, and wiped out the heirs of the Baasha family. Omri, the army commander, who was out fighting Philistines, was proclaimed king by the army in the field. He led the troops to Tirzah, where he torched the city and the citadel, burning Zimri to death.

All this is the subject of a rapid-fire report in the biblical text. Afterwards we learn that Omri faced a rival, one Tibni, to whom half of the people were loyal, and that it took several years to resolve this clash in Omri's favor. Omri then "reigned for twelve years, six of them in Tirzah" (1 Kings 16.21–23). The Chronicler never mentions Omri. There are two noteworthy gaps in our information about Omri. We hear nothing about his origins within the tribal system. And there is no report of a prophet at work; if anything, the military seems to be the instigating factor, and neither the sources nor the editor give any hint of divine approval or disapproval. This is odd in a historical presentation that has already used prophetic narrative to account for transitions in government and that will do so again in what follows. Only one notice appears about Omri's activities as king: how he acquired the hill of Samaria, fortified it, and named it after its preceding owner, Shemer. Shechem and Tirzah recede into the shadows, and Samaria takes over as capital.

Other historical sources, however, suggest that with Omri and his son Ahab, Israel entered upon an era of strong leadership and political—even international—prominence. The Mesha inscription on the Moabite Stone credits the Omri dynasty with regaining control of Moab, all the way south to the midpoint of the Dead Sea at the Arnon River. And as we have already seen, Ahab, Omri's son, is named by the Assyrian king Shalmaneser as a major player in the confrontation at Qarqar in 853 BCE, with a substantial military force. The nomenclature *house of Omri* will in Assyrian records continue to be a designation for the northern kingdom, long after the dynasty ended.

There is substantial archaeological evidence of Omri's and Ahab's activities. At Samaria, clarification of the stratigraphy and pottery is emerging from a meticulous analysis by Ron E. Tappy, employing the field diaries and sketches of Kathleen Kenyon as she explored the region of the "ivory house," dug in 1932–35. Confirming the biblical mention of Omri's purchase of the estate of Shemer, archaeology reveals that Omri built the first structures of a citadel on the remains of a preceding establishment. He constructed an enclosure wall, laid a yellow plaster flooring as living surface within it, and built a complex of rooms. Ahab then extended the citadel's size with a casemate wall (cross-walls joining two parallel wall lines to form chambers, or "casemates") outside the line of Omri's structure, laid a new white surfacing that in some cases displaced Omri's yellow one, and expanded the interior complex of rooms. Ahab's citadel covered some 1.6 hectares (4 acres), measuring 89 meters × 178 meters (290 feet × 584 feet).

The walls of major structures in both the Omri and Ahab phases were built of finely squared blocks of stone, called ashlars, fitted together so well that no chinking was needed. They were laid up in "header-stretcher" style, a hallmark of royal building technique in both Israel and Judah throughout the monarchy. Another hallmark is the use of "proto-Aeolic" capitals, six of which were uncovered along the east limit of the citadel; at Samaria they cannot be dated securely to the Omri-Ahab phases, but they may have topped pilasters at an eastern entrance during this period. Quarrying and shaping these ashlars and capitals required skilled workers, as well as large numbers of people to haul and lift; they lived, presumably, elsewhere on the hill of Samaria, outside the citadel, in homes that have not been the target of archaeological study. Within the citadel compound, the earlier Harvard excavations revealed parts of the palace complex that also show two phases of construction, probably attributable first to Omri and then to Ahab.

In the DH's standard evaluating verses describing Ahab (1 Kings 22.39–40), mention is made of an "ivory house that he built." Kenyon's excavations found quantities of burned ivory furniture inlay, as well as figures carved in the round, in the debris of the structure designated "ivory house" on the plan. Tappy's scrutiny of Kenyon's diaries has raised serious doubts about whether any of the ivories belong to Omri-Ahab layers, and Tappy has shown that Jehu reused the Omri-Ahab structures without destroying them. The ivories come, with one possible exception, from layers higher in the stratigraphy; more will be said about them in the section on Jeroboam II.

"And all the cities that he built," says 1 Kings 22.39 of Ahab. It is Ahab to whom archaeologists assign major building projects at other key northern sites, notably Dan, Hazor, Megiddo, and Tirzah (Tell el-Farah [N]). He expanded the sanctuary platform at Dan to form a square of ashlar masonry 19 meters × 19 meters (62 feet × 62 feet), with steps leading down from it to an enclosed precinct, in addition to building fortifications and a planned city with cobbled streets. Apparently, Ahab continued the Jeroboam religious arrangement of two sanctuary centers; one "horn" of a large altar has turned up in the precinct.

Ahab seems also to have expanded greatly the settlement at Hazor (Stratum VIII), constructing a citadel at the neck of the bottle-shaped mound. Two proto-Aeolic capitals found there support archaeologists' suppositions about pilastered entrances to public structures dating from the time of Ahab at Samaria. The citadel stands at the opposite end of town from a storage complex with a granary, on a terrace at the east; this suggests that Hazor was both a military strong point and a store-city for agricultural supplies, either for military or for public consumption.

A more spectacular find at Hazor is the elaborate shaft and tunnel cut deep into the mound's interior, which gave access to the water table beneath. The work attests to the builders' technical knowledge of hydrology, as well as to their sensible recognition that it is safer to protect the city by not opening a tunnel to an outside spring and thereby giving an enemy possible access (recall David's capture of Jerusalem in 2 Sam. 5.8). Presumably much of the workforce that built Hazor lived in the houses and thrived in the shops that fill the rest of the hilltop, a total space of roughly 6.5 hectares (16 acres) with a population of perhaps 1,500.

At Megiddo the Iron Age stratigraphy is disputed, but a majority of scholars still tend to assign the origin of Stratum IVA to Ahab, including the laying out of huge areas as chariot parks adjacent to pillared buildings identified as stables for the horses. Another large amount of space within the massively fortified city was given to the water system, which in this case involved a tunnel leading outside the fortifications to the spring. A major public building at the east edge of town has been proposed as a palace, although it does not occupy the usually favored location—upwind, at the west edge of town. Megiddo does not manifest changes in layout during the ninth and eighth centuries BCE as Samaria and Hazor do; its Stratum IVA plan persists until the end of the Divided Monarchy.

Tirzah shows similar continuity throughout the ninth and eighth centuries, although there is tantalizing evidence of an unfinished phase of building (Stratum VIIc) that might belong to the rapid series of events in the transition from Baasha's dynasty to Omri. The next phase (Stratum VIId) is a well-planned city; Ahab may have been its founder.

Ahab, then, was a builder, and, to judge from Megiddo and Hazor, part of what he built was military. The most explicit indication of his military strength comes from the report of a crucial battle to which the Bible makes no reference, the battle of Qarqar in 853 BCE. Information about it comes from Assyrian sources. Assyria had begun looking westward, seeking control of trade routes to the Mediterranean, under Ashurnasirpal, who ruled Assyria from near the beginning of Omri's reign through much of Ahab's. Successor to Ashurnasirpal was Shalmaneser III, who came to Assyria's throne about 858 BCE. Early in his reign, he began to threaten northern Syria.

In his sixth year, according to the boastful "Monolith Inscription" on which are recorded his early successes, he campaigned westward across the upper Euphrates, past Aleppo (which capitulated) into the Syrian state of Hamath along the east side of the Orontes River, well north of Damascus. At Qarqar on that river, which his inscription designates the royal city of Hamath's ruler, Irhuleni, he met a coalition of forces from twelve locales that included Hamath, Damascus under Hadadezer, and Israel under Ahab. Ahab's force consisted of 10,000 men and 2,000 chariots, outnumbering the 1,910 chariots supplied by all the other allies together and equaling what Shalmaneser himself threw into the battle. The Assyrian king claims to have utterly devastated his foes and captured all their chariots, cavalry, and horses—but seems himself to have stopped at Qarqar. The clash may indeed have stalled Assyrian moves westward for a time, since Shalmaneser waited four years before returning. Three further campaigns in 849, 848, and 845 are known from more formulaic records, which name the two Syrian kings and in one case speak of the twelve-king coalition. All the attacks stall in the Orontes Valley. No Israelite presence is mentioned in these accounts.

Military forces mean many men and the disruption of many families. Building enterprises imply many workers, mostly men. Both may have meant income or largesse for Israelite families, but both would have exacted hardships. In an economy based on agriculture carried out by extended families on patrimonial holdings, and on cottage industries in homes and local shops, how were human resources deployed? The Bible provides little direct information, but analogies from social and cultural anthropology cast some light. Family property rights passed from father to son (or occasionally to daughter). While high infant mortality and somewhat restricted birthrates may have prevented rapid population growth, some families found themselves with too many heirs for the system of land inheritance within the family to sustain. A family with several sons would have had to parcel out small holdings, eventually resulting in tiny, irreducible plots. In the monarchic period, no new land could be added to a family's holdings by "pushing back the frontier," and apparently new acquisitions by military conquest became crown property. The army, then, was probably made up of younger sons of families that could no longer divide their land. The priesthood, too, may have been drawn from this resource, and it may also have supplied the workforce that built Ahab's cities. We cannot know whether and to what extent this process would have begun to cause the typical Israelite family hardship; presumably things went well most of the time, but prospects for economic and social difficulties loomed.

Against this background, let us try to understand the biblical depiction of the Omri-Ahab dynasty. In it the kings are not at the fore; it is the prophets who dominate the scene. The material in DH begins with a diplomatic marriage between Ahab and the daughter of King Ethbaal of Sidon. Her name is Jezebel. Apparently in accord with this alliance, Ahab is reported to have placed an altar and a temple for Baal worship in Samaria, together with an *asherah*—a pillar representing the tree sacred to the goddess Asherah, a consort of Baal. Jezebel was the patron of this establishment, Ahab the accomplice.

Onto this scene came Elijah and the divine decision to bring drought upon the land. A series of wondrous stories about the prophet's care of the poor widow of

Zarephath removes him from contact with the king as the drought unfolds and
famine strikes the land. Meanwhile it is noted that Jezebel has been killing off Yahweh's prophets. Elijah reappears to tell Ahab that the drought will end, but in doing
so he puts the blame for the drought on Ahab's worship of the Baals. Since Baal is,
among other things, deity of fertility and storm, irony pervades the unfolding drama.
There ensues the mighty contest on Mount Carmel, with Elijah standing alone
"against the four hundred fifty prophets of Baal and the four hundred prophets of
Asherah, who eat at Jezebel's table" (1 Kings 18.19). The immediately succeeding
chapter then shows Elijah's flight to Mount Horeb, where his success as the lone
faithful Yahwist on Mount Carmel reverses into his desolate sense of failure at the
place where he will meet his divine recommission:

> Go, return on your way to the wilderness of Damascus; when you arrive, you shall
> anoint Hazael as king over Aram. Also you shall anoint Jehu son of Nimshi as king
> over Israel; and you shall anoint Elisha son of Shaphat of Abel-meholah as prophet
> in your place. And whoever escapes from the sword of Hazael, Jehu shall kill; and
> whoever escapes from the sword of Jehu, Elisha shall kill. Yet I will leave seven
> thousand in Israel, all the knees that have not bowed to Baal, and every mouth that
> has not kissed him. (1 Kings 19.15–18)

The DH and the Chronicler present the prophets as wonder-workers. In these
accounts the prophets are shown as occupying a particular office and playing an
accepted role in the public life of ancient Israel and Judah, including the life of the
general populace. Being confronted with prophets surprises neither king nor people.
In the stories of prophets whom the DH sets in the ninth-century BCE, notably Elijah,
Elisha, and Micaiah, these men appear as lone actors—especially in conflicts with
other prophetic figures saying the opposite. It is inappropriate to describe prophets
as isolated eccentrics and malcontents operating as free agents. Rather, they are part
of a social phenomenon, the bands and groups of prophets, such as those whom
Jezebel tries to kill off as well as those who eat at her table. Even the seven thousand
who have not bowed the knee to Baal appear as a part of a support system, about
whom Elijah has perhaps forgotten. Regularly, Elijah and Elisha use members of their
prophetic groups as agents to carry out their prophetic tasks.

Individually or in groups, the prophets' allegiance is to the will of Israel's deity,
to whom they have access when the deity wishes. Their visits force decision upon
their audience: Is this person a true spokesperson for deity, or a fake? There is no
way to avoid the recognition that the ancient historians, DH and the Chronicler, take
prophets and their role as part of historical reality, whether what they have to say is
palatable or not.

Were prophets agents of revolution? Ahijah commissioned both Jeroboam and
Baasha to rebel against existing authority. Omri received no such prophetic warrant,
but Jehu did. Yet the prophet is not pictured as a revolutionary. At most, the prophet
speaks for a combination of divine displeasure and human disillusionment. No complete contrast separates the prophets' commissionings of Jeroboam, Baasha, and Jehu
from the commissioning of Omri by a popular movement of the army. At the
Shechem assembly, Jeroboam's divine commissioning by Ahijah is wedded to the
human circumstance of outcry against unjust rule. Both sets of circumstances reveal

the central issue of good governance and the pursuit of justice for people, a check upon royal prerogative. And good governance fundamentally means the practice of loyalty to God.

The prophetic story in 1 Kings 21 stands out. Ahab has a palace in a town called Jezreel (see 1 Kings 18.45–46), lying at the edge of the valley of the same name some 50 kilometers (30 miles) north of Samaria. (The spot is prominent enough in the biblical record to have suggested to some scholars that it was the second capital of the country during the Omri dynasty, perhaps the one where Ahab expressed his loyalty to Israel's deity through a shrine, while Samaria served as the seat of Baal worship.) At Jezreel, Ahab had a family holding.

Naboth also held property in Jezreel, a vineyard that Ahab wanted in exchange. The scenario is based on a patrimonial land tenure system. Naboth's response to Ahab expresses it: this land is inalienable, ancestral. Naboth holds the upper hand, and the king knows it; kings in Israel are bound by the same system as everyone else. Queen Jezebel, however, has a different perspective: "Are you the king of Israel or not?" Using the royal seal, Jezebel then contrives Naboth's downfall and death, and the king takes the land he wanted. Perhaps Ahab and Naboth were related, and Ahab became heir as next in line; or perhaps an otherwise unknown practice allowed the crown to confiscate land owned by a convicted criminal.

Ahab goes to take possession, and Elijah is there to greet him. The end of the dynasty is announced, on the pattern that had ended Jeroboam's and Baasha's dynasties, but because Ahab humbles himself, the divine decision is deferred until Ahab's son's days. But Jezebel, and Ahab through her, will be used by the DH as the symbolic violator of norms.

Other episodes in the cycle of stories about Elijah and Elisha provide information that we cannot take as a record of political history, but which does presume social custom and thus yields insight into social history. An instance comes from 2 Kings 8.1–6. Elisha has lodged with a family in Shunem in the Jezreel Valley; in a story in 2 Kings 4.8–37, he has brought the family's dead son back to life. In that story, the woman of the household, pictured as wealthy, is clearly the active agent, and her husband an aging foil. In 8.1–6, the same woman has been told by Elisha to resettle in Philistia because of an impending seven-year famine in Israel. Upon her return, she appeals to the king for the return of her house and land, and he sends an official to see that she gets her holdings back, together with the revenue her fields yielded to whoever took them over in her absence. The glimpse here of a system of redress, and the fact that women held property and maintained usufruct, are factors in Israelite social practice that do not appear clearly if one takes as guides the collections of law preserved in Exodus, Leviticus, and Deuteronomy. In the common life of Israel, custom and system delivered justice, in this case apparently for a now-widowed person. And the prophetic role includes seeing that such justice is done.

Obscure events of the year 843/842 BCE brought the Omri-Ahab dynasty to an end. According to the Assyrian evidence, Hadadezer has been the king in Damascus; Shalmaneser's inscriptions record him as an opponent in battles on the Orontes between 853 and 845. Another Shalmaneser text reports that he defeated Hadadezer and that Hadadezer died; Hazael, a usurper, took the throne. The text seems to connect the death and the usurpation but says nothing about a murder.

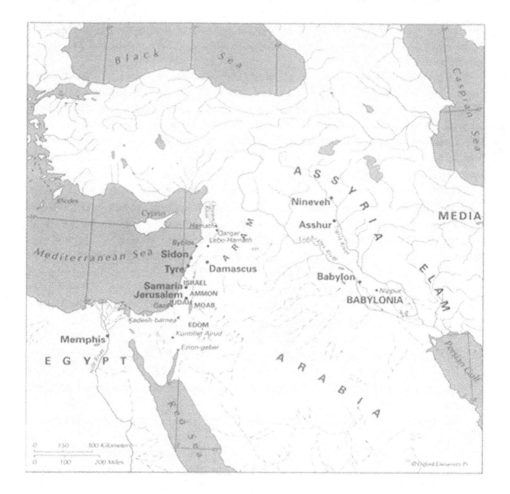

The Near East during the Assyrian Empire

The DH's selection of materials about relations with Syria during Ahab's reign (1 Kings 20; 22; 2 Kings 6.24–7.20) speaks instead of a Ben-hadad, king of Aram (chapter 22 gives the Syrian king only his title, no name). The series culminates in 2 Kings 8.7–15, which reports a visit of Elisha to Damascus during an illness of Ben-hadad. Hazael, in attendance upon Ben-hadad, goes to meet Elisha, and Elisha tells Hazael he will be king of Aram. Hazael thereupon smothers his master and becomes his successor.

As we have already noted, there is legitimate reason to doubt the names of the participants in the stories of Israelite-Syrian battles in 1 Kings 20 and 22 and to suspect that the events belong to a later period. The episode in 2 Kings 6–7 has similar problems: Ben-hadad appears in 6.24, but otherwise no royal figure in the chapter is named. The assertion that Hazael killed Ben-hadad in 2 Kings 8.15 is plain, however, so the discrepancy in the Assyrian and biblical evidence remains.

Proposals to resolve the discrepancy abound. One is to assume that Hadadezer and Ben-hadad are names for the same person, the latter perhaps a typical Syrian throne name. Both sources would then be accurate. A more elaborate theory is that since Shalmaneser's words are ambiguous about a murder and supplanting by Hazael, there was a son of Hadadezer named Ben-hadad, "Ben-hadad II," who reigned for two or three years after Hadadezer's death and before Hazael's usurpation. A third proposal is to claim that Ben-hadad's name is a late addition to the 2 Kings 8 depiction of the death of the king of Aram, which originally had Hadadezer or gave no king's name; thus the biblical account would now be in error. The upshot is that there is a Ben-hadad of Damascus who reigns throughout the early ninth century, then Hadadezer whom Shalmaneser encountered at Qarqar, contemporary with much of Ahab's reign, possibly a Ben-hadad II for a couple of years, and finally Hazael.

The DH gives the overall impression of protracted strife between Israel and the Syrian state of Damascus, with periods of cooperation interspersed (note the three-year respite in 1 Kings 22.1). The alliance for the battle at Qarqar would be one such interlude. The short story of Naaman, the Syrian army commander with leprosy whom Elisha treats with the medicine of the waters of the Jordan (2 Kings 5), suggests both conflict—an Israelite slave girl in Naaman's house—and benign interaction. And whatever decision scholars may reach about the historical settings of the battles in 1 Kings 20 and 22, the account in 20.31–34 speaks of the relationship between the Israelite king and the Syrian king as one of "brotherhood"—that is, treaty-connection—and the placement of bazaars in Damascus and Samaria means reciprocal commercial activity. Less certain is the frequent proposal that ninth-century destruction levels at Dan or Hazor or Shechem result from Syrian military incursions.

The stela from Dan is a case in point. Hazael has clashed with Jehoram of Israel and Ahaziah of Judah in 843 BCE, according to 2 Kings 8.28–29. These two met their deaths either at the hands of Jehu (9.14–28) or at the hands of Hazael himself (the stela, if correctly read). Both the stela and the DH, with the Chronicler in substantial agreement (2 Chron. 22), picture the period leading up to 842 as a time of cooperation between Judah and Israel.

Few sources outside the Bible say much about Judah in the ninth century BCE. No Judean king figures in the Assyrian records, and the Dan stela is the only nonbiblical evidence about relations between Judah and Israel. This led a few historians to wonder whether a Davidic royal establishment and a "covenant with David" might be a fiction, retrojected into the past from Josiah's time or even from the time of the Babylonian exile—that is, from the late seventh or sixth centuries BCE. But this hypothesis has been destroyed by the discovery of the Dan stela, with its inescapable reference to the "house of David."

At Arad, guarding the Judean southern frontier, 25 kilometers (15 miles) west of the Dead Sea, the date of the Solomonic fortress (Stratum XI) has been disputed and may belong to the early ninth century BCE. Beer-sheba, west of Arad in the central northern Negeb, was a fortified Judean town substantially to the south of Rehoboam's string of frontier fortifications, suggesting that Asa's or Jehoshaphat's control extended farther to the south than had Rehoboam's.

Asa's long reign (roughly 908–867 BCE) extended into the opening years of the Omri dynasty, but it was his son Jehoshaphat who ruled Judah throughout Ahab's reign. The DH ushers Jehoshaphat onto the scene in 1 Kings 15.24, in Asa's death notice; it includes him in the Micaiah story and the battle to recover Ramoth-gilead of 1 Kings 22.1–28; and then it gives a brief summation of his reign in 1 Kings 22.41–50. As with Asa, the Chronicler presents significantly more about Jehoshaphat, while giving alternative angles on two of the features the DH had included. The Chronicler criticizes Jehoshaphat for his participation with Israel's king in the Ramoth-gilead battle (2 Chron. 19.1–3), and his narrative about a maritime venture of Jehoshaphat and Ahaziah, son of Ahab, differs strikingly from the DH's account.

This maritime venture involved an effort to build and deploy a mercantile fleet at Ezion-geber, the port at the northern tip of the Red Sea. In 1 Kings 22.47–49, the information is as follows:

> There was no king in Edom; a deputy was king. Jehoshaphat made ships of the Tarshish type to go to Ophir for gold; but they did not go, for the ships were wrecked at Ezion-geber. Then Ahaziah son of Ahab said to Jehoshaphat, "Let my servants go with your servants in the ships," but Jehoshaphat was not willing.

The Chronicler has it this way:

> After this King Jehoshaphat of Judah joined with King Ahaziah of Israel who did wickedly. He joined him in building ships to go to Tarshish; they built the ships in Ezion-geber. Then Eliezer son of Dodavahu of Mareshah prophesied against Jehoshaphat, saying, "Because you have joined with Ahaziah, the LORD will destroy what you have made." And the ships were wrecked and were not able to go to Tarshish. (2 Chron. 20.35–37)

Manifestly the Chronicler opposed Judean alliances with kings of Israel; the story is retold to make the maritime venture a disapproved cooperative one, and it implies that Israel took the initiative, perhaps already having access to Ezion-geber.

The brief notices about this venture suggest that if Judah and Israel could cooperate, working out (by either treaty or submission) arrangements with Phoenicia to the north and Edom to the south, then they could develop on the land bridge from the Mediterranean to the Red Sea a lucrative and mutually beneficial commercial program. The note from 1 Kings 22.47 affirms Edom's compliance, forced or otherwise. The northern end of the trade route was secure with Ahab's relationship to Sidon and Tyre.

Probably the commercial program worked. Current understanding of the archaeological sequence at Tell el-Kheleifeh confirms its identification as the site of Ezion-geber. It still supports Nelson Glueck's original assignment of a stratum to the first half of the ninth century BCE—Jehoshaphat's time. But the only notice about its role as a factor in the economic life of Judah at this time has to do with the wreck of the fleet, apparently before it ever set sail. And for the Chronicler the story provides an object lesson in Jehoshaphat's wickedness.

Ingredients such as these two "reversals" of DH materials have led historians to question whether the Chronicler can be trusted for historical information. But a strong theme in the Chronicler's account commends itself as historical: the twin efforts at administering justice and instructing in just practice. Jehoshaphat's name, probably a throne name, means "Yahweh has judged," or better, "Yahweh has seen to justice." In 2 Chronicles 17.7–9 and 19.4–11, Jehoshaphat is reported to have dispatched officials and Levitical educators throughout Judah. They had "the book of the law of the LORD with them," which sounds like an anachronism consistent with the time of Ezra and Nehemiah, but their task was to inculcate justice in the land and to deal with cases in Judah's fortified cities. Reference is also made to a Judean "court of appeals" in Jerusalem. Consistent administration of law under the royal aegis is plausible enough and may even have been an improvement on local administration. What such efforts to ensure justice would have run up against is perhaps best seen from Ruth 4. Here, a complex set of issues involving land ownership, land transfer, inheritance, and marriage are interwoven in a case requiring the elders of the town and two disputants to work out a satisfactory resolution. Another instance, with a far less benign outcome, forms part of the drama in the Naboth vineyard story, where a trumped-up charge brings down a local notable. There is good reason to credit the tradition of judicial reform under Jehoshaphat, and to connect it with the introduction (or reinstitution) of a district system in Judah suggested by Joshua 15.21–62 and in Benjamin in Joshua 18.21–28. Solomon had districted the north, but there has been no report of a similar administrative move in the south. Jehoshaphat's construction of store-cities and fortresses (2 Chron. 17.12) would have been part of such an administrative reform.

Jehoshaphat's military development, as reported (with improbably large numbers) in 2 Chronicles 17.14–19 clashes with the presumed weakness depicted in 20.5–30. Given Ahab's control over Moab and probably Ammon to its north, victory over these neighboring states and even over Edom strains credulity.

One crucial feature of the relations between Israel and Judah, at least by the end of Ahab's and Jehoshaphat's reigns, does stand out: apparently the two arranged the marriage of Ahab's daughter Athaliah to Jehoshaphat's son Jehoram (2 Kings 8.18)— a potent signal of cooperation between the realms.

The kings who succeeded Jehoshaphat and Ahab would reign only about eight years in each kingdom. Here again, problems arise with the number of years assigned to each. In Israel, Ahab's successors were his sons Ahaziah (parts of two years) and Jehoram (roughly seven, though the DH gives him twelve). In Judah, Jehoram son of Jehoshaphat reigned for seven-plus years and Jehoram's son Ahaziah for less than a year. The duplication of the name *Jehoram*, even if in reverse order, is startling and has led to speculation that the kingdoms were really under one rule, but Athaliah's position is evidence enough of close association.

Each of the short-term successions faced an international problem. Ahab's death seems to have given King Mesha of Moab an opportunity to try to end his subservience to Israel. Notice of this is given in the first verse of 2 Kings, and a remarkable story in 3.5–27 follows it up. Ostensibly, it is another in the series of prophetic stories, in this case involving Elisha, set in the context of a battle plan bringing together Israelite, Judean, and Edomite forces to crush Moab's rebellion. The prophet promises success, and a ruse leads to an ambush of the Moabite army. But the final verse of the account has the Moabite king sacrifice his son on the wall at Kir-hareseth, his last remaining stronghold. Then "great wrath came upon Israel, so they withdrew

from him and returned to their own land" (3.27). Whose wrath? Yahweh's? The
Moabite deity Chemosh's? Whatever is meant, this account is the only one available
to correlate with the words on the Moabite Stone:

> Omri, king of Israel, humbled Moab many days because Chemosh was angry at his
> land. And his son succeeded him, and he also said, "I too will humble Moab." During
> my days he said this, but I have triumphed over him and over his house, and Israel
> has perished forever.

Moab had released itself from Israel's dominance.

For Judah, it was Edom that worked free, during Jehoram's reign (2 Kings 8.20–
22). It was the two rulers in alliance who are reported to have tried to resist Hazael,
in the clash at Ramoth-gilead where Jehoram of Israel was badly wounded (8.28–30).
Into all this rode Jehu.

Jehu's Legacy

Two of the nine chapters the DH devotes to the next 120 years of history concern
themselves with the Jehu purge, and a third is given over to Athaliah's brief queenship
in Judah. Then the DH skips rapidly through events of the Jehu dynasty. This was
the longest-reigning dynasty, at just about a century, that Israel would ever have—
roughly from 842 to 745—and through the fateful final decades of Israel's life as a
nation. By contrast, the Chronicler gives four verses to the Jehu purge and presents
episodic coverage of the period's events in Judah in seven chapters. Complicating
historical reconstruction is the fact that the regnal spans given for Judah's five rulers
for this 100-year period add up to 144 years.

On the other hand, the literary portrayal of the period is enriched by three collections of material belonging to the genre of books named for prophets—Amos,
Hosea, and Isaiah of Jerusalem. These books present not only the prophets' words
but also minimal accounts of their adventures.

Jehu's move had been commissioned through prophetic word, presented to Elijah
but carried out by Elisha. It commenced at the military post in Ramoth-gilead, where
Jehu was holding council with his top army command. Israelite presence at Ramoth-
gilead presumes an advance position in the to-and-fro conflict with Damascus. Once
again, a military leader was selected, and Jehu is given a two-generation patronymic,
son of Jehoshaphat, son of Nimshi (see 2 Chron. 22.7)—which may indicate only
that he was "somebody," though his status is not made clear. The emphasis on
prophetic designation is unusual in the DH, since the outcome is disastrous for Israel
and Judah, and it does not take a prophet or a DH editorial comment to make that
apparent.

Jehu was proclaimed king by his army colleagues and at once set out for Jezreel,
where King Jehoram was recuperating. It was a mark of disenchantment with the old
regime that the messengers who were sent to meet Jehu as he approached joined his
cause. In quick order, Jehoram of Israel, Ahaziah of Judah, Queen Jezebel, and finally
seventy sons of Ahab in Samaria were wiped out. In reporting the demise of the
seventy, the DH offers a sardonic explanation. Jehu gives an intentionally ambiguous
order—"bring me the heads of the royal house" (2 Kings 10.6; my translation)—
which the people of Samaria dutifully obey by decapitating the victims. This allows

Jehu to absolve himself of complicity in the massacre of the king's family, but the report goes on to tell of the sweeping removal of Ahab's entire government: priests, friends, leaders, cronies—together with the whole religious establishment dedicated to the worship of Baal. The Baal temple was turned into a latrine. Moreover, Jehu's force encountered kin of Ahaziah of Judah en route to Samaria, whom Jehu instructed to "take alive." The report is that all forty-two were slaughtered—a curious account, which again implies that Jehu's intent and the sequel are out of accord (2 Kings 10.12–14).

As for the effects of Jehu's purge, the evidence comes in from all directions. Jehu had killed Ahaziah of Judah, leaving Athaliah, Ahab's daughter, a path to the Judean throne, which she quickly secured by wiping out the rest of Ahaziah's family. Any rapport between Israel and Judah ended. The slaughter of Jezebel must have meant the end of association with Phoenicia. Stresses had already developed with Damascus, as the Dan stela makes plain, and now they escalated; the DH mentions this in an expanded summation of Jehu's reign in 1 Kings 10.32–33, reporting Hazael's capture of all the Transjordanian holdings of Israel from Gilead to the Arnon River (Ammon and Moab).

In 841 BCE by Assyrian reckoning, and hence very soon after Jehu's purge, Shalmaneser III campaigned westward again. He left an account of his successes on the Black Obelisk, depicting Jehu groveling before him and recording the tribute he exacted: "Tribute of Jehu, son of Omri: silver, gold, a golden bowl, a golden beaker, pitchers of gold, lead, staves for the hand of the king, javelins. . . ."

The economic impact of closing off the flow of commerce over the Palestinian land bridge from Phoenicia to the Red Sea can only be guessed. Most farmers and herders, probably 85 percent of the population, would have hardly noticed. Their lot was largely fixed, except that they could elect to turn some of their terraced strips and even valley floors to the raising of surplus olives and grapes if there were consumers with resources to make it worthwhile doing so—and if it seemed worth the risk of turning away from grain staples. Given the uncertainty of sufficient rain from one year to the next, they probably stayed with their survival base, although some would have taken the risk of growing for profit. Presumably, a merchant and commercial element developed, when there was peace along the line of commercial flow. They would have been the ones to feel hardest the impact of choking off trade, as would the royal court, their consumers.

Archaeology indicates that iron smelting and forging to produce agricultural tools was done locally, but the iron ore sources were in the south, on both sides of the Dead Sea and on down into the Arabah. These sources were inaccessible without an entente with Edom and (for Israel) passage through Judah. The importing of more exotic commodities (such as spices, incense, and gold) would have stopped. If the absence of such luxury (and ritual) items marks an economic downturn, both Israel and Judah would have suffered from it during the Jehu aftermath. The DH and the Chronicler gave only the barest of hints about these matters. Prophetic writings and archaeological artifacts point out social and economic conditions more explicitly.

The biblical historians treat Athaliah's reign in Jerusalem sparely, but the story of court intrigue dominates what we hear. A sister of Ahaziah and daughter of Jehoram—that is, a woman specifically identified as being in the direct line of the

Davidic monarchy—Jehosheba (in Chronicles Jehoshabeath) by name, was able to hide one surviving son of Ahaziah, Jehoash, within the royal palace for six years. A priest named Jehoida, whom the Chronicler identifies as Jehosheba's husband, engineered this seven-year-old's placement on the throne. The ceremony and the language marking that placement recall themes both of a royal covenant with the Davidic line and a covenant between deity and community based in the commitments associated with Sinai (compare 2 Kings 23 and the activity of Josiah).

Especially important in this narrative is the appearance of a segment of the population designated "the people of the land" (2 Kings 11.14, 18, 20) who ratified and rejoiced over what had happened. This societal ingredient was important to the DH's account of reform and the implementation of traditional values throughout the remainder of the Judean monarchy. These people were some sort of landed gentry, a group with tangible political influence. Given what has been said about land tenure and patrimony, they were probably heads of households with landholdings who retained political influence, the younger sons serving in the military and the priesthood. Some such interlock between the people and the monarchy would mean that this was a popular movement, not merely the activity of a small elite, but for such an interpretation much depends on the degree to which land tenure had moved out of the hands of the many and into those of a few. The narrative in 2 Kings 11.4–21 seems to be depicting a popular overthrow of the current rule.

Note that the queen could assert control, and note further that the story does not suggest her gender being the primary factor in DH's negative judgment on her reign. Instead the focus falls on the existence of a temple to Baal in Jerusalem—the first reference to such an institution there—implying that the fault lay in Athaliah's membership in the Omri-Ahab line, sharing its religious perspective. When the clash came that ended her reign, she could cry "Treason!" (2 Kings 11:14). Implicitly her rule is conceded by the DH to have been considered legitimate at least by parts of the Jerusalem establishment. The story provides a rare glimpse of the people and institutions of Judah—a cycle of guards captained by military leaders which went on and off duty on the Sabbath; a priest of Yahweh's Temple who could bring to bear sanction and equipage; a pillar that emblemized royal designation and/or authority; a group called the Carites who formed a kind of praetorian guard; the action of the "people of the land." For the DH to narrate so much about the Judean monarchs is unusual. The chapter is a unique resource for institutional history. The Chronicler's account of the incident presents other details, including replacing the cycle of military with Levites from throughout Judah and designating the participants as "the whole assembly." These are hints of other ideologies at work, but they still indicate a popular movement.

The result of the intrigue was the ascendancy of Jehoash (Joash) for a forty-year reign. We need to adjust this span because it is a round number and because the time frame for the Jehu dynasty must, as previously noted, be compressed; 836 to 798 BCE is a sensible proposal. The DH approved Jehoash because Jehoida was his mentor (the Chronicler augmented this motif), but he still did not meet the DH's ultimate test: the removal of the high places. DH focused on the repair of the Temple and the noteworthy claim that, once started, the repairs were carried out with integrity. What that signals in the way of a restoration of popular consciousness hints at recovery of political and social will. If so, it did not last. Disenchantment with Jehoash set in by the end of his reign, and he was assassinated by his own servants—no talk here of a popular movement—with his son Amaziah succeeding him.

At this point the DH notes that "Hazael set his face to go up against Jerusalem" (2 Kings 12.17). This isolated bit of information, and Jehoash's response—to buy Hazael off with gifts—is paralleled by the report that Jehoahaz king of Israel, Jehu's son and successor after a twenty-eight-year reign, also had to deal with Hazael (2 Kings 13.3) and indeed did so for his whole reign (13.22). Hazael, then, had a long reign, from about 842 to almost 800 BCE. The mention of the threat to Jerusalem places Hazael at Gath in Philistine territory; unencumbered by any constraint from an Assyria that was now tied up with concerns closer to home, he had both Israel and Judah at his mercy. According to 2 Kings 13.7, Jehoahaz was left with a symbolic parade guard of fifty horsemen, ten chariots, and ten thousand foot soldiers (perhaps to be read as ten contingents from various households, or about a hundred men).

This is the period to which many authorities now assign the narratives of encounters with Syria contained in 1 Kings 20 and 22 (see above). In any case, the depiction of the two small kingdoms incapable of coping with Syria applies to the second half of the ninth century BCE. The diversion in 2 Kings 13.14–19 to the report of Elisha's death, which includes Elisha's instruction to King Jehoash about victories over Syria (Aram) but portrays an omen of an insufficient three victories instead of the needful five or six, coheres with this hypothetical proposal as well. Three successful clashes with Syria were not enough.

One side or the other of the year 800 BCE, Assyria's return to the scene had a direct impact on Syria's power. By that time, Adad-nirari III was on the Assyrian throne and was old enough to begin anew the drive to the west. Probably in 796, but perhaps even earlier, he crushed Damascus and defeated Hazael's son, Ben-hadad (the third ruler of that name, if the Syrian succession has been correctly reconstructed here). Adad-nirari received tribute from Israel as well, according to his "summarizing inscription" on the Tell er-Rimah stela; but Syria's threat had been reduced, and Damascus and Hamath apparently returned to fighting one another. The note in 2 Kings 13.25, that Jehoahaz's son Jehoash recovered territory from Ben-hadad, fits with all this. The most plausible meaning of 2 Kings 13.5, according to which "the LORD gave Israel a savior," is that Adad-nirari was perceived as the hidden agent of divine relief.

Relief from external danger there may have been, but conflict resumed between Judah and Israel. Amaziah had succeeded Jehoash (Joash) of Judah; Jehoash (Joash) had succeeded Jehoahaz of Israel. The DH reports briefly a Judean defeat of Edom, followed by a clash with Jehoash of Israel, brazenly invited by Amaziah but disastrous for him. Jehoash captured Amaziah at Beth-shemesh west of Jerusalem, advanced to his capital and broke down a segment of the city wall, pillaged the Temple, took hostages—and departed. Then, for the third time in as many reigns, the Judean monarch was assassinated, to be succeeded by a son. With Amaziah, as for his father, Jehoash, the ancient historians give no reason for the conspiracies that removed them. Meanwhile, in Israel, Jehoash's reign completed its course very soon after Amaziah's death. It had been roughly sixty years since Jehu's purge. To the ancient historians it had been an undistinguished time. Except for Elisha's final intervention with

Jehoash of Israel and a note from the Chronicler about a confrontation between a prophet and Amaziah over the Edomite venture, the historians gave their accounts without including the prophetic voice.

In the course of the second decade of the eighth century BCE, around 788 for Jeroboam ben-Joash (perhaps a throne name recalling the first Jeroboam, who was ben-Nebat) and 785 for Azariah/Uzziah, the fortunes of Israel and Judah took a turn for the better. Both reigns were lengthy; the DH gives Jeroboam II forty-one years and Azariah/Uzziah fifty-two. But neither historian dwelt on their accomplishments. Jeroboam II is the subject of seven verses in the DH, and he does not appear in the narrative account of the Chronicler at all. One interesting fact does appear in 1 Chronicles 5.17: "All of these [the tribal family of Gad in Transjordan] were enrolled by genealogies in the days of King Jotham of Judah, and in the days of King Jeroboam of Israel." Jotham was Azariah's successor, and most chronological reconstructions place his reign after the end of Jeroboam's. The text does not have to mean that they overlapped. More important is the suggestion that a census of at least the Transjordan population was carried out in the mid-eighth century, because a census is taken for tax and/or military purposes. Jeroboam may have conscripted for military action; military might, and "how he fought," are features of the DH's summation in 2 Kings 14.28–29. The collocation of the two kings' names may hint at cooperation between Israel and Judah.

The seven verses in 2 Kings 14.23–29 about Jeroboam II are tantalizing, their wording unusual. The DH gave him the usual negative assessment of failing to depart from the ways of the northern kings since his distant predecessor of the same name. Then:

> He restored the border of Israel from Lebo-hamath ["the access to Hamath"] as far as the Sea of the Arabah, according to the word of the LORD, the God of Israel, which he spoke by his servant Jonah son of Amittai, the prophet, who was from Gath-hepher. For the LORD saw that the distress of Israel was very bitter; there was no one left, bond or free, and no one to help Israel. But the LORD had not said that he would blot out the name of Israel from under heaven, so he saved them by the hand of Jeroboam son of Joash.

The restoration of the territorial boundaries reached to the ideal northern extent of the land promised to Israel in Numbers 34.7–9 and implicitly attained by Solomon (1 Kings 8.65). To the south, it reached to the east coast of the Dead Sea, the limit sometimes attained by the kingdom of Israel. Confirmation that Jeroboam actually held all this territory derives from the sarcastic words in Amos 6.13–14. There the prophet scoffs at people's rejoicing over victories in Transjordan, at "Lo-debar" ("nothing") and Karnaim ("horns")—actual locations in Gilead and Bashan mentioned with fair frequency in the Bible, but here with their names bearing double meanings along the lines of "not-much" and "two horns of pushing people around—big deal!" Amos then threatens the arrival of a nation that "shall oppress you from Lebo-hamath to the Wadi Arabah"—the same spread of territory that Jeroboam had reclaimed.

The DH's passage about Jeroboam goes on to speak of lamentable conditions in Israel (a motif unique to this passage) and portrays the attention of the national deity to the bitterness of life. What "no one left, bond or free" suggests can only be imag-

ined. The verb *to save* (the Hebrew root is the one used about the relief provided by
Adad-nirari III, the "savior" of 2 Kings 13.5) expresses both the need and the relief
under Jeroboam. Jonah, known otherwise only from the comic prophetic legend that
bears his name, was the prophetic announcer. The highly theological assessment in
14.26–27 combines with the cry and the hope of Amos and Hosea.

The DH also claims that Jeroboam "recovered for Israel Damascus and Hamath,
which had belonged to Judah." The first clause is best understood as recovery of
commercial access and treaty relationship with the two Syrian states. The second
claim, about Judah, remains puzzling.

Azariah/Uzziah (it is not clear which was the throne name and which the given
name) also receives seven verses from the DH, but the only historical information
we have about him concerns his illness, a skin disease that caused his quarantine in
a separate house and led to his son Jotham becoming regent. The Chronicler gives
the disease an etiology—it is punishment for his participation in illegitimate rituals—
but also offers political information. Uzziah, he says, rebuilt Eloth (Elath), the Red
Sea port; he defeated the Philistines; he secured the Negeb; he received tribute from
the Ammonites; and he fortified Jerusalem and armed it with new military machinery.

Together, Israel and Judah had reestablished circumstances that would let commerce flow and employ many people and their skills, bringing a time of prosperity.
Archaeological evidence throws light on the scene. Deep in the Negeb, the oasis of
Kadesh-barnea, 80 kilometers (50 miles) south-southwest of Beer-sheba, lay along
the road from Elath to Gaza, a key trade route. Destroyed by Shishak in the late tenth
century, it reemerged as a fortress around 800 BCE, whether at the instigation of
Uzziah or one of his predecessors cannot be determined. The fortress measures 60
meters by 40 meters (200 feet by 130 feet) with salients at the corners and midway
along each side of a ramparted wall 4 meters (13 feet) thick. Fifty kilometers (30
miles) south and east, not far off the Gaza-Elath road, lay another rectangular structure that may have been a fortress or a rest stop, at a site called Kuntillet Ajrud,
excavated in the mid-1970s. Efforts have been made to determine, from the kinds of
pottery found, who would have lived at these outposts. Kadesh shows "Negebite"
pottery styles otherwise thought to be from local dwellers in the wilderness, combined
with Judean styles; Ajrud has none of the local Negebite styles, but combines Judean
styles with styles identified as Israelite. Tentatively, this is another indication of
Judean-Israelite cooperation, as well as of the use of local populations as part of
military garrisons.

From Ajrud comes evidence of the religious life of the time, in the form of ink
graffiti on the doorjambs and painted drawings with graffiti on walls and Judean-
style storage vessels. Some inscriptions are blessing formulas invoking the god of
Israel. One noteworthy graffito runs across the headdress of a crowned, dwarfish,
bovine-headed figure standing in front of another such figure; adjacent to the upper
right is a seated female playing a lyre. Interpretation of all the ingredients is difficult.
The forward crowned figure clearly has a penis with testicles or a tail, while the one
behind him has indications of breasts but no penis or tail, despite earlier reconstructions that supplied her with what looks like a penis. The two then may be a male
deity and his consort. The text, probably added subsequently, identifies them as
"Yahweh of Samaria and his *asherah*." The seated lyre player may also be a depiction

of the goddess Asherah, drawn by still another hand. Very likely the whole collection indicates a mixture of religious motifs, pointing to Canaanite worship and to a linking of Yahweh with the goddess Asherah. What "his *asherah*" means is uncertain, because in the Semitic languages a possessive suffix is not added to a personal name. All in all, a picture emerges of mixed religious piety, something of a kind that official religious policy, not to mention the "true" prophets of Yahweh, would have abhorred. The reference to Yahweh of Samaria and the spelling of Yahwistic names in the blessing formulas again point to northern participation in trade activity and possibly defense deep in Judean territory.

With Jeroboam's reign in the north, there emerge the earliest of the "writing" prophets, those for whom books of their sayings were gathered by their followers and edited into a tradition of their words and work. Hosea was a native northerner, whereas Amos's home was in Judah. Both aim what they have to say at the population of the north, designated as Ephraim by Hosea. For Amos it is seldom possible to tell when he is addressing Israel as a state and when as the whole people of God, but some of his words name Samaria, while other passages are directed to Bethel. Aid in sensing the targets of their vehement critique comes from archaeological evidence, including the Samaria ostraca and the Samaria ivories, from analogies of other developed agrarian societies provided by comparative sociology, but most of all directly from their pungent words and symbolic actions.

The Samaria ostraca sketch a picture of a capital peopled by the king's retinue and mulcting the neighboring countryside. The locations mentioned in the ostraca suggests that the region from Samaria southward to Mount Gerizim, above the city of Shechem, was the main source of supply for the capital; other regions probably supplied royal and military centers at cities such as Megiddo, Aphek, Hazor, Bethel, and Dan, along with lesser centers like Shechem and Tirzah.

Amos's prophecy stressed social injustice. His main target was the families living in Samaria, whom he portrayed as wallowing in luxury and leisure at the expense of the populace in the towns and villages of the countryside, and probably even those living around the citadel of the capital itself. Those exploited in this way are designated not only the "poor" and the "needy," but also "the righteous" (2.6; 4.1; 5.11–12). Amos, from the village of Tekoa south of Bethlehem, himself a landed person with social standing (according to his answer to the priest at Bethel who challenges his credentials [7.1]), was indignant at economic and social conditions in the north. But since his tradition was doubtless carried south and augmented after Samaria fell, his critique must have fit conditions there as well.

The proposal of sociologists that Israelite society in the time of Jeroboam II and his successors be analyzed as an "advanced agrarian society" is convincing. The principle of patrimonial inheritance had largely given way to a system in which gifts (prebends) of land from the throne had produced estates held by people who lived most of the time at the court. As part of the same development, lands in the hands of common folk were acquired by the large landowners when small landholders could no longer survive economically. A system of "rent capitalism" is likely to have come into play whereby the landed peasantry had to sell land in bad seasons in order to buy seed to plant what land they retained, and a cycle began that ended in peasantry operating as tenant farmers, owing their livelihood to their patrons. An economic elite came to possess most of the land; more and more people became landless. In the midst would have been people of commerce, who traded in necessities like tools and seed, as well as in luxury items.

One of the symbols for the life of luxury is the use of carved ivory, either as furniture inlay ("beds of ivory" in Amos 6.4) or as figures carved in the round. The impressive collection of ivory pieces found at Samaria, all belonging to the eighth-century BCE layers of the "ivory house," illustrates this aesthetic dimension of life at the capital. The style of carving is a thorough mixture of Egyptian, Phoenician, and Syrian motifs, in some cases involving inset lapis lazuli imported from Egypt. The ivory probably came from the elephants indigenous to the river valleys of Syria. No more graphic indication can be cited of the cosmopolitan influences at play among the wealthy of Samaria. While few motifs can be specifically connected to Baal iconography, the worship of Baal at the capital is best illustrated by the proportion of Baal-compounded names in the Samaria ostraca.

Amos and Hosea are better seen not as themselves downtrodden and thus protesting "from below," but as informed and empathic observers from the ranks of the well-to-do, indignant at the effects of the unfolding social and economic structure. Amos is appalled by unfair trade practices (2.6), by fines imposed on and levies taken from the indigent (2.8, 11), by the violation of the rights to adjudication for those who protest and the bearing of false witness (5.10). Corollary to these injustices are the lavish expenditures at the court or among the gentry: houses of hewn stone, summer homes, overstocked pantries, and the high living that goes with the binge of overindulgence translated "revelry" (6.4–7)—a social and religious ritual (in Hebrew, *marzeah*) that appears in texts from the second millennium BCE to the Byzantine period.

Exploitation of the righteous was interwoven with religious injustice, combining hollow if punctilious practice (4.4–5) with the likelihood that participation in worship, a valued aspect of all Israelite life, was denied the poor because they had no time or resources. For Hosea the dimension of worship was paramount; unjust practices combined with a lying interpretation of tradition and of worship. Hosea laid the practice of injustice and of disillusionment at the door of the priests (Hos. 4.4–10; 5.1–2; 6.9). An unholy alliance of king and religion, resulting in a violation of the ideology of northern kingship and worship, will result in the rejection of the calf of Samaria (8.5). Hosea's words and agenda accord with those of Deuteronomy and of E.

While Amos and Hosea were excoriating royal, priestly, and judicial leadership, they laid equal responsibility on the people. Recalling the standards of social justice claimed as foundational for the people Israel, both appeal to the norms and terminology of the Sinai covenant (Hos. 4.1–3; 8.1–3; Amos 3.1–2). Amos in particular, in the litany that critiqued the nations with whom Israel and Judah have been involved in foreign relations across the centuries (1.3–2.3), invoked a theme of desired covenantal peace among the nations—also an ingredient in the ancient hopes of Israel. These indications of the wider pertinence of the prophetic message suggest that the audience of Amos and Hosea extended outward throughout the land. The message may have been carried by their followers. We must not assume that the prophets were heard by very few and dismissed as disgruntled killjoys.

What was the common lot of people in the towns and villages away from the capital and the cities of royal patronage? Tirzah and Shechem are towns near Samaria, which at this time probably did not fall under the direct aegis of the court. At Shechem in Stratum VII, the layer that ended with the Assyrian destruction of 724–722, a well-preserved "four-room" house and its surroundings have been excavated. This typical architectural plan involves a central room entered at one end, with rooms along the other three sides; the side chambers can be subdivided into various combinations. A hundred or more examples of the layout have been found from Hazor to Beer-sheba, at Mizpah, Tirzah, Tell Qasile, and across the Jordan River—in short, in virtually every excavated Iron Age town.

The Shechem house had two full stories and probably an upper partial story. On the ground floor, in addition to cobbled rooms housing the family's donkeys and perhaps their fatted calves, were rooms for their provender as well as for food and fuel storage. The central room contained at first a food-processing (grapes? olives?) or dyeing installation, later supplanted by a huge hearth for some such industry as the preparation of lime. The family practiced diverse agriculture and cottage industries.

At a secondary construction stage, rooms were added along one side wall, probably to accommodate an expanding family. The addition encroached upon a spacious yard next to the house where bread was baked, but where there was also space for recreation. Another similar house lay across the yard, perhaps combining with the first one to make up a family compound.

This complex was sited near the western perimeter of town, near what is likely to have been one of the town gates. In construction and in extent of surroundings, it contrasts with contemporary housing closer to the center of town—more closely compacted, and farther from the gate where business was transacted and justice administered. A similar pattern has been noted at Tirzah. An interesting question is whether this indication of relatively small social distinction means social stratification, and whether people such as those who lived in House 1727 at Shechem or the "good" homes in Tirzah had the discretionary resources and power sufficient to engage in the unjust practices Amos denounced.

Assyria and the End of Israel

Close to the year 745 BCE, Jeroboam II in the north and Uzziah in the south reached the end of their reigns. In that year Tiglath-pileser III, referred to as "Pul" in the Bible, entered upon his reign over Assyria. From as early as about 738, Tiglath-pileser's tribute lists give the name of a ruler of Syria, which equates with Rezin of the Bible. In the south, Egypt was experiencing a period of internal strife; one power center was at Sais in the delta, whose ruler Tefnakht is probably the king called "So" in 2 Kings 17.4. Israel and Judah were in the midst of a brewing storm.

Turmoil in Samaria must have arisen over how to participate in the constantly changing power game. Six kings sat on the throne of Israel between 747 and 722, only three of them for any length of time and none for over a decade. Precise chronological details are elusive; for example, the twenty years assigned Pekah cannot be squared with Assyrian information. The sequence: Jeroboam's son Zechariah lasted six months, struck down by the usurper Shallum, who lasted one month. Menahem ousted Shallum and reigned close to ten years; Menahem's son Pekahiah succeeded him, only to be overthrown by a military captain named Pekah. (Pekah and Pekahiah are forms of the same name; did Pekah assume his predecessor's throne name?) Hoshea killed Pekah and reigned for nine years, to the fall of Samaria.

Things were more stable in the south; Jotham, regent for Uzziah, continued on the throne until about 735 BCE and was succeeded by his son Ahaz, who held the throne until about 715. (There is controversy about the chronology; Ahaz's reign may have fallen a decade earlier, and Hezekiah may have begun his reign about 727 to 725—no synchronisms for this period help resolve the question.)

Tiglath-pileser III ruled Assyria from 745 to 727. He campaigned westward repeatedly during that time. Assyrian policy of conquest took one of three tacks, all of them ruthless. Frequently the policy worked on a three-stage progression: seek voluntary submission of local rulers; conquer by force if voluntary submission does not happen; punish any recalcitrance or rebellion by taking over governmental control and deporting local leadership, while substituting populations drawn from other locales. Menahem voluntarily submitted and sent tribute to Tiglath-pileser, as at this stage did Tubail (or Hiram—Assyrian annals and inscriptions differ on the name) king of Tyre and Rezin of Damascus in 738/737.

The account in 2 Kings 15.19–21 indicates the economic impact. Menahem's tribute was 1,000 talents (a talent was roughly 50 kilograms [110 pounds]) of silver, which "he exacted from Israel, that is, from all the wealthy" at the rate of 50 shekels a head. Since 50 (or perhaps 60) shekels is a mina and there are 60 minas in a talent, this computes to at least 60,000 people who had to contribute. If we take Jeremiah 32.9 as the guide, 50 shekels was three times what Jeremiah had to pay for his family's field in Anathoth—no paltry amount. That 60,000 people could be thought of as "wealthy" in Israel raises its own set of issues. If it means there were that many landholders in mid-eighth-century BCE Israel, we must be cautious in estimating the proportion of "wealthy" to "poor and needy." What is more likely is that everybody ("Israel" in 2 Kings 15.20) was reckoned "wealthy" for the purposes of exaction, an economic hardship disastrous for those on the margin. That alone would have created popular opposition, which doubtless played its part in Pekah's conspiracy against Menahem's son Pekahiah.

Tiglath-pileser enlisted voluntary submission, or compelled it, in the west until about 738 BCE, and contended with threats to his north and east for three to four years after that. Assyrian public records combine with biblical accounts to portray what happened between 735 and 732. Rezin assembled a rebellious coalition including Pekah of Israel, and sought to involve Judah. The DH places their first efforts at the end of Jotham's reign (2 Kings 15.37), but the pressure came when Ahaz had succeeded Jotham during 735 (16.5–9). The coalition attacked Jerusalem, probably in 734, but Ahaz took the course of sending an advance tribute to Tiglath-pileser, requesting him to intervene.

Tiglath-pileser probably never intended otherwise. In 734 he campaigned across the middle of Syria to the Phoenician coast, conquering city after city from Byblos southward and ending by securing the frontier city of Gaza and the boundary with Egypt. That in itself may have been enough to frighten the Syrian-Israelite coalition into pulling back from Jerusalem. The Chronicler presents an alternative picture, claiming that Syria and Pekah separately wrought havoc in Judah, but that Ahaz's invitation to Assyria was occasioned by attacks from Edom in the south and Philistia on the west. Whatever the precise course of events in Judah, Tiglath-pileser's annals combine with 2 Kings 16.9 to report fighting with Syria in 733 and 732, ending with the fall of Damascus and the death of Rezin.

For Pekah, the end came at this time also. Hoshea killed him and silenced the anti-Assyrian voice in Samaria. Meanwhile, Tiglath-pileser applied the third stage of Assyrian policy to the entire north of Israel's territory, turning them into the Assyrian provinces of Megiddo, Dor, and Gilead (2 Kings 15.29) and deporting their populations. Hoshea was left with the central hill country, over which the Assyrian king claimed to have appointed him.

The impact on Judah, notably on Ahaz and his "pro-Assyrian" circle, was brought home to Jerusalem by Isaiah. Isaiah is presented in the book named for him as a figure of prominence in Jerusalem. As with other prophets, he has a following (8.16) and enjoys customary access to the king. The book's superscription, and the retrospective in chapter 6 of his inaugural prophetic vision, dates his first activities to the end of the reign of Uzziah; but narrative encounters show him at work with Ahaz and then, after a gap of time, with Hezekiah. The account of his confrontation of Ahaz served as the gathering point for chapters 7–11.

With "the house of David" (7.2) quaking before the threat of the alliance of Pekah and Rezin, Isaiah realized that he was divinely commissioned to confront King Ahaz. Isaiah bore a message and a symbolic act, the latter taking the form of Isaiah's son Shear-jashub, whose name has a deliberately ambiguous meaning: "a remnant shall return/only a remnant shall return," both a threat and a promise. Isaiah's message: the conspiracy being developed by Rezin and Pekah will not succeed; neither fear nor resist it. If you want reassurance that this is so, ask for a sign—and if you are too pious to ask for a sign, you will get it anyway. A son has already been conceived by one known to us both (the queen? the prophet's wife?) whose name is the assurance, Immanuel, "El is with us." By the time that child has been weaned, the threat of the Syro-Ephraimite conspiracy will have been put down by Assyria.

Isaiah's message would have amounted to counsel not to take such measures as sending to Assyria for help. As noted above, Assyria would probably have come to punish rebels anyway, and to set the boundary with Egypt. The rest of the collection in Isaiah 7–11 is a rich amalgam of prophetic interpretation of what went on from 732 to 722 and a projection of the prophet's commitment to the political control of Israel's deity, even over Assyria itself. To unravel the dates of the various oracles in this portion of the book would be futile, but one point is inescapable: what is about to happen, or has happened, to Samaria is a direct lesson to the kings of Judah. Failure to heed the lesson brings disaster on Judah as well. Accounts of the progression of disaster in the north serve as warnings to Judah (9.8–10.4). Portrayals of what a truly faithful king and kingdom would look like are positioned to fortify warning with hope (9.2–7; 11.1–9). Interwoven with all this we hear the prophet's personal frustration as warnings go unheeded—hence his decision to lapse, with his disciples, into silence and waiting (8.16). Whether or not the prophetic counsel worked to change the policy of Judah's king Ahaz, the option proclaimed by the prophet and cherished by those who thought like him is as much a part of Judah's history as is the reality of what the pro-Assyrian party opted to do.

The conspiracy did fail, and within a decade the axe fell on Samaria. For a while, into the reign of Shalmaneser V (727–722 BCE), Hoshea paid tribute to Assyria. But at some point Hoshea sensed an opening and sought help from the Saite dynasty of Egypt (2 Kings 17.4). The move cost him his throne and his people their land. The rebellious act brought Shalmaneser roaring back to the west to besiege Samaria. For over two years, Samaria held out, while Assyria ravaged the countryside. Then, in 722, the city fell—probably to Shalmaneser, although neither the DH nor the Assyrian record is quite clear on the agent of destruction and deportation. Shalmaneser's successor Sargon II claims credit in his own inscriptions, and possibly a sequence of events unfolded complex enough to involve several stages of conquest. The DH here reaches one of its climactic points, and pauses to draw the lessons in 2 Kings 17.7–18. A second historian in the Deuteronomic tradition added verses 19–20 to bring the point to bear upon Judah. Then, in verses 21–23, the first DH summarizes the whole: from Jeroboam I to Hoshea, the course of events had been developing disastrously, never reversing Jeroboam's religious sin, and, though challenged by prophetic voices, had finally led to exile.

The epitaph of the northern kingdom was augmented by the remarkable portrayal in 2 Kings 17.24–33, which depicts the Assyrian policy of population exchange and provides a valuable vignette of religious phenomenology. The new populations did not know the governing religious reality of the territory and needed instruction from the indigenous priesthood. A knowledgeable priest, who had been taken into captivity, was sent back to live at Bethel. "He taught them how they should worship the LORD." The result for the DH was built-in syncretistic religion as a way of life.

The year 722 BCE brought an era to an end. Judah stood in suspended animation, awaiting what Assyria would have in store for it. Israel was in ruins, its leadership deported and its remaining population left to the agonies of deprivation and of occupation by people alien to their ways. Sargon's accounts speak of either 27,280 or 27,290 exiles and of the capture of chariots (50 in one inscription, 200 in another). He also claims to have rebuilt Samaria "better than it was before." The archaeological evidence suggests the devastation: at Tirzah, Shechem, and Samaria the wreckage speaks eloquently, emblemized by the fine Assyrian seal found in the collapsed ruins of House 1727 at Shechem. The silence of the written sources for what followed in the north is deafening. The consequences for Judah become the story of the next chapter of this volume.

It was just two centuries from Rehoboam's action at Shechem to the fall of Samaria. A monarchic experiment under David and Solomon had envisioned a realm of peace and prosperity stretching from Dan to Beer-sheba, in harmony with surrounding peoples. The Deuteronomic Historian portrays the division of this unity with deep sadness, a tone of bewilderment. The fault lies with the people's unfaithfulness to a deity who sought justice and peace. Israel bears the brunt of the critique, while Judah bears its share. The Chronicler, giving more attention to Judean failures, clings to hope in the Davidic promise, but shares the sadness.

The events alone, even without the prophets' yearnings and the editors' evaluations, convey a sense of lost opportunity. Justice and rectitude might have prevailed. More perhaps than is usually recognized, the ways in which the division of the monarchy is presented in the Bible and even in the annals of other nations of the period—the Moabite Stone, the Assyrian inscriptions, the Dan stela—inform the reflections of historians of other eras and places as they ponder the human pilgrimage.

Select Bibliography

Alt, Albrecht. "The Monarchy in the Kingdoms of Israel and Judah." In *Essays on Old Testament History and Religion*, trans. R. W. Wilson, 241–59. Oxford: Blackwell, 1966. The classic statement on differing ideologies of monarchy in Israel and Judah.

Boling, Robert G., and Edward F. Campbell. "Jeroboam and Rehoboam at Shechem." In *Archaeology and Biblical Interpretation: Essays in Memory of D. Glenn Rose*, ed. Leo G. Perdue, Lawrence E. Toombs, and Gary Lance Johnson, 259–72. Atlanta: John Knox, 1986. A study of text variations in 1 Kings 12 in conversation with the archaeology of Shechem in the tenth century.

Bright, John. *A History of Israel*. 3d ed. Philadelphia: Westminster, 1981. A history that takes the biblical accounts as generally reliable, the prophets as making a historical difference, and archaeology as a signal resource.

Coote, Robert B. *Amos among the Prophets*. Philadelphia: Fortress, 1981. A reconstruction of Amos's message and the way it was augmented to apply to Judah, with special attention to socioeconomic conditions.

———. *In Defense of Revolution: The Elohist History*. Minneapolis: Fortress, 1991. An interpretation of E as the ideological apologia for Jeroboam's monarchic style.

Cross, Frank Moore. *Canaanite Myth and Hebrew Epic: Essays in the History of the Religion of Israel*. Cambridge, Mass.: Harvard University Press, 1973. Valuable essays on Israel's religious history, notably on the priestly houses and the ideologies of monarchy.

Dearman, J. Andrew. *Religion and Culture in Ancient Israel*. Peabody, Mass.: Hendrickson, 1992. Resource for the material and religious culture, including a chapter on Deuteronomy's agenda.

King, Philip J. *Amos, Hosea, Micah—An Archaeological Commentary*. Philadelphia: Westminster, 1988. Resources from archaeology for interpretation of the eighth-century prophets.

Knoppers, Gary N. *Two Nations under God: The Deuteronomistic History of Solomon and the Dual Monarchies*. 2 vols. Atlanta: Scholars Press, 1993–94. Fresh attention to the purposes of the Deuteronomic History in portraying the monarchy.

Miller, J. Maxwell, and John H. Hayes. *A History of Ancient Israel and Judah*. Philadelphia: Westminster, 1986. Miller's chapters on the Divided Monarchy give lucid treatment of the interpretive problems, extended quotations of nonbiblical texts, and helpful maps.

Pitard, Wayne T. *Ancient Damascus: A Historical Study of the Syrian City-State from Earliest Times until Its Fall to the Assyrians in 732 B.C.E.* Winona Lake, Ind.: Eisenbrauns, 1987. A detailed presentation of Syria's history; the second half deals with Syria in relation to Israel.

Stager, Lawrence E. "The Archaeology of the Family in Ancient Israel." *Bulletin of the American Schools of Oriental Research* 260 (1985): 1–35. A stimulating exploration of archaeological and anthropological clues to Israelite family life.

————, and Samuel R. Wolff. "Production and Commerce in Temple Courtyards: An Olive Press in the Sacred Precinct at Tel Dan." *Bulletin of the American Schools of Oriental Research* 243 (1981): 95–102. An analysis of the industry that produced fine-grade oil for cultic use.

Tappy, Ron E. *The Archaeology of Israelite Samaria*. Vol. 1, *Early Iron Age through the Ninth Century BCE*. Harvard Semitic Studies, 44. Atlanta: Scholars Press, 1992. A fresh analysis of the stratigraphy at Samaria, making use of Kathleen Kenyon's unpublished daybooks from the 1932–35 excavations.

Wilson, Robert R. *Prophecy and Society in Ancient Israel*. Philadelphia: Fortress, 1980. A thorough investigation of the social role of the prophets and their place in Israelite life.

CHAPTER SEVEN

Into Exile

From the Assyrian Conquest of Israel
to the Fall of Babylon

MORDECHAI COGAN

B y all accounts, Judah's century-long vassaldom to Assyria had its beginnings in the reign of Ahaz (743–727 BCE). After half a century of sporadic appearances in Syria, Assyria had renewed its sustained westward drive to the Mediterranean coast under the vigorous leadership of Tiglath-pileser III (745–727). The Assyrian monarch was clearly bent on a policy of imperial expansion and incorporation. His early wars were confined mostly to northern Syria, but by 734 Tiglath-pileser was drawn to campaign against a coalition of rebellious vassals that included Tyre, Aram-Damascus, and Israel. Ahaz had come under pressure to join the rebel cause, but as he wavered the coalition set out to force the issue, laying siege to Jerusalem with the intention of replacing him with a more compliant ruler (2 Kings 16.5, 7–9; Isa. 7.1–6). The neutrality urged on him by the prophet Isaiah (Isa. 7.4–6; 8.1–8) seemed ill-advised, and in the end Ahaz decided to submit to the Assyrian yoke. Ahaz's abject message to Tiglath-pileser says it all: "I am your servant and your son. Come up, and rescue me from the hand of the king of Aram and from the hand of the king of Israel, who are attacking me" (2 Kings 16.7). This move, and the king's responsibility for Judah's new status, are strongly criticized in the biblical book of Kings: it was the servile plea from Ahaz to Tiglath-pileser for protection that was Judah's undoing. But from the Assyrian point of view, Tiglath-pileser would have moved against the anti-Assyrian element even without Ahaz's submission. Intimidation and the fear of entanglement, exhibited so markedly by Ahaz, were to dominate relations between Judah and Assyria over the next hundred years. And the gifts that accompanied the plea for aid were only the first of a continuous stream of tax and tribute payments exacted by Assyria's rapacious rulers.

A side feature of Israel's new political status was the opening of the kingdom to the cultural trends and fashions of other regions of the Near East. We are told that Ahaz had an altar erected in the Solomonic Temple in Jerusalem, modeled after one he had seen in Damascus during an audience with Tiglath-pileser. The traditional offerings were transferred to the new, larger altar, and the original bronze altar was set aside for the king's private use (2 Kings 16.10–16). This has sometimes mistakenly been seen as an act of compliance, either imposed or desirable, with Assyrian imperial norms. But Assyria did not impose its forms of worship on vassal states, nor did it interfere in their internal affairs, as long as imperial obligations were acknowledged and met. Incorporation into the provincial system of the empire was another story, to be recounted below in connection with Samaria.

A Note on Sources

As these introductory remarks imply, re-creating so tempestuous a period calls for critically reading a variety of sources. Their assessment, combined with sound judgment and a modicum of imagination, stands modern historians in good stead as they face knotty questions, including the ever-so-many undocumented years during the century of Assyria's domination.

Our most important sources, in addition to the Bible, are the texts recovered from the mounds of the ancient Near East. In several instances these texts supplement the Bible by reporting events or specifying dates that biblical writers did not include in their accounts. When they overlap with a biblical account, the nonbiblical texts provide a valuable comparison with the views expressed by Israelite writers, even though most of their comments are restricted to matters of war and its aftermath. In the end, however, for Israel and Judah—especially in light of their relative insignificance from a geopolitical perspective—the Bible remains the main and often the only resource at the disposal of historians.

Two historical works, the book of Kings and the book of Chronicles (later divided by tradition into two books each), survey the monarchic age in Israel. Kings is by and large a product of the late seventh century BCE, whereas Chronicles seems to have been written in the fourth century, toward the close of the Persian period— some three hundred years after the last king reigned in Judah. Each bears the distinctive stamp of its author(s), and of the two, Chronicles is less serviceable, being a didactic explication of Kings with little in the way of additional documentary material from preexilic days.

Not to be slighted are the large prophetic collections of Isaiah, Jeremiah, and Ezekiel, as well as the smaller tracts of Micah, Zephaniah, Nahum, and Obadiah. Their rich lode of inspired preaching and reflections on the moral state of Israelite society pose serious problems for modern historians. Questions of source evaluation hinder our every step. How are we to distinguish between the authentic words of the prophet and those of his disciples and of the later editors and compilers responsible for the final shape of the prophetic "book"? In only one instance do we learn how a prophet's words were collected: Jeremiah dictated them (from memory or from written notes) to his scribe Baruch, the son of Neriah (Jer. 36.4), under circumstances and with an outcome that are discussed below.

The relevant source material from Assyria consists of historical inscriptions and administrative documents, originally deposited in the state archives in the capital,

Nineveh, whose recovered items number in the tens of thousands. Annalistic texts record the victorious military pursuits of Assyria's monarchs, at the same time praising their loyalty to the gods and their good works in building temples and palaces. These annals may be classified as royal propaganda, highly selective in their presentation, careful to justify the king's deeds before both the gods and his subjects. For modern researchers they open a window into the world of the court scribes, their goals and techniques, and are suggestive of similar literary phenomena in Israel. Complementing these "official" texts is the vast correspondence received by the palace from all corners of the empire, together with business and judicial records and oracular and magical texts, to name just a few of the types of texts available. This wealth of material adds to our understanding of the daily pursuits of those who lived at the center of the vast and imposing Assyrian empire.

From Babylonia, the most valuable historical source is the Neo-Babylonian Chronicle Series, only a small portion of which has been recovered. It presents the summary record, year by year, of the major military undertakings of the reigning king, with little editorial bias. The Babylonian scribe, unlike his Assyrian counterpart, could describe the defeat of the sovereign without apology, and often does. (The Assyrian scribe turned every setback of the imperial army into a victory.) As for Egypt—that ever-present threat to the Mesopotamian powers lying just beyond the Sinai Peninsula and the Nile Delta—relevant source material is rare. When available, it focuses on internal affairs, so that it is only from non-Egyptian sources that we know of even such key moves as the appearance of Egyptian forces in fulfillment of pledges of aid to Israel and Judah against Assyria and Babylonia, or Egypt's support of Assyria itself.

Finally, archaeological remains from Israel during the latter part of the Iron Age (Iron IIC, ca. 722–586 BCE) illuminate aspects of life not touched on by written sources. Out of the jumbled ruins of destroyed cities emerge the outlines of rooms and buildings, streets, walls, and gates, together with the artifacts that served their dwellers. These are the silent witnesses to ancient life that await interpretations and integration into the historical picture. To our delight, embossed Assyrian wall reliefs preserve contemporary illustrations of several cities in Israel and Judah. From the palace of Tiglath-pileser at Nimrud, depictions of the attack on the city of Gezer in the foothills of Judah and on Ashteroth in Transjordan have been recovered. And from Sennacherib's "palace without rival" at Nineveh are the wonderfully detailed reliefs of his siege of Lachish, from which we learn not only about the techniques of ancient warfare but also observe the very exit of Judeans from their city on the long road to exile. Their story and that of their compatriots follows.

The Age of Hezekiah: Glory and Defeat

Ahaz's son Hezekiah (727–698 BCE; this is an alternate chronology to that used in chapter 6) came to the throne in Jerusalem just about the time that Samaria embarked on the path of rebellion against Assyria that would eventually lead to its demise. After several encounters and a lengthy siege, Shalmaneser V (727–722) brought Samaria to its knees in the winter of 722. Only in 720, however, was the city's rebellious military and political leadership finally subdued by Sargon II (722–705); he retook the now largely destroyed city, deported its population, and organized the territory into an Assyrian province. Sargon then moved down the coast and fought off an

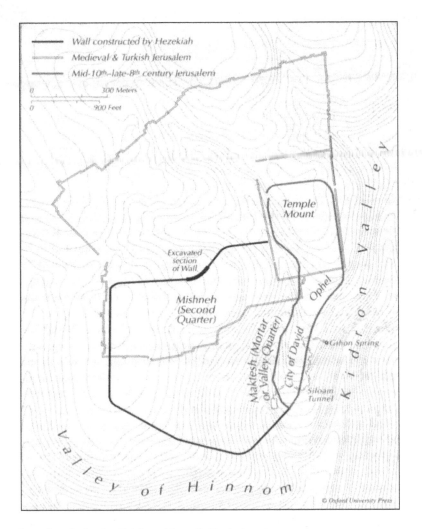

Jerusalem during the Eighth and Seventh Centuries BCE

Egyptian corps that had arrived at Raphia at the gateway to the northern Sinai Peninsula, razing the town and carrying off thousands.

The kingdom of Judah was spared the direct effects of the Assyrian onslaught on Israel, but the harsh measures meted out were not lost upon Hezekiah, who for the present adopted the policy of compliance with the vassal demands of Assyria that had been adopted by his father, Ahaz, less than a decade earlier. Yet despite the tax and tribute payments—which must have been onerous (even though no records survive of the amounts involved)—the kingdom of Judah seems to have enjoyed the benefits of association with an imperial power. Judah after all bordered the Philistine entrepôts on the southern Mediterranean coast, the transshipping hub of the Arabian trade that passed through the Negeb desert. Hezekiah amassed great wealth, a process fostered by a sweeping reorganization of his kingdom. Newly constructed or refortified royal store-cities gathered in the produce of herd and field, and in the capital state reserves of spices and aromatic oils and of silver and gold, not to mention the well-stocked arsenal, won international renown. Evidence of this vital economic and military activity can be found in the many jar handles impressed with stamp seals, which have been unearthed at dozens of sites in Judah. The seals consist of the phrase *belonging to the king* (in Hebrew, *lmlk*), the name of one of four administrative centers (Socoh in the Shephelah, Hebron in the hill country, Ziph in the Judean wilderness, and Mamshet [pronunciation uncertain] in the Negeb), and the royal insignia, the two-winged solar disk or the four-winged beetle that Judah's kings had borrowed from Egypt. The storage jars on which these sealings appear presumably contained provisions that had been dispensed from the royal stores.

There are also indications that this period was one of rapid demographic growth in Judah. Archaeological surveys of the Judean hill country have uncovered several dozen new settlements founded toward the end of the eighth century BCE, and excavations in Jerusalem have shown that the capital's developed area tripled or even quadrupled at the same time. Two of the city's new neighborhoods are known by name, the Mishneh ("Second" Quarter) and the Maktesh ("Mortar" or "Valley" Quarter). Many if not most of the new settlers were probably refugees from the territories to the north and west that had been annexed to the Assyrian empire.

In religious affairs as well, Hezekiah took an active role as a reformer. Though the evidence is disputed, it seems that for the first time in Judah's history the king, with the tacit support of the priesthood, set out to concentrate all public worship in the Jerusalem Temple. Local sanctuaries throughout the kingdom, the infamous "high places" that had served as the focal points of local ritual since earliest times, were shut down. An indication of what must have taken place at these sanctuaries was recovered by the excavators of ancient Beer-sheba, where the large stone blocks of a sacrificial altar were found embedded within the wall of a building; they had been used secondarily as construction material after the dismantling and desanctification of the altar. But whether the closure of the high places actually made the populace more dependent on the capital is questionable. Moreover, the king's reform seems to have had another focus. His acts included the removal of ritual accoutrements that, though long associated with Israelite traditions, seemed to the authors of the reform essentially pagan. Stone pillars and Asherah-poles that had often been planted alongside the altars were eliminated, and even the *Nehushtan*, the venerated brazen serpent with a putative Mosaic pedigree that stood in the Jerusalem Temple, was removed from its honored position and smashed to pieces. All of these moves may have been inspired by a spirit of repentance urged by the reformers, who could point to the destruction of the northern kingdom as an object lesson: only by observing the demands of the Mosaic law for worship devoid of all images and concentrated at a single chosen site could Judah's future be secured. These radical changes did not meet with universal approval, and with Hezekiah's passing the status quo ante returned.

Not to be overlooked in all this activism is the literary output that flowed under royal sponsorship. Wisdom teachers had had entrée to the Jerusalem court from its earliest days, and now at Hezekiah's direction this circle set about copying and collecting Solomonic sayings, thus preserving for later generations the image of Solomon as the wisest of men (see Prov. 25.1). Other literature, with roots in northern Israel, made its way south with the Israelite refugees who fled the Assyrian wars in search of a new home in Judah. Among these were such works as the popular tales of the wonder-working prophets Elijah and Elisha, collections of the sayings of prophets such as Hosea, and the nucleus of the material that was to become the book of Deuteronomy. In Jerusalem these traditions were accommodated and eventually included in the canon of sacred scripture that grew up there. It may have been during these heady days of Hezekiah's first decade of rule that there was composed an early version of the Deuteronomic History, the narrative history of Israel in the land that eventually comprised the books of Joshua, Judges, Samuel, and Kings.

Prophets of another kind were active in Judah in the last quarter of the eighth century, the most prominent being Isaiah son of Amoz. This proud Jerusalemite served as the occasional counselor of both King Ahaz and King Hezekiah, but his pronouncements were directed for the most part to Israel in its entirety, the "house of Jacob." Like his contemporary Micah from the lowland town of Moresheth, he introduced Judeans to the kinds of teachings developed by Amos and Hosea, prophets who had been active in the northern kingdom prior to the fall of Samaria. A hallmark of these literary prophets—a more apt designation than the customary "classical prophets"—was their call for societal reform. A new kind of idolatry had taken root in Judah: the worship of material gains. Isaiah observed that a great rift had opened between Judah's influential wealthy and the neglected populace, whose cause he took up:

> Ah, you who join house to house,
>   who add field to field,
> until there is room for no one but you. . . .
> Ah, you who call evil good and good evil . . .
> who acquit the guilty for a bribe,
>   and deprive the innocent of their rights! . . .
> Therefore the anger of the LORD was kindled against his people.
>   (Isa. 5.8, 20, 23, 25)

The prophet decried the piety of the privileged who had been led to believe that correct ritual observance was all that was needed; in God's name he rejected their pretense:

> Trample my courts no more;
> bringing offerings is futile. . . .
> When you stretch out your hands,
>   I will hide my eyes from you;
> even though you make many prayers,
>   I will not listen;
>   your hands are full of blood. . . .
> Cease to do evil,
>   learn to do good;
> seek justice,
>   rescue the oppressed,
> defend the orphan,
>   plead for the widow.
>   (Isa. 1.12–17)

Micah put it succinctly:

> He has told you, O mortal, what is good;
>   and what does the LORD require of you
> but to do justice, and to love kindness,
>   and to walk humbly with your God?
>   (Mic. 6.8)

Sacrifice could no longer guarantee the common weal. The new prophetic standard for national well-being elevated morality to the level previously occupied by ritual obligations alone; the responsibility of the individual to pursue justice as taught in the Mosaic law was extended to the entire nation, henceforth seen as collectively accountable for the ills of society.

Isaiah's message also had a universal aspect. In his vision of a new world in days to come, all nations would make pilgrimage to the Temple in Jerusalem. There, in this house of instruction, they would be taught the ways of the Lord, thus ushering in an age of universal peace:

> They shall beat their swords into plowshares,
>   and their spears into pruning hooks;
> nation shall not lift up sword against nation,
>   neither shall they learn war any more.
>   (Isa. 2.4)

For the present, Assyria's victories were prophetically interpreted as God-sent punishments for the godless. But that rod of the Lord's anger would in turn be punished for its shameless pride and boasting self-acclaim. In his mind's eye, Isaiah foresaw a time when the Assyrian empire would be united in the worship of the one God:

> On that day there will be a highway from Egypt to Assyria, and the Assyrian will come into Egypt, and the Egyptian into Assyria, and the Egyptians will worship with the Assyrians. On that day Israel will be the third with Egypt and Assyria, a blessing in the midst of the earth, whom the LORD of hosts has blessed, saying, "Blessed be Egypt my people, and Assyria the work of my hands, and Israel my heritage." (Isa. 19.23–25)

Because of their unorthodox message, more than once these visionaries found themselves confronting a hostile audience. Amos was banished from Bethel by its high priest, who branded as sedition his prophecy of the impending punishment of Israel's leaders (Amos 7.10–12). On the other hand, Isaiah seems to have remained a keen social critic of his compatriots for over three decades, continually calling Judah's ruling classes into line. Micah too fared well; Hezekiah was won over by the prophet's somber prediction of Jerusalem's destruction. A century later, when the mob threatened Jeremiah for his message of doom, some people still remembered the similar words of Micah and their positive effect on Hezekiah (Jer. 26.1–19).

Throughout most of Hezekiah's reign, tensions remained high between Assyria and the states along the Mediterranean. Sargon continued to consolidate his hold. The Assyrian presence on the coast, as far as the border of Sinai, was reinforced by resettling foreign captives in an emporium in which Assyrians and Egyptians "would trade together" (Sargon prism inscription from Nimrud, col. 4, ll.46–50), a remarkable free-market policy for its time. Even the nomads of the desert, who were major players in the movement of overland trade, were integrated within the imperial administration.

Yet significant as these developments may have been, they did not bring stability; rebellion, an ever-ready option, broke out whenever the Assyrian overlord seemed inattentive or weak. In 713 Sargon replaced Azur, the upstart ruler of Ashdod (an important Philistine city on the southwest coast of the Mediterranean), with his brother, an Assyrian loyalist. He in turn was ousted by Yamani, who sought to lure other vassal kingdoms in the southern region, among them Judah, to his side. At about this time, emissaries of Merodach-baladan (the biblical rendering of Marduk-apal-iddina), the Chaldean king of Babylonia, arrived in Jerusalem; ostensibly, they had come on a courtesy visit to inquire of Hezekiah's health, which had recently been failing. Merodach-baladan was a known foe of Assyria with a record of rebellion, and conceivably while in Jerusalem his envoys discussed diplomatic and perhaps even economic relations between Judah and Babylonia. Sargon himself did not lead the army that came to restore order in Ashdod; rather, it was his army commander who in 712 attacked and captured Ashdod as well as several neighboring Philistine towns, carrying off rich spoil and numerous prisoners. Ashdod was reorganized as an Assyrian province, a first for the region. There is reason to believe that Azekah, a town on the border of the Shephelah of Judah, was also attacked; a fragmentary Assyrian report describes the storming of this well-positioned fortress. Whatever the details, Hezekiah survived this blow and somehow avoided more serious Assyrian reprisals. He had to bide his time as a humbled vassal a bit longer before he would try again to free his kingdom.

His moment came in 705 BCE, when the Assyrian empire was shaken by Sargon II's death on the battlefield while campaigning in distant Anatolia. That mighty Assyrian king, infamous for his merciless use of force, a man who redrew the map of the Near East by uprooting entire populations, was himself denied a final resting place. He is the only ancient Assyrian monarch not to have been interred in royal fashion. In a mock eulogy, the Israelite prophet Isaiah expressed the relief surely felt by many upon receiving the news:

> Is this the man who made the earth tremble,
>   who shook kingdoms,
> who made the world like a desert
>   and overthrew its cities,
>   who would not let his prisoners go home?
> All the kings of the nations lie in glory,
>   each in his own tomb;
> but you are cast out, away from your grave,
>   like loathsome carrion,
> clothed with the dead, those pierced by the sword,
>   who go down to the stones of the Pit,
>   like a corpse trampled underfoot.

> You will not be joined with them in burial,
>   because you have destroyed your land,
>   you have killed your people.
>   (Isa. 14.16–20)

In the wake of Sargon's untimely end, rebellions erupted throughout the empire, from Babylonia as far as the Persian Gulf and along the Mediterranean coast down to the Egyptian border. As the new Assyrian ruler Sennacherib (705–681 BCE) fought to subdue the Chaldean rebels and their Elamite allies directly south of Assyria, Hezekiah took the lead in organizing the southern Syrian states against him. These included the Phoenician port of Sidon and its holdings down the coast to Acco, as well as Philistine Ashkelon and Ekron and the smaller towns under their rule. As on many previous occasions, Egyptian aid was promised, this time by the new pharaoh Shebitku (702–690 BCE) of the Nubian Dynasty 25, who was ready to pursue an active role in western Asia against Assyria. Hezekiah pressed for maximum participation in the rebel cause, to the point of using military force against holdouts. At Ekron, where those who called for armed resistance were in the majority, its pro-Assyrian king Padi was removed and imprisoned in Jerusalem. Other small kingdoms, such as Ashdod, Ammon, Moab, and Edom, may have toyed with the idea of joining the rebels, but they promptly dissociated themselves when Sennacherib finally appeared on the scene.

Preparations in Judah for the anticipated Assyrian reprisal concentrated on reinforcing Jerusalem's defenses, especially the residential quarter that had recently grown up on the city's western hill. Isaiah looked askance as the king's engineers "counted the houses of Jerusalem and . . . broke down the houses to fortify the wall" (Isa. 22.10). A short run of the massive (7 meters [23 feet] wide) fortification wall constructed at that time has been excavated in the Old City of Jerusalem. In the "lower city," the "city of David," the Siloam Tunnel project was completed, guaranteeing a sure water supply in case of a siege. A winding tunnel running 533 meters (1,750 feet) from the Gihon Spring in the Kidron Valley to the "Lower Pool" within the city's walls was dug through the limestone bedrock of the hill beneath the city. An appreciation of the difficulties encountered by the workmen can be read in the inscription chiseled on a wall within its recesses:

> While [   ] (were) still [   ] the axe(s) toward one another, and while there
> were still three cubits to be [tunneled, there was heard] a voice calling to his fellow,
> for there was a fissure (?) in the rock on the right [and on the left]. And on the day
> when the tunnel was cut through, the stonecutters struck toward one another, ax
> against ax. The water flowed from the source to the pool for 1,200 cubits, and the
> height of the rock was 100 cubits above the heads of the stonecutters.

Not until 701 BCE, more than three years after he had ascended the throne, did Sennacherib set out to quell the rebellions in the west. Unlike most chapters in Israelite history, the events of that year are particularly well documented. The sources consist of biblical texts from both royal and prophetic sources, an account in Sennacherib's annals, and an inscribed wall relief from the Assyrian royal palace in Nineveh; this rich trove, together with archaeological evidence, enables us to reconstruct the course of events in considerable detail.

Sennacherib marched his troops down the Mediterranean coast, meeting little resistance from the rebels in Sidon. The latter's king having fled to a safe haven in one of the city's overseas colonies, Sennacherib installed a new king, who shouldered Assyrian vassaldom. Continuing south toward Philistia, the Assyrians took Ashkelon and its environs and deported the royal family; a member of a rival line was set on the throne. At this juncture an Egyptian expeditionary force under the command of Taharqa, later to become pharaoh, engaged the Assyrians. The combined Egyptian and Nubian cavalry and chariot corps were no match for Sennacherib's army; many were taken prisoner before they could escape the rout. The cities of Eltekeh, Ekron, and Timnah in the Shephelah were the next to fall, setting the stage for the attack farther inland on the line of fortresses that guarded the roads up to the Judean hill country. Sennacherib's scribes described the scene:

> As for Hezekiah the Judean, who had not submitted to my yoke, I besieged forty-six of his fortified walled cites and surrounding smaller towns, which were without number. Using packed-down ramps and by applying battering rams, infantry attacks by mines, breeches, and siege machines, I conquered (them). I took out 200,150 people, young and old, male and female, horses, mules, donkeys, camels, cattle, and sheep, without number, and counted them as spoil.

Among the walled cities to fall to Sennacherib was the mighty fortress at Lachish, whose storming has been immortalized on an engraved relief that was prominently displayed in the king's palace at Nineveh. The expansive montage depicts the multiphased Assyrian assault on the city, whose defenders are shown desperately hurling stones and torches on the attackers from the wall. Excavations at the site have recovered the remains of a counterramp within the city opposite the Assyrian ramp on the outside, heaped up just in case the wall would be breached by the attacking forces. The Assyrian artist included later stages of the battle in his relief; engraved below the besieged city is a row of impaled Judeans, suffering the punishment meted out for treason. A long line of refugees is shown exiting the city gate on their way to pass in review before Sennacherib, who had set up his command post at the foot of the high mound of Lachish.

While these battles for control of the Judean Shephelah raged, Sennacherib also set about negotiating with Hezekiah for his submission, no doubt in an attempt to cut his losses and to complete the campaign in the quickest possible time. As a warning of things to come, Jerusalem was brought under siege:

> As for Hezekiah the Judean . . . I locked him up within Jerusalem, his royal city, like a bird in a cage. I surrounded him with earthworks, and made it unthinkable for him to exit by the city gate.

Simultaneous with the physical pressure, Sennacherib dispatched a high-level team of ranking Assyrian officers to meet their Judean counterparts at the upper pool on the Fuller's Field road to the north of Jerusalem's city walls. In the carefully crafted speech reported in 2 Kings 18.19–35, the Rab-shakeh, an Assyrian official who is presented as having more than just a working knowledge of Hebrew, turned to the defenders on the city wall and warned them of the consequences they would suffer if they continued to resist. Nothing and no one, he claimed, could thwart Assyria's sure victory, especially since the God of Israel had ordered the attack! In his shock over these uncompromising demands, Hezekiah sought the advice of Isaiah, whose counsel urged calm confidence in the Lord's protection of the city and its Davidic king.

In the end, it seems that negotiations led to a formula of surrender. Hezekiah would retain his throne, with Judah resuming its vassal status and the yearly payment of dues and tribute; a large indemnity, beyond the normal spoils of war, was to be transferred to Sennacherib; extensive sections of the kingdom—those captured during the fighting—were to be parceled among the Philistine city-states loyal to Assyria (Ashdod, Ashkelon, Gaza, and Ekron). An onerous settlement, but one that saved Hezekiah and Jerusalem.

Later generations, looking back on the attack on Judah in that year, viewed it as perhaps the most fateful event in the kingdom's three-hundred-year history to that point. Had Jerusalem fallen, Judah would have gone the way of the northern kingdom of Israel and especially its capital, Samaria—to exile and extinction. That Sennacherib struck a compromise with Hezekiah, given the strategic upper hand held by the Assyrian army throughout the land, seemed inconceivable. Sennacherib was not beyond the most ruthless punishment of rebellious cities: a decade or so later he would literally wipe Babylon from the map. Some Judahites (as Byron illustrates in his poem "The Destruction of Sennacherib") understood this break with the customary imperial practice as a miracle: the hand of the Lord, the God of Israel, had saved Jerusalem. Champions of Jerusalem's cause told of the annihilation of the vast Assyrian army that had camped outside the city's walls (2 Kings 19.35), and they pointed to Sennacherib's assassination, though some twenty years after the siege of Jerusalem, as just due for the blasphemous words he had uttered against the Lord.

The seventh century opened for Judah with its monarch and its population in the most dire straits. The prophet Isaiah is once again our informant, as he addressed the nation:

> Your country lies desolate,
>   your cities are burned with fire;
> in your very presence
>   aliens devour your land.
>   (Isa. 1.7)

The most that the man of God could promise those who daily faced the ravaged countryside was that, within three years, life would resume its regular cycle of sowing and reaping, planting and eating (Isa. 37.30). Within three years, Hezekiah died, the despair of defeat and the destruction that he brought on Judah accompanying him to his grave.

Survival under Assyrian Vassalage

Hezekiah's son Manasseh ascended the throne at the young age of twelve, and went on to reign in Jerusalem for fifty-five years (698–642 BCE), longer than any other dynast of the house of David. Historians as a rule vilify Manasseh, adopting the evaluation of the biblical sources that censure the king for his deviation from the religious reforms instituted by his father and for introducing idols into the Temple.

Manasseh is further accused of instituting a reign of terror, shedding the blood of many innocent persons in the capital; postbiblical tradition holds that the venerable prophet Isaiah was among those martyred. The report of Manasseh's evil deeds and apostasy was transparently worked up by the editors of the oldest history of Israel, the book of Kings, to rationalize the later demise of the monarchy and the exile of the nation in terms of God's just management of the world. In the editors' view, Judah's violation of the Mosaic covenant brought deserved punishment, Manasseh's acts being the breaking point. But a more balanced view of Manasseh and his policies can be achieved by setting them against the backdrop of the Near East during the century of Assyrian domination when Judah was subject to Nineveh.

Sennacherib did not return to the west again; the political settlement imposed at the conclusion of the campaign of 701 held for close to a quarter century, into the reign of his son Esarhaddon (681–669 BCE). In 679, the second year of his reign, Esarhaddon marched unchallenged to the border with Egypt in the Sinai Peninsula, in a show of force meant to demonstrate Assyria's continuing interest in those distant reaches of its empire. An uprising in the Phoenician port of Sidon several years later tested this policy, and the revolt was decisively put down—the city was despoiled and leveled, and its population was deported. A new commercial center named after the king, Kar Ashur-ahi-iddina ("Port Esarhaddon"), was built to replace the former town, settlers from abroad were brought in, and all were placed under the direct administration of a governor appointed by Nineveh. Clearly Assyria would brook no interference with its rule.

All the while, however, the Egyptian king Taharqa (biblical Tirhakah; 690–664 BCE), who may have harbored memories of his defeat in 701, when as a young commander he led the Egyptian forces against Sennacherib, was bent on supporting those elements in Phoenicia and Philistia who were prepared to take a more independent position vis-à-vis Assyria. Esarhaddon saw no other means to protect Assyrian interests in the Mediterranean area than direct confrontation with Taharqa, and he invaded Egypt in 674, only to be repelled. Such a defeat could not be left unanswered—to do so could have meant loss of the west altogether. In fact, while Esarhaddon reorganized for another attempt at taking Egypt, Baal of Tyre, who was bound by treaty to Assyria, and Mitinti of Ashkelon made common cause with Taharqa. Other petty monarchs may also have been enticed into revolt against what they perceived as a weakened Assyria. Three years later, as a prelude to his second invasion of Egypt, Esarhaddon laid siege to Tyre and forced its surrender. Proceeding south, he crossed the desert of the northern Sinai with the help of local Arab rulers and entered Egypt. There he triumphed. Taharqa fled Memphis, leaving behind family and officials, who were taken prisoner and, together with great wealth, carried off to Assyria. The victorious Assyrians established their rule throughout the Nile Valley.

This was the world that Manasseh faced during his first three decades as king, and it is little wonder that as ruler of the diminutive mountain kingdom of Judah he fulfilled his vassal duties on command. Esarhaddon mentions Manasseh among the "twenty-two kings of the west, the sea coast, and overseas" who were called up to provide material for the reconstruction of the royal storehouse at the Assyrian capital of Nineveh; these same vassals took part in the building of Port Esarhaddon. But as expressive of obedience as these activities may seem, there is one blemish on this picture of Manasseh as loyal servant of the empire. A late, reworked biblical passage (2 Chron. 33.11) tells of Manasseh's incarceration by Assyrian troops in Babylon and his subsequent return to Jerusalem. Manasseh may have been enticed by Baal of Tyre and by Pharaoh Taharqa to join in their revolt, and when Esarhaddon set out for Egypt, his route took him through the coastal plain of Philistia, very close to the border of Judah. Like the other rebels, Manasseh was arrested on the charge of treason; he was subsequently pardoned and returned to his throne, as were several of the minor rulers in the Nile Delta after the Assyrian victories in Egypt. Less than a decade later, Manasseh appears in Assyrian records once again, together with the twenty-one other western vassal kings, this time providing armed contingents for the Egyptian campaign of Esarhaddon's son and successor, Ashurbanipal (669–627 BCE).

On balance, vassal obedience, which was based on economic submission to imperial goals, had its rewards. The archaeological record contains signs that during the seventh century BCE the Judean countryside recovered under the watchful eye of the Assyrian army. Throughout the territory of the Philistine kingdoms to the west and south of Judah, in areas that had at one time been Judean, fortresses and structures were built following Mesopotamian architectural design; some of their brick walls— as much as 4 to 5 meters (13 to 16 feet) thick—still stand as evidence of Assyria's investment in this vital border zone. In the excavated rooms at several sites, imported Assyrian palace ware points to the luxurious lifestyle of the area's residents. Particularly striking is the example of Ekron on Judah's western border, which had been taken by force during Sennacherib's campaign. Excavation at Tel Miqne, the site of ancient Ekron, has shown that the city developed into the region's largest center for olive oil production (the annual yield is estimated at more than a thousand tons) and its domestic residential quarters mirror the city's prosperity. The local religion at Ekron flourished as shown by a recently discovered royal inscription, the first of its kind from a Philistine city, that commemorates the dedication of a shrine to a hitherto unknown goddess by Ikausa son of Padi, king of Ekron. (Padi had been reinstalled by Sennacherib when hostilities ended in 701.) Manasseh, too, was able, no doubt with imperial license, to rebuild Judah's defenses and reconstruct Jerusalem's walls and gates.

The written record complements this picture of growth and resurgence with its own point of view. Especially among the upper class, Judeans adopted foreign customs wholesale. Outlandish dress became fashionable in Jerusalem, as did such alien folkways as "leaping over [the Temple?] threshold" in Philistine manner (Zeph. 1.4–5, 8–9). Merchants from Judah plied the routes to Mesopotamia, where the unit weight of Judah, the shekel, was recognized currency in those distant markets; luxury items, along with the profits of this trade, accompanied them on the journey home. Considering the multifarious daily contact with the Assyrian administration and the mixed populations settled throughout the land, it would have been surprising indeed had Judahite culture not absorbed some of the signs of the dominant Assyro-Aramean culture. At Gezer, for example, business transactions were conducted according to standard Assyrian legal practice, as is made clear by the cuneiform sale document of a parcel of land: the owner of the field in question, an Israelite named Netanyahu, impressed his personal seal decorated with typical Mesopotamian lunar symbolism.

King Manasseh seems to have been taken up by this new cultural wave, which

found its most glaring expression in the introduction of unorthodox forms of worship
at the national shrine:

> He erected altars for Baal, made a sacred pole, as King Ahab of Israel had done,
> worshiped all the host of heaven, and served them. He built altars in the house of
> the LORD. . . . The carved image of Asherah that he had made he set in the house. (2
> Kings 21.3–7)

More than anything else, this royal sponsorship of what from the perspective of the
biblical historians was idolatry determined Manasseh's negative reputation. Some
modern commentators have constructed a case partially in Manasseh's defense, jus-
tifying the king's acts by invoking the supposed Assyrian policy of requiring subject
peoples to adopt the official religion of the empire. According to this view, whether
it be the introduction of a new altar in the Temple courtyard by King Ahaz, Manasseh's grandfather, or Manasseh's stationing of sculptured images in the Temple itself,
the kings of Judah were in reality following Assyrian dictate. *Cuius regio eius religio*:
a region follows its ruler's religion.

But this exculpatory argument does not survive close examination. Assyrian imperialism was noncoercive in religious matters; vassal kings were not required to
worship the imperial god Ashur, and local religions suffered no interference. In fact,
Assyria's kings often made public display of their respect for non-Assyrian gods by
acknowledging their divinity, and on occasion by offering sacrifice to them. As for
the kingdom of Judah, despite its checkered history of relations with Assyria, it remained a vassal state for over a century, free to pursue its native religion.

Manasseh's acts, then, are best understood as representative of the climate of
cultural assimilation that swept over many areas of the Near East in the wake of the
Assyrian conquest. While the restoration of local sanctuaries throughout Judah may
have stemmed from a conservative reaction to the reforms of Hezekiah and his failed
political policies, the foreign rituals reportedly introduced during the reign of Manasseh were voluntary adoptions. They were of mixed origin: Baal and Asherah were
of Canaanite-Phoenician affinity, whereas the veneration of astral deities and the
dedication of horses and chariots to the sun-god had links to Assyro-Aramean practice. Possibly Judah's sorry state throughout most of Manasseh's reign engendered a
disenchantment with native Israelite traditions, which in turn abetted the assimilation
of foreign ways. Yet this is not to imply that all Judeans subscribed to the king's
innovations. Though there is a distinct lack of prophetic composition from this period, the brutal silencing of the opposition—"Manasseh shed very much innocent
blood" (2 Kings 21.16)—teaches otherwise.

Toward the end of Manasseh's long reign, in the sixth decade of the seventh
century, Assyria became entangled in an uninterrupted series of wars that put to a
severe test its hankering for imperialism. Ashurbanipal had to face his rebellious
brother in Babylon and that city's Elamite allies, as well as the ever-restless Arab
tribes in the south and west. Egypt, under Psammetichus I (664–610 BCE), aided by
Greek mercenaries, freed itself from Assyrian vassalage without encountering miliary
reprisal, and may have come to an agreement on the management of imperial interests in Syria. This would account for the tradition, reported by Herodotus, of a
twenty-nine-year siege of Ashdod by Psammetichus. At the same time, Assyria faced

increasing threats on its northern border as the nomadic Cimmerians and Scythians pushed westward toward Syria. There is, however, evidence for Assyrian military activity in Transjordan and on the Phoenician coast as far south as Acco during this decade; Samaria once again became home to a group of deportees. The Assyrians had not quite yet withdrawn to the Tigris-Euphrates Valley. But from a modern vantage point, the sudden interruption of cuneiform documentation after 639 does read like a sign that victorious Assyria had come upon bad times.

Manasseh died in 642 BCE, and his son and successor Amon (641–640) reigned just two years before being assassinated by his courtiers. There is no way of knowing just what prompted this mutiny, and equally strong cases can be made for either foreign or internal affairs. Judah did not lack for political tensions and intrigues. The uprising was soon put down by "the people of land," that influential segment of the population of Judah, mostly the wealthy, who appeared in times of dynastic crisis to protect the succession rights of the house of David. In the present instance, this conservative grouping of landowners and merchants nominated Amon's son Josiah, who was only eight years old when he ascended the throne, and during the new king's minority the "people of the land" continued to manage the affairs of state.

Samaria as an Assyrian Province

The Israelite polity came to its end with the conquest of Samaria by Sargon II of Assyria in 720 BCE. After some two hundred years of the independent monarchy established by Jeroboam I, tens of thousands of Israelites found themselves exiled to distant regions of the Assyrian empire—to Gozan in northern Syria, to Halah farther east, even to the distant Iranian frontier. Sargon speaks of deporting 27,290 persons from Samaria and enlisting up to 200 skilled charioteers as a separate unit in his royal corps. The presence of only occasional stray references to individual Samarians in later Assyrian documents seems to confirm the view that within a few generations these exiles lost their national and ethnic identity in Assyria's melting pot. True, prophets such as Jeremiah and Ezekiel held out hope that both houses of Jacob, Judah and Israel, would take part in the promised restoration. But tradition has done right in dubbing the Israelite exiles in Assyria "the ten lost tribes."

As for the conquered territories, an Assyrian prism inscription has Sargon boasting that he "restored the city of Samaria and settled it more densely than before, and brought there people from the lands of my conquest. I placed my eunuch over them as governor and counted them as Assyrians." The resettlement of the city proceeded in many stages, continuing well into the seventh century; people arrived from as far away as Babylonia and the city of Susa in Persia, as well as from relatively nearby Hamath in Syria. Under Sargon's regional economic reorganization, nomadic Arab tribesmen moved into the province, where they probably continued to serve as a link in the overland trade. Thus the ethnic admixture of the population to be found in Samaria mirrored that to be found in many areas of the empire. For the Israelites who remained in the land—some modern estimates consider their number to have been considerable—and for the newcomers resettled in the province the Assyrians called Samerina established by Sargon in the hill country of Ephraim, life reorganized itself around the model dictated by the conqueror. An Assyrian governor oversaw the collection of tax and tribute payments, and experts trained the new Assyrians in proper conduct, "to revere god and king."

Were it not for religious developments among the residents of Samerina reported by the editor of the book of Kings, there would be little to include in a history of Samaria—or, for that matter, of the other provinces Assyria created out of the former kingdom of Israel—for lack of written sources. Only fragments of the commemorative stelae proclaiming Assyrian victories, which were erected in Samaria and Ashdod, have been recovered; a more substantial piece of a monument left in the Sharon coastal plain by Esarhaddon awaits publication. The names of two governors of Samerina and of a governor of the province of Megiddo are known, as they served as year eponyms in the Assyrian system of calendric reckoning. These officials oversaw an administration that operated on models imported from the homeland. Documentary evidence from Samaria and Gezer shows that commercial transactions were drawn up following cuneiform legal tradition. The Assyrian presence has also left its mark in the archaeological record. Public buildings copied Assyrian architectural design, and the imported ceramics known as "Assyrian palace ware" recovered at a number of sites in Israel and in Philistia indicate the good life enjoyed by provincial officials.

The required reverence of god and king, a civic duty of all Assyrian citizens, did not abrogate the worship of other, non-Assyrian divinities, which the Samarians continued uninterruptedly. But of more than passing interest to the biblical historians was the development in Samaria of what they viewed as an aberrant form of Israelite worship. According to 2 Kings 17.25–33, soon after their arrival the settlers in Samaria suffered repeated lion attacks, which were interpreted as punishment by the local god for failure to worship him properly. For want of a local priest—all of whom had apparently been exiled—a priest of the God of Israel was repatriated by imperial order to Bethel in order to instruct and lead the provincials in the correct forms of worship. But the newcomers erred in their belief. Although they served the God of Israel, at the same time they continued to serve the deities they had worshiped in their former homelands, creating improper, even dangerous, religious mingling. Such is the biblical account, which later history shows to be flawed.

Toward the end of the seventh century BCE, all traces of the non-Israelite forms of worship imported by the foreign settlers seem to have disappeared from Samaria. One report, in 2 Kings 23.15–20, notes that the reform measures carried out by King Josiah in Samaria (see below) were focused on the worship of the God of Israel at Bethel, an ancient Israelite sacred site. A second report, a survey of the century-long Assyrian rule by a Chronicler living in the Persian period, tells of the Israelites living in the north as having been welcomed to take part in the festivities in Jerusalem marking the Temple rededication (2 Chron. 34.9, 33; 35.18). Neither of these reports acknowledges the presence of foreign rituals in Samaria; even the foreigners themselves have disappeared from the record. Considered from a critical point of view, these sometimes polemical biblical descriptions suggest that within three to four generations of their arrival in Samaria the foreign settlers were on their way to being absorbed by those Israelites who had escaped deportation and still lived in the land. Assimilating Israelite customs, the foreigners became virtually indistinguishable from the autochthonous population. And by the mid-sixth century, the residents of Samaria had developed into a community of faithful who worshiped the God of Israel and who pressed to participate in the rebuilding of the Temple in Jerusalem alongside the Judeans who had returned from Babylon. These Samarians must have been scrupulous enough in their religious practice, for some of them married into the families of the high priesthood in Jerusalem. But that development is best left for the next chapter.

King Josiah and the Great Reform in Judah

King Josiah (639–609 BCE) is one of the heroes of the editor of the book of Kings; he is depicted as a second David, who displayed loyalty to God as no other king had done before or afterward. Though he ruled at a time of major changes in the political map of the Near East, the biblical record speaks only tangentially of Josiah's position in the international arena; the focus is on his religious reforms and the renewal of the covenant between Judah and its God. Extrabiblical documentation, mostly from Babylonia, is not much more informative on affairs in distant Judah.

Even before the death of Ashurbanipal in 627 BCE, dispute had broken out over the succession to the Assyrian throne pitting against one another several rival brothers and their supporters in the army. Babylonia seized the occasion of the king's passing, and under the leadership of the Chaldean Nabopolassar, rebelled and achieved independence. The Babylonian Chronicle records several failed Assyrian attempts to contain the loss. Within a decade, the once mighty empire had to be propped up by Egyptian aid, as the forces of Babylonia, now allied with the powerful Median army under Cyaxeres, carried the battles into the Assyrian heartland. In 614, the ancient religious capital Ashur fell, and in 612 the imperial capital Nineveh was overrun, its magnificent palaces and temples sacked and set ablaze in an act of fury and revenge. The Hellenistic historian Berossus adds a dramatic detail: Sin-shar-ishkun, the penultimate Assyrian king, "dismayed at this attack, burned himself together with his palace." The Israelite prophet Nahum caught the mood of many who rejoiced over the empire's collapse when he intoned:

> Your shepherds are asleep,
>   O king of Assyria;
>   your nobles slumber.
> Your people are scattered on the mountains
>   with no one to gather them.
> There is no assuaging your hurt,
>   your wound is mortal.
> All who hear the news about you
>   clap their hands over you.
> For who has ever escaped
>   your endless cruelty?
>   (Nahum 3.18–19)

Though some of the army managed to escape to Haran in Syria and tried to regroup under Ashur-uballit, the last Assyrian monarch, Assyria effectively ceased to exist.

Given this picture of imperial dissolution, one wonders whether any of the territory of the Assyrian provinces in Israel was formally transferred to Josiah, as may
have been the case with the Philistine city-states on the coast given over to Egyptian
governance. Many historians have seen Josiah as reestablishing Israelite rule over
most parts of territory of the former northern kingdom of Israel, though the extension
of his rule beyond Judah cannot readily be established. Josiah did carry his reform
measures into Bethel and the other cities of the province of Samerina at about the
same time that Assyria was fighting for its life, but this need not have meant the
formal annexation of Samerina to Judah. Often cited as relevant in this regard are
discoveries at a site on the Mediterranean coast, Mesad Hashavyahu, just south of
Yavneh. In this small fortress of some 6 dunams (1.5 acres), local as well as imported
Greek pottery was excavated; a small number of ostraca in Hebrew were also recovered. One of these, a letter of fourteen lines, illuminates the administration of justice
in everyday life: a complaint by the corvée worker Hoshayahu is submitted to his
commander, in which he claims to have been wronged by his work supervisor, his
cloak confiscated. While the ceramic styles and the Hebrew inscriptions fit the period
of Josiah, drawing conclusions from them as to Josiah's control of the vital coast road
and his engaging of Greek mercenaries in Judah's army is unwarranted. After all, the
fate of Judah was dependent on Egypt's determination to assert its authority over the
western kingdoms freed from Assyrian control, and Psammetichus was bent on just
that.

It is more likely that an arrangement prevailed whereby the dominant Psammetichus, who himself employed Greek soldiers, permitted Josiah a sphere of influence
in nonstrategic areas, while retaining overall authority for himself. This might well
have included the frontier fortress of Arad in the eastern Negeb, where documents
record the issue of rations to *Kittiyim*, a Hebrew term for Greeks. Throughout, the
Egyptian army enjoyed unhampered movement on its way north to prop up the
tottering Assyria until Josiah's final year.

During this turbulent period Josiah's home-front reputation was made. Jeremiah
praised him as the dispenser of "justice and righteousness . . . [who] judged the cause
of the poor and the needy" (Jer. 22.15–16), but it is the reform of Judah's worship
that is most often associated with the king's name. Just from the amount of space
given to the report of Josiah's reform activities in the book of Kings, one learns that
in official circles Josiah was touted as the ideal Davidic king. What began as a routine
royal duty, the repair of the Temple building, turned into a major milestone in
Judah's history. One of the duties and prerogatives of ancient Near Eastern monarchs
was the upkeep of temples and the maintenance of worship that took place in them,
through gifts and dedications, notably after military victories. Inscriptions from as
early as the third millennium BCE record such royal benefaction and voice the hope
that reciprocal divine blessing will be showered upon the donor and his offspring.
Josiah's initiative vis-à-vis the Temple of Jerusalem falls within the category of periodic repair and remodeling. But unlike the instances where the expenses were covered by royal donation, the present work was underwritten by public contributions
specially earmarked for the purpose. This procedure was not new; King Jehoash (early
eighth century BCE) is already credited with having instituted a regulation by which

the repair funds were to be collected separately from the priestly revenues, then checked and distributed by a joint committee of two, the king's scribe and the high priest (2 Kings 12.7–17).

What distinguishes Josiah's enterprise is the reported discovery during the repair work in the Temple of a "book of law [Hebrew *tôrâ*]," which stimulated the movement for religious reform. Our sources depict Josiah as deeply moved by the message of the "book of law," when it was read to him, that violators of Israel's covenant with God would be severely punished. After due consultation and encouragement from the prophetess Huldah, he convoked a kingdomwide assembly to renew the covenant between Judah and God based on the "law." This commitment in hand, Josiah ordered a thoroughgoing purge of all non-Israelite forms of worship—the residue of centuries-long accommodation to foreign influence. Everything associated with these rituals was removed and burned, and the priests who attended them banned. And, like Hezekiah in his day, Josiah outlawed worship at the local shrines and high places, redirecting all ritual to the newly cleansed Temple; the priests who had served at the rural sites were accommodated in Jerusalem, though they were not granted equal status at the altar as the "book of law" stipulated (see Deut. 18.6–8).

Josiah also moved against the sites of worship in Samaria where, to his mind, aberrant Israelite ritual was practiced; of particular note is his dismantling the high place at Bethel constructed by Jeroboam at the time of the founding of the northern kingdom of Israel, a symbolic act of reprisal against the long-defunct rebel monarchy. To mark the completion of this year-long activity, the Passover was celebrated in Jerusalem as it had not been celebrated for generations.

A major difficulty in evaluating the foregoing description of the reform, which is based solely on biblical narrative, is the identity of the "law book" that stirred Josiah to action. The discovery of a law book in the Temple is not implausible, for as dwellings of the gods temples often became the repository of documents of state as well as of religious interest, their divine residents often being called on to defend and protect the agreements deposited with them. In the present instance, many identify the "book of law" with the biblical book of Deuteronomy or a significant part of it. The demand for centralization of worship at a single site and its purification from all foreign forms pervades Deuteronomic law. Deuteronomy 28's threats of frightening punishments for nonobservance of the law would surely spur a pious king to action. Furthermore, it is thought that Deuteronomy is not, as the book itself claims to be, a work of Mosaic origin, which supposedly had been secreted away during the dark years of Manasseh's rule. Rather, it was the ideological platform of the Josianic reform movement. Indeed, Deuteronomy is marked by a specific phraseology and rhetorical style in promoting a number of teachings, which distinguish it from the other books ascribed to Moses. It is hard to claim that Deuteronomy, as a pseudepigraph, was a wholly new creation of the late seventh century. Because it seems to include materials from an older age, the book of Deuteronomy might conceivably have been created by the reformers in anticipation of its "discovery." It thus represents the first stage in the process of collection and canonization of Israelite law and tradition, which would culminate several centuries later under the direction of Ezra the scribe in the completed Torah that we know today. For certain, ascribing legal and sermonic material to Moses lent the reform program the justification needed to win vigorous royal support and public acceptance. King Josiah, with priests and prophets at his side, rallied the people of Judah behind the call for a renewal of the covenant, at a time when the kingdom was emerging from long years of Assyrian subjugation.

These days of glory on the home front did not stand him well on his day of reckoning, for Josiah met a sorrowful end. A single laconic sentence tells of his meeting at Megiddo the Egyptian pharaoh Neco II (610–595 BCE), who was rushing north with aid for Assyria, and of Josiah's being killed there (2 Kings 23.29). The circumstances behind this tragic encounter can in the main be reconstructed. The retreat of the Assyrians from Nineveh to Haran in 612 was followed by their ouster from that city two years later, despite continued Egyptian support, and for the next few years it was Egypt that thwarted the advance of Babylonia into the former Assyrian holdings in the west. These continuing Assyrian losses, as well as the death of the aged Psammetichus during the summer of 610, may have been interpreted by Josiah as a chance to advance Judean independence. At the same time, he may have reckoned that the future lay with Babylonia, and so sought to check further Egyptian moves. The modus vivendi that had marked Judah-Egypt relations for several decades became an open question now that the untried Neco sat on the throne.

The meeting at Megiddo did not end well; though a full-scale military encounter may not have taken place, Neco succeeded somehow in killing Josiah. From there, he hurried to his base camp on the Euphrates, where the combined Assyrian-Egyptian armies failed to retake Haran from the Babylonians. Meanwhile, the body of Josiah was returned to Jerusalem for burial. Tradition tells of a lament composed by the prophet Jeremiah in commemoration of the king's passing (2 Chron. 35.25) that, centuries later, was still recited as part of the standard liturgy, so enduring was the sense of great loss.

The true literary monument to Josiah, however, is the biblical book of Kings (in its first, preexilic edition). It was composed in Deuteronomic reform circles as the encomium for the king whose faithfulness to the "law of Moses" gave Israel a new lease on life. To prove that Josiah had indeed saved the nation from doom, the Deuteronomic author-editor of Kings surveyed the history of the monarchy from Solomon until his own day, judging each ruler on a simplistic, pragmatic scale: he did what was pleasing or displeasing to the Lord by observing the law of Moses. This author-editor utilized a number of sources in his work—palace and temple records, popular prophetic tales, perhaps even an earlier historical composition that used judgment formulas—and refers the reader to the "Book of the History of the Kings of Judah [or Israel]" for more detailed information on royal activities. While the audience for whom the editor of Kings wrote is unknown (perhaps it was the literati and official circles at court), the message of his synthesis of Israel's history is unmistakable. Disobedience and rebellion led to the inevitable punishment of Samaria, its destruction and exile; loyalty and a returning to the Lord as enjoined by Josiah spared Judah a similar fate.

Given such praise, it is proper to inquire after the immediate and long-range success of Josiah's reform, before pursuing Judah's political history after the Megiddo debacle. In truth, the evidence is meager and sometimes contradictory. The book of Kings is not helpful; its author reverts to the use of standard formulas and tells of

Josiah's successors as behaving to the displeasure of the Lord without providing any details. Among the prophets who were active during the postreform decades, Jeremiah spoke out mostly against popular fetishes and forms of worship that he observed in his travels around Jerusalem. Only Ezekiel, from his place of exile in Babylonia, envisioned the Temple of Jerusalem as rife with idolatry, but his portrayal may have been based, at least in part, on a retroversion of the excesses of Manasseh's age. Thus, all that can be said with any assurance is that as long as Josiah reigned, his reform enjoyed wide support. With his death and the rapid decline in Judah's political fortunes, many Judeans seem to have adopted the stance quoted by the prophet—"The LORD does not see us, the LORD has forsaken the land" (Ezek. 8.12)—as an explanation for their worship of other deities.

The Final Decades of the Judean Monarchy

The unforeseen death of Josiah had left Judah without a designated heir. Once again the "people of the land" stepped into the breach, appointing Josiah's son Jehoahaz to the throne in 609 BCE. But because Judah was now effectively under Egyptian hegemony, this independent move was rejected. Neco removed Jehoahaz after just three months and exiled him to Egypt. Jehoiakim (a throne name, given by his overlord), another son of Josiah, was elevated as king, and a crushing indemnity of one hundred talents of silver and a talent of gold was imposed on the "people of the land."

The decade of Jehoiakim's reign (608–598 BCE) saw Judah shifting back and forth between allegiance to Egypt—to whom Jehoiakim owed his throne—and the new Babylonian overlord, who in due course arrived on the scene. The struggle between the two powers continued for a number of years, until Neco was worsted at Carchemish on the Euphrates in 605; the Egyptian army reeled back to the Nile Delta, driven by the superior Babylonian forces under the crown prince Nebuchadrezzar (a form of the name *Nebuchadnezzar* etymologically closer to the original and found in some biblical passages). In the summer and winter of the following year, Nebuchadrezzar, now king of Babylonia, marched his troops south. Underscoring the desperate straits of Egypt's former vassals in Philistia, a letter written in Aramaic from King Adon of Ekron to Neco urgently asks for aid inasmuch as the forces "of the king of Babylon have reached Aphek [in the coastal plain]." The heavy fighting reported to have taken place at Ashkelon and the city's destruction show that Egypt had abandoned the area, preferring, for the time being at least, to bolster its soon-to-be-tested home defenses. "The king of Egypt did not come again out of his land, for the king of Babylon had taken over all that belonged to the king of Egypt from the Wadi of Egypt [Wadi el-Arish] to the River Euphrates" (2 Kings 24.7).

At this juncture Judah submitted to Babylonia, but not without bitter internal controversy. The voices of those who urged surrender to Nebuchadrezzar, most prominent among them the prophet Jeremiah, were antagonistically received. The high drama of those days can be grasped by a chapter from the biography of Jeremiah (Jer. 36). No newcomer to Jerusalem, the prophet had been expounding the word of his God since the days of Josiah. His warning that continued disregard of the covenant demands for justice and righteousness in public life would lead to God's punishing his people was more than once met with scorn and outright hostility. The antagonism

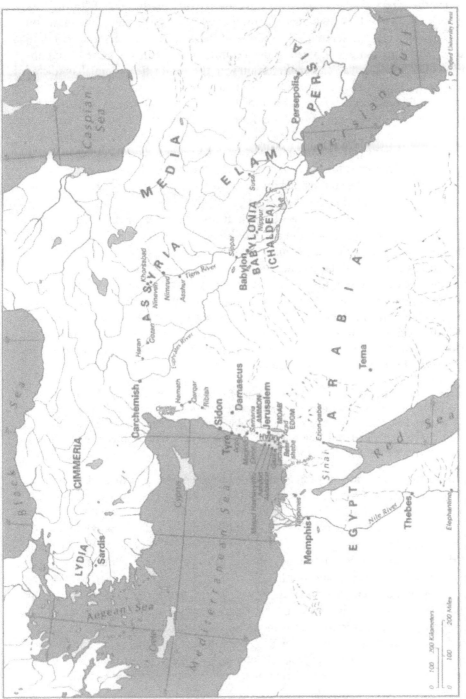

The Near East during the Neo-Babylonian Empire

between the king and Jeremiah must have been particularly great following the prophet's censure of his sanguineous extravagances. Not surprisingly, therefore, on this particular occasion, Jeremiah chose to send Baruch, his secretary and friend, to read his words to those assembled at the Temple; he himself was barred from appearing there because of an earlier altercation with the authorities. Jeremiah predicted dire consequences if they resisted Babylonia. It was a chimera to believe that the Temple would offer them refuge, for it, too, was forfeit, just as the old premonarchic sanctuary in Shiloh had been handed over for destruction to the Philistines. His words were immediately brought to the king's attention, and though some ministers supported the prophet's stand, Jehoiakim derisively consigned Jeremiah's scroll to the fire section by section as the scroll was read, and ordered both the prophet and his secretary arrested. In the end, Jehoiakim did submit to Nebuchadrezzar, although he soon found reason to switch loyalties.

Nebuchadrezzar suffered a major setback in his attempt to invade Egypt in 601 and was forced to return to Babylonia to refit his army. This information is recorded in the Babylonian Chronicle as the main event in Nebuchadrezzar's fourth year, and it is a striking example of the evenhandedness of that ancient source. In the wake of his victory, Neco moved against Gaza, thus moving Egypt's border to the northern Sinai once again; Jehoiakim returned to his pro-Egyptian stance. Babylonian garrison troops stationed in the west took the lead in trying to bring Judah back into line, until Nebuchadrezzar himself appeared on the scene. Despite Egypt's proximity, Neco lent no support to his erstwhile client in Jerusalem. The outcome is reported in the Babylonian Chronicle in summary fashion:

> Year 7 [of Nebuchadrezzar]. In the month of Kislev [December 598], the king of Babylonia mobilized his troops and marched to the west. He encamped against the city of Judah [Jerusalem], and on the second of Adar [16 March 597], he captured the city and he seized [its] king. A king of his choice he appointed there; he to[ok] its heavy tribute and carried it off to Babylon.

Sometime during the Babylonian siege of Jerusalem, Jehoiakim died under unknown circumstances—there is even suspicion of assassination. His son Jehoiachin assumed the throne, but within three months he submitted and threw himself upon the mercy of Nebuchadrezzar. The young Jehoiachin was indeed spared, living out his life in exile. Deported together with the king were members of the royal household and the court, as well the city's elite—officers of the army and its premier fighting units and skilled craftsmen and smiths all found themselves on the road to Babylon, where they would be employed in state service. Their total number reached some ten thousand persons, more than enough for the start of what was to become a flourishing community in exile. Foremost among the spoils were the state and Temple treasuries, including golden vessels dedicated by King Solomon. Thus, when Zedekiah, Jehoiachin's uncle and the last son of Josiah to attain the throne, was installed as a Babylonian vassal king, he took over a land much impoverished, depleted of both human and material resources.

Zedekiah's eleven-year reign, as tumultuous as any in Judah's recent history, would be the kingdom's final decade as a sovereign state. Rather than maintaining loyalty to his liege and overlord, as might have been expected, Zedekiah seized every opportunity to break free from Babylonia. To suggest youth and inexperience as the causes of this policy would be to engage in modern psychohistory. On the other hand, it is understandable that observers in the west might have thought that Babylonia was going into decline. After his victory at Jerusalem, Nebuchadrezzar faced several serious threats to his rule. During the next three years, he met Elam on the eastern front and put down a rebellion among army officers at home. In each case, Nebuchadrezzar overcame his enemies, but to some, these events suggested that the time was ripe to regain independence. Thus, in the late summer of 594 BCE, a regional conclave convened in Jerusalem to plan joint action against Nebuchadrezzar. Among the participants were delegates from Edom, Moab, Ammon, Tyre, and Sidon. Egypt stood conspicuously aloof, Neco having died the previous winter and his successor, Psammetichus II (595–589), finding himself engaged in strengthening his southern border.

Talk of rebellion was everywhere, and the leadership in Judah was clearly divided over the issue. Once again, Jeremiah found himself confronting the anti-Babylonian faction in heated debate. He demonstrated his disapproval of their actions by appearing before those assembled at the Temple wearing a yoke of straps and bars on his neck, symbolic of the yoke of the king of Babylon that God had placed on the nations, not to be removed. The prophet also warned against the false hopes spawned by other prophets that the exiles would soon return. Through his contacts with that community, he knew that the unrest had reached them, and that several of their leaders had been executed by Nebuchadrezzar. Among those present at the Temple when Jeremiah spoke was Hananiah, son of Azur from Gibeon, who to the dismay of the crowd and the prophet himself removed the yoke from Jeremiah's neck. Breaking the yoke, Hananiah prophesied that just so would God "break the yoke of King Nebuchadnezzar of Babylon from the neck of all the nations within two years" (Jer. 28.11).

In the end, the rebellion did not come off. Apparently a decision could not reached by the delegates, but Zedekiah was summoned that winter to appear personally before Nebuchadrezzar while the Babylonian king was on campaign in northern Syria, in all likelihood to explain his conspiratorial activities and to pledge renewed loyalty.

In 592, Egypt reappeared on the stage. Fresh from his victory in Nubia, Psammetichus II planned and executed a triumphal visit of his court and army to Philistia, Judah, and the Phoenician cities of Tyre and Sidon: "Let the priests come with the bouquets of the gods of Egypt to take them to the land of Kharu [Syria] with Pharaoh" (Papyrus Rylands IX, 14.16–19). Babylonia's failure to react to this irruption into its holdings most likely stoked the smoldering embers of rebellion among its Syrian vassals, although the lengthy illness and death of Psammetichus delayed open uprising. But in early 589 the new pharaoh Apries (589–570 BCE; called Hophra in the Bible) showed his intention to continue the vigorous policy of his predecessor, launching a foray into the mountains of Lebanon. With the promise of Egyptian support in matériel and an auxiliary fighting force, Zedekiah finally broke with Nebuchadrezzar.

Only the final stages of the Babylonian retaliation against Judah can be discussed, and this merely in outline. Biblical sources focus on the siege of Jerusalem, and the parts of the Babylonian Chronicle covering these years no longer exist. Archaeological investigation, however, adds perspective: excavations at many major sites in Judah have uncovered destruction levels of burnt debris and ruins properly ascribed to the Babylonian army, either in its campaign of 598 or in that of 587. On the other hand, a number of Judean sites, particularly north of Jerusalem, show evidence of continuity, with undisturbed occupation levels into the sixth century BCE. In the key fortress of Lachish in the Judean lowlands, a collection of over twenty Hebrew ostraca was found in the rubble by the gateway; they are part of the correspondence received by Yoash, apparently commander of this strategic post, during the period of the Babylonian operations in Judah, and they hint tantalizingly at matters known to the addressee but hidden from the modern reader. One letter informs Yoash that "we are watching for the signal fires of Lachish according to signs which my lord set, for we cannot see Azekah." Yoash was also apprised that "the army officer Coniah son of Elnathan came down in order to go to Egypt and he sent to take from here Hodaviah son of Ahijah and his men. And your servant is sending you the letter of Tobiah, the king's servant, which came to Shallum son of Jaddua through the prophet, saying 'Beware!'"

Jerusalem came under siege in January 587, holding out for eighteen months until the summer of 586. The arrival of Egyptian forces did provide a short respite as the Babylonian army withdrew to meet them, but not for long. After the defeat of the Egyptians, who had once again shown themselves to be an unreliable "broken reed of a staff" (2 Kings 18.21), the siege resumed. In the end, severe hunger brought the city to its knees. The walls of Jerusalem were breached, probably on the north, where the topography lends itself to the setting up of siege machinery, and where a great quantity of Babylonian-style arrowheads have been recovered. Zedekiah tried to escape to the Jordan Valley and from there abroad, but he was captured and hauled before Nebuchadrezzar, who was encamped at Riblah in central Syria. After watching his sons' execution, the king was blinded—a common punishment of rebellious slaves—and sent off to exile. Meanwhile, the order was given to complete the deportation and to destroy the city. The ringleaders of the rebellion were rounded up, shipped off to Riblah, and summarily put to death, and the final destruction took place:

> In the fifth month, on the seventh day of the month—which was the nineteenth year of King Nebuchadnezzar, king of Babylon [16 August 586]—Nebuzaradan, the captain of the bodyguard, a servant of the king of Babylon, came to Jerusalem. He burned the house of the LORD, the king's house, and all the houses of Jerusalem; every great house he burned down. All the army of the Chaldeans who were with the captain of the guard broke down the walls around Jerusalem. Nebuzaradan the captain of the guard carried into exile the rest of the people who were left in the city and the deserters who had defected to the king of Babylon—all the rest of the population. (2 Kings 25.8–11)

> How lonely sits the city
>   that was once full of people!
> How like a widow she has become,
>   she that was great among the nations!
> She that was a princess among the provinces
>   has become a vassal.
>   (Lam. 1.1)

In this verse, the opening line from the book of Lamentations, one feels the great sense of personal and national loss that the destruction of Jerusalem engendered. Laments over destroyed cities and sanctuaries form a distinct literary genre in ancient Mesopotamia, with roots reaching as far back as the early second millennium BCE. The poems collected in the biblical book of Lamentations probably belong to this genre, and they may have been recited at the site of the ruined Temple as part of a ritual of commemoration on designated fast days. The book is traditionally ascribed to Jeremiah, but this cannot be established; similar style and language are common to several of the prophet's contemporaries, and the viewpoint expressed in Lamentations is most unlike his pronouncements. Rather, the impression is that the poet (or poets) was a member of Zedekiah's court, a veteran Jerusalemite, overcome with remorse by the grievous suffering of the city and its population. The poet acknowledges Israel's guilt, for which God had brought on her deserved punishment, but beyond this he mentions no specific sin. One wonders whether this indefiniteness results from the lament style or from the poet's inability to comprehend the enormity of the tragedy. Like the author of the book of Kings, the poet points to the nation's leaders as the culprits:

> Your prophets have seen for you
>   false and deceptive visions;
> they have not exposed your iniquity
>   to restore your fortunes,
> but have seen oracles for you
>   that are false and misleading.
>   (Lam. 2.14; see also 4.13)

In the end, however, God's justice holds out hope for forgiveness and renewal. And with such confidence as their support, many exiles endured the hardships of life in distant Babylonia.

One might expect, or at least regard it as understandable, that Judah's conquerors would have been the prime focus of vengeful fulminations on the part of the survivors as they vented their grief and anger over the destruction. Yet surprisingly it is not the Babylonians but the Edomites who are most reviled for their behavior at the time:

> Your iniquity, O daughter Edom, [the Lord] will punish,
>   he will uncover your sins.
>   (Lam. 4.22)

Were it not for the oracle of Obadiah, the smallest of the prophetic books, the role of Judah's southern neighbor in her misfortune would still be clouded. At the time of the Babylonian hegemony over the west, there had flared up centuries-long strife between Judah and Edom over the southern Negeb desert down to the Red Sea port of Elath (modern Eilat), whose trade routes were its chief asset. Illustrative of the tension of this period is a memorandum, recovered at Arad, addressed to the commander of the outpost there and ordering him to transfer troops to reinforce another position, "otherwise Edom will arrive there." Judah regarded Edom as close kin—the Genesis narratives depict Jacob and Esau, the traditional ancestors of Israel and

Edom, as rival twin brothers—and so when Edom did not support the rebellion against Nebuchadrezzar, but rather took advantage of Judah's downfall, the reaction was one of anger over familial betrayal and a call for revenge:

> For the slaughter and violence done to your brother Jacob,
>   shame shall cover you,
>   and you shall be cut off forever. . . .
> You should not have rejoiced over the people of Judah
>   on the day of their ruin. . . .
> You should not have entered the gate of my people
>   on the day of their calamity. . . .
> You should not have looted his goods. . . .
> You should not have stood at the crossings
>   to cut off his fugitives;
> you should not have handed over his survivors
>   on the day of distress.
>
>   (Obad. 10, 12–14)

There is an epilogue to the history of the Judean monarchy, not only in the two surviving kings who lived out their lives in Babylon, but also in the organization of the "poorest people of the land [who had been left] to be vinedressers and tillers of the soil" (2 Kings 25.12). The Babylonian monarchs, unlike their Assyrian predecessors, did not make use of population exchange as a tool of imperial rule. To administer those Judeans still on the land (their number cannot be determined), a native Judean, Gedaliah son of Ahikam, from a prominent Jerusalem family and formerly in the royal service, was appointed governor of Judah, with headquarters in the city of Mizpah, just north of Jerusalem. Refugees drifted back, and so did some of the fighting forces who had been in hiding. The prophet Jeremiah was released by his captors, and he, too, joined the coterie at Mizpah as a close adviser of Gedaliah. But the road to recovery was short-lived, no more than a few months. After the fall harvest was in, a small band of conspirators led by Ishmael son of Nethaniah, a member of the royal family, with the backing of King Baalis of Ammon (whose name can be restored to its original form *Baal-yisha*, from a seal impression recently discovered in Jordan), murdered Gedaliah and his entire entourage. They probably acted more out of rancor against the perceived collaborator than as rebels against Babylonia. The frightened survivors of the massacre hurriedly departed for Egypt, Jeremiah among them. Whether the Babylonians retaliated is unknown; the only record from the period tells of a further deportation from Judah five years later. The day of Gedaliah's death (the third of Tishri [October]) entered the cultic calendar of the Judeans as a day of fasting, together with the day of the Temple's destruction (the ninth of Ab [August]). These two days marked the tragic endpoints of Judah's national existence.

It is often suggested that after the Gedaliah debacle the administration of Judah was transferred to Samaria, and that this political arrangement was subsequently carried over into the Persian period. This would explain, in part, the tensions between Judah and Samaria over the appointment of a native governor in Jerusalem in the mid-fifth century BCE. It is also argued that parts of southern Judah and the Negeb were taken over by Edomites who had begun their push northward toward the end of the Judean monarchy. At a number of sites, such as Khirbet Qitmit in the Negeb and En Haseva in the Arabah Valley, impressive Edomite remains vouch for their foothold in the region. But there is a total documentary blackout for the half century of Babylonian rule, and reading back from the Persian period, when our sources resume, is full of pitfalls. Nevertheless, a few notes on life under the Babylonians can be appended to the sorry tale of opportunity given and lost. From the archaeological perspective, numerous sites, especially north of Jerusalem, bear evidence of continuous settlement during the sixth century, with Israelite culture remaining intact until the Persian period. Judah was neither totally devastated nor depopulated, as some biblical writers would have us believe. The rural population held on, eking out a living for several generations until their fortunes took another turn. For all we know, they may have adopted the viewpoint, reported of them by Ezekiel, of considering themselves the rightful heirs of the property left behind by their exiled brethren and neighbors (Ezek. 33.23–24). They were on the scene fifty years later when the early returnees from Babylon to Jerusalem arrived, and they were powerful enough to frighten those who came with royal authorization to restore the Temple. Even in this matter, the populace in Judah saw themselves as the legitimate successors of the exiles; it was they, after all, who had continued to make pilgrimage, "bringing grain offerings and incense to present at the [ruins of the] temple of the LORD" (Jer. 41.4–5). Jeremiah may have disparaged their fathers by labeling them "bad figs" (24.8), but those who had remained in the land rejected the claim that only those who had suffered in exile could take part in the promised renewal.

The Babylonian Exile: Continuity and Change

The exile represented the first foreign experience for vast numbers of Judeans. It saw the creation of countless emigré communities scattered throughout the Near East, safe havens where some semblance of their former lives might be maintained. The half century of Babylonian rule remains a virtual dark age due to the paucity of contemporary documentation. Still, a partial sketch can be made of life outside Judah by comparing the relatively well-known beginning and end stages of the exile, especially as reflected in prophetic texts.

Jehoiachin, the royal household, and Jerusalem's elite who had surrendered in 597 BCE were transferred to the city of Babylon, where they became state pensioners. Cuneiform documents from Nebuchadrezzar's thirteenth year (592) record that "Jehoiachin, king of the land of Judah," and his five sons, together with other foreign dignitaries confined to Babylon, received food rations. Other Judeans besides the former king were on the same roster; Nebuchadrezzar's bookkeeper noted that among the artisans transferred from Jerusalem (whom the Bible leaves unnamed) were Gaddiel, Qoniah, Semachiah, and Shelemiah the gardener. They were just a few of the many skilled workers from conquered countries employed to Babylon's advantage.

At some point, Jehoiachin fell on bad times and was imprisoned, a punishment often meted out to those guilty of treason. It was not until 562, in an act of amnesty upon the accession of Amel-marduk (the biblical Evil-merodach), son of Nebuchadrezzar, that Jehoiachin was pardoned and his pension restored. Yet despite such vicissitudes in the king's fortunes, the exiles continued to hold him in high respect; they numbered their years in Babylonia from the start of Jehoiachin's exile, and some may even have entertained the hope for an eventual restoration of the monarchy upon their return to Judah. Such an eventuality must have seemed more palpable when Zerubbabel, a grandson of Jehoiachin, was appointed by the Persian authorities as governor of Judah in the first repatriation in 538 BCE.

The main body of exiles, perhaps numbering in the tens of thousands, were settled in the border area between Assyria and Babylonia that had been heavily damaged during the wars between the two powers, in towns whose names suggest that it was official policy to reclaim wastelands, such as Tel-abib ("Mound of the Flood"; Ezek. 3.15) and Tel-harsha ("Mound of Potsherds") and Tel-melah ("Mound of Salt"; Ezra 2.59). These communities of Judeans seem to have been self-governing units; the elders of Judah and the heads of families took over communal duties with the blessing of the Babylonian authorities. Not only Judeans, but also deportees from Tyre, Ashkelon, Gaza, and other cities are known to have maintained a semblance of their former national identities in communities that were organized along ethnic lines. In this respect, Babylonia contrasts sharply with Assyria, where the forced mingling of exiles had been the rule. Generations later, when return to Judah was an option, the list of Judeans who made the trek home (a copy of the register is preserved in Ezra 2) shows that the exiles had held on to genealogical records as well as oral family traditions, so that even the various orders of liturgical personnel could take up their positions when given the chance. Thus Jeremiah's picture of a comfortable exile, described in his letter to those who were clamoring for a quick return home, was not mere wishful thinking:

> Build houses and live in them; plant gardens and eat what they produce. Take wives and have sons and daughters . . . multiply there, and do not decrease. But seek the welfare of the city where I have sent you into exile, and pray to the LORD on its behalf, for in its welfare you will find your welfare. (Jer. 29.5–7)

Yet at the same time, the maintenance of ethnic identity by the exiled Judeans was tempered by their contact with Babylonian society. Language, for example, was always a ready vehicle for assimilation. Aramaic, the lingua franca of the Near East, replaced Hebrew in daily discourse and commerce; and though Hebrew seems to have remained the preferred literary vehicle, parts of Ezra-Nehemiah and of the late biblical book of Daniel are written in Aramaic. Babylonian month-names, in their Aramaic renditions, replaced the common Hebrew ones, and epigraphic finds indicate that the Hebrew script, which had been in use during the period of the monarchy, gave way to Aramaic script. Later tradition credits Ezra the scribe with transcribing the five books of Moses into the new script, at the same time preserving the original Hebrew text. Furthermore, the Judean onomasticon underwent a profound change, and in just one generation, Babylonian personal names, some including the names of Babylonian deities, were adopted by the exiles; even among the family of the Davidides, one finds names like Zerubbabel ("seed of Babylon") and Shenazzar ("the god Sin protects"). For sure, fashions did change in another generation or two, when Hebrew names were again given to children as national feelings revived, as can be seen in the female name Yehoyishma ("the Lord will hear"), bestowed by a father with the Babylonian name Shawash-shar-usur ("the god Shamash protects the king"). But a divide had been crossed. A telling measure of the cultural changes that the exile engendered can be seen in the description of the New Year's convocation held in

Jerusalem a century and a half after its start: Ezra read aloud from the scroll of the Torah in Hebrew to the assembled crowd, and was assisted by Levites who translated the text into Aramaic "so that the people understood the reading" (Neh. 8.1–8).

Perhaps the greatest issue facing the exiles was the lack of organized public worship. Because Israelite ritual law prohibited sacrifice outside the borders of the Promised Land, as all other lands were considered "unclean" (defiled by idolatry), the exiles could not reestablish communion with their God through traditional means. A psalm of lament recalls their plight:

> By the rivers of Babylon—
>   there we sat down and there we wept
>   when we remembered Zion.
> On the willows there
>   we hung up our harps.
> For there our captors
>   asked us for songs,
> and our tormentors asked for mirth, saying,
>   "Sing us one of the songs of Zion!"
> How could we sing the LORD's song
>   in a foreign land?
>   (Ps. 137.1–4)

The solution reportedly contrived by the Syrian army commander Naaman sometime in the late ninth century when he adopted the God of Israel as his god—he constructed an altar to the Lord in Damascus on soil brought from the land of Israel (2 Kings 5.15–19)—was an impractical answer for the multitudes living in Babylonia. Besides, prophets such as Jeremiah and Ezekiel taught that the Lord's distancing himself from his people by the destruction of the Temple was part and parcel of their punishment. Only a contrite heart could win them forgiveness. Under these circumstances certain ritual acts, whose observance was not restricted to the national home, properly acquired new significance. The weekly Sabbath rest and the covenant of circumcision developed into clear ethnic markers of the exiles. It is just possible that an institution that might be termed a "protosynagogue" took its first steps. At public gatherings on fast days, the exiles lamented the loss of their former homeland and prayed for a speedy return. On such occasions the teachings of prophets and the reading of sacred texts from preexilic times may also have filled the spiritual void.

We can experience a fair measure of the spiritual climate among the exiles by turning to the book of Ezekiel, the collected oracles of a prophet who was among those deported with Jehoiachin. In exile, Ezekiel ministered to the Judeans living in Tel-abib, a town in southern Babylonia on the Chebar canal (which ran through Nippur), for close to thirty years. He was visited regularly by the elders of Judah, who came to hear his pronouncements on matters concerning national destiny. From the start the fate of Jerusalem was uppermost in their minds. Ezekiel assured his listeners that the city was doomed: he had seen its people's errant ways and insisted on the justice of the punishment awaiting them. Many of his listeners still held to the view that their suffering was the consequence of inherited guilt, the sins of the fathers being visited on the children and grandchildren. But the prophet countered with a lesson in the doctrine of individual responsibility—"It is only the person who sins that shall die" (Ezek. 18.4)—urging each one to consider their ways "with a new heart and a new spirit" (18.31). And as sure as he was of the punishment, so he was of the restoration. Once the news of the city's fall reached the exiles, Ezekiel turned his attention to the future. Though Israel remained undeserving of God's mercy, he envisioned the revival of the dry bones of both houses of Israel, forcefully repatriated to the land of Israel in a new Exodus. The prophet's utopian program for rebuilding Jerusalem and the Temple remained an unrealized dream; at the same time, it most certainly contributed to keeping the hope of redemption alive.

In contrast to this picture of life as it developed among the Judeans in Babylonia is the one that can be pieced together concerning the exiled community in Egypt. Only scant information is available on the refugees who had fled southward after the murder of Gedaliah at Mizpah. The military leaders responsible for the assassination considered Egypt a safe haven from Babylonian reprisal, and towns in both Upper and Lower Egypt became home to many of them. They may have joined other Judeans already living in the Nile Valley; besides those who during hard times looked to Egypt as a natural sanctuary, one should not forget that soldiers from Judah had fought in the ranks of the Assyrian army when it invaded Egypt close to a century earlier, and some of their number may have stayed on and settled there. Jeremiah settled in Tahpanhes in the eastern delta, where he continued to provoke the anger of his fellow Judeans, on one occasion over their continued worship of the "queen of heaven" (Jer. 44).

Nothing is known of this southern Diaspora scattered about Egypt, save for the small community at Elephantine, an island in the Nile just north of the First Cataract, near modern Aswan. A collection of Aramaic ostraca and papyri dating from the end of the fifth century BCE discovered on the island contains the records of a military garrison of Judeans in the employ of the Persians. In addition to legal deeds concerning the private affairs of individuals (marriage and divorce, sales and purchases), a memorandum discussing the proper observance of the Passover and the Festival of Un-leavened Bread is of particular note. Unlike their former compatriots in Babylonia, however, the Judeans at Elephantine served the God of Israel at a temple where animal sacrifices were offered, and there is also some evidence that they reverenced Aramean deities. Yet this significant difference in religious practice did not alienate them from the leaders in Judah and Samaria, to whom they appealed to intercede on their behalf before the Persian authorities concerning the reconstruction of their house of worship. Still, the ex-Judeans at Elephantine were passed over by history until their rediscovery in modern times, when their affairs were reconstructed as an exotic footnote.

The Fall of the Neo-Babylonian Empire and

the Hope of Return to Zion

For the most part, the Neo-Babylonian empire was dominated by two outstanding rulers, Nebuchadrezzar (604–562 BCE) and Nabonidus (556–539). While the former took up the challenge of reestablishing Mesopotamian rule over the entire Near East after the demise of Assyria and left a record of conquest abroad and of building at home, the latter forsook his capital for a desert oasis, then lost it without a battle to

Cyrus the Persian. Among the Judean exiles, it was Nebuchadrezzar whose name was incised in the collective memory. Around this king who had razed Jerusalem and had deported Judah to Babylonia, a store of derisive and derogatory tales inevitably grew up, though some of them had originally been associated with Nabonidus.

The last Babylonian monarch, Nabonidus, was probably not of Chaldean ancestry. His energetic support of the moon-god Sin and his cult center in the Syrian city of Haran suggest Aramean extraction. His mother had been a lifelong devotee of Sin. That this outsider could take the throne points up the instability in post-Nebuchadrezzar Babylon. During his first years, Nabonidus fought in northern Syria and the west, after which he abruptly departed Babylon for Tema in the north Arabian Desert. There he tarried for at least ten years of self-imposed isolation. Crown Prince Bel-shar-usur (the biblical Belshazzar) administered affairs in Babylon during his father's absence. One official duty, however, he could not fulfill. The annual New Year's festival, during which the king "took the hand of Marduk," Babylon's chief deity, had to be postponed in his absence, to the displeasure of the god's priesthood.

While the Babylonian king seems to have busied himself with protecting and even developing trade centers in the west, a new power that would eventually challenge Babylonia arose on the Iranian plateau. Under the leadership of Cyrus of Parsua, who had rebelled against his Median overlord, the combined armies of Persia and Media fought their way across the entire Anatolian peninsula to conquer the Lydian capital of Sardis, not far from the Aegean Sea. By 546 BCE, the Babylonian empire had been surrounded, and the choice of time and place to strike belonged to Cyrus.

These geopolitical developments may have spurred Nabonidus's return to Babylon, though no answer to Cyrus's ascendancy was forthcoming. The rupture between the king and the city's leaders, especially the priests of Marduk, widened when he set about completing the constructions to Sin in Haran. For the year 539 BCE, the Babylonian Chronicle records that the Persians defeated the Babylonian army at Opis and Sippar in late summer, after which "the army of Cyrus entered Babylon without a battle" and Cyrus declared peace to all. Biblical tradition associated Babylon's fall with Belshazzar in particular: the inscrutable handwriting on the palace that he observed was interpreted for him by Daniel as a message from God that his kingdom would be handed over to the Persian king (Dan. 5). From the tenor of the propagandistic inscription prepared for Cyrus by the priests of Marduk who welcomed the Persian in the name of their god, one wonders whether they had not acted in the end as a fifth column: Marduk "beheld with pleasure [Cyrus's] good deeds and his upright heart, and therefore ordered him to march against his city Babylon. . . . Without any battle, he made him enter his town Babylon, sparing Babylon any calamity. He delivered into his hands Nabonidus, the king who did not worship him." Such was the eloquent apologia signaling the orderly transfer of power to the Persian conqueror.

Among the Judean exiles in Babylonia, expectations ran high for the imminent fall of Nabonidus; they, too, looked to Cyrus as their deliverer. The emotion-charged words of an anonymous visionary, who held out hope for a speedy end of the exile, are preserved in the collection of speeches now appended (from chapter 40 on) to the prophecies of the eighth-century BCE Isaiah of Jerusalem. This "Second Isaiah" spoke of Cyrus as God's "anointed," raised up to subdue the nations so that in the end Israel might be set free and Jerusalem rebuilt. Although Jeremiah's predicted seventy-year enslavement to Babylon had not run its full course—the number was, in any case, a typologically large one indicating completeness—Second Isaiah offered comfort and solace to his audience, that Israel "has served her term, her penalty is paid" (Isa. 40.2). God will lead his people safely home through the desert, in a stunning reenactment of the Exodus. It was not unusual for Israel's prophets to interpret contemporary events in terms of God's plan for Israel. Isaiah and Jeremiah in their days had referred to Assyria and Babylonia as instruments of judgment; in like manner, the exilic Isaiah greeted Cyrus as the God-sent liberator of Israel.

Along with his consoling message to the exiles, the prophet addressed a challenge to the nations: only the Lord had announced in advance what the future had in store, and its execution would be proof of his Godhead. His call to give up idolatry, the futile worship of wood and stone "that cannot save" (Isa. 45.20), held out the promise that those who would embrace Israel's faith would be welcomed in the new Zion:

> And the foreigners who join themselves to the LORD,
>   to minister to him, to love the name of the LORD,
>   and to be his servants,
> all who keep the sabbath, and do not profane it,
>   and hold fast my covenant—
> these I will bring to my holy mountain
>   and make them joyful in my house of prayer . . .
> for my house shall be called a house of prayer
>   for all peoples.
>
> (Isa. 56.6–7)

Just how many foreigners, if any, actually took up the call and attached themselves to the community of exiles cannot be determined. But one pole of the ideological debate that was to divide Judeans over the next several centuries had been staked out: no longer the exclusive preserve of Israel alone, her faith now opened its doors to converts from all the nations to worship the Lord in a rebuilt and resplendent Jerusalem. Some of these grand visions draw on landscape images which suggest that Second Isaiah himself may have been one of the early returnees who responded to Cyrus's call:

> The LORD, the God of heaven, has given me all the kingdoms of the earth, and he has charged me to build him a house in Jerusalem, which is in Judah. Whoever is among you of all his people, may the LORD his God be with him! Let him go up. (2 Chron. 36.23)

Select Bibliography

Avigad, Nahman. *Discovering Jerusalem.* Nashville: Thomas Nelson, 1983. A firsthand account of the excavation of the Western Hill of Jerusalem and the important discoveries of occupation levels from the First and Second Temple periods.

———. *Corpus of West Semitic Stamp Seals.* Jerusalem: Israel Academy of Sciences and Humanities, 1997. The most comprehensive collection to date of Israelite seals. Analyzes over 1,100 seals, shedding light on ancient onomastics, popular beliefs, and artistic styles.

Cogan, Mordechai, and Hayim Tadmor. *II Kings.* Anchor Bible, vol. 11. Garden City, N.Y.: Doubleday, 1988. A translation of the biblical text, with philological and historical commentary.

Cogan, Morton. *Imperialism and Religion: Assyria, Judah and Israel in the Eighth and Seventh Centuries B.C.E.* Society of Biblical Literature Monograph Series, 19. Missoula, Mont.; Scholars Press, 1974. Investigation of the religious policy practiced by Assyria's rulers in the territories annexed to empire and in autonomous vassal states.

Cross, Frank Moore. "The Themes of the Book of Kings and the Structure of the Deuteronomic History." In *Canaanite Myth and Hebrew Epic,* 274–89. Cambridge, Mass.: Harvard University Press, 1973. Discussion of the major Israelite historical work of the First Temple period, its composition and double edition.

Eph'al, Israel. "The Western Minorities in Babylonia in the 6th–5th Centuries B.C." *Orientalia* 47 (1978): 74–90. Cuneiform documents from the Neo-Babylonian age show that self-organization and national identity were features common to many ethnic minorities who resided in Babylonia, not only the Judeans.

Greenberg, Moshe. "The Design and Themes of Ezekiel's Program of Restoration." *Interpretation* 18 (1984): 181–208. An incisive study of the concluding section of the exilic prophet's vision of the new Israel—the future Temple, its rules and activities, the land and its people—seen as a purposeful revision of existent priestly legislation.

Malamat, Abraham. "The Twilight of Judah: In the Egyptian-Babylonian Maelstrom." *Supplements to Vetus Testamentum* 28 (1975): 123–45. The shifting loyalties exhibited by Judah's kings during the final decades of the monarchy are studied against the background of volatile international politics.

———, ed. *The Age of the Monarchies: Culture and Society.* The World History of the Jewish People, vol. 4, part 2. Jerusalem: Massada, 1979. Summary examinations of various aspects of Israelite life: literary creativity, language, religion, society, state administration, trade, crafts, home life.

Porten, Bezalel. *Archives from Elephantine: The Life of an Ancient Jewish Military Colony.* Berkeley: University of California Press, 1958. Reconstruction of the life of a Diaspora community in the upper Nile Valley during the Persian period.

Stern, Ephraim. "Israel at the Close of the Monarchy: An Archaeological Survey." *Biblical Archaeologist* 38 (1975): 26–54. Assemblage of the material evidence from archaeological excavations in Israel and Jordan for the considerable cultural influence exerted by Assyria, and, to a lesser degree, by Babylonia, on the area.

Tadmor, Hayim. "Propaganda, Literature, Historiography: Cracking the Code of the Assyrian Royal Inscriptions." In *Assyria 1995,* ed. S. Parpola and R. M. Whiting, 325–38. Helsinki: Helsinki University Press, 1997. A critical review of the methods employed by historians in studying the style and structure as well as the ideology of Assyrian texts.

Ussishkin, David. *The Conquest of Lachish by Sennacherib.* Tel Aviv: Institute of Archaeology, Tel Aviv University, 1982. Richly illustrated album containing a survey of the archaeological finds from Lachish, as well as analysis of Assyrian reliefs depicting the siege of the city.

Weinfeld, Moshe. *Deuteronomy and the Deuteronomic School.* Oxford: Oxford University Press, 1972. A linguistic and theological analysis of the Israelite school of thought responsible for most of the Bible's historical literature.

Israel among the Nations

The Persian Period

MARY JOAN WINN LEITH

n the Persian period the concept of "Israel" changed. Before the Babylonian exile,
Israel was defined not by worship but by its independent geopolitical existence, by
occupying its own land. Exile and Diaspora forced a new, evolving sense of identity.
The Persian period (539–332 BCE) constitutes an era of both restoration and innovation. The religious attitudes and practices characteristic of postexilic Judaism
did not originate in the Persian period. The centrality of the Jerusalem Temple and
of public worship at its sacrificial altar are only the most obvious in a list of continuities from preexilic Israel; others include the priestly families, the practice of circumcision, Sabbath and Passover observance, and prohibitions against mixed marriage. At the same time, however, with the figures of Ezra and Nehemiah we reach
the end of biblical Israel.

In leading Jewish circles during this period, written words perceived as having
originated in Israel's distant past came to assume a primacy previously uncontem-
plated—if not unanticipated (see 2 Kings 22–23)—in legitimating the practice of
worship and for determining social and ethnic identity. The movement toward com-
piling a biblical canon accelerated. The Psalms, the editions of the prophetic books,
and, most important, the Torah or Pentateuch (the first five books of the Bible)
approached their final shape during the Persian period. The period is also rich in
literature by Yahwistic prophets, poets, priests, and philosophers whose names often
elude us; they wrote pseudonymously, claiming the names of ancient Israelite heroes
or sages, covering their creations with a validating veneer of antiquity. Late biblical
works frequently quote from older Israelite writings (now become scripture) and
contain early examples of traditional Jewish biblical exegesis. One of the era's most
arresting images is that of Ezra the scribe, a contemporary of Socrates, reading aloud

the "book of the law of Moses" (Neh. 8.1) to women and men assembled at the gates of rebuilt Jerusalem. Ezra's reading, however, is supplemented by interpreters (Neh. 8.7–8)—or possibly translators—whose task is to ensure that all the listeners correctly understand the meaning of the Torah.

Formerly a nation with fixed borders, postexilic Israel became a multicentric people identified not geographically or politically but by ethnicity—an amorphous cluster of religious, social, historical, and cultural markers perceived differently depending on whether the eye of the beholder looks from inside or from without. The identity of this Israel could not be threatened by the Persian hegemony over the homeland or by military aggression. Rather, the danger to this new Israel lay in a different sort of boundary transgression: ethnic pollution, an offense variously defined.

The pronounced Jewish sectarianism of the Hellenistic and Roman periods, embodied in such groups as the Samaritans, the Qumran community, the Pharisees, and the earliest Christians, has its roots in the Persian period. Typically for this period, while Ezra and Nehemiah attempted to restrict membership in the privileged group they considered to be "Israel" (Ezra 10.2, 7, 10), the Bible itself preserves traces of rival Jewish groups engaged in an ideological struggle against the vision of Ezra and Nehemiah. During the Persian period Jewish communities—Yahweh worshipers— flourished not only in Judea, but also in Babylonia, Persia, and Egypt, in neighboring Samaria to the north, and in Ammon to the east.

The term *Jew* originates as an ethnic label for a person whose ancestry lay in the land of Judah (see 2 Kings 16.6); the earliest occurrence of the term to designate a religious community is in Esther 2.5, a Hellenistic novel set in the Persian court. The word is used in a broad sense in this chapter to designate Yahweh worshipers—be they exclusive or syncretistic—in the Persian period.

Cultural Influences

To what extent were Jews, whether in the Diaspora or the Levantine homeland, influenced by Persian or Greek culture? The Persian period encompasses, after all, the Greek Classical Age. (Conventionally spanning the years 479–323 BCE, this age is the time of Periclean Athens: the Parthenon, Phidias and Praxiteles; Aeschylus and Sophocles and Euripides; Socrates and Plato and Aristotle, the tutor of Alexander before he became "the Great"; the historians Herodotus, Thucydides, and Xenophon.) In the eastern Mediterranean world, including the western territories of the Persian empire, the era sees the increasing presence of Greek artists, writers, doctors, adventurers, and especially mercenary soldiers, frequently in the pay of non-Greeks (including Persians).

What did cultural assimilation entail, specifically in the case of the Jewish encounter with Hellenism? The assumption that a Jew's adoption of Greek culture meant a renunciation of Judaism is refuted by the example of Philo, the great Jewish philosopher of the first century CE. Judaism in the later Second Temple period became deeply hellenized without any loss of communal historical consciousness or national culture.

How deeply Greek culture might have penetrated Judah and Samaria—or the Diaspora, for that matter—in the Persian period is difficult to determine. Students of fourth-century BCE cultural history have increasingly recognized a pre-Alexandrine Hellenic *oikumene* of sorts in the western Persian empire. During this period the Phoenicians were the primary conduit of Hellenism to the Levant, although less in terms of political and religious thought than of material culture and artistic taste. Evidence of extensive trade with Greece and the west in the form of imported high-prestige-value eastern Greek and Attic pottery appears in the Phoenician cities of the coast and in the Shephelah, but far less of such pottery is found at poor inland sites in Judah and Samaria. Eastern influences (Babylonian, Assyrian, Egyptian) still dominated the material culture of inland Palestine.

Any exposure to Greek culture in Judah and Samaria must have been indirect. There are no references, biblical or otherwise, to Greek natives in Judah or Samaria before the arrival of Alexander, although Greek mercenaries might have served in Persian garrisons in Palestine, including Nehemiah's fortress in Jerusalem. The coinage of Judah and Samaria in the fourth century includes devices in imitation of Greek coins. But the adoption of Greek images such as the Attic owl or the head of the goddess Athena need not be interpreted religiously. Provincial mints copied foreign issues, particularly the ubiquitous and trustworthy Athenian tetradrachm.

In small ways, such as their predilection for seals with Greek subjects (probably from Phoenician workshops), Samarians (if not the Judeans) seem to have been attracted to Greek culture, even if they had no firsthand experience of it. Nevertheless, there can be no cultural receptivity unless the receiving culture has receptors attuned to new influences. Without a degree of hellenizing groundwork already having been accomplished by cultural interactions, the world conquered by Alexander, including Syria-Palestine, would have been far more resistant to the Greek ways that took root with such ease.

The paucity of Persian artifacts in the archaeological record of western lands subject to the great king led earlier scholars to deny significant Persian artistic, religious, or cultural influence. They assumed that the Persians were interested only in maintaining the flow of tribute into the national treasuries but otherwise allowed their subjects to go their separate religious and economic ways. More recently scholars have interpreted the Persian art that has been found in the western satrapies as evidence of a conscious imperial propaganda program. We now consider the Persian impact on the western reaches of the empire to have been subtle but assertive, with more cultural interaction than had been previously supposed.

Beginning with Darius I (522–486 BCE), Zoroastrianism was the national religion of the Achaemenids, the official name for the Persian royal family. This religious tradition included purity laws (to prevent pollution by corpses and bodily emissions) and the belief in a cosmic struggle between Justice, upheld by the great god Ahuramazda ("Lord of Wisdom"), and the "Lie." The struggle would climax in a final, apocalyptic battle. Zoroastrian priests, called magi, officiated at all sacrifices, usually on mountaintops. There is no evidence for any imperial proselytizing, nor was the adoption of Zoroastrianism a necessary condition of advancement for a nonnative official in Persian service. There is little if any effect of Zoroastrian elements on Judaism in the Persian period. Most discussions of Persian influence on Judaism now look to the Hellenistic and Roman periods as the era of significant cross-fertilization.

One effect of Persian domination was the spread of the Aramaic language throughout the empire. Originally the native tongue of small Syrian and Mesopotamian states, Aramaic became the international commercial, administrative, and diplomatic language of the Assyrian empire in the eighth century. Aramaic's alphabetic script was more flexible than Akkadian cuneiform. Second Kings 18.26 (= Isa. 36.11) shows Aramaic in diplomatic use, as well as the general Palestinian populace's ignorance of it in the eighth century. During the Neo-Babylonian period, however, Aramaic became the main spoken language of the Neo-Babylonian empire, and subsequently the Indo-European Persians adopted this Semitic cousin of the Hebrew language for all aspects of their written communications and records. Eloquent testimony to this fact appears in the book of Ezra, which employs Aramaic for official Persian documents (Ezra 4.8–6.18; 7.12–26) and some narrative.

After the exile the use of Aramaic was on the increase in Palestine. Preservation of Israel's ancestral language was a particular concern of Nehemiah, who complained that the children of mixed marriages did not know Hebrew (Hebrew *yehudit*, literally "Judahite"; Neh. 13.24; see Isa. 36.11). Hebrew did not die out, but it was gradually replaced by Aramaic as the language most commonly spoken. The biblical texts attributed to the Persian period were written in Hebrew, attesting to its continued use as a literary language, but late biblical Hebrew—in Chronicles, for example—contains numerous Aramaisms. Hebrew and Aramaic inscriptions on coins and seals of the Persian period from Judah and Samaria alike show both languages being employed in official governmental contexts. Hebrew names also occur in Aramaic texts.

Chronology and Sources

The two centuries of the Persian period (the early Second Temple period) in Syria-Palestine are framed by two dates. Achaemenid Persian control began in 539 with the conquest of Babylon by the army of King Cyrus II ("the Great," 559–530). It ended in 332, when Alexander the Great (336–323), having defeated the Persian king Darius III Codomanus (336–330) in the battle of Issus (in Cilicia near the Syrian border), marched into and took possession of the Levant. In 539 Cyrus's capture of Babylon meant that the territories of the Babylonian empire, including Syria-Palestine, now belonged to the Persian empire. Two centuries later, by his victory at Issus, Alexander annexed the western Persian empire including Syria-Palestine, formerly the fifth Persian satrapy of Abar Nahara ("Across the [Euphrates] River"). Archaeologists divide the era into two phases, Persian I (539/8–ca. 450) and Persian II (ca. 450–332). These chronological anchors, however, belie the often frustrated attempts by modern historians to make sense of the erratic textual and archaeological evidence, not only for chronology but even more crucially for Jewish religious and social history in the shadowy intervening years.

The starting point for our discussion of the Persian period as it relates to biblical history is actually 586 BCE, when the Babylonians looted and destroyed the Jerusalem Temple, razed much of the city along with its walls, and exiled an indeterminate number of Judah's ruling elite to Babylonia (2 Kings 25.8–21). The exiles of 586 joined other Judahites, among them King Jehoiachin and the priest-prophet Ezekiel, who had previously surrendered to Nebuchadrezzar II in 597 (2 Kings 24.12–17; Jer. 52.28–30). A second significant group of Jews were exiles by choice in Egypt, where they had dragged the reluctant prophet Jeremiah (Jer. 43). Their fate is unclear, but

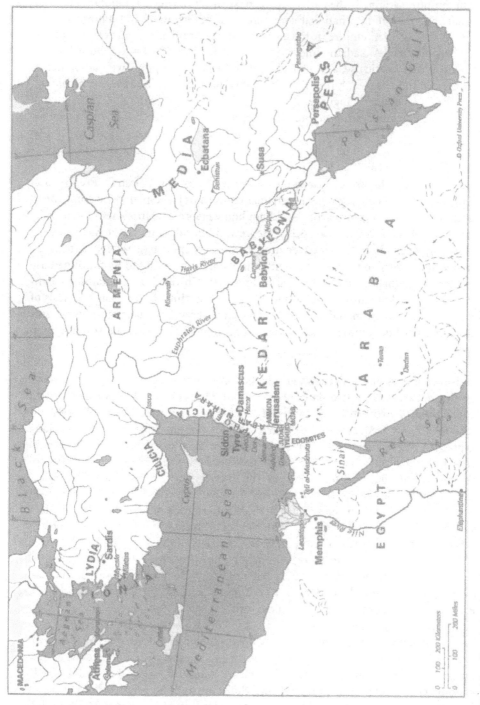

The Near East during the Persian Empire

the exilic revision of the Deuteronomic History could have occurred in this community, out of which grew the large Jewish population of Hellenistic Egypt.

Clearly, intense theological ferment brewed among the exiles in Babylon, seeking as they did to find meaning in the inexplicable series of tragedies they had suffered and at the same time trying to address the future of their relationship with Yahweh. How were they to "sing the LORD's song in a foreign land" (Ps. 137.4), and what place should their ruined city and Temple have outside the confines of their tenacious memories? Genesis 1–2.4, which envisions the entire created universe as God's sanctuary, where worship occurs in sacred time (the Sabbath) rather than space, can be read as one exilic response. An important element of the exiles' theology, however, also involved hope for a return to Judah and Jerusalem and for restoration of the Temple (programmatically outlined in Ezek. 40–48)—not unexpectedly so in view of the close link before the exile between the upper class of Judah and the Temple establishment. The theme of a restored people, city, and active Temple is central to the narrative of Ezra-Nehemiah, the biblical text that provides the most extensive treatment of the Judean restoration in the Persian period. These books are supplemented by parallel material in the prophetic books of Haggai and Zechariah, the apocryphal book 1 Esdras, some data in Chronicles, and Book 11 of Josephus's *Antiquities*.

Scholars dispute the history of composition of the three important historical books—Chronicles, Ezra, and Nehemiah—for this period, although a cautious consensus exists around a date in the fourth century BCE for each. A final editor—perhaps the author or final editor of Chronicles—may have shaped the received texts of Ezra and Nehemiah, although originally each book probably was an independent composition. Ezra and Nehemiah include older, reworked material, such as official Persian imperial documents (originally in Aramaic), a Nehemiah memoir, perhaps an Ezra memoir, and miscellaneous archival lists. But these texts that describe the early Second Temple period are not (and were not written to be) straightforward reports of historical events. They idealize heroes, foreshorten historical events, make use of typology and recurring narrative patterns, and contain inner contradictions because the "facts" are less important as empirical data than as subtle symbolic literary elements in the service of ideology.

Nor does the Bible treat the first half of the Persian period systematically. It ignores the half century between the completion of the Temple around 515 BCE and the reforms of Ezra and Nehemiah. A still vexing question is the biblical ordering of the missions of Ezra and Nehemiah. The Bible places Ezra first, then Nehemiah. Nehemiah's arrival in Jerusalem in 445 BCE is likely. Ezra is the problem. The two leaders seem to have no knowledge of each other; their missions do not overlap (Neh. 8 is transposed for rhetorical reasons; Neh. 8.9 is almost unanimously considered to be a scribal harmonization); and no reflection of Ezra's activity appears in the Jerusalem of Nehemiah. These facts have prompted the influential theory that Nehemiah preceded rather than followed Ezra, whose dates then become 428 or 398, rather than 458 as implied by the Bible. Today authoritative scholars line up on both sides of the issue, with the biblical order (putting Ezra first, in 458) enjoying a small edge; a few minimalists even doubt Ezra's existence. This chapter diffidently retains the priority of Ezra.

After Nehemiah's second term as governor of Yehud (Judah) (ca. 430), the Bible is silent about events through the fourth century down to 332. Except for allusive references in Daniel and the books of the Maccabees, the Bible never mentions Alexander the Great's usurpation of the Persian satrapy of Abar Nahara. Nor does the archaeological evidence from Judah and Samaria indicate notable changes in settlement patterns or material culture immediately after 332.

Some nonbiblical texts supplement the biblical picture of Jewish history in the Persian period, although they are not without their own difficulties; most concern Jewish communities outside the territory of the Persian province of Yehud. Three groups of documents are of particular importance. First are the Elephantine papyri, written in Aramaic, which come from a Jewish military colony in Elephantine (on the Nile opposite Aswan) and cover the period from the beginning to the end of the fifth century; they include letters, lists, legal contracts, and literary-historical texts, and tell of a Yahweh temple in Egypt whose functionaries were in contact with both Yehud and Samaria. Second, from Nippur in Mesopotamia come over 650 cuneiform tablets belonging to the archives of the Murashu trading house, written between 455 and 403 BCE. Approximately 8 percent of the names mentioned are Jewish, and the fortunes of these Diaspora Jews can be traced for several generations. Third, the foremost documentary source for fourth-century Palestine is the Samaria papyri, a group of fragmentary Aramaic legal documents from upper-class circles in Samaria, dating between 375 and approximately 335 BCE. Their importance lies in the historical data gleaned from them and the names they contain. Most of the theophoric names are Yahwistic, indicating continued devotion to Yahweh and hence the persistence of Judaism in the territory of the former northern kingdom.

Cyrus and the Restoration

In the joyous anticipatory oracles (Isa. 44.24–45.13) of Second Isaiah (Isa. 40–55), Cyrus erupts onto the biblical stage even before his victory procession into Babylon on 29 October 539 BCE. The anonymous prophet, perhaps an exile in Babylon, astoundingly refers to Cyrus the Persian as "messiah" (Isa. 45.1), the only instance in the Bible where a non-Jew bears this resonant title of the preexilic Davidic kings. As the instrument of Yahweh "the Redeemer" (Isa. 44.24), Cyrus will repatriate the exiles (45.13), who are called collectively Yahweh's "servant" (44.21), and sanction the restoration of Jerusalem and worship in the Temple (44.28). Second Isaiah's oracles, like the oracles of the preexilic prophets, are rooted in the historical circumstances of the prophet's audience. In this case we see exiled Jews in mid-sixth-century Babylonia witnessing with satisfaction the death throes of the Babylonian empire.

For the rise of Cyrus and the Persian empire (the historians' usual adjective is "meteoric") and the fall of Babylon there are several important nonbiblical sources. In addition to the *Histories* of Herodotus, three contemporary documents from Babylonia are particularly valuable. The Nabonidus Chronicle describes in a relatively objective manner the deeds of Nabonidus (556–539), the last king of Babylon. The "Verse Account of Nabonidus" is a fascinating piece of pro-Cyrus propaganda composed soon after the arrival of Cyrus by elements among the Babylonian priesthood hostile to their former king. The famous "Cyrus Cylinder" is a Babylonian foundation

document of Cyrus himself describing his restoration of Mesopotamian temples supposedly neglected by Nabonidus.

The Persians were an Indo-European people who by the sixth century BCE had
settled in Parsa (Greek *Persis* [modern Fars]), the mountainous land east of the
Persian Gulf's northern coastline. Practically undocumented in the historical record
before the advent of Cyrus, by the sixth century the Persians were vassals of the
Medes, another Indo-European group who occupied the Iranian plateau north of the
Zagros Mountains and established their capital at Ecbatana (modern Hamadan). The
Medes are comparatively better known to history, appearing in Assyrian texts as early
as the ninth century. By 600 the Medes had captured the former Assyrian capital,
Nineveh. There, watched uneasily by Babylon, they controlled an empire that ex-
tended from eastern Anatolia and Armenia in the west to Turkestan in the east and
Parsa in the south.

Cyrus's career began in 560/559 when, as the heir to the ruling Persian Achaemenid dynasty, he inherited the kingship of the Persians. In 550 Cyrus rebelled against
his overlord, the aging Median warrior-king Astyages. His successful uprising won
for Cyrus the territories of the Medes and provided him with a substantial pool of
army recruits. Cyrus's next target was the Lydian kingdom of Croesus, an ally of
Babylonia. Herodotus recounts a famous story of Croesus's visit to Delphi, where he
was delighted to hear from the Delphic Oracle that if he attacked the Persians as
planned, he would "destroy a great empire." But in 546 Cyrus effectively destroyed
Lydian sovereignty by a surprise winter assault on Sardis, Croesus's supposedly im-
pregnable capital. By a combination of hard combat, self-interested leniency, and
propaganda, Cyrus brought the Greek cities on the Ionian coast of Asia Minor into
his realm. Cyrus briefly turned his attention to his eastern front, but soon aimed his
military might at the principal unconquered power in his path, Babylonia and its
king Nabonidus.

As neighbors of the Medes and formal allies of Croesus, the Babylonians (and
their Jewish populations) could hardly be unaware of Cyrus's relentless accumulation
of territory. While the Persian conquest of Babylonia in 539 was not the quick and
easy victory suggested by some of the sources, the capital Babylon fell without any
casualties. Cyrus's success is credited to military acumen, to judicious bribery, and
to an energetic publicity campaign waged throughout Babylonia, which portrayed
him as a lenient and religiously tolerant overlord. Second Isaiah's prophecies fit perfectly into this context and suggest that the author absorbed the essence of Cyrus's
carefully crafted image.

By 539 the Neo-Babylonian empire was experiencing severe inflation exacerbated
by plague and famine. But the Cyrus Cylinder and the Verse Account of Nabonidus—
both generated by the Persian propaganda machine—blamed the impious religious
innovations of Babylon's unpopular king Nabonidus for reducing the people to
"corpses" until Cyrus, Marduk's "friend and companion," arrived to return the gods
to their proper places and to restore the land. According to Cyrus's publicists, Nabonidus had blatantly disregarded the duty of the Babylonian kings of old to honor
Marduk and the other gods of Babylon, callously concentrating his religious energies
on the worship of Sin, the moon-god of Haran (on the upper Euphrates), where his

formidable mother, Adad-guppi, was a priestess. And rather than foster Babylonian business and political interests—so the Persians claimed—Nabonidus chose to exile himself to faraway Tema in northwestern Arabia. There for ten years he frittered away his time and forced a cessation of the Babylonian New Year festival (Akitu). Babylon was left in the care of Nabonidus's son, Belshazzar. Even the neutral Nabonidus Chronicle confirms that the "king did not come to Babylon in the month of Nisan. . . . The Akitu festival did not take place." Nabonidus did finally celebrate the Akitu festival in 539; but by then, it would seem, Marduk had given up on him. The Cyrus Cylinder claims that Cyrus prevented his army from terrorizing the populace; his "numerous troops walked around in peace"; happy Babylonians "kissed his feet, jubilant . . . with shining faces."

It is important to assess these narratives judiciously. Our sources for Nabonidus's impious religious innovations and disregard for his empire are pro-Persian, perhaps generated by the influential priests of Marduk, with whom Cyrus consciously ingratiated himself. An equally strong claim could have been made by elements of the Babylonian populace living outside the capital for Nabonidus as a penitent, reverent ruler with respect for the past. His sojourn in Tema has been interpreted not as an unconsidered whim but as an attempt to create for Babylon a commercial empire founded on the fabulously lucrative spice trade of Arabia. Still, Nabonidus was a Babylon outsider who suffered the consequences of flouting the social and religious expectations of the empire's capital.

No independent evidence confirms the report in Ezra 1.1–11 that in 538 BCE the first of several waves of Judean exiles returned home. According to Ezra 1.2–4 (Hebrew; see 2 Chron. 36.23; and Aramaic, Ezra 6.2–5), Cyrus decreed that "the LORD, the God of heaven," who had given him "all the kingdoms of the earth," had charged him to build a temple in Jerusalem and to that end all of God's people could return to Jerusalem. In its present wording this decree of Cyrus does not correspond to known official Persian documents or inscriptions; it has been called a free composition, possibly written to evoke the Cyrus oracles of the exilic Isaiah. Furthermore, the Aramaic reference to the decree in Ezra 6.1–5 does not mention any return from Babylon.

Still, the contents of the Cyrus Cylinder correspond closely to the spirit of the putative decree, especially in its Hebrew version (Ezra 1.2–4), which concentrates on the divinely chosen status of Cyrus. According to the cylinder, Cyrus entered Babylon at Marduk's command, protected its temples, and allowed the (statues of the) gods, whose dwelling places had been abandoned, to return to their native centers in the company of their human associates, their priests. In both texts Cyrus credits the god of the intended audience for his success, and both texts sanction the return of displaced people to their home and native sanctuaries.

The claims of restoration of worship, piety, and religious tolerance that Cyrus makes for himself in the cylinder (seconded by the compiler of Ezra-Nehemiah, working in the shadow of the Persian authorities) must be viewed in the context both of Persian imperial policy and of Mesopotamian royal traditions. The cylinder belongs to a specific Mesopotamian literary genre, the royal building inscription; no such genre is known in Old Persian literature. By publishing such a document, Cyrus cannily manipulates local traditions to legitimate his claim to Babylon; he is doing what a good and pious Babylonian ruler (in contrast to bad Nabonidus the blasphemer) was expected to do. Concerned with Marduk and the return of Babylon and cities in Mesopotamia to normal, the cylinder never calls for a general release of deportees or a universal restoration of centers of worship that had suffered at Babylonian hands. Furthermore, the term *restore* is ambiguous; we do not know how much religious innovating Nabonidus actually did that needed undoing, and there is no evidence for any rebuilding or repair of Mesopotamian temples during the reign of Cyrus. Life in Babylonia proceeded much as before.

The Cyrus Cylinder was meant for Babylonian consumption, to enhance Cyrus's popularity in Babylonia. It cannot confirm the authenticity of Cyrus's decree in Ezra. It is possible that Cyrus issued such a decree, however. The evidence of the cylinder suggests that in "restoring" the Jerusalem Temple, as in "restoring" Babylon, Cyrus was following the lead of earlier Mesopotamian rulers by strategically granting privileged status to some cities, often in sensitive areas, whose support and cooperation could benefit the empire. Cyrus might wish to cultivate loyalty in a territory close to Egypt, which he firmly intended to conquer.

Only recently have the implications of the pro-Persian bias of many Persian period sources been addressed. The near-unanimous, even automatic, characterization by historians (which goes as far back as Herodotus) of the Achaemenid Persians as enlightened and tolerant rulers should have aroused suspicion. Revisionist assessments acknowledge the pro-Persian bias of the key sources and also of the Western scholarly tradition, which can fall prey to biblio- or Eurocentrism. Have Western scholars been more willing to believe the best of Indo-European Persians and the worst of Semitic Assyrians and Babylonians? The historical record indicates that the "civilized" Persians were as capable as their supposedly barbarian predecessors of destroying sanctuaries and deporting peoples. The most judicious approach acknowledges both the tyrannical and the tolerant policies. Texts dating to the reigns of later Persian kings do confirm a pattern of Persian religious tolerance and noninterference in the cultural traditions of subject peoples. But in return—and this is essentially a Persian innovation—the temples were obliged to pay taxes to the Persians in kind. Food, livestock, wool, and laborers were regularly requisitioned by the Persians from their subordinate temple communities, which were expected to support local officials of the empire with food rations. It was not high-minded respect for individual peoples, ethnic groups, and foreign religions that motivated Persian policy. Rather, Persian policy was driven by enlightened self-interest. By reconciling the central power with local subjects, the Persians strengthened their empire.

Another way of assessing the decree of Cyrus is to look at the visual arts. Cyrus's appeals to Marduk in the cylinder and to Yahweh in the biblical decree demonstrate the Persian tendency to co-opt local religious and political traditions in the interest of imperial control. The artistic record corroborates this. Margaret C. Root has outlined the Persians' carefully calculated imperial program, designed to convey a vision of hierarchical order and imperial harmony over which presided the benevolent but omnipotent great king. To communicate this ideology the Persians brilliantly synthesized history and art according to the traditions of their subject peoples.

One outstanding example of this is the over-life-size granite statue of Darius I discovered in 1972 by French excavators at Susa in the Persian heartland. Made in and intended for Egypt, the statue remarkably mixes linguistic and artistic vocabularies. Darius stands in a conventional Egyptian pose but wears a Persian robe; the cuneiform text inscribed on the robe glorifies Darius as a conqueror. By contrast, the accompanying hieroglyphic inscription on the base tactfully dispenses with the conqueror references, proclaiming Darius as pharaoh, "King of Upper and Lower Egypt," with additional titulary. Tellingly, beneath Darius's feet appear not the traditional bound enemies of Egypt but personifications of Darius's subject peoples raising their hands in an Egyptian gesture of reverential support previously reserved for divine beings. Just as Cyrus speaks only of Marduk to the Babylonians and of Yahweh to the Judeans, for the Egyptians Darius becomes the pharaoh. Darius is also, however, a Persian pharaoh, less intent on calling attention to his dominating power over Egypt than in publishing the idea that all his various peoples are engaged in the harmonious support of his sovereignty.

The decree, or something like it, might have existed, along with the copy later found by King Darius's archivists in the Persian summer capital Ecbatana (Ezra 6.1–5 [Aramaic]). At some point, whether 538 (the date could be symbolic) or somewhat later, an indeterminate number of exiles returned to Jerusalem. Their leader was the Persian province of Yehud's first governor and a "prince of Judah," Sheshbazzar (a Babylonian name), who had been entrusted with the financial contributions raised by the Babylonian Jews and with the 5,400 gold and silver Temple vessels returned by Cyrus (Ezra 1.6–11). The first group of returnees is said to have laid the foundations of the new Temple (Ezra 5.14–17), although Ezra 4.5 reports that attempts to build the Temple were frustrated until the second year of Darius (520) and the governorship of Zerubbabel. Likewise, the second quotation of Cyrus's decree (Ezra 6) is silent on the subject of any exilic return to Judah in Sheshbazzar's time, prompting the suggestion that no notable return of any sort occurred before 520, when Zerubbabel and Joshua began their building program. Josephus reports that Jews in Babylon were "unwilling to leave their possessions" (*Antiquities* 11.1.3). Any returnees accompanying Sheshbazzar constituted only a portion of the Babylonian Jewish community, whose religious practices and beliefs were possibly heterogeneous.

The Homeland: People and Land

Yehud (Judah) was but one subprovince in the Persian fifth satrapy (Abar Nahara), which comprised Babylon (until 482), Syria-Palestine (including the coastal Phoenician city-states), and Cyprus. Unlike the Assyrians, the Babylonians had not brought deportees from elsewhere into Palestine. But Palestine was nevertheless the home of peoples who had been displaced and whose national identity had been threatened during the unrest of the sixth century: Philistines, Judahites, Samarians (both ethnic Israelites and settlers brought in by Assyria), Moabites, Ammonites, Edomites, Arabs, and, growing ever more influential, the Phoenicians, who dominated the entire Levantine coastal plain.

Over the two centuries of Persian rule the already mixed Phoenician culture absorbed increasingly greater doses of Cypriot and Aegean (Greek) elements as well. Impoverished inland areas such as the mountainous region of Judah, parts of Samaria, and perhaps Transjordan, whose economic life was based on grazing and agriculture, avoided heavy Phoenicianizing and consequent hellenization far longer

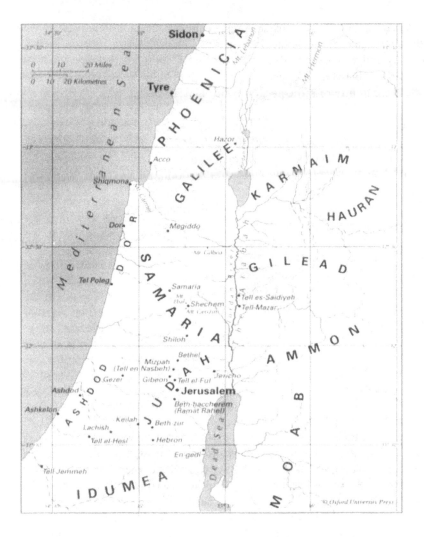

Palestine during the Persian Period

than areas on the coastal plain or along trade routes, where industry and commerce
flourished in the international common market of the Persian period. At the beginning and for much of the Persian period, Judah was poorer, less populous, and more
isolated than the surrounding territories. Besides Jerusalem, other Judean sites, especially fortress cities, bear the marks of the Neo-Babylonian king Nebuchadrezzar's
campaigns of destruction and conquest. Many urban sites, such as Hazor, Megiddo,
Tell Jemmeh, Lachish, and Ashdod, although not abandoned now supported smaller
unwalled settlements, often dominated by a large administrative building variously
identified as a "fortress," "residence," or "open-court house." Throughout the Persian period Jerusalem occupied only the eastern hill (the Ophel, originally captured
by David) and the Temple Mount.

Most of the inhabitants mentioned in Ezra-Nehemiah are clustered in northern

Judah and Benjamin, areas which archaeological evidence shows suffered least at the hands of the Babylonian invaders (at sites such as Tell en-Nasbeh, Gibeon, Bethel, and Tell el-Ful) and where some degree of prosperity endured. Perhaps this area surrendered early to Babylon. Likewise, farther north in Samaria archaeological surveys indicate a continuity of settlement into the Persian period with no decline in population. In particular, small groups of farmhouses found in a number of regions in the Samarian countryside, even on marginal and rocky lands, attest to a flourishing, even growing, population in the province. Beyond Samaria, Galilee became heavily Phoenician, densely settled, and prosperous during the Persian period. And crowded along the coastal plain were numerous cities of a predominantly Phoenician nature, with the associated inland plains, especially the Shephelah, densely settled.

The nature of the Persian administration of Palestine, as well as the place within that system of Samaria and Judah, are still obscure. Because Persia took over the Babylonian empire at one stroke by conquering Babylon, it is supposed that in the early years of Persian control the Babylonian provincial and subprovincial framework remained in place. The Persian administrative center nearest to Jerusalem was at Mizpah (Tell en-Nasbeh; Neh. 3.7), formerly the seat of the Babylonian authorities (2 Kings 25). Actual Persian presence in Syria-Palestine is difficult to pinpoint in the archaeological record. The Persian authorities lived in widely scattered enclaves or military strong points linked by the remarkable Persian system of communication. The best known such enclave is the "Persian residency" at Lachish. Other such sites include Tel Poleg and Shiqmona on the coastal plain, Tell el-Hesi, whose fortification system is one of the largest known mud-brick structures of the Persian period in Palestine, Ramat Rahel (Beth-haccherem) south of Jerusalem, En-gedi near the Dead Sea, and (in the Jordan Valley) Tell es-Saidiyeh and Tell Mazar.

The political designation applied by Persia to Judah and translated as "province" or "subprovince," as well as the title *governor,* applied, for example, to Zerubbabel and Nehemiah, have a range of meanings. Neither term proves the autonomous status of Judah as a territory of the Persian empire or the exact hierarchical level of the Judean governor. Nevertheless, the terms are official ones in Achaemenid imperial administrative contexts. Sheshbazzar is the first in a series of governors of Yehud known variously from the Bible and from Judean seals and sealings. The cumulative evidence suggests that Yehud was an autonomous administrative unit and not part of the province of Samaria. The Neo-Babylonians did not collapse previously distinctive political territories (such as Judah and Israel [Samaria]) into new provinces, nor did they subsume one territory under the power of the authorities governing another, so it is unlikely that the Persians inherited such an unusual type of province.

The Shephelah west of the Judean hill country may have been under the control of the coastal city of Dor. Samerina (Samaria) was administered from its capital in Samaria by a series of governors belonging to the Sanballat family. Archaeological remains at sites in the Jezreel plain and southern Galilee show an orientation toward coastal Phoenician culture, but their administrative center is uncertain; perhaps Megiddo remained as the provincial capital, as it had been under the Assyrians and Babylonians. Northern Galilee may have been administered separately, from Hazor.

The capital of Idumea, south of Judah, is unknown. Idumea was settled primarily by Edomites but also perhaps by some Judeans (Neh. 11), the Edomites having been forced out of their ancestral territory farther east by advancing Arab tribes. Beyond Idumea, Arabs, called "Kedarites" according to inscriptions from Tell el-Maskhuta in Egypt and from ancient Dedan (modern al-'Ula) in the north Arabian Hijaz, controlled northwest Arabia, southern Transjordan (former Edom), the Negeb and Sinai, and the coast around Gaza. The same inscriptions mention Geshem (known also from Neh. 2.19; 6.6) and later his son as leading the Arab federation. Herodotus reports that these Arabs were allies, not tributaries, of the Persian king. Across the Jordan, from north to south lay the provinces of Hauran, Karnaim (Bashan), Gilead, Ammon, and perhaps Moab. Excavations in Jordan suggest that in the sixth and fifth centuries BCE the land continued to be occupied and in some cases to flourish. On the coast clustered the Phoenician city-states, and the quasi-autonomous city-states or provinces of Acco, Dor, and Ashdod.

The Bible's interest is restricted essentially to Jerusalem and the Judean hill country immediately around it, about 2,000 square kilometers (770 square miles). Compared to its preexilic extent, postexilic Yehud was sadly diminished. Reconstructions of the boundaries of the Persian province of Yehud have been based on a correlation between lists in Ezra-Nehemiah (Ezra 2.21–35; Neh. 3.2–22; 7.25–38; 12.28–29), the distribution of Judean seals and coins, and the results of archaeological surveys. All of these sources are problematic. Some towns in the biblical lists, particularly those in the Shephelah (the fertile low hills west of the Judean hill country), may not have belonged to Yehud but were instead places to which the returnees had ancestral connections. Some of the seals and coins used to determine boundaries come from the Hellenistic era, and some of the sites that had been interpreted as boundary fortifications may have been built to secure trade and communication routes rather than borders. Yehud's northern boundary matches the preexilic tribal boundary line north of Mizpah and Bethel. The east was bounded by the Jordan River, thus including Jericho and En-gedi; and the southern edge followed a line from En-gedi to the Shephelah, running north of David's first capital, Hebron (now in Edomite territory). According to Nehemiah 3, the province of Yehud was divided into five districts: Mizpah, Jerusalem, Beth-haccherem, Beth-zur, and Keilah (and some scholars add Jericho to the list). Precise district borders are disputed.

Not surprisingly, there are fewer sites in Judah in the Persian I period (539/8–ca. 450) than in Persian II (ca. 450–332). By the later period, the prosperity of the thriving eastern Mediterranean economy had begun to trickle down to Judah. The Egyptian revolt of 460 transformed Judah into a more strategically significant Persian possession, and the missions of Ezra and Nehemiah (second half of the fifth century), which were probably related to Persia's Egyptian problems, marked the province's rise in the Persians' scale of importance. Exceedingly low population figures for Judah have been arrived at by recent demographic studies, based on the number of excavated and surveyed sites occupied in the Persian period. New modes of analysis have produced a tentative estimate of 32,250 for the population of Judah in the late preexilic years. In the Persian I period the population had dramatically fallen to 10,850, one-third Judah's former size. By Persian II the number increases to 17,000.

These figures help put the biblical picture in perspective. For instance, Jerusalem's population in Persian I has been calculated at a minuscule 475 to 500, which more than trebles to a still meager 1,750 in Persian II. There was no sizable population in

Jerusalem or Judah until the second century BCE. Numbers like these recall the biblical descriptions of exilic and postexilic Judah as devastated (Jer. 52.15–16; Zech. 7.7, 14). They also explain the concerns expressed by Zechariah (8.4–8), Nehemiah (11.1–2), and Second Zechariah (Zech. 9–14, composed well into the Persian period) with repopulating Jerusalem and the land by means of exilic return and by divinely ordained human fruitfulness (Zech. 10.7–10).

A casual reading of the Bible, particularly Ezra-Nehemiah, could leave the impression that the land to which the exiles returned was utterly abandoned and depopulated. On the contrary, archaeology, common sense, and even the Bible indicate that part of the Judean population, although markedly diminished, had continued to live in Judah after the Babylonian deportations and flights of refugees to Egypt. There are a few scattered biblical allusions to Judeans who were never exiled. Jeremiah 39.10 mentions that after the destruction of Jerusalem the Babylonians gave vineyards and fields to poor Judahites. Perhaps the Jewish families assigned in Nehemiah 11 to cities south of Beth-zur (and thus technically outside the borders of Judah) had remained there during the exile.

In Ezra-Nehemiah the "empty land" is a literary theme, reflecting the interest of Jewish circles preoccupied with asserting privileged ethnic boundaries—with defining "Israel" by a policy of exclusion, particularly of nonexiles whose existence Ezra-Nehemiah often ignores. For the authors of Ezra-Nehemiah, "Israel" was restricted to the returned exiles who had established themselves in Jerusalem and Judah in the first generations of the restoration, along with (presumably) those sympathetic Jews remaining in Babylonia and Persia who provided the returned exiles with moral and financial support. Ezra and Nehemiah themselves come from the Jewish communities in Babylonia and Persia, respectively. Accordingly, in Ezra "Israel" is equated with more frequently encountered terms, such as *exiles, the exile,* and *the congregation of exiles.* To this true Israel alone belonged the land of their forebears. Nevertheless, according to Ezra 6.21 and Nehemiah 10.28, which allude to people who have separated themselves from the "pollutions of the people of the land," some nonexilic native Judeans—in other words, Jews technically excluded from the Israel of Ezra-Nehemiah—did receive admittance into the exclusive "exilic Israel" community.

Another significant population of local Yahweh worshipers inhabited the Persian province of Samaria and possibly southern Galilee. The Bible suggests that after the Assyrian deportation (722) only foreign immigrants populated this area (2 Kings 17; Ezra 4). But the Assyrians did not deport the entire Israelite population, and 2 Chronicles 34.9 implies that some urban Israelites not of the ruling class, as well as rural Israelites, remained in the land. Just as the Judean "people of the land" are viewed with contempt by Ezra-Nehemiah as impure and unworthy, so the Samarian Yahwists, led by the Samarian governor Sanballat, are presented as spiteful enemies of the true Israel, not as another group of Jews with a variant understanding of religious matters and ethnic definitions.

Both Chronicles (see 2 Chron. 30.5–11, 18; 34) and Zechariah convey a more conciliatory and inclusive attitude toward the inhabitants of Samaria. The brief period of a reunited monarchy under Josiah in the late seventh century BCE may have reinforced social and religious connections between north and south. Jeremiah 41.4–5 is intriguing in this regard; after the destruction of Jerusalem and the Temple, eighty worshipers bearing the marks of deep mourning came south from Shechem, Samaria, and Shiloh to make offerings at the site of the destroyed Temple.

Aramaic letters from Elephantine also attest to Samarian Yahwism. For example, they show that Nehemiah's Samarian nemesis, Governor Sanballat, gave his sons Yahwistic names. Moreover, when the Jews of Elephantine in the late fifth century needed help rebuilding their temple, they appealed for aid to Jerusalem and Samaria alike as if both cities had some claim to their religious allegiance. And while many of the names mentioned in the Samarian Wadi ed-Daliyeh papyri (fourth century BCE) are foreign (Edomite, Aramaic, Moabite, Phoenician, and Babylonian), the largest percentage of names with divine elements is Yahwistic, confirming the notion that, among the ruling elite at least, Yahwism persisted and even flourished in the Persian period. Moreover, the Zadokite priestly family of Jerusalem and leading Samarian families were allied by diplomatic marriages (Neh. 13.28; Josephus, *Antiquities* 11.8.2). Reassessments of sectarian Samaritanism have demonstrated that its feasts, its conservatism toward the Torah, and its version of the Pentateuch indicate more derivation than deviation from Judaism of the Second Temple period.

North of Samaria the ancient Israelite territory of Galilee included prosperous coastal cities that were subject, politically and culturally, to the Phoenician powers of Tyre and Sidon. But the cultural and ethnic affinities of inland Galilee's population during the Persian period remain enigmatic. Can a Jewish (Yahweh-worshiping) population in this formerly Israelite land be assumed during the Persian period? The usual answer to this question, if even asked, has been "no." Archaeologically, the evidence suggests that Phoenician culture dominated inland regions. Moreover, Galilee is never mentioned in biblical sources describing the Persian period, and Galilee appears to have been predominantly Gentile in sources describing it in Hellenistic times. Nevertheless, a case can be made for the existence of a significant Jewish community in Galilee during the Persian period, based partly on the evidence of deep-rooted Galilean Jewish traditions in late Hellenistic times that cannot be explained if the population had been entirely ignorant of or antagonistic to Judaism.

In addition to nonexiled Judeans, the inhabitants of Samaria, and possibly Galileans, there may have been an additional group of local Yahwists. In Nehemiah's time, a prominent family with a Yahwistic name, the Tobiads, lived across the Jordan in Ammon (Neh. 2.19). They intermarried with members of the Jerusalem priestly family (Neh. 6.19) and participated in some way in the Jerusalem Temple (Neh. 13.4–9). Some scholars see a connection between Nehemiah's Tobiah and the large "family of Tobiah" (Ezra 2.60; Neh. 7.62; 1 Esd. 5.37), which returned with Zerubbabel from exile but could not prove an Israelite pedigree. Because a Tobiah is also mentioned in Zechariah (6.9–15) as a returned exile who participated in the symbolic crowning of Joshua, the mention of an imperfect pedigree in Ezra and Nehemiah may be a tendentious attempt, made long after the reestablishment of the Temple, to cast aspersions on a losing group in a Temple power struggle. This family continued to be important; the archaeological record supports the evidence from Josephus (*Antiquities* 12.4.2) and the Zeno papyri for a powerful Jewish landowning family called the Tobiads in third-century BCE Ammon.

Thus, the Palestinian (as opposed to Diaspora) "Jewish" population throughout the Persian period consisted of local, nonexiled Jews of Judah; exiled Jews who had returned to Judah; Samarians; Galileans; and at least one family in Ammon across the Jordan. These local Jewish communities maintained contacts with Jews who remained in Babylonia, Persia, and Egypt.

The Empire and the Restored Community

Many questions surround the earliest Judean restoration. Is Judah's first governor, the fatherless Sheshbazzar (ca. 538) in Ezra 6.14 (a book that downplays the role of the house of David), the same as Shenazzar, a son of Judah's captive King Jehoiachin (1 Chron. 3.18)? His title *prince* merely indicates high status, not royal blood. Perhaps he was not a Judean. Sheshbazzar is also the first of several important Judean officials who vanish mysteriously from the biblical record. Was his role in the restoration suppressed for theological reasons by the editors of Ezra-Nehemiah, or did he fail in his mission to complete the Temple? The suggestion that he took part in a thwarted Judean independence movement against the Persians is likewise only a guess.

Little is known of events in Judah or Samaria in the generation after the disappearance of Sheshbazzar. Temple building came to a halt, if it had ever begun. Haggai 1 suggests that any early movement toward Temple restoration quickly ran out of steam. Considered realistically, to exiles intent on building homes and organizing a subsistence system, the fields, the "well-roofed houses," and the wage earning described so bitterly by Haggai could well have mattered more than the Temple.

One decade after Sheshbazzar's time, Cyrus's son Cambyses (530–522 BCE) realized his father's dream of conquering Egypt. In 526 the Persian army, its ranks augmented by Greek mercenaries, invaded Egypt via northern Sinai. A Kedarite king provided camel trains bearing water skins for the desert crossing. The Persian fleet, largely Phoenician ships, penetrated the Nile mouths, and together these land and sea forces defeated the pharaoh Psammetichus III, the last king of Dynasty 26. When Egypt submitted to him in 525, Cambyses also gained Cyprus for the Persian empire. Judah and Samaria as inland territories lacked the strategic value of coastal cities like Acco, the staging area for the invasion, and were unaffected by invasion activities.

Cambyses's policies in Egypt mirrored those of his father in Babylon. Just as Cyrus added "King of Babylon" to his titulary, his son was formally crowned the first pharaoh of Dynasty 27. Like Cyrus, Cambyses presented himself as the restorer of a land suffering sad misrule, in this case, from the late usurper Pharaoh Amasis and his heir Psammeticus III. And, like his father, Cambyses was careful to cultivate good relations with important priestly establishments, although he alienated other priests by diminishing their income. In sum, the first two Persian kings set a pattern for culturally informed flexibility in ruling diverse foreign subjects.

With the reign of Darius I (522–486 BCE), Persian and Jewish history takes a new turn. Darius was probably a usurper, and he spent his first year and a half quelling rebellions on multiple fronts. To consolidate his control and to further integrate the political and social order of conquered territories into his imperial system, Darius embarked on a series of administrative reforms. He organized the empire into twenty tributary satrapies, large territorial units that included provinces usually following the former boundaries of conquered lands.

Darius did not create the satrap system, but he did bring to it a new level of systematized administrative practices. In charge of each satrapy was the satrap (Median *Khshathrapan*, "Protector of the Realm"), a Persian aristocrat who was the king's personal representative. The satraps were responsible for justice and security and most especially for ensuring carefully specified tribute payments. Important satrapal centers such as Memphis in Egypt and Sardis in Lydia were fortified by permanent imperial garrisons, whereas in other centers only household troops were regularly billeted. Large numbers of native Persians also received land in the satrapies; if called on, they were required to lead local recruits in battle. Like the great king, the satrap had a chancery staffed with Aramaic-speaking scribes to maintain communication with the royal court and with local authorities subject to the satrap. The provinces within individual satrapies had no uniform mode of government: sometimes they were headed by a native dynast, sometimes by a local or a Persian appointee, sometimes by a city prince or priest.

Darius also introduced imperial coinage and a postal system, and he greatly expanded the network of royal roads connecting all parts of the Persian empire. Inns along the way provided travelers on imperial business with free board and lodging. In addition to facilitating communications among the satrapies, the well-maintained roads ensured the efficient movement of troop convoys wherever they were deployed.

Darius's ambitious building projects included a short-lived Suez Canal. Its purpose may have been to enhance Red Sea trading enterprises, or, as a royal project in the pharaonic tradition, to emphasize continuity with Egypt's past and to impress Darius's subjects. The archaeological record confirms that Darius improved or built new palaces in the old royal capitals of Babylon and Susa and in Cyrus's city, Pasargadae. But most notably, Darius planned and began the construction of Persepolis in the heart of the Persian homeland, a city whose magnificence served well the ideological program that informed its creation and whose impressive remains still stand today in southern Iran.

Darius sagely kept an eye on religious matters in his empire. In Egypt the satrap, on Darius's behalf, personally confirmed and dismissed appointees to the priestly post of temple superintendent. Darius sent his Egyptian physician Udjahorresnet back to Egypt to reconstitute the old Saite temple-colleges, which taught priestly learning, ritual procedure, and medicine. Another project personally initiated by Darius and entrusted to Aryandes, satrap of Egypt, was the codification of Egyptian "laws" (probably temple endowments, privileges, and immunities) and their translation into Aramaic and Egyptian Demotic.

In 520, Darius's second year and almost twenty years since the exile had ended, two Judean prophets, Haggai and Zechariah, began a spirited campaign to convince Judean leaders and the citizenry that the time was ripe to rebuild the Temple. Haggai's first oracle (Hag. 1.1–11) directly challenges Zerubbabel the governor and the high priest Joshua to remedy the deleterious consequences of letting God's Temple remain a rubble heap. Both Zerubbabel and Joshua (Jeshua) may have been born and raised in Babylonia; Zerubbabel was the grandson of Judah's captive Davidic king Jehoiachin (Hag. 1.1; Ezra 3.2; Neh. 12.1; 1 Chron. 3.19). Joshua is described as the son of J(eh)ozadak (Ezra 3.2), the last preexilic chief priest (not high priest) according to 1 Chronicles 6.15. (However, 2 Kings 25.18–21 instead names Jehozadak's father, Seraiah, as chief priest and does not explicitly say that his family went into exile. Nevertheless, it is likely that surviving members of Seraiah's family were exiled.)

Under Zerubbabel and Joshua, presumably the governor saw to secular affairs and the high priest attended to matters of ritual, but whether they always shared equal power or one at first outranked the other is uncertain. One of Zechariah's visions (Zech. 6.9–15) alludes to friction between high priest and governor over jurisdictional questions. Perhaps in this period of imperial and provincial administrative restructuring, the heretofore rare title *high priest* (more common was *chief priest*) was assumed by Joshua in recognition of new, expanded powers. This diarchy may also reflect the restoration program described in Ezekiel. On the other hand, that prophet's allusions to a future leader from the priestly Zadokite family (Ezek. 43.18–27) that had dominated preexilic Temple ritual and to a pious Davidic prince (Ezek. 37.24–28) need not imply a formula for diarchy. Although the status of Judean governors may have fluctuated during the two centuries of Persian rule, for the most part it is accurate to call Judah's form of government in this period a theocracy, with the deity's representative the high priest assuming an increasingly dominant role, possibly even filling the post of governor on occasion.

Ezra 2–3 (see also Neh. 7) describes the return to Judah of Zerubbabel and Joshua with a huge company of Babylonian exiles. They immediately establish an altar in Jerusalem, resume sacrifices, and begin the rebuilding. Ezra's dates for this event are vague, and the historicity of the Ezra narrative is called into question by the virtual silence of both Haggai and Zechariah (but note Zech. 6.10) on the subject of exiles or the expectation of a large-scale return. Perhaps the Temple-building activities did not involve any significant group of recent arrivals, or perhaps returned exiles were only one of several Jewish parties originally involved in the Temple restoration.

From the ideological perspective of the Ezra-Nehemiah narrative, the only legitimate Israelites are the "exiles." But it is clear from the same narrative and elsewhere in the Bible that as the Persian period progressed other Jewish groups challenged the "exiles." Some of these Judeans were probably responsible for the so-called Solar Temple at Lachish, which has been dated to the time of Darius I. Similarities between Ezra's descriptions of exilic "return" and the story of the Exodus (compare Ezra 1.6 with Exod. 12.35–36) suggest that typological and ideological considerations may be obscuring historical data about the activities and motivations of Zerubbabel and Jeshua. Still, just because a story conforms to a literary pattern is not reason for total skepticism; tablets found in Syria attest that early in Darius's reign at least one other exiled ethnic group returned from Babylonia to its ancestral home. Whenever it was that they arrived in Judah, returned exiles were an important Judean interest group by the time of Zerubbabel, in close communication with supportive like-minded exiles in the Diaspora. Ultimately the "exiles" or their ideological heirs gained the upper hand in Jewish political and religious affairs, and their version of the events of the restoration dominates the biblical record.

Attempts to understand the Temple restoration movement of 520 focus both on the rebellions of subject nations against Darius in his early years and on the implications for Judah of Darius's imperial reorganization. Did the upheavals in the Persian empire associated with Darius's rise to the throne suggest to the Judahites that the time had come for a political and spiritual renewal in Judah, even the restoration in some form of its preexilic identity? The close conjunction of Darius's accession with the dated activities of Haggai and Zechariah, who use messianic language associated with preexilic Davidic kings to extol David's descendant Zerubbabel and the high priest Joshua (Hag. 2.20–23; Zech. 3.8; 6.11–14), has suggested a short-lived movement to overthrow Persian hegemony in Yehud. Like Sheshbazzar (and later, Ezra and Nehemiah), Zerubbabel and Joshua drop inexplicably from the biblical record, even before the Temple is completed in 516/5 (Ezra 6.15–16). Were they punished as rebels? Or recalled to Darius's court? Recent scholarship is turning away from the rebellion theory; perhaps Zerubbabel died a natural death around 516–515, or he may have succumbed to opponents in an internal Judean power struggle.

Precisely when Zerubbabel became the second attested governor of Yehud is unclear. If Zechariah is prophesying in expectation of Zerubbabel's arrival in Jerusalem he would have to be a Darius appointee, but in Ezra 5.2 Zerubbabel is already governor when Zechariah begins his ministry, perhaps appointed recently by Darius or even earlier by Cambyses. Viewed in the context of Darius's reforms, the presence of a governor of the Davidic line could reflect a new imperial attitude toward the region. Zerubbabel would not have been the only local dynast administering a minor satrapal province. Darius made a regular practice of deputizing native experts on provincial affairs, including religious matters, as in the case of the Egyptian Udjahorresnet.

According to Ezra 6.6–12, in his second year (520) Darius gave orders that the work already begun on the Temple could proceed with the added incentive of financial support from district revenues (6.8). Thanks to imperial endorsement, perhaps some limited imperial funding, donations from wealthy exiles (Zech. 6.10–11), and the exhortations of Haggai, Zechariah, and additional unnamed prophets (Ezra 5.2; Zech. 7.3; 8.9), the Temple was completed in 516 or 515 (Ezra 6.15). Ezra 6.16 describes the dedication ceremony celebrated by the priests, Levites, and the rest of the returned exiles followed by observation of the Passover (6.17). The date of 516–515 for this joyous event (in Ezra 6.15 only) cannot be confirmed. By including this date notice, the Ezra narrative can claim that the seventy-year desolation Jeremiah had predicted (Jer. 25.11–12; 29.10) ended almost exactly on prophetic schedule.

Once again, animal sacrifices could be burnt by the priests on the altar each morning and afternoon. But in spite of the Temple's symbolic, religious, political, and economic centrality, the Bible contains no descriptions of its actual dimensions despite its duration for five centuries, the longest surviving Jerusalem Temple. Herod's Temple (begun in 20 BCE) was a wholly new structure, technically the "Third Temple," and can provide no information about its immediate predecessor. The archaeological evidence for the destruction of Jerusalem is abundant, but the site of the Temple has not been excavated. In constructing their new Temple the rebuilders would have returned to the site of the original structure, thus conforming to traditional practice in which sacredness of place persists through time. They would have followed the plan of the old Temple, whose foundations and dimensions could probably be seen in the ruins. They also had the Pentateuchal tabernacle texts and the Deuteronomic Historian's descriptions of the First Temple.

There is no way to ascertain the nature of Sheshbazzar's earlier "foundation" or of the altar raised by Zerubbabel and Joshua as a prelude to their successful rebuilding. The stylization and allusiveness of the narratives concerning the Temple limit their historical and descriptive value. The narration about this period stresses the newness—hence the purity—of the new building, as well as its continuity with the

Table 8.1 Governors, Davidides, and High Priests of Yehud in the Persian Period (538–433 BCE)

DATES	GOVERNORS	DAVIDIDES	HIGH PRIESTS
538	Sheshbazzar (*phh*, Ezra 5.14; "prince," Ezra 1.8)	Sheshbazzar b. before 592 (uncle of)	Jehozadak b. before 586 (father of)
520–510?	Zerubbabel (*pht yhwdh*, Hag. 1.1, 14)	Zerubbabel b. 558–556 (?)	Joshua (Jeshua) b. ca. 570
510–490?	Elnathan (*phw'*, bulla and seal)	Shelomith ('*mh* of Elnathan) b. ca. 540	
		Hananiah b. ca. 545	Joiakim b. ca. 545 (brother of)
490–470(?)	Yehoezer (*phw'*, jar impression)		Eliashib I b. ca. 545
		Shecaniah b. ca. 520 (father of)	Johanan I b. ca. 520 (father of)
470–	Ahzai (*phw'*, jar impression)	Hattush b. ca. 495 (father of)	Eliashib II b. ca. 495 (father of)
445–433	Nehemiah (*hphh*, Neh. 5.14; 12.26)	Elioenai b. ca. 470	Joiada I b. ca. 470

First Temple. It underscores that the vessels of the First Temple were once again being put to use in the traditional sacrificial rituals. Rabbinic tradition, however, lamented that the First Temple possessed five things the Second lacked: "the sacred fire, the ark, the urim and thummim, and the Holy Spirit (prophecy)" (P. *Taanit* 2.1 [65a]).

The Jewish rebuilders of the Temple clearly subscribed to the ancient Near Eastern—and preexilic Jerusalem—worldview (see Ps. 68.34–35) that a nation's well-being depended on the maintenance of the central sacrificial cult (Hag. 2.9). This explains why Haggai and Zechariah were so anxious to energize the dispirited population that had allowed the Temple to remain in ruins (Hag. 1.2–6). Both these postexilic prophets use language reminiscent of Ezekiel and Second Isaiah in their message of God's imminent action in the lives of Judah's people. The return to the

Temple of God's glory (Hag. 2.8–9; Zech. 8.3), of God's manifest presence (Ezek. 43.1–5), would reverse Yahweh's curse on the land, the prophets' explanation for the poor harvests, blight, drought, poverty, and stagnant economy (Hag. 1.5, 10–11; 2.16–17; Zech. 8.10–12). The presence of God's glory would usher in a new era of prosperity (Hag. 2.9; Zech. 8.12–15). Zechariah's extravagant vision of the golden lampstand flanked by olive trees (Zech. 4.1–6, 10–14) calls to mind ubiquitous ancient Near Eastern tree-of-life symbolism (see Gen. 2.9; Prov. 3.17–18; 11.30). The visions of Zechariah 1.7–6.15 in particular may be viewed as an essay on early postexilic Temple symbolism. Echoing standard ancient Near Eastern as well as biblical literary and visual imagery, Zechariah refers to the Temple as the sacred mountain (Zech. 4.7; 8.3), which connects earthly and heavenly realms. As such it is the locus of God's covenantal law and justice (Zech. 3.7; 5.1–4).

Curiously, despite their shared purpose, the contemporary prophets Haggai and Zechariah do not make reference to each other, and their rhetorical styles differ. Unlike other prophetic books, the book of Haggai is written entirely in the third person, as a historical narrative rather than a first-person delivery of Yahweh's word. Nonetheless, both prophets address the corollary principle of preexilic Temple ideology, namely, the Zion/David theology. Most notably expressed in Psalms, this theology proclaimed that the king rather than the priesthood bore primary responsibility for protecting and promoting the national worship. Haggai more than Zechariah retains the older monarchical ideals, specifically in association with Zerubbabel. Repeating God's description of exiled King Jehoiachin (Jer. 22.24), Haggai (2.23) dubs Zerubbabel God's "signet ring," a mark of honor and of the governor's function as God's divine representative. By contrast, the book of Zechariah makes more guarded references to Zerubbabel and kingship (Zech. 3.8; 4.6–10; 6.12–13), preferring to stress a joint messiahship of prince and priest. Zechariah wants to reassure the citizens of Judah that their quasi-national status, newly reembodied in the restored Temple ritual, did not depend on the old preexilic form of monarchy. Both Haggai and Zechariah, however, avoid mentioning an important part of the priestly mandate throughout the empire, namely, prayers and sacrifices for the well-being of the Persian king and his sons. Ezra-Nehemiah pragmatically accepts the necessity for the prayers without question (Ezra 6.10).

For Zechariah, who came from a priestly family (Zech. 1.1, 7; Ezra 5.1; 6.14; Neh. 12.4, 16), Davidic kingship lives most compellingly in Israel's memory and in eschatological expectation. Real power belonged in the hands of the Zadokite priesthood, whose exclusive claim to administer the Temple appears earlier in a programmatic text in Ezekiel 44. This apparent expansion of priestly power is a postexilic phenomenon, and, in fact, convincing evidence for the anointing of a high priest is only found in postexilic literature. By the Hasmonean period (mid-second century BCE) the high priest was exercising the function of the king. The fading of kingship from actual Judean experience accompanies the gradual disappearance of prophets in the classical mode and the growing power of the high priest.

From a symbolic standpoint, where the new Temple differed most from the old was in having no royal palace immediately adjacent to it. This difference signaled the adjustments to Judean royal ideology alluded to in Zechariah 1–8. However, a measure of continuity between old and new may be exemplified by the citadel that Nehemiah apparently built just north of the Temple precinct around 445 BCE (Neh. 2.8; 7.2). Probably garrisoned by troops of the Persian military establishment, this citadel adjacent to the Temple would have constituted the Persian-period equivalent of the preexilic royal compound. The citadel signified monarchical control of the land's institutions, though now the monarch was the Persian king. Similarly, the biblical books least resistant to the Persian presence in Jewish lives (Haggai, Zechariah, Ezra, and Nehemiah) date events as a matter of course by the Persian king's regnal year.

Inclusion and Exclusion in the Restored Community

The community of returned exiles was frequently at odds with the indigenous population, among them nonexiled Judeans and Samarians, who also professed allegiance to Yahweh. Biblical references to the comparative wealth of these immigrants from Babylonia (Ezra 2.68–69; 8.26–27; Zech. 6.9–11) reinforce the suspicion that they had to be well-off in order to finance their return in the first place. The Ezra-Nehemiah narrative suggests that even some sixty years after Zerubbabel the families of returnees had maintained their identity as social and economic elites, distinct from the local population, who were poorer farmers and peasants. Did the returned exiles, who were, after all, strangers to their ancestral lands, clash with indigenous Judeans and foreign opportunists (such as Edomites) who had taken over their property in their absence? Did the returnees settle down only in unpopulated land, perhaps just south of Jerusalem? Did they force wholesale evictions? Dominated by an "exilic" perspective, the Bible is virtually silent on these embarrassing questions.

From a sociological perspective, Judah like other agrarian societies was characterized by social inequality. A class-based breakdown of the population and distribution of wealth illuminates both the social tensions and the inner-Temple struggles to which the biblical record alludes. The majority of the population consisted primarily of peasants and artisans, along with petty criminals and underemployed itinerant workers who lived by their wits or off charity. Ethnographers and historians suggest that the governing class—particularly the priestly families in postexilic Judah—averaged about 1 percent of the population but controlled as much as a quarter of the national income. Together, the ruler (the Persians) and the governing class (primarily the Zadokite priestly families) in general could have received not less then half the national income.

According to the theology of the exiles, bluntly expressed in Ezekiel 11, Yahweh had deserted Judah and joined the people in exile. According to Ezekiel, God has no patience with "inhabitants of Jerusalem"—in other words, nonexiled Jews who make the counterclaim that the land is theirs because God was punishing the exiles. Ezekiel speaks for his constituency and promises that once the returnees have cleansed the land of the supposedly syncretistic religious practices of the indigenous Judahites, Yahweh will restore their lands to the true people of Israel—the exiles—whether those remaining liked it or not. In Ezekiel's chronology the syncretistic horrors described in Ezekiel 8 occur before the destruction of the Temple, but the passage may be a polemical accusation composed by the Babylonian exiles in a long-distance contest with the nonexiled population over the authentic worship of Yahweh.

From the Persians' standpoint, the Temple in Jerusalem, like temples elsewhere, contributed various forms of tribute to the state—revenues, goods, and services.

Persia's Judean proxies in control of the Temple were responsible for raising this tribute from a local population already struggling to pay the tithe and annual levy they owed the Persians (Neh. 5). High-priestly families also administered the material and fiscal resources that accrued to the Temple as part of the sacrificial system. Thus, whoever controlled the Jerusalem Temple also participated significantly in the economic activity of the land and enjoyed high social and economic status. As the social elite, the Temple community could dictate the terms by which an outsider could qualify for membership in their group and thereby share its privileges.

Three episodes of local conflict are described in Ezra 4–6. According to Ezra 4.6–23, the "people of the land" and Persian officials in league with foreigners resettled in Samaria and elsewhere in the Trans-Euphrates satrapy wrote a letter to the king protesting against the Temple builders in the reigns of Xerxes I (Hebrew Ahasuerus, 486–465; Ezra 4.6) or Artaxerxes I (465–424; Ezra 4.11). There are serious textual and chronological difficulties with this notice. The episode has been associated with the unrest right after Xerxes' assassination in 465, or with the activities of Ezra or Nehemiah. Whatever the opposition, they successfully put a stop to some sort of building activity in Jerusalem by informing the king that the Jews were "rebuilding that wicked and rebellious city."

The wording of Ezra 4 suggests that the shadowy "people of the land" and the "foreigners" of Samaria and elsewhere in the satrapy are spitefully subverting pious Jews intent on restoring their city and Temple. Samarians may have feared that restoration of the Jerusalem Temple would result not in religious rivalry, but rather in a latent claim by Jerusalem for political hegemony over the northern tribal territories of the Davidic/Solomonic and Josianic monarchies. But the historical, social, and political dynamics behind the episode(s) remain obscure. From a literary point of view, the story acts as a foil for the successes of Nehemiah, the exilic Jew who rebuilds the walls of Jerusalem in the face of similar opponents with similar accusations.

Ezra 5.1–6.15 tells of an investigation by Tattenai, governor of Abar Nahara (mentioned also in a tablet dated to 502), and by Shethar-bozenai into the authority by which the Jews under Zerubbabel (ca. 520) are rebuilding the Temple. The Temple builders invoked the eighteen-year-old decree of Cyrus, for which Tattenai requested verification by letter from Darius. Work on the Temple proceeded while Tattenai's questions were processed through the royal chancelleries, and a confirming copy of the decree was finally run to ground in far-off Ecbatana, the Persian capital. Tattenai may have been stirred to ask his questions by rivals of Zerubbabel's party in a neighboring province or provinces, possibly Samaria. In Ezra 4.1–3, "adversaries of Judah and Benjamin" attempt to join in Zerubbabel's rebuilding project; their offer is rejected. Although they worship "the same God," they are supposedly descendants of peoples resettled in Samaria by the Assyrians, and hence as foreigners they are ethnically disqualified. Because Ezra-Nehemiah shows an intense interest in separating legitimate from illegitimate Israelites, this passage may be tendentious in presenting the "adversaries" as foreigners. Perhaps over two centuries the distinction between foreign and native Israelite had broken down. Perhaps the Yahweh worship of the adversaries was syncretistic, but, conversely, perhaps they had become exclusive Yahwists. Perhaps they were not foreign at all; Jeremiah 41 hints that northerners devoted to the Jerusalem Temple, possibly the same group whose help was turned down by Zerubbabel's followers, continued to make pilgrimages there even after its destruction.

In Ezra 4.4, the "people of the land," who may be the same as Zerubbabel's "adversaries" in 4.1 or an entirely different group, impede the rebuilding by bribing officials to cause trouble. The first-century CE Jewish historian Josephus's identification of the rival group(s) of Ezra 4.1–5 as "Samaritans" is anachronistic; Josephus's assumptions about Persian-period Samarians arise from the extreme alienation of Jews and Samaritans in his own time. The decisive break by sectarian Samaritans from Judaism occurred only in the second century BCE. According to various hypotheses, the enigmatic "people of the land" here could be residents of Judah of foreign, mixed, or doubtful lineage, or they could be "ethnically pure" Jews who had remained in the land during the exile, or they could be a combination of such groups.

Behind these troubles lie power struggles over control of the Temple, early manifestations of a key element in Second Temple period sectarianism. If the Jerusalem Temple enjoyed Persian support, then whoever controlled the Temple stood to accrue collateral financial and political benefits. In theological terms, a conscientiously administered Temple ensured the prosperity of the land by honoring the demands of the Temple's chief inhabitant, Yahweh. The exiles could claim with Ezekiel that knowledge of proper ritual practice belonged to the exiled priestly elite, of whom Ezekiel was one, not to the humbler levels of Judean society who had been beneath the notice of socially discriminating Babylonian deporters. On a more pragmatic level, a well-run sacrificial ritual collected and redistributed the land's produce and, ideally, fostered prosperity and political stability.

Postexilic Prophecy

The concern of Haggai and Zechariah for the proper maintenance of worship is typical of postexilic prophecy and marks a change in emphasis from earlier prophecy, which had often been critical of ritual. Prophetic speech more and more follows liturgical forms used in public worship. The postexilic age did have charismatic prophets, but their activities and words were often suppressed in theocratic circles as the work of renegades. Moreover, postexilic prophetic authors writing in both the theocratic and the charismatic vein pseudonymously clothed themselves in the garb of eminent classical forebears, giving a new text validity by embedding it in the words of a venerated ancient prophet.

In addition to specific, if obscure, biblical references to sociopolitical opposition to the Temple rebuilders, there are in Isaiah 56–66 (Third Isaiah), Ezekiel 38–39, Isaiah 24–27, and Zechariah 9–14 (Second Zechariah) allusions to additional internal Jewish protest against the ruling establishment. Such protests come from a group or groups who reject Zadokite priestly claims and propose an alternative religious program in which direct vindication from God of the aggrieved party is a central element. But, as will become increasingly the case with postexilic Jewish writing, these texts assiduously avoid chronological notices and authentic autographs. If they do criticize those in power, the source of the disagreements remains vague, in part because ancient Judaism, like all other ancient religions (except, perhaps, Christianity) was not based on a doctrinal creed whose tenets were under fire from opponents outside the faith. By the Hellenistic period, inter-Jewish dissent was seldom if ever expressed in theological terms, turning instead on matters of religious practice.

The interest group behind "Third Isaiah" remains shadowy. Perhaps its composition stems from disfranchised Levites who viewed the political accommodations of the dominant Zadokite priesthood as compromising "pure" Yahwism. Without specific dates in the text, attempts to associate this visionary group with particular rivals of Joshua and the Zadokites mentioned in Ezra-Nehemiah founder. Passages in Isaiah 57, 65, and 66 do repudiate Haggai's and Zechariah's call for Temple restoration. Nevertheless, this is not a repudiation of Temple ideology. Rather, it is a rejection of the current Temple authorities in favor of a now-marginalized group with claims of superior priestly qualifications. The intent of the hybrid "salvation-judgment" oracles of Isaiah 59 and 65 to condemn wicked Judeans, but to affirm eschatological salvation for the righteous few, provides a good indication of the rifts in postexilic Judean society.

Protoapocalyptic visions of Ezekiel 38–39 may also belong to the circle of Third Isaiah, as eager as their Zadokite rivals to co-opt the great exilic prophet for their own ends. These chapters suggest that the Babylonian destruction was nothing compared to the future horrors intended for a still-wicked Israel, presumably those Jews in control of the Temple. Only divine intervention would enable the restoration program of Ezekiel 40–48 to proceed.

People harboring visionary expectations of vindication by cataclysmic divine irruptions into history are, or at least feel, disfranchised, and they occupy the margins of mainstream society. But without a secure sociohistorical matrix we must be careful not to create a rigid theoretical framework for such protoapocalyptic passages as Isaiah 56–66, Ezekiel 38–39, Isaiah 24–27, and Zechariah 9–14. They cannot all be attributed to the same period, much less to the same ideological groups. Even the well-entrenched Zadokites could have fostered a visionary or two.

What these texts do illustrate is a movement away from classical prophecy, which located God's judgment firmly in history. Instead, these visionaries saw punishment and redemption in terms of otherworldly categories, which ultimately became central in fully formed apocalyptic thought. The timescale for God's judgment begins to expand, as does the sphere of divine judgment, which now includes all the nations, a more universalist view of God's interest, perhaps, than that of Ezra-Nehemiah. Some expect God to personally intervene in history (Zech. 14); dreams and visions abound, often populated by angelic interpreters, a form of assistance that earlier prophets seldom required. The roots of Jewish apocalyptic do not lie in Zoroastrian (Persian) dualism, with its vision of a climactic war between the cosmic forces of good and evil. The symbolism and rhetoric of early Second Temple protoapocalypticism has an unquestionable Israelite pedigree, even to the extent of reviving such ancient mythic motifs as Yahweh the divine warrior and Yahweh's battle with the chaos dragon. The common characteristics that Yahweh shared with Canaanite Baal were no longer a source of confusion or polemic, and they could profitably be brought again to the fore.

The book of Malachi is usually assigned to the early fifth century, just before the period of Ezra and Nehemiah. Like other postexilic writings, its authorship is anonymous; the reference in 3.1 to "my messenger" (Hebrew mal'ākî) gives the book its title. Malachi synthesizes priestly and prophetic themes. Its bitter attack on the reigning Temple priesthood has been viewed as merging the interests of dissident Levites and Third Isaian circles. Here, too, is a dramatic eschatological denouement, but the writer also appeals to sacred antiquity, appropriating for the prophet's constituents God's covenant with Levi, a more ancient and thus more authoritative covenant than that of the Zadokites.

A corollary to this resurgence of ancient lore is the Persians' encouragement, beginning with Darius I, of the collection and preservation of their subjects' religious learning. Both the work of Aryandes and Udjahorresnet in Egypt and of Ezra the Israelite scribe attest to this policy. The Priestly strand of the Pentateuch or even the Pentateuch itself could belong to this same incipient antiquarianism.

But ultimately the single most important stimulus to Persian-period Israel's interest in and reverence for its history is the exile. The prophets having proved themselves by correctly predicting disaster for both Israel and Judah, their oracles were now sought out and edited, complete with chronological notices, for purposes of edification and future warning. Faced with the loss of national identity, priests and sages set about collecting and codifying religious laws and preserving Israel's epic lore and its national history (the Pentateuch and "Former Prophets"). They collected the songs sung in the Temple, the Psalms. And they composed a new history, the book of Chronicles, whose stress on the sole legitimacy of the Jerusalem sanctuary and its rituals colors every episode from creation to exile. This process of collecting and amplifying led to the final canonization of the Bible, and may have been stimulated by an attempt to reconcile conflicting factions in the Jewish community.

From Zerubbabel to Ezra-Nehemiah

After the successful completion of the Jerusalem Temple around 516–515 BCE, the Bible is virtually silent about events in Judah during the seventy years between Zerubbabel and Nehemiah—that is, between the reigns of Darius I (522–486) and Artaxerxes I (465–424). Despite hints of internal religious dissent in Judah, the self-interested tolerance of the Persians who gave their blessing to the rebuilding of the Temple perhaps resulted also in some thirty years of relative political stability in Judah before a return to unsettled times. Lack of mention of Persian interference in Judah in itself is noteworthy, since the Persians are known to have intervened in religious disputes elsewhere that threatened local peace.

Political stability cannot guarantee economic or social well-being, however. The book of Malachi belongs to this period. The Temple is operating, and the prophet tries to assure doubting Judeans of Yahweh's continued love in spite of infestation, drought (Mal. 3.10–11), and general social ills and inequities (Mal. 3.5). If Third Isaiah (Isa. 56–66) can be assigned to this period, it confirms Malachi's portrayal of economic struggle and religious uncertainty.

According to the prophet in Malachi, who speaks from within the priestly establishment, Judah's misfortunes are Yahweh's punishment for breach of the covenant in both ritual and ethical terms. Priest and people alike offend God by improper practices in the Temple and by their cruel treatment of each other, particularly by casual divorce. A much discussed passage (Mal. 2.11–12) warns against marriage to "the daughter of a foreign god"; it is unclear whether the writer means intermarriage with foreigners, later a prime concern of Ezra and Nehemiah, or whether instead the offense is syncretistic religion. By repentance and reform, Yahweh's people must ready themselves so that the coming "day of the LORD" (Mal. 4.5–6) will be one of salvation.

While Judah's problems are only hinted at in Third Isaiah, and Malachi's listing of misfortunes is stereotypical, signs of a spiritual and moral malaise appear in the archaeological record of early fifth-century Judah. The decades following the construction of the Temple did not bring the abundance promised by Haggai and Zechariah. Persian I sites in Judah are distinctly smaller and poorer than coastal cities, towns in the adjacent Shephelah, and particularly the Phoenician centers to the north, whose thriving commercial activities expanded continuously in the eastern Mediterranean under Persian rule.

The question of the degree of provincial independence that Judah might have enjoyed before the governorship of Nehemiah in 445 remains unresolved in modern scholarship. The Bible portrays Nehemiah's governorship as unprecedented, and no governor is mentioned between Zerubbabel and Nehemiah. This has led some scholars to conclude that during this period Judah was subject to Samaria, and that when Nehemiah refers to "former governors" (Neh. 5.15) he means Samarian governors with authority over Judah, not former governors of Judah. By this theory, Nehemiah's arrival signals Judah's independence from Samaria; his commission from the Persian king is to set up the governing apparatus of a new Persian province. It is equally likely, however, that Judah was autonomous from at least the time of Zerubbabel and probably all the way back to Sheshbazzar. Had the Samarians controlled Judah before 445, they could have exercised their governing authority and put a stop to the wall-building in Ezra 4 instead of appealing for permission from faraway Persian administrators. It seems, thus, that the Persians dispatched Nehemiah to Judah not to supervise a newly autonomous province but to tighten the empire's grip on a province with newly perceived strategic importance.

A key to the argument for pre-Nehemian autonomy rests on two tiny objects recently purchased on the antiquities market: a stone seal and a clay seal impression (*bulla*). As part of a significant cache of early postexilic seals and sealings, these objects unfortunately lack archaeological context, but the cache is believed to come from the Jerusalem area. The clay seal impression refers (in Aramaic script of the Persian period) to "Elnathan the governor," the stone seal to "Shelomith the maidservant of Elnathan the governor." One difficulty lies in the word translated "governor." Did Elnathan enjoy the same status as governor Nehemiah? The term might even refer to some other office. Also problematic is the dating of the scripts, which some assign to the early Persian period and others to later in the era.

If Shelomith can be identified with Shelomith the daughter of Zerubbabel in 1 Chronicles 3.19, then the conjunction of the names *Shelomith* and *Elnathan* raises the probability that Elnathan followed Zerubbabel as governor of Yehud sometime after 515. Were Shelomith the wife or concubine (a possible interpretation of "maidservant") of Elnathan, then a governor not of Davidic descent would have strengthened his position by marrying into the royal family, an astute move in a transitional period when the civil authority of the governor was giving way to the ascendant power of the priesthood.

In addition to the Shelomith and Elnathan seals, jar-handle sealings found at
Ramat Rahel and Tell en-Nasbeh help close the Yehud "governor gap." They supply
the names of two Judean governors, Yehoezer and Ahzai, possibly bringing us down
to the governorship of Nehemiah. Neither appears to have any connection with the
family of David. For Shelomith to possess a seal in her own name shows that she
held a high administrative position; the seal, along with her presence in a male-
dominated genealogy, indicates that she must have been a memorable woman. With
Shelomith we have reached the end of the Davidic dynasty's hold over Judah, but
the list of Davidic descendants in 1 Chronicles 3.17–24 continues to the end of the
fifth century, attesting to an ongoing regard for David's line in some Jewish circles.
The cryptic references in Zechariah 12.7–10 to David's line may also come from the
period following Elnathan and Shelomith.

Backwater Judah was not where Darius's interests lay. His sights were set north,
across the Bosporus and west to the Greek mainland. In 499 BCE, rebellions aided by
Athens in the Ionian Greek cities and Cyprus set in motion decades of Greco-Persian,
east-west conflict, a fateful clash with deep ramifications for biblical—and world—
history. Following the Greek naval disaster at Lade, Ionian Miletus was retaken in
494. The Persian destruction of the city and deportation of half its population became
a byword among fifth-century Greeks in their struggle against Persia. Herodotus
reports that Phrynichus had to pay a fine when his play *The Capture of Miletus* caused
the audience to burst into tears. A rough guess of around 490 for the end of governor
Elnathan's term coincides with the year of Darius's most humiliating defeat, inflicted
on him by the Greeks at Marathon. Darius's death in 486 put an end to his plans for
another go at the Greeks. Instead, his successor Xerxes I (486–465) was forced to
quash first a minor Egyptian attempt at secession (486–483) and then a Babylonian
uprising that began in 482 with the murder of the satrap Zopyrus. With Egypt and
Babylon pacified, Xerxes attended to affairs in Anatolia and to avenging his father's
disgraceful defeat by the Greeks. But after Xerxes repeated his father's mistakes in
Greece at Salamis (480) and Mycale (479), he turned his attention to building pro-
grams at Persepolis. He died in a palace coup in 465 and was succeeded by Artaxerxes I.

Surveys of biblical history describe the decades leading up to Ezra and Nehemiah
as turbulent, noting the uprisings against Xerxes by Egypt and Babylon, as well as
the more serious Egyptian revolt of 460 early in the reign of Artaxerxes I. Judah,
some scholars propose, took advantage of the Egyptian independence movements to
do some rebelling of its own. Unrest in Palestine explains an essentially unresolved
issue, namely, the Persians' reasons for sending Ezra (458 or 428) and Nehemiah
(445) to Judah. Their missions, which mark a turning point in Jewish self-definition,
must first be placed in the context of Persian imperial policies.

It would not be surprising if Judah had tried to revolt at some point during this
period, given the tendency of lands on the fringes of empires to do so. Both the Bible
and the archaeological record have been cited for evidence of political unrest, but
both sources have been overinterpreted. There is the biblical story of Nehemiah's
shock on hearing, seventy-five years after the completion of the Temple, that the
walls of Jerusalem are broken, its gates burned (Neh. 1.3). And there is the variously
dated episode(s) in Ezra 4.7–23 in which Jerusalem's attempts to repair its walls are

reported by Persian officials as an act of rebellion and are halted by imperial edict. Perhaps Xerxes I visited Jerusalem on his way to Egypt in 485 to intervene personally. Or Ezra 4.7–23 could be set in the reign of Artaxerxes I, associating it with the Egyptian revolt of 460 or with Ezra himself, who was exceeding his imperial brief by attending to the walls. Unfortunately Ezra 4.7–23 continues to resist attempts at secure dating and has been assigned to the reigns of every Persian king from Cyrus to Artaxerxes I. The fallen walls of Nehemiah 1.3 could have been caused by an isolated event, such as a raid by an Arab tribe from the south. As the biblical text now stands, Nehemiah 1.3 is a literarily shaped story that falls in the center of a three-step thematic movement, commencing with the disheartening wall episode of Ezra 4.7–23 and reaching a triumphant climax with Nehemiah's completion of the walls (Neh. 6.15–16).

Archaeological evidence for a possible Judean revolt is equally ambiguous. Modern accounts of the Persian period mention widespread destruction and thus social unrest around 480 in areas of Benjamin and southern Samaria, most notably at Shechem, Bethel, Tell el-Ful, Tell en-Nasbeh (Mizpah), and Gibeon. Reexamination of the relevant strata at these sites shows that at Shechem abandonment, not destruction, was more likely, and that this occurred in the mid-fifth, not early fifth, century. Tell el-Ful was abandoned, not destroyed, about 500. The destruction of Bethel cannot be dated later than the sixth century, and Tell en-Nasbeh shows signs of continuous occupation well into the mid-fifth century. The picture of disturbances in Judah at the end of the first quarter of the fifth century can no longer be affirmed or denied. In the succeeding quarter century, however, Judah became entangled in the epic struggle between Greece and Persia.

The tempestuous first half of Artaxerxes I's forty-year reign included a protracted revolt in Egypt (460–454?), in which Persians and Greeks again clashed. The Athenians allied themselves with Egypt as a step toward their ultimate goal of supplanting the Persians as masters of the eastern Mediterranean; and it was not so much the Egyptians who worried the Persians as the Athenians, whose presence in Egypt represented a direct military threat to Persia's holdings in the Levant. If the city named "Doros" on Delian League tribute lists for 454 is the coastal city of Dor just south of the Carmel range, then the Greeks had gained a strategic foothold on Palestinian soil. The participation of the Greeks in the Egyptian revolt of 460 has been described as the most serious challenge to imperial control the Persians faced in the fifth century.

Megabyzus, satrap of Abar Nahara, led Artaxerxes I's forces to eventual victory in Egypt. With substantial help from Phoenician ships the Persian navy obliterated the fleet of the Delian League led by Athens in 454 at Prosopitis in Egypt. Three years later, the Greek admiral Cimon's naval expedition to oust Persia from Cyprus, while not well understood, is a good example of Athenian determination to take over Persia's western holdings. Athens may have been successful enough to achieve a stalemate, which was formally recognized by a treaty with Persia. The existence of the "Peace of Callias" (449) has been disputed since antiquity, but for several decades after 450 there are no recorded Greek efforts against Persian interests in the eastern Mediterranean or Persian attacks on the Greek cities of Asia Minor. Nevertheless, even after the signing of the putative Peace of Callias, tensions and plotting between Athens and Persia continued.

In the light of the Greek threat to Persia in the decade between 460 and 450, a secure hold on the Levant became more important to the Persians than ever before. The missions of Ezra and Nehemiah can be understood as part of the Achaemenids' altered practices in the administration and control of the region. We lack nonbiblical documentary sources directly relevant to this period, but the archaeological record indicates that as part of their strategy for guaranteeing Levantine loyalty the Persians proceeded to garrison imperial troops in a new series of fortresses scattered throughout the region. Distinctive square courtyard buildings dated to the mid-fifth century BCE have been discovered in the Negeb, on the southern coast, in the Judean hill country, in Samaria, and in the Jordan Valley. Their uniformity and contemporaneity suggest a standardized imperial blueprint for small Persian garrisons. Rather than being border fortresses or centers for tribute collection, their wide distribution and often remote locations along ancient roadways suggest that they were deployed to maintain and control the famous Persian road system, which bound the empire closely together and ensured rapid military deployment. The abandonment of many of these sites not long after their construction also suggests that the specific strategic problem prompting their establishment had come to an end. By the late fifth century, mainland Greece had exhausted itself in the Peloponnesian War (431–404) and had no energy for campaigns in the Levant.

Ezra and Nehemiah

The missions of Ezra and Nehemiah were part of a conscious imperial strategy for strengthening the empire's hold on Yehud, as Persia responded to threats resulting from the Egyptian revolt and Greek expansionism. But the books of Ezra and Nehemiah gloss over the possibility that the reformers were acting primarily in the interests of Judah's Persian overlords. Instead, the Bible tells us, the two leaders come to Judah full of concern for the moral and material well-being of the people and with the express purpose of forming an exclusive holy community. As representatives of the influential and wealthy Diaspora Jewish community, their attitudes—which met resistance among Palestinian Jews—were influenced by the strict Yahwism found in the Deuteronomic laws. Ezra and Nehemiah are remembered in Jewish tradition as religious heroes whose reforms shaped and secured the future of Judaism.

Ezra's very existence has been doubted. In the stylized presentation of the books of Ezra and Nehemiah, Ezra is a leader and lawgiver patterned after Moses. The similarity between Ezra the priest-scribe (but not high priest) and Nehemiah the secular governor on the one hand and Joshua and Zerubbabel on the other has been observed. Writing in the early second century BCE, Jesus ben Sirach praises Nehemiah (Sir. 49.13), but makes no mention of Ezra. The Ezra narrative has obviously been carefully shaped, but this does not mean that Ezra is a fictional character. The "historical Ezra" has simply been given a theological buildup, ancient "star treatment." It is impossible to state conclusively when he operated and what he did for the twelve months covered in the biblical account, but attempts to reject Ezra's historicity have been unsuccessful.

The defective and probably fictional priestly genealogy for Ezra (Ezra 7) is not meant to mislead but rhetorically to convince the reader that Ezra's mission should be viewed in continuity with preexilic legal and ritual traditions. Ezra's commission (Ezra 7.12) from the Persian king Artaxerxes (I?) calls him "the priest . . . [and] scribe of the law of the God of heaven," the official Persian name for Yahweh. While Ezra's title has been cited by those who claim that Ezra served as the imperial official in charge of Jewish affairs, there is scant evidence for such a post elsewhere in the empire. The title "scribe," however, does suggest that Ezra had some official function. Ezra is sent to Judah and Jerusalem to inquire concerning the "law of your God, which is in your hand" (Ezra 7.14). Of what Ezra's "inquiry" was to consist is also a difficult question. The Judean priesthood and community were not bereft of religion nor ignorant of Israel's legal traditions, many of which had long ago been set down in writing. The Temple ritual had been restored, a theocracy well established. There is no reason to think the people were hearing anything startlingly new. The account of Ezra's public Torah reading (Neh. 8–9) follows a liturgical pattern also found in the account of Josiah's reform in the seventh century (2 Kings 23); the narrative is shaped to impress readers with the theological momentousness of the event.

Rabbinic tradition attributed to Ezra the creation of Judaism (*m. Abot* 1.1), and claimed that "Ezra and the Torah surpassed in importance the building of the Temple" (*b. Megilla* 16.b). The author/editor of Ezra 7–10 and Nehemiah 8, the ancient rabbis, and many modern scholars have believed Ezra's "law" to be the completed Pentateuch (Torah). But it is almost impossible to correlate any aspect of Ezra's commission in Ezra 7 with specific Pentateuchal legislation, and the few quotations that we have from Ezra's Torah do not match the wording of the received Pentateuch. Biblical references to the Torah need not refer to the Pentateuch at all. For example, the word *tôrâ* in Psalm 119 (roughly contemporary with Ezra and Nehemiah) refers not so much to a written text as to a fluid principle of God's commandments and teaching, received from teachers and sages and by charismatic revelation.

Some scholars maintain, with justification, that the editing and promulgation of ancient Pentateuchal traditions occurred in an "Ezra school." The Ezra-Nehemiah narrative, like the book of Chronicles, does contain numerous allusions to Pentateuchal legal traditions—Deuteronomic, Priestly, and the Holiness Code. For example, in the list of peoples excluded from Israel (Ezra 9.1), we see Deuteronomic laws undergoing a process of exegetical development, in other words, early Jewish biblical interpretation. The Ezra narrative drops some groups from the traditional Deuteronomic seven peoples (Deut. 7.1) and adds others, including Ammonites, Moabites, and Egyptians. Notably, the list does not include Samarians, with whom the Jerusalem priesthood continued to intermarry into the next century. To complicate the picture there are also practices that accord with neither Deuteronomic nor Priestly law. By the mid-fifth century, then, the Pentateuch was on its way to completion but not yet fully formed.

Clearly, some of Ezra's tasks are quite worldly. He is charged with distributing gifts and Temple vessels to the "God of Israel, whose dwelling is in Jerusalem" (Ezra 7.15). And in accordance with the wisdom of Ezra's god (Ezra 7.25–26), he is ordered to appoint magistrates and judges to uphold "the law of your God and the law of the king" and to ensure that all the people observe them. The close association of the law of God and the law of the king suggests that Ezra's task may have involved replacing existing officials with new appointees charged with enforcing a new legal order in a region of new strategic importance.

Whatever the nature of his imperial mission, in the biblical text Ezra's main interest is the problem of mixed marriages and consequently of defining the boundaries of Israelite ethnicity. Because some of Judah's leaders, namely, priests, head the list of guilty persons (Ezra 10.18), Ezra may represent an exclusivist faction of Yahwism battling a more assimilationist local priestly or lay-priestly governing faction. Ezra 10.15 describes Jewish leaders as resisting Ezra's orders.

Another approach to assessing Ezra's actions against mixed marriage is to consider the marriages as other than a purely religious crime that causes the community's "great guilt" (Ezra 9.13). The penalties for staying away from the great assembly (Ezra 10.7), where the guilty will be dealt with, are not religious but economic and social: loss of both property and membership in the assembly of "the exiles," the dominant group of the restoration community.

Ezra, we must always remember, was a representative of the Babylonian Diaspora and the bearer of an official Persian mandate. While the Bible suggests that Ezra came to Judah to root out corrupting influences on the purity of ancient Jewish law, as a Persian agent, Ezra might well have channeled the interpretation of that law into new areas. Political theorists note that law in imperial systems is used to maintain the relationships between groups in a subject territory and the imperial center. Broadly based reforms of the legal system occur when the relationship between subject and imperial center changes enough to require new legal structures. In the mid-fifth century Persia's fear of Greek expansionism enhanced Judah's strategic value. Ezra's mission may have resulted in the creation of a legal apparatus for defining an ethnically circumscribed community, the Bible's "community of exiles," or "Israel." Such a community could gain privileges from the Persian authority; according to the imperial view, all conquered land was the great king's to distribute. Returning exiles or local loyalists could hope to benefit from such tangible expressions of royal patronage. At the same time, however, they would constitute a loyal elite, socially and economically bound to the empire.

Beginning with Cyrus, the Persians carefully coordinated imperial policy with local religious laws to foster political stability. Persian officials, for example, intervened several times in the religious lives of the Elephantine Jews; the Elephantine papyri include a letter dated 419 BCE to the Egyptian satrap concerning regulations for the Jewish Festival of Unleavened Bread in the Elephantine community. Like Udjahorresnet, Darius I's Egyptian legal and ritual reformer, Ezra was probably the agent not of imperial condescension but of strengthened imperial control mechanisms.

In the short term, Ezra's actual success appears limited. The Bible's Ezra, however, colored by hindsight (even if the composition date of the books of Ezra and Nehemiah remains elusive), shapes both the future and the sacredness of God's holy people by bringing them (back) to the Torah of Moses. Like important postexilic Jewish leaders before him, he then recedes into the historical obscurity from which he emerged. Josephus's report that Ezra died at an old age and was buried in Jerusalem is formulaic, a detail appropriate to a biblical figure. But Josephus's need to account for Ezra's death also demonstrates the honor accorded him at the end of the Second Temple period.

Despite Ezra's centrality to the biblical account of the Persian period, Nehemiah's is the dominant personality. Nehemiah, the king's cupbearer (not a eunuch), left the Persian court and Susa to begin his mission to Judah in "the twentieth year of Artaxerxes" (Neh. 2.1). He served for at least twelve years, returned to Persia, and was back in Judah again around 430 BCE. References to "Sanballat the governor of Samaria" in a letter of 408 from the Jewish community of Elephantine to Bagoas, the then-governor of Yehud, have led to a consensus that Nehemiah served under Artaxerxes I, beginning in 445. Scholars identify the Sanballat of the Elephantine letter with Nehemiah's archenemy (Neh. 2, 10, 19).

Nehemiah is one of the most colorful figures in the Bible, thanks to the lively first-person voice of the "Nehemiah memoir." This memoir does include Nehemiah's own words, but it is more rhetorical than factual. Nehemiah could not have been privy to many of the events and the motivations he describes. Not an autobiography, the "memoir" has affinities with royal inscriptions and votive texts (it is addressed to God), prayers of the falsely accused, a self-justification addressed to an angry monarch, and biographical tomb inscriptions such as that of Udjahorresnet. Whatever its original form, it was revised and reworked in the light of later events.

Nehemiah's emotional, strong-willed—some have said vain—character emerges vividly from the pages of his story. It opens with the hero weeping at the news of Jerusalem's fallen walls and then artfully inducing his royal master to send him to the rescue of his ancestral city. Once in Jerusalem, he physically separates the holy city from the profane peoples around it by rebuilding the walls under difficult circumstances. A wall identified as Nehemiah's lies higher up the slope from the preexilic fortifications, circumscribing a relatively small area and possibly explaining the brief period of fifty-two days for the work. Religiously, too, he walls off the holy community by sternly enforcing regulations derived from Deuteronomic law concerning the Sabbath and intermarriage.

From an imperial perspective, Nehemiah's job was to build a city wall and an imperial fortress (the citadel of the Temple, Neh. 2.8) just outside the city. The fortress and the fortifications of Jerusalem may have been part of the general Persian deployment of garrisons suggested in the archaeological record. The Persians did not encourage the building of walls in Levantine cities, probably considering them symbolic of civil independence; Samaria, for example, never had an urban wall system in the Persian period. The unusual nature of Nehemiah's wall-building with the blessing of the great king is highlighted in the biblical narrative.

Explanations for the fortification of Jerusalem include the suggestions that the Persians were hoping to foster or to reward Judean loyalty. Alternatively, in a region where Persian control was threatened by international military adventurism, Jerusalem became an inland defensive city and possibly a new center for the collection and storage of imperial revenues (delivered in kind and not in coin before the late fifth century). The latter is suggested by the account of the people's economic distress in Nehemiah 5. When Nehemiah lightened the tax burden, rather than aiming at some sort of rapprochement between peasant and aristocracy he may have been trying to minimize an increased tax burden caused by the need to maintain the new garrisons. The implied criticisms of Persian rule by the later author/editor of Ezra-Nehemiah (Ezra 9.8–9; Neh. 5.1–19; 9.37) may reflect Persia's tightened grip on Judah and the economic consequence of Ezra's and Nehemiah's work. The Samarian governor Sanballat's obstructionist behavior suggests that he understood that Jerusalem's walls announced for that city a status higher than Samaria's, ensuring greater royal favor. Judean national revival would not have appealed to a citizen of the former northern kingdom, aware of Judah's ancient claims on his territory. Sanballat must have sensed that Nehemiah's official privileges could only be diminished by addressing directly to the king himself insinuations about Nehemiah's disloyalty (Neh. 2.19).

Always Nehemiah struggled against opposition. This opposition is difficult to characterize and is multifaceted, but its sources are political and economic, not religious. He helped Judean peasants by suppressing excesses of usury and remitting the taxes paid for his own maintenance, but he was also willing, as an upper-class member of the influential eastern Diaspora, to exclude them from his definition of Israel. He may have pleased the Levitical families by giving them an enhanced role in the Temple while alienating some priestly officials. Whereas biblical tradition depicts Sanballat, the Ammonite Tobiah, and the Arab king Geshem as mean-spirited pagans, it is more likely that their disagreements with Nehemiah were political. Sanballat and Tobiah were probably Yahweh worshipers, and before the new governor arrived all three men had enjoyed friendly relations with Jerusalem. After Nehemiah's return to Persia we find Tobiah, a relative of Eliashib the high priest and other Judean nobles, in possession of an office in the Temple (Neh. 6.18; 13.4–9). A number of Jerusalemites also disagreed with Nehemiah's activities. These included the Jerusalem district administrator Shallum (Neh. 3.12), Shemaiah (Neh. 6.10–13), and the influential female prophet Noadiah and her fellow prophets (Neh. 6.14). Nehemiah all but accuses Noadiah of waging psychological warfare (Neh. 6.14).

As with Ezra, even marriage regulations can be viewed as a mechanism for imperial control. Regardless of whether Nehemiah's attention to matters such as the Sabbath regulations and mixed marriages stemmed from Deuteronomic principles, Persian policy, or both, they may have been seen as extreme by local leaders. His expulsion of the high priest's son from Jerusalem for refusing to divorce his Samarian Sanballatid wife would not have endeared him to either family (Neh. 13.28). Some of the "foreign" women could have been Yahweh worshipers; the marriage habits of Jerusalem's priestly elite show that what Ezra and Nehemiah condemned as mixed marriages were considered within the bounds of good Yahwism by others. No difficulties are expressed over mixed marriages in the Chronicler's history, a work thoroughly informed by the ideology of postexilic Judah. The book of Ruth, although resistant to dating, may contain a postexilic call for inclusiveness in its positive depiction of King David's great-grandmother, Ruth the Moabite.

The restricted definition of Israel in Ezra and Nehemiah and the xenophobia of postexilic oracles against the nations (Isa. 46–47) hang in dynamic tension with the trend toward greater universalism in prophetic writings of the Persian period, most notably in Third Isaiah (Isa. 56.3–8) and Zechariah (Zech. 8.20–23). Malachi gives Gentiles credit for sincere worship (Mal. 1.11–14), and by acknowledging that even foreigners (Ninevites) can receive God's favor, the book of Jonah rejects the exclusion of other nations from membership in the people of God.

With the arrival on the scene of Ezra and Nehemiah in the mid- to late fifth

century, the boundaries between Jew and non-Jew began to be defined more narrowly. The reforms were controversial, but the Persian empire stood on the side of
Ezra and Nehemiah, and resistance could have been risky. Even so, in view of the
continued relations between Jerusalem and Jews of Samaria, Ammon, and Egypt in
the decades after Ezra and Nehemiah, the new restrictions were not immediately
enforceable.

The prevailing heterodoxy of Persian-period Judaism with which Ezra, Nehemiah,
and their followers struggled is illustrated by two controversial items, a coin of Judah
engraved with an image that must have been someone's idea of Yahweh, and the
subversive book of Job. The coin, a unique silver quarter-shekel now in the British
Museum, is inscribed *yhd*, Yehud, in Aramaic lapidary script and assigned to the
early fourth century. On the reverse a bearded deity carrying a falcon or eagle on his
outstretched left hand sits on a winged wheel. If not for the inscription, the iconography would suggest a Greek deity such as Zeus or an eastern Mediterranean god
identified with him. The inscription, however, demands a Jewish context for the
image, and the winged wheel naturally evokes Ezekiel's vision of Yahweh's "glory"
(Ezek. 1.4–28). Attempts to relegate the drachma to the hand of some ignorant
Persian official in Judah disregard the reality of Persian religious policy toward its
subject peoples. If Judah issued the coin, the Jerusalem priesthood would have had
veto power over the imagery.

The author of the biblical book of Job deliberately created a character who is not
Israelite, does not live in Israel, seldom refers to God as Yahweh, and makes no
allusions to Israel's history or its covenant with God. Job is Everyman, his innocent
suffering a challenge to retributive ideas of God's justice especially favored in exilic
and postexilic meditations on the catastrophe of 586 BCE. In particular, this book
engages in an eloquent and disturbingly open-ended dialogue with the Deuteronomic, prophetic, and wisdom traditions that dominate the Bible. Even if the book
was composed before the exile, as some propose, its presence in the canon testifies
to its continued life into the Persian period and beyond.

In the end, Nehemiah's exclusivistic vision may have resulted in a Judah that
looked inward and viewed the outside world with suspicion, but that same vision
helped a tiny, impoverished community preserve itself in the coming centuries of
tumultuous change.

Diaspora Judaism

Jews in the eastern Diaspora had opportunities for advancement under the Persians,
as one sees in such romantic, didactic tales of Jewish life in the Diaspora as Daniel
1–6, Esther, Tobit, and 1 Esdras 3–4. The Murashu tablets contain the names of Jews
acting as agents for the Persian government or for Persian nobles. Ezra and Nehemiah
came from the Babylonian and Persian Diaspora, respectively, and Nehemiah's position of trust at the Persian court illustrates how proximity to the centers of Achaemenid power enhanced the religious authority of these Jewish communities of upper-
class ancestry at the expense of Jewish leaders in Palestine. While many in the
Diaspora did not enjoy great wealth—some Jews in Nippur were slaves—economic
conditions in Judah were far worse; the Bible mentions Diaspora Jews sending money
to underwrite Temple expenses (Ezra 7.16; 8.25; Zech. 6.10).

The religious life of Babylonian Jews is illuminated by a trend in the nomenclature of the Murashu tablets. A century after the exile (ca. 480) a large number of fathers with Babylonian names began to give their sons names with *Yahweh* as the theophoric element. The suggestion has been made that this phenomenon reflects the gradual dominance of a "Yahweh alone" party in the Diaspora, to which Ezra and Nehemiah belonged. Daniel's categorical resistance to any form of assimilation contrary to Jewish practice (Dan. 1–6) reflects eastern Diaspora concern for maintaining Jewish identity in a later period.

Egyptians are among the peoples Jews are forbidden to marry according to the marriage legislation of Ezra (Ezra 9.1). The Elephantine papyri give a fascinating picture of life during the fifth century in a Jewish military colony on Egypt's southern frontier. When this community of mercenaries in the service of Persia first came to Egypt is unclear, perhaps as early as the seventh century. Their local temple, whose construction antedated the Temple of Zerubbabel, was dedicated to Yahweh, but they also worshiped a god Bethel and the Canaanite goddess Anat. Despite their apparently syncretistic worship, these Egyptian Jews were not isolated. They corresponded with Jerusalem and Samaria on religious matters, appealing to both cities for assistance in rebuilding their temple when it was burned in local riots and promising as a condition of aid not to sacrifice animals in it. The monotheism that characterizes rabbinic Judaism evolved slowly. Rather than being Judaism of a sadly degenerated form, the Yahwism of Elephantine may preserve ancient elements of Israelite Yahwism, frozen in time. Elephantine Judaism no less than Samarian Judaism must be viewed within the broad parameters of early Second Temple Judaism.

By the late Second Temple period the synagogue had become a common element in Jewish life, both in the Diaspora and in the Jewish homeland. On the basis of logic and the indirect testimony of Ezekiel 11.16, it has been assumed that such an essential Jewish institution must have arisen among the exiles in Babylon. Unfortunately, neither archaeological nor epigraphic evidence supports this theory. The term *synagogue*, meaning "house of assembly," is Greek, and it did not become current until the turn of the era. The earliest undisputed reference to a synagogue comes from Egypt in the third century BCE, where it is called a "prayer house." Synagogues do not seem to have been part of Palestinian Judaism until the Roman period.

Rather than assume a single line of development, one should conceive of the gradual convergence of several Jewish institutions: a prayer hall, an assembly hall or community center (see Jer. 39.8), a Torah study hall and school, and perhaps also the preexilic city gate where elders gathered to render judgment. Synagogues were a product of the Hellenistic Diaspora, but they were not Temple substitutes. They were not built on sacred ground; they were a lay, not a priestly, institution; and they were not the sites of animal sacrifice. Furthermore, while the Jerusalem Temple remained central in the religious consciousness of Diaspora Jews, this did not prevent some Jewish communities from erecting their own local temples in fifth-century Elephantine (Egypt), on Mount Gerizim in the fourth century, at Leontopolis (Egypt) in the Hellenistic period, and elsewhere. Thus, synagogues, whenever they originated and in whatever form(s), belong to a wide spectrum of possible venues and contexts for communal worship in Second Temple Judaism.

Events to 332

After Ezra and Nehemiah, the historical record again becomes obscure. Both Judah and Samaria maintained their autonomous status within the empire; no evidence for a parallel Persian administrator over the subprovinces beyond the satrap has come to light. The Bible provides the names of high priests (Neh. 12.10–11, 22) and Davidides (living in Judah? 1 Chron. 3.17–24) down to the end of the fifth century. (See table on p. 296.) With additional data gleaned from Josephus, the Elephantine and Wadi ed-Daliyeh (Samaria) papyri, and inscriptions on seals, sealings, and coins, attempts have been made to fill out the list of Judean high priests and the governors of both Judah and Samaria down to 332 (see table 8.2). If these reconstructions are accurate, the firm dynastic grip on the Judean high priesthood and governorship of Samaria indicates a level of stability in the two regions. But dynastic tenacity cannot prevent family quarrels or the backing of different political factions (pro- or

Table 8.2 *Governors of Samaria; Governors and High Priests of Judah (445–335 BCE)*

GOVERNORS OF SAMARIA	GOVERNORS OF JUDAH	HIGH PRIESTS OF JUDAH
ca. 445, Sanballat I (the Horonite) founder of the Sanballat dynasty	ca. 445, Nehemiah	ca. 470, Joiada I
ca. 410, Delaiah son of Sanballat I; acted for aged father	ca. 408, Bagoas	ca. 410, Johanan II
? Shelemiah possibly cogovernor with Delaiah		before 400, Joiada II
early fourth century, Sanballat II grandson of Sanballat I		
? Jeshua son of Sanballat II		? Johanan II
by 354, Hananiah son of Sanballat II		
ca. 335, Sanballat III governor in time of Darius III	ca. 335, Hezekiah	ca. 335, Joiada III

Source: Created from data from F. M. Cross Jr., "Aspects of Samaritan and Jewish History in Late Persian and Hellenistic Times," *Harvard Theological Review* 59 (1966): 201–11.

anti-Persian, for example). Josephus mentions the murder by the high priest Johanan of his brother in the Temple, bringing down on Judah a punishment of seven years of extra tribute (*Antiquities* 11.7.1), probably during the reign of Darius II.

Let us end by returning to the larger stage of history. Artaxerxes I died peacefully in 424 BCE. After a period of violent intrigue, Artaxerxes' son Ochos emerged the winner and took the throne name Darius II (424–404). The Elephantine papyri concerning the Festival of Unleavened Bread (419) and the ruined temple (410) come from his reign. Aided by the capable diplomats and satraps Tissaphernes and Pharnabazus, Darius II intrigued to foster Greek disunity, even intervening in the Peloponnesian War. Then Darius II was succeeded by his son Artaxerxes II (Memnon; 404–359), a long-lived monarch whose reign was marked by continuous revolts, particularly by Greek city-states. A potentially dangerous attempt to unseat Artaxerxes by his brother Cyrus was thwarted in 401 at Cunaxa (Babylonia), despite the formidable Greek mercenary army assembled by Cyrus and immortalized by Xenophon. By the terms of the King's Peace (386–376), the Ionian Greek cities for a time acknowledged Persian control.

The loss of Egypt in 405 was more serious. Several times the Persians launched campaigns to regain Egypt, but without success until 343. Although coastal Palestinian cities served as staging points for Persian campaigns, it is unclear whether Samaria and Judah were involved. A move by independent Egypt at the turn of the century up the coast and into the Shephelah as far as Gezer came to an end around 380, when the Persians regained the territory.

Throughout the second half of the 360s the Satraps' Revolt upset affairs in the Persian empire, but any repercussions for interior regions of Syria-Palestine elude us. Judah is unlikely to have participated in a rebellion of Phoenician cities against the next Persian king, Artaxerxes III (Ochos; 359–338), initiated around 350 by Tennes the king of Sidon. Destruction layers are found at numerous sites, but most of them lie outside Judah, and distinguishing between mid-fourth-century and later Alexandrian destructions has proved impossible. First Tennes (345) and then Egypt (343/2) capitulated to Artaxerxes III.

But disaster soon fell upon Persia. The short, unhappy reign of the Achaemenid puppet king Arses (338–336) was followed by that of Darius III (Codomanus; 336–331), whose even unhappier fate it was to lose his empire to the Greek forces of Alexander of Macedon. After his victory at Issus (333), Alexander marched south into Phoenicia, where all but Tyre submitted to him. A seven-month siege ended in victory for the Greeks, and slavery or crucifixion for the Tyrians. After Tyre, only Gaza dared resist Alexander, who took it before conquering Egypt. There the people hailed him as their liberator from the hated Persians.

No reflexes of Alexander's arrival appear in the Bible, although Josephus tells a transparently legendary tale of Alexander's visit to the Temple (*Antiquities* 11.8.5) on his way to Egypt. The first explicit reference to Alexander appears in 1 Maccabees. According to Josephus, after submitting to Alexander in 332 the nobles of Samaria revolted and burned Alexander's prefect to death. Alexander's army marched north, and the rebels were delivered up to them. The Samaria papyri belonged to these rebels and were deposited with other valuables in the cave where the unfortunate plotters were found and massacred. Samaria was reorganized and resettled as a Greek colony, while the surviving Samarians rebuilt the city of Shechem as their center. According to Josephus, the Samaritan temple on Mount Gerizim was built in the late fourth century; he attributes to Alexander the commissioning of the temple (*Antiquities* 11.8.4). Recently, excavators at Tell er-Ras, the temple site, claimed to have found the remains of this fourth-century temple.

Much of the biblical material suggests that during the Persian period, both in the Diaspora and in the ancient homeland, Jewish communities were more intent on preserving their past than recording their present. A correct interpretation of their past, they felt, would determine their future fate for good or ill. Chronicles taught lessons based on Israel's past. The same impulses contributed to the final redaction of the Pentateuch. However, other texts and objects suggest a less retrospective mood. For example, large numbers of locally minted fourth-century BCE coins—including coins from Judea and Samaria—have been appearing on the antiquities market. Their small denominations would be useful only for local commerce, not for tribute or international trade. These coins, considered alongside the commercial interests expressed in Ecclesiastes and the buying and selling recorded in the Samaria papyri, suggest a lively local economy.

Archaeological discoveries combined with new analytical approaches to existing information have improved our understanding of the two centuries of Persian rule and have led to reassessments of long-held assumptions and generated new questions. The Persian period's elusiveness persists, but scholars in search of the roots of Judaism can no longer dismiss it as a negligible interim between exile and Alexander.

Select Bibliography

Ackroyd, Peter R. *Exile and Restoration*. Philadelphia: Westminster, 1968. The classic study.

Boyce, Mary. *A History of Zoroastrianism*. 2 vols. Leiden, The Netherlands: E. J. Brill, 1975, 1982. The definitive study.

Briant, Pierre. *Darius, les Perses et l'empire*. Découvertes Gallimard, 159. Paris: Gallimard, 1992. A tiny paperback by a renowned French scholar, which contains the best illustrations of any book on the Persian period, almost all in sumptuous color.

———. *From Cyrus to Alexander: A History of the Persian Empire*. Winona Lake, Ind.: Eisenbrauns, 1998. An impressive new two-volume history.

Cook, J. M. *The Persian Empire*. New York: Schocken, 1983. Basic and engagingly written history.

Davies, W. D., and Louis Finkelstein, eds. *The Cambridge History of Judaism*. Vol. 1, *Introduction: The Persian Period*. Cambridge: Cambridge University Press, 1984. A pioneering work on the period.

Gershevitch, Ilya, ed. *The Cambridge History of Iran*. Vol. 2, *The Median and Achaemenian Periods*. Cambridge: Cambridge University Press, 1985. Numerous scholars contributed to this comprehensive survey of the Persian empire. Good attention to archaeological evidence.

Grabbe, Lester L. *Judaism from Cyrus to Hadrian: Sources, History, Synthesis*. Vol. 1. Minneapolis: Fortress, 1992. An extremely helpful survey, with judicious summaries of the primary sources, specific critiques of recent scholarly work, and extensive bibliographies. Little attention to canonical issues.

Hoglund, Kenneth G. *Achaemenid Imperial Administration in Syria-Palestine and the Missions of Ezra and Nehemiah*. Atlanta: Scholars Press, 1992. Summarizes the historical questions, reassesses textual and archaeological assumptions about the period, and provides some helpful new perspectives.

Hornblower, Simon. *The Greek World 479–323 BC*. New York and London: Methuen, 1983. Brief, readable history, which gives more attention than most histories of Greece to the non-Greek world.

———. *Mausolus*. New York: Oxford University Press, 1982. A model study that explores in depth a small Persian-period province.

Kugel, James L., and Rowan A. Greer. *Early Biblical Interpretation*. Philadelphia: Westminster, 1986. The first part of the book, by Kugel, describes the roots of Jewish biblical criticism.

Olmstead, Albert T. *History of the Persian Empire*. Chicago: University of Chicago Press, 1948. Still the most in-depth study of the Persian period.

Root, Margaret Cool. "From the Heart: Powerful Persianisms in the Art of the Western Empire." *Achaemenid History* 6 (1991): 1–29. Vividly demonstrates the visual component of Persian propaganda.

Smith, Morton. *Palestinian Parties and Politics That Shaped the Old Testament*. New York: Columbia University Press, 1971. A trailblazing analysis of the religious tensions underlying Persian-period Judaism. Although Smith's theories have been criticized as overly schematized, most scholars have accepted his basic approach.

Stern, Ephraim. *Material Culture of the Land of the Bible in the Persian Period 538–332 BC*. Jerusalem: Israel Exploration Society, 1982. Monumental survey of the archaeological evidence.

Yamauchi, Edwin M. *Persia and the Bible*. Grand Rapids, Mich.: Baker, 1990. Fundamentalist viewpoint, but covers the basic biblical questions in tandem with a good overview of Persian history.

CHAPTER NINE

Between Alexandria and Antioch

Jews and Judaism in the Hellenistic Period

LEONARD J. GREENSPOON

A lexander the Great's arrival in the east in 333 BCE—along with hordes of Macedonians and Greeks whose cause he was championing—had a major impact on subsequent developments for the Jews, as for countless other peoples. But it is important not to overemphasize the extent of Alexander's impact. Greeks and other Westerners had been traveling through the east, primarily as traders and mercenaries, for centuries before the great Macedonian warrior launched his army. The interests of such individuals undoubtedly ran more in the direction of popular rather than high culture, but their cumulative influence was considerable. At the other end of the socioeconomic spectrum, the complex of cultural, economic, philosophical, religious, and social factors called "Hellenism" reached some groups, such as city-dwellers and some artisans, before others, and it penetrated such geographical areas as the Mediterranean coast and major cities more rapidly than it did other, more rural or remote places. For these reasons we have to nuance statements about the spread of Hellenism.

Modern interpretations of this era are frequently colored by their authors' views of Hellenism, especially in comparison with the monotheistic faith of Israel. Those who evaluate Hellenism positively tend to see its encounters with Judaism, at least initially, as a coming together of forces that could have produced a reinvigorated and strengthened faith, better able to face the realities of the new world. Those for whom Hellenistic incursions into Jewish religious life and culture represent a clash of incompatible systems, however, tend to limit the degree of Greek influence among those Jews who represented the best of their inherited tradition. In large part, these judgments by modern historians mirror opinions expressed by ancient writers: in the last few centuries before the Common Era it was difficult to be neutral on the issue of Hellenistic influence within the Jewish community, both in Israel and in the Diaspora.

As bearers of the only pre-Christian monotheistic tradition, Jews had often faced extinction by more powerful polytheistic peoples. The Bible is filled with accounts of such clashes; some the Israelites overcame, others temporarily overwhelmed them. In that sense the attractions, as well as the perceived dangers, of Hellenism were no different from Israel's earlier experiences with Egyptians, Assyrians, Babylonians, and Persians.

But in a larger sense Hellenism posed a unique challenge. It incorporated a world-view and way of life that appeared to avoid the excesses and unacceptable features of earlier outsiders' religions and cultures; at the same time it offered elevated concepts that would join Jews to the rest of the culturally and economically advantaged of the known world. As a result, this period saw unprecedented ruptures that pitted group against group, even among the priestly families. This is easy to chronicle, but more difficult to evaluate. In any case, the world of Judaism in 63 BCE was a very different place than it had been three centuries earlier, when Alexander appeared on the scene.

Alexander and the Jews

After the assassination of his father, Philip, in 336 BCE, Alexander quickly solidified his position as Macedonian monarch. Like his father, his vision extended far beyond his kingdom to the Greek city-states to the south. He succeeded in establishing himself as the savior of the Greek-speaking world, whose shame at the hands of the Persians it had never properly avenged. Although almost every aspect of Alexander's personality, including his motives, have elicited widely varying judgments ever since his own lifetime, there is little debate concerning his military prowess and battlefield leadership. The heartland of Judea, relatively isolated and away from the main routes of transport and troop movement, was not a major concern to Alexander as he marched south from Phoenicia to Egypt. Legendary tales that portray Alexander acknowledging the power of Israel's deity have little historical value. But the development of such legends among almost all Near Eastern peoples, including Judea's neighbors and frequent antagonists the Samaritans, testifies to the imprint that Alexander left on the region. Whether by design or not, he was a unifying force through the sheer greatness of his personality as perceived by those he encountered and conquered.

At the oasis of Siwa, deep in the Egyptian desert, Alexander is said to have received an oracular response that established (or perhaps confirmed) his own sense of divinity. Whatever Alexander himself may have thought, there is no indication that he sought to impose worship of himself or any particular pantheon of deities on his subjects. He seems to have been genuinely open to all sorts of inquiries and willing to entertain non-Greek ideas about the gods, as his experience with the Persians indicates. If he ever heard anything about the monotheistic faith of the Jews, he took no action against them. Nor can we ascertain, beyond the realm of legends, what the Jews thought of Alexander during his lifetime. Since their life under Persian domination was on the whole good, it is not clear that they would have welcomed him as a liberator. To the extent that he championed new ideas and a new way of life, he may have been feared as much as admired. But all this is speculative. If the accounts of a Samaritan revolt against Alexander are credible, we can at least say that the Judeans were wise enough to avoid such disastrous actions.

The Period of Ptolemaic Dominance

Alexander's sudden death in 323 BCE plunged the lands he had conquered into decades of uncertainty, as his generals and would-be successors fought it out for territory and power. In the scale of things, the land of Judea itself was not worth fighting for, but its location was sufficiently close to the major thoroughfares connecting or dividing Egypt and Mesopotamia that Alexander's close friend Ptolemy experienced satisfaction when Judea and neighboring lands at last fell into his hands.

Ptolemy and his immediate successors adopted a policy toward their northern possessions that was on the whole mutually rewarding, largely mirroring previous Persian practice. Unless they saw a specific reason to intervene, the Ptolemies allowed the Jews considerable self-rule under the leadership of the high priests and the bureaucracies the latter maintained. Taxes of all sorts were collected in support of the Jerusalem Temple and the vast Ptolemaic government centered in Alexandria. Friction probably arose on occasion, but there is no record of far-ranging attacks on the central institutions that supported Israel's monotheistic faith. Presumably sacrifices were regularly offered on behalf of the Ptolemaic monarch, as they had been in the past and would be in the future. Throughout most of the third century such sacrifices would most often have been sincere expressions of gratitude for genuinely benign governance rather than simply politically expedient actions.

Paradoxically, we are better informed about life in Judea for earlier times than for the period of Ptolemaic dominance, the third century BCE. Archaeological remains, including hoards of coins, along with a handful of historical documents and accounts provide scant, if valuable, information. We have, for example, a cache of letters written by and addressed to Zenon, who was the chief aide to Apollonius, finance minister in the court of the first Ptolemy. A powerful figure in his own right, Zenon toured Judea and neighboring areas for several years during the mid-third century on a fact-finding mission for both his immediate master and the king. His reports support the picture of Ptolemaic rule as widely, if not firmly, established throughout this region. Along with coins probably minted in Jerusalem as well as along the Mediterranean coast, these letters demonstrate the extent of Egyptian/Macedonian bureaucratic incursions into all areas and all aspects of life. Still, Hellenistic influence was less prominent in Jerusalem and its immediate environs than elsewhere.

The Jewish historian Josephus, writing in the first century CE, provides information on this period as well. He is often the major source for many incidents, but modern scholars remain divided on the reliability of Josephus's work. Moreover, since Josephus himself depended on earlier sources, his accounts are bound to vary considerably in their trustworthiness. Nonetheless, even taking into account the conditions under which he labored and the biases he regularly displays, Josephus's record remains an invaluable resource to be fully but critically mined.

Josephus preserves what appears to be a domestic saga, taking in several generations of the Tobiad family. Well-connected to the ruling Jerusalem priesthood, the Tobiads stood equally close to their Egyptian rulers. Their fortune seems to have originated from their lucrative tax farming in Transjordan and perhaps elsewhere. Through the practice of tax farming, individuals or consortia bid for the right to collect government revenue in a certain area. Whatever they gathered above that bid was their profit, which throughout the Greco-Roman world could be considerable. So successful were the Tobiads in this enterprise that they constructed a veritable mini-empire near present-day Amman, Jordan, one that survived the change in power from Egyptian Ptolemies to Syrian Seleucids. At the same time, the Tobiad saga provides interesting as well as entertaining data on the question of assimilation and maintenance of distinctive Jewish identity.

Another source for this period is the Letter of Aristeas, which like the more extensive history of Josephus has been both promoted and reviled as a reliable historical source. The Letter of Aristeas is most often cited as a witness to the earliest Greek translation of the Hebrew Bible, known as the Septuagint. It also reports that the second Ptolemy, surnamed Philadelphus, early in his reign freed thousands of Judeans who had been brought to Egypt as slaves by his father. If correct, this contradicts the view that Ptolemaic rule over Egypt's northern territories was always peaceful and that a considerable number of Jews had voluntarily migrated to Egypt, and in particular to its capital city, Alexandria. But there is good reason to give this report considerable credence. During the several decades after Alexander's death, when the fate of Syria-Palestine hung in the balance, there were undoubtedly many Judeans who favored Seleucid control, just as many others supported Ptolemaic claims. Ptolemy's forcible deportation of those who had given aid to his enemy is not surprising, nor would it be difficult to imagine that he actively encouraged some of his supporters to join groups of Jews who had earlier settled in Egypt. Philadelphus's freeing of members of the former group and their eventual amalgamation into the growing Jewish population of Alexandria is in character with this monarch, who regularly lived up to his epithet ("man of brotherly love").

It is also consistent with Philadelphus's intellectual curiosity that he would have given strong royal support to his chief librarian's request for a Greek translation of the sacred texts, especially the laws, of his Jewish subjects. At the same time, such a version would have been promoted and widely accepted in the Alexandrian Jewish community, among whom knowledge of Hebrew was growing rarer. Although the Letter of Aristeas narrates the arrival from Jerusalem of seventy-two elders as translators, Alexandria itself probably supplied the group responsible for this earliest foreign-language version. As indicated in the letter, this first translation effort covered the Pentateuch, or Torah, only; the term *Septuagint* (meaning "seventy") was later expanded as other portions of the Hebrew Bible were subsequently translated into Greek.

According to the Letter of Aristeas, the process by which the translators produced their Greek text was a collaborative effort, with the work of individuals and subcommittees revised and reshaped by their colleagues into a finished product. There is little, if any, of the miraculous in Aristeas's account. Later accounts added details, such as the picture of seventy-two scholars working in isolation and yet producing identical versions. Modern scholars have detected sufficient distinctions in the Greek translations of each of the five books of the Torah to cast serious doubt on the view that the Greek Pentateuch was the product of one group at one time. Nonetheless, the high quality of this work served as a model for many later translations, both in Greek and in other languages both ancient and modern.

No precise precedents guided these earliest Greek translators. They seem to have constructed their own path, which lay closer to a literal rendering than to a free one. Although their choice of Greek vocabulary and syntax was partially conditioned by the Semitic text they were translating, in general the language they chose was the *koine*, or common Greek, then in wide usage throughout the Hellenistic world. Greek papyri from Egypt form the closest parallels to the language of the Septuagint and point to a date in the first half of the third century for the Pentateuch at least. Most if not all of the translators were bilingual. Such was clearly not the case for their intended audience, and misunderstandings and misconceptions would have arisen on the part of those who read or heard the original or Old Greek version of the Septuagint. Additionally, differing interpretations of the sacred text abounded, and some readers of the Greek, even if ignorant of the Hebrew language, were conversant with interpretations other than those in the Septuagint. These considerations would have led to calls for revising or recasting of the Greek.

But there was a more pressing issue. Even a cursory examination of the Old Greek reveals instances where this text reflects wording at variance with the established Hebrew version that came to be known as the Masoretic Text. Although it would be anachronistic to project the work of the Masoretes, vowels and all, back to this much earlier period, it is appropriate to imagine a Hebrew text close to it, at least in the Torah, at home in Jerusalem. When differences between this text and the Greek version became known, inevitably there would be calls to revise the Septuagint to reflect more closely what was regarded as the authoritative Hebrew, and revisions of that sort are known.

The author of the Letter of Aristeas was opposed to such calls for revision. In his view the Septuagint possessed an authority equal to that of any Hebrew text, even one located in Jerusalem. He makes this clear near the end of his letter, where he describes the Septuagint's tumultuously positive acceptance by the Jews of Alexandria, using language reminiscent of that used in the book of Exodus to characterize the Israelites' approval of the law of Moses. The first-century CE Jewish philosopher Philo held that the Septuagint translators, no less than the Bible's original authors, were inspired prophets. Augustine championed a similar view, which to this day is the position of Orthodox Christianity.

It is not surprising that Hebrew fell out of general usage among the Jews of the Diaspora, especially in an intellectual and cultural center such as Alexandria. We might think, in contrast, that the ancestral tongue or perhaps its close kin, Aramaic, held sway against a similar linguistic incursion into Judea. But this was not always the case. Although it is demonstrable that the Semitic languages continued in use among portions of the population throughout the Hellenistic period, Greek was a practical necessity not only for those who wished to succeed in occupations involving trade and commerce, but also for bureaucrats and political functionaries of all sorts. There does not appear to have been any organized reaction against the speaking of Greek as such during the first part of the Hellenistic period. It could not have escaped notice that foreign notions and patterns of thought went hand in hand with the introduction of a new language; but the new idiom might also be useful for expanding the representation of older, even venerated concepts. And with no outside power actively pressuring the Jews to give up their ancestral ways, the trade-offs probably seemed, at least to those who considered them, more positive than negative.

Esther, Judith, and Tobit

Before constructing a detailed time line of events and personalities that lead up to the decisive events associated with Antiochus IV and Judah Maccabee, we turn again to the question of written sources and in particular to three biblical books generally understood to originate in and reflect conditions of the Hellenistic period. These three books, listed in order of their familiarity among the general public rather than in chronological order of composition (which is extremely difficult to determine), are Esther, Judith, and Tobit. For modern Protestants and Jews, the designation of at least the last two of these works as biblical may seem puzzling, since they are not among the canonical literature for those communities. But just as all three of these works are authoritative in the Catholic and Orthodox Christian communities today, they were also highly regarded in many, if not most, Jewish communities during the period under discussion.

Prior to a brief examination of each of these works as individual entities, we should discuss their genre. At least in their finished form, these books are Jewish novels, much like the book of Daniel, to be discussed below. As such, their authors or compilers were not intent on relating actual events of the past, nor did they expect their audience to understand these works as historical. On the one hand, this characterization has a negative result: we do not make use of novels to fill in details of historical narrative or flesh out the meager evidence of historical documents from the ancient world. There was no Queen Esther, the heroine Judith did not live, the exciting adventures associated with Tobit and his family did not occur. On the other hand, we may ask different but equally valid and valuable questions: Who composed these works? What were their purposes and how well did they achieve them? Who was the audience for these works, and how do they (audience and work alike) compare to similar phenomena in the Greco-Roman world? Answering these questions gives us enormous insight into the lives of real people, especially in the Diaspora, even if their names and the particularities of their lives remain beyond our grasp.

By and large, these works address the question of how a Jew (understood here primarily in terms of his or her adherence to the monotheistic faith of Israel) should live, especially when faced with a seemingly endless array of attractions offered by society at large. In the case of Esther, a Jewish queen in the Persian empire, she must put aside concerns for personal safety to safeguard the continued communal existence of her people. Judith must likewise place complete trust in God and risk her very life to overcome the danger posed by an enemy general. Tobit must continue to do what he knows is correct, including burying the dead and maintaining other ritual requirements, even though his only rewards for his good deeds are anguish and animosity. Although these works are fictional, we ought not thereby to regard them as addressing issues of no importance for their audience. Jews of this period would have identified with these stories' heroes and heroines and would have identified within their own context individuals as villainous as, say, Haman or Holofernes (from Esther and Judith, respectively). And it would not have taken the threat of extinction by decree or military engagement for Jews to recognize that their own circumstances were dramatically mirrored in these novels.

The dramatic nature of these literary works is one of the keys to their genre. They are filled with clever reversals of fortune on a personal and grand scale; they delve deeply into personal motivation and character development (something largely absent in other biblical material; adding such developments is a major goal of several of the Greek additions to the earlier Hebrew story of Esther), and they are filled with delightful irony of the sort we often seek, but seldom find, in real life. In short, they are literary masterpieces, aimed at a wide audience. Some of the special appeal for this audience can be detected in the elevated and central role played by women. The books of Esther and Judith take their names from heroic females, but even in the book of Tobit women play decisive and independent parts in the narrative flow. Readers are given an opportunity, unparalleled in other biblical literature, to enter into the often anguished minds of the protagonists, from whom they learn that all Jews, being underdogs (for it was not just Jewish females who labored in disadvantaged circumstances), needed to take a stand and that each instance of danger needed to be faced decisively. Ultimate success would come in no other way.

Another characteristic shared by these novels (and the book of Daniel as well) relates specifically to their historicity. They contain what appear to be historical notices that contradict the historical record preserved elsewhere. So, for example, we know of no Jewish queen in Persia, the forces said to have massed against Judith's hometown come from different periods, and Daniel is replete both with otherwise unknown—and impossible—personages and with a collapsed or convoluted chronological framework. Although some fundamentalists have sought to expand or correct the generally accepted historical record on the basis of their interpretation of these "historical" details, such efforts must be judged misguided when we realize that their authors were not writing history. They were aware that these things never happened and that these individuals never lived, and their audience had the same knowledge. The overall effect was one of irony, and it added both to their readers' enjoyment and to their enlightenment in terms of moral and theological instruction.

This is not to say that the authors of these works lacked any knowledge of the societies or cultures they were describing. Quite the contrary, they are masterful in their ability to evoke a general sense of court life or travel-adventure or military preparations. But their primary goal in such descriptions was to lay the scene for the novels' actions, not to prepare a backdrop for a historical account. The genre thus entails limitations as well as possibilities.

Under the First Two Seleucid Kings

The historical sources, such as the Zenon papyri and the narrative of Josephus, present a micro view of the situation in Judea and the rest of Syria-Palestine during the third century BCE. From other records we derive a larger picture of struggle between the two great Hellenistic powers that divided up the Near East after Alexander's death, the Ptolemies and the Seleucids. Although the Ptolemies maintained their control over the area, which could be conceived as either their northernmost territory or the Selucuids' southern border, there were no fewer than a half dozen separate military campaigns in this period. Slowly but noticeably the advantage began to shift in favor of the Seleucids. Aggressive, if prolonged, actions by Antiochus III resulted ultimately in their gaining decisive control of the area by century's end.

Jews, under the leadership of the high priest Simon (widely known as Simon the Just) and members of the Tobiad family, played an active role in favor of Antiochus III, and they were appropriately rewarded for their support. (Those Jews who had fought alongside the Ptolemies left Judea, finding refuge in Egypt.) Among the specific benefits the Jews received were Seleucid aid in efforts to rebuild Jerusalem's Temple and to maintain its ritual of daily offerings, official support for the special status of Jerusalem and its Temple (for example, foreigners were forbidden to enter the sanctuary), reduction or elimination of some taxes, and recognition of the right to live according to their ancestral laws. These actions were intended to establish an era of peaceful relations between Seleucid overlords and Jewish subjects. On the whole such mutually desirable results were achieved and sustained during the remainder of Antiochus III's reign, down to 187 BCE, and the rule of his son Seleucus IV, who governed until 175.

Antiochus III was far less astute in dealing with a rising western European power that was making its initial forays into the Hellenistic East. The Romans, who until now had been content to flex their muscles on the Italian peninsula and elsewhere in the western Mediterranean, were drawn to the East at about the same time Antiochus had succeeded in capturing Syria-Palestine from the Ptolemies. Although their immediate goal, successfully pursued, was to stop a Macedonian king from enlarging his holdings, the Romans were quick to view aggressive Seleucid activities as equally alarming. A Roman victory over Seleucid forces in Asia Minor resulted in the imposition of harsh, if deserved, penalties, including the requirement that Antiochus and his successors pay Rome a huge sum of money over a decade or so. When the usual sources of revenue proved inadequate for this purpose, Seleucid leaders resorted to the forcible extraction of funds from religious sanctuaries in their territories. In antiquity, temples and similar institutions regularly served as banks, where people felt it safe to leave large sums of money, and they were also the recipients of often lavish gifts from grateful worshipers. We are told that Antiochus III died in an attempt to take wealth by force from such a sanctuary. Throughout his reign the Temple in Jerusalem was spared this ultimate indignity, but its lucrative coffers were to attract the attention of his successors.

During the first part of his reign, Seleucus IV, Antiochus's son and successor, found it expedient to follow his father's policies toward the Jews. They had worked in achieving their twin goals of producing peace and revenue. If they also pleased Jewish religious sensibilities, all the better. But just below the surface lay pent-up rivalries and antagonisms among influential families in Jerusalem's leadership, all of which rose to the surface during the final year or so of Seleucus's rule and grew in severity during the kingship of his brother and successor, the infamous Antiochus IV Epiphanes. By this time Onias III had succeeded to the office of high priest after the highly regarded tenure of Simon the Just. One of his officials, also named Simon, was stung by the high priest's refusal to allow him to expand the scope of his responsibilities, and he appealed to the Seleucid governor of the region. While such an appeal was not yet normal procedure for their Jewish subjects, Seleucid officials did regularly intervene in the internal affairs of subject peoples and in extraordinary

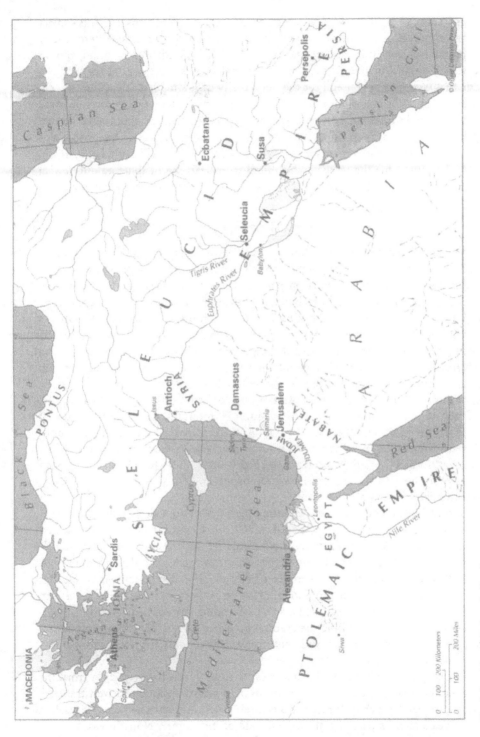

The Seleucid and Ptolemaic Empires

circumstances. Since the very appointment of the high priest of Jerusalem was subject to their approval, the Seleucids would not have hesitated to intervene here if they thought it sufficiently important and to their benefit. With this in mind, Simon sweetened the deal by pointing out that substantial funds were kept at the Temple, funds that would be very useful for the perpetually cash-strapped Seleucid monarch. When Seleucus's prime minister, Heliodorus by name, attempted to force his way into the Temple treasury, he was thwarted by the miraculous appearance of two angels—at least that is the story told in Jewish sources. Whatever happened, this much is clear: Heliodorus returned empty-handed to the Seleucid capital of Antioch, but at the same time the Seleucids benefited from learning of splits among Jewish leaders that they could exploit and of treasures they could confiscate when a more propitious occasion arose.

Antiochus IV and the Jews

The Seleucids did not have to wait long for such an occasion. When Onias III realized that Simon still enjoyed the support of much of the Jerusalem populace, he judged that his only recourse was a direct, in-person appeal to the king. At about the same time Onias set out for Antioch, Heliodorus murdered Seleucus IV, setting the stage for the succession of one of the king's younger brothers, Antiochus IV. Onias's brother, who had taken the Greek name *Jason*, reacted more quickly and successfully to these changed circumstances and through bribery obtained the high priesthood for himself; the subsequent whereabouts of Simon are unknown. Jason followed up his initial success by further bribing the king to allow him to establish a Greek-style gymnasium in Jerusalem and to draw up a list of the "Antiochenes" in that city. Although the exact nature of this latter request is uncertain, there can be no doubt that Jason's requests and their approval by Antiochus marked a turning point both in Seleucid-Jewish relations and in the internal workings of the Jerusalem leadership. Since Antiochus IV had only recently returned from Rome, where he had long been a hostage for his father's and brother's good behavior, he may not have fully understood the likely results of his actions.

Jason had bribed his way into becoming high priest, an action—which unfortunately became a precedent—that could have been viewed as debasing the sacred office. From the Seleucid perspective the Jerusalem high priest was probably no different from any other local leader whose power and very existence depended on royal goodwill. Even if Antiochus were aware of any of these distinctions, it would not have dissuaded him from an appointment that was otherwise so lucrative. Jerusalem "Antiochenes" probably constituted a group of leading citizens dedicated to the promotion of Hellenism, including the cultural activities associated with a gymnasium. Such a development Antiochus could enthusiastically support, despite the probability of opposition from Jerusalem traditionalists.

Surprisingly, Jason's efforts did not meet with an immediate rejection from the Jerusalem populace. The first few years of his high priestship were relatively tranquil, so much so that Antiochus IV received a favorable welcome when he visited Jerusalem several years later as part of a triumphal tour of his empire. Nonetheless, this appearance of tranquility was soon shattered when the high priest was done in by individuals who had learned from Jason himself how to bribe their way to the top.

Three or four years after his succession Jason sent Menelaus, a brother of his brother's former opponent Simon, to Antioch on official business. Seizing the opportunity, as Jason had done earlier, Menelaus offered a larger bribe to Antiochus, who appointed him as the new high priest. This led to Jason's hasty retreat across the Jordan River, where he may have sought the support of the Tobiads (who, however, eventually came down on the side of Menelaus).

Antiochus IV's decision to intervene in high-priestly politics, which may be viewed as a logical extension of his earlier activities, was bound both to worsen Seleucid-Jewish relations and to exacerbate difficulties among Jews. First, Menelaus was not a member of the family that had traditionally provided the Jews with their high priest. The Oniads traced their lineage back to Zadok, whom Solomon had secured in this position, and Jews worldwide generally agreed that Zadok's descendants had been chosen by God for the priestly leadership. As noted above, during both Persian and Hellenistic times the office of high priest had expanded to the point that he was leader in secular and economic matters, as well as in religious affairs. Was the issue of Zadokite pedigree, which from the Jewish perspective was crucial, brought to Antiochus's attention? And would he have cared if it had been? We simply do not know, but apparently here again financial concerns dominated his thinking.

It was in the realm of finances that Menelaus managed to run afoul of both his Seleucid overlords and his Jewish subjects. Having promised Antiochus IV more than he could deliver even through increased taxation and further diversion of Temple revenues, Menelaus resorted to bribery, with golden vessels providing the resources and a Seleucid tax collector as the chief beneficiary. Onias III, still alive and in Antioch, sought to expose these activities, but was killed by Menelaus and his Syrian allies. When Antiochus IV learned that his tax collector was seeking to enrich himself at royal expense, he had his official executed, but no action was taken against Menelaus. Menelaus even managed to regain the king's favor when a delegation from Jerusalem, enraged by the actions of Menelaus and his supporters, took their complaints against him directly to Antiochus. Again, his success was due in part to bribery.

Jerusalem could not have been a happy place when it was learned that members of its delegation were condemned to death, while Menelaus got off scot-free. Presumably most Jews, apart from those closely allied to the current high priest and dependent on his largesse, were growing increasingly dissatisfied with Seleucid rule, which had begun so auspiciously only thirty years earlier. Perhaps there was also widespread dissatisfaction with the rate and direction of hellenizing among the Jerusalem Antiochenes and others.

Antiochus too may have been angered that the high priest he had appointed could not maintain both a steady flow of income and a tranquil populace. As he planned his next major campaign, against Egypt, he was probably more concerned about the former, but he could not ignore the latter. Trouble in Judea would divert needed attention and resources.

Antiochus achieved notable victories in his first campaign against a weakened Ptolemaic empire. Returning triumphantly north from these initial successes, he stopped in Jerusalem during the fall of 169 BCE and used this as an opportunity to expropriate huge sums in gold and silver from the Temple treasury. From the perspective of almost all the Jewish community, this was an illegal and impious action.

From Antiochus's point of view, he was only helping himself to what was lawfully his, with the active support of the Jewish high priest Menelaus. Antiochus had high hopes for a repeat performance when he embarked on his second Egyptian campaign the following year. At first, everything went his way, as he and his victorious troops marched up the banks of the Nile toward Alexandria. But at that very moment, as if on cue, a Roman envoy arrived on the scene and demanded that Antiochus immediately halt his advance and return home. A humiliated Antiochus, unwilling to oppose a force that had humbled his father some years earlier, could only acquiesce.

During this second Egyptian campaign word spread through Judea that Antiochus had died. Emboldened, the exiled Jason returned at the head of a small army to retake Jerusalem. When he and his followers embarked on the systematic slaughter of their enemies, the populace, which otherwise would probably have taken Jason's side, turned against him and moved to restore Menelaus. Antiochus IV, on his way home from Egypt and in no mood to put up with a rebellion, also actively intervened. The result was further bloodshed and the permanent installation of royal officials who would be able to look out for Antiochus's and Menelaus's best interests at close range.

This brings us to 167 BCE. In hindsight we might think that the course of events from late in the reign of Seleucus IV to this point in Antiochus's had been leading inescapably to confrontation. For those on all sides who were living through these events, it probably appeared much more mundane. Antiochus needed money, loyalty, and occasionally troops from his subject peoples. At any given moment, there were bound to be problems as well as bright spots throughout his empire. For those in Jerusalem who supported Antiochus, there was a sense that the major source of difficulty lay with their fellow Jews, who stubbornly held on to outmoded ideas and customs and refused to embrace the opportunities that greater participation in the Hellenistic world would afford. No one was talking about the complete abandonment of Judaism, only its modification and updating. Among those who opposed Antiochus, there were many who saw great value in Hellenism, but wished to pursue it in other directions, at different speeds, or under the governance of their earlier overlords, the Ptolemies, who probably looked better as conditions under the Seleucids grew worse. At this point, there were probably few who felt that the very existence of Judaism was at stake.

All of this changed during the second half of 167. The events of those months are easy enough to narrate; explaining them is more difficult. It began when Antiochus sent his general Apollonius to Jerusalem at the head of an army of mercenaries, ostensibly to end feuding among the city's factions. But he soon initiated a series of more permanent changes. First, he tore down the defensive walls of Jerusalem, allowing for the creation of a single fortified portion within the city called the Akra ("citadel" in Greek). There were gathered Syrian and mercenary forces, foreign residents, and those Jews who allied themselves with Antiochus, including the high priest Menelaus, who along with his associates provided the Seleucids with the detailed knowledge they needed to proceed. Antiochus then imposed a harsh new system of taxation on the Jews.

Such onerous actions were but a prelude to the unprecedented ones that followed. Another Seleucid official arrived in Jerusalem with a decree that struck at the very heart of Judaism. All distinctive Jewish customs and ceremonies were forbidden, including Sabbath and festival observance and circumcision. All Torah scrolls were to be seized and burned. All sacrifices and offerings to God at the Jerusalem Temple were abolished. Anyone who persisted in carrying out these or other Jewish rites was subject to the death penalty. To demonstrate that the provisions of these decrees were not empty threats, those in charge of Seleucid forces, together with their allies among the Jews, began a concerted and public effort to implement them. Nowhere were their actions more provocative than at the Temple itself, which they turned into a place of worship for the Greek god Zeus Olympius. The altar on which daily sacrifices had been offered to the God of Israel was desecrated, and in its place an altar to Zeus was erected. On 25 Kislev 167 BCE (during the first part of the winter) a pig was sacrificed on this altar, a direct insult to the traditions of Judaism. Statues of Greek gods appeared in the Temple and elsewhere in Jerusalem. Throughout Judea, into Samaria, and to a lesser degree elsewhere in his empire Antiochus IV seemed determined that the monotheistic faith of Israel be utterly destroyed and that those brave or foolish enough to resist be killed.

It is impossible to determine what percentage of Jerusalem's population actively supported such efforts. Beyond the high priest and his associates, that number may have been small. It is also difficult to know how many actively opposed Antiochus's decrees. For many of those who did, the initial action was to abandon Jerusalem for the countryside. Most of the populace probably did nothing, the demands of family and business dictating a policy of noninvolvement. When active resistance arose, it originated in the small towns of Judea, not in Jerusalem. This was the Maccabean revolt. Its beginnings, initial successes, and varied results constitute major elements in the final century of the Hellenistic period in Judea. But before turning to these events, let us consider the enigma that is Antiochus IV.

What was anomalous about Antiochus IV's activities was his determined effort to wipe out a religion. By and large, ancient polytheists were tolerant of the beliefs and practices of other peoples. In a world populated by a large number of divine beings, there was no sense that any of them needed to be forcibly eliminated. Deities might show themselves to be weak, ineffectual, fickle, unpredictable, or otherwise problematic. In such cases, adherents might choose to cease worshiping specific gods or alternatively to show their devotion in different ways. The only precedent to Antiochus's actions is found more than a thousand years earlier in Egypt, when Pharaoh Akhenaten attempted to eliminate all gods except the Aten (the solar disk)—and, of course, himself. But Akhenaten's unsuccessful example, even if known to Antiochus IV, could hardly have constituted the major impulse that drove him.

The classic scholarly explanation seeks the primary impetus in Antiochus's desire to promote a pan-Hellenistic culture, including religion, that would harmoniously unite all of his subjects under one banner. It is argued that Antiochus saw himself as a veritable incarnation of Zeus, especially Olympian Zeus. This would explain his order to turn the Jerusalem Temple into a center for the worship of Zeus Olympius and would clarify his epithet, *Epiphanes*, or "God-manifest." But the evidence indicates that such long-range, long-term goals far exceeded whatever Antiochus had in mind. At the other extreme is the idea that Antiochus had nothing in mind, that in fact he was out of his mind, driven by delusions or caught up in the eccentricities of an unstable personality. Many stories that circulated about Antiochus pointed up odd features in his personality and his actions. Not without cause did punning satirists of the day change the solemn epithet *Epiphanes* into *Epimanes*, meaning "madman." But such an appeal to the irrational is also at odds with the recorded facts of Antiochus's reign. After all, this Seleucid monarch could claim many accomplishments, and his assault on the Jewish religion was not capricious or mindless.

Other explanations attribute Antiochus's actions primarily to interest in money or in politics. According to one, Seleucid financial obligations had all but bankrupted the empire, and Antiochus needed to get additional funding in any way possible. But in fact Antiochus's circumstances were not so dire as commonly portrayed, and even if they were, an attack on the Jewish religion seems an odd and ineffectual way to achieve solvency. Antiochus's interest in political stability may have led him to support Menelaus at all costs and against all enemies. But if that were the primary goal of Seleucid policy toward the Jews, less provocative means could have been devised to achieve it.

Perhaps Antiochus had learned the value of suppressing potentially rebellious religious cults during his stay at Rome. In 186 BCE, while he was there, the Roman senate had attempted to suppress the worship of Dionysus/Bacchus on the grounds that its reportedly orgiastic excesses and foreign practices posed a threat to the stability of the self-consciously sober society of the day. This incident, however, is a dubious parallel to Antiochus's more far-reaching efforts to uproot the Jewish religion from its native soil. Or it could be that Antiochus was primarily motivated by a desire to erase the stigma attached to him and his reign by his utterly humiliating defeat by the Romans in Egypt. Other subject peoples might exploit this apparent weakness unless he showed, dramatically and decisively, that he was in charge. His decrees and subsequent actions against the Jews were no doubt dramatic, but it is difficult to ascribe their primary motivation to the realm of public relations. In short, there is no evidence that he planned to use the Jews as an example in this way.

Still another view is to place the burden not on Antiochus but on Jewish leaders, especially Jason, Menelaus, and their supporters. They are to be seen as the primary instigators in the efforts to hellenize Jerusalem and its rituals, and they are the ones who counseled Antiochus to adopt increasingly extreme policies in this regard. But again, the evidence does not support the view of Hellenism and Judaism as mutually exclusive allegiances or that their supposed opposition fueled the internal strife in Jerusalem, at least prior to 167 BCE. Nor can it be demonstrated that a Seleucid ruler during this period took his marching orders from the very people he ruled, even if their leaders had aligned themselves with him.

In short, we have no single answer to the question of what motivated Antiochus IV to promulgate and enforce the decrees of 167. More likely the solution lies in a combination of all these suggested factors. Brilliant but inconsistent, methodical yet brash, generous and cruel, Antiochus was a complex individual living in dangerous times. History would have been very different had he followed his loftier instincts.

Jewish Resistance under Judah Maccabee

As we have seen, the majority of Jerusalem's population silently acquiesced to even the harshest of Antiochus IV's decrees. In addition to the understandable desire to survive, there was a widespread belief that rebellion against a king, even a harsh foreign king, was against God's will. The biblical text records numerous instances of Israel's refusal to recognize that the Assyrians, Babylonians, and other powerful foes were in reality the rods of divine anger, to punish them for their sins. Perhaps the same was also true of the Seleucids.

But when had an enemy struck at the very heart of Israel's monotheistic faith? What would the heroes of old have done in such a circumstance? Would they have quietly accepted Antiochus's actions as the result of divine inevitability? Would they have simply abandoned Jerusalem for the relative security of the countryside? At least one family found inspiration for active opposition through their interpretation of the biblical record. In the town of Modein, not far from Jerusalem, lived the priest Mattathias and his five sons. One of his ancestors had been named Hashmonay, the origin of the collective designation of Mattathias and his descendants as the Hasmoneans. Around this family gathered a small band who initiated their armed conflict with the Seleucids through a series of guerrilla raids. Since they were vastly outnumbered and had only limited support from their fellow Jews, confining themselves to guerrilla operations was wise. In addition, the Hasmoneans could take advantage of their superior knowledge of the area's topography. After the death of Mattathias, who was elderly when the conflict began, his son Judah (Judas), also known as the Maccabee (Maccabeus; the name means "hammer"), assumed the leadership and continued the series of military successes that the Hasmoneans had enjoyed almost from the beginning.

At first, Seleucid officials did not take seriously the threat posed by Judah. But his string of victories brought him increasing fame and increasing numbers of soldiers. Syria's leaders could no longer afford to ignore them, especially because of Judea's strategic location near the northern border of the weakened but still dangerous Ptolemaic empire. More substantial armies, commanded by experienced generals, were sent against the Maccabees, but the results were the same: Jewish victory, Seleucid defeat. As the situation grew graver, it attracted the personal attention of Lysias, whom Antiochus IV had placed in charge of the western portions of his kingdom while he himself headed east. Lysias marched at the head of a massive army, but could do no better than fight to a draw against Judah's outnumbered but energized troops.

In early 164 BCE negotiations opened between the Seleucids and the Jews. The Seleucid offer extended the promise of amnesty to all who renounced their rebellious activities and returned to their pre-rebellion lifestyle. Henceforth Jews could once again carry out the commands of the Torah, but they could not punish those Jews who chose not to. Moreover, the Jerusalem Temple remained in Seleucid hands, effectively barring the Jews from practicing the system of sacrifices that was central to communal worship. Equally upsetting to many was Menelaus's confirmation as high priest. Nonetheless, this "Peace of Lysias" was accepted by large numbers of those who had fought alongside Judah, as well as by Menelaus and his supporters.

Judah and his numerically reduced band, refusing to lay down arms, continued their struggle against what they saw as the oppression of their fellow Jews. Confident of doing God's will, Judah and his soldiers retook the Temple against only token opposition, and cleansed it from the physical and spiritual filth it had suffered. On the twenty-fifth day of the month of Kislev in 164 BCE, according to tradition exactly

Palestine under the Hasmoneans

three years from the day when a pagan sacrifice was first offered at the Temple, priests were again able to make offerings to God in accordance with biblical commands. This event became the basis for the holiday of Hanukkah or Rededication, which continues to be celebrated for eight days by Jews throughout the world.

For most of those who celebrate Hanukkah today, the rededication of the Temple marks the end of the Maccabean revolt or at least the end of their knowledge of the revolt. In fact, the three years thus far covered constitute only the first part of a prolonged period marked by continued Syrian-Jewish fighting and increasingly bitter internal Jewish squabbling. The dangers inherent in hellenization became clearer at least for some, even as others made their peace with it. Judah, the only Hasmonean well known to the general public today, was followed by a succession of brothers, nephews, and other relations. The history of this Hasmonean period is complex.

Under the leadership of Judah and his brothers, the Maccabean forces continued to win an almost unbroken series of victories in their efforts to punish those who had persecuted Jews. As important as the cleansing of the Temple was, it was not their ultimate goal. They probably also drew strength from reports that Antiochus IV had died far away in the east at about the same time they were rededicating the Temple to God. Was that not another sign of divine approval?

Sometime in 163 Judah tried but failed to storm the Akra in Jerusalem, the garrison that housed foreign soldiers and civilians as well as Menelaus and his supporters. Lysias, who now controlled the Seleucid empire in the name of Antiochus IV's young son Antiochus V, recognized that Judah was still a force to be reckoned with, but calculated that he could neutralize this force by deposing the increasingly unpopular and ineffectual Menelaus as high priest. In his place Lysias arranged for the appointment of Alcimus (his name in Greek; Yaqim was its Semitic version), who had a reputation for personal piety that contrasted favorably with Menelaus's. Although Alcimus came from a priestly family, he was not a Zadokite. At this time Onias IV, son of Onias III who had been the last of the line of Zadok to occupy the high-priestly office, left Judea for Egypt, where he founded a temple at Leontopolis.

Other reverses followed Judah's unsuccessful attempt to take the Akra. He met other military defeats, and one of his brothers, Eleazar, died in battle. Judah's forces narrowly averted forcible eviction from the Temple. Apparently Lysias's balanced policies were effectively diminishing Judah's power and would eventually lead to the abandonment of his cause by all but his most die-hard followers. As it happened, however, Lysias's power rather than Judah's soon collapsed, as the Romans successfully promoted a brother of Antiochus IV as the new Seleucid monarch, deposing both Lysias and the young king he had more or less served. As Demetrius I, this ruler confirmed Alcimus as high priest and, like his predecessor, sought to gain decisive military advantage over Judah. What began as another series of Maccabean routs ended sometime later with the tragedy of Judah's death in battle.

Shortly before his death Judah managed to engineer an extremely important alliance with the Romans. As friends and allies of the major world power of the day, the Jews could feel secure against further incursions by the Seleucids. At the same time, as witnessed by the very Syrian attack in which Judah died, the Seleucids were not deterred by the threat of Roman force in defense of their new Jewish allies. Jonathan, Judah's oldest surviving brother, became leader of the remaining Hasmonean forces; their chief nemesis was Bacchides, the Seleucid governor of the region under whose command Judah had been killed. Things continued to look dire for the Maccabees when another of the brothers, John, fell in battle against Arab tribesmen. But thereafter the tide of battle turned again.

Jonathan and Simon as Jewish Leaders

Enemies of the Jews, knowing of their refusal to fight on the Sabbath, often launched their attacks on that very day. Imagine Bacchides' surprise when his Sabbath sortie against Jonathan's forces was answered by defensive actions by the Jews, who in this way succeeded in extricating themselves from what would otherwise have been sure defeat. This bold reinterpretation of the traditional understanding of biblical law was not accepted by all Jews; some undoubtedly judged it an arrogant power play by the

Maccabees. In their defense Jonathan, or his father Mattathias before him, could have argued that obedience to God's law was intended to result in life, not death. Perhaps more forceful than the abstract theological argumentation was the interpretation of Maccabean victory, won at the price of self-defense on the Sabbath, as signifying divine approval for such activity. In any event, the main lines of later Jewish exegesis sided with the Maccabees and even went beyond their practice to allow for offensive attacks on the Sabbath. The seventh day, when Joshua and his forces stormed the city of Jericho, was identified with the Sabbath, providing the required biblical precedent. The Maccabean period thus saw the beginnings of this line of development, when questions arose not only about the substance of this interpretation but also the authority of Mattathias and his family to formulate and impose their interpretation on others. When in mid-year 159 BCE the high priest Alcimus suffered a painful death, this seemed another sign that the Hasmoneans were charting a course in accordance with the divine will.

With Alcimus out of the way, Bacchides felt it safe to withdraw his strong military presence from Judea. Throughout most of the remainder of the decade an uneasy but largely uneventful peace prevailed between the Seleucids and the Hasmoneans. Curiously, Bacchides did nothing to secure a successor for Alcimus, and the office of high priest fell vacant for approximately seven years.

In 152 a challenge to Demetrius I arose in the person of Alexander Balas, whose claim to the Seleucid throne was buttressed by his claim to be a son of Antiochus IV. In the bidding that followed, Jonathan prospered and set an example for later Hasmoneans who found themselves in similar circumstances. Demetrius made the first bid for Jonathan's support: the Jewish leader could legally assemble and equip an army, those held hostage in the Akra would be released (although the Akra itself would remain as a foreign garrison), and Jonathan would be recognized as leader of the Jews. Thus equipped, Jonathan was able to enter Jerusalem, rebuild its walls, and provide for new construction on the Temple Mount. Alexander Balas raised the ante by confirming everything Demetrius had offered plus naming Jonathan as high priest and one of the "king's friends." Jonathan readily assumed the high priesthood in the fall of 152, during the festival of Sukkot. Demetrius's counteroffers were ineffectual, and his defeat by Alexander Balas two years later confirmed the validity of Jonathan's appointment. The Hasmoneans, although priests, were not from the line of Zadok. In their defense it could be added that non-Zadokites had already served as high priests, so that Jonathan's acceptance was not unprecedented. Nevertheless, it aroused opposition and may even have precipitated the development of one or more of the sectarian movements to be discussed below. Opponents of Jonathan who voiced their concerns to Alexander Balas received no support from the Seleucid monarch. Quite the opposite: he heaped additional honors on Jonathan, further solidifying his position as the leader of Judea.

Alexander Balas's confidence in Jonathan was not misplaced, although it was several years before the Jewish leader had to demonstrate his loyalty. At that time Demetrius II, son of Demetrius I, rose to challenge Alexander Balas. When the governor of the region deserted Alexander Balas in favor of this challenger, Jonathan and his brother Simon took the lead in inflicting a punishing defeat on him. By now Jonathan was a "kinsman of the king," several rungs higher up the royal ladder than his earlier rankings as one of the "king's friends" and "first friend."

But Alexander Balas's days were numbered. Not long after Jonathan received the last batch of honors from his royal patron, Ptolemy VI intervened on behalf of Demetrius II, who was crowned as Seleucid king following the defeat of Alexander. Taking advantage of the uncertainty associated with such changes in leadership, Jonathan launched another attack on the Jerusalem Akra. Demetrius II was not about to allow this challenge to go unanswered, and he summoned Jonathan before him. Since neither side wished to risk a full-scale conflict at this time, they reached a compromise whereby the Akra remained in Seleucid hands and Jonathan retained most of his power over a newly enlarged Judea.

Although Jonathan showed himself as loyal to Demetrius as he had to his predecessor, the current monarch did not reciprocate with the generosity that had characterized Alexander's dealings with the Jewish leader. Jonathan repaid Demetrius in kind by offering his full support to a rival claimant to the throne, Antiochus VI. This young son of Alexander Balas was championed by a man named Tryphon. Jonathan fought bravely on behalf of Antiochus and against Demetrius's supporters, taking this opportunity to launch an expanded assault on the Akra. In Jonathan's eyes, its continued existence was a major irritant.

Jonathan also used his increased power and prestige to enlarge the scope of his diplomatic activity. Not only did he take steps to ensure that his alliance with the Romans remained intact, but he also initiated official contacts with the Spartans, with whom he claimed a long kinship. Such a claim, although dubious, gives insight into the way Jonathan perceived the Jews in relation to other peoples of the ancient world.

Like many other regents before him, Tryphon aimed not so much to safeguard the throne for his young charge as to ascend it himself. Because he discerned that Jonathan would block such a move on his part, he lured the Jewish leader into a trap that resulted in the slaughter of his substantial bodyguard and his own capture. Leadership of the Jews now fell to Simon, the last remaining son of Mattathias. He ably parried every attempt by Tryphon to follow up his treachery with military success, but in the end Tryphon thwarted Simon's attempts to gain his brother's freedom. When Simon reluctantly accepted Tryphon's offer to free Jonathan in return for ransom money and two of Jonathan's sons, the disreputable Tryphon took all that Simon gave but refused to keep his part of the bargain. Soon after, Tryphon killed Jonathan on his way out of Judea.

These actions probably elevated Simon's stature among his own people, some of whom declared him the new high priest. That status was later confirmed by Demetrius II, who also exempted the Jews from the payment of those taxes associated with subservience to the Syrian empire. For all practical purposes Demetrius had granted independence to his former Jewish subjects. Documents dated to this period, in the autumn of 142 BCE and later, refer to Simon as high priest, commander, and chief of the Jews.

In general, the eight years of Simon's leadership were positive and successful for the new Jewish state. Early on he succeeded in finally expelling foreign troops, foreign civilians, and their Jewish sympathizers from the Akra. When Demetrius II was succeeded by Antiochus VII, the latter left in place all of the provisions agreed to by his predecessor and even allowed the Jews to mint their own coins (a privilege later rescinded). But like several of his predecessors, Antiochus VII soon grew suspicious of the power of his Jewish allies; his moves against them were, however, countered by Simon and his sons Judas and John.

Hyrcanus, Aristobulus I, and Janneus

Simon, who had survived so much, was done in—along with his sons Judas and Matthias—by the treachery of one of his sons-in-law, named Ptolemy. Presumably Ptolemy, from whose perfidy only Simon's other son John escaped, was driven by a desire to find favor with Antiochus VII. But it was John, succeeding Simon as high priest, who would lead his people through the final decades of the second century BCE.

John, also known as Hyrcanus, probably took action against Ptolemy as soon as possible. Such action was bound to be popular with most of the Jews. But Ptolemy had two formidable assets of his own: support of Antiochus VII and possession of Simon's widow, John's mother. John wisely sought to shore up his position by renewing his people's alliance with the Romans. Antiochus VII, like Syrian monarchs since Antiochus III, was not overly impressed by Rome's guarantees, and he laid siege to Jerusalem, which John and his followers were defending. The compromise that averted further bloodshed left Jerusalem and its defenders intact, but required the Jews to pay substantial tribute and reduced them to Seleucid subjects once more.

When Antiochus VII died while fighting on his eastern borders, John took the military initiative. Among his first steps was to eliminate the threat posed by the murderous Ptolemy, who was in control of Jericho and its environs. John's success in this enterprise was bittersweet, since it came at the cost of his mother's life and since he failed to capture Ptolemy. But at least Ptolemy no longer had a base of power in Judea. The throne now reverted to Demetrius II, whose weakness John exploited through an impressive series of victories in Moab, Samaria, and Idumea, to name only the most prominent territories he conquered. With respect to the Idumeans, John reportedly allowed them to become Jews, in which case they would be able to retain their place in the land. Circumcision would have been required of all Idumean males and would signify their acceptance of the monotheistic faith of Israel. Herod the Great, installed by the Romans about a century later as king of the Jews, could trace his family's connections with Judaism to this event.

A rival claimant to the Seleucid throne, who took the name of Alexander, challenged Demetrius. Demetrius and Alexander each had the support of one of the feuding factions in Ptolemaic Egypt. But neither Alexander nor Demetrius could win the upper hand, and they both fell in rapid succession. Demetrius's son ruled as Antiochus VIII for about a decade (ca. 123–113). As during the years when Demetrius and Alexander fought it out, John was generally left alone to continue his conquest of neighboring territories and to reap the benefits of his and his people's labors. When a new king, Antiochus IX, arose to threaten this relative tranquility, John successfully appealed to the Romans, who issued a stern warning. As it was, Antiochus IX's energies were more than taken up in conflict with his brother, who still reigned as Antiochus VIII. Perfecting a technique that had been profitably used by himself

and other Hasmoneans before, John Hyrcanus used this opportunity to further enlarge his already extensive territory.

The city of Samaria had thus far resisted conquest, although most of the surrounding land had earlier fallen into John's hands. John judged this prize so significant
that he entrusted the campaign against it to two of his sons, Antigonus and Aristobulus. The siege of Samaria was long and difficult. In response to an appeal from
Samaria's residents, Antiochus IX joined the battle, but to no avail. The Hasmonean
capture of Samaria, near the end of John Hyrcanus's long tenure, resulted in the
city's demolition. The thoroughness with which the Jewish forces carried out their
task is reminiscent of the earlier Roman treatment of Carthage at the conclusion of
the Third Punic War.

Much of the populace admired John and was grateful to him for the relative peace
and prosperity he secured through his conquests and alliances. Although he may not
have scrupulously observed Torah commands, he had established himself as leader
of the Jewish religion, as well as of the Jewish people. His numerous building projects
in and around Jerusalem are best understood in this light. Though he faced some
internal opposition, we cannot be sure of its nature or of its seriousness. All and all,
these were decades that could be remembered with nostalgia by later generations who
had to endure notably deteriorated circumstances.

In common with the first generation of Hasmoneans, John bore an additional
name, and he also bestowed such names on his sons. We know of three: Aristobulus,
Antigonus, and Janneus. Unlike earlier appellations, these three are Greek. But since
they appear to express sentiments completely at home in Israel's monotheistic faith,
we should not make too much of this linguistic distinction.

Aristobulus, more fully Judas Aristobulus I, succeeded his father, only to be followed shortly by his brother Alexander Janneus. Either Aristobulus or Janneus was
the first Hasmonean to take for himself the title *king*. In either case, such a move was
significant not only for its political implications, but also for its theological overtones.
The restoration of a king on the throne in Jerusalem would evoke memories, fond
and otherwise, of the distinctive relationship that God established with the house of
David. Aristobulus was known to have initiated a new round of conquests that might
have been aimed at further enlarging the boundaries of his kingdom to "biblical"
proportions. But the historical sources also report that he was guilty of immense
cruelty to members of his own family, his mother and brothers included. After only
a year in power, death brought an end to this Hasmonean's rule.

Aristobulus's widow, Alexandra, bestowed the kingship on her brother-in-law Janneus, who in turn took her as his wife. Such a union accorded with the biblical
practice of levirate marriage, whereby a brother married his childless sister-in-law in
order to keep their line alive. Both documentary and numismatic evidence confirms
that for at least part of his reign Janneus actively assumed the role of king with its
attendant regalia such as the diadem. If he was not the first Hasmonean to mint his
own coins, he was among the most prolific and astute producers of such numismatic
materials.

But Janneus aimed too high when he sought to capture the major Phoenician city
of Ptolemais. This attempt embroiled him in an intra-Egyptian family feud that
threatened to undermine Janneus's stature and credibility among his subjects. Only

the intervention of Egypt's queen Cleopatra III saved the Jewish king from an inglo-
rious and total defeat. In determining her course of action, Cleopatra is said to have
followed the advice of Onias IV's two sons. Onias had founded a Jewish temple at
Leontopolis, and his family had established itself within the highest circles of Egyptian
political life and had on this occasion chosen to aid the Hasmoneans, whom they
might otherwise have regarded as rivals for the religious leadership of the Jewish
people. Thwarted at Ptolemais, Janneus turned his attention elsewhere.

Although from Janneus's perspective the ensuing record of military engagements
was largely positive, these victories cost his nation many lives and cost him personally
much of the goodwill he had built up. Accusations spread that Janneus was unfit to
be high priest, and these ill feelings spilled over into hostile acts on more than one
occasion. In response, Janneus brought in mercenaries to first bully and then kill
thousands of those Jews who protested. The sense that God had abandoned this
Jewish king grew all the more intense when Janneus's army suffered a major reversal
in Transjordan. So repugnant had Janneus become in the eyes of some Jews that they
invited the Seleucid monarch Demetrius III to deliver a crushing blow against their
own ruler. Although without precedent, this request did conform in general to the
biblical teaching, supported by narrative accounts, that God could use foreign rulers
to punish Israel—or in this case its king. In the struggle that followed Demetrius
succeeded in striking the first blow, and it was heavy. But Janneus managed to rally
his troops. Faced with the prospect of a protracted Judean campaign and the reality
of further losses, Demetrius withdrew his forces. From his perspective, this was only
a sideshow; the main event was the threat posed by rival claimants to his throne.

Janneus ordered the crucifixion of almost a thousand Jewish men who had fought
against him alongside Demetrius. We are told that the king compelled these men,
even as they were suffering a long and painful death, to endure further anguish: to
witness the massacre of their own wives and children. Not surprisingly, a considerable
number of Jews went into exile, and Janneus was the recipient of hateful epithets
that rivaled those given to Antiochus IV. These events occurred midway through the
quarter century of Janneus's rule (103–76 BCE). He faced no further internal threats
for the remainder of his reign, but it is doubtful that things were so tranquil below
the surface.

Janneus did continue to pursue his policy of territorial conquest and expansion,
with mixed results. Faced with an increasingly aggressive challenge from the Nabatean
Arab king Aretas III, Janneus constructed and fortified several sites, probably including Masada of later fame. To Janneus's reign can also be dated several important
literary works, including 1 Maccabees (discussed below) and the expanded Greek
version of Esther that is canonical for Roman Catholic and Orthodox Christians.

We will shortly discuss in detail the origins and early history of the Sadducees,
Pharisees, and Essenes. Josephus is our chief source for these "sects," and he wrote
many years after the events we are now narrating. Rabbinic materials in their written
forms also date from a much later period. And it must be admitted that the Dead
Sea Scrolls are often difficult to interpret. Nonetheless, judicious use of these several
sources leads to one conclusion: at one time or another members of all of these
groups opposed, often with great vehemence, Alexander Janneus and his policies.

Presumably such hostility mirrored in general the stance of the vast majority of Jews who identified with no specific group. Especially dramatic is a scene set by Josephus. Bedridden, chronically ill, and near death, the king summoned his wife Alexandra and pleaded with her to listen to the Pharisees. He had not treated them with respect, but now repented of his actions against them. Whether or not this story is historically reliable, the incident points to the reality of Hasmonean-Pharisaic opposition during Janneus's reign.

From Queen Alexandra to General Pompey

As queen, Alexandra appears to have followed her husband's advice with respect to the Pharisees. The Sadducees also seem to have given her their support during the nine years of her rule. In foreign affairs, the reign of Alexandra was likewise tranquil, with only a handful of military engagements, for the most part successful. Janneus and Alexandra had two sons: John Hyrcanus II and Judas Aristobulus II. Hyrcanus, the elder, succeeded his father as high priest, while Alexandra maintained royal power and prerogatives for herself. This unusual arrangement sufficed so long as the queen remained in good health. Only near the time of her death in 67 BCE did fraternal rivalry threaten to tear apart the Jewish kingdom. From the perspective of the Hasmonean dynasty it was unfortunate indeed that this threat became a reality only four years after Alexandra's death.

While the queen was still alive, but noticeably weakened, Aristobulus took aggressive steps to ensure that he, and not his elder brother Hyrcanus, would succeed their mother as king. Shortly after Alexandra's death, armed forces loyal to the two brothers clashed. Aristobulus had the military advantage, and Hyrcanus, bowing to reality, proposed a face-saving compromise compatible with his own chief interests: Aristobulus would be both king and high priest; Hyrcanus would retire from public life, but retain considerable prestige and wealth. Aristobulus instantly accepted.

With this agreement in place, it was possible to envision continued peace and prosperity for the Jewish state. But such was not to be. The irritant was the Idumean leader Antipater (Herod the Great's father). Antipater's father had for many years served Hyrcanus's parents, and Antipater himself threw his support behind Hyrcanus. Perhaps he thought him easier to manipulate than his younger brother Aristobulus, or perhaps he feared for his life if Aristobulus gained too much power. In any event, Antipater persuaded Hyrcanus to break his fraternal pact and seek support from the Nabatean monarch Aretas III, whom Janneus had earlier opposed. Encouraged by Antipater, Aretas raised a huge army and marched against Aristobulus. Hyrcanus joined in this effort, which resulted in a massive defeat for his younger brother. Aristobulus and his supporters retreated to the Jerusalem Temple and maintained the traditional rituals of sacrifice while staving off the attacks of their opponents.

Both brothers sought the advantage by appealing to the Roman leader Pompey, who was then in Asia Minor. At first, one of Pompey's aides declared in favor of Aristobulus. This was enough for the Nabateans, who had no desire to challenge Roman power. Aristobulus now had the upper hand and rapidly took advantage of his vastly improved circumstances. Pompey decided to look into these matters himself and summoned both Hyrcanus and Aristobulus to Damascus. A third party to this dispute was also given the chance to make its case. This third party consisted of a delegation from the general populace of Judea. Pompey listened to all sides, but adjourned the session without announcing his final disposition of the matter.

In the interim Aristobulus acted in what Pompey interpreted as a hostile manner. As a result, Pompey attacked Aristobulus's forces, predictably compelling the Jewish leader to surrender. It must have occasioned surprise on Pompey's part when he learned that Aristobulus's supporters, still in control of the Jerusalem Temple, desired to keep up the struggle. Hyrcanus's group gave its full support to Pompey's continued efforts, but only after a protracted and bloody siege did the Romans succeeded in capturing the heavily fortified Temple Mount. As victorious general, Pompey had no scruples against entering the Temple's innermost chamber, the holy of holies, but he was well advised not to steal anything from the Temple's great store of wealth. This occurred in 63 BCE.

The Romans were now firmly in charge. This was obvious to all through the imposition of tribute and the submission of Judea to the direct control of the Roman governor of Syria. Aristobulus and his family were taken to Rome as captives. Jewish freedom was a thing of the past. In these circumstances it is difficult to imagine that most Jews took much solace in Pompey's reinstatement of Hyrcanus as high priest.

For over a century prior to Pompey's triumph, Hasmoneans had dominated Jewish religious, cultural, and political life. Individual Hasmoneans varied greatly in terms of personal characteristics and fitness to lead the Jewish people. On the whole, members of that dynasty were probably more willing to reach compromises with the forces of Hellenism than was the general populace. But it is not clear that they consciously courted foreign favor at the expense of Judaism as they understood it, or that they consistently promoted policies that favored Hellenizers over more traditional Jews. In this regard, it is instructive to point out that the last Hasmonean defenders of the Temple, Aristobulus's supporters, refused to fight against the Romans on the Sabbath, and many Jews were slaughtered by the Romans in the very midst of their performance of Temple ritual.

Daniel, 1 and 2 Maccabees

In our discussion of the third century BCE, we explored the nature and extent of evidence provided by three biblical books: Esther, Judith, and Tobit. Likewise there are three biblical books among our sources for the second and first centuries: Daniel, 1 Maccabees, and 2 Maccabees. In considering the term *biblical*, we observed that only one of the earlier three, Esther, belongs to the Hebrew canon that constitutes the Jewish Bible and the Protestant Old Testament. For Catholics and Orthodox Christians, the Old Testament also encompasses Judith, Tobit, and an expanded form of Esther that has been preserved in Greek. Exactly the same configuration holds true for the three biblical books we are now discussing. Daniel is found in all canons, whereas 1 and 2 Maccabees are canonical for the Roman Catholic and Orthodox Churches, but apocryphal in the Jewish and Protestant traditions. Moreover, the Hebrew text of Daniel, preserved or translated as part of Jewish and Protestant Bibles, was augmented in Greek and in this form was taken up by Catholics and the Orthodox. In terms of genre there is an important difference: Esther, Judith, and Tobit are novels; of the latter triad, only Daniel can be so designated.

The Hebrew form of Daniel neatly divides into two parts: chapters 1 through 6 consist of a collection of tales, in which Daniel and his companions demonstrate the superiority of their God and those who obediently follow him over the worshipers of false, empty, and powerless deities. Set loosely in the period of the Babylonian exile, most of these stories appear to have circulated independently in oral form before being committed to writing. As with Esther, Judith, and Tobit, there are several deviations from the historical record as known elsewhere. Their utilization in a fully ironic, even mocking, manner makes it unnecessary to charge either ancient author or modern reader with ignorance or carelessness. The author and his initially intended audience fully understood and appreciated Daniel's novelistic context. What was most important was Daniel's steadfast loyalty to God in the face of imminent disgrace and death. The same held true for his three colleagues. The reversal of fortune, whereby they were all rewarded for refusal to obey royal command, was fully prepared for by the knowledge that such commands stood diametrically opposed to the will of God, the ultimate king and lawgiver. The sudden changes of heart, through which foreign rulers acknowledged the sovereignty of God, did not really happen, but exemplify what should be the reaction of all people when confronted by the monotheistic faith of Israel.

These exemplary tales are augmented by three others in the Greek version of Daniel. The first deals with Susanna, a Jewish woman of flawless virtue, who is the victim of base and groundless accusations by two elders. Young Daniel leads the judicial charge to free her and remove these blotches from the blameless maiden's reputation. Of course, virtue—in the form of God's justice, its pleader (Daniel), and its exemplar (Susanna)—triumphs at tale's end. Susanna's relatively brief role parallels the more extensive treatment lavished on Esther, Judith, and other female characters in Jewish literature of the Hellenistic period. In Bel and the Dragon, Daniel steps forward to expose the utterly foolish trappings that underpinned much pagan worship. For all but the most credulous there ought to be no contest in the struggle between God and other deities.

But there was a struggle, a crucial one, between the followers of God and those, including some of the Jews, who worshiped many gods. The apocalyptic nature of this struggle, which dominated the world scene and involved angelic hosts as well as human enemies, is the subject of the series of visions that make up chapters 7 through 12 of the book of Daniel. All but the most conservative interpreters agree that these chapters date from the time of the Maccabean revolt, specifically to the period between Antiochus's decrees of 167 BCE and Judah's cleansing of the Temple at the end of 163. The visions contain many veiled allusions to Jewish history, and these allusions are often attributed to the visionary Daniel. Traditionally, these visions and their interpretation have been understood as prophecies or predictions of the future and dated to the Babylonian exile. Today we understand them as prophecies after the fact, a characterization often troubling to Bible readers until they realize that this is exactly what the author or compiler of Daniel intended. God has not lost control of history, and the victory of the forces of evil over the supporters of good is more illusory than real, temporary and not permanent. The final chapter of this part of Daniel, chapter 12, contains the Hebrew Bible's first and only unequivocal statement concerning reward and punishment after death. The postresurrection rewards of those Jews who die in obedience to God's commands are as sure as the eternal punishment of those who achieve earthly success at the expense of their fellow Jews.

With respect to the books of Maccabees, we will discuss 2 Maccabees first because its genre and teachings are closer to Daniel's. We designate 2 Maccabees as a historical novel because its author, while making effective use of many techniques in common with Daniel, Esther, Tobit, and Judith, fully intended his audience to understand his narration as based on events that actually occurred and on people who really lived. Composed in Greek, 2 Maccabees is an unnamed writer's effort to summarize a longer history by the otherwise unknown Jason of Cyrene. This abridgment covers the decade and a half from approximately 175 BCE to 160, when Judah Maccabee successfully faced the Syrian commander Nicanor. Judah, a fully realized character like Judith or Daniel (especially in the longer, Greek version), is clearly the hero of the story. Appeal to the emotions is a prominent feature of the author's style, nowhere more evident than in his narration of martyred Jews, who willingly chose death rather than profaning divine command. Whether these individuals are the first martyrs known from history, their memorable portrayal served as a paradigm for other Jews and later for Christians who undoubtedly did choose death at human hands rather than disobey the Lord God. Also instructive in these portrayals is the characters' insistence that the pain they have chosen to endure on earth is as nothing when compared with the rewards they will enjoy for all eternity after death. By extension, the price of earthly rewards is frequently eternal damnation. These are themes that receive full, if distinctive, development in later Jewish and early Christian literature.

By comparison, 1 Maccabees—although it covers a considerably longer period of time, concluding with the death of Simon and the imminent elevation to the throne of John Hyrcanus—is rhetorically inferior, though of great value as a historical source. Originally composed in Hebrew but preserved in Greek, 1 Maccabees glorifies the three sons of Mattathias who led their people and seeks to legitimate the powers exercised by John and his sons. As noted above, the work probably dates from the reign of his second son, Alexander Janneus. Overall, 1 Maccabees has the look of other biblical books of history, such as 1 and 2 Kings.

These two books of Maccabees cover much the same ground, but not always in the same way. Matters of fact and especially matters of emphasis and judgment differ. The same is true when Josephus adds his witness. Careful modern historians avoid reliance on blanket characterizations when assessing the historical validity or reliability of these three works, as well as others that provide occasional references to this period; every narrative section or list must be judged on its own merits. In the end, each of these works is a useful source that must be critically evaluated. Even when the contents of a given narrative are not historically valid, we can appreciate an author's theological perspectives as evidence of patterns of belief or faith. Since no one, either in antiquity or in the modern world, writes history in a vacuum, such subjectivity even in the most reliable of historical witnesses is hardly surprising.

Pharisees, Sadducees, and Essenes

We now turn to several groups within the Jewish community already mentioned in passing. The first three of these, the Pharisees, the Sadducees, and the Essenes, are generally considered together by modern scholars, as they also were by one of our most important ancient sources, Josephus. But scholarly consensus is rare on almost all aspects of the history and development of these groups, in part because the best evidence either dates from a later period or is susceptible to different interpretations. To be sure, we are not dealing with movements that originated or developed in a vacuum, that were monolithic in character, or that regarded themselves or their opponents with calm detachment. The individuals who identified with these groups did so in a committed, even impassioned, way. So it is not surprising that both ancient writers and modern scholars have come up with widely divergent portrayals.

There is general agreement that all three of these groups or sects originated before or during the Maccabean revolt. According to one view, members of the group that became known as the Pharisees were earlier (originally?) called the *Hasidim*, from the Hebrew root meaning "pious" or "righteous." Their primary concern was scrupulous observance of Mosaic law, and they willingly took up arms to defend it. When the course of the Maccabean revolt turned to more nationalistic goals, so the argument goes, these Hasidim separated themselves from its leaders and either failed to support or actively opposed later developments, until they gained a considerable degree of power, particularly under Queen Alexandra. The Hebrew word underlying *Pharisees* is generally understood to mean "to separate." This term probably connotes physical as well as ritual and spiritual separation from other Jews; to put it another way, they distinguished themselves from other Jews by their style of life and system of beliefs. If we are correct in identifying the Pharisees as lay leaders and teachers of organizations similar to what we today would call synagogues, then we have a picture of a movement that actively sought to influence Jewish society at all levels.

For the Hellenistic period it is difficult to know exactly which beliefs or practices characterized the Pharisees. Not all Pharisees agreed on all matters. There was presumably a core of accepted rituals and beliefs by which the group achieved a sense of self-identity, as there was a core of practices and ideas that most, if not all, Pharisees opposed. Two of the former are resurrection and the oral law. We have already mentioned the belief in resurrection of the dead, along with the concept of postmortem judgment that resulted in reward or punishment. The fully elaborated view of the oral law held that God had revealed more to Moses at Sinai than had been committed to writing in the Torah. Knowledge of the oral law, passed down by word of mouth from generation to generation, was necessary for proper interpretation and implementation of the written law. The Pharisees undoubtedly developed both pedagogical and judicial systems that centered on the law. The totality of their discussions and decisions could be incorporated in the term *halakah*, which encompassed a comprehensive way of life the Pharisees attempted both to exemplify and to promote. When they had the ear of the powerful, they exerted enormous influence. At other times, they had to content themselves with a more marginalized social status. It is unlikely, however, that they ever considered such marginalization as anything more than a passing phenomenon. In a sense they were correct, since there is a direct, but not unambiguous, line to be drawn from them to later rabbinic Judaism.

The Sadducees, whenever they developed as a distinctive movement, must be understood—and must have understood themselves—as preservers or carriers of a set of beliefs and practices associated with the biblical figure Zadok. During the reign of King David there were two high priests, presumably reflecting sectional differences of the divided peoples whom David had succeeded in uniting. As David lay near death, both Solomon and one of his brothers claimed the throne, each supported by a high priest. Zadok's support for Solomon ensured that he and his family would have the sole privilege of providing Israel's high priests from then on. In theory, if not in practice, that was the case for many hundreds of years. With the end of the monarchy at the time of the Babylonian conquest of Judah or in the early years of the return—in any case sometime during the sixth century BCE—the office of the high priest assumed even greater importance. Throughout the Persian and early Hellenistic periods the high priest was the leader of the Jews not only in the sphere of religious ritual, but in every aspect of life. He was, in short, his people's representative to the ruling powers, responsible for such matters as the maintenance of peace and the collection of taxes. Only with the capture of Syria-Palestine by the Seleucids did this change. It may be then that a distinct self-identity developed among the descendants of Zadok and their supporters.

In ancient Israel, as elsewhere in the Mediterranean world, priestly concerns revolved around the temple (or temples), at which sacrifices and other forms of communal worship took place. Maintenance of such rites was often considered crucial for the preservation of a positive relationship between humanity and the divine. Because all life depended on such a relationship, the priests could view themselves as the central players in their people's national drama. Some priests from the line of Zadok undoubtedly followed Onias IV when he founded his temple at Leontopolis in Egypt. He may have intended this not as a rival to the Jerusalem Temple, but rather as its Diaspora counterpart. As we have observed, Onias's sons gave considerable support to Hasmonean rulers contemporary with themselves, in spite of the Hasmonean claim to the high priesthood, although other descendants of Zadok may not have been so understanding.

In any event, a priestly tradition that could maintain its sense of integrity in dealing with alien occupation forces could probably accommodate itself to internal changes. Moreover, the Sadducees' experience in dealing with foreign leaders would be valuable in protecting valid Temple interests against further incursions from competing or even hostile domestic forces. So it appears that many, if not most, Sadducean priests accepted their diminished status. In much of the modern literature the Sadducees are characterized as wealthy accommodationists who would do almost anything to maintain their privileged position. This characterization is unfair, reflecting as much as anything else the anticlerical bias of many scholars. There existed in Israel, as elsewhere in the ancient world, a temple theology or ideology that could be as sincerely articulated and defended as any other.

Likewise, the Sadducees are often criticized for having a narrow view of the law. Because they considered only the five books of the Torah as authoritative, they refused to support beliefs or rituals that in their opinion were not found there. Thus, to take the best-known example, Sadducean interpreters found no biblical support for the doctrine of resurrection, and therefore they found no place for that doctrine in their belief system. They viewed many Pharisaic interpretations, based on the oral law, as unwarranted innovations, but that is not to say that the Sadducees lacked their own interpretative devices or, for that matter, their own halakah. The Sadducees may not have countenanced as much diversity of opinion and practice as did the Pharisees, but it is mistaken to assume that they were rigidly monolithic.

An even greater distaste for diversity probably characterized the third group of this triad, the Essenes. Josephus is virtually our only source for them. There is no generally agreed-upon etymology for the word *Essene,* nor are we sure what the underlying Semitic term was. More than the Pharisees and Sadducees, the Essenes developed what we might today call a sectarian consciousness. Even when they dwelled among the general populace, they lived a life apart. According to Josephus, some Essenes married and had dealings with their fellow Jews, while others did not marry and cut themselves off from the mainstream. Although they accepted new members, they did not actively seek them nor did they welcome just anyone. An elaborate system of probation and initiation preceded full acceptance into their fellowship, an acceptance that could be revoked for failure to follow the distinctive system of beliefs and practices they constructed.

When the Dead Sea Scrolls were discovered and read in the late 1940s and early 1950s, a consensus arose that the Qumran settlement responsible for these scrolls was an Essene community. Although the doctrines and rites outlined in the scrolls did not agree in every detail with Josephus (nor do the scrolls always agree with each other), the Essene hypothesis was attractive. Despite challenges to this consensus in recent years, the Essene hypothesis still retains its value as a reasonable interpretative tool.

The Qumran community seems to have been founded sometime in the Maccabean or Hasmonean period. Because the community styles itself the "sons of Zadok," its founders felt some connection or kinship with the priestly group out of which the Sadducees also arose. These "sons of Zadok" were unwilling or unable to make their peace with the authorities in Jerusalem and therefore effected a physical separation into the remote area just west of the Dead Sea. From there they waged a prolonged and often impassioned campaign against those in power in Jerusalem, whom they regarded as unworthy of such offices and influence. Although they rarely named names, preferring instead code terms like "Wicked Priest" and "Teacher of Righteousness," much of their hatred was clearly directed at the Hasmonean dynasty and its supporters. In fact, the Qumran community implacably opposed not only foreign countries, but also all Jews outside their group. They identified themselves as the "sons of light," destined by God to be victorious in apocalyptic battle against the "sons of darkness." They considered that even the angelic hosts were entering the battle on their side. Human beings had to make a choice between light and darkness, and that choice led directly to eternal reward or its opposite.

The community at Qumran was tightly structured, dedicated to the study and interpretation of Mosaic law, and stood poised to take over the now debased organization of the Temple when the Messiah (or Messiahs) should appear to lead them. Their criticisms of the Temple were not aimed at the authentic Temple of the past or future, but only at the present structure and its unclean priesthood. According to their literature, they believed that Jerusalem worship was further invalidated because it relied on a faulty calendar and a false calculation for the observance of festivals and holidays. Josephus does not mention this calendrical dispute, but its existence would have been crucially important for two groups, both of which claimed to be the true Israel.

Because they designated themselves as the "sons of Zadok" and had unmistakable ties with priestly concerns and practices, it has been proposed that the Qumran community's members were Sadducees. But the Qumran group's belief in resurrection stands in stark contrast with everything known of Sadducean beliefs on this subject. The founders of the Qumran community may, however, have been closer to Sadducean belief and practice than later generations of their followers. It may also be that Sadducean tenets in these matters become normative only in the later period that we know from Josephus and other sources. In any case, Josephus did not intend to present an exhaustive listing and discussion of all the sectarian groups that he knew.

Jews and Samaritans, Jews and Non-Jews

In the Samaritans we encounter a group that had similarities with—but also more significant differences from—the triad discussed above. Like the Sadducees, the Samaritans accepted as authoritative only (a form of) the Torah, or five books of Moses. They shared with both the Sadducees and the Essenes of Qumran a conviction that there was only one temple at which communal worship should be centralized. Unlike the Sadducees, but again in common with the Essenes, the Samaritans did not consider the Jerusalem Temple as valid. And perhaps of greatest significance, their claim to be the true Israel, aimed primarily against the Jerusalem leadership, parallels the self-identity of the Qumran community.

But the differences are striking. The Essenes' hatred for Jerusalem and its Temple was limited to the present. As in the past, in the messianic future Jerusalem would be the site for the true priesthood and the authentic sacrificial worship of Israel. For the Samaritans, on the other hand, the Jerusalem Temple was not and never could be that sacred place ordained by God for his worship. Instead, the territory of Samaria, with its capital at Shechem and its temple on Mount Gerizim, was the intended focus for priest, cult, and worship. The Samaritans traced their lineage back to the same twelve tribes as the Judeans or Jews. While the Davidic monarchy and Jerusalem as the city of David were crucial for Judean self-understanding, the Samaritans could point to other ancient traditions associating Shechem and other Samaritan sites with centralized and sacrificial worship of God. In effect, supporters of the Samaritan claim to be the true Israel were drawing from the same traditional sources as the Judeans, but with vastly different interpretations and consequences.

From the Judean or Jewish perspective, two things were clear: God had chosen Jerusalem to be the site of his Temple, and, despite their claims, the inhabitants of Samaria were a culturally and religiously mixed people, not the homogeneous monotheistic community they claimed. A Judean text, 2 Kings 17.24–44, provided crucial support for this position.

These differences in interpretation had practical consequences. When exiled Judeans or Jews returned from Babylon to rebuild their city, they brusquely rejected offers of help from the Samaritans, whose words of friendship they regarded with utmost suspicion. Nehemiah viewed with horror intermarriage between the son of a priestly family from Jerusalem and the daughter of a leading Samaritan family (Neh.

13.28–29). As the book of Nehemiah and subsequent history make abundantly clear, not everyone shared Nehemiah's distaste for such unions. Around the time of Alexander the Great's conquest of Syria-Palestine, another marriage between these leading families was forged. This time the governor of Samaria, who bore the apparently common name *Sanballat*, chose to ensure his son-in-law's happiness by constructing a temple, on the model of Jerusalem's, atop the sacred Mount Gerizim. Archaeological, historical, and epigraphical evidence confirms at least the general contours of this story. This temple had not been standing for long when the Samaritans, for reasons unknown to us, rebelled against Alexander the Great's representative in that area. Although Alexander's reprisals were swift and severe, the temple was apparently spared destruction.

Throughout the remainder of the fourth century, the third century, and most of the second century, the Samaritans maintained their central cult on Mount Gerizim. They escaped the wrath of Antiochus IV, although it is difficult to determine the exact nature of the compromise they reached with him. The effects of hellenization among the Samaritans are also difficult to gauge, but as in Jerusalem there must have been many who did not view all Greek influence as incompatible with the distinctive features of their beliefs and practices. In any case, the Samaritans were not the target of Hasmonean expansion until the time of John Hyrcanus. Early in his reign, in 128 BCE, he destroyed the temple on Mount Gerizim, ransacking Shechem in the process. Two decades later he returned to effect the complete destruction of that city and of the city of Samaria.

Given the centuries of hostility between Jews and Samaritans, it is surprising to learn of the basic compatibility between the beliefs and practices of these two feuding groups. The Samaritan Pentateuch and the form of the Torah accepted in Jerusalem had hundreds of minor differences between them. But apart from the former's insistence that God had chosen Shechem as the place for his worship, there are few theologically crucial contradictions in these competing texts. Even after the destruction of its temple, the Samaritan priesthood retained much of its power and prestige. To this day, a small group sustains the distinctive core of Samaritan teaching: we, not they, are the true heirs of Moses.

One other group needs mentioning: non-Jews, especially Greek and Roman non-Jews. Even a cursory discussion of the relationship between Jews and non-Jews in antiquity is a daunting task. We have discussed relations between the Jewish state and the Ptolemies, the Seleucids, neighboring Syro-Palestinian peoples, the Romans, the Spartans, and others. We have seen that some Jews eagerly embraced Hellenism and with equal alacrity abandoned all distinctive aspects of Judaism, while others felt that only by intractable opposition to even the slightest hint of insidious Hellenism could they preserve their Jewish way of life. Between these two extremes, individual Jews made their way through daily rounds of trade and commerce, heated discourse, friendly transactions, habit, and ritual, with most people forming their opinions about others on the basis of personal contact, hearsay, and preconceptions.

Yet even in antiquity, when the degree of literacy and the technology of mass communication were undeveloped in comparison with today, there were influential voices, whose words—preserved for us in written form—carried weight. Throughout the Hellenistic period the Jews were the subject or object of observation and analysis by interested writers. Sometimes these observations were firsthand; on other occasions, they were based on a less than clear understanding of sources that may themselves have been obscure. Were Greco-Roman writers favorably disposed or antagonistic toward Jews and Judaism as they understood them? The answer depends in part on chronology. By and large, observations dating from earlier in the Hellenistic period are more favorable than those composed later. Particularly influential in this regard were the Maccabean revolt and its aftermath. However we assess the factors that motivated Antiochus IV, it is difficult to deny that his Judean policy was important to him and that his lack of success there was a severe embarrassment. We must assume that he mobilized not only military armies, but masses of propagandists in his efforts to discredit, if not completely destroy, Judaism. His scribes would have been given free rein to incorporate every anti-Jewish remark they had ever read or heard and additionally to create new stories that would denigrate the distinctive beliefs and practices of the Jews. To this period may date the origins or more likely the popularity of tales concerning ritual homicide and ass worship among Jews. This contrasts with earlier praise of the Jews as a nation of philosophers who shunned the crudities of belief and expression that marred so many other peoples.

Sources of information, especially when not firsthand, were another determining factor in the tone of statements about Jews. From the very beginnings of Ptolemaic rule, even before Jews had been welcomed into Egypt and allowed for the most part to compete on an equal footing for the wealth that flowed into and out of Alexandria, there were all sorts of occasions for friction on social, cultural, economic, and religious levels, and such animosities were severe and frequent enough to find their way into writings that originated in Egypt. Because Egypt was held in high esteem by many in the Greco-Roman cultural elite, these views were widely circulated and provided a filter through which even eyewitnesses viewed Jews and Judaism. Nonetheless, we ought not to underestimate the talents, energy, and curiosity of individual writers in the Greco-Roman world. Even when they used secondhand or second-rate material, such writers frequently give evidence of an enviable ability to perceive and even to appreciate.

Given these factors, another question often arises: Were there many non-Jews who became Jews, and if so, did this result from an active proselytizing by Jews? The available evidence allows for more than one interpretation. Clearly most if not all Jewish literature from the Hellenistic period was aimed at Jewish audiences. On the other hand, even in such literature there is evidence that its authors were not unaware that non-Jews might also be reading it. Individual examples of conversion are not absent. More numerous are statements in praise of one or more of Judaism's distinctive features. Although such positive statements would not necessarily or even regularly lead to conversion on the part of author or audience, they could create a context for such action. Most likely those interested in Judaism would have seen it as an addition to rather than as a substitute for whatever religion, philosophy, or combination of both they were then practicing.

Population figures have also played a role in attempts to answer this question. According to some, the Jewish population increased so dramatically in the Hellenistic period that no explanation other than successful missionary activity can explain it. But in the view of others, the increases cited are within what could be expected given what is known of life span, mortality rates, and similar factors in the ancient world. In fact, there is as much uncertainty on just this point as there is in trying to arrive at reasonable estimates of population for a given area.

Still, throughout the Hellenistic period a number of writers commented on the Jews—some favorably, some unfavorably, and still others in a mixed vein, all influenced by a variety of cultural and social factors and by their source of information. A few of those who wrote or who read these words formed an attachment, formal or otherwise, to Judaism. Unfortunately, the hostile words and characterizations were more often preserved, and they influenced later generations to think and act antagonistically toward the descendants of the Hellenistic Jews we have been discussing.

Conclusion

We began this chapter by articulating the view that the Hellenistic world is a difficult but rewarding period to write about. Many of its primary characters, both historical and fictive, passionately embraced the positions they held and invested their actions with universal, if not cosmic, significance. The very future of the Jewish people, of the Jewish state, of the Jewish god seemed to be at stake. When viewing such events centuries later, it is perhaps wisest to be as dispassionate as possible, recognizing that subjectivity neither can nor should be entirely eliminated. Is it not best to remain neutral?

And yet we feel impelled to state our position. A creative and mutually beneficial synthesis between Judaism and Hellenism was not only desirable, but possible; not only possible, but attainable; not only attainable, but attained. Much of the Jewish-Greek literature we have examined, both that originally composed in Greek and that translated from a Semitic language into Greek, achieved a high level of cultural, artistic, and aesthetic synthesis. The same is true in the realm of architecture. This was not the old-time religion of previous eras, but neither was it a diluted form of the tradition.

With these thoughts in mind, we may look at one other biblical book from the Hellenistic period, Qoheleth, or Ecclesiastes. Its very name is an enigma, but it apparently refers to an individual who calls others together in solemn assembly. In the first chapter the author is identified as David's son, whom we understand to be Solomon. The entire linguistic and literary structure of the work makes it clear that it originated not in the tenth century BCE, in the days of the United Monarchy, but in the Hellenistic age. The author of Ecclesiastes did not intend to confuse anyone with this designation; rather, he was emphasizing the role of tradition in this most untraditional book. Through its chapters almost every mainstay of tradition seems to be rejected: the very value of life, not to mention ritual and social norms, is questioned, weighed, and found wanting. Everything is transitory, and death is seen as part of the problem and not the solution. This author shows an openness to all sorts of concepts, images, and experiences. At the same time, he evinces little desire to reconcile the contradictions that are part of his thinking and most likely of his life.

In many ways, "Ecclesiastes" speaks for the Hellenistic Jew, who seeks to synthesize the variety of stimuli to which he has been exposed. At the same time, his readers are alerted that all Jews must go on their own quest. He recognizes that the end results of these quests will not be equally satisfying when strictly viewed from the norms of tradition. But he and his audience lived in an age when life's largest questions had no single answer and tradition was only one of several authorities that could be appealed to. Go your own way, experience life fully, remember your roots, make God your master. This is the contradictory, but surprisingly appealing, advice Qoheleth imparts to his readers and to his fellow Jews with whom he shared the Hellenistic age.

Select Bibliography

Bickerman, Elias J. *The Jews in the Greek Age.* Cambridge, Mass.: Harvard University Press, 1962. A classic work by one of the acknowledged masters in Hellenistic studies.

Cohen, Shaye J. D. *From the Maccabees to the Mishnah.* Philadelphia: Westminster, 1987. An excellent account by a leading scholar in the field.

Davies, W. D., and Louis Finkelstein, eds. *The Cambridge History of Judaism.* Vol. 2, *The Hellenistic Age.* Cambridge: Cambridge University Press, 1984. This standard reference work contains impressive analyses and syntheses by a distinguished group of experts.

Feldman, Louis H. *Jew and Gentile in the Ancient World: Attitudes and Interactions from Alexander to Justinian.* Princeton, N.J.: Princeton University Press, 1993. An impressive array of evidence dealing with non-Jewish attitudes toward Jews and the question of Jewish proselytism.

Goldstein, Jonathan A. *1 Maccabees* and *2 Maccabees.* Anchor Bible, vols. 41 and 41A. Garden City, N.Y.: Doubleday, 1976, 1983. These commentaries are essential reading for anyone interested in these books.

Grabbe, Lester L. *Judaism from Cyrus to Hadrian: Sources, History, Synthesis.* Vol. 1. Minneapolis: Fortress, 1992. The author of this recent study is judicious and perceptive in his analysis of primary documents.

Gruen, Erich S. "Hellenism and Persecution: Antiochus IV and the Jews." In *Hellenistic History and Culture,* ed. Peter Green, 238–74. Berkeley: University of California Press, 1993. An excellent summary and discussion of various proposals to explain Antiochus IV's actions against the Jews.

Hengel, Martin. *Judaism and Hellenism: Studies in Their Encounter during the Early Hellenistic Period.* Trans. John Bowden. 2 vols. Philadelphia: Fortress, 1974. One of the most influential studies of the past three decades.

Kraft, Robert A., and George W. E. Nickelsburg, eds. *Early Judaism and Its Modern Interpreters.* Atlanta: Scholars Press, 1986. A collection in which experts discuss the status of research in their areas of specialization, with excellent bibliographies.

Modrzejewski, Joseph M. *The Jews of Egypt: From Rameses II to Emperor Hadrian.* Trans. Robert Cornman. Philadelphia: Jewish Publication Society, 1994. An elegant discussion of Ptolemaic (Hellenistic) Egypt as the zenith of Jewish life in that land.

Momigliano, Arnaldo. *Essays on Ancient and Modern Judaism.* Chicago: University of Chicago Press, 1994. This posthumous publication contains several characteristically erudite and creative articles on Hellenistic Judaism.

Nickelsburg, George W. E. *Jewish Literature between the Bible and the Mishnah.* Philadelphia: Fortress, 1981. In-depth analysis by an acknowledged expert.

Peters, F. E. *The Harvest of Hellenism: A History of the Near East from Alexander the Great to the Triumph of Christianity.* New York: Simon and Schuster, 1970. A dependable historical survey of the Hellenistic period.

Schiffman, Lawrence H. *Reclaiming the Dead Sea Scrolls: The History of Judaism, the Background of Christianity, and the Lost Library of Qumran.* Philadelphia: Jewish Publication Society, 1994. A fine overview of the topic that emphasizes the Jewish context(s) of the scrolls and their authors.

Tcherikover, Avigdor. *Hellenistic Civilization and the Jews.* Philadelphia: Jewish Publication Society, 1959. An influential study that is considered indispensable even by those who disagree with it.

Wills, Lawrence M. *The Jewish Novel in the Ancient World.* Ithaca, N.Y.: Cornell University Press, 1995. A sustained treatment of Daniel, Tobit, Esther, and Judith as Jewish novels.

CHAPTER TEN

Visions of Kingdoms

From Pompey to the First Jewish Revolt

AMY-JILL LEVINE

rom the time they suppressed the revolts led by Sertorius in Spain and Spartacus in Italy in the 70s BCE to their defeat of King Mithradates VI of Pontus in 66 BCE, Roman forces under the capable leadership of Pompey increasingly consolidated their power over Europe and extended their control eastward to the Euphrates River. By 65, Pompey began to focus on Syria, and in 64 the former Seleucid empire became an imperial province. Since the region included Judea and Galilee, the territory once ruled independently by the Hasmonean dynasty would soon come under Roman control, inaugurating a new chapter in the history of Israel.

The Arrival of Roman Rule

To some extent, the Romans' assertion of control over Judea was the direct outcome of the empire's expansionist policies, but strife within the Hasmonean family helped the Romans achieve their goals. At the end of the relatively peaceful reign of the widow of Alexander Janneus, Salome Alexandra (76–67), her son Aristobulus began to position himself for the throne. Aided not only by his father's allies but also by some Sadducees whom the queen had removed from royal influence, he soon occupied twenty-two fortresses in Judea. This action aroused the concerns of his mother's allies, the Pharisees, and of his older brother Hyrcanus II, the heir-apparent and high priest.

After the death of their mother, Alexandra—whose Hebrew name *Shalom-zion* ironically means "the peace of Zion"—the brothers and their supporters fought near Jericho. Routed by Aristobulus and his Sadducean allies, Hyrcanus II fled to the Akra, the old Jerusalem citadel, and there he finally surrendered. In their treaty, Aristobulus received the throne and probably the high priesthood, and Hyrcanus retained his possessions and his income.

This uneasy relationship did not remain untouched by outsiders. Antipater, the son of a rich Idumean who had been a governor under Alexander Janneus, attempted to return Hyrcanus to power and so increase his own. He convinced the passive Hyrcanus to make a treaty with Aretas III, the king of Nabatea (85–62). The pact guaranteed the Nabateans the return of lands taken by Janneus in return for support for Hyrcanus. Aretas defeated Aristobulus and attacked his troops, who had attempted to gain shelter in the Jerusalem Temple. At this point, both Aristobulus and Hyrcanus II sought help from Rome.

Pompey, then campaigning in Asia Minor, turned his attention to the entreaties, and the bribes, offered by the warring brothers. In 63, Pompey came to Damascus, where he met with Aristobulus and Hyrcanus II. The royal entourages were not alone: the people of Judea also sent representatives, who requested that neither brother receive the throne but instead that Pompey replace the Hasmonean royal dynasty with rule by priests.

Rather than make an immediate decision, Pompey deferred all requests until he could settle the Nabatean situation. Aristobulus, taking advantage of the delay, secured his forces in the fortress of Alexandrion. This military move did not please Pompey, who promptly invaded Judea. Aristobulus surrendered almost immediately, but his supporters, who took refuge in Jerusalem, did not. Pompey then attacked the city; there the ever-hopeful Hyrcanus opened the gates to Rome. After a three-month siege, the Temple held by Aristobulus's allies fell to the Romans, and Pompey impiously entered the holy of holies, the innermost chamber of the Temple. There he found not an idol but an empty room.

Thus the Hasmonean dynasty ended. All that remained of the Hasmonean lands were Judea, Galilee, Idumea, and Perea. Signifying their vassal status, these territories had to pay Roman tribute. Gone from Jewish governance were the coastal cities and all non-Jewish cities east of the Jordan. Pompey reestablished Hyrcanus as high priest, but without that office's formerly substantial political power. Rome had no interest in promoting the Hasmoneans; the family's nationalistic aspirations coupled with their dynastic difficulties had fully compromised their position. The only effective local power was held by that Idumean political opportunist Antipater, whose son would become known as Herod the Great.

Pompey returned to Rome, bringing with him several hundred Judean prisoners, including Aristobulus. These slaves, and their freed descendants, contributed to the formation of the large Roman Jewish community, among whom the nascent Christian church would later find both support and enmity. The presence of Jews in Rome, and indeed throughout the Diaspora at this time, in turn contributed to the Hellenistic ethos that permeated formative Judaism.

From the Negeb to Jerusalem and on to the borders of Galilee, Greek and Roman influences could be found. Although the vernacular remained Aramaic, and although most of the Dead Sea Scrolls are in Hebrew, many local people had some skill in Greek, increasingly the language not only of politics but also of trade. Greek inscriptions on coinage and monuments were common; two native authors, Justus of Ti-

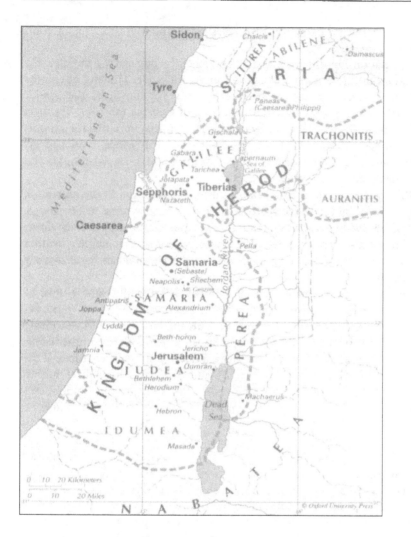

Palestine under the Herods

berias and Josephus, both wrote in Greek, as did one of the principal sources for
Josephus's history of this period, Herod's court historian Nicolaus of Damascus. And
Greek-speaking soldiers and merchants became common figures. From the cache of
manuscripts discovered at the Dead Sea come Greek fragments of the Hebrew Bible,
suggesting that as early as the Herodian period some local Jews used a Greek version
of the scriptures that they thought to be closer to the Hebrew than the Septuagint
version used by Diaspora communities.

As for Pompey, in 60 BCE he formed, along with Julius Caesar and Crassus, the
First Triumvirate. This political union was complemented by a personal one: Pompey's wife was Caesar's daughter, Julia. Following the death of Crassus and the several
military triumphs of Caesar, eventually the coalition broke apart. Caesar crossed the
Rubicon, civil war ensued, and Pompey, who had escaped to Egypt, was killed.

Pompey's actions in Jerusalem and his political fate in Rome and Egypt are described not only by the historians of the period but also by the Jewish poet who penned the Psalms of Solomon. This collection of eighteen poems, surviving in Greek and Syriac translations but probably originally written in Hebrew, testifies not only to the literary heritage of Israel but also to its hope for a savior and for the restoration of the land to the people of Israel. Psalms 18 and 19 speak of a new monarch in the image of King David, anticipating the increasing messianic fervor that would grip much of the first century CE.

From the Hasmoneans to the Herodians

After Pompey's death in 48 BCE, Hyrcanus II and Antipater allied themselves with Julius Caesar, Pompey's rival in the Second Civil War. For encouraging the Egyptian community to support Caesar's campaign there, as well as for sending Jewish forces to Egypt, Hyrcanus was granted the title "ethnarch of the Jews," which he added to his rank as high priest. The political title symbolized his role of representative of all Jews, both in Judea and throughout the Diaspora. Although Hyrcanus thus gained status, Antipater, appointed "procurator of Judea" by Caesar, retained the political power.

Antipater engineered for his son Phasael the governorship of Jerusalem, and over Galilee he placed his younger son Herod. There Herod would face local popular as well as juridical opposition. In 47 he suppressed the guerrilla war being waged in the north by the local leader Hezekiah (Ezechias). Having executed the rebel after a mock trial, Herod was summoned by Hyrcanus to appear before the Sanhedrin to defend his actions. Yet he by no means capitulated; he arrived in royal purple, accompanied by an armed guard. Hyrcanus disbanded the session, perhaps on Roman orders, and expelled Herod from Jerusalem.

Humiliated, Herod's immediate impulse was to attack Jerusalem, but he was restrained by his calmer brother and father, who feared a potential civil war. Herod's status was in fact enhanced following this confrontation with the Sanhedrin: Sextus Caesar, the Syrian governor, appointed him governor of Coele-Syria, and probably Samaria as well. In 43, Antipater was poisoned by his one-time ally Malichus, whom Herod then had assassinated.

Ever dependent on the fortunes of the empire, both Herod and Judea found themselves caught in the web of Roman internal politics. In 42, Octavian, Mark Antony, and Lapidus defeated the old republicans Brutus and Cassius at the battle of Philippi in Thrace. Antony assumed responsibility for the eastern provinces. Within a year, two Jewish delegations complained at separate times to Antony about their local governors, Phasael and Herod. But Herod, who had been a supporter of Cassius, not only managed to neutralize the charges by appealing directly to Antony; he and his brother consolidated their positions when the new ruler, acting against the wishes of a substantial delegation of Jewish leaders, named them tetrarchs of Judea.

Antony, Phasael, and Herod were at least momentarily content; the general population of Judea was not. To the contrary, already opposed to Herod, they were now responsible for contributing to Antony's lavish lifestyle. Taxes became more and more burdensome. The army too would demand increasing support.

In 40 BCE the Parthians again took up arms against Syria and Judea. Among their allies was Antigonus, the son of Pompey's captive Aristobulus II. Antigonus offered the Parthians support in exchange for their placing him on the throne in Judea. His campaign also received substantial backing from the Jewish population unhappy with Antipater's sons. By the end of the campaign, the Parthians had captured Phasael and Hyrcanus II. Herod, the most politically astute of the local rulers, fled. To prevent Hyrcanus II from serving again as high priest, the Parthians mutilated his ears (see Lev. 21.17); Phasael committed suicide. The Parthians then honored their treaty and installed Antigonus as king in Judea.

While the Parthians were hoisting the Hasmonean heir into power in Jerusalem, the Roman senate, with the support of Antony and Octavian, appointed Herod king of Judea. Herod then began his own military campaign. In 39 he took Galilee, Samaria, and Idumea; in 38 he received substantial help from the Roman general Ventidius, who defeated the Parthians and thereby cut off Antigonus's military support. With the aid of Ventidius's successor, Sosius, Herod gained the rest of the kingdom by the spring of 37. Antigonus was captured, taken to Antioch, and beheaded on Antony's orders. Herod married Mariamme, the granddaughter of Hyrcanus II and the sister of Aristobulus III. He settled down to a reign of grandeur, economic and architectural expansion, and familial intrigue that lasted more than three decades (37–4 BCE).

The Reign of Herod

Through a combination of political cunning, good luck, and an occasional murder, King Herod retained his Roman support, his throne, and his life. Presenting a Hellenistic, assimilated image to the empire while emphasizing a more Jewish perspective to his local constituency, Herod survived and prospered during the battle between Octavian and Antony. Domestically, he had to withstand unrest caused by overtaxation, famine, and religious zeal, as well as continuing threats from the surviving Hasmoneans. He also had to control a mixed and not always friendly population consisting not only of Jews and Greeks but also of Samaritans, Syrians, and Arabs. It was a formidable challenge.

The first major crisis began in 36 when Herod's patron, Antony, still living lavishly as the ruler of the eastern part of the empire, married his equally lavish lover, Queen Cleopatra VII of Egypt. This marriage was deplored by most of Italy, and especially by Octavian, for it suggested not only a lack of loyalty to Rome and its traditions, but also a repudiation of Antony's wife Octavia, Octavian's sister. Herod himself was not particularly well liked by the Egyptian queen, who wanted his lands. Cleopatra obtained Judea's coastal cities as well as Jericho during Herod's early time in office, but she did permit him to lease these territories.

The animosity between Rome and Egypt, and between the erstwhile brothers-in-law, escalated until 31, when Octavian defeated Antony at the battle of Actium. Antony and Cleopatra committed suicide, and Egypt fell directly into Roman hands. Octavian lost an in-law, but he gained the grain of Egypt for his empire, and a new title (Augustus—the "exalted one") for himself. During his rule, the Roman Empire extended its borders and brought peace to its territories (the *Pax Romana*).

Among Octavian's earliest acts was to receive Herod. Although previously Antony's ally, Herod courageously admitted his past errors and pledged his loyalty to the new emperor. Following his practice of leaving client kings in place, and impressed by Herod's political acumen, Octavian accepted his support and granted him not only the lands he had leased from Cleopatra but also her holdings in Samaria and east of the Jordan.

Herod rebuilt Samaria, which he renamed Sebaste (from the Greek word for Augustus), and he erected there a temple to the emperor. He also built a port city, which he named Caesarea in the emperor's honor. Other projects included creating an elaborate winter palace in Jericho, reinforcing the former Hasmonean complex on Masada, and opening several areas for agricultural cultivation. To fund such enterprises as well as his extensive building in Jerusalem, Herod adapted the Hasmonean taxation system. Much of the population, particularly in Galilee, was overburdened with the taxes due to Herod and to Rome as well as the smaller contributions made to the Temple, although archaeological investigation has yielded evidence of ornate homes in the suburbs of Jerusalem. Nevertheless, Herod may have improved parts of the economy with his various projects. The construction provided substantial employment opportunities, and the increase in agricultural production offset some of the exactions due in taxes.

Within Jewish territory, Herod showed considerable sensitivity to his population's religious concerns. His coinage did not depict human images, he refrained from placing statues in public buildings, and he began the remodeling of the Second Temple, although in Hellenistic style. Not completed until 64 CE, during the reign of Herod's great-grandson Agrippa II, this project employed thousands, from artisans to priests. Even within Jerusalem, however, Herod's primary allegiance was to Rome; thus he affixed a golden eagle to the gate of the Temple. When the scribes Judas and Matthias, hearing a rumor that the terminally ill Herod was dying, attempted to remove it, the king had them and their associates tortured to death.

Herod the Great not only engaged in extensive Temple renovations, he also controlled the high priesthood. By appointing members of the priestly families of Babylonia and Alexandria, he sought to bolster his support from the Diaspora population. Unfortunately, his appointments did little to enhance the reputation of the office or peace within his own household.

The high priesthood would remain a point of tension. Herod first appointed Ananel, from a Babylonian priestly household. The decision did not please Mariamme's mother, Alexandra, who attempted to have her son Aristobulus III succeed to the office; aided by Cleopatra she convinced Herod to fulfill her wishes. But Aristobulus gained great popularity with the people, so in 35 Herod arranged to have him drowned. A pattern was set: charging them with treason (perhaps rightly), Herod executed his beloved Mariamme in 29 and Alexandra in 28. By the end of his reign, he had also executed numerous nobles who either in fact or in his imagination challenged his status, his sons by Mariamme, Alexander and Aristobulus, and his son Antipater by his first wife, Doris. Such activities prompted Augustus's quip that "I would rather be Herod's pig [hys] than his son [huios]." Although the historicity of the "slaughter of the innocents" in Matthew 2 is questionable in the absence of other testimony—the story probably arose out of the evangelist's strong interest in connecting Jesus to Moses (see Exod. 1–2 on the deaths of the Hebrew children) and reflects the folkloric motif of endangered heroes—doing such a thing would not have been out of character for Herod.

Beset by Nabatean conflicts and domestic disputes, Herod's final years granted him no peace. According to Josephus, his death brought no quietude either. Aware he was dying, Herod arranged to have many political prisoners executed at the time of his death, so that there would be general mourning.

Temple, Synagogues, and Sanhedrin

The Temple had been the central concern of the Maccabees and a focus of continuing Hasmonean politics, and it was central to Herod the Great's domestic politics. Built by Solomon, destroyed by Nebuchadrezzar, rebuilt during the Persian period, and remodeled by Herod, the Temple served mythologically as the link between heaven and earth, ritually as the locus of sacrifice and domain of the priesthood, economically as the national bank, and politically as the focus of many who sought the rule of heaven as opposed to the rule of Rome. The center of worship for all Jews in the formative period—either because they participated in it or because they defined their movement as an alternative to it—the Temple would remain, long after its destruction in 70 CE, a major focus of Judaism's religious imagination.

The Temple's centrality for Judaism, both locally and throughout the Diaspora, is indicated in various ways. One was Jewish fidelity to paying a Temple tax of a half-shekel annually, a practice based on Exodus 30.11–16 and mentioned in Matthew 17.24. Another manifestation of the Temple's importance were the annual pilgrimages during the festivals of Booths (Sukkot), Passover (Pesach), and Weeks (Shavuot), which brought Jews from throughout the empire to the capital (see Acts 2.5–11). Still other signs of the Jews' attachment to the Temple are the extensive renovations undertaken by Herod and his successors; the fight for control of the Temple and Temple Mount during the First Revolt; the extensive discussion of the Temple and its sacrifices within the documents of early Christianity and rabbinic Judaism; the depiction of the Temple menorah on the Arch of Titus; the image of the Temple on the coins minted by Bar Kokhba in the Second Revolt, more than sixty years after the Temple's destruction; and the ongoing references to the Temple in Jewish liturgy. Yet permutations of this centrality emphasize as well the diversity of practice and belief among the people called "Jews."

Within the Temple, daily sacrifices were offered by the priests, both on their own behalf and for the Jewish community. The priests themselves, who inherited their position, were divided into twenty-four courses; each course served for a set period. Aiding the priests in the Temple were members of a second hereditary group, the Levites.

Priests and Levites were not the only figures in the Temple. Pilgrims could purchase animals for sacrifice from local sellers, and those wishing to pay the Temple tax or make monetary offerings could exchange their own currency for the Tyrian shekels that alone were accepted by the institution—hence the employment that the Temple offered to money changers.

The Temple itself consisted of areas of increasing holiness. Outermost was the court of the Gentiles, which anyone could enter. Proceeding farther in, one reached the court of the (Jewish) women, the court of the (Jewish) men, and finally the holy of holies—entered only by the high priest on the Day of Atonement. Participation in the Temple was open to everyone: women could make offerings, as Jesus' account of the widow's offering (Mark 12.42–43) and Josephus's narrative of Queen Helena of Adiabene, the proselyte, clearly indicate.

For Jewish groups, the Temple had diverse meanings. Some Sadducees, who were priests, saw it as their livelihood; when the Temple was destroyed in 70 CE, the priestly Sadducees for all practical purposes lost their public role and disappeared. For the Pharisees, it provided the model of holiness which they then extended to the home; after 70, members of this group clung to the hope for the Temple's reconstruction while at the same time claiming that deeds of loving kindness took the place of sacrifice. For the authors of one of the Dead Sea Scrolls, the "Temple Scroll," a new Temple would replace the corrupt present one. Early Christians presented Jesus as disrupting the Temple's daily activities, and although Jesus' Jewish followers remained involved with Temple worship, Christian theology eventually replaced Temple sacrifice with the sacrifice of Jesus, a shift articulated in the letter to the Hebrews. Thus, with the exception of the Sadducean priests, the various Jewish groups of the final centuries BCE and the first centuries CE were prepared to continue their worship apart from the Temple.

Because the Temple was a place of sacrifice, it was also a place of sanctification. Worshipers in the Jerusalem Temple, as in most temples of Greco-Roman antiquity, had to be in a state of ritual purity before entering the sacred precincts. The Temple courts were therefore inappropriate places for men who had just had an emission of semen, or for women who were menstruating. Such traditions—many of the regulations are outlined in Leviticus and Numbers—concern the sanctity of the site, not the sinfulness of the person. To menstruate was not sinful, and sexual intercourse was mandated by God's command to "be fruitful and multiply." Many Temple-based purity regulations were extended to their homes by several communities of Jews, and each group determined both which rules to emphasize and how to interpret them. For example, *havurah* (fellowship) groups insisted on eating only food that was scrupulously tithed and prepared. For the majority of Jews during the early Roman period, however, purity concerns such as restrictions on menstruants or ejaculants were not emphasized; apart from the Temple, there was little need to maintain a state of ritual purity.

In the absence of the Temple, the synagogue—the word itself is a Greek term that means "bring together"—became the most recognizable public Jewish institution. The synagogue and the Temple were not ultimately comparable institutions. The Temple was a place of sacrifice and pilgrimage; synagogues were not. Officially there was one Temple—although others did exist, prior to the time of Pompey, in Elephantine and Leontopolis in Egypt and, for the Samaritans, on Mount Gerizim—and it was controlled by priests. There were many synagogues, but they were apparently not, especially before 70 CE, dominated by the Pharisees, despite suggestions by the Gospels. The book of Acts (6.9) mentions synagogues of freed slaves, of Cyrenians, Alexandrians, and Cilicians. Synagogue activity included the reading and interpretation of scripture, and the institution also served as a meeting place and a house of study. From the first century CE comes this inscription from Jerusalem: "Theodotus, son of Vettenus, priest and leader of the synagogue, built the synagogue for the reading of the law and the teaching of the commandments, and the guest house and the rooms and the water supplies as an inn for those who come from abroad, which [synagogue] his fathers had founded and the elders, and Simonides." Comparable to the synagogue is the *proseuche*, or place of prayer; the term appears in reference to Jewish gathering places in the Diaspora as well as in Galilee, and Acts 16.11–15 refers to a proseuche in Philippi, the Thracian city where Paul finds several women gathered and where Paul makes his first convert on European soil, Lydia, a dealer in purple cloth.

Judea's principal judicial body, the Sanhedrin, took its name and probably its form from the Greek institution known as the *Synedrion*, the "sitting together" or "assembly." Rabbinic writings (especially Tractate Sanhedrin in the Mishnah) describe the seventy-one-member Great Sanhedrin that met in the Temple; this institution was headed by the high priest. The Gospels, which with some major discrepancies describe a trial of Jesus before the Sanhedrin, suggest that its membership included Sadducees, Pharisees, and priests. According to Josephus, the Sanhedrin met occasionally, whenever the high priest convened it for the major task of providing him guidance. Apparently it was rendered powerless under Herod, who remembered how it had once humiliated him, for there are no records of any action undertaken by it during his kingship. The Sanhedrin regained some authority under direct Roman rule. By that time its concerns included implementing religious law on such issues as agriculture and trade as well as maintaining peace with local Roman authorities.

From Herodian Tetrarchs to Roman Governors

Given Herod's proclivity for removing both real and perceived threats to his power, succession upon his death in 4 BCE was less complicated than it might have otherwise been. The territory was divided among the king's surviving sons: Archelaus, the heir according to Herod's final wish, was appointed by Rome as ethnarch of Judea, Samaria, and Idumea; Antipas became tetrarch of Galilee and Perea; and Philip was named the tetrarch of Auranitis, Trachonitis, and probably Iturea. Only Philip would complete his rule.

The transition began inauspiciously. Upon Herod's death, the people of Jerusalem rebelled in reaction to the executions of the scribes Judas and Matthias. Archelaus sent in troops, and a massacre of the local population ensued. When he left for Rome with his brothers to confirm the distribution of territory, another revolt erupted in Judea. This time Varus, the Roman governor of Syria, quelled the conflict and left a legion in Jerusalem as insurance against further outbreaks. Yet the legion's commander, Sabinus, oppressed the local population, and sporadic outbreaks continued. Concurrently, in Galilee and Perea new rebellions brewed. In response, Varus returned, crushed the resistance, and crucified over two thousand rebels.

This presence of Roman troops in Judea facilitated Archelaus's removal from office in 6 CE. Hearing substantial complaints by a delegation from Judea and Samaria, and perhaps concerned as well with Archelaus's internal policies with respect to the trade route between Syria and Egypt, Augustus banished Herod's first heir to Gaul. Judea and Samaria were incorporated into the province of Syria and consequently fell under the authority of a succession of Roman governors.

In the absence of a local king, Rome permitted the Jewish population substantial political autonomy; the arrival of the Roman governor coincided with the reestablishment of the Sanhedrin with the high priest as its leader. Among the twenty-eight priests who held the office between Hyrcanus II and the destruction of the Temple, the most famous is also the one with the longest tenure, Joseph Caiaphas, who served from 18 to 36 CE. To avoid rebellion under this local authority, Rome reserved the right to name the high priest and to control the priestly vestments needed for the celebration of major holidays.

Unlike the Herodian rulers, the governors had no sympathy for the population's economic situation or religious sensibilities. Their policies of raising taxes, bringing Roman standards into Jerusalem, raiding the Temple treasury, and other such provocations would eventually lead to a full rebellion against Rome. Problems began almost immediately with Rome's demand for a census. Inaugurated by Augustus for all provinces, this practice enabled the empire to determine taxation rates for land, material goods, and individuals. Josephus mentions the census under P. Sulpicius Quirinius, which he dates to the thirty-seventh year after the battle of Actium, or 6/7 CE. Luke's story of the birth of Jesus records: "In those days a decree went out from Caesar Augustus that all the world should be registered. This was the first registration and was taken while Quirinius was governor of Syria" (Luke 2.1–2). By this device, Luke explains why Joseph, together with his very pregnant wife, Mary, made the journey from Galilee to Bethlehem; thereby, Jesus is born in Bethlehem and the prophecy from Micah 5.2 can be fulfilled. (The Gospel of Matthew depicts Mary and Joseph as already living in Bethlehem; they relocate to Nazareth after the death of Herod the Great for fear of persecution by Herod Archelaus.)

The dates provided by Josephus and Luke are not easily reconciled. Luke 1.5 depicts the census as occurring during the reign of Herod the Great, who died in 4 BCE. Possibly Luke's "first" is incorrect, and there was an earlier census under Herod the Great, prior to the incorporation of his territory into the provincial system, but direct attestation is lacking. For Luke the census, historical or not, serves as a dramatic apologetic device. Joseph and Mary, and therefore Jesus, are seen as adhering to the demands of the Roman government: travel anywhere when one is about to give birth, let alone by donkey over the rough terrain between Galilee and Bethlehem, surely proves dedication to duty. This loyalty is contrasted with another event, and another Galilean, mentioned by both Luke and Josephus in conjunction with the census, and this other reference illustrates the problems created by the Roman policy.

Acts 5.37, in a speech attributed to Gamaliel I, states that "Judas the Galilean rose up at the time of the census and got people to follow him; he also perished, and all those who followed him were scattered." According to Josephus, Judas, originally from Gamala in Galilee, protested against the census held by Quirinius. In this he was joined by a Pharisee named Zadok. Whether these leaders called for open revolt or simply urged noncooperation is unclear, but the premise for the protest is certain. Judas and his followers believed that the local population should not be forced to relinquish the freedom they had struggled to attain during Maccabean times, that there is "no king but God," and that obeying Augustus would be a violation of the First Commandment. Probably killed for his views, Judas was survived by his equally zealous sons, James and Simon, who were to be executed during the reign of Tiberius for revolutionary activities, and Menahem, a leader of the revolt in Jerusalem just before the war of 66–70. The family line, and its legacy of zeal, continued until the fall of Masada.

The Roman governor at the time (6–9 CE), Coponius, faced additional problems. According to Josephus, during this time a group of Samaritans entered the Temple during the Passover celebration and profaned its sanctity by scattering human bones. This is one of many episodes that testifies to the enmity between Samaritans and Jews; the phrase "good Samaritan," based on the parable of Jesus in Luke 10.30–37, would have seemed to most Jews an oxymoron.

Meanwhile, in Galilee, Antipas was continuing the building practices of his father, Herod the Great, by creating the city of Tiberias in honor of Augustus's successor, Tiberius. Like his father, Antipas also faced problems within his own household: rejecting his wife, the daughter of the Nabatean king Aretas IV, the tetrarch married Herodias, the sister of Agrippa I. This did not please the Nabateans, who successfully battled Antipas's troops. Nor, according to the Gospels, did it please John the Baptist, a Jewish prophet who condemned the remarriage as a violation of biblical law, for Herodias had been the wife of Antipas's half brother Herod. (She was not, contrary to Mark 6.17, the wife of Philip; he was married instead to Herodias's daughter, Salome.)

As both popular leader and political prophet, John presented a danger to Antipas. According to the authors of the Gospels, he was beheaded at the instigation of Herodias and her daughter. Josephus confirms the execution, but not the Gospel story of the daughter's dance, the silver platter, or the condemnation of the marriage. According to Josephus, John the Baptist was killed because his enormous popular support threatened Herod's rule. He states that John was a pious man who immersed Jews "for the purification of the body when the soul had previously been cleansed by righteous conduct. Others joined crowds about him because they were aroused to the highest degree by his sermons. . . . His eloquence had so great an effect on the people that it might lead to some form of sedition, for it looked as if they would be guided by John in everything that they did" (*Antiquities* 18.5.2).

Following the death of Tiberius in 37 CE and in light of the subsequent friendship of Herod Agrippa with Gaius Caligula, Antipas fell out of favor with Rome. In 39, the emperor banished him to Gaul, or possibly Spain, where he was accompanied by Herodias.

Philip, the third brother, inherited a region populated almost entirely by non-Jews. Thus the particular problems caused by conflicting cultural and religious norms that brought unrest to the rules of Archelaus and Antipas did not affect him. Continuing the family's interest in reconstruction, Philip rebuilt the city of Panias near the head of the Jordan River and renamed it Caesarea Philippi; here, according to the Gospels, Peter confessed Jesus to be the Messiah (Mark 8; Matt. 16). Upon Philip's death, his territory was annexed to Syria.

The extent to which various members of the population resisted Roman occupation and colonialism is unclear. The overarching power of the empire, while antithetical to the sensibilities of Jews like Judas the Galilean, was to some extent buffered by the continuing role of the Herodian household, now represented in Rome by Herod's grandson Agrippa I (called Herod Agrippa in Acts 12), and his son, Agrippa II. The relatively homogeneous population, as well as the lack of strong, consistent policies either from the procurator's palace at Caesarea or from the imperial throne itself, also limited Roman oppressiveness. Between the death of Augustus and the First Jewish Revolt of 66 CE, Rome was ruled by Tiberius (14–37), Gaius Caligula (37–41), Claudius (41–54), and Nero (54–68). It is not known how often Jews came in direct contact with representatives of Rome; the experiences of the metropolitan population of Caesarea would have been different from that of residents of a village like Nazareth. Also unknown is the extent to which various Roman social services, such as fighting bandits, building roads, and constructing aqueducts, might have been appreciated. But for many the financial drain of Roman exactions substantially outweighed the benefits of these services.

When the situation did become intolerable, either the governor would be recalled by the emperor or the emperor himself would be involuntarily recalled to his ancestors. The ineptitude, if not the sheer malevolence, of the governors is epitomized by their most famous representative, Pontius Pilate (26–36 CE), who deliberately provoked the local population by bringing Roman shields, probably decorated with images of the emperor, into Jerusalem. The population protested the action by baring their throats to the soldiers; rather than risk a bloodbath, Pilate sent the standards back to Caesarea. But his problems with the locals continued. Attempting to raid the Temple treasury for funds to construct an aqueduct in Jerusalem, Pilate provoked another protest that ended when he sent his soldiers into the unarmed crowd, massacring them.

Pilate's difficulties, and those of other Roman officials, were not only with Jewish groups. In 36, Pilate learned of a Samaritan prophet who promised his people that he would show them the vessels of the wilderness tabernacle; local tradition taught that the sacred implements were buried somewhere on Mount Gerizim, where the Samaritan temple had stood. Pilate sent his troops to intercept the crowd, even though the people involved may not have had revolutionary goals. When the news of the Roman attack reached Vitellius, Pilate's superior in Syria, the governor was finally, after ten years of hatred by and for the local population, recalled. His replacements, Marcellus (36–37) and Marullus (37–41), did little to appease the Jewish population but also little to antagonize them.

During Roman rule, heavy taxation and the economic stratification of rich and poor intensified. Under the authority of the procurators, the Sanhedrin was responsible for collecting taxes on agricultural produce, which had been paid since 63 BCE, and the poll tax, which began in 6 CE after the annexation of Judea and Samaria. This latter tax is probably referred to in the question put to Jesus: Is it lawful to pay taxes to Caesar? Jesus' answer, "Give to the emperor the things that are the emperor's, and to God the things that are God's" (Mark 12.17), is, perhaps characteristically, ambiguous: either pay the tax, the traditional interpretation, or do precisely the opposite, if one assumes that all things belong to God.

The contradictory interpretations of Jesus' answer reveal the contradictory ways that taxation was viewed by the local populations. For the rich and for the tax collector, it was, respectively, tolerable and possibly lucrative, if socially unacceptable; for the poor, it was, well, taxing. Tolls, a second form of tribute, were levied on imports and exports, and for the use of roads, ports, and markets. To collect funds, the Romans contracted with wealthy locals, who in turn subcontracted to tax collectors. Condemned by the population as agents of an oppressive government, liable to corruption, and badly paid as well, the tax collector—the "publican" of the King James Version—was generally despised. Compounding his problems was the system itself: given the siphoning of funds by various Roman officials, more taxes had to be collected than what imperial records mandated, simply to meet demands.

Social Movements

As taxation increasingly oppressed ordinary people, and as famine and drought reduced substantial portions of the population to poverty, the wealthy—including many members of the high priestly families—were filling their own coffers. Meanwhile farmers, forced to sell their land at reduced prices, found themselves reduced to tenant laborers often working for absentee landlords. The landlords themselves had substantial representation among the high priestly families. Worse was the situation of the day laborer, and worse still that of individuals forced to sell themselves or their relations into slavery in order to pay their debts. Unemployment in some areas ran high, and beggars were common sights.

Between laborers and landowners came a social stratum of artisans and traders. Neither impoverished nor financially secure, this middle stratum—members of the retainer class, scribes, minor priests, small farmers, and merchants—may well have given the impetus to social and religious reform. It was perhaps from this group that the Pharisees and the followers of Jesus both gained adherents, and from this group as well may have come the Zealots of the revolt against Rome in 66–70 CE.

Other movements and leaders gained members and sympathizers from various social and economic strata. The Qumran community, John the Baptist, and several charismatic leaders in one way or another addressed the spiritual and material needs of the population, by variously promising revolt against Rome, the deity's direct intervention in human affairs, or the assurance of life after death. How individual Judeans and Galileans reacted depended on such issues as personal concerns, economic circumstances, familial responsibilities, and their view of Rome. There was no monolithic theological system and no single reaction to occupation.

Josephus describes four prominent philosophic schools, or *haireseis*, in Judea in the early decades of the first century CE. In the context of discussing the reign of Jonathan the high priest (ca. 145 BCE), he records the origins of the first three:

> Now at this time there were three *haireseis* among the Jews, which held different opinions concerning human affairs; the first being that of the Pharisees, the second that of the Sadducees, and the third that of the Essenes. As for the Pharisees, they say that certain events are the work of fate, but not all; as to other events it depends upon ourselves whether they shall take place or not. The sect of Essenes, however, declares that Fate is the mistress of all things, and that nothing befalls people unless in accordance with her decree. But the Sadducees do away with Fate, holding that there is no such thing and that human actions are not achieved in accordance with her decree, but that all things lie within our own power. (*Antiquities* 13.5.9)

Josephus repeats these descriptions in the context of the Herodian monarchy a century and a half later. For this cosmopolitan Jew living in Rome, the Judean movements are philosophic schools divided principally over the perennial question of fate and free will. Josephus goes on to compare the Pharisees with the Stoics, the Essenes with the Pythagoreans, and, implicitly, the Sadducees with the Epicureans. Unfortunately absent from his descriptions are such concerns of modern historians as detailed reports of lifestyle, views of the Torah, and attitudes toward the Temple.

The Sadducees and Pharisees are also mentioned by the Jewish philosopher Philo of Alexandria, by early Christian texts, and by the later rabbinic documents. The Essenes appear in the writings of the Roman naturalist Pliny, and many scholars associate one group of Essenes with the people responsible for the various scrolls located near the Dead Sea settlement of Qumran. While the Greek texts (Josephus, the Gospels, Philo) emphasize philosophic and theological differences, the Hebrew and Aramaic documents (the Qumran scrolls, the rabbinic documents) focus on issues of practice. Only through comparison of all the data can we reconstruct the practices and beliefs of these groups and their histories.

Even more amorphous were what Josephus labels a "fourth philosophy," the Zealots. To these movements can be added various revitalization and reformist groups, including the followers of John the Baptist, the growing movement known for its claim that Jesus of Nazareth was the Messiah, the diverse congregations of Diaspora Judaism, and various "proselytes" and "sympathizers."

Sadducees

Although the Temple was the most important and influential institution of the second commonwealth, contemporary comments on its priests and the party most closely connected with them, the Sadducees, are—not unexpectedly—scant. The Sadducees lost power with the onset of the revolt against Rome. All sources describing their beliefs and practices both postdate their fall and are composed by individuals who define themselves in opposition to Sadducaic practice: Josephus, the early Christians, and the rabbis.

The origin of their name is not clear. Perhaps it derived from Zadok, the high priest appointed by King David. Yet the Sadducees are also associated with the Boethusians, a high-priestly family from Alexandria in Egypt, who gained ascendancy under Herod the Great, perhaps because Herod needed them as a counter to the high-priestly claims of the Hasmonean household.

The various sources provide a composite view of the Sadducees: they were predominantly wealthy and aristocratic; their social interests were therefore not surprisingly in preserving the status quo. Such a conservative agenda also extended to their religious preferences. They apparently did not accept such theological innovations as resurrection or angels (see Acts 23.8), and they believed strongly in free will. While many were priests, not all were.

As Temple officials, the Sadducees in the first century CE also dominated the Sanhedrin. The high priest was its president, and its senior leaders were members of the Sadducaic party. Pharisees also served in the Sanhedrin, but not infrequently the two groups disagreed.

Pharisees

Although the origins of the Pharisees are not clear, their name apparently comes from a Hebrew root that means "to separate." The Pharisees may thus have separated themselves from other Jews in order to practice particular forms of personal piety, or they may have separated themselves from the Gentiles (see 1 Macc. 1.11). According to Josephus, they were immersed in Hasmonean politics, first as enemies of Janneus and later as friends of his wife, Salome Alexandra. The queen promoted the Pharisees, but her action was later reversed by her son Aristobulus. The group found itself again empowered under Herod, in part because the Pharisee Pollio advised the people to accept his rule.

Under Herod the Great, the Pharisees numbered about six thousand (so Josephus). Herod apparently provided them some support, and they in turn appear to have shifted from their strongly political orientation during the reign of Alexander Janneus to a greater emphasis on inward religiosity. Their political activities did not cease, however. At the time of the First Revolt against Rome, the Pharisee Simon ben Gamaliel, along with several Pharisaic colleagues, strongly supported the rebels.

Josephus also remarks upon the Pharisees' influence with the women of the Herodian court and among the Jewish population at large. Because these comments appear in the *Antiquities*, written in the last decade of the first century CE, but are not recorded in his *Jewish War*, written at least a decade earlier, it is plausible that Josephus rewrote history to the advantage of the movement that survived the revolt. Nevertheless, the Pharisees were influential even before 70, as Christian texts also indicate. Paul, writing before the First Revolt, proclaims himself to have been a Pharisee (Phil. 3.5–6), and Acts 22.3, written after, adds that Paul was educated "at the feet of Gamaliel . . . strictly according to our ancestral law" (see also Acts 5.34–39 on Gamaliel's view that the followers of Jesus should be tolerated). Regardless of the accuracy of the statements in Acts, their testimony to the importance of the Pharisees remains. For all the Gospels, and especially for Matthew, the Pharisees represent the standard of piety even as they present the greatest challenge to the nascent church.

From the writings of Josephus, early Christian texts, and rabbinic sources, the Pharisees' beliefs can be tentatively reconstructed. This confederation of like-minded individuals valued both the Torah and their own elaboration of its contents to fit the new questions and circumstances of the changing world. Josephus notes that they "handed down to the people certain regulations from the ancestral succession and not recorded in the laws of Moses" (*Antiquities* 13.10.6). This tradition of interpretation, which came to be known as the "oral law," thus took its place alongside the "written law," the Torah. The Pharisees extended the holiness of the Temple and its functionaries to domestic life: for them the home became a focal point for religious practice, and the household table matched the Temple altar in sanctity. Doctrinally expanding beyond scripture, the Pharisees also promoted such non-Pentateuchal concepts as the resurrection of the dead, and they coupled belief in free will with an acknowledgment of divine omnipotence.

To accomplish their extension of Torah and practice, the Pharisees engaged in ritualized eating practices, insisted that their food be tithed according to scriptural mandate, and sought to live their daily lives in conformity to the will of heaven. They apparently fasted, a practice shared by many in early Judaism (see Mark 2.18). Some may have practiced private prayer. Yet how specific laws and beliefs were to be interpreted and implemented differed among Pharisaic groups. Rabbinic texts suggest that by the mid-first century CE, divisions arose within the movement itself, the most famous being the "house of Hillel" and the "house of Shammai." Hillel and Shammai themselves were teachers during the end of the first century BCE and the beginning of the first century CE. Their debates concerned such matters as Sabbath observance, table fellowship, and purity regulations. Shammai is best known today for his impatience. Hillel—whose spiritual heirs, the rabbis, are responsible for telling the stories about him and about his rival—is remembered as having told the Gentile who asked to be taught the Torah while standing on one foot, "What is hateful to you, do not do to others. This is the whole Torah; the rest is commentary. Go and learn!" Despite the several rabbinic references to these figures and their schools, it is extremely difficult to peel away the layers of legend to find the real Hillel or Shammai, much as it is difficult to find the "historical Jesus" beneath the Gospel texts.

The Essenes and the Dead Sea Scrolls

The origins of the word *Essene* are unknown; it may been connected to the Hebrew *Hasidim,* or "holy ones," or it may have some relation to the Greek term for "healers." Josephus makes the earliest known reference to the group, describing a movement in existence at least by the mid-second century BCE. Like Philo, Josephus also indicates that the number of Essenes was comparably small, perhaps only four thousand, and that members lived throughout Judea.

But Philo and Josephus's Gentile contemporaries, Pliny the Elder and Dio Chrysostom, state that the Essenes lived on the shore of the Dead Sea. From this evidence comes impetus for the conclusion, accepted by the majority of scholars today, that the group responsible for the copying and preservation of the scrolls discovered in the caves near the Dead Sea settlement of Qumran were Essenes. Other scholars, however, have suggested that the composers and copiers of the scrolls were instead a group of Sadducees disenchanted with, if not disfranchised from, the Temple. A third view holds that the scrolls were composed and copied elsewhere and brought to Qumran for safekeeping.

Were the Essenes exclusively male and celibate? The Qumran scroll 1QS suggests that members were celibate men. (Scrolls are identified with a number representing the cave in which the document was found, with "Q" for Qumran, and a final element identifying either the contents of the document or the number of the manuscript. In this case, the "S" stands for *Serek ha-yahad,* Hebrew for "rule of the community.") But the Essenes known from external sources as well as the group represented by another scroll associated with but not found at Qumran, the Cairo-Damascus Document (abbreviated "CD," and sometimes called the "Zadokite fragment"), included married members and children. Apparently, some were celibate and some were not.

Reconstruction of the Qumran community on the basis of archaeological investigation and from the Dead Sea Scrolls themselves suggests that the community began as early as the time of the Maccabean revolt. Excavations indicate a settlement from approximately 140 BCE that was substantially expanded about 100, abandoned about 31 BCE because of an earthquake, and repopulated at the turn of the era.

The scrolls locate the origins of the community with a figure known only as the "Teacher of Righteousness" or "Righteous Teacher." Probably a contender for the high priesthood but deposed by the "Wicked Priest" (the Hasmonean kings Jonathan and Simon are plausible candidates), the Teacher led his followers out of Jerusalem and eventually to the shores of the Dead Sea. Accepting the centrality of the Temple but rejecting its present practices and leaders, the scrolls unique to Qumran propose an alternative to Sadducaic control, as well as to the Pharisaic response.

From the fourteen caves around Qumran come numerous manuscripts in Hebrew, Aramaic, and even Greek. These include copies of books from the Hebrew scriptures (with the possible exception of Esther) and from the Old Testament Apocrypha (such as Tobit; the Wisdom of Jesus ben Sirach, also known as Ecclesiasticus; the Letter of Jeremiah); pseudepigraphical works known also from external sources (sections from 1 Enoch; the Testaments of the Twelve Patriarchs; Jubilees); commentaries on the Hebrew scriptures (called *Pesharim*); Targums (Aramaic translations) of Job and Leviticus; and various documents unique to Qumran, such as the War of the Sons of Light against the Sons of Darkness (1QM), the Hymn Scroll (1QH), the Temple Scroll (11QTemple), the Genesis Apocryphon (1QapGen), and the awkwardly titled "Collection of Works of the Torah" or (more succinctly) 4QMMT.

In addition to documents, the caves near Qumran also yielded a substantial number of *mezuzot* and *tefillin* (phylacteries) that contain texts from Exodus and Deuteronomy. *Mezuzot* were, and still are, attached by Jews to the doorposts of the house in conformity with Deuteronomy 6.9. Following Deuteronomy 6.8, *tefillin*, also still used in Judaism, are small boxes ceremonially worn on the left hand and forehead during prayer.

The individual manuscripts of the Hebrew scriptures, as well as the *tefillin* and the *mezuzot*, sometimes match the Hebrew versions now standardized in synagogue worship. Sometimes they conform to the version familiar from the Septuagint, the early Greek translation of the Hebrew scriptures. Sometimes they differ from both. The Psalms scroll contains several songs absent from the canonical collection. Thus the Qumran documents reveal that at the turn of the era the biblical text was not yet fully standardized.

A highly ordered society as indicated by the scrolls, the Qumran covenanters had a council of twelve members (one for each tribe of Israel) and three priests. They required candidates to endure a three-year probationary period, held property in common, dressed in white, practiced table fellowship, and believed in predestination. These practices, as well as their utilization of a solar calendar (in contrast to the lunar calendar of the Pharisees and Sadducees), ensured their distinction from those they considered corrupt. Josephus remarks of the Essenes that "although they send votive offerings to the Temple, they do not offer sacrifices because of the difference in the purity regulations which they practice" (*Antiquities* 18.1.5).

Highly eschatological in their outlook and dualistic in their theology, the scrolls represent a community anticipating the imminent end of the world and a style of life designed in preparation for that end. They attest to the expectation of two Messiahs: one, the son of Joseph, would fall in battle; the other, the son of Aaron, would lead the community to its final reward. The covenanters, the "sons of light," would accompany the angels in battle. Their enemies, the "sons of darkness," would eventually fall.

The end came, but not as the covenanters expected. Not the heavenly hosts but the Roman army appeared in 68 CE. Some members may have escaped to Masada, where they awaited their fate with the Zealots who fled from Jerusalem. Josephus speaks of "John the Essene," who may or may not have had an association with Qumran, as active in the early campaigns of the revolt; excavations of Masada have yielded at least one scroll with connections to the Qumran documents. Others may have joined the early Jerusalem Christian movement, with whom Qumran shared such beliefs and practices as a charismatic leader, scriptural interpretation, communal meals, common property, messianic interests, and the coming judgment.

Charismatic Prophets, Teachers, and Visionaries

The community responsible for the Qumran scrolls was by no means the only group of first-century Jews with messianic expectations. Numerous, and quite diverse, portraits of the Messiah and the messianic age flourished: for some Jews, the savior would be a human warrior; for others, an angel; for others, the age to come would be inaugurated not by a savior figure but directly by divine command. Apparently, many Jews did not expect a messiah at all. Still others may have seen divine agency manifested by charismatic prophets, reformers, and teachers. One such figure was John the Baptist.

A popular figure in the early part of the first century CE, John the Baptist was one of a number of Jewish reformers who attracted disciples and crowds, and consequently the attention of local authorities, both Jewish and Roman. Although the Gospels suggest that Herod Antipas was coerced by Herodias's daughter into decapitating John, it is more likely that the tetrarch recognized John's threat to his authority and, following his father's practice, executed someone who challenged his rule. To be a religious leader during the Second Temple period was thus, as epitomized by John, also to be a political figure.

Jesus and his followers may be placed in the context of various reformist groups—Pharisees, Qumran covenanters, urban Essenes, political revolutionaries, and John the Baptist, whose follower Jesus appears to have been at one time. The Gospels indicate that Jesus had much in common with various other charismatic teachers, healers, and sages of the period. All sought to live the way God intended, but they emphasized different lifestyles, interpretations of scriptures, relations to the occupying Roman government, and views of the Temple.

Jesus was probably born during the reign of Augustus (27 BCE–14 CE). The Gospels of Matthew and Luke indicate, through quite different stories, that he was born in Bethlehem, conforming with Micah 5.2, but all four Gospels also identify him as being from Nazareth in Galilee. Consequently, more skeptical readers suggest that the birth in Bethlehem is a "theological truth" rather than a historically accurate statement. The evangelists recount that as the result of his healings and teachings Jesus gathered a crowd substantial enough to worry the Jewish officials responsible for maintaining peace with Rome. At some point in his ministry, he engaged in an incident in the Temple (Mark 11.15–19; John 2.13–22) that brought him to the attention of the Sadducaic authorities, as well as of Roman officials who took an equal interest in maintaining peace. He was executed by crucifixion as a Roman criminal on the orders of Pontius Pilate, the governor from 26 to 36, during the reign of Tiberius (14–37). Some of his followers proclaimed that after three days he was raised from the dead.

Aside from these few conclusions, neither the chronology nor the central message of Jesus' preaching nor the reason for his crucifixion can be given with certainty. The sources for his life, principally the Gospels but also other writings from inside and outside the Christian communities, lead to various reconstructions. Nor can he be securely located in a single social class (peasant, artisan, retainer), cultural environment (urban, rural; Galilee or Jerusalem), or even religious orientation (conservative, liberal). Jesus has been viewed, by followers and detractors, historians and theologians, in diverse roles: a Jewish reformer anticipating the end of the world and the beginning of the reign of God; a Hellenistically inclined Cynic-sage seeking to subvert conventional expectations; a Pharisaic interpreter of biblical law; a proponent of the Temple and of ritual practice; an opponent of the Temple and ritual practice (both conclusions can follow from how one interprets the "cleansing"); a revolutionary preaching a kingdom to replace that of Rome; a pietist who sought peaceful coexistence with the occupation forces; a sexual ascetic; a glutton and a drunkard; a proponent of family values; an underminer of precisely those values and the instituter of a new family connected not biologically but by faith. As Albert Schweitzer observed nearly a century ago, portraits of Jesus often reveal as much, if not more, about the painter as about the subject of the painting.

Compounding these problems in constructing a biography of Jesus is the nature of the sources themselves. First, we lack any autographs—that is, the original manuscripts—of the Gospels. The documents we have today are composites based on various ancient manuscript traditions. Both the ancient texts and the modern translations of them represent various philological, historical, aesthetic, and ideological judgments. Second, while Jesus' native language was Aramaic, the Gospel texts are written in Greek. Jesus may have been bilingual, but it is more likely that the Gospels derive from collections of teaching material translated from Aramaic. Third, although Jesus lived during the early part of the first century CE, and although stories about him circulated both during his lifetime and after his crucifixion, the Gospels date from the second half of the century.

Moreover, the evangelists are addressing the concerns of the early Christian communities, most likely outside Palestine. Theological statements written by passionate believers rather than unbiased outsiders' recollections, the Gospels present, each in its own way, the story of Jesus adapted to meet the needs of the diverse Christian groups in the early years of the church. Theology and history need not be mutually exclusive, but even so how we read the stories of Jesus preserved from antiquity will to a great extent be determined by our own religious orientation. If we believe that the Gospels recount events exactly as they are recorded, then little reconstruction needs to be done: Jesus disrupted Temple activities once at the beginning of his ministry (John) and again at the end (Matthew, Mark, and Luke); he delivered the same talks on more than one occasion (the Sermon on the Mount in Matthew's Gospel; the Sermon on the Plain in Luke's); and so forth. But different pictures emerge if we see the Gospels as the stories told by Jesus' followers to aid the church in its mission to both Jews and Gentiles, as it was rejected or persecuted by representatives from those groups, as it sought its own place in the world and its relation to the traditions of Israel.

Two examples illustrate the difficulty of historically reconstructing the story of Jesus. First, to a great extent, the Gospel accounts are garbed in the images of the

Hebrew scriptures. The way his story has been told, what has been preserved, is influenced by the way those early Christians read their Bibles. For example, the crucifixion scene in Mark echoes Psalm 22, almost verse for verse. The infancy material, temptation scenes, and location of the Sermon on the Mount in Matthew recollect the story of Moses from his birth to the Exodus to the wandering in the wilderness to the Sinai theophany. Second, the Gospels in various ways present Jesus in conflict with his contemporaries, identified either simply as "the Jews" (or "the Judeans"— the Greek term is the same) as the Gospel of John puts it, or with Pharisees, Sadducees, high priests, and others. Regardless of the episode, from controversies over practice to the events of Jesus' final days in Jerusalem, these Jewish figures almost invariably appear at best as completely misguided, usually as malevolent, and even as children of the devil (John 8.44). If we recognize that the Gospels come from groups who define themselves in opposition to the thriving Jewish communities who identify themselves as "true Israel," who have their own program of scriptural interpretation to support that self-designation, and who in turn reject the Christian proclamation, we can also recognize that the Pharisees and Sadducees of the Gospels are less objective portraits than caricatures. One might compare the portraits of contemporary political parties as painted by their bitterest enemies.

Just as individuals bring different experiences to their studies of literature and history, just as they interpret events variously, so too did the "proclaimers of the good news," the "evangelists" who composed the Gospels. The Christian canon has four Gospels, and each provides a different picture of its central character. According to early tradition, Mark was the interpreter of Peter, and Luke of Paul, while Matthew and John were members of Jesus' inner group of disciples. Yet not only do the Gospels themselves not make these claims, but the names Matthew, Mark, Luke, and John were assigned only later to the texts. Moreover, the Gospels themselves present differing views of the course of Jesus' mission, the names of his disciples, the content and style of his preaching, the events surrounding his birth, and the date of his death. Although this diversity shows the richness of the early tradition (one might compare, for example, the different accounts of creation and the Flood in Genesis, or of the monarchy in the Deuteronomic History and Chronicles), it also creates problems for historians.

The four canonical Gospels are not the only texts about Jesus that have come down to us from antiquity. Some scholars argue as relevant to the historical Jesus such texts as the Gospel of Thomas, a collection of sayings many of which resemble material in the Synoptic Gospels; the Gospel of Peter, a fragmentary text containing the trial of Jesus, the crucifixion, and the beginnings of a resurrection account; and even a text whose antiquity is debated, the "Secret Gospel of Mark," which depicts a shamanlike Jesus who practices esoteric initiation rites.

The value of non-Christian sources is likewise debated. In discussing Pilate's rule, Josephus notes:

> About this time there appeared Jesus, a wise man, if one should even call him a man. For he was a doer of striking deeds and was a teacher of such people as accept the truth gladly. He gained a following both among many Jews and among many of the Greeks. He was the Messiah [Greek *christos*]. When Pilate, upon hearing him

accused by leading men among us, had condemned him to be crucified, those who had in the first place come to love him did not give up their affection for him. On the third day he appeared to them, living again, for the prophets of God had prophesied these and countless other marvelous things about him. And the tribe of Christians, so called after him, still to this day has not disappeared. (*Antiquities* 18.3.3)

Not surprisingly, this statement has provoked much controversy. Of the three surviving manuscripts of the *Antiquities* in Greek, the earliest dates to the eleventh century, and all are preserved by the church. Thus, some suspect that the monks engaged in editorial elaboration. Supporting this view are three other factors: the tenth-century version of the Christian Arab Agapius lacks this testimony (of course, later Muslim copyists may have omitted it); unlike other comments of Josephus on early Christian leaders, this passage is not cited by the church fathers prior to the fourth century; and nowhere else, including in his autobiography, does Josephus indicate any Christian confessionalism. Finally, even if we assign the entire passage to Josephus, we still cannot account it as independent testimony, since Josephus is recounting the information second- or even thirdhand.

Rabbinic sources are even further removed from the historical Jesus. The Babylonian Talmud, a product dating several hundred years after the first century CE, reports: "On the eve of Passover they hanged Yeshu of Nazareth. And the herald went before him forty days, saying, 'Yeshu of Nazareth is going forth to be stoned, since he has practiced sorcery and cheated, and led people astray. Let everyone knowing anything in his defense come and plead for him.' But they found no one in his defense, and they hanged him on the eve of Passover" (*Sanhedrin* 43a). The composite nature of the material (stoning and hanging are both mentioned) and the date of the text, which is from the time of Christian ascendancy and attendant persecution of the Jews, suggest that this is less an independent witness than a product of Jewish reflection on church teaching.

Given the problems with these outside sources for reconstructing the life of Jesus, scholars turn primarily to the canon, and specifically to the first three Gospels. The accounts of Matthew, Mark, and Luke—called "Synoptic" since "seen together" they present a generally similar chronology and description of Jesus' life—highlight the proclamation of the "kingdom of God" through parables and healings. Mark, usually viewed as the earliest of the canonical Gospels, is dated by most biblical scholars to sometime around the First Revolt against Rome, either immediately before or just after 70 CE. Matthew and Luke, which appear to use Mark as a source, are dated toward the end of the first century. Matthew and Luke are also seen as having used additional traditional material, both shared and independently. Most scholars suggest that Matthew and Luke used, along with Mark, another text comprised mostly of sayings attributed to Jesus; this collection, known as Q (from the German word *Quelle*, meaning "source"), accounts for material Matthew and Luke both contain but Mark lacks, such as the Beatitudes (Matt. 5.3–12; Luke 6.21–26; the form was well known in both Jewish and Gentile sources) and the "Lord's Prayer" (Matt. 6.9–13; Luke 11.2–4). Matthew alone provides such material as Jesus' statement that divorce is permitted in cases of unchastity and the description of Pilate washing his hands. Luke alone offers the well-known parables of the good Samaritan and the prodigal son.

Some scholars do not agree with this reconstruction of the interrelationship of the Synoptic Gospels. They argue instead that Matthew was the first Gospel, that Luke expanded on Matthew, and that Mark is a conflation of Matthew and Luke. Consequently, the dating of the sources differs, the sayings source, Q, disappears, and the reconstruction of Jesus' own life and teaching necessarily changes. Thus, even within studies of the Synoptic Gospels, scholars do not see eye to eye; the picture of Jesus therefore remains blurry.

Offering a substantially different vision of Jesus is the Gospel of John. Here Jesus speaks more about himself than the kingdom of God. He identifies himself as the true vine; the bread of life; the way, the truth, and the life; and he teaches primarily by means of extended speeches rather than short parables or pithy sayings. And even the Synoptics offer distinct portraits: Matthew has Jesus' earthly mission restricted to "the lost sheep of the house of Israel" (Matt. 15.24; see also 10.5–6) and emphasizing obedience to and preservation of biblical law. Mark, however, opens the mission to Gentiles and suggests the abrogation of the dietary regulations mandated by the Torah. And Luke, whose work is supplemented by a second volume called Acts of the Apostles, emphasizes Jesus' innocence in the eyes of Rome. As for chronology, all four Gospels begin Jesus' public career with an encounter with John the Baptist. The Synoptics then depict teaching and healing activities in Galilee, a trip to Jerusalem marked by an incident in the Temple, and crucifixion on the first day of the Passover holiday. John, however, locates the Temple incident very early in Jesus' career, depicts several trips to Jerusalem, and dates the crucifixion to the "day of preparation," at the time that the lambs for the Passover meal were being sacrificed in the Temple.

In current Jesus research, some view Jesus as a reformer prophet in the tradition of Jeremiah or the Teacher of Righteousness known from the Dead Sea Scrolls, and perhaps John the Baptist. They see him as exhorting the fellow Jews with whom he comes in contact to strengthen their adherence to traditional practices and beliefs even as they await the inbreaking of the rule of God. Other scholars, however, see Jesus more as a sage interested less in the end of the world and the rituals of Judaism than in the creation of a new community. This Jesus advocates solidarity with peasants and open-table fellowship, with an attendant disregard for biblical dietary regulations. Anything in the Gospels that suggests apocalyptic warning or division between those to be saved and those to be damned is by this interpretation usually assigned not to Jesus but to his early followers, who are reacting against the rejection of their original message. Equally debated are questions of Jesus' own messianic self-consciousness. Did he think he was the messiah, and if so, what sort—political/Davidic, eschatological, or social? Did he anticipate or plan his death? Did he anticipate his return from the dead? Was there a resurrection?

How we interpret Jesus' message in turn influences how we view the lives of his earliest followers in Jerusalem and Galilee. For example, when they prayed (probably originally in Aramaic) what has come to be translated as "Give us this day our daily bread," were they asking for the bread of the heavenly kingdom and thus the end of the world, or were they asking for shared food, or both? When they spoke of not serving both God and *mammon* (Aramaic for "wealth"), were they speaking from a position of poverty or of riches? Did they take a this-worldly focus and add an emphasis on the end of the world, or did they take an apocalyptic message and deemphasize it once the end did not follow directly upon the cross? Or was there some of both?

Similarly problematic is the attempt to determine how Jesus' earliest followers viewed him. Considering the number of messianic views prevalent in first-century Jewish culture, Jesus would have evoked a variety of responses, even from those who knew him. Some saw him as a political figure who would liberate the land from the Romans; some perhaps saw him as a priest who would restore the Temple; some saw him as a prophet and others as a sage; still others saw in him the promised return of Elijah or the new Moses. Some first-century Jews may well have regarded Jesus as a divine figure (for example, Wisdom incarnate), others as a human being divinely anointed. Thus, even in the proclamation of Jesus as "Messiah," one still needs to ask what that term connotes.

The Early Church

After the crucifixion, Jesus' followers did not disband. To the contrary, they began to teach that after three days in the tomb he had been raised from the dead. Since the idea of resurrection was current in Judea and Galilee, in part because of Pharisaic teaching, the message was not entirely anomalous. Luke's second volume, the writings of Paul of Tarsus, and various non-Christian sources provide some indication of the church's organization in Palestine in the years prior to and during the First Revolt against Rome.

According to Luke, Paul, and Josephus, the leader of the Jerusalem church was James, the brother of Jesus. How he attained this prominent position is unclear. He is not depicted in the Gospels as one of his brother's disciples. Both Paul, who disagrees with James (see Gal. 2.12), and Josephus, who appears to have respected him, suggest that James was interested in preserving the practices enjoined upon Jews by the Torah—as, apparently, was the predominantly Jewish group of Jesus' earliest followers. Thus, for example, they participated in Temple worship and retained Levitical dietary practices. In Acts 15, Luke presents a mediating position, assigning a speech to James in which he successfully proposes that Gentiles in the church need not conform to such practices; they need only behave much like the "resident aliens" of Leviticus 17–18: avoid unchastity in any form, not consume animals that had been strangled, not eat meat that had been offered to an idol, and not eat anything with blood in it.

Acts records that the leaders of this early Jerusalem-based movement included, along with James, also Peter and John. Acts 6.1 also mentions groups to which Luke refers as Hebrews (local, Aramaic-speaking Jews) and Hellenists (probably Diaspora Jews who spoke Greek). The comments on the local leadership are confirmed in Paul's letter to the Galatians, but apart from a reference to the "poor" there he does not describe the social situation of the Jerusalem church.

Acts of the Apostles also provides the most detailed evidence for the organization of this group of Jesus' followers. But as with the story of Jesus itself, the evangelist's presentation of the early church has historical gaps. For example, although Acts describes the persecution and dispersion of the Hellenists, it does not explain why the Hebrews were left in peace. Luke has particular emphases, demonstrated already in the Gospel, that continue in this depiction of church history. For Luke's Jesus, the possession of riches is not conducive to entry into the kingdom of God. This model holds as well for Acts, where Luke depicts the Jerusalem community as sharing property.

Others among Jesus' followers may not have been based in Jerusalem. The Synoptic Gospels suggest that some took to the road as wandering preachers. Jesus tells his twelve disciples: "Take nothing for your journey, no staff, nor bag, nor bread, nor money" (Luke 9.3), and he exhorts seventy more followers (Luke 10.1; only Luke recounts this mission) to bring neither sandals, nor bag for provisions, nor purse. These missionaries are to leave their families and travel from town to town, finding welcome and support where they can.

Diaspora Judaism

When representatives of the early Jesus movement left the borders of Judea and Galilee and ventured to Alexandria, Rome, and Antioch, they found there a vibrant Judaism represented by Jewish neighborhoods, civic associations, and schools. Distinct in varying degrees from their Gentile counterparts in terms of ethnic identification, religious practice, and participation in local civic and cultural practices (such as the refusal to offer sacrifices to the emperor and to worship local or imperial gods, for which non-Jews accused them of "atheism"), Diaspora communities often formed individual semi-independent governmental structures. It is unlikely that the majority of Jews had Roman citizenship (as Paul of Tarsus did). On occasion, however, privileges were given to them; for example, Julius Caesar exempted Jews from military service, given the impossibility of their complying with either dietary or Sabbath practices when in the army.

Not infrequently these distinctions led to social intolerance. From 38 to 41 CE in Alexandria, Antioch, Asia Minor, and Rome, civil disturbances between Jewish and Gentile residents erupted. Alexandrian propagandists such as Apion published extensive tracts delineating the Jews' ostensible ignominious beginnings, silly superstitions, and heinous practices; in rebuttal, Josephus later wrote his *Against Apion*.

On the other hand, conversion to Judaism was not uncommon even though for men this required circumcision. Josephus recounts the story of Helena, the queen of Adiabene, who along with her sons and many in the royal court converted to Judaism in the first century CE and even made pilgrimage to the Jerusalem Temple.

Along with converts, many in the Hellenistic and Roman periods admired the Jews' ethical norms, ritual practices, and ancient roots. Some, known as "God-fearers," did not take the step of conversion but practiced affiliation with Judaism. From this group Christianity may have found its earliest members both in the Diaspora (see Acts 13.16, 26; 16.14; 17.4; 18.7) and in Palestine. God-fearers participated in various Jewish activities, from Sabbath observance to attending synagogue to worshiping the Jewish god. It remains debated whether Jews actually engaged in any organized, formal missionary efforts to attract Gentile affiliates (as Matt. 23.15 may suggest) or whether the proselytizing effort was more passive—through the public presence of Jewish institutions such as synagogues and prayer houses, through literary

products, through explanation of Jewish practices, through occasional individual in-
itiatives, and the like.

Records of Jewish communities in the Diaspora, responses to anti-Jewish propagandists, and explications of Jewish history, philosophy, and practices are most fully
known today from writings preserved not by Jews but by Christians, the works of
Philo and Josephus. Philo provides the major source for the various forms of Judaism
thriving in Alexandria in the first century CE. These include the Therapeutae and
Therapeutrides, men and women living celibately, in communal fashion, dedicated
to philosophical and spiritual exercises. For them Philo has nothing but compliments,
so much so that some scholars even question their existence. They also include the
group Philo refers to as "extreme allegorists," who proclaimed that the various biblical instructions concerning such physical matters as circumcision and dietary regulations were meant only as metaphors and therefore need not be practiced (comparable are the Hellenizers, against whom the Maccabees struggled, as well as some
members of early Christianity). For them, Philo has nothing but condemnation.
Finally, among the Jews in Alexandria was Philo's nephew, Tiberius Julius Alexander,
who renounced his Jewish background for a career in politics, became procurator of
Judea, and finally was an aide to Vespasian. Ethnically Jewish, his case demonstrates
the possibilities for assimilation as well as the flexibility of the term *Jew*.

Philo himself, a member of one of the most prominent and wealthy Jewish families
in Alexandria, sought a synthesis between Greek philosophy and Jewish tradition,
between Plato and Moses. For example, Philo suggested that the *Logos*, God's "reason" or "speech," served as a mediating principle between divine transcendence and
the material world. Similar to the figure of Wisdom in Proverbs 8—which he specifically cites—the *Logos* for Philo is actively present during creation. A similar construction may be found in the opening of the Gospel of John, where the Christ is
identified with the *Logos*, who was "with God, and . . . was God" (John 1.1).

While Philo was dressing Judaism in the clothing of Greek philosophy in Alexandria, so Josephus, his slightly younger counterpart, was doing the same in Rome.
Josephus, although more a politician than a philosopher, similarly presented Judaism
as philosophically based, compatible with if not superior to the best of Greek and
Roman culture and ethics. When in 39 CE the Greek citizens of Alexandria began to
persecute the local Jewish population, which was also seeking citizenship rights, it
was Philo who led the Jewish delegation to Rome. The emperor at the time was Gaius
Caligula.

On the Eve of Revolt, 41–66 CE

The political and economic situation in Judea, Samaria, and Galilee became increasingly intolerable by the middle of the first century. In addition to the problems caused
by famine and occupation, more difficulties sprang from Rome itself. At first, the
ascension of Gaius Caligula in 37 looked promising for the local population. Not
only did Caligula early in his tenure entrust to his friend Agrippa I, the grandson of
Herod the Great and Mariamme, the tetrarchy that had been held by Philip, but two
years later he added the territory of Antipas. Thus two parts of Herod the Great's
massive holding remained, nominally, in Jewish rather than imperial hands. Agrippa
also received the right to appoint the high priest.

This friendship did not, however, lead to the emperor's appreciation for Jewish sensibilities. In 40/41 Caligula determined that his statue would be erected in the Jerusalem Temple. The action may have been one of many signs of his increasingly erratic behavior, or Caligula may have wished to punish the Jewish population for their refusal to allow Gentiles to erect a statue of the emperor in Jamnia. Even though they recognized the potential for mass slaughter, the Jewish population of Judea mobilized to protest this desecration. Caligula was killed before the order could be carried out. Agrippa, who had attempted to keep the population of Judea calm during this crisis, and who then had worked toward the accession of Claudius, was fittingly rewarded: the new emperor severed Judea and Samaria from the province of Syria and so from direct Roman rule, and he appointed Agrippa king over the whole area once held by Herod the Great. To Agrippa's brother Herod, Claudius granted Chalcis in Lebanon.

Because Agrippa presented himself as an adherent of Torah and because of his Hasmonean connections, he was well received by the Judean and Galilean populations. He also appears to have begun construction on a wall on the north side of Jerusalem; but since Rome withheld sufficient funding, the project remained incomplete. Finally, Agrippa convinced Claudius to grant various political privileges to Jewish communities, first in Alexandria and then throughout the empire. Such local concerns were, however, belied by his more cosmopolitan interests outside Jerusalem. In Caesarea, Agrippa erected statues of his daughters Berenice and Drusilla, minted coins bearing his portrait, and sponsored games.

And, in Caesarea, in 44 CE, he died. Josephus recounts that when Agrippa appeared dressed in resplendent clothes, the local crowd proclaimed him divine; he immediately saw an owl, which reminded him of earlier predictions about his death. He then declared his demise to be the will of heaven, suffered excruciating abdominal pain, and died five days later. Acts 12.20–23 recounts a similar story:

> Now Herod [Agrippa] was angry with the people of Tyre and Sidon. So they came to him in a body, and after winning over Blastus, the king's chamberlain, they asked for a reconciliation, because their country depended on the king's country for food. On an appointed day, Herod [Agrippa] put on his royal robes, took his seat on the platform, and delivered a public address to them. The people kept shouting, "The voice of a god, and not of a mortal!" And immediately, because he had not given the glory to God, an angel of the Lord struck him down, and he was eaten by worms and died.

Josephus recounts that the populations of Samaria and Caesarea rejoiced at his passing. There is no similar testimony from Judea, where his reign had been a rare beneficial interlude for the population during the first century CE.

Agrippa I had died, but social problems and political machinations continued as usual. Instead of bestowing the kingdom on Agrippa's son, Agrippa II, who was only seventeen, Claudius annexed the territory as a Roman province, as he had several others. Then came a series of governors, each contributing to increasing domestic unrest. Cuspius Fadus (44–46) had the misfortune of ruling at the time the prophet Theudas attempted to part the Jordan River (and so, symbolically, represent Joshua conquering the land held by enemy hands). Many people followed him—as did the cavalry of Rome, under the governor's orders. Fadus was replaced by Philo's nephew, Tiberius Julius Alexander. His term (46–48) witnessed a bad famine, partially alleviated by generous gifts of Egyptian grain from Helena of Adiabene, and, from her son Izates, funds for purchasing food. This governorship also witnessed the revolts of the sons of Judas the Galilean, James and Simon, whom Alexander had crucified. The governor would return to Jerusalem in 70 to fight more rebels; Vespasian appointed him as adviser to Titus.

Third came Ventidius Cumanus (48–52), an inept ruler responsible for many of his own problems. In 52, when a Galilean was murdered in Samaria and conflict between the two populations subsequently broke out, Cumanus did nothing. The conflict spread to Judea, from which two Jews mounted a raid into Samaria. Claudius, spurred on by Agrippa II, finally intervened: he found in favor of the Jews, penalized the Samaritans, and exiled Cumanus.

The next governor, Antonius Felix (52–60), faced increasing incidents of rebellion, particularly attacks from the Sicarii (from *sica*, a curved dagger, used to assassinate Jews seen as cooperating with Rome). Felix was also ruling when a Jew known only as the "Egyptian" led a large number of people to the Mount of Olives, having promised them that he would bring down the walls of Jerusalem. The governor's heavy-handed approach to squelching these incipient revolts only exacerbated local tension. His greed is attested by Acts 24.26; he had hoped to relieve Paul of his funding. Felix's personal life, no less suspect, demonstrates the interconnection of Roman rule and Judean royalty. His wife, Drusilla, was the daughter of Agrippa I. Although she was betrothed to Epiphanes of Commangene, that contract ended following Agrippa's death, when Epiphanes recanted on his promise to be circumcised. Drusilla was then betrothed by her brother, Agrippa II, to Azizus of Emesa, who did agree to the ritual operation. The queen would later dissolve her marriage in order to wed Felix, who had been courting her by proxy.

Personal scandal also touched Agrippa II. Rome did not approve of his living with his other sister, Berenice; rumors of incest spread. Berenice was the widow of, first, the son of the Jewish leader of Alexandria, and second of Herod of Chalcis; she would later become the wife of the king of Cilicia and finally the partner of the emperor Titus. Yet Agrippa's personal life does not appear to have interfered substantially with his political career. Appointed by Claudius king of Chalcis in 49, when his uncle Herod died, Agrippa II also received control of the Jerusalem Temple and the power to appoint the high priest. In 53, Claudius granted him both Herod Philip's former holdings and Abilene. In 54/55, Nero would increase these holdings with the addition of two cities in Perea and two more in Galilee.

In turn, Agrippa II remained faithful to the empire. From the time of his enthronement in 49 to his death in 92, his coins depict the reigning emperor. Nevertheless, he also tried to do well by his Jewish citizens. He continued the construction of the Jerusalem Temple, and when the massive unemployment that resulted from its completion threatened Jerusalem's peace, he provided jobs for many of the workers. When the First Revolt broke out in 66, he sought to quell the rebellion; but once hostilities increased, he sided with Rome. Although his loyalties were to the empire, and although he did have a dispute with the Jerusalem priests mediated by the next governor, Porcius Festus (60–62), over his desire to tear down a wall that blocked his view of the Temple (Nero decided in favor of the priests), Agrippa II is well regarded in rabbinic sources.

Festus is also known for sending another dispute to Nero. It is Festus to whom Paul appeals in Acts 25.11. Although an able and cautious administrator, Festus could not resolve the heightened tensions and increasing Jewish antipathy toward Rome. Between Festus's death in office and the arrival of his successor, Albinus (62–64), the Jerusalem church began to face increasing local pressure.

That the early followers of Jesus faced opposition is certain; Paul himself admits in his letter to the Philippians that he had been a persecutor of the church. Yet it is much less clear why and to what extent it was harassed—by Jewish kings, Sadducees, representatives of the synagogues, Roman authorities, and members of the general populace. Although much of the evidence for the persecution of the church locates the difficulties outside Judea, Acts does record several local incidents. For example, Acts 12.1–2 mentions that James the son of Zebedee and brother of the apostle John was ordered executed by Agrippa I. And in 62, during the interim between governors, James the brother of Jesus perished at the command of the Sadducean high priest, Annas II. But then, prompted by complaints from the Pharisees, Agrippa II deposed the priest. The timing of the incident indicates that the high priest's action was illegal; both Roman and Christian sources suggest that local governments in occupied territory lacked the right to carry out capital punishment.

Such persecution of the church occurred sporadically outside Judea as well. Although the origins of the Christian communities in such locations as Rome and Egypt are not known, it is nevertheless likely that the movement was spread by Jewish evangelists, who used private homes and perhaps synagogues as bases for proselytizing. Among these missionaries, the best known is Saul of Tarsus, a Pharisee who himself once persecuted the church. Following a conversion experience, Saul—or, as he became known to the Greek-speaking world, Paul—established churches throughout Asia Minor and Greece. Through his efforts and those of his fellow missionaries, Gentiles were brought into the church by means of baptism. They were not required to follow the rituals of the Jewish scriptures, such as dietary regulations, circumcision for males, or particular forms of Sabbath observance. Instead, their principal ritual appears to have been the Eucharist, practiced as a fellowship meal. Yet Paul, who advised cooperation with the government (see Rom. 13.1–7), was, according to legend, beheaded by Nero.

As a new religious movement, the Christians were already suspect in the eyes of their neighbors. Their preaching of a crucified savior, the sexual asceticism practiced by some of them (especially women), their Eucharistic language, their strong eschatological orientation, and their insistence (like the Jews') that there was only one deity—all these contributed to various outbreaks of violence against them. The most famous of these occurred in Rome, when Nero accused the local Christian community of starting the great fire of 64 CE. Moreover, whenever Jews were targeted for specific governmental action, Christians, especially those who were ethnically Jews, were likely to find themselves under attack in the wake of that action. Thus, when Claudius expelled the Jews from Rome in 49, the Jewish Christians were banished as well; one missionary couple involved in this expulsion, Priscilla (Prisca) and Aquila, is known from both Paul's letters and Acts of the Apostles.

The Fall of Jerusalem

Albinus (62–64), together with the last governor prior to the revolt, Gessius Florus (64–66), confirmed for much of the local populace that independence from Rome was essential. Each took bribes, looted treasuries, and served only himself. Simmering hatred of the governors reached the boiling point in 66 CE, heated by growing nationalism, religious enthusiasm, increasing strife between Jews and Gentiles in various areas of the country, major economic problems caused by droughts and famines as well as by taxation, massive unemployment in Jerusalem in the early 60s occasioned by the completion of Herod's Temple, the inability of the upper classes either to provide leadership or to evoke popular support, and a series of local incidents. Adding even more heat were the diverse interests of peasants from the rural areas of Galilee and urban merchants from the cosmopolitan centers, of those who expected divine intervention and those who relied on their own skill with weapons, of those who hated the Romans and those who hated the rich. As Richard Horsley has aptly observed, a "spiral of violence" eventually enveloped the entire country.

The incident that sparked the revolt may have been the blocking of a synagogue in Caesarea in 61 by a building erected by Greeks. Nero judged in favor of the Greeks; Jewish tensions began to rise, and by 66 fighting erupted in the streets between the Jewish and Greek populations. Concurrently, Florus—following an old procuratorial practice—attempted to remove funds from the Temple treasury. Although his predecessors had faced little direct opposition to this action, Florus provoked Jerusalem's anger. The population, disgusted by his plan but aware of their limited political power, mocked him by holding a public collection. The governor ordered his soldiers to break up the protest, but the opposition became so intense that he retreated to Caesarea, leaving behind in Jerusalem only one cohort of soldiers.

The absence of the governor and the limited number of troops provided the final impetus. Rebellion broke out in Judea; shortly it swept Galilee; within a year it had spread to Samaria. The Sanhedrin, comprised primarily of Sadducees and Pharisees, became the de facto governmental organ. Those in rebellion quickly took various fortresses, including Masada and the Antonia, and even the Temple Mount. Led by Eleazar, the son of the high priest, they stopped the daily offerings to the emperor. Many priests, recognizing that their positions now depended on their support of the revolt, joined the alliance.

Among the various groups engaged in active resistance against Rome, the best known are the Zealots and the Sicarii. Josephus connects the Zealots with the philosophic schools of Pharisees, Sadducees, and Essenes, but he lists this "fourth philosophy" as an "innovation and revolution in the ancestral ways" (*Antiquities* 18.1.1). The term *Zealot* appears first in the context of the revolt itself, and should not be confused with either the "bandits" (Greek *lestai*) or the Sicarii. The *lestai* probably came from rural or village settings and were involved in social banditry. Their primary motivation seems to have been economic rather than ideological. In contrast, the Sicarii were urban-based revolutionaries who shared the ideals of Judas the Galilean and Zadok. One of their leaders, Eleazar, was the grandson of Judas. The Zealots, perhaps peasants who headed toward Jerusalem from the north even as the Romans were advancing into Galilee, had various agendas: economic, political, even personal.

Nor should the Zealots be equated with others involved in the first days of the war, including various revolutionaries from among the priestly houses and the rich who hated the Zealots and Sicarii, and even some Jews from Idumea, who scorned the priests and the upper class.

That the revolt was not merely an uprising against Rome but was also fueled by local political and economic concerns is clearly indicated by the Zealots' more destructive activities. They torched the palaces of Agrippa II, Berenice, and the high priest, as well as the city archives. This latter event is particularly telling, since the debt and tax records were stored there. For the Zealots, elimination of debt would end the economic imbalance of the country, allowing land and wealth to be distributed according to the more egalitarian model suggested by the Torah. The fighting was especially intense in areas of mixed Jewish and Gentile population, as earlier in Caesarea. In such cases, nationalism rather than economics served as the primary catalyst. From Josephus, one might conclude that in Galilee part of the unrest was caused by cultural and geographical rivalries; he recounts that the urban populations were much less in favor of the revolt than the rural peasants.

To what extent the revolt represented the sentiments of the full population is not known. Agrippa II sought peace; sailing immediately from Alexandria to Jerusalem, he sent three thousand soldiers to attempt to remove the Zealots, but receiving almost no help from the inept Florus, he failed. Unlike his son, the high priest as well as the majority of the Sadducees could see no benefit from the revolt. Yet the lower-ranking priests did have reason to rebel. According to Josephus, their superiors had begun taking the people's tithed offerings directly from the threshing floor of the Temple; the lower priests, who depended on these offerings for their livelihood, were thereby being reduced to impoverishment and starvation. One leader of the Jewish forces in Galilee was John the Essene. Pharisaic views are less clear, since they are recorded only by Josephus, if not already then at least later himself a Pharisee with strong apologetic interests. Some Pharisees appear to have counseled peace or at least caution; Rome's willingness to sponsor Pharisaic interests in the aftermath of the war may imply at least some Pharisaic sponsorship of Roman interests prior to the revolt. But others, including Simeon ben Gamaliel, joined the struggle.

For many in Galilee, the war was unwanted. Much of the territory remained prosperous despite famines, taxation, occupation, and memories of Judas and the census. The major cities, Sepphoris and Tiberias, had substantial economic and cultural ties to Rome. Josephus, at first the leader of the Galilean resistance, announces in his *Jewish War* (the major source for the reconstruction of the events of 66–73) that rebellion is not desired by God.

The varied responses to the call for revolt are epitomized by two residents of Galilee who, during the war, found themselves in Jerusalem. Johanan ben Zakkai, who had lived in Gabara just prior to 66, counseled peace; John of Gischala was at the forefront in defending Jerusalem against the Roman troops. How the Jerusalem church reacted is unclear. According to the fourth-century church historian Eusebius, the church relocated to Pella, across the Jordan River, early in 66. Yet this account has its problems. Much of the sixty miles between Jerusalem and Pella would already have been under Roman control; Pella itself was then in the hands of Jewish revolutionaries, and the reports of the relocation may well originate from Pella itself.

Rome was clearly unhappy with this turn of events. In the autumn of 66, the governor of Syria, Cestius Gallus, headed for Jerusalem. Facing strong opposition, he had to retreat, and during the withdrawal, over half of his military support perished at Beth-horon. This initial victory brought even more of the Jewish population over to the Zealot side. Soon local coins with the inscription "Year 1" began to appear.

Nero next sent his general Vespasian to restore order. Supported financially and materially not only by the emperor but also by Agrippa II and Malchus II of Nabatea, Vespasian embarked for Galilee in 67. There he would meet Josephus, whom the Sanhedrin had appointed commander of the revolutionary troops. Josephus by his own account fortified Jotapata, Tarichea, Tiberias, Sepphoris, and Gischala; he also claims to have mustered a hundred thousand soldiers, an improbably high number. Distrusted by the Zealots, and in particular by John of Gischala, Josephus was accused of negotiating with Rome. Once Vespasian arrived, Josephus recounts that many of the Jewish resistance fighters fled, and he himself retreated to Tiberias while his own troops moved to Jotapata.

The siege of the fortress in Jotapata lasted forty-seven days in June and July of 67. Then, through internal betrayal, the fortress finally fell. The population was either killed or enslaved, and the city was leveled. Josephus claims that he fled to a cave and then, after both a convenient miracle and his opportune prediction that Vespasian would become emperor, his life was spared. He joined the general's entourage, took Vespasian's household name—Flavius—as his own, and spent the rest of his life under Rome's aegis.

Distrusted during and after the revolt by many of his fellow Jews, Josephus is not entirely trusted by modern historians either. His various accounts of Roman political activities in Judea and Galilee, of the actions of the Jewish revolutionaries, of the general political climate in Jerusalem, of the role of the Pharisees and Sadducees, and of the extent of Gentile attitudes toward Jews during the first century CE must be viewed in the context of his apologetic motives. Yet regardless of the extent of his exaggeration, it remains the case that by the end of the year 67, Rome had retaken not only Jotapata and Tiberias, but all of Galilee. John of Gischala fled to Jerusalem, and the Roman army soon followed.

Under Vespasian, the tenth Roman legion next headed for the Dead Sea. Probably expecting the war of the sons of light against the sons of darkness, the Qumran covenanters found instead the army of Rome. Their light remained extinguished until 1947, when their scrolls were rediscovered; Rome turned their settlement into a barracks. Some members of the group may have fled to Masada, but their fate too was sealed.

As the Roman forces marched on toward Jerusalem, the various revolutionary groups in the city recognized the need to consolidate their power. With help from Idumean allies, they replaced the weak Sanhedrin government with their own. They also deposed the high priest, in favor of Phanni (or Phanassus) ben Samuel, not from one of the high-priestly families but chosen by lot. Still, factionalism began to sap both their strength and their spirit. Simon bar Giora, who left Idumea following Vespasian's incursion, headed for Jerusalem in the summer of 69. There he found himself in rivalry not only with John of Gischala, but also with the priest Eleazar ben Simeon, who had split from John's party. Each group formed its own base: bar Giora directed the upper city and parts of lower Jerusalem; John of Gischala held the Temple Mount; Eleazar controlled the Temple's inner forecourt. The rival groups burned much of the grain stored in the city, a move that gave different factions temporary political advantage but ultimately doomed Jerusalem.

Recognizing the toll internal fighting was taking, Vespasian had left the Zealots in Jerusalem to weaken each other and turned instead to Idumea, Perea, Antipatris, Lydda, and Jamnia. Quickly advancing, he took Shechem, and thus the Samaritans who had begun to fight Rome in 67 were subdued. Soon Jericho fell, and Vespasian was ready for the last major rebel stronghold, Jerusalem. Yet again, however, Jerusalem was spared. On the ninth of June 68, Nero committed suicide, and the general's attention was redirected westward. Given this sudden lull in Roman activities, bar Giora recognized an opportunity to attack southern Judea, including Hebron. Vespasian naturally then mounted a campaign against Hebron, which fell quickly. By mid-June, he held all points except for Jerusalem and the fortresses of Herodium, Machaerus, and Masada.

Apparently during this time, perhaps as late as the summer of 69 when the Idumeans also fled Jerusalem, the Pharisaic leader Jochanan ben Zakkai escaped from the city. Rabbinic accounts suggest that he had received permission from Vespasian to establish a school in Jamnia. These accounts also depict ben Zakkai—like Josephus—as predicting that Vespasian would both destroy the Temple and ascend the imperial throne. A minor episode during the war, ben Zakkai's relocation would have a major effect on the survival, and configuration, of Judaism.

Attentive to power struggles both in Rome and in Jerusalem, Vespasian bided his time. On 1 July 69, the Roman armies stationed in the eastern part of the empire proclaimed Vespasian emperor. Leaving his army in the control of his capable son, Titus, Vespasian returned to Rome, where he began his ten-year reign as emperor. Titus, aided by (among others) the Jewish-born former procurator Tiberius Julius Alexander, the former rebel leader in Galilee Josephus, and four legions of soldiers, began the siege in early 70, a few weeks before Passover. The timing perfectly coincided with the increasing tension among the internal factions. When Eleazar the priest opened the gates of the Temple for the celebration of the festival, John of Gischala stormed the inner court. Now only two Zealot factions remained. With Titus laying siege to the northern wall of Jerusalem, the groups inside finally united. Their effort failed, and in only three weeks Titus controlled the entire inner city.

The fortress of Antonia capitulated in three days, but the Temple, better defended and less accessible, took longer to fall. Yet the cessation of the daily sacrifices, caused by the food shortage, signaled the inevitable. This cessation, which demoralized the religious population remaining in the city, reduced the Temple to a Zealot stronghold. After a fierce battle and numerous losses to his own troops, Titus succeeded in capturing it. Sometime in August 70, the ninth day of the month of Ab according to Jewish tradition, the Temple was burned. We do not know whether Titus was responsible (Josephus asserts that the general wanted to spare the Temple, but the claim itself is questionable) or whether it was torched by the remaining Zealots.

John of Gischala and his followers escaped and continued their resistance from various locations in the upper city. Lack of food ended this last Jerusalem holdout within five months. Titus marched seven hundred prisoners to Rome for his victory procession, including John of Gischala and Simon bar Giora. Josephus recounts that the former spent his life in prison, while the latter was executed. Titus's arch, depicting many spoils from the Temple including the famous menorah and the altar table where the showbread were displayed, commemorates the Roman conquest. But the conquest was by no means complete. Symbolically, the remaining western wall of the Temple, the Kotel, can be seen to represent the refusal of the Jewish population to surrender completely to Rome. Historically, there remained yet a few pockets of resistance whose story would also be preserved through archaeological remains.

The task of taking Masada, Herodium, and Machaerus fell to Sextus Lucius Bassus, who was appointed procurator of Judea in 71 by Vespasian. Herodium fell quickly in 71, and Machaerus, after a longer battle, was taken in 72 when Bassus promised amnesty for the rebels. Bassus died shortly thereafter; his successor, Flavius Silva, began the siege of Masada in early 73.

Masada had been held by the Sicarii since 66. During the war, Eleazar ben Jair, his troops, and their families accumulated abundant stores of food and water. Their resources gave them an initial advantage over Silva's troops, since the Romans had to bring in supplies from a considerable distance, and since in the late spring and summer the heat in the region is intense. But the fall of Masada was inevitable. Eventually, the Roman troops broke through Masada's defenses, set fire to the wooden barricade erected by Eleazar to protect the wall, and prepared to enter the fort.

What happened next is a matter of some debate. According to Josephus, Eleazar recognized that Masada would fall and persuaded his followers to kill their own families and then commit suicide. The victorious Romans then entered, but found more than nine hundred corpses; only two women and five children, who told the conquerors what had happened, had escaped by hiding in cisterns. Some scholars doubt this story, believing that Josephus made it up in order to satisfy both his Jewish sympathies and his Roman loyalties, allowing the Jews to appear heroic and sparing the Romans the infamy of having slaughtered whole families.

The Aftermath of the War

In the sixth century BCE the Jewish people, having experienced the destruction of their Temple, survived by turning internally to their traditions, their theological beliefs, their community. These same factors contributed to their perseverance after 70 CE. To some extent ideal models for the Temple were already in place. The Temple Scroll from Qumran already indicated a vision of an alternative Temple system. Similarly, pietists (perhaps Pharisees), who ate fellowship or *havurah* meals in ritual purity and thereby treated the domestic table as the Temple altar, were to some extent prepared for the loss of the sacrificial cult. Synagogues and schools in both Palestine and the Diaspora moved into the gap created by the lack of a central location for community worship. Further, Diaspora Jews, although contributing to the Temple through the annual tax and although connected to it through pilgrimage, had long lived without its immediate presence.

Theological concerns and rereadings of biblical texts provided additional comfort. For Josephus, for the rabbis, and for the authors of such apocalyptic texts as 2 Baruch and 4 Ezra, the destruction was in part the result of the people's sin. This Deuteronomic perception was, however, coupled with a return to the perspective of Jeremiah. That prophet, who had lived at the time of the Babylonian onslaught, had explained that through divine plans some nations rise and others fall. Now the Roman Empire was ascendant, but in time it too would fall. According to some early Christians, the destruction of the Temple was punishment on the Jews for the death of Jesus (see Matt. 27.25) and a fulfillment of a prediction Jesus himself had made (Mark 13.2).

The Romans themselves probably did not want the Temple system reestablished. Given the controversies earlier appointments to the high priesthood had caused and the potential of both priesthood and Temple to serve as rallying points for another revolt, they would not have wanted another high priest. Their instincts would have been correct: the Bar Kokhba coinage depicts the Temple, a symbol of nationalism and independence. To attempt the reconstruction would have also been politically unwise. Rome replaced the annual two-drachma or half-shekel Temple tax with the humiliating *Fiscus Judaicus*, now to be paid by all Jewish men over the age of twenty for the reconstruction of the temple of Jupiter Capitolinus in Rome. This policy was abolished by the emperor Nerva in 97.

Roman coins inscribed with the legend "Judea Capta" and depicting a woman weeping beneath a willow tree proclaimed the people's defeat even as they silently but eloquently displayed their grief. The Jewish population of Judea in 73 found themselves surrounded by death—without the Temple, without a clear leadership from among their own people, and without any semblance of local political and economic infrastructure. The Sanhedrin was disbanded. Jerusalem now lacked the revenues that came into the city from pilgrimages (although some Jews continued to make the trip), from the Temple tax, and from the general mechanisms by which the sacrificial system functioned. The Temple would become for the people an ideal; its rituals and practices, description and fate, would be recorded in the rabbinic documents, reviewed in schools, and recited in liturgies. But the various attempts to rebuild it, from the Bar Kokhba rebellion to the initiative in the fourth century, during the reign of Emperor Julian the Apostate, would all fail.

The war also gave rise to a new relationship between Jews and non-Jews in the land. Judea was proclaimed a separate Roman province, which entailed stationing troops. The Tenth Legion, comprised of soldiers who had already fought in the war, was permanently located to Jerusalem; together with their families, these soldiers substantially increased the Gentile population of a city that before 70 had been almost entirely Jewish. Major tracts of land were given to Roman officials and imperial favorites, and Rome constructed new cities for the growing imperial presence. Vespasian, for example, built Neapolis (modern Nablus) near the site of Shechem. Jews were, in turn, expelled from several cities, such as Caesarea. Galilee and Transjordan, which had always had significant non-Jewish populations, also saw demographic shifts.

To survive these various challenges to religious practice and cultural integrity, many Jews turned to their scriptures, and to the teachers who studied them. The Gospels and Josephus both suggest that the Pharisees gained dominance at this time. They were the logical successors to the previous leaders. Although Zealotry would flare up again in the Diaspora revolts at the beginning of the second century and, more completely, in the Bar Kokhba rebellion of 132–35, the principal Zealot leaders were either dead, in prison, or in exile. The Sadducees, many of whom had collaborated with the Romans early in the war, and who with the destruction of the Temple had lost their raison d'être, had neither the numbers nor the influence to unite the community. The Essenes living in the towns had no political structure on which to rely, and apparently no inclination to enter politics; whether they even survived as a coherent group after 70 is doubtful.

The Pharisees, now leaders in the political as well as in the religious sphere, also underwent changes. Together with the scribes, who prior to 70 represented a separate class of Torah scholars (the Gospels mention Sadducaic and Pharisaic scribes, as well as scribes as a group distinguished from both), they became known as "rabbis." The term literally means, in Aramaic, "my teacher" (see John 1.38); originally a title for someone in an authoritative position, it came to signal a member of the group responsible for development and codification of specific sets of literature (Mishnah, Tosefta, Talmud, Midrashim). These "rabbinic" writings refer to individuals as *rabbi*, as *rab* (teacher), and as *rabban* (our teacher), the collective being *ha-hakamim*, "the sages" or "the wise." No longer would this group be "Pharisees" in the sense of "separated ones"; they would be teachers.

And teach they did. Emphasizing personal piety and study of the Torah over the practices of the Temple, they continued to develop their interpretation of scripture, which came to be known as the "oral law." While the rabbis were united in their desire to live according to the way they believed the Torah taught and God wanted, they were not united around specific beliefs and practices. Nevertheless, during the period between the First and Second Revolts (70–135 CE) they apparently did work to establish greater harmony than they had prior to the First Revolt. For example, the houses of Hillel and Shammai appear now to be united. From their school in Jamnia, led by Jochanan ben Zakkai immediately after the revolt and then, from approximately 80 to 120, by Gamaliel II, their teachings spread gradually throughout Judea. Their establishment of a "house of judgment" (*bet din*) filled the gap left by the loss of the Sanhedrin. Meanwhile, other such centers developed, as at Tiberias.

Judaism thus continued, but in a much different form. Gone were the Temple, the power of the Sadducees, the challenge of the Essenes; only latent now were impulses toward political revolt. The Christian movement was increasingly turning toward the Gentile world, separating itself from both Jewish people and Jewish practice. The Diaspora communities continued, but they too faced religious changes occasioned by the loss of the Temple and political changes occasioned by the repercussions of the revolt. Yet through the teachings of the rabbis, the preservation of scripture, the ongoing practice of tradition, and continuing faith in God, Judaism would persevere.

Select Bibliography

Cohen, Shaye J. D. *From the Maccabees to the Mishna.* Library of Early Christian Classics, 7. Philadelphia: Westminster, 1987. Accessible thematic guide to formative Judaism's history, society, and politics, notable for discerning the unity among various religious expressions.

Goodman, Martin. *The Ruling Class of Judaea: The Origins of the Jewish Revolt against Rome*

A.D. 66–70. Cambridge: Cambridge University Press, 1987. Concise summary of the political, economic, and social issues leading to the First Revolt which posits the inability of the upper class to rule as a major cause of the unrest.

Grabbe, Lester L. *Judaism from Cyrus to Hadrian: Sources, History, Synthesis.* Vol. 2, *The Roman Period.* Minneapolis: Fortress, 1992. Detailed, well-annotated study with excellent discussions of primary sources, a helpful time line, and a superb bibliography.

Horsley, Richard A. *Galilee: History, Politics, People.* Valley Forge, Pa.: Trinity Press International, 1995. A focused study, substantially informed by a social-scientific approach, on the effects of Roman rule on village culture and economics.

Jagersma, Henk. *A History of Israel from Alexander the Great to Bar Kochba.* Philadelphia: Fortress, 1986. A concise, lucid summary of major political events.

Kraft, Robert, and George W. E. Nickelsburg, eds. *Early Judaism and Its Modern Interpreters.* Atlanta: Scholars Press; Philadelphia: Fortress, 1986. Essays on the literature, history, and religious beliefs and practices of Judaism in the Hellenistic and Roman periods.

Neusner, Jacob. *From Politics to Piety: The Emergence of Pharisaic Judaism.* Englewood Cliffs, N.J.: Prentice-Hall, 1978. Systematic analysis of Roman, Jewish, and Christian sources accompanied by cogent warnings about how one does "history."

Safrai, S., and M. Stern, eds. *The Jewish People in the First Century: Historical Geography, Political History, Social, Cultural and Religious Life and Institutions.* 2 vols. Assen, The Netherlands: Van Gorcum; Philadelphia: Fortress, 1974–76. Critical, accessible essays from American and Israeli scholars.

Saldarini, A. J. *Pharisees, Scribes, and Sadducees in Palestinian Society: A Sociological Approach.* Wilmington, Del.: Michael Glazier, 1988. A well-balanced study informed by social-science methodology.

Sanders, E. P. *Judaism: Practice and Belief 63 BCE–66 CE.* Philadelphia: Trinity Press International, 1994. An attempt to define "common Judaism" as represented by personal and communal observances and views.

Schürer, Emil. *The History of the Jewish People in the Time of Jesus Christ (175 B.C.–A.D. 135).* Rev. by Geza Vermes et al. 3 vols. Edinburgh: T. & T. Clark, 1973–87. Substantially updated version of a classic work.

Segal, Alan A. F. *Rebecca's Children: Judaism and Christianity in the Roman World.* Cambridge, Mass.: Harvard University Press, 1986. Readable treatment of both religious movements as responses to similar social situations.

CHAPTER ELEVEN

Churches in Context

The Jesus Movement in the Roman World

DANIEL N. SCHOWALTER

The Jesus movement consisted at first of a small group of Jews who held the unorthodox view that their teacher was the expected Messiah of Jewish tradition. Few non-Jews would have understood the importance of this peculiar point of view or why it was contested so intensely. Certainly, most Romans would not have been able to distinguish between followers of Jesus and the other unusual groups within Judaism. Officials of the vast empire had little interest in making this distinction, caring only about collecting taxes and maintaining order. If social unrest arose out of this internal Jewish conflict, both sides were liable to punishment regardless of their perspective on Jesus.

In its earliest stages, few Romans would even have been aware of the Jesus movement. Had events veered only slightly, the movement might have remained a mere blip on history's radar screen. Instead, it evolved into a system of belief and an ecclesiastical structure that would profoundly affect the Western world. This chapter covers the beginning of that evolution up until the middle of the second century CE. By then, many changes had occurred in the movement, and several characteristics of later Christianity had begun to develop.

By the middle of the second century, the majority of Jesus followers were non-Jews who were widely known as Christians. Although the title *Christ* (from the Greek for "anointed one," translating the Hebrew *mashiah*, or "messiah") had been incorporated into the group's name, the original issue—whether Jesus was the Messiah/Christ—had become peripheral. Jesus was still referred to as Christ, but the term now served more as a surname than as a title. By the middle of the second century, the Christians stood apart from other sects within Judaism. They were increasingly recognized and distrusted by Roman officials, who were prepared to suppress individuals and groups of believers, and to execute them when necessary.

How did the Jesus movement develop from an obscure Jewish sectarian group into an independent religion with a wide spectrum of followers and adversaries? The answers must rest on careful consideration of the religious, political, and social realities of the Roman world of the first century CE, along with the standard means of communication and expression in that world. Within the context of first-century society, one can examine the evidence for the evolution of the Jesus movement in the New Testament, as well as in early Christian writings outside the canon. These works provide information on how a variety of early believers in Jesus viewed the world around them and tried to respond to it.

The dominance of Christianity in later centuries makes it hard to comprehend how vulnerable these early groups of believers were. A tiny minority, they were surrounded by people who recognized a very different political, social, and religious reality—a reality based on the overwhelming power of imperial Rome.

Augustus Caesar: Savior, Founder, and Son of God

Gaius Octavius Augustus Caesar, emperor and princeps of the Roman people, died in the forty-first year of his reign, at the age of seventy-six. In that same year, 14 CE, Jesus son of Joseph was in his middle teens, past the age of maturity for a Jewish male of his time, and would have been fully engaged in his chosen career. Augustus had no reason to be aware of the existence of Jesus, but the latter would certainly have known about the great emperor. Coins commemorating the death of Augustus circulated in Galilee, where Jesus lived, and other coins, statues, official decrees, and even milestones provided a regular reminder that the Roman emperor was in control.

On the surface, Jesus and most other Jews in Palestine were numbered among the great majority of people in the empire who were subjugated by the Romans and either apathetic or antagonistic toward them. At a deeper level, however, no thinking person in the empire could ignore entirely the emperors and their representatives in the provinces. Even local officials might have seemed distant to an average resident of the empire, but these governors, generals, legates, and others had the authority to enact far-reaching social and economic policies, not to mention life-and-death powers over individuals. Understanding the influence of Roman authority, even at the farthest extent of the empire, is essential to tracing the development of the Jesus movement. The basis for much of the power and influence of Rome in the first century CE was the long and eventful reign of Augustus Caesar—Julius Caesar's grandnephew, originally named Octavian.

Julius Caesar had laid the foundations of Augustus's empire. After successfully waging war in Gaul during the 50s BCE, Caesar was voted dictator for life over the expiring Roman republic in 49 BCE. Despite his continuing military successes, Caesar's opponents soon tired of his autocratic rulership and divine pretensions, and they assassinated him on the "Ides [15th] of March," 44 BCE.

To many aristocratic Romans, Caesar's demise vindicated the republic, the form of government that had served the Romans since 509 BCE. Roman military forces had been expanding the republic's influence over ever-wider territories. Beginning with central Italy, Roman power eventually extended westward to Baetica in southern Spain, southward to parts of North Africa, and eastward over Macedonia, Greece, and parts of Asia Minor, all the way to Syria and Palestine at the eastern end of the Mediterranean Sea.

The republic was an oligarchy controlled by an elite, self-perpetuating body of Roman citizens, the senators. Two consuls were elected for one-year terms to lead the senate and, through it, all of Rome. Magistrates were also elected to rule the captured territories, known as provinces, although sometimes the provinces were controlled through special arrangements such as client kings. It was with this kind of Roman approval and support that Herod the Great was appointed by the senate as king of the Jews in 40 BCE. Thus, the Roman republic had long functioned as an effective system of government, especially for the aristocratic segment of society that controlled it. When Julius Caesar usurped the power of the senate on the basis of his prowess as a military general, he offended others in the ruling class, and eventually perished at their hands.

After Caesar's death in 44 BCE, his grandnephew and adopted son, Octavian, joined with two other military leaders, Mark Antony and Lepidus, to form a coalition to rule the empire. This triumvirate broke down quickly, however, and a major civil war erupted between the forces of Mark Antony in the east and those of Octavian in the west. In 31 BCE, at the battle of Actium off the coast of western Greece, Octavian prevailed, and Mark Antony fled to Egypt, ruled by his consort Cleopatra VII. Their suicides quickly followed, and the victorious Octavian gained sole control of Egypt and the entire Roman Empire. From that time on, Egypt remained the personal property of the emperor and the source of much wealth for him.

Octavian was also quick to reinforce the imperial boundaries. In Judea he confirmed Herod's rule as client king, even though Herod had sided with Antony in the civil war. Octavian knew that control of the eastern frontier was essential, and Herod had shown that he would go to great lengths to maintain peace in his region.

Octavian consolidated his power in Rome by celebrating a triumphal procession (29 BCE) and adopting the name *Augustus* (27 BCE), a venerable religious title emphasizing his regard for Roman traditions. He bore this title for the remainder of his reign, and in his honor every emperor after him was also called Augustus. Because his accession ended a bloody civil war, Augustus won support from most of Roman society. The *Pax Augusta* ("Peace of Augustus") was celebrated with festivals, coin issues, statues, and monuments around the empire. The most famous of these was the ornate Ara Pacis ("Altar of Peace") set up for Augustus in Rome.

The *Pax Augusta* brought stability to the empire as a whole, but its benefits were not spread evenly. While some enjoyed freedom and prosperity, subject peoples and those on the fringes of society experienced oppression. Such inequity often leads to unrest and even insurrection, and some scholars have viewed the ministry of Jesus as a hostile response to oppression by the Romans and their representatives in the east. Certainly the Roman treatment of Jesus and later of his followers indicates that they were considered a threat to the peace.

Although the senate recognized the importance of order and stability, it tended to look with suspicion on the success of any individual. Senators watched nervously as Augustus used his control over the armies to enhance his own authority and prestige. Having learned from the fate of his adopted father, Augustus gave the appearance of attending to senatorial concerns. He maintained traditional forms of leadership, while restructuring the government in a way that made the republic little more than a quaint memory. In the *Res gestae divi Augusti*—an extensive statement of his accomplishments inscribed in public places throughout the empire—Augustus says, "I accepted no authority given to me unless it was according to custom" (1.6). Augustus avoided inflammatory titles, preferring to be known as "princeps," a traditional designation for a leading senator. "I presided over all in official rank, but I held no more power than my fellow magistrates" (*Res gestae* 6.34). Notwithstanding such modest professions, the rule of Augustus went unchallenged. The senate could confirm his honors and titles, but this meant little more than recognizing the status quo: Augustus's absolute control of the armies gave him absolute control of the empire.

Generally, Augustus avoided direct claim to divine status, but he found other ways of using the gods to enhance his authority. In the Greco-Roman world, the vast majority of people believed that life was controlled by innumerable divine forces. To ensure a happy life, these divinities had to be appeased through sacrifices and other acts of devotion. Some gods remained aloof from human beings; others intervened directly in everyday affairs. Even human beings could manifest different levels of divinity. Military or athletic heroes and exceptional rulers were acclaimed as gods posthumously, and sometimes while still alive.

Thus it is not surprising that after his death the followers of Jesus struggled with the connection between their leader and God. Given his accomplishments, it is natural that the Jesus movement quickly came to understand Jesus as son of God, and eventually as God incarnate. But although the faith in Jesus developed in the polytheistic Roman world, its roots were firmly planted in Jewish monotheism. Calling Jesus "God," then, raised significant questions about how there could be more than one god. For three centuries there were many attempts to resolve this issue, until the Council of Nicea in 325 CE developed a credal formulation and declared all others heretical.

Augustus, on the other hand, contended with the issue of divine honors during his own lifetime. Since his adopted father, Julius Caesar, had been posthumously proclaimed to be a god by the senate (42 BCE), Augustus had used the title *son of god* (*divi filius*) as part of his official nomenclature on coins and inscriptions throughout the empire, announcing to all that the reign of Augustus enjoyed divine sanction. Augustus also promoted his special connection to the god Apollo, who was famous for using his chariot to pull the sun across the sky each day. The establishment of a temple of Apollo on the Palatine Hill in Rome (28 BCE) served both to honor the god and to remind the people that he was the patron of Augustus.

To solidify support in the provinces for himself and for Roman rule, Augustus allowed worship of himself as part of the honors given to the deified city of Rome. Gradually, new temples to Roma and Augustus arose in cities throughout the empire. The Roma and Augustus temple in Athens was erected on the Acropolis, close to the Athenians' most sacred buildings, symbolizing the powerful role that the emperor had come to play in Greece. In some places, Augustus himself came to be worshiped as a god, although officially he was reluctant to accept such honors.

Scholars often associate extravagant honors for the emperor with the eastern provinces, but Augustus also received spectacular tributes in the west that suggested a
connection with the divine. Excavations in Rome have revealed the remains of an
enormous sundial system inscribed on the pavement of the Campus Martius, a military assembly ground, arranged so that on Augustus's birthday the sundial's shadow
moved along the center of the grid and ascended the steps of the Ara Pacis, suggesting
that the sun-god was leading the celebration in the emperor's honor.

In many ways, Augustus owed his success as princeps to the use of a variety of
popular media to promote loyalty among his far-flung subjects. Whether minted on
coins, chiseled in sculptured images, or written into the latest literature, messages
promoting the emperor came to the attention of anyone living under Roman control.
Coins announcing the vast array of imperial accomplishments flooded the empire.
Some were minted in Rome and distributed, others served as statements of loyalty
from local officials. Many coins highlighted a connection with the divine by depicting
Augustus on one side, with a scene symbolizing a deity on the other. Coin issues
commemorated major events, including the building of roads and aqueducts, military
victories, the founding of temples, and travels of the emperor. Because coinage came
in a variety of denominations, from small copper coins to large commemorative
medallions, the emperor's images found their way into the hands of a wide cross-
section of residents of the empire. These images portrayed a variety of imperial activities, but their purpose was always to elicit support for the emperor and his policies
by promoting his extraordinary deeds.

The emperor's accomplishments were also celebrated in a variety of sculptural
materials and formats. Many busts of Augustus, standing figures, and even equestrian
statues have been discovered. Often such representations were originally rendered in
bronze, but few have survived (the value of the material to later generations meant
that most metal statues were melted down).

Remains of marble statuary are much more common. Carved relief panels preserve
a glimpse of Roman life and ritual. The famous reliefs on the reconstructed Ara Pacis
in Rome include images of the gods and of a procession, most likely the one commemorating the dedication of this altar to the Augustan peace. Numerous marble
statues and sculptural fragments of Augustus indicate the extent to which his image
was used as a reminder of Roman presence and power. Displays from imperial statuary also permitted subjects to show respect and loyalty. The fixed media of carved
statues allowed for a degree of control of the emperor's image unavailable in a modern
multimedia culture. When Augustus died in 14 CE, he had ruled for over forty years
and was almost eighty years old, but his image as portrayed on works of art throughout the empire was still that of a powerful and energetic young princeps.

Augustus also benefited from the literary works of supportive authors. Gaius Mae-
cenas, his close friend and political ally, is credited with financing the efforts of
authors like Virgil and Horace, who used the written word to extol the virtues of
Rome and especially of Augustus. Although Virgil's epic *The Aeneid* tells the story of
the mythical founding of Rome, it also looks forward to: "Augustus Caesar, offspring
of a god, who will establish again the golden age in the fields where Saturn ruled, and
will extend his empire . . . to a place beyond the stars" (*Aeneid* 6.792–95). Written

at the outset of the reign of Augustus, this work can be read as a prophecy of the greatness to come, and also as a contribution to its fulfillment.

The *Carmen saeculare* by Horace was also sponsored by Augustus to mark the beginning of a new era in Roman history in 17 BCE. As part of the three-day celebration, a children's chorus sang Horace's hymn and amplified the glory of Rome: "Now Faith and Peace and Honor and venerable Modesty and disregarded Virtue have courage to return, and prosperous Plenty appears with her cornucopia" (*Carmen saeculare* 57–60). Credit for this prosperity goes to Augustus, a point Horace makes explicitly elsewhere: "Your reign, O Caesar, has brought abundant produce to the fields . . . has removed crime and recalled the ancestral ways by which the Latin name and the strength of Italy were distinguished, and the reputation and power of our empire extended from the resting place of the sun to its rising" (*Odes* 4.15.4–16).

This remarkable ancient "media blitz" contrasts sharply with how the message of the Jesus movement was transmitted. Although written words about the significance of following Jesus are attested by the mid-first century CE in Paul's letters, we have no record of anything being written about the life and teachings of Jesus until several decades after his death. Without the benefit of accomplished authors, coins and statues bearing his image, or impressive monuments, the stories of Jesus circulated from person to person. Against all odds, those stories and the faith they engendered survived periods of obscurity, times of tribulation, and even the threat of persecution and death. As uncovered and reconstructed by modern scholars, the remnants of the propaganda efforts for Augustus are impressive, but considering the limited resources they had to work with, the first followers of Jesus should be credited with an even more successful public relations campaign.

In 12 BCE, Augustus assumed the position of pontifex maximus, the chief of the official priests of Rome, who was responsible for ceremonies intended to ensure the well-being of the Roman state. This was a concentration of power in which the unchallenged political strength of Augustus was combined with ultimate religious authority. Until the fourth century CE, all succeeding emperors served as pontifex maximus.

Augustus also set a precedent for most of his successors when he received the title *pater patriae* ("father of his country") from the senate in 2 BCE. The title, which earlier had been awarded to Julius Caesar and to the great Roman orator Cicero, emphasized that Rome was indebted to the holder as to a father. It also had to bring to mind the absolute power of the father (*patria potestas*) within the Roman family. Under Roman law, the *paterfamilias* had life-and-death control over family members.

During his later years, Augustus promoted social legislation aimed at encouraging childbirth and securing the future of the empire. He himself, however, was not to have the satisfaction of a natural male heir. Instead, he adopted as his successor the general Tiberius, also a member of the Julio-Claudian family, who ruled after the death of Augustus in 14 CE.

Some of Augustus's titles and appellations continued to be used by his successors, and several came to be shared by other figures of great authority. A number of these titles were later applied to Jesus. The Jesus followers were not equating their leader with Augustus; they would have thought such a comparison inappropriate. But the influence of Augustan power pervaded the empire, and similarities of usage did not go unnoticed. Many of those who referred to Jesus as "son of god" knew perfectly well that a Latin form of the phrase was among the most frequent designations for Augustus and his successors. Another example of shared terminology was the Greek term *euaggelion* ("good news"), often used to introduce announcements about the emperor and his deeds. The same term—usually translated as "gospel"—was used by the earliest followers of Jesus to describe the message they preached, and later as the designation for written stories about Jesus' life and teachings.

When Augustus died forty-five years after his victory at Actium, the Roman people celebrated his memory and the Roman senate recognized that their deceased princeps had become a god. In Palestine the young Jesus and his friends probably paid little attention. The death of Augustus did nothing to relieve the smothering effect of Roman oppression on the Jews and other subject peoples. Later, of course, the imperial power established during the long reign of Augustus would profoundly influence the followers of Jesus, but ultimately their movement would transform the empire.

Ruling in the Shadow of Greatness: The Reign of Tiberius

In the institutions he had created and supported, Augustus left little doubt that the precedent of a single omnipotent ruler would continue. But it was unclear who the successor would be, and how the transition from one ruler to another would take place.

Augustus's relationship with his successor Tiberius had been tumultuous. They shared in glorious military successes and together mourned the death of an infant born to Tiberius and Augustus's daughter, Julia. But in the end there were suggestions that Tiberius was at best Augustus's reluctant choice as successor. The second-century historian Suetonius is aware of these reports, but his comments on Tiberius include quotations from Augustan correspondence that indicate a more positive attitude: "I beseech the gods that they will preserve you for us and allow you good health now and always, unless they despise the people of Rome" (*Lives of the Caesars, Tiberius* 21.6). Tacitus, who also wrote in the early second century, claims that Tiberius was chosen only because Augustus had "observed in him pride and ferocity, and sought to reflect honor to himself by the comparison" (*Annales* 1.10).

Whatever his motivation in choosing Tiberius, once Augustus died, his authority was transferred with relative ease. Tiberius had received a share of imperial power before the death of Augustus, and thus was the apparent successor. Both Suetonius and Tacitus speak of Tiberius's supposed reluctance to accept power, but after observing the proper rituals for the death of Augustus, the senate proclaimed Tiberius emperor. Opposition came from several of the northern legions, whose soldiers put forward their own general, Germanicus. Apparently Germanicus chose not to take advantage of his troops' support and pledged loyalty to his new emperor, thereby stemming the uprising. The incident did highlight the dependence of the emperor's power on control of the Roman army, and foreshadowed the significant role that the legions would play in choosing future rulers.

Tiberius took power amid expressions of joy and hope across the empire. So great were the accomplishments of Augustus that there was a naturally high level of expectation for his successor. In some provinces, that expectation was translated into spectacular divine honors. The Athenians honored Tiberius by rededicating to him a large monument in their central market (*agora*). An inscription on the monument base refers to the emperor as "the god Augustus" and "a benefactor of the city" (*Inscriptiones Graecae* II² 4209). For his part, Tiberius appears to have refused such honors for himself, but he did emphasize his divine connections by minting coins to the divinized Augustus that highlighted his own status as "son of god."

Unfortunately, Tiberius did not fulfill these hopes. He succeeded in the sense of continuing the office and the practices of Augustus, but accomplished little on his own initiative. Suetonius describes him as a reluctant ruler who began by making sincere attempts to appease all his constituencies. But gradually, he succumbed to the pressures of governing such a vast empire. By the end of his reign, Tiberius was so obsessed with himself and his power that he reportedly engaged in all manner of immoral and depraved activities. At the same time, like Herod in Judea, he suffered from a destructive paranoia and ordered that all potential successors be put to death, including members of his own family. Eventually, Tiberius retreated permanently to the island of Capri.

Tiberius is also remembered for his cruelty toward religions outside the Roman mainstream. According to Suetonius, he went to great lengths to suppress Judaism and the Egyptian mystery rites, "ordering any who held such superstitious beliefs to burn all their religious vestments and instruments" (*Tiberius* 36). This opposition reflects a long-standing Roman suspicion of unusual religious activity, especially toward groups whose religious views tempered their enthusiasm toward the various expressions of piety that made up Roman religion. In this case, Egyptian cults eventually became a widely accepted part of the diverse religious practice in the empire, but the monotheistic Jews continued to be suspect.

The movement of Jesus followers that grew out of Judaism was in its infancy during Tiberius's later years. Tiberius and his representatives would have had neither the ability nor the desire to distinguish between Jews who believed in Jesus as Messiah and the vast majority of Jews who did not. Any suppression of Judaism would have been felt equally by Jewish believers in Jesus, unless they had withdrawn from all of their traditional practices, which is unlikely at this early stage in the movement.

On the other hand, later Jesus followers were anxious to place their accounts of the early movement within the historical and chronological context of the Roman Empire. The Gospel of Luke was probably written around 90 CE, but the author was careful to detail the Roman power structure of an earlier age: Augustus as emperor and Quirinius as governor of Syria at the time of Jesus' birth, and Tiberius ruling when John the Baptist began his ministry (Luke 2.1–2; 3.1).

Whether Tiberius was as harsh with the Jews as Suetonius indicates, he and his advisers no doubt deliberately selected Pontius Pilate as governor in Judea. A governor's main duty was to oversee the emperor's interests in the territory, which included maintaining order and dealing with potential sources of sedition. Whatever else Jesus might have been saying and doing in Pilate's domain, his ability to keep a regular group of followers and to attract large crowds warranted close scrutiny. Although the New Testament condemns the Jewish authorities as responsible for Jesus' death, Pilate as the local voice of Roman authority would have needed little encouragement to eliminate any source of potential insurrection. Pilate's role in the execution of Jesus is recounted in vivid detail by the Gospel writers, but it is unlikely that a Roman governor would have become so directly involved in the execution of a criminal. Possibly, Pilate's deputies dealt with Jesus and notified their superior. In any case Pilate would have noted the elimination of a potential revolutionary and included Jesus' death in a regular report on activity in Judea. Tiberius, for his part, might have noted with satisfaction that the governor in Judea was doing his job.

Immediately after the death of Jesus, his followers must have been in a state of confusion and shock. Although the expectations for his mission differed, none could have anticipated the failure and death of their leader. Luke's portrayal of two disciples on the road to Emmaus captures this mood of disappointment. For Luke this disappointment is ironic, since the disciples are discussing their uncertainties in the light of Jesus' death, all the while talking with the resurrected Christ but not recognizing him (Luke 24.13–35). The belief that Jesus had risen served as the catalyst for the disciples to recover from their grief and begin spreading the good news throughout the Mediterranean world.

Luke also provides the only known record of this early mission in his second volume, Acts of the Apostles. Like the Gospels, Acts was written at least forty years after the death of Jesus, and decades of development within the movement influenced its account. It is impossible to know exactly what took place in those first years after the death of Jesus. Luke himself admits that he was not reporting as an eyewitness, but conveying oral tradition (Luke 1.1–2). What is clear is that the spreading of the message about Jesus was immensely successful. The combination of intentional proselytizing by individuals like Paul and the natural movement of believers meant that by the middle of the first century churches had been established in most of the major cities of the empire, including Rome.

Runaway Power: The Reign of Gaius

If the Roman legions had had their way, Germanicus rather than Tiberius would have succeeded Augustus. Germanicus died in 19 CE, but his son Gaius Julius Caesar inherited his position as heir to the empire. Nicknamed "Caligula," the term for the small military boots he wore as a child, Gaius had inherited his father's popularity with the armies and the people. According to later records, however, his tendency toward cruelty was apparent even before he came to power. Tiberius himself felt that allowing Gaius to live would prove the ruin of himself and of all people. Because of his immense popularity, however, Gaius was the unanimous choice of the senate as emperor when Tiberius died in 37 CE. Suetonius reports that he was welcomed by 160,000 sacrifices during the first three months of his reign (*Gaius Caligula* 11, 14).

Gaius came to power at the age of twenty-five, and although he is credited with extensive achievements, his attitude and actions proved to be a disappointment to the troops and others who had supported him. Caligula quickly embraced a more absolute sense of his authority and severely punished anyone who challenged it. The image of the princeps as a first among equals gave way to a sense of the emperor as monarch. There was probably little difference between Gaius's power and that wielded by his predecessors, but Gaius was unwilling to feign humility.

Gaius claimed that being emperor made him equal with the gods and deserving of divine worship. Suetonius mentions that Gaius imported famous statues of the gods and ordered that likenesses of his head be substituted for the divinity's. Gaius also set up a temple to his own divine spirit, complete with priests and exotic sacrificial victims (*Gaius Caligula* 22). The claim to divine honors outraged some Romans, so most emperors attempted to maintain a balance between modesty and offending those who wanted to pay homage to them. Gaius, however, had no such inclination to moderation.

Demanding and receiving divine honors, Gaius raged against anyone who refused to offer them. Thus the Jews, who would not worship any god but their own, were frequently the targets of the emperor's wrath. The Jewish philosopher Philo of Alexandria details what transpired when Gaius proposed to force the Jews to worship him by installing his statue in the Temple in Jerusalem (*Legatio ad Gaium* 30–42; a shorter and slightly different account of the same story is found in Josephus, *Jewish War* 2.10). Philo uses this account to illustrate the mental instability of Gaius, who had suffered a life-threatening illness in the eighth month of his reign. In Philo's view, this illness caused a "turning to wildness, or rather bringing to light the savagery that he had hidden under the actor's mask" (*Legatio ad Gaium* 22).

In trying to convince Gaius to abandon his plan to desecrate the Temple, Philo cites the example of the moderation of the deified Augustus in dealing with the Jews: "So highly did he regard our concerns that he and almost his whole family furnished our sanctuary with the richness of his offerings, commanding that perpetual burnt offerings should be made each day at his own expense as a tribute to the most high God" (*Legatio ad Gaium* 157). Although this description of respect for the Jews might be hyperbole, Philo wrote it only twenty-five years after the death of Augustus, so it could reflect a genuine level of tolerance. Philo cites examples from Tiberius as well, and records that Gaius was eventually persuaded to abandon his plan to install his statue in the Temple, without changing his fundamentally negative disposition toward the Jews.

Philo concludes his discussion of Gaius with a description of an audience that he and other Jewish leaders from Alexandria had with the emperor. This embassy meets with Gaius in hope of defending their right to live peacefully in the city. Instead, Gaius becomes the accuser of the Jews in general: "Are you the god-haters who do not know me as a god, a god acknowledged by all others, but not named by you?" The Jewish delegation responds that they show their loyalty by offering regular sacrifice on behalf of the emperor, but Gaius is unmoved: "You have made offerings, but to another, even if it was for me. What good is it then, for you have not sacrificed to me." Eventually, Gaius dismisses the Jewish embassy with an uncharacteristically mild rebuke, saying that they seemed "to be unlucky rather than evil, and to be foolish in not believing that I have been allotted the nature of a god" (*Legatio ad Gaium* 353, 357, 367).

Jewish followers of Jesus would have received the same harsh treatment. At this time the development of a mission to "the nations" began to bring non-Jews into the Jesus movement. This inclusion of Gentiles led to internal debates about whether one needed to be a Jew before being a follower of Jesus (Acts 10–11; 15; Gal. 1–5). The participation of non-Jews must also have raised the profile of the movement considerably. Paul makes it clear that he suffered persecution both from Jewish authorities and because of his efforts to bring Gentiles into the church (2 Cor. 11.24–26). When people who all their lives had worshiped the Greco-Roman gods and given due homage to the emperor suddenly refused to do so, social unrest arose. This no emperor could tolerate, and Gaius responded with brutality.

While the Jews and the Jesus followers lay at the mercy of the divine emperor's moods, Gaius's pretensions were also infuriating to more powerful members of society. After less than four years as emperor, Gaius Caligula was assassinated by soldiers of the Praetorian Guard assigned to protect him.

To Be or Not to Be a God: The Reign of Claudius

When Gaius Caligula died in 41 CE, some in the Roman senate sought to restore the republic. The military, on the other hand, saw an advantage in having only one ruler if he could be easily influenced. Having eliminated the uncontrollable Gaius, the Praetorian Guard felt that they had found a potential puppet in his fifty-year-old uncle, Tiberius Claudius Nero Germanicus. The troops took Claudius to their camp and declared him to be emperor. Eventually the senators capitulated and voted power to Claudius, who began a thirteen-year reign that would be more productive than either the senate or the army had anticipated.

After voting appropriate honors and titles to the new emperor, the senate attempted to dishonor Gaius Caligula officially. Claudius blocked this legislation, but on his own removed the name and image of his predecessor from all civic records. Remembering the reasons for Gaius's downfall, the new emperor was especially careful about accepting honors that could be construed as excessive. In a letter to the citizens of Alexandria in Egypt, Claudius responded to the offer of honors by accepting some, such as a formal celebration of his birthday and statues erected to his family and to the peace secured by his reign (Pax Claudiana), but rejecting others. He adamantly refused the dedication to him of temples and priesthoods, saying that these were to be reserved for the gods. Claudius thus showed both an awareness of his own humanity and a respect for the consequences of claiming excessive honors.

This letter (Corpus papyrorum Judaicarum II 153) illustrates the carefully balanced power relationships that held together the empire. When Claudius came to power, governing bodies in provincial cities like Alexandria rushed to show loyalty to the new emperor. After passing various honorific decrees, leaders in each city would send representatives to pay tribute and pledge support. It remained for the emperor to endorse these gestures, thereby ratifying the local actions. Through this reciprocal action, the emperor established a reliable contingent of powerful persons in the main cities, which in turn hoped to ensure future benefactions from the emperor.

This relationship made the cities dependent on the emperor's approval for many of their actions. In his letter, Claudius responds to other questions that the Alexandrians raised about the local political and social structure. One concerns the institution of a lottery system for selecting priests for the temple of the deified Augustus. Ever since Augustus's postmortem deification, cities had set up sacred structures and instituted religious rituals to honor the divine Augustus. At the same time, various religious rites involving the emperor were an important means of articulating the mutual relationships that held the empire together.

The structures, statuary, and other images associated with the emperor tangibly represented Roman power, even in distant provincial cities. At the same time, the rituals associated with the emperor allowed people to demonstrate their loyalty and pay honor to the power of Rome as manifested through the emperor. Priests of the divine Augustus stood at the intersection of this relationship, mediating the bonds of loyalty and patronage. As such, the Augustan priesthood was a highly significant and coveted position in the city. Citing earlier practice, Claudius stipulated that the priest should be chosen by lot, eliminating the possibility of divisive competition or the monopolization of the office by powerful families or groups.

The letter from Claudius to the Alexandrians also sheds light on a long-standing social conflict involving the Jewish population in the city. Representatives of both parties had defended their actions before the emperor, but Claudius was upset with everyone involved, and he used harsh language to express his anger. Claudius affirmed the rights of the Jews, who had lived in the city for many years, and, citing precedent from Augustus, insisted that they be allowed to follow their traditional religious customs. On the other hand, he reminded the Jews that they were aliens in the city, and warned them against trying to participate in civic functions where they were not welcome.

Apparently, some Jews were attempting to improve their status by joining in games and other activities. This intrusion prompted some Alexandrians to attack the Jewish community, at times violently. Claudius threatened to punish both sides if the dispute was not resolved, but he imposed extra restrictions on the Jews. Most notably, in order to relieve the xenophobic fears of the Alexandrians, the emperor prohibited further Jewish immigration into the city. These actions illustrated the Roman desire to maintain order, whatever the cost. Unlike Gaius Caligula, Claudius displayed no animosity toward the Jews or their religion, but he would not tolerate any activity that might upset the social order in this important provincial city. The same lack of tolerance is demonstrated in an incident involving Claudius and Jewish residents of Rome.

The second-century historian Suetonius notes in passing that Claudius expelled the Jews from Rome because of a continuous disturbance caused by *Chrestus* (*Claudius* 25). It is possible that this refers to conflict within the Jewish community over the claims that Jesus fulfilled expectations for the anointed one, the Messiah, or *Christos* in Greek. If so, then by the mid-40s CE the Jewish population of Rome included some followers of Jesus. Exactly how the message of Jesus reached Rome is not clear. It may have been brought by missionaries, or by Jewish members of the movement who traveled or relocated to Rome. Apparently, these Jesus followers were willing to argue for their belief, creating a disturbance in the Jewish community and in the capital city. Moreover, if *Chrestus* does refer to Christ, this is the earliest reference to the activity of the Jesus movement outside Christian literature. The report is sketchy, but Suetonius seems to be describing a dispute involving the Jewish community, with no mention of the problems associated with Gentiles joining the churches.

For most Jews, Jesus had simply not lived up to what Jewish scriptures predicted for the coming Messiah. Jewish followers of Jesus, however, read many biblical passages as prophecies that Jesus had fulfilled. Those who did not see Jesus as the Christ were not persuaded by such interpretations. They remained unconvinced by promises

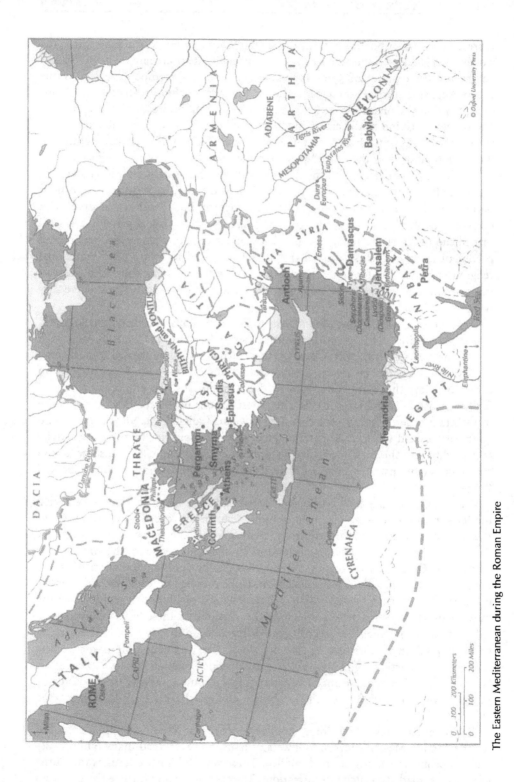

The Eastern Mediterranean during the Roman Empire

that Jesus would return to earth to complete the messianic work of setting up God's kingdom. This disagreement about Jesus as Christ was the fundamental difference that eventually isolated the Jesus followers from Judaism, and caused the creation of a separate religion known as Christianity. During the reign of Claudius (41–54 CE), however, this complete separation still lay in the future. Claudius did not care at all about the details of the dispute over *Chrestus*, but once it led to social disorder, he acted swiftly and decisively to end it. The report by Suetonius may be exaggerated, but the expulsion order it describes was well within character for a Roman emperor.

After a reign that included many effective and harsh efforts to maintain order, Claudius died from other than natural causes. Agrippina, the wife of Claudius and mother of Nero, was the prime suspect, accused by Roman historians of assassinating her husband with poisoned mushrooms. Nero came to power and shortly thereafter eliminated his one rival, Britannicus, Claudius's fourteen-year-old son.

Neither Tiberius nor Gaius had been deified after death, but the senate recognized Claudius as a god despite opposition. After the senate's action, someone—probably Seneca, the philosopher and teacher of Nero—wrote a satirical account of Claudius's deification. Known as the *Apocalocyntosis* ("pumpkinification"), this imaginative piece recorded a controversy among the gods as to whether the newest god, Claudius, should be admitted to the heavenly court. After rancorous debate, the divine Augustus himself spoke against Claudius because of his murderous cruelty, and the gods dispatched Claudius to Hades to stand trial for his crimes.

Times of Terror: The Reign of Nero

Nero came to power amid great hopes. A Greek document from Egypt records the proclamation announcing the death of Claudius and painting an optimistic picture for the reign of his successor: "The Caesar [Claudius], god manifest, who had to pay his debt to his ancestors, has joined them, and the expectation and hope of the world has been declared emperor, the good spirit of the world and source of all things, Nero, has been declared Caesar. Therefore, wearing garlands and with sacrifices of oxen, we ought all to give thanks to all the gods"(*Papyrus oxyrhynchus* 1021). By the time of Nero's accession, the imperial family was poised to ensure smooth transition of power after the death of an emperor. This kind of proclamation was meant to reassure people all around the empire and to begin the immediate shift in loyalty to the next Caesar. In spite of the treachery surrounding the death of Claudius, Nero began his reign by paying homage to his predecessor in ritual acts and by new coin issues. Nero wanted to emphasize his connection to the divinized Claudius, although he was now free to rule as he liked.

In the proclamation, Claudius is referred to as god manifest, and Nero is called "good spirit of the world and source of all good things." The term *spirit* here (Greek *daimon*) refers to a wide range of semidivine entities thought to be present in the world. The same word is used in the Gospels to describe the evil spirits cast out by Jesus, but here it is specified as a good spirit and applied to the new emperor. Most likely the reference is to the divine element (Latin *genius*) perceived to be part of Nero's makeup.

Initially, the seventeen-year-old Nero seems to have lived up to the high hopes of his admirers, missing no opportunity "for acts of generosity and mercy" (Suetonius,

Nero 10). Before long, however, the people's confidence in the new princeps was shattered. Shortly after coming to power, Nero began to devote much of his time, effort, and treasury to fulfilling his desires for music, theater, and sport. He took advantage of a trip to Greece to compete in contests of all sorts against the greatest of Greek performers and athletes. Not surprisingly, the emperor won all the contests he entered, receiving the prize for a chariot race even when he fell out of his vehicle and did not reach the finish line (Suetonius, *Nero* 24.2).

So anxious were the Greeks to please the emperor that they rescheduled contests, including the Olympics, to permit him to participate in all of them during his visit. The cities of Greece also poured out lavish honors on the emperor. In Athens, an inscription in large bronze letters was affixed to the architrave blocks on the east side of the Parthenon (*Inscriptiones Graecae* II² 3277). Thus, the most famous structure in all of Greece now served as a signboard to honor "the emperor supreme, Nero Caesar Claudius Augustus Germanicus, son of god."

After winning his sham victories in Greece, Nero returned triumphantly to Rome and continued his performing career at the expense of other duties. The extent of Nero's distraction is captured by Dio Cassius, who tells how Nero was responsible for the destructive fire that ravaged the city for nine days during the summer of 64 CE. To emphasize his point, the historian describes Nero standing on the roof of the palace singing and playing a small harp, or cithara (Dio Cassius 62.18.1).

Nero was suspected of setting the fire to create open space for his building projects. The most striking part of the "new city" created in the aftermath of the fire was an extravagant palace complex. The Golden House, as it was called, was really a spacious country villa covering 50 hectares (125 acres) in the middle of the crowded city. Suetonius is both awed and disgusted by the structure that demonstrated how "ruinously prodigal" Nero was:

> The courtyard was of such a size that a colossal image of Nero, 120 feet high, stood in it, and so wide that it had a triple colonnade a mile long. There was a pond, like a sea, with buildings representing cities surrounding it; and various landscapes with tilled fields, vineyards, pastures, and woodlands, and great numbers of every kind of domestic and wild animal.

Underlining his contempt, Suetonius reports that Nero dedicated his new structure by saying that "he was finally beginning to dwell like a human being" (*Nero* 31).

Although the Golden House was never completed, Tacitus makes it clear that the building had a tremendous impact on the long-term development of Roman architecture (*Annales* 15.43). The immediate impact on the city, however, was devastating, and the people of Rome held Nero responsible for the blaze. In the early second century Tacitus wrote that to deflect blame, Nero accused a group of people, "known for their shameful deeds, whom the public refers to as Christians" (*Annales* 15.44).

It is significant that Tacitus—making one of the earliest direct references to Jesus' followers outside the New Testament—uses the popular name *Christiani* to describe them. The name *Christian* is not used in the earliest New Testament literature, the letters of Paul and the Gospels. The authors of these documents considered belief in Jesus as the Messiah to be a fulfillment of Judaism and saw no need to identify themselves as a group apart from that tradition. The term *Christian* appears twice in the book of Acts and once in 1 Peter. In all three instances, the context of the usage implies that the title was given to the Jesus followers by others, and (as in Tacitus) in 1 Peter the title is a term of approbation: "But if one among you should suffer as a 'Christian,' do not be ashamed, but glorify God on account of this name" (1 Pet. 4.16; my translation). This supports the claim of Tacitus that it was the crowds who gave the name *Christian* to the believers, and suggests that only later did it become a term of self-identification.

In reporting on the reaction to the fire of Rome, Tacitus also provides a brief history of the Jesus movement, mentioning that "Christus," the founder, had been executed in Judea by the procurator Pontius Pilate during the reign of Tiberius. He adds that the "deadly superstition" was temporarily repressed, but eventually revived and spread to Rome, "the city where horrible and shameful things from all over the world flow together and are praised" (*Annales* 15.44). The Christians were accused of practicing superstition because their refusal to worship the traditional gods of Rome seemed to jeopardize the stability of Roman society. Thus it would have been natural to blame them for the tragic conflagration.

Nero's punishments were said to be so horrible, however, that pity for the Christians replaced initial popular anger. Some condemned believers were covered with wild beast skins and torn to death by dogs; others were crucified and burned as human torches (*Annales* 15.44). These atrocities are said to have taken place in Nero's garden and racecourse (*circus*).

In describing this repression of Christianity under Nero, Tacitus is influenced by concerns over the movement in his own time, when the church was increasingly a force to be reckoned with and when this kind of literary attack was just one of the weapons used against it. During the first decade of the second century, the correspondence between Pliny the Younger and the emperor Trajan (98–117) reveals anxiety about private associations in general and Christianity in particular. Trajan tells Pliny not to allow the formation of an association of firefighters at Nicomedia out of fear that it might turn into a political club. Pliny also asks for confirmation of his handling of persons accused of being Christians in the regions of Pontus and Bithynia (*Epistulae* 10.34, 10.96). It is possible that Tacitus reads this contemporary concern back into earlier history when describing Nero's response to the fire at Rome.

Nero was capable of this kind of evil, but it is strange that the brutality went unreported for fifty years. If Nero did execute followers of Jesus in such horrible ways, it did not become common practice. In the early second century, Pliny the Younger mentions that he had never been present at the trial of a Christian. Since Pliny had spent the previous thirty years deeply involved in legal and political matters in the capital, this comment implies that few trials of Christians took place in Rome during the second half of the first century.

In the wake of the fire, Nero could have lashed out at a particularly vulnerable group, but there is no evidence that imperial officials sponsored systematic or widespread persecution of Jesus followers for the rest of the first century or well into the second. Occasional points of conflict, like the arrest and execution of Bishop Ignatius of Antioch and the tribulation inspiring the book of Revelation, occur around the end of the first century but appear to be isolated incidents. Some scholars see the book of Revelation as a response to persecution of Jesus followers during the reign of Nero rather than under Domitian (81–96 CE). There is no other evidence, however, that Nero's attacks on believers in Jesus went beyond the response to the fire reported by Tacitus. Later church tradition blaming Nero for the execution at Rome of Paul and Peter may be based in large part on the emperor's reputation.

A further clue to the extent of imperial persecution under Nero can be found in Paul's letter to the community of Jesus followers in Rome in which Paul encourages his readers to cooperate with the empire: "Let every person be subject to the governing authorities; for there is no authority except from God, and those authorities that exist have been instituted by God. Therefore whoever resists authority resists what God has appointed, and those who resist will incur judgment" (Rom. 13.1–2). This admonition reveals Paul's desire to see the community of believers operating within the Roman political apparatus. He argues that the political authority "is God's servant for your good." The only people who have reason to fear this servant are those who do evil rather than good. Paul must know that this is not always true, since he himself had suffered at the hands of authorities during his ministry (2 Cor. 11). Nevertheless, Paul advises the church in Rome to acquiesce to the usual demands of the governing body: "Pay to all what is due them—taxes to whom taxes are due, revenue to whom revenue is due, respect to whom respect is due, honor to whom honor is due" (Rom. 13.7). Later writers will be even more explicit in telling the community how to react in the face of authorities who threaten them (see 1 Peter). Given the ultimate power of Roman officials, it is not surprising that Christian leaders such as Paul counseled their followers to conform to the expectations of political authorities.

Even allowing for historical exaggeration regarding his misdeeds, Nero did not deserve the sort of respect Paul urges. His life was one of destructive debauchery. In addition to drinking and sexual depravity, he is reported to have committed crimes ranging from battery to robbery and murder (Suetonius, *Nero* 26.1). By the end of his reign, he had alienated or assassinated most relatives and close associates. It is telling that the list of his victims includes his teacher Seneca, who had counseled Nero early in his reign to rule with a sober and merciful attitude, not "by anger to excessive punishment, nor by youthful passion, nor by human rashness and stubbornness which have often wrung patience from even the most quiet of hearts, nor even with the arrogance which shows authority by means of terror" (*De Clementia* 1.1.2–3).

In June 68 CE, when the same crowds who had welcomed his accession were now calling for his head, Nero was forced to commit suicide. His final words as reported by Dio were "O Zeus, what an artist is being destroyed" (Dio Cassius 63). Before his death, the senate had already convicted Nero of treason (*maiestas*) and declared that he was an enemy of the people (Suetonius, *Nero* 49). The punishment for such a crime included *damnatio memoriae*, which meant that all traces of the individual would be erased from the Roman public record. This included both inscriptions and visual portrayals, and ensured a great deal of erasure work for stone carvers. In the east, however, the legacy of Nero lived on in some circles, and the prediction of Nero returning (*redivivus*) after death became a popular myth.

This expectation of a return of the deceased emperor developed at about the same time as an increase in hopes for the imminent return of Jesus. Not everyone in the early church was convinced that belief in the second coming of Jesus was essential. In 1 Corinthians Paul goes to great lengths to persuade some readers that faith in Jesus is meaningless without belief in the second coming and the concomitant resurrection of the dead (1 Cor. 15). John's Gospel stresses the community receiving the Holy Spirit, rather than the return of Jesus. But Mark's Gospel, written shortly after the death of Nero in 68, emphasizes the second coming. Its author seems concerned to provide sound teaching on the topic so that his audience will not be led astray by false messiahs proclaiming the end times (Mark 13.21–27). In Mark, discussion of the second coming is connected to the turmoil caused by the destruction of the Jerusalem Temple in 70 CE. The expectation for a return of the deceased Nero, however, may have resulted from the struggle to fill the power vacuum created by that emperor's demise.

A General Victorious: The Reign of Vespasian

Nero's execution of his rivals, coupled with similar actions by his predecessors, meant that when he died no member of his family could claim power. Thus with Nero the Julio-Claudian dynasty, in power for more than a century, died out. The question of succession was more open than ever before, and the Roman legions became even more influential in determining who would be the next emperor.

In 68 CE, Servius Sulpicius Galba was serving his eighth year as Roman governor of Hispania Tarraconensis (eastern Spain). Even before the death of Nero, Galba's troops declared him to be a special representative of the senate. Once Nero had died, other legions followed suit, and Galba was acclaimed as Caesar. He ruled for six months, but was betrayed by his associate Otho, who conspired to have him killed and then became emperor with the support of the Praetorian Guard in Rome and several other legions. At the same time, however, troops loyal to Vitellius had already proclaimed him to be Caesar, so a tense battle was played out between the troops of Otho and those of Vitellius. After three months Vitellius forced Otho to commit suicide, but his victory proved short-lived.

The Roman legions had come to appreciate their own power in determining who would be emperor. Troops in the east put forward the commander of Roman forces in Palestine, Titus Flavius Vespasianus, who appeared reluctant to take power. Suetonius reports that Vespasian's position was strengthened when two thousand soldiers from Moesia (modern Bulgaria) decided to support him. This bold move was said to be motivated by the realization "that they were not inferior to the Spanish army which had appointed Galba, or to the Praetorian Guard which had elected Otho, or to the German army which had appointed Vitellius" (*Vespasian* 6.2).

Vespasian's popularity with the troops was due in no small part to his successful campaigns against the Jews in Palestine who had rebelled against Roman control in 66 CE. Vespasian managed to repress the revolutionaries elsewhere in the territory, leaving the final defeat of the Jewish forces in Jerusalem to his son Titus. Vespasian's victories are described in great detail by the Jewish general Josephus, who gained the future emperor's favor after the rebel forces he commanded were defeated at Jotapata in Galilee. On the basis of his prediction that Vespasian would soon be emperor, the captive Josephus became a guest of the imperial family in Rome, where he lived out the last third of the century, writing histories of the Jewish people. Not surprisingly, his accounts highlighted Roman beneficence.

Given the high level of intrigue and instability in the empire following the death of Nero, it was not far-fetched to predict in 68 CE that Vespasian would become Caesar, however preposterous such a prediction would have been at his birth, given the stratification of Roman society. Vespasian's family was of the equestrian order and therefore would have had limited access to the path of civic offices (*cursus honorum*) that led to imperial power. His uncle, however, had gained access to the senate, and this connection put Vespasian in a position to exercise military leadership. Suetonius remarks that one reason Nero selected Vespasian for the high-profile task of putting down the rebellion in Judea was that Vespasian's humble family made him no threat to Nero's rule, even as a conquering general (*Vespasian* 4.5). Nero's death and the end of the Julio-Claudian dynasty, however, created a situation in which boundaries between the upper classes in Rome could be breached solely on the basis of military strength.

After learning that his son Domitian was in control of affairs in Rome, Vespasian left his other son, Titus, in command of the troops in Judea and began his journey to the capital. On the way he stopped in Alexandria to ensure that the Egyptian troops would support his imperial claim. He also visited the famous temple of the Egyptian mystery deity Serapis to read the omens surrounding his coming to power. While in the temple, he was welcomed by an unknown presence, and after exiting he miraculously healed a blind and lame man (Suetonius, *Vespasian* 7.2–3). These and other signs provided further assurance that Vespasian had divine approval to be emperor. When news came that Vitellius was dead, Vespasian moved on toward Rome to inaugurate a new imperial dynasty for himself and his sons. This Flavian dynasty would not last as long as the Julio-Claudian, but it would have a great impact on the history of the later empire and on the developing Christian churches.

Once in power, Vespasian proved to be a ruler of stature and effectiveness. Suetonius claims that both his foreign policy and his care for Rome and her citizens were great. The historian is especially impressed by Vespasian's humility, saying that "he was civil and merciful from the beginning of his principate until its end" (*Vespasian* 12). Dio's assessment is likewise positive: "He was considered emperor because of his concern for the public good, but in all other things he lived equally and in common with the people" (Dio Cassius 65.11.1). Suetonius does complain about Vespasian's greed, which led him to impose heavy taxes and even confiscate riches, but even this is excused due to "the desperate state of the treasury" (*Vespasian* 16.3). The ancient historians also point out the many good works done by Vespasian, including the establishment of endowed chairs of Latin and Greek rhetoric in Rome.

Vespasian is remembered especially for working to rebuild parts of the city of Rome damaged during the upheaval following Nero's reign. The emperor himself is said to have "carried away a basket of debris on his own neck" (Suetonius, *Vespasian* 8.5). Along with construction of the Temple of Peace, Vespasian's most spectacular architectural accomplishment was the Flavian amphitheater in Rome, later known as the Colosseum.

This marble-covered structure reached four stories high, and the top was fitted with mastlike devices that could support a canopy to shade spectators. It also featured an elaborate substructure with cages for wild animals and passageways that allowed for the movement of animals, personnel, and equipment to different spots in the arena. The longest axis of the elliptical structure measured 188 meters (616 feet), and it could hold up to fifty thousand spectators. Vespasian began the construction, but the amphitheater was dedicated by Titus in 80 CE and not fully completed until the reign of Domitian (81–96 CE).

To commemorate the dedication of the amphitheater, the poet Martial wrote a series of epigrams, fragments of which have survived. From these we know that the amphitheater was constructed on the site of Nero's Golden House. Martial also stresses the international appeal of the events taking place there: "What race is so distant, what race so barbaric, Caesar, from which a spectator is not in your city," and he comments on the exploits of performers in the amphitheater, like the hunter Carpophorus, who "dispatched a magnificent lion of unheard of size, worthy of the strength of Hercules" (*Spectacula* 2–3, 15). Elsewhere Martial describes the accomplishments of gladiators and the men who drove chariots in the racecourse (*circus*). His contemporary the poet Juvenal laments that all that was needed to satisfy the average citizen of Rome was "bread and circuses" (*Satires* 10.81).

The popularity of public spectacles in Roman cities is attested by a proliferation of amphitheaters around the empire. Theaters in Greek cities were often remodeled to accommodate more spectacular and violent events. This usually meant that a wall was erected around the orchestra of the theater to separate the audience from the gladiators, wild animals, and other exotic entertainments. In some cases, as in the theater of Dionysus in Athens, this wall was waterproofed so that the orchestra could be flooded for mock naval battles.

Some of these spectacles also involved humans being devoured by animals, as a letter to the churches in Rome from Ignatius, the bishop of Antioch in the early second century CE, illustrates. Ignatius uses graphic language to convey his anticipation of a martyr's death as an imitator of the suffering of Christ: "Allow me to be eaten by the beasts, through whom I can attain to God. I am God's wheat, and I am ground by the teeth of wild beasts that I may be found pure bread of Christ" (*Romans* 4.1). As such punishment for Christians became more common in the second and third centuries, the martyrological writings became even more vivid.

Compared with the dramatic deaths of the martyrs, or even with the harsh endings endured by some of his predecessors, the passing of Vespasian (79 CE) was mundane. Suetonius reports that after being weakened by a slight illness, the emperor succumbed to a gastrointestinal problem. His demise is remembered mostly for an offhand remark shortly before his death: "Woe, I think I'm becoming a god" (*Vespasian* 23.4). This quip is often taken as both a sign of Vespasian's humility and at least a slight mocking of the custom that a deceased ruler could become a divinity. Whatever the comment meant for Vespasian, the prospect of deification after death did have an impact on his successors.

A Heroic Older Son: The Reign of Titus

Once Vespasian had returned to Rome, his son Titus continued to battle the Jewish rebels in Palestine. Josephus records in great detail the compassion shown by Titus in battle, highlighting his reluctance to press the siege against Jerusalem because of his respect for the famous Temple of the Jews. Despite exaggerations in the account, Titus is remembered as a considerate leader. He found such favor with his troops that after his capture of Jerusalem his soldiers hailed him as emperor and wanted him to lead them in an armed challenge to his father (Suetonius, *Titus* 5.2). Instead, Titus took only the moral support of his forces with him when he returned to Rome in late 70/early 71 CE, and Vespasian welcomed him back, effectively making him coruler.

Titus's victories in the east also made him popular in Rome, where he and his father celebrated a triumph to recognize the long-awaited victory. For centuries the triumphal procession had been a means of honoring Roman leaders who had defeated foreign enemies. Originally, strict requirements had limited who could be a *triumphator*, and in what circumstances. By the imperial period, triumphs were reserved for emperors or members of the imperial family. The procession gave the conqueror a chance to display the fruits of his military prowess, including captives and spoils of war. It also permitted the senators, officials, and citizens of Rome to celebrate the power of the empire.

To preserve the glory of the moment, triumphal arches were erected throughout the empire as permanent commemorations. Evidence for earlier arches is found mostly on coins minted to celebrate a triumph. The triumphal arch of Titus, which still stands in Rome, was actually erected posthumously in 81 CE, more than ten years after the victory over the Jews. Sculptural relief panels on the interior passage of the arch portray details of the triumphal procession. One panel shows soldiers carrying a menorah and other furnishings from the Temple. The other side features the emperor driving a four-horse chariot, being crowned by a victory figure, while he gestures to the assembled crowd. Prominently placed in the Forum of Rome, the arch is both a recognition of Titus's achievements and a challenge for emperors to come. Anyone who passed through the Arch of Titus was reminded immediately of the great deeds Titus had done in order to deserve deification by the senate after his death. Of course, any Jews who viewed the arch would have been shaken by this vivid reminder of the destruction. Followers of Jesus, on the other hand, would have had mixed reactions to the fall of the Temple: the destruction was a tragedy perpetrated by the oppressive Romans, but the loss of the Temple could also be seen as retribution for the Jews who had failed to believe that Jesus was the Messiah (Matt. 22.1–7).

The reign of Titus is also notable for one of the most famous natural disasters of ancient times. In 79 CE, Mount Vesuvius erupted, burying the nearby towns of Pompeii and Herculaneum, large sections of which have been excavated by modern archaeologists. Titus could do little more than provide imperial support to the survivors, but according to Suetonius, he did so with such generosity that the historian states that Titus "showed not only the concern of a princeps, but also the unique love of a parent" (*Titus* 8.3). This kind of positive view of the emperor dominates the reports of his reign, and makes it easy to understand why the senate moved quickly to honor him after his death in 81 CE. Because his reign as sole emperor was brief, the destruction of the Temple in Jerusalem remains the major historical legacy of Titus. This single event precipitated major changes in Judaism, and also served to widen the growing chasm between Judaism and believers in Jesus as the Christ.

In each of the Synoptic Gospels (Matthew, Mark, and Luke), Jesus is said to predict the downfall of the Jerusalem Temple: "As he came out of the temple, one of his disciples said to him, 'Look, Teacher, what large stones and what large buildings!' Then Jesus asked him, 'Do you see these great buildings? Not one stone will be left here upon another; all will be thrown down'" (Mark 13.1–2; see also Matt. 26.61; John 2.18–22). Most scholars interpret Jesus' remark as a prophecy after the fact, written after the destruction of the Temple, but presented as a prediction that the event would occur. In this case, the author of the Gospel of Mark, writing around the time of the destruction (70 CE), develops a saying of Jesus that was influenced by the actual or impending fall of the Temple. For those Jews who had been convinced that Jesus was the Messiah, the one who had come to usher in the new kingdom of God and set up a new understanding of atonement for sins, the destruction was neither unexpected nor especially tragic. To most Jewish believers in Jesus, the promise of new life in Christ rendered inessential the traditional means of atonement, Temple and Torah. In addition, the proportion of Jewish believers in Jesus was diminishing as the movement attracted larger numbers of Gentiles, for whom the issue of whether Jesus had fulfilled the expectations for the Jewish Messiah was unimportant. If they believed that following Jesus would lead to eternal life, then they could join without hesitation. The mission to bring Jews into the church could never overcome that point of contention, so the churches continued to attract predominantly Gentiles, and questions about how the Jesus movement was related to Judaism became less significant.

Even as the connection with Judaism was ebbing, voices within the churches attempted to retain or reinterpret that bond. The author of the Gospel of Matthew wrote some ten years after the destruction of the Temple, using Mark's Gospel as a source. This author knew that the church was becoming a Gentile institution. The Gospel of Matthew, however, emphasized the ways in which Jesus as the Messiah had provided a sound interpretation of the Torah, and had fulfilled prophecies of Judaism in both his life and his death. The author of Matthew wanted to show belief in Jesus as the true continuation of Judaism. The letter to the Hebrews promoted Jesus as high priest and as sacrifice for the sins of the people. The second-century author of "The Preaching of Peter" accused Paul of being an apostle of Satan, since he had led the churches away from Judaism. Paul, however, had argued with Gentiles in the church at Rome who were claiming that God had rejected the Jews. He claimed the Jews' refusal to believe in Jesus resulted from God's temporarily hardening their hearts to allow the "full number" of Gentiles a chance to come into the church, but that God would eventually end the hardening and "all Israel will be saved" (Rom. 11.25–26). Paul's vision was not realized, and after the Temple was destroyed, Judaism began to develop in new directions under rabbinic leadership. Meanwhile, the churches continued to attract mostly Gentiles. Ten years later, after Titus's death in 81 CE, the churches and Judaism were evolving differently, but they both faced new challenges under the repressive policies of Vespasian's other son, Domitian.

A Younger Brother's Revenge: The Reign of Domitian

Many Romans greeted the accession of Domitian skeptically. Residing in Rome since before his father came to power in 69 CE, he had been instrumental in maintaining power until Vespasian returned to the city. In doing so, he had raised concerns about his leadership abilities. Once his father began to rule, Domitian was quickly relegated to a secondary status, and his eclipse was exacerbated when his victorious brother Titus returned to Rome. Suetonius suggests that Domitian had plotted against Titus after Vespasian's death, but that Titus was too compassionate to deal harshly with him (*Titus* 9.3). After Titus died, Domitian came to power and at least went through the motions of honoring his predecessors, dedicating his boyhood home as a temple to the Flavian family and building the Arch of Titus (*Domitian* 1.1).

Although the common interpretation of Domitian's reign is decidedly negative, Domitian may have been popular with the people and especially with the troops, whom he treated with great generosity. He regularly clashed with senators and other elites, and his terrible reputation reflects the upper-class bias of the sources for his reign—writers like Tacitus, Suetonius, and Pliny the Younger. An anti-imperial perspective is evident in these sources, but the horrors they describe were not reserved only for senators. Suetonius also mentions harsh actions taken against the Jews (*Domitian* 12.2), including a heavy tax burden and physical inspection for circumcision to determine who was liable to pay the tax. Dio tells of Domitian's execution of the consul Flavius Clemens for atheism, mentioning that this was the same charge "on which many others who had veered into the ways of the Jews had been condemned" (Dio Cassius 67.14.10). The book of Revelation is often cited as evidence for Domitian's persecution of another marginal group, the followers of Jesus.

Throughout the history of Christianity, the apocalyptic imagery of Revelation has been interpreted to refer to a variety of situations, both ancient and modern. The messages or "letters" at the beginning of the book, however, are all addressed to cities in western Asia Minor, and symbolic references within the letters have led scholars to date Revelation to the close of the first century, when important aspects of civic life in western Asia Minor coincided with the situation described in the book. Particularly significant is the heightening of a rivalry among the leading cities of Asia—Pergamon, Smyrna, and Ephesus.

Pergamon had gained the upper hand more than a century earlier, when it was awarded the honor of building a provincial temple to Roma and Augustus. From then on, being allowed to build an imperial temple was important in the rivalry among these cities. Sometime during the Flavian period, the Ephesians were finally able to challenge Pergamon and Smyrna by constructing a temple dedicated to Domitian and his family. This increased attention to civic honors for deified emperors also led to a heightened emphasis on individual citizens paying ritual honors to the emperor. If followers of Jesus in these cities refused to participate in sacrifices to the Augusti, they could have been subjected to persecution.

The images of the beast from the sea and the beast from the earth in Revelation 13 probably refer to the emperor and his representatives in the province, either officials sent out from Rome or local elites who administered the honors offered to the emperor. The second beast "exercises all the authority of the first beast on its behalf, and it makes the earth and its inhabitants worship the first beast . . . and by the signs that it is allowed to perform on behalf of the beast, it deceives the inhabitants of earth, telling them to make an image for the beast . . . so that the image of the beast could even speak and cause those who would not worship the image of the beast to be killed" (Rev. 13.12–15). This description may foreshadow the kind of loyalty test used by Pliny the Younger when, about 110 CE, he confronted people accused of being Christian in Pontus and Bithynia. Those who refused to give honor to the statue of the emperor were endangering the well-being of society as a whole. Such refusal would have been even more dangerous if the city had just erected a new temple to the imperial family, which stood as a source of great civic pride. Persons with power in the city could easily lose privileges, and people would be risking their lives if they refused to worship the "image of the beast."

The phrase *imperial cult* is often used in discussion of honors paid to emperors. Unfortunately, the term is usually interpreted as a set religious system with uniform beliefs and practices. On the contrary, there was great diversity in where, when, and how honors were offered to the emperor. One variation focused on whether a living emperor could receive honors as if he were a god. The usual assumption is that living emperors were readily given divine honors in the undisciplined eastern provinces, but not in Rome and the west, where cooler heads prevailed. This view needs to be questioned.

In the eastern provinces, divine honors do seem to have been offered to emperors. These offerings were not an irrational reaction by superstitious residents of the east, but rather part of a larger social matrix that connected people with the powers (human and divine) that controlled their world. Simon Price has pushed scholars to a more sophisticated understanding of how honors offered to the emperor should be seen as societal phenomena: "Using their traditional symbolic system they [the Greeks] represented the emperor to themselves in the familiar terms of divine power. The imperial cult, like the cults of the traditional gods, created a relationship of power between subject and ruler" (*Rituals and Power: The Imperial Cult in Asia Minor*, Cambridge University Press, 1984, p. 248). Although he refuses to look at these honors in strictly political terms, Price emphasizes that honors offered to the emperor also enhanced the civic power of those who controlled them, the local elite.

It is also necessary to modify the view that divine honors offered for the emperor in the east stood in sharp contrast to those in Rome and the west. During his lifetime Domitian demanded honors as a god in the city of Rome. Suetonius reports that the emperor insisted on being addressed as *dominus et deus* ("lord and god"), and he describes how priests wore crowns with Domitian's image alongside those of Jupiter, Juno, and Minerva (*Domitian* 13.2, 4.4). Pliny the Younger laments that traditional religious ritual had been selfishly usurped by Domitian: "Enormous herds of victims [intended for sacrifice at the temple of Jupiter Optimus Maximus] were intercepted on their way to the Capitolinum and large parts of them were forced to be diverted from their path, because to honor the statue of that atrocious master, as much blood of victims had to flow as the amount of human blood he had shed" (*Panegyricus* 52.7).

Pliny complained about these excesses in order to encourage the current emperor, Trajan, to expect more moderate honors during his lifetime. He was grateful that under Trajan the senate no longer needed to waste time deliberating on "enormous arches and inscribed titles too long to fit on temples" (*Panegyricus* 54). Pliny also laments the excessive "shows and riotous entertainment" that were performed in honor of Domitian: "He was a madman, ignorant of his true honor . . . who thought himself to be equal to the gods yet raised his gladiators to be equal to himself" (*Panegyricus* 33.4). However loudly they protested after the fact, Pliny and other senators who survived Domitian's reign played a role in bestowing these honors. Even if they did not participate in rites honoring Domitian as a god, they must have swallowed their disgust and looked on silently.

Like Gaius Caligula, Domitian perished at the hands of servants and friends. Upon his death in 96 CE, Domitian was mourned by the soldiers whose wages he had increased substantially (Suetonius, *Domitian* 23.1; see also 7.3). The majority of the population, however, was either unmoved or relieved that his reign had ended. Pliny reports that statues of the emperor were viciously destroyed in the streets, as a "sacrifice to public delight" (*Panegyricus* 52.4). Domitian's cruelty had been directed mainly against senators like Pliny. It was hoped that Domitian's passing would inaugurate a more civil form of government in which the senate would wield considerably greater power. As for the Jesus followers, they had weathered persecution under Domitian, but now the empire was clearly aware of their existence and would increasingly pressure them to conform to Roman standards of behavior. The spectacular events predicted in the book of Revelation had not occurred, and the church would face escalated levels of persecution and martyrdom for the next two centuries.

A Caretaker's Accomplishments: The Brief Reign of Nerva

The Flavian dynasty ended with the death of Domitian. Those who had plotted to kill him did not carry out their plan until they had agreed on a suitable successor. According to Dio Cassius, the elder statesman Nerva was chosen in part because he was "of the best lineage and most reasonable." An astrologer had also foretold that Nerva was destined to become emperor, and Domitian would have wanted him to be killed. Dio, however, relates that Domitian's belief in astrology led him to trust a second soothsayer who told him erroneously that Nerva would soon die of natural causes (Dio Cassius 67.15.5–6). But it was Domitian who perished first, and not of natural causes.

Once in power, Nerva was quick to compensate for the damage done by Domitian. He returned unlawfully confiscated property and canceled many extravagant sacrifices and spectacles instituted by his predecessor. Nerva also set out to curb the informants (*delatores*) who had advanced themselves under Domitian by offering incriminating testimony against others. Domitian encouraged such behavior, for it gave him a pretext to convict Roman citizens and seize their property. Information on senators and other wealthy Romans was especially desirable to Domitian, so it became common practice for slaves and other servants to betray their masters. Nerva put to death these informants and acquitted those who had been convicted with such evidence (Dio Cassius 68.1.2; 2.1–2). Pliny the Younger rejoices that Trajan went beyond the actions of Nerva by sending into exile boatloads of informers who were rightfully cut off "from the lands devastated by their informing" (*Panegyricus* 34.5).

Dio's comments on these informers include the charges on which their victims were usually convicted. "No one was permitted to accuse anybody of impiety or of living the Jewish life" (Dio Cassius 68.1.2). The first charge of treason (*maiestas*) was a plausible accusation for an informer to bring. The second, however, is a surprising indication of the extent to which Judaism was restricted during Domitian's reign. As already mentioned, Dio had reported that Domitian's cousin, Flavius Clemens, was executed for atheism and adopting "ways of the Jews." Dio's tone makes it clear that these charges were often spurious, but they would not have been made unless concern about the spread of Judaism existed. Apparently Jewish proselytizing had interested some Romans in the teachings of the Jewish law.

It is difficult to know how common this practice was, or to assess how the Romans would have understood what "living the Jewish life" meant. For instance, would Romans who joined the Jesus movement have been considered Jews at this time? By the time Dio writes in the late second century, the distinction between Jews and Christians would have been clear, but the same cannot necessarily be said for the late first-century society on which Dio was reporting. Evidence about the church in Rome can be found in the late first-century document known as 1 Clement. Scholars have long speculated that the author of this letter to the church in Corinth was related to Flavius Clemens. If true, this would support the contention that families of prominent Roman senators were involved in the Roman church during the late first century.

Nerva ruled effectively but briefly, and he is reported to have said that "I have done nothing to make it impossible for me to resign from office and live safely in retirement" (Dio Cassius 68.3.1). Unfortunately, his advanced age and ill health made him an easy target for those who sought to gain power during the tumultuous times following Domitian's death. To strengthen his position and maintain the peace, Nerva adopted Marcus Ulpius Trajan and appointed him Caesar and coruler. Trajan had recently won a major military victory over the Germanic tribes, and some have suggested that Nerva did not willingly delegate power. If Trajan and his troops were a threat, it is understandable why Nerva chose to make him coruler and thereby avoid a bloody rivalry. This would also explain how Trajan, who was born in Spain, came to control the Roman Empire.

A New Ruler for a New Century: The Reign of Trajan

After his adoption in 97 CE, Trajan remained in Germany, and even after Nerva's death in 98 CE delayed his return to Rome until he had completed an inspection of his troops along the northern frontier. According to Pliny, Trajan's arrival at Rome in 99 CE was met with an outpouring of adoration and devotion from the people (*Panegyricus* 23.5). The brief principate of Nerva had done little to erase the terrible memories of Domitian's reign. Pliny and other Romans were hoping for great things when the general Trajan arrived in the city.

The reign of Trajan (98–117 CE) is usually recognized as a time of stability and prosperity in the empire. Much of this reputation rests on the positive assessment of Trajan in Pliny's *Panegyricus*. Far from being a gushing piece of flattery, however, the *Panegyricus* was carefully worded political rhetoric, in which Pliny used every possible means to encourage the moderation Trajan exhibited in his first few months in office. He was especially pleased about Trajan's temperateness in military matters and, as mentioned above, in not demanding excessive honors: "Never should we flatter him as a god or a divinity. We are speaking not of a tyrant but of a citizen, not of a master, but of a parent. He himself is one of us, and this is especially eminent and stands out, that he thinks he is one of us; even though he presides over human beings, he remembers that he is a human being" (*Panegyricus* 2.3–4). As senatorial propaganda, the *Panegyricus* held up the standard of the emperor as princeps, a first among equals in the ruling class of Rome. The title *optimus princeps* ("greatest prince") became an important part of Trajan's nomenclature, appearing on coins and inscriptions throughout his reign.

Information about the reign of Trajan can also be gleaned from the letters that Pliny wrote to the emperor while serving as his personal representative (*legatus*). Pliny was assigned to the regions of Pontus and Bithynia along the southern coast of the Black Sea. Even before he left, Pliny was obsessed with gaining Trajan's approval. "I hope that you will judge my action to be reasonable, for I desire that all my actions and words be acceptable to your most sacred standards" (*Epistulae* 10.3). The collected letters make it seem as if Pliny tried to report back on almost every word and deed. Pliny's assigned task was to investigate the imperial finances in these territories and rectify discrepancies, but he consulted with Trajan on a wide variety of concerns.

The best-known surviving letters in Pliny's correspondence with Trajan concern people accused of being Christians. Coming at the end of Pliny's extant correspondence, these were written around 110 CE, a year or two before his death. The allegations took Pliny by surprise, and he conducted a quick investigation to learn about the Christians: "By custom they had come together before sunrise on a set day and took turns singing songs to Christ as a god, and later to bind themselves in an oath, not for some criminal purpose.... After this they separated and assembled again to take food of a common and harmless kind. But they themselves had put a stop to these things after my edict, which followed your mandate" (*Epistulae* 10.96). Pliny confirmed these reports by torturing two Christian slave women who were called deacons and concluded that, though misguided, the Christians were not involved in treasonous activity.

In spite of having found no evidence of wrongdoing, Pliny used his authority as legate of the emperor to execute any suspects who refused to renounce Christ by invoking the Roman gods and offering wine and incense to a statue of the emperor. The rationale for this action was that "whatever the nature of their confession, I am certain that their stubbornness and inflexible obstinacy deserves punishment" (*Epistulae* 10.96.3). Trajan approved of Pliny's actions without commenting on the specifics of the legal process. The emperor's main concern was that accusations against alleged Christians not become another means by which informants could get rid of rivals. Trajan was especially adamant that anonymous accusations be prohibited, since "they are the worst sort of example and not appropriate for our age" (*Epistulae* 10.97).

The letters of Pliny do not reveal any systematic oppression of Christianity during the age of Trajan. What they do show is that in society as a whole, the name *Christian* had developed a negative connotation. It is tempting to read the admonitions in 1 Peter 4.14 and 16 in this context; the answer of 1 Peter to those who were suffering was different from the book of Revelation's apocalyptic vision. Although concern for the end times was part of 1 Peter's message (see 1.5, 13; 4.7), the author was more interested in advising people about how to live in their present circumstances: "For the Lord's sake accept the authority of every human institution, whether of the emperor as supreme, or of governors, as sent by him to punish those who do wrong and to praise those who do right" (1 Pet. 2.13–14). Right behavior toward political powers was seen as the appropriate way to respond to the negative pressures felt by the churches.

According to 1 Peter and other authors, this attempt to conform to society also required harmony and good order within Christian households. Wives were told to accept the authority of their husbands and to be an example of good and holy women (1 Pet. 3.1–6). The same combination of respect for political authorities and restrictions placed on women was also an important element in the Pastoral Epistles. Although 1 Timothy, 2 Timothy, and Titus are written as letters of Paul, most scholars read them as pseudonymous documents from the early second century. The admonition to pray "for kings and all who are in high positions, so that we may lead a quiet and peaceable life in all godliness and dignity" (1 Tim. 2.2) reflected a desire to avoid political alienation by appeasing the government.

At the same time, the author of the Pastorals commanded that a woman may not teach or have authority over a man, and used the image of Eve to state that "she will be saved by childbearing, provided they continue in faith and love and holiness, with modesty" (1 Tim. 2.12, 13–15). The message to women in the churches was clear: find your proper place and stay there. Such a warning would have been unnecessary unless women were doing the opposite, involving themselves in leadership roles at the expense of the reputation of the churches. The undisputed letters of Paul provide ample evidence for women as active and vocal leaders in the churches (see 1 Cor. 1.11; 11.5; Rom. 16.1–7), and apocryphal writings from the second century such as "The Acts of Paul and Thecla" make it clear that women apostles were viewed as heroes in some churches. The Pastoral Epistles attempted to use the authority of Paul to limit the rights and roles of women in the churches, and for most of Christian history they have been successful. It is no accident that this effort to domesticate the Jesus movement and make it more socially and politically acceptable coincided with Trajan's nineteen-year reign of order and prosperity.

The only area in which Pliny's expectations for moderation in Trajan's reign were disappointed concerned military matters. At the outset Pliny urged Trajan to exercise restraint and not to emulate Domitian, who fought wars for the sake of gaining honors at home (*Panegyricus* 16–17). Trajan did, however, fight two successful wars against the Dacian tribes along the Danube River, finally defeating them in 106 CE. Trajan died in 117 CE while waging a major campaign in the east against Rome's longtime nemesis, the Parthian empire.

Trajan used the spoils of his military campaigns to finance major building projects. In addition to construction in the provinces, such as the Temple of Zeus Philios and Trajan in Pergamon, there were also substantial developments in Rome, including a market area, a bath complex, and an elaborate forum of Trajan, which stood as a monument to the Dacian victories. A central feature of the forum complex was a column on which was engraved a continuous spiral relief frieze detailing the Dacian conflicts. Including its base and a statue of Trajan at the top, the piece towered 40 meters (131 feet) above the ground.

Although it stands alone in the middle of a plaza today, the column was originally surrounded on at least three sides by structures that would have provided a vantage point for viewing the upper level and statue. Dedicated in 112 CE, the forum complex also included an equestrian statue of Trajan, large ground-level relief panels of the

Dacian conflict, numerous statues of captured Dacians, and a podium temple. This temple was perhaps dedicated first to the deified Nerva, but then rededicated to the deified Trajan by his successor, Hadrian. The structure made a powerful visual effect. When the emperor Constantius II visited the site in the fourth century, he was awestruck, and he is reported to have hoped that he "could breed a horse equivalent to the bronze horse on which Trajan was riding" (Ammianus 16.10.16). This spectacular structure gave fitting testimony to the successful reign of Trajan and the prosperity of his times. But it is only a prelude to the impact of Hadrian on the empire, which was monumental far beyond his architectural accomplishments.

Rebuilding the Empire: The Reign of Hadrian

Like his predecessor, Hadrian was a Spanish-born aristocrat who gained power and influence in Rome through his military leadership in the provinces. Hadrian was serving as governor of Syria in 117 CE when Trajan died during his Parthian campaign. The report was sent to Rome that Trajan had adopted Hadrian as his heir shortly before his death, but rumors circulated freely that Hadrian's adoption was the work of Trajan's wife Plotina, who withheld news of her husband's death until after Hadrian's succession was assured (*Scriptores historiae Augustae, Hadrian* 4.4.9–10). Whatever the details of his coming to power, Hadrian did not waste time in setting his own agenda. Armenia and Mesopotamia, taken by Trajan in the Parthian campaign, were abandoned, and Hadrian attempted to secure the borders of the empire and unite its disparate elements. Central to these efforts was an ambitious campaign of travel, reorganization, and building by which Hadrian left his mark throughout the empire.

Hadrian came to power convinced by his experience in the provinces that the empire had grown too large and complex to be ruled by decree from Rome. Despite his absence from the capital for more than half of his reign, Hadrian did have a significant impact on Rome and its environs. Most notably, he constructed a greatly expanded and redesigned Pantheon in the city and developed a sprawling villa complex near Tivoli. His travels took him throughout the empire, as a rough itinerary for his first extensive tour in 120 (or 121) to 128 CE reveals (*Scriptores historiae Augustae, Hadrian* 10–13).

Passing through Gaul, he continued into the Germanic regions, where he lived with the troops guarding the borders, reinvigorating discipline among the legion and instituting numerous military reforms. These included regulating leaves of absence, clearing the camps of banqueting rooms and other places of leisure, and ordering that no one should serve as a soldier "younger than his strength allows, or older than humanity permits" (*Hadrian* 10).

From Germany, Hadrian crossed to Britain, first invaded by Julius Caesar in 55–54 BCE and then partially conquered by the Romans under Claudius in 43 CE. As he had done in the east, Hadrian first withdrew forces to a reasonable point. He then ordered the construction of a frontier wall to protect against barbarian incursion. The wall ran 117.5 kilometers (73 miles) across what is now northern England, and parts of it and an adjacent defensive system are still visible. Returning to the Continent, Hadrian traveled south through Gaul and stayed for some time in Spain before going to Syria, probably by sailing the length of the Mediterranean Sea. The *Scriptores historiae Augustae* claim that Hadrian's personal intervention in negotiations with the Parthians helped prevent another conflict in the East (*Hadrian* 12.8). Returning from Syria, the emperor traveled through Asia Minor to Greece and back to Rome. Along his route, material remains and evidence from inscriptions reveal that he founded new towns, built monuments, and made numerous other dedications.

It was in Athens, however, that Hadrian's generosity and love of Greek culture were most vividly displayed. Pausanias, who traveled extensively in Greece during the later second century, marveled at the sanctuary of Olympian Zeus, which was completed by Hadrian (1.18.6). The huge temple, 44 meters × 110 meters (144 feet × 361 feet), featured a forest of over 100 columns, 10 meters (33 feet) high. The gold and ivory statue of Zeus was complemented by statues of Hadrian at the entrance and all around the expansive temple precinct (129 meters × 206 meters [423 feet × 676 feet]). Many inscriptions have been found in Athens dedicated to Hadrian as "founder" by cities from all over the Greek world. These provide evidence for the Panhellenic league, which Hadrian established as a means of uniting Greek cities and cities that had been colonized by the Greeks.

While staying in Athens, Hadrian made a connection with the ancient past of Greek mystery religions by being initiated into the venerable mystery cult for Demeter and Persephone with its shrine at nearby Eleusis. By this time, however, other mystery religions were steadily gaining popularity. Sanctuaries of the Egyptian deities Isis and Serapis and of the youthful Persian god Mithras have been discovered throughout the empire. Because the adherents of these cults were offered mystical access to divine power, they were popular across a wide spectrum of society. The Mithras cult especially appealed to men from the lower strata of society. It is striking that both the Mithras cult and the early Jesus movement could develop strong followings in the religious climate of the first three centuries CE.

Conclusion

By Hadrian's time, Christianity had begun to assert itself as an increasingly significant social force, and reaction against the churches had grown correspondingly. The monotheistic belief system of Jews and Christians set them apart from the rest of the Greco-Roman world, and by the mid-second century the Jesus followers had broken ties with their roots in Judaism. From the Roman perspective the Christians were an unconventional group, outside any long-standing tradition. As such they were potentially dangerous and subject to a variety of criticisms, many unwarranted. The second-century Roman orator Fronto described in vivid detail Christian gatherings in which young children were eaten and participants were driven by "unspeakable lust" to engage in illicit sexual activities (cited in Minucius Felix, *Octavius* 9.5–6).

In response to such criticism and to harsh, repressive actions, some Christians attempted to put forward a logical defense of their faith. Eusebius, a fourth-century church historian, mentions Quadratus, who addressed a defense of the faith to the emperor Hadrian (*Historia ecclesiastica* 4.3). Such later second-century apologists as Justin Martyr and Athenagoras directed some of their writings to the emperor, answering charges and seeking relief from persecution. Justin even cited a rescript from Hadrian to the proconsul of Asia that warned against false claims being lodged against Christians "merely as slanderous accusations" (*Apologia* 1.69). The document portrayed the emperor as approving of punishment for people who had broken the laws, but unwilling to bring to trial people who were accused only of being Christians. Whether the rescript is authentic or not, this more open attitude toward believers was not characteristic of society at large, where persecution of the churches continued to accelerate.

At the same time, internal conflict was also becoming an increasing problem for the churches. Near the end of Hadrian's rule (he died in 138 CE), church leaders in Rome became concerned about the teachings of Marcion, who advocated a sharp separation between the Gospels' principles of love and the law of the Jewish Bible. His attempts to organize his followers and to limit their reading to ten letters of Paul and an edited version of the Gospel of Luke led to his excommunication in 144 CE. Marcion's canon, however, was the first recorded attempt to establish an authoritative list of documents within the churches. Eventually, after two hundred more years of debate, the churches would for the most part agree on the twenty-seven books of the New Testament canon.

The book of 2 Peter is often considered the last of those twenty-seven documents to be written. Some scholars date it as late as 150 CE, in the reign of Hadrian's successor, Antoninus Pius (138–61 CE). Second Peter attempted to counter destructive teachings of "false prophets" among the people (2.1). The book ends with a reference to the letters of Paul, parts of which are said to be hard to understand, and a return to a Pauline-like emphasis on the second coming of Jesus. According to 2 Peter, believers should not be led astray by teachers who claim that the Lord is slow in fulfilling his promise to return. Rather, he "is patient with you, not wanting any to perish, but all to come to repentance" (3.9).

Whether through renewed expectation of Jesus' second coming or through the reasoned words of the early apologists, second-century believers found reason to hope despite growing opposition from the society around them. Over a century and a half of persecution lay ahead before Christianity gained official acceptance within the empire (312 CE). By the middle of the second century, the churches were already beginning to create the ecclesiastical structure and common doctrine that would eventually enable Christianity to dominate the empire that had tried to destroy it. On the basis of this structure and doctrine, the Roman world would become the Christian world in the Mediterranean region and beyond.

Select Bibliography

Campenhausen, Hans von. *The Formation of the Christian Bible.* Trans. J. A. Baker. Philadelphia: Fortress, 1972. Classic analysis of the transmission and canonization process for the Old and New Testaments.

Dunn, James D. G. *Unity and Diversity in the New Testament: An Inquiry into the Character of Earliest Christianity.* 2d ed. Philadelphia: Trinity Press International, 1990. Dunn elucidates a variety of issues and approaches found in the New Testament documents, but he also argues for particular thematic points of unity.

Georgi, Dieter. "Who Is the True Prophet?" In *Christians among Jews and Gentiles: Essays in Honor of Krister Stendahl,* ed. George W. E. Nickelsburg and George W. MacRae, 100–126. Philadelphia: Fortress, 1986; also *Harvard Theological Review* 79 (1986): 100–126. A provocative look at the interplay of imagery between Roman imperial propaganda and the earliest Jesus movement.

Harris, Stephen L. *The New Testament: A Student's Introduction.* 3d ed. Mountain View, Calif.: Mayfield, 1998. A good, basic introduction to the Greco-Roman world and New Testament literature.

Henig, Martin, ed. *A Handbook of Roman Art: A Comprehensive Survey of All the Arts of the Roman World.* Ithaca, N.Y.: Cornell University Press, 1983. An insightful collection of essays.

Horsley, Richard A., ed. *Paul and Empire: Religion and Power in Roman Imperial Society.* Harrisburg, Pa.: Trinity Press International, 1997. An illuminating collection of essays on Roman social, political, and religious realities, and the development of the church within that context.

MacMullen, Ramsay. *Paganism in the Roman Empire.* New Haven, Conn.: Yale University Press, 1981. Building on extensive literary evidence and material remains, MacMullen explores fundamental questions about what the Romans believed and why.

Millar, Fergus. *The Emperor and the Roman World 31 BC–AD 337.* Ithaca, N.Y.: Cornell University Press, 1977. Emphasizes the increasing significance of the emperor's relationship with the provinces throughout the imperial period.

Price, S. R. F. *Rituals and Power: The Roman Imperial Cult in Asia Minor.* Cambridge: Cambridge University Press, 1984. A fundamental reassessment of scholarly approaches to honors offered to emperors in Asia Minor.

———. "From Noble Funerals to Divine Cult: The Consecration of Roman Emperors." In *Rituals of Royalty: Power and Ceremonial in Traditional Societies,* ed. David Cannadine and Simon Price, 56–105. Cambridge: Cambridge University Press, 1987. Price surveys and interprets evidence for the deification of Roman emperors.

Roetzel, Calvin J. *The Letters of Paul: Conversations in Context.* Louisville, Ky.: Westminster, 1991. A solid introduction to Paul, his world, and his letters.

Safrai, S., and M. Stern, eds. *The Jewish People in the First Century: Historical Geography, Political History, Social, Cultural and Religious Life and Institutions.* 2 vols. Assen, The Netherlands: Van Gorcum; Philadelphia: Fortress, 1974–76. A sweeping consideration of formative Judaism.

Schüssler Fiorenza, Elisabeth. *In Memory of Her: A Feminist Theological Reconstruction of Christian Origins.* New York: Crossroad, 1983. A fundamental work of feminist New Testament criticism, highlighting the ways in which stories of women's involvement in the earliest churches have been lost and hidden in the transmission of traditions.

Stark, Robert. *The Rise of Christianity: How the Obscure, Marginal Jesus Movement Became the Dominant Religious Force in the Western World in a Few Centuries.* Princeton, N.J.: Princeton University Press, 1996. A leading sociologist examines the origins of the church and its rise to prominence.

Suetonius. *The Lives of the Twelve Caesars.* Trans. J. C. Rolfe. 2 vols. Cambridge, Mass.: Harvard University Press, 1979. Latin text with facing English translation, with introduction and limited notes.

Zanker, Paul. *The Power of Images in the Age of Augustus.* Trans. Alan Shapiro. Ann Arbor: University of Michigan Press, 1988. Explores the use and effectiveness of political and religious imagery in Augustan art.

Transitions and Trajectories

Jews and Christians in the Roman Empire

BARBARA GELLER

A mid great upheaval in Palestine, the first century witnessed the emergence of Christianity and rabbinic Judaism. Both were survivors of what was, before the Roman-Jewish War of 66–73/74 CE, a more diverse Judaism. Shared characteristics contributed to their survival. First and foremost, neither the Pharisaic-rabbinic nor the Christian communities fought as organized groups against the Romans. Second, neither required for its survival the Jerusalem Temple, which the Roman army destroyed in 70, although both continued to maintain an attachment to the city. Moreover, both were portable and as such were not location-dependent. Each offered its adherents the identity of "Israel" and an understanding of Torah that enabled it to adapt readily to changing times, and each developed its own authoritative scriptural canon. Finally, both rabbinic Judaism and Christianity offered believers a retributive afterlife and the possibility of right relationship with God and eternal salvation, and they encouraged their devotees to develop mechanisms to care for the needy and the oppressed.

The Gospel of Matthew, a late first-century Jewish-Christian document, likens the scribes and Pharisees (the antecedents of the rabbis) to hypocrites, paradoxically acknowledging the similarities between the Matthean and the Pharisaic-rabbinic communities. In terms of doctrine, the differences between the Pharisee-rabbis and the Matthean community may have been modest, especially from the Roman perspective. Nor was it clear at the time that a belief in Jesus as the risen Messiah would evolve as a permanent boundary marker between Judaism and Christianity. By the close of the century, however, the process of separation was well under way. This may be the context for the Gospel of John's use of the term *the Jews* as a multipurpose designation for the opponents of Jesus. The language of John 8.44 is especially forceful: in response to the Jews' assertion that they have one father, God, Jesus says, "You are from your father the devil, and you choose to do your father's desires." Such language probably reflects the pain and anger of the Jewish-Christian Johannine community, a tiny group within a small minority community, as it became separated—divorced in a sense—from the larger Jewish community, and as it sought to develop its own identity outside this "other" Judaism in the often hostile environment of the Roman Empire.

The Jewish Revolts of the Second Century

In the aftermath of Titus's capture of Jerusalem in 70 CE, the Roman senate honored Titus and his father, the emperor Vespasian (69–79), with a grand triumphal procession, later memorialized in the Arch of Titus, which still stands in Rome. However, although the Roman army had succeeded in crushing the Jewish rebels, it failed to crush the spirit of rebellion, fueled in part by anti-Roman and militant messianic sentiments, which exploded again during the reigns of Trajan (98–117) and Hadrian (117–38). Papyri, inscriptions, and archaeological data, as well as the writings of Appian and Dio Cassius and of the later Christian historians Eusebius and Orosius, provide evidence of a massive uprising of the Jews of Egypt, Cyrenaica, and Cyprus.

The revolt probably began early in 115 and was quelled roughly two and a half years later. Although its causes are uncertain, long-standing tension between the Jewish and Greek communities of the region, especially in Alexandria, was a factor, and Palestinian Jewish refugees who had fled to Egypt and elsewhere after 70 may have fanned nationalistic and messianic sentiments. Even if the revolt began as a conflict between the Jewish and non-Jewish populations, however, Rome was soon involved. Trajan sent Marcius Turbo, one of the leading generals from his ongoing campaign against the Parthians, to suppress the rebellion. Dio names one "Andreas" as the leader of the uprising in Cyrenaica; Eusebius may be referring to the same individual as "Lucuas their king." The significance of the designation *king* is unclear, but the uprising may have had messianic underpinnings, and, if so, Lucuas may have been regarded as a messianic figure by some. In either case, the data clearly reveal the widespread and devastating character of the revolt, including not only the deaths of thousands of Jews and non-Jews but also the great destruction by Jewish rebels of land and property, including many temples and sacred precincts. In its aftermath, the Jewish communities of Cyrenaica and the formerly populous Jewish communities of Alexandria and the Egyptian countryside decreased in number and significance. The situation in Cyprus was only slightly better.

Although the data are sketchy, it is likely that the Jews of Mesopotamia, newly annexed by Rome, participated in an anti-Roman rebellion that began in 116. It was suppressed by another of Trajan's leading commanders, Lusius Quietus, who was awarded with an appointment as the first consular legate of Judea. Quietus also took steps to suppress unrest among the Palestinian Jewish population.

This unrest probably in turn contributed to the outbreak of the third and final major Jewish anti-Roman rebellion, the war of Bar Kokhba. This uprising centered in southern Judea, the region of biblical Judah, and lasted from 132 to 135 CE. Here, too, the causes, character, and course of the revolt are imperfectly known. The pagan, Christian, and rabbinic sources are mostly later, are often inconsistent, and have their respective biases and concerns. But recent discoveries at sites in the Judean desert, including coins and letters from the rebel forces, have allowed historians to look anew at the revolt.

The leader of the revolt was Simeon bar Kosba, or Kosiba, referred to in Christian sources (and perhaps by those Jews who regarded him as the Messiah) as Bar Kokhba—literally, "son of a star." Rabbinic sources portray the venerable Rabbi Akiba as having regarded Bar Kokhba as the Messiah, although many other sages did not. Indeed, the belief in Bar Kokhba's messiahship was not necessarily widespread among his followers. The coinage of the rebels identifies him as the *nasi,* or head, of Israel, and his letters further substantiate the scope of his authority among the rebels to whom he issued orders concerning military, economic, and religious matters.

The strength and early successes of the rebels alarmed the Roman government. Hadrian went so far as to summon, from the opposite end of the empire, one of his top generals, Julius Severus, then serving as governor of Britain. And Hadrian himself, writing from the front, failed to greet the Roman senate with the customary opening, "If you and your children are in health, it is well; I and the legions are in health"— another indication of the severity of the situation. According to the historian Dio Cassius, Hadrian's lapse was due to the great losses suffered by his troops. But the Roman army finally prevailed, defeating the rebels decisively at Bethar, southwest of Jerusalem.

The revolt had many causes. Anti-Roman nationalistic unrest and militant messianic sentiments were key factors, as probably was the confiscation of Jewish land by the Roman government in the aftermath of the First Jewish Revolt. The latter contributed to the growing impoverishment of the Judean peasantry, many of whom may have participated in the uprising. If Dio is correct, Hadrian's plans to build a Roman city on the site of Jerusalem precipitated the revolt, while a later source attributes it to the emperor's prohibition of circumcision.

In the aftermath of the revolt, the Roman government changed the name of the province from Judea to Syria Palaestina. Jews may have been banned from Jerusalem and its vicinity, although the degree to which such a ban was enforced by later emperors, as well as its duration, are unclear. Jerusalem was transformed into the Roman city of Aelia Capitolina, and it was given the coinage and architecture typical of Greco-Roman cities of this era, continuing Hadrian's policy of hellenization in the Roman east.

Jews in the Pre-Christian Roman Empire

The War of Bar Kokhba resulted in great loss of life and in the destruction of many Judean towns and villages, and the heartland of the Jewish population shifted to Galilee, which became the center of the emerging rabbinic movement. The militant anti-Roman agitation and messianism that had fueled the Jewish revolts of the first and second centuries CE quieted. Antoninus Pius (138–61) modified Hadrian's ban on circumcision to allow Jews to resume its practice. Overall, later rabbinic literature reflects a kind of rapprochement with pagan Rome, an attitude of "live and let live," and an appreciation as well of the perils of imminent messianic expectations and of false messiahs. Rabbinic literature preserves contradictory assessments of Bar Kokhba, depicting him both as the false messiah, a son of lies (Bar Koziba) who brought ruin to his people, and also as an almost larger-than-life military and national hero.

There is relatively little information on Roman-Jewish relations of the latter half of the second and the third centuries CE. Rabbinic literature, with its focus on the interests and concerns of the rabbis, yields only scant data on nonrabbinic Jews or on the presence of Rome, even in Palestine. The overall silence of the sources probably bears witness to an effective modus vivendi between Rome and its Jewish communities. Jews were not singled out but shared the burdens of beleaguered provincials throughout the empire. These included oppressive taxation, resulting not infrequently in the loss of one's land, and the billeting of soldiers stationed in the area.

In 212, Emperor Caracalla (211–17) issued his "Constitutio Antoniniana," which granted Roman citizenship to all free inhabitants of the empire. Roughly a century later, the emperor Constantine prepared to do battle at the Milvian Bridge, setting in motion a chain of events that would radically alter the empire's religious landscape. The emerging Christian state, with its dual identity both as the continuation of the Rome of Caesar and Augustus and now also as the patron and promulgator of Christianity, would wrestle with the challenges posed by the existence of communities of Jewish citizens located on three continents and a tradition that, since the days of Caesar, had accepted Judaism as legal religion.

The Triumph of Christianity

If the Pliny-Trajan correspondence of the early second century suggests Rome's growing understanding of Christianity as distinct from Judaism, the literature of the church fathers indicates that as late as the close of the fourth century, many Christians, most of them new Christians, blurred the boundaries between the two religious communities, despite efforts by church leadership to prevent such misunderstandings. The Roman government, generally tolerant of religious diversity in the empire, for the most part ignored Christians and growing Christianity. Episodically, however, the government unleashed severe anti-Christian persecutions, finding in the Christians a convenient scapegoat for the empire's ills, and seemingly hoping to restore prosperity by attacking those perceived as threatening the gods, and thus the very foundations of the Roman state.

The final persecution began during the reign of Diocletian (284–305 CE) and extended even to Palestine, the birthplace of Christianity. Thus the fourth-century Palestinian church father Eusebius could describe the interrogation of his mentor, the Christian scholar Pamphilus, by a Roman magistrate at the provincial seat of Caesarea. When asked to identify his city, Pamphilus responded, "Jerusalem." Eusebius assumed that Pamphilus was referring to the heavenly Jerusalem. But the official appeared to be familiar with neither the earthly nor the heavenly Jerusalem and was concerned that the Christians had established a city "hostile to the Romans." Pamphilus was subsequently executed in 310. This episode is a reminder not only that Christians were persecuted well into the fourth century but also that roughly three centuries after the birth of Christianity, and despite its substantial growth throughout the empire, a Roman official in Palestine could claim never to have heard of Jerusalem. (Undoubtedly, he would have recognized "Aelia," the very earthly city built on the ruins of Jerusalem by Hadrian and given his family name.)

Less than seventy-five years after the martyrdom of Pamphilus, Egeria, a Christian pilgrim from the west who spent the years 381–84 in Palestine and Egypt, could marvel at the jewels, gold, and silk of the decorations of the "Great Church on Golgotha" and the "holy church of the Anastasis" in Jerusalem. She wrote of the magnificence and solemnity of the liturgy in Jerusalem, with its interweaving of prayer, place, and sacred event, especially powerful during the Easter celebrations and the eight-day festival of Encaenia, which commemorated the consecration of the church on Golgotha and the Anastasis, built on the very sites where, it was believed, Jesus had been crucified and resurrected. These edifices, and the wave of fourth-century pilgrims who visited them so that they might see and touch the very places in which the saving events of biblical history had taken place, bore witness not only to a transformed Jerusalem but also to the transformed status of Christianity. Having entered the century as a persecuted and illegal faith, by the close of the century Christianity was the official state religion of the Roman Empire. The persecuted had become the powerful, and the persecutor, the Roman state, had become the promulgator of Christianity. One of the watershed events for this transformation was the conversion to Christianity of the Roman emperor Constantine, the sole emperor in the west from 312 and in both east and west from 324 to 337.

In the aftermath of Diocletian's abdication in 305, the tetrarchic system of rule that he had established failed to ensure a stable succession. Rival claimants to the throne battled for almost twenty years. In 312 Constantine and his troops found themselves at the Milvian Bridge outside Rome, facing the numerically superior forces of his adversary Maxentius. According to the Christian author Lactantius, writing a few years after this decisive event, during the night before the battle Constantine was commanded in a dream to place on the shields of his soldiers "the heavenly sign of God." Later, in his "Life of Constantine," written shortly after the emperor's death in 337, Eusebius claimed that sometime before the battle Constantine had seen a cross in the heavens and the inscription "In this sign, you will conquer." Although the factual basis of these legends is uncertain, it is clear that Constantine and others attributed his victory to the Christian deity. In good Roman fashion, a god had communicated to the emperor in a dream or a vision, had promised victory, and had delivered. Twelve years after the battle of the Milvian Bridge, Constantine defeated the last of his rivals, Licinius, at Adrianople in Thrace and again at Chrysopolis in Asia Minor. Whereas Licinius had placed his hope for victory in the old gods of the Roman state, Constantine's forces had gone into battle bearing the Christian standard, called the *labarum*, with its chi-rho monogram, the first two letters of "Christ" in the Greek alphabet.

Although, as was common in the fourth century, Constantine was not baptized until he was near death, throughout his years of rule he acted as a patron of the church. One of his earliest and most significant acts on its behalf was the promulgation in 313 of the Edict of Milan, with his then ally, the coemperor Licinius. The edict, which, to be sure, followed the Edict of Toleration issued by Emperor Galerius in 311, promised freedom of religion to Christians and, indeed, to all, whatever their religion. It also promised to restore Christian property seized during the persecutions or, barring that, to provide compensation for lost property.

In edicts and letters, in the financial largesse showered on the church, and in

Constantine's interest and intervention in church affairs, such as his leadership at the Council of Nicea in 325, the emperor made clear his role as patron of the church. Whether as part of or in addition to his concerns about Christian unity, Constantine also expressed an interest in Jerusalem. This would have an immediate and dramatic impact on the city. Constantine permitted Bishop Makarios of Jerusalem to destroy the temple of Aphrodite, built over the presumed tomb site of Jesus, expecting that the tomb itself would be unearthed. According to Eusebius, Constantine commanded that the place be purified and that the soil, to some depth, be taken far away inasmuch as it had been "polluted" by "demon worship." The excavations met the expectations of the emperor and the bishop. Not only did they yield the tomb of Jesus; they also yielded Golgotha, the hill of the crucifixion. Constantine commissioned the building of the Anastasis rotunda, dedicated in 335, over the tomb site, and the nearby basilical prayer hall. The Byzantine Holy Sepulcher complex, with its rotunda, Holy Garden (including the hill of Golgotha), basilica, and atrium, lay on the Cardo, the main street of Roman Aelia. As in Jerusalem's earlier history, religion, politics, and monumental architecture were inextricably intertwined. By acts of destruction and rebuilding, Christianity, with imperial patronage, had taken a giant step in marking its ascendancy in the heart of Jerusalem. And as for Jews and Judaism, the Temple Mount remained in ruins, a visible proof, from the perspective of the church, of the "New Israel's" victory over the "Old."

Roughly contemporary with the Christian "conquest" of the Holy City was a change in the value accorded to the earthly Jerusalem. Before the fourth century, Christian theologians had paid little heed to the earthly city, preferring to focus on its heavenly counterpart. But from the time of Constantine, pilgrimage to Jerusalem would be valued as part of a spiritual quest for perfection and as a means of confirming and validating one's faith. Early pilgrims included Helena, Constantine's mother, who, according to legend, uncovered the true cross while in Jerusalem. Indeed, pilgrimage would flourish throughout the years of Christian rule, bringing not only visitors but also increased prosperity to the city, and to all of Palestine, as the region developed the infrastructure needed to support this holy tourism. For most pilgrims, the high point of their sacred journey was a visit to the Church of the Holy Sepulcher in the holy city of Jerusalem, despite the admonitions of some fourth-century fathers of the church. After visiting Jerusalem, Gregory of Nyssa observed in his "Letter on Pilgrimages" that the sinfulness of the people of Jerusalem must be proof that God's grace could not be more abundant there than elsewhere. Likewise, Jerome, although he settled near the city as part of his quest for perfection, wrote in a letter that the people of Jerusalem, like those of other crowded cities, included actors, prostitutes, and clowns. These sentiments do not seem to have deterred pilgrims, but they testify to the ancient and ongoing tension between Jerusalem the ideal and Jerusalem the real, a city of religious visions and visionaries, and a city of the everyday, filled with people struggling to meet the demands of daily life in a city haunted by its history.

Although his building projects in Jerusalem were only one of numerous activities that he undertook on behalf of the church, Constantine remained, despite his growing identity as a Christian, a transitional figure in the empire's slow and gradual process of Christianization. Throughout his reign, not only were the old Roman rites left intact and functioning, but Constantine himself retained the traditional title, honors, and responsibilities of the pontifex maximus. During his early years of rule, his older allegiance to the sun-god seems to have coexisted, or perhaps became fused, with his new allegiance to the son of God. This is reflected in some of his early coinage.

Unlike Constantine, all but one of his successors acted decisively not only to enhance the status of Christianity in the empire but also to delegitimate pagan worship. Moreover, while maintaining Judaism's status as a legal religion, they significantly altered the status of Jews and Judaism, destroying the "entente" that had functioned so effectively since the close of the war of Bar Kokhba in 135 CE.

Julian the Apostate

The imperial promotion of Christianization was interrupted only by Julian, a nephew of Constantine, who in his brief reign (361–63) sought to restore the primacy of pagan worship and to reverse the tide of Christianization in the empire's governing classes. Having survived the bloodbath in the royal family that followed Constantine's death, Julian was eventually appointed as Caesar in 355 by his cousin and brother-in-law, Constantine's son the emperor Constantius. When Constantius died in 360, Julian openly declared himself to be a worshiper of the ancient gods and thanked them for his accession with many public sacrifices. He also provided funds for the restoration and building of temples and sought to encourage large-scale pagan charitable giving.

For Julian, Christianity was undermining the Roman state, and with it the gods and classical culture, both of which were essential to the state's well-being. Julian could not accept the appropriation of that culture by the Christian elites, including the bishops, since Hellenism, for him, was a gift and a legacy of the gods and thus synonymous with paganism. This sentiment lies behind an edict of 362 that demanded that teachers excel in morality and eloquence and that the municipal councils submit nominations of teachers to the emperor. He did not want the Galileans, as he called the Christians, to teach grammar or rhetoric, the foundations of a classical education. How could Galileans teach Homer or Hesiod when they argued that the Greek gods did not exist? Let them expound Matthew and Luke in their churches, declared Julian. He claimed that he did not seek to harm Christians, but rather to show preference to pagans.

Julian's view of, and policies concerning, both traditional religion and Christianity had their counterpart in his policies toward Judaism when he decided to rebuild the Temple of the Jews in Jerusalem. He knew that this would enable the Jews to resume sacrificial rituals, a practice Julian sought to restore throughout the empire. He also knew that the rebuilding of the Temple would undermine the Christian belief that Jesus had prophesied its destruction (Matt. 24.2), the absence of which was, for the church, a sign of divine disapproval of Judaism—a testimony to its defeated and false character.

Julian's project to rebuild the Jerusalem Temple failed. Work ceased not long after its inception, in the aftermath of a fire probably associated with the powerful earthquake of 363. Christian sources viewed the fire as divine intervention; many claimed that the fire was accompanied by other miraculous portents, including a giant cross in the sky. God's anger against Julian, his Christian adversaries claimed, was also evident in his death at the age of thirty-one in his campaign against the Persians that same year. Still, as the historian Peter Brown has eloquently observed, the very survival of the writings of Julian the Apostate bear witness to the "compromise" between Hellenism and Christianity, preserved as they were by medieval churchmen.

The Defeat of Paganism

Any imperial sympathy for pagan or Jewish worship ended with Julian's death, and antipagan and anti-Jewish legislation continued throughout the fourth and into the fifth and sixth centuries. Beginning in the decades before Julian's accession to power, the imperial campaign against paganism escalated gradually. By the end of the fourth century, both antipagan and anti-Jewish legislation would serve as licenses for the increasing number of acts of vandalism and violent destruction directed against pagan and Jewish places of worship carried out by Christian mobs, often at the instigation of the local clergy.

In 383, Gratian (emperor in the west, 367–75; joint emperor in the west, 375–83), one of whose mentors was Ambrose, the powerful and aggressively antipagan bishop of Milan, had relinquished the title and remaining responsibilities of the pontifex maximus, ordering also the removal of the altar of Victory from the senate. This action further widened the breach between the state and the old Roman religion. In 391, Theodosius I (379–95; joint emperor, 379–92) ordered that all temples be closed and that all forms of pagan worship cease. In the aftermath of the emperor's edicts, the bishop of Alexandria ordered the destruction of the city's main temple, the great Serapeum. This pattern of destruction continued, in Alexandria, Carthage, Gaza, and elsewhere, as the severe legislation directed against temples, pagan worship, and the old priesthood increased.

The repetitive nature of antipagan legislation bears witness to the persistence of traditional worship. Thus in 435, Emperors Theodosius II (emperor in the east, 408–50) and Valentinian III (emperor in the west, 425–55) ordered the destruction of all temples and shrines "if even now any remain entire." As late as the sixth century, legislation was promulgated demanding the death penalty for the practice of sacrifice.

The policies of Emperor Justinian (527–65) were especially instrumental in the final phase of the Roman government's struggle against paganism. Justinian's policies were repressive not only toward pagans but also toward Jews, Samaritans, Manichaeans, and heretics. In 529 he closed the Neoplatonist school at Athens—an action consistent with his policy of prohibiting pagans from teaching, proclaimed in the same year, although not enforced consistently throughout the empire. Justinian also issued an edict demanding that all who were not yet baptized receive instruction in the "true faith of Christians" to become eligible for baptism. Failure to comply could result in confiscation of property or the loss of the right to an inheritance. Pagan worship was punishable by death.

Organized traditional worship seems to have persisted in the east somewhat longer than in the west. The dissolution and division of the western empire in the fifth and sixth centuries by the now Christian "barbarian" tribes of Europe was not fertile ground for the continuation of paganism in any organized form. Some pockets of paganism survived, especially in the countryside, and some pagan practices coexisted with Christianity, especially in the lives of new Christians. Astrology and the use of amulets for healing would have been especially difficult to eradicate. In fact, paganism continued to be of concern to church councils into the seventh century, though sources for organized pagan worship are spotty after the sixth. Christianity triumphed, but only after incorporating and then promulgating much of the classical culture formerly identified with paganism.

Many historians of religion also argue that the triumph of Christianity was facilitated by its ability to adapt, transform, and internalize facets of the religious traditions with which it had competed during its formative centuries in such areas as its calendar and its evolving understanding of its key personages. Thus, even as Justinian was endeavoring to suppress in its entirety the worship of the goddesses who for millennia had been believed to sustain the recurring seasonal cycles of death and rebirth, he was building magnificent churches to Mary, mother of God and God-bearer, a more powerful, complex, and significant figure than the Mary of the New Testament, who receives relatively scant attention in the four Gospels. Although officially a focus of veneration and not worship as such, Mary shared, well before the sixth century, some of the features of the old goddesses such as Athena and Artemis, who, like her, were both virgins. Like Isis, the Egyptian goddess whose worship had spread throughout the empire, Mary was also the queen of heaven and an intercessor for humankind, whose love for her son had brought her honor and adoration; in both hymns and statuary Mary and Isis share attributes.

Christian Diversity

Although the concept of "orthodoxy" is anachronistic before the fourth century, and notwithstanding the great diversity of the early church, there was an emerging mainstream. During the second and third centuries, however, it had to respond to the challenges posed by the divergent views of a number of groups and systems of belief, prominent among which were those of the Christian Gnostics. Before the 1945 discovery in Nag Hammadi (Egypt) of more than forty Christian writings, many of them Gnostic, our understanding of Gnosticism was largely dependent on the writings of its adversaries, who included such prominent church figures as Irenaeus, Hippolytus, Origen, and Justin Martyr. The origins of Gnosticism, which existed in both Christian and non-Christian contexts, are obscure, and Christian Gnosticism is itself diverse. Still, as Robert McL. Wilson writes, developed Gnostic systems shared several features: "(1) a radical cosmic dualism that rejects this world and all that belongs to it: the body is a prison from which the soul longs to escape; (2) a distinction between the unknown transcendent true God and the creator or Demiurge, commonly identified with the God of the Hebrew Bible; (3) the belief that the human race is essentially akin to the divine, being a spark of heavenly light imprisoned in a material body; (4) a myth, often narrating a premundane fall, to account for the present human predicament; and (5) the saving knowledge [gnosis] by which deliverance is effected and the gnostic awakened to recognition of his or her true nature and heavenly origin" (*The Oxford Companion to the Bible*, New York, 1993, p. 256). Similar to the beliefs of the Gnostics were the teachings of the second-century writer Marcion, who viewed the God of the Jews as an evil and inferior deity and would have excluded the Hebrew Bible from Christian scripture.

Other divergent views appeared, for example, in late second-century Phyrgia in

Asia Minor, where Montanus and two women, Priscilla and Maximilla, proclaimed a "new prophecy." Apocalypticists, they heralded the second coming, announcing that Christ would return imminently to the Phrygian villages of Pepuza and Tymion. Despite Christ's failure to do so, the movement persisted. Two centuries later, Emperor Theodosius commanded that the books of the Montanists be burned and that those who hid them be put to death. In their unbridled eschatological expectation, ecstatic prophesying, and claim to be instruments of the Holy Spirit, the Montanists challenged the growing authority of the church's episcopal structure.

Women in Early Christianity

The Montanist movement was also noteworthy for the prominent role of its female prophets. However, just as the existence of powerful goddesses in the great civilizations of the ancient Near Eastern and Mediterranean world had not yielded societies with gender equality, so too in the church the growing importance of Mary, the mother of Jesus, was not accompanied by an increasing role for women in its ecclesiastical life.

The study of women in the earliest phase of Christianity is largely the study of Jewish women; indeed, the New Testament is a major source for Jewish women's history, reminding us that the original followers of Jesus were Palestinian Jews. Not long after the death of Jesus, however, as non-Jews began to enter the community "in Christ," debate arose concerning the role of Jewish law in God's scheme for salvation. With his position that followers of Jesus had been "discharged from the law . . . which held us captive" (Rom. 7.6), Paul represented one end of the theological spectrum. James, the brother of Jesus and the leader of the Jerusalem church, represented the other in maintaining that the Jewish law in its entirety remained valid. By the second century, the majority of Christians were non-Jews, and the church adopted the Pauline position that the law was no longer a vehicle for salvation. Jewish Christians, diverse groups who followed Jewish law and accepted Jesus as the resurrected Messiah, were condemned by both the church fathers and the rabbis. At a time when the emerging church and the emerging synagogue engaged in a rigorous process of self-definition, Jewish-Christian groups blurred the boundaries that both sought to erect. Still, rabbinic and patristic sources hint that as late as the fifth century, Jewish-Christian communities persisted in such areas as Galilee, Jordan, and Syria. It is likely that eventually they were assimilated into the Christian community.

During the Byzantine era, female leadership was exercised largely within the hierarchical structures of women's monastic communities. However, the letters of Paul and the book of Acts suggest that in the earliest phase of emerging Christianity, the opportunities for women were far greater. The closing chapter of Paul's letter to the church at Rome, following the epistolary conventions of that period, includes greetings and personal commendations. Paul mentions ten women, the first of whom is Phoebe, described in Greek as a *diakonos* and a *prostatis*, correctly translated in the New Revised Standard Version as "deacon" and "benefactor" (Rom. 16.1–2). Older translations erroneously rendered these words as "deaconess" and "helper"; thus, generations of translators ignored the plain sense of the text because of their assumption that women could not have exercised significant roles in the early church, and here and elsewhere produced translations that could be used both to reinforce that point of view and to limit contemporary women's ecclesiastical activities. To be sure, Romans was written before the institutionalization of church offices; one cannot describe with certainty the activities of a first-century deacon. But the inaccurate translation "deaconess" suggests a role of less importance than that of "deacon." During the following centuries, the former developed into a position of circumscribed responsibilities, distinct and limited relative to those of a deacon.

Ancient inscriptions suggest, moreover, that the *prostatis* or *prostates* was not only a benefactor or patron, but frequently the president or head of an association. Phoebe was probably one among many of an increasing number of wealthy upper-class Roman women who could control and dispose of their property as they wished, and who often chose to act as donors and benefactors, participating in the Roman system of euergetism or benefactions in the same manner as their male counterparts.

Later in Romans 16, Paul describes the activities of other women mentioned in the chapter using the same vocabulary he employs with respect to his own work and to that of his male colleagues. The husband-and-wife couples Prisca and Aquila (mentioned also in 1 Cor. 16 and Acts 18) and Andronicus and Junia, along with Mary, Tryphaena and Tryphosa, and Persis, are all greeted as coworkers in Christ, and, notably, in the case of Andronicus and Junia, as missionary colleagues (the Greek word is *apostoloi*, "apostles"). Paul also extends greetings to the mother of Rufus, to Julia, and to the sister of Nereus, who must also have been prominent in the community at Rome. Elsewhere Paul takes for granted that women pray and prophesy in church (1 Cor. 11). Similarly, Luke, the author of Acts, mentions women who are prophets, patrons of house churches, prominent converts, missionaries, and teachers.

Both the theological concerns and the highly stylized literary character of the Gospels are such that the historical significance is unclear of those passages in which women are portrayed as the discoverers of the empty tomb and the first post-resurrection witnesses, or as understanding Jesus' true nature when his male disciples fail to do so. The Gospels do, however, provide evidence that Jesus' followers included both men and women. Mary of Magdala was almost certainly among his innermost circle of disciples.

Perhaps the varied and important roles available to women in the earliest phase of Christianity were the church's equivalent of the "Rosie the Riveter" phenomenon in the United States during World War II. That is, in times of political, social, and spiritual revolution, women have often had exceptional ranges of opportunities. However, during the periods of increasing stabilization that typically follow, many of these opportunities tend to shrink or be lost. The "household codes" of some of the later books of the New Testament advocate a subordinate and submissive role for women, and reflect what the pioneering feminist New Testament historian Elisabeth Schüssler Fiorenza has termed "repatriarchalization." Thus the author of 1 Timothy, writing in the name of Paul decades after his death, decreed: "Women should dress themselves modestly and decently in suitable clothing, not with their hair braided, or with gold, pearls, or expensive clothes, but with good works, as is proper for women who profess reverence for God. Let a woman learn in silence with full submission. I permit no woman to teach or to have authority over a man; she is to keep silent" (1 Tim. 2.9–12). The household codes are embedded in documents written at a time of fading apocalyptic expectations within the church, as it was beginning to develop the institutions and the structure of authority that would facilitate its stability and self-perpetuation. Although the church would view itself as "outside" its Roman environment, at the same time it had set out to evangelize this same Roman world. Respectability could serve its goals.

In the Roman culture, "honor" and "shame" could be acquired on the basis of the behavior of the females in the household. The well-run household was both a microcosm of and the foundation of the well-run state. The images of the "ideal" woman in the household codes, in later rabbinic documents, and in the works of Roman orators, elegists, and historians are strikingly similar. They can be summed up in the epitaph of a Roman housewife of the first century BCE: "Here lies Amynome, wife of Marcus, best and most beautiful, worker in wool, pious, chaste, thrifty, faithful, a stayer-at-home" (*Inscriptiones Latinae selectae* 8402). But the image of Amynome must be balanced against sources that depict women participating in a broad range of occupations and activities outside the home, including serving as priestesses and holding offices in religious associations. Upper-class women attended dinner parties and the theater, and as noted above, some participated in the Roman system of benefactions. Thus models both for women's leadership roles and for the subordination of women in the church existed in the larger Roman environment of which the church was part.

During succeeding centuries, debate continued within the church concerning the proper roles for women. In some circles, women taught, prophesied, baptized, and administered the Eucharist, rousing the ire of such Christian authors as Tertullian and Epiphanius. Collections of church rules such as the fourth-century Apostolic Constitutions barred women from priestly activities. Early on, however, women created a place for themselves in communities of female ascetics. The letters of the church father Jerome inform us about an ascetic circle of Roman aristocratic women of the second half of the fourth and the early fifth centuries. These include Marcella, Melania, Paula, and Paula's daughter Eustochium. Both Melania and Paula established women's monasteries in Palestine. Paula's monasteries were located in Bethlehem, near the men's monastery, which Jerome headed and which was built through Paula's largesse.

Jerome is well known for his disparaging comments about women despite his close friendships with several female ascetics who lived as virgins or celibates. For Jerome, sexual renunciation had spared them the taint of femaleness, enabling them to acquire holiness. Mary, a second and vastly improved Eve, had brought life and had preserved her virginity; a woman could do no better than to imitate her. In a letter to Eustochium, Jerome also listed some of the practical advantages of the life of the unmarried virgin: no pregnancy, no crying baby, no jealousy, and none of the worries of managing a household. Although Jerome was especially ardent in his advocacy of female virginity, the Byzantine church would accept that the most attainable lot for the majority of women was that of the honorable wife. But contrary to paganism and rabbinic Judaism, Christianity's highest praise was reserved for the virgin. Women such as Paula and Eustochium anticipate the powerful and pious female ascetics of medieval Europe.

The "Fall of Rome"

Throughout the fourth century CE, the proponents of paganism had warned that the well-being of Rome was dependent on the proper maintenance of the old imperial religion. Conversely, such church leaders as Eusebius had seen in the Christianization of the ruling house the effective union between church and state. The glory and power of the latter provided evidence of the triumph of the church. These ideas would be challenged when, in 410, the Visigothic Arian king Alaric and his army sacked Rome. While pagan authors saw in this traumatic event the gods' punishment for their neglect, Augustine (354–430), bishop of Hippo Regius in North Africa, responded with his magisterial *City of God*, penned in twenty-two books between 413 and 426. For Augustine, the "universal way" of salvation was through Christ and the Catholic church, the earthly point of access to the eschatological and eternal "city of God."

In today's language, *City of God* is a multidisciplinary work, intertwining, as the Roman historian Averil Cameron has observed, not only theology but also political theory, history, and philosophy to argue that pagan culture and, indeed, the Roman state were fundamentally flawed. Thus for Augustine the sack of Rome did not undermine the belief that God was the agent of human history as it moved toward the final judgment and, for some, life in the Heavenly Jerusalem.

As Augustine lay near death in 430, the "barbarians" stood literally at the gates of his beloved city. Had he lived another year, he would have witnessed the partial destruction of Hippo by the Arian Vandals, who would rule North Africa for roughly the next century. In 476, well before their departure, the paradoxically named Romulus, the last Roman emperor in the west, was deposed by his master of the soldiers, a Visigoth, constituting the date often serving to mark the "fall" of the Roman Empire. But the previous century had already provided ample evidence that, in the west at least, the empire was splitting at some of its seams. At the same time, the "barbarian" kingdoms that evolved in the fifth and sixth centuries, some of which shaped the map of medieval Europe, displayed much continuity with their Roman and Christian pasts. The Latin language, the Christian religion, and the Late Antique culture of the eastern elites were adopted and transmitted by the "barbarian" elites, resulting in a kind of "romanization."

In the east, although Justinian and his successors understood themselves to be Romans, modern historians typically refer to them as Byzantines. Historians differ in their date for the beginning of the Byzantine era. Some date it to the reign of Justinian, others to 330 when Constantine dedicated his new capital at Constantinople, the former Byzantium. The end of the Byzantine empire is usually dated at 1453, when, under Mehmet the Conqueror, the Ottoman Turks captured Constantinople.

Justinian's lust for power and glory in both secular and sacred spheres was reflected not only in his territorial ambitions but also in his building projects. They included the rebuilding of the magnificent Hagia Sophia church in Constantinople, whose extraordinary interior prompted Byzantine clerical sources to observe that it embraced the divine cosmos, enabling worshipers through their senses to contemplate and celebrate God. At its dedication in 537, Justinian is said to have uttered, "Solomon, I have surpassed you."

Its enduring grandeur notwithstanding, the circumstances in which Justinian rebuilt Hagia Sophia are reminders of the hardships and tensions of urban life in the Late Antique empire. Justinian began his building project in the aftermath of the Nika riot of 532, in which the older church had been destroyed by fire. The revolt had left many thousands dead and much of Constantinople in ruins. Anger at Justinian's officials probably fueled the riot. Indeed, exorbitant taxes, government mismanagement, occasional interruptions in the food supply, and mass poverty contributed to the unrest, which exploded at times in devastating riots in the cities of the empire. Of course, the fate of the city-dwellers was inextricably linked to the countryside. Rural unrest, whether the outcome of natural disasters or political and economic strife, exacerbated by the rural populace's disproportionate tax burden, could affect food production and transportation with devastating consequences for civic life. Disease was also a ubiquitous specter haunting the cities. Only six years after the dedication of Hagia Sophia, as much as one-third of Constantinople's population may have died in an epidemic of bubonic plague.

The Church in Late Antiquity

The fourth to sixth centuries CE witnessed the church's adaptation to empire, as well as its increasing institutionalization and associated efforts at doctrinal clarification. Begun centuries earlier, the process of scriptural canonization, which would yield a fixed and authoritative listing of the books of the New Testament, reached a milestone in the fourth century. In a festal letter written in 367, Bishop Athanasius of Alexandria listed all of the twenty-seven books of today's New Testament. By the early fifth century, his canon had been largely accepted in both the east and the west.

The process of canonization cannot be reconstructed with certainty. In the second and third centuries many Christian writings were regarded as authoritative, but not all of them ended up in the New Testament canon or even exist today. The degree to which a text was regarded as authoritative often varied both regionally and among different factions and figures in the church. Indeed, the second century was an era in which many gospels were composed, containing traditions about and sayings of Jesus not found in the canonical Gospels. By the close of the century, the four canonical Gospels and the letters of Paul had already acquired a widespread authoritative status. But the Epistle of Barnabas, 1 Clement, the Shepherd of Hermas, and the Apocalypse of Peter are examples of texts that were widely known and viewed as authoritative by many, and yet did not achieve canonical status. Many historians hold that the process of canonization was in part a response to what key figures in the early church regarded as threats, including in the second and third centuries Gnosticism, Marcionism, and Montanism. The opinions of, and rivalries among, various sees and prominent clerical figures also played a role, both shaping and reflecting the evolving regional consensus concerning a writing. Moreover, as New Testament scholar Harry Gamble has observed, canonicity demanded that a writing be considered apostolic, catholic—of relevance to the universal church, orthodox, and in wide usage. Significantly, only in the fourth century, when the canon emerged, did the technology of codex production make possible the manufacture as one book of a collection as large as the New Testament.

The fourth and fifth centuries witnessed also the growing power and authority of the bishop of Rome, even as, during the fifth century, Roman imperial power was in decline. To be sure, the title *pope* (Latin *papa*) had been appropriated not only by the bishop of Rome but also by the bishops of other major cities. However, from the time of the papacy of Damasus (366–84), the Roman bishops had argued increasingly forcefully and explicitly that they were, as the inheritors of the authority of the apostle Peter, the rightful leaders of the church. Strong and able fifth- and sixth-century popes such as Leo I (440–61) and Gregory the Great (590–604) contributed to the growing power, especially in the west, of the Roman papacy, an office that would facilitate greater church unity in the west and add to the growing tensions between eastern and western Christendom.

During this period there were seven church councils whose decisions on the nature of the Trinity and the nature of Christ were regarded as binding for all Christians: Nicea (325), Constantinople (381), Ephesus (431), Chalcedon (451), Constantinople II (553), Constantinople III (680–81), and Nicea II (787). The church also developed the belief that the decisions of these councils had been guided by the Holy Spirit. From a sociological perspective, this served to legitimate the majority-rule decision making of the conciliar bishops, an emerging power elite, and to better position them against others who claimed authority to act in God's name.

The bishops are paradoxical figures. Many emerged from the upper-class urban elites who had appropriated and adapted the traditional system of *paideia*, or learning, which had also been the domain of the pagan elites. They had close ties with the state, exercised much authority in their locales, and stood at the top of a very wealthy institution that the state had endowed with great privileges. For example, by the early fifth century, church lands were exempt from most taxes. Most of the bishops were part of the empire's privileged "handful," supported by and generally supportive of a social, economic, and political structure oppressive to the vast majority of people, who, overwhelmingly, were dreadfully impoverished. At the same time, the bishops presented themselves as the protectors of the poor. In an era of growing civic unrest, this enabled them to accrue power vis-à-vis the imperial government and to serve as mediators between the populace and the government, at times intervening with the latter on behalf of the former. The bishops' appropriation of the roles of civic patron and benefactor, institutions essential to the functioning of the cities, was facilitated by the privileges that the imperial government allocated to them, even as these privileges contributed to the bishops' increasing wealth, power, and popularity among the populace.

Their frequent alliances with the monks contributed to the popularity of the bishops. In contrast to bishops, monks represented, at least in theory if not always in fact (some monks were themselves from the elite), the uneducated and simple man of the lower classes who understood and indeed embodied the fundamental truths and teachings of Christianity, and for whom the culture of the upper classes was inferior and superfluous. The bishops were able both to participate in and to benefit from the prominence and power that the monks enjoyed with the populace, while retaining the advantages of their upper-class status. The monks, in turn, were separate from the larger society and distinct from its ruling classes. Yet simultaneously, by virtue of this separateness and distinctiveness (especially as exemplified in the widespread belief in their extraordinary holiness, reflected in their sexual renunciation, asceticism, and withdrawal from ordinary life), monks could play a significant role in influencing the outcome of events in both the clerical and the civic realms—and in making peace between local communities and the state.

Monasticism drew on a long-standing belief in many religious and philosophical traditions of the Roman world that the path to the holy rested in subduing the body, especially sexual desire, and in withdrawing from the everyday world. By the early fourth century CE, both male and female ascetics populated the Egyptian deserts. These monks and solitaries claimed to experience the divine outside the institutions and the locales that the bishops controlled. This threat to the hierarchy's authority was curbed in part by the growing institutionalization of monasticism. Even in the lifetime of the earliest solitary, Anthony (ca. 270–356), about whom traditions survive, communities of monks had been established in the deserts of Egypt. The evolution of communal monasticism with its rules and orders, increasingly under the supervision of bishops and abbots, brought the monks under institutional authority. For most Christians, the veneration of those to whom extraordinary holiness was ascribed, and who might intercede with God on one's behalf—monks, martyrs, and saints—played a greater role in their religious lives than did the doctrinal disputes that preoccupied the bishops. Yet the distinction between "popular" religion and the religion of the elites should not be overstated, for one of the strengths of the institutional church has been its capacity to organize, regularize, and thus domesticate the practices and customs of its adherents.

Christian Rome and the Jews

Although the legislation of the earliest Christian emperors did not significantly alter the rights and privileges of the empire's Jews, the laws reflected the desire of the government to limit the spread of Judaism. The language of some of the legislation, even from the reign of Constantine, was harsh, a marked change from the neutral tone of laws promulgated by pagan Rome, and a reflection of the government's changing perception of Jews and Judaism. For example, Constantine issued legislation that both imposed penalties on anyone who converted to Judaism and forbade Jews to disturb those who had been converted from Judaism to Christianity. Constantine also issued an edict, similar to earlier legislation, demanding that a Jew forfeit any slave whom he had purchased and circumcised. Under such conditions, the slave would receive his freedom.

The legislation of Constantine II (337–40) and Constantius (337–61), sons of Constantine, reiterated and developed that of their father. In a law issued in 339, Jews were again prohibited from purchasing non-Jewish slaves. Such slaves would be immediately forfeited. If a Jew circumcised a slave, he would both forfeit him and be subject to capital punishment. Although this edict was similar to the law issued by Constantine only four years earlier, now the punishment for circumcising a non-Jewish slave was death. Also, a non-Jewish slave was to be forfeited, even if he were uncircumcised.

Another decree commanded that women converts to Judaism who had formerly been bound to the imperial weaving factory be returned to the factory. Jews who converted Christian women to Judaism were subject to capital punishment. Finally, in 353, Constantius issued legislation ordering that the property of Christian converts to Judaism be confiscated. The language of the latter two decrees was again harsh in its identification of Judaism with turpitude, villainy, and sacrilege.

By the close of the fourth century, marriages between Jews and Christians had been prohibited; such marriages were to be treated as adultery. During the fifth and sixth centuries, legislation designed to limit the spread of Judaism continued to be promulgated. As in the earlier fourth-century legislation, decrees were issued to eliminate both Jewish proselytism and the Jewish ownership of non-Jewish slaves. Also, the building of new synagogues was repeatedly prohibited. To be sure, the degree to which such legislation was enforced is unclear. In fifth- and sixth-century Palestine, for example, despite the prohibitions, new synagogues were built, and in fifth-century Capernaum, a grand synagogue and church stood in close proximity. Jews were also excluded from most imperial offices, with a few lowly and burdensome exceptions, including service in the financially oppressive municipal councils. Increasingly, much of the legislation concerning Jews and Judaism was embodied in laws that also addressed pagans and heretics, and that limited the rights of individuals in these groups in a number of venues, including the courts.

In contrast to pagan worship, however, the practice of Judaism was never banned. A decree issued by Theodosius in 393 and addressed to the supreme military command in the east stated: "It is sufficiently established that the sect of the Jews is prohibited by no law. We are therefore gravely disturbed by the interdiction imposed in some places on their assemblies. Your Sublime Magnitude shall, upon reception of this order, repress with due severity the excess of those who presume to commit illegal deeds under the name of the Christian religion and attempt to destroy and despoil synagogues" (*Codex Theodosianus* 16.8.9, trans. A. Linder, *The Jews in Imperial Roman Legislation*, Detroit: Wayne State University Press, 1987, p. 190). Similar protective legislation would also be issued in the early fifth century, reflecting not only the state's concern with law and order and its desire to assert its power in relationship to the church, but also, even if in weakened form, the acceptance of Judaism as a "licit religion."

The Church and the Jews

The legislation of the fourth through the sixth centuries thus represented a marked deterioration in the status of Jews and Judaism, especially in their relationship to the Roman state. The laws echoed the sentiments and concerns expressed at the roughly contemporary church councils, whose canons included prohibitions against marriage with Jews, adultery with Jewish women, the blessing of fields by Jews, the participation in feasts with Jews, and the observance of the Jewish Sabbath and Passover. Yet both the church canons and the imperial legislation assumed that Jews and Christians were interacting, and that Judaism remained a powerful attraction to Christians and to potential pagan converts to Christianity.

Although anti-Jewish sentiments in the writings of the church fathers antedate the fourth century, they assumed greater significance in the emerging Christian state. Like the ecclesiastical canons, many of the patristic texts were a response to the presence of thriving and vibrant Jewish communities and to the perceived threat Judaism posed as an alternative to Christianity. We should recall that during the early centuries of Christianity, most Christians were new Christians for whom the evolving boundaries between Judaism and Christianity were likely to have been blurred. The church remained concerned about "Judaizing" tendencies among its adherents, as it continued to erect boundaries and to define itself, in large part, in contrast to the Judaism out of which it had emerged—a Judaism that continued to thrive and that not only competed with the church for members but whose very existence challenged the church's self-understanding as the "true Israel" and, as such, the sole legitimate interpreter and possessor, in a sense, of the Jewish scriptures, the Old Testament.

As early as the second century, a genre of Christian apologetic literature emerged, aptly described as "Against the Jews," titles first used by Pseudo-Cyprian and Tertullian during the last quarter of the century. This literature, contributions to which were also made by such prominent figures as Justin Martyr in the second and Augustine in the fifth century, sought to demonstrate that in the aftermath of the coming of Christ and the destruction of the Jerusalem Temple, Jewish religious practice was obsolete and that the "old Israel" had been superseded by the "new." The Old Testament itself, when properly understood, bore witness both to the life of Christ and to the emergence of the church and the displacement of the Jews.

Similar anti-Jewish teachings were also expressed in a broad range of patristic writings, including sermons, biblical commentaries, and works that sought primarily to refute paganism or Marcionism. Augustine's position concerning the Jews would become the dominant view of the medieval church. Like biblical Cain, the Jew was to be both protected and condemned to the life of a pariah. Jewish misery would testify, in turn, to the victory and truth of Christianity. The language of the patristic anti-Jewish writings was often harsh. Jews were accused, in some texts, of the paramount religious and moral crime of deicide; they were also charged with activities that society in general condemned—sacrilege, impiousness, drunkenness, lasciviousness, thievery, and disease.

All of these sentiments are present in John Chrysostom's eight forceful homilies to the Judaizing Christians of Antioch, delivered in 386 and 387, which drew on stock rhetorical images and on what by the fourth century had become stereotyped Christian invective. John's sermons must be understood, as Robert Wilken has observed, both in the context of the vibrance and attractiveness of the Antiochene Jewish community to which many local Christians were drawn and in the context of his ongoing struggles against Arian Christians as well as against those pagans who saw in the continuation of Jewish ritual practice a challenge to the claims of Christianity. For John, Jewish ritual practice had been permanently invalidated by the destruction of the Jerusalem Temple within a generation of the death of Jesus and in fulfillment of his prophecy in Matthew 24.2. Julian's failed attempt to rebuild the Temple confirmed this view. Thus John declared, "If the Jewish rules are holy and venerable, our way of life must be false" (*Adversus Iudaeos* 1.6).

Of course, early rabbinic Judaism, like early Christianity, evolved in the aftermath and responded to the destruction of the Temple and the cessation of ancient Israel's sacrificial system. Each, in its way, developed its own identity and forms of self-legitimization independent of the Temple and its rituals. The church maintained not only that Jesus had prophesied the destruction of the Temple but also that Jesus was the final and perfect atoning sacrifice, after whom no more sacrifices were necessary. Although rabbinic Judaism would develop liturgical and other expressions of remembering the Temple, and even hoped for its rebuilding, at the same time it maintained that in the absence of the Temple equally effective means of attaining a right relationship with God were present. In a statement attributed to Rabbi Yohanan ben Zakkai, depicted as comforting a colleague who was mourning the destruction of the Temple, the place of Jewish atonement, he uttered that another atonement, equally effective, was "deeds of loving-kindness." Whereas the early church would understand itself as the sole and universal vehicle for salvation, early rabbinic Judaism envisioned salvation as open not only to Jews, who were mandated to adhere to God's commandments as interpreted by the rabbis, but also to righteous non-Jews who were required to follow the laws of Noah. The rabbis debated the number and content of these laws, generally numbered as seven. To be sure, one of the laws was a prohibition of idolatry, which would have excluded those who engaged in pagan religious practices.

Today, when Christians number close to two billion and Jews are fewer than 1 percent of that total, it is easy to forget that Christian anti-Jewish polemics evolved during the period when Christianity was a small, powerless, illegal, and at times persecuted minority, seeking to develop its own identity apart from and often in contrast to the Judaism that had given birth to it. In vastly different times, patristic anti-Jewish teachings, loosed from their historical moorings, would contribute to the demonization of the Jew in medieval and modern Europe, with terrible and tragic consequences.

Judaism in Late Antiquity

The surviving sources yield little information concerning Jewish responses to evolving Christianity and to the Christianization of the empire with the concomitant deterioration in the legal status of Jews and Judaism. Some Jews and Christians probably engaged in debates, and both Origen and Jerome, roughly a century apart, apparently studied with Jewish sages, a reminder that Jewish-Christian relations could be positive as well as negative. Perhaps the standardization of the Jewish calendar, which probably occurred in the mid-fourth century, and the completion of the Palestinian Talmud and such midrashic works as Genesis Rabbah and Leviticus Rabbah in the late fourth and early fifth centuries, were responses to the challenges posed by now Christian Rome, as the eminent scholar of rabbinic Judaism Jacob Neusner has suggested. Both in their doctrines of history, Messiah, and Torah and in their depictions of Rome, these works appear to respond implicitly to Christian dominance, notwithstanding the absence of explicit reference to Christianity in them.

The same period was also formative in the evolution of such institutions as the synagogue, the patriarchate, and the office of rabbi. Today the intimate association between the rabbi and the synagogue is taken for granted; but in the earliest centuries of the rabbinate and the synagogue, they functioned largely independently of each other. The origins of the synagogue are unclear. It is apparent from archaeological data and from Jewish and non-Jewish literary sources, including the writings of Josephus and the New Testament, that the synagogue, as a Jewish communal association

and as an actual building or place, existed in Palestine and in the Diaspora before 70
CE, when the Jerusalem Temple was destroyed. In the aftermath, the roles and importance of the synagogue would increase in Jewish communal and religious life.
These roles were neither static nor uniform, varying regionally and over time. The
evolving synagogue appears to have assimilated what, at least in some places, were
originally separate institutions, to become a multipurpose institution whose activities
included the reading of the Torah, organized prayer, study, and, most likely, a variety
of communal endeavors such as education and charitable work.

The earliest archaeological evidence for the synagogue dates from third- and
second-century BCE Egypt, where inscriptions for "prayer houses" have been found.
At Delos the remains of a first-century BCE synagogue have been excavated. Diaspora
synagogues have also been identified in such places as Ostia, Sardis, Stobi, Priene,
and Dura-Europos on the Euphrates, where a third-century CE synagogue contained
wall frescoes depicting biblical scenes, some of which have parallels in rabbinic midrashic texts.

Although there is evidence for first-century CE synagogues at Gamla and Migdal
and at the fortresses of Masada and Herodium, the florescence of Palestinian synagogal architecture dates from the third century CE. Most of the more than one hundred remains of synagogues that have been identified are located in Galilee and in
the Golan. Typically oriented toward Jerusalem, synagogue buildings consisted of
apsidal and nonapsidal variations of the Roman basilical structure, as did Christian
churches. The art of the synagogue was diverse, and included both relief sculpture
and mosaics, and secular and distinctly Jewish symbols, the most common of which
was the menorah. Several of the mosaics include depictions of the pagan sun-god
Helios surrounded by the signs of the zodiac. Although the significance of these
mosaics is unclear, they are testimony to the participation by local Jewish communities in facets of the larger Greco-Roman culture. Similarly, synagogal donor inscriptions provide evidence of Jewish participation in the Greco-Roman practices of
communal benefactions. Inscriptions and imperial legislation both provide some information on synagogue offices, especially that of the *archisynagoge*, or "head of the
synagogue." The rabbi seems to have had no authority over the synagogue; his domain was the academy or disciple circle, and the rabbinic court.

The synagogues of the fourth to sixth centuries are also indicative of the vitality
of the Palestinian Jewish community, despite the changing legal status of Jews and
Judaism. The fourth and fifth centuries were overall a period of growth and prosperity
for all of the communities of Palestine, not only because of that region's special status
as Holy Land but also because it shared in an overall economic recovery in the east,
facilitated by the radical administrative, economic, and financial reforms of Diocletian, which were continued by Constantine and Constantius. Although the economic
situation was far from optimal, it was better than it had been during the political
and economic anarchy of much of the third century.

Although it is commonplace to refer to "the rabbis" and to "rabbinic Judaism,"
each of these terms subsumes significant diversity. Not only do each of the foundation
documents of rabbinic Judaism, completed between the third and seventh centuries,
preserve diverse opinions on a given topic, but each document has its distinctive
concerns, perspectives, and methods.

The earliest rabbinic writing, the Mishnah, was completed about 200 CE. Later rabbinic works attribute its editing to Rabbi Judah the Patriarch, although the Mishnah makes no mention of this. The Mishnah is arranged by topic. It consists of six divisions or orders: *Zera'im*/Seeds (agricultural laws), *Mo'ed*/Appointed Times (festivals), *Nashim*/Women (marriage law), *Neziqin*/Damages (civil law, contracts, torts), *Qodashim*/Holy Things (sacrifices), and *Toharot*/Purities (sources of impurity, means of purification). The orders are divided further into sixty-three tractates. With the exception of the tractate *Pirqei Abot*/Sayings of the Fathers, which may slightly post-date the remainder of the Mishnah, the latter is a kind of book of laws, albeit one that preserves diverse and often contradictory opinions on a given topic.

The degree to which the contents of the Mishnah reflect or are rooted in the life of third-century Palestine varies. Much of the Mishnah concerns Temple ritual, although at the time of the Mishnah's promulgation the Temple had been absent for more than a century. The Mishnah is also striking in that it rarely endeavors to justify its positions through scriptural citations. This would be left to the two Talmuds—the Palestinian Talmud, also referred to as the Jerusalem Talmud or the Talmud of the Land of Israel, and the Babylonian Talmud. The former was completed around 400 CE, whereas the latter, the product of the rabbinical academies of the Sassanian empire, dates from a century or so later. Both are essentially commentaries on the Mishnah and consist of mishnaic passages followed by elucidations of the Mishnah passage. The Talmuds include not only legal or halakic material but also haggadic texts, which are narratives of nonobligatory material, often presented in the form of didactic stories.

In addition to the Mishnah and its commentaries, the rabbis of the first seven centuries also produced compilations of scriptural exegesis known as Midrashim. The process of *midrash*, or inquiry, and its outcome in the form of exegetical collections, were the vehicle by which the rabbis explored the meanings of various books of the Hebrew Bible.

During the same period in which the formative documents of rabbinic Judaism were produced, the rabbis developed the belief that their teachings, embodied in these documents, had the same authority as scripture. The rabbis even went a step further to articulate the central distinctive tenet of rabbinic Judaism—that is, the Torah itself consisted of both the oral Torah and the written Torah. According to rabbinic belief, at Mount Sinai God had revealed the dual Torah to Moses. But whereas the written Torah had been revealed to all of Israel, the oral Torah had been transmitted from one generation of sages to the next, by means of memorization and recitation, in a chain of tradition that linked the revelation at Sinai to the rabbis of the Mishnah, the foundation document of the oral Torah.

For the rabbis, a scholarly elite of Late Antique holy men, the most worthwhile activity was the study of Torah, a holiness-producing activity. Insofar as one could know God or imitate God, it was through the study of his Torah. Through the mastery of Torah, the rabbi came to embody Torah. His activities on earth echoed the activities in heaven, where not only Moses but also God studied Torah.

With the exception of the religious systems of such groups as the Jews of Ethiopia and the Samaritans and Karaites (the latter two having been treated at times as part of, and at other times as separate from, the Jewish community), all the varieties of modern Judaism are forms of rabbinic Judaism. But during the formative centuries of rabbinic Judaism, it is unclear how much authority the rabbis exercised outside their own circles, especially over the Jewish communities of the Roman Diaspora. As the historian Shaye Cohen has aptly summarized, the Diaspora communities probably celebrated the Sabbath, followed Jewish dietary laws, and worshiped God quite independently of the rabbis.

In Palestine, the rabbinic presence and rabbinic authority seem to have increased significantly from the second to the seventh centuries. The major arena of rabbinic authority was probably the rabbinic court. But whereas rabbinic literature provides some information concerning the kinds of cases that may have been adjudicated, it yields little information about who, when, where, and at whose bidding Jewish men and women resorted to those courts, whether in place of or in addition to the Roman courts. The situation in Sassanian Babylonia was similar, although the rabbinic presence there begins slightly later than in Palestine, where the movement emerged. Eventually, the Babylonian rabbinic academies surpassed the Palestinian academies in importance, and the Babylonian Talmud became the foundation document for succeeding centuries of Jewish learning.

Whereas the office of rabbi survived and evolved, imperial legislation provides evidence that the patriarchate had ceased by 429. The reasons for this cessation are unknown, but it may have been abolished by the Roman government. Still, both rabbinic literature and Roman law reveal the growing authority of the patriarchate as it developed from the second through the close of the fourth centuries. The patriarch (Hebrew *nasi*) functioned initially as the head of the major rabbinic academy and of the Sanhedrin in Palestine, but by the late fourth century Roman law had granted the patriarch jurisdiction over all of the empire's Jewish communities, including the right to collect taxes. Most of the increase in power occurred under Christian rule. During the reign of Theodosius (379–95), Roman law granted the patriarch the titles of *clarissimus* and *illustris*, typically bestowed on the highest magistrates and on members of the senatorial order. The letters of Libanius include correspondence, dating from 388 to 393, between him and the patriarch Gamaliel V, suggesting that Gamaliel, like Libanius himself and the Christian bishops, was part of the cultured and powerful elite described above.

Although Gamaliel was typical neither of the rabbis nor of the larger Jewish population, he reminds us that the Jewish communities of Late Antique Palestine did not exist in isolation from a larger eastern Mediterranean Greco-Roman culture. Literary sources, as well as regional surveys and excavations, especially in lower Galilee, suggest that even the predominantly Jewish cities had mixed populations and were linked by trading patterns and the Roman road system to the predominantly non-Jewish cities of the coastal area and elsewhere.

Jewish Women in the Roman Empire

Until recently most studies of Jewish women in the Roman Empire were confined to their depictions in the formative documents of rabbinic Judaism. Rabbinic literature, however, reveals much more about the roles of women in the intellectual landscape of the rabbis than it does about the opportunities and restrictions of the flesh-and-blood women of late antiquity.

As Jacob Neusner has demonstrated, rabbinic interest in women focused on such aspects as marriage and divorce (which necessitated transfer of the woman and her property) and on women as purveyors of uncleanliness because of menstruation—aspects that threatened the rabbis' constructions of an ordered and sanctified world. Analogously to the depictions of women in the writings of the roughly contemporary church fathers, the rabbis bestowed honor and praise on the mother, wife, and daughter who functioned within the framework of rabbinic law. Outside its constraints, the female was a source of chaos and disorder.

Rabbinic literature, of course, is largely interested in the activities of the rabbis, for whom holiness was acquired through the study of Torah and the performance of the commandments preserved in the dual Torah. In general, rabbinic law exempted women from the study of Torah and from the performance of commandments that were positive and time-bound. Nevertheless, the rabbis did not treat women as a seamless group. The Mishnah and Talmuds distinguish between dependent and autonomous women, the latter including unmarried adult daughters, widows, and divorcées. Unlike their dependent counterparts, they could arrange their own marriages, as well as control and dispose of their property. Thus rabbinic literature provides the framework in which some women could amass wealth and power.

The existence of such women has been confirmed by the pioneering studies of Ross Kraemer and Bernadette Brooten. Their examination of inscriptions, almost all of which are from the Roman Diaspora, indicate that at least some women served as synagogue officials and as donors, participating in the system of benefactions discussed earlier. To be sure, these women, like their pagan and Christian counterparts, were exceptional. The majority of women lived in poverty and labored from sunup to sundown in child care and the production of food and clothing. But the inscriptions suggest that high socioeconomic status may have been a more decisive factor in determining the opportunities and restrictions of the empire's women than was religious identity and, at times, even gender.

The nonrabbinic evidence for Palestinian Jewish women is frustratingly small. One can only speculate, for example, about the range of options that women exercised in seeking a divorce. Whereas Roman law allowed both men and women to initiate divorces, rabbinic law limited this to males—although mechanisms were devised to persuade recalcitrant husbands, under some circumstances, to grant divorces to their wives. Did such women turn to the Roman courts? The second-century CE archive of Babata, a cache of thirty-five legal documents found in the Judean desert and belonging to a young and wealthy widow, suggests that at least some women made use of the Roman courts in their legal affairs.

The cache, which consists of documents in Greek, Nabatean, and Aramaic, includes property deeds, documents concerning lawsuits brought by and against Babata, and marriage contracts. Many of these documents conform to Roman law. We cannot determine the degree to which Babata was representative of Palestinian Jewish women of her era, a time when the rabbinic movement was still in its infancy. However, the Babata archive raises again the questions concerning the degree to which Palestinian Jews participated in the larger Greco-Roman culture of which they were part and from which, at least in some ways, they were distinct.

Islam and Jerusalem

Not only Palestine but the entire Roman east as well would be shaken by the resumption of the perennial warfare between Byzantium and Sassanian Persia during the latter half of the sixth and the early seventh centuries. Perhaps exhausted by warfare, the Byzantine emperor Maurice (582–602) and the Persian king Chosroes II (590–628) made an "eternal" pact of peace. The peace lasted approximately a decade, but was shattered when Maurice was murdered by the usurper Phocas. In 614 Chosroes conquered Jerusalem, from which he is said to have taken the true cross and transported it to Persia. Persian rule was short-lived. The Byzantine emperor Heraclius (610–41) left Constantinople in 622 to launch a major counterattack, triumphantly returning the cross to Jerusalem eight years later.

Weakened, however, by decades of conflict, neither the Sassanian nor the Byzantine armies were any match for the forces of Islam, which between 634 and 644 would conquer the Sassanian empire and much of Byzantium as well. In 638, under the leadership of Umar, the second caliph, Muslim forces peacefully entered Jerusalem, following the surrender of the city by the Christian patriarch Sophronius. With the exception of the periods of Crusader rule (1089–1187, 1229–44), Jerusalem would remain in Muslim hands until 1917.

At about the same time that Chosroes II was invading Byzantine territory, Islam holds that the prophet Muhammad was beginning to receive revelations from God, mediated by the angel Gabriel and eventually embodied in the Quran. Islam understands Muhammad as the seal of the prophets, bringing to humankind a final and perfect form of monotheism. In this sense, Islam can be understood as a continuation of and a correction of the older monotheistic traditions of Judaism and Christianity. Like Judaism and Christianity, Islam views Abraham as the ancestral figure and as the perfect man of faith.

To be sure, historians disagree over the precise nature of the relationship between early Islam and contemporary Judaism and Christianity. It is clear, however, that Jerusalem, identified as the city of the prophets and the site of Solomon's Temple, occupied a place of profound importance in emerging Islam. For a brief period, before Muhammad's *hijra*, or emigration, from Mecca to Medina in 622, the direction of prayer was toward Jerusalem; the Quran notes the change in the direction of prayer to Mecca.

Unlike many earlier conquerors of the Holy City, Umar's forces would neither massacre its inhabitants nor destroy the religious monuments of the vanquished. Later sources describe Umar's interest in the Temple Mount, the "Noble Sanctuary" (Arabic *Haram al-Sharif*). Horrified by the state of ruin and filth in which the Byzantine Christians had kept the Temple Mount, thereby testifying to the victory of the "new Israel" over the "old," Umar ordered that it be cleaned in its entirety. Sometime thereafter a modest mosque was built at the southern end of the old Herodian platform.

In 691/692 the magnificent Dome of the Rock, a rotunda on an octagonal base built by the Umayyad caliph Abd al-Malik, was completed. The Dome, which dominates the Haram today, affirmed the triumph of Islam in the Christian showplace of Jerusalem. Early Muslim authorities would identify Jerusalem as the destination of the prophet Muhammad's "night journey," and the rock as the place from where he ascended to heaven, thus strengthening for Islam the sanctity and significance of Jerusalem. So, too, as in Judaism and Christianity, Jerusalem would assume an important role in Muslim beliefs concerning the end time.

Although the name *Jerusalem* probably originally meant "foundation of [the god] Shalem," it has often been interpreted to mean "city of peace" (Hebrew *'ir shalom*). Tragically, peace has eluded Jerusalem for most of its history. Today Jerusalem often seems to embody that which separates the children of Abraham. News stories bear daily witness to the enduring tensions between Jerusalem the ideal and Jerusalem the real.

Roughly a millennium ago, Muqqadisi, a Muslim geographer and historian and a native of Jerusalem, would describe it as a place oppressive to the poor, lacking in learned men, "a golden basin filled with scorpions." However, he would also celebrate Jerusalem as "the most illustrious of cities," where the advantages of the present and the next world meet. Perhaps the visions of and yearnings for Jerusalem the holy, the ideal Jerusalem, embedded in centuries of Jewish, Christian, and Muslim literature, can serve as a reminder of that which brings together the children of Abraham and all of humankind.

Select Bibliography

Armstrong, Karen. *Jerusalem: One City, Three Faiths.* New York: Alfred A. Knopf, 1996. A thoughtful history of Jerusalem from the Bronze Age to the present.

Bowersock, Glenn W. *Julian the Apostate.* Cambridge, Mass.: Harvard University Press, 1978. An authoritative study of the last pagan Roman emperor.

Brooten, Bernadette. *Women Leaders in the Ancient Synagogue: Inscriptional Evidence and Background Issues.* Brown Judaic Studies, 36. Chico, Calif.: Scholars Press, 1982. A pioneering study of inscriptions that provide evidence for the communal leadership roles of some Jewish women in late antiquity.

Brown, Peter. *The World of Late Antiquity AD 150–750.* New York: Harcourt Brace Jovanovich, 1971. A pioneering, elegant, and lavishly illustrated historical and cultural survey.

Cameron, Averil. *The Later Roman Empire AD 284–430.* Cambridge, Mass.: Harvard University Press, 1993.

———. *The Mediterranean World in Late Antiquity AD 395–600.* New York: Routledge, 1993. Excellent companion volumes on the history of late antiquity with special attention to issues of cultural change.

Chuvin, Pierre. *A Chronicle of the Last Pagans.* Trans. B. A. Archer. Cambridge, Mass.: Harvard University Press, 1990. A study of the persistence and the ultimate defeat of paganism in the context of the ascendance of Christianity in the Roman Empire of the fourth to sixth centuries.

Fox, Robin Lane. *Pagans and Christians.* New York: Alfred A. Knopf, 1987. A comparative study of the complex intellectual and historical relationships between paganism and Christianity through the reign of Constantine.

Gager, John G. *The Origins of Anti-Semitism: Attitudes toward Judaism in Pagan and Christian*

Antiquity. New York: Oxford University Press, 1985. A balanced examination of pagan and early Christian views on Judaism, including those in the New Testament and in the writings of the church fathers.

Gamble, Harry. *The New Testament Canon: Its Making and Meaning.* Philadelphia: Fortress, 1985. A helpful study of the evolution of the New Testament canon and the complex issues in reconstructing its history.

Grabar, Oleg, ed. *The Shape of the Holy: Early Islamic Jerusalem.* Princeton, N.J.: Princeton University Press, 1996. A valuable recent study with special attention to the significance of early Islamic monuments, especially the Dome of the Rock.

Grant, Michael. *The Roman Emperors: A Biographical Guide to the Rulers of Imperial Rome 31 BC–AD 476.* New York: Charles Scribner's Sons, 1985. Sketches of the lives and reigns of the Roman emperors from Augustus to Zeno.

Kee, Howard Clark, et al. *Christianity: A Social and Cultural History.* New York: Macmillan, 1991. A sociologically grounded history of Christianity from its origins to the present.

Kraemer, Ross Shepard, ed. *Maenads, Martyrs, Matrons, Monastics: A Sourcebook on Women's Religions in the Greco-Roman World.* Philadelphia: Fortress, 1988. A valuable collection of primary sources on Jewish, Christian, and pagan women's religious practices and opportunities in the Hellenistic and Late Antique Mediterranean world.

———. *Her Share of the Blessings: Women's Religions among Pagans, Jews, and Christians in the Greco-Roman World.* New York: Oxford University Press, 1992. Historical and anthropological study of women's religious practices and opportunities.

Levine, Lee I. *The Ancient Synagogue: The First Thousand Years.* New Haven, Conn.: Yale University Press, 2000. A monumental and comprehensive study of the development of the institution of the synagogue.

MacMullen, Ramsay. *Christianizing the Roman Empire (A.D. 100–400).* New Haven, Conn.: Yale University Press, 1984. An analysis of the growth and ultimate triumph of Christianity in the Roman Empire and the concomitant conflict between paganism and Christianity.

———. *Christianity and Paganism in the Fourth to Eighth Centuries.* New Haven, Conn.: Yale University Press, 1997. A sequel to the preceding volume.

McManners, John, ed. *The Oxford Illustrated History of Christianity.* Oxford: Oxford University Press, 1990. A comprehensive and lavishly illustrated history of Christianity from its inception to the present, with contributions by nineteen leading scholars.

Meyers, Eric M., and James F. Strange. *Archaeology, the Rabbis, and Early Christianity.* Nashville: Abingdon, 1981. A helpful introduction to the importance of material culture in reconstructing the evolving histories of Judaism and Christianity in Roman and early Byzantine Palestine.

Neusner, Jacob. *Rabbinic Judaism: Structure and System.* Minneapolis: Fortress, 1995. A thoughtful analytical study of the key characteristics of rabbinic Judaism as present in its formative documents.

Pelikan, Jaroslav. *Mary through the Centuries: Her Place in the History of Culture.* New Haven, Conn.: Yale University Press, 1996. A thoughtful study of the changing depictions of the mother of Jesus from the New Testament to the present.

Peters, F. E. *Jerusalem: The Holy City in the Eyes of Chroniclers, Visitors, Pilgrims, and Prophets from the Days of Abraham to the Beginnings of Modern Times.* Princeton, N.J.: Princeton University Press, 1985. A superb collection of primary sources from the Bronze Age to the nineteenth century, with helpful accompanying comments.

Schüssler Fiorenza, Elisabeth. *In Memory of Her: A Feminist Theological Reconstruction of Christian Origins*. New York: Crossroad, 1983. A pioneering feminist analysis of women in the New Testament and early Christianity in historical context.

Shanks, Hershel, ed. *Christianity and Rabbinic Judaism: A Parallel History of Their Origins and Early Development*. Washington, D.C.: Biblical Archaeology Society, 1992. A valuable introduction by nine leading scholars to Christianity and rabbinic Judaism, in historical context, during their first six centuries.

Smallwood, E. Mary. *The Jews under Roman Rule: From Pompey to Diocletian*. Leiden, The Netherlands: E. J. Brill, 1976. A political history of the Jews in the pagan Roman Empire.

Wegner, Judith Romney. *Chattel or Person: The Status of Women in the Mishnah*. New York: Oxford University Press, 1988. A careful analysis of the Mishnah's categories of women, and the opportunities and restrictions that it envisioned for women.

Wilkinson, John. *Egeria's Travels*. London: SPCK, 1971. The text of the itinerary of the fourth-century Christian pilgrim with an accompanying helpful discussion.

———. *Jerusalem Pilgrims before the Crusades*. Warminster, England: Aris & Phillips, 1977. An overview, with selected texts of early Christian pilgrims to the Holy City.

Chronology

DATES	PERIOD	SYRIA-PALESTINE	EGYPT	MESOPOTAMIA	ASIA MINOR
CA. 43,000–18,000 BCE	UPPER PALEOLITHIC				
CA. 18,000–8500 BCE	EPIPALEOLITHIC				
CA. 8500–4500 BCE	NEOLITHIC				
CA. 4500–3300 BCE	CHALCOLITHIC	Early stages of urbanization throughout the Near East			
CA. 3300–2000 BCE	EARLY BRONZE AGE				
3300–3100 BCE	Early Bronze I		Earliest forms of writing	Full urbanization / Sumerian culture develops	
3100–2700 BCE	Early Bronze II	In Egyptian sphere	Political unification / Early Dynastic period	Floruit of Sumerian culture	
2700–2300 BCE	Early Bronze III	Flourishing city-states	Old Kingdom / Dynasties 3–5	Sargon of Akkad / Naram-Sin of Akkad / Gudea of Lagash	
2300–2000 BCE	Early Bronze IV	Decline/abandonment of city-states	First Intermediate Period	Third Dynasty of Ur	

Chronology (*continued*)

DATES	PERIOD	SYRIA-PALESTINE	EGYPT	MESOPOTAMIA	ASIA MINOR
CA. 2000–1550 BCE	MIDDLE BRONZE AGE				
2000–1650 BCE	Middle Bronze I–II	Revival of urbanism Invention of alphabet	Middle Kingdom Dynasties 11–12	Amorite kingdoms Shamshi-Adad of Assyria (ca. 1813–1781) Hammurapi of Babylon (ca. 1792–1750)	Rise of Hittites
1650–1550 BCE	Middle Bronze III		Second Intermediate/ Hyksos Period		
CA. 1550–1200 BCE	LATE BRONZE AGE	In Egyptian sphere Rise of Mitanni in north Ugarit flourishes Collapse of city-states	New Kingdom Dynasties 18–19 Thutmose III (1479–1425) Akenhaten (1352–1336) Seti I (1294–1279) Rameses II (1279–1213) Merneptah (1213–1203) Sea Peoples invasions begin		Hittites challenge Egypt for control of Syria Hittite empire collapses Trojan War
CA. 1200–586 BCE	IRON AGE				
CA. 1200–1025 BCE	Iron I	Israel emerges in Canaan Philistines settle on SW coast Small city-states develop in Phoenicia, Syria, Transjordan	Rameses III (1184–1153)	Resurgence of Assyria Tiglath-pileser I (1114–1076)	

DATES	PERIOD	SYRIA-PALESTINE	EGYPT	MESOPOTAMIA
CA. 1025–586 BCE	Iron II			
CA. 1025–928 BCE	Iron IIA	United Monarchy in Israel Saul (1025–1005) David (1005–965) Solomon (968–928)		
CA. 928–722 BCE	Iron IIB	Divided Monarchy Israel — Judah Jeroboam I (928–907) — Rehoboam (928–911) Omri (882–871) capital at Samaria Ahab (873–852) — Jehoshaphat (867–846) Jehu (842–814) — Athaliah (842–836) Jehoash (836–798) Jehoash (800–788) Jeroboam II (788–747) Hoshea (732–722) — Ahaz (743/735–727/715)	Shishak I invades Palestine (925) Tiglath-pileser III (745–727) Assyrian conquest of the Levant	Rise of Neo-Assyrian empire Shalmaneser III (858–824) Battle of Qarqar (853) Adad-nirari III (811–783) Shalmaneser V (727–722) Samaria captured (722)

Chronology (*continued*)

DATES	PERIOD	SYRIA-PALESTINE	EGYPT	MESOPOTAMIA
CA. 722–586 BCE	Iron IIC	Judah Hezekiah (727/715–698/687)		Sargon II (722–705) Sennacherib (705–681) Attack on Judah and siege of Jerusalem (701)
		Manasseh (698/687–642) Josiah (639–609)	Egypt conquered by Assyria (671) Psammetichus I (664–610)	Esarhaddon (681–669) Ashurbanipal (669–627) Rise of Babylon
		Jehoahaz (609)	Neco II (610–595)	Assyrian capital of Nineveh captured (612) Nebuchadrezzar II (604–562) of Babylon
		Jehoiakim (608–598) Jehoiachin (597) Zedekiah (597–586) Capture of Jerusalem (586)		
CA. 586–539 BCE	NEO-BABYLONIAN			Nabonidus (556–539)

DATES	PERIOD	SYRIA-PALESTINE	EGYPT	MESOPCTAMIA	GREECE AND ROME
539–332 BCE	PERSIAN	Some exiles return from Babylon (538) Second Temple built (520–515) Nehemiah governor of Judah (ca. 445–430)		Cyrus II (the Great) (559–530) Capture of Babylon Cambyses (530–522) Capture of Egypt (525) Darius I (522–486) Xerxes (486–465) Artaxerxes I (465–424) Artaxerxes II (405–359)	Greeks repel Persian invasions Peloponnesian War (431–404)
332–63 BCE	HELLENISTIC	Seleucus I (312/311–281) controls Syria and Mesopotamia Ptolemy I (323–282) controls Egypt, Palestine, Phoenicia Antiochus III (223–187) gains control of southern Syria, Phoenicia, and Judea from Ptolemy V (202–198) Antiochus IV Epiphanes (175–164) Revolt of the Maccabees (167–164) Hasmonean rule of Judea (165–37) John Hyrcanus (135–104) Alexander Janneus (103–76) Salome Alexandra (76–67)			Alexander the Great (336–323) Defeats Persians at Issus (332) Occupies the Levant and Egypt Rome gains control over Greece (ca. 188–146; 146: sack of Carthage and Corinth)

Chronology (*continued*)

DATES	PERIOD	EASTERN MEDITERRANEAN	ROME
63 BCE–330 CE	ROMAN	Pompey conquers the Levant (66–62) Enters Jerusalem (63) Herod the Great king of Judea (37–4) Rebuilds Second Temple (Herod) Antipas (4 BCE–39 CE) Life of Jesus of Nazareth (ca. 4 BCE–30 CE) Pontius Pilate governor of Judea (26–36) (Herod) Agrippa I (39–44) (Herod) Agrippa II (49–92) First Jewish Revolt in Judea against Rome (66–73) Jerusalem captured (70) Jewish revolts in Egypt, Libya, Cyprus (115–118) Second Jewish Revolt in Judea against Rome (132–135) Constantinople becomes capital of empire (330)	Julius Caesar named dictator (49); assassinated (44) Octavian (Augustus) defeats Antony at Actium (31) (emperor 27 BCE–14 CE) Tiberius (14–37 CE) Gaius (Caligula) (37–41) Claudius (41–54) Nero (54–68) Vespasian (69–79) Titus (79–81) Domitian (81–96) Nerva (96–98) Trajan (98–117) Hadrian (117–38) Diocletian (284–305) Constantine (324–37)
330–638 CE	BYZANTINE	Julian the Apostate (361–63) Theodosius I (379–95) Christianity official religion of empire Justinian (527–65) Life of Muhammad (ca. 570–632) Arab conquest of Jerusalem (638)	Rome falls to Visigoths (476)

General Bibliography

The works listed here are applicable to the volume as a whole, or to more than one chapter. Our intention has been to provide interested readers with accessible sources for some of the ideas contained in this book, as well as with current reference works dealing with the biblical world. More detailed bibliographies will be found after each chapter, as well as in most of the works that follow.

ENCYCLOPEDIAS AND ENCYCLOPEDIC DICTIONARIES

Achtemeier, Paul J., ed. *The HarperCollins Bible Dictionary*. Rev. ed. San Francisco: HarperSanFrancisco, 1996. A current and comprehensive handbook.

Cross, F. L., and E. A. Livingstone, eds. *The Oxford Dictionary of the Christian Church*. 3d ed. New York: Oxford University Press, 1997. A recent revision makes this standard current.

Freedman, David Noel, ed. *The Anchor Bible Dictionary*. 6 vols. New York: Doubleday, 1992. The standard reference both for the Bible and for the biblical world. (Also available on CD-ROM from Logos Research Systems, Oak Harbor, Wash.)

Hornblower, Simon, and Anthony Spaworth, eds. *The Oxford Classical Dictionary*. 3d ed. Oxford: Oxford University Press, 1996. Recently revised and expanded, this is the place to start for information about the Greco-Roman world.

Metzger, Bruce M., and Michael D. Coogan, eds. *The Oxford Companion to the Bible*. New York: Oxford University Press 1993 (also available on CD-ROM).

ARCHAEOLOGY

Ben-Tor, Amnon, ed. *The Archaeology of Ancient Israel*. Trans. R. Greenberg. New Haven, Conn.: Yale University Press, 1992. A detailed survey by a number of scholars, with excellent plans and photographs.

Levy, Thomas, ed. *The Archaeology of Society in the Holy Land*. New York: Facts on File, 1995. A collection of essays covering a wide chronological span from earliest times through the Ottoman period.

Mazar, Amihai. *Archaeology of the Land of the Bible 10,000–586 B.C.E.* New York: Doubleday, 1990. A useful synopsis of the archaeological history of ancient Israel.

Meyers, Eric M., ed. *The Oxford Encyclopedia of Archaeology in the Ancient Near East*. 5 vols. New York: Oxford University Press, 1997. A comprehensive work that is especially valuable for its coverage of sites outside Israel and for its thematic discussions.

Stern, Ephraim, ed. *The New Encyclopedia of Archaeological Excavations in the Holy Land*. 4 vols. New York: Simon & Schuster, 1993. Lavishly illustrated with photographs and plans, this is the best resource for sites in Israel.

Stillwell, Richard, ed. *The Princeton Encyclopedia of Classical Sites*. Princeton, N.J.: Princeton University Press, 1976. Although dated, a useful resource.

PRIMARY SOURCES

Barrett, C. K., ed. *The New Testament Background: Selected Documents*. Rev. ed. San Francisco: Harper & Row, 1989. A handy anthology of historical and literary primary sources.

Ehrman, Bart D. *The New Testament and Other Early Christian Writings: A Reader*. New

York: Oxford University Press, 1998. A collection of all known Christian writings up to 130 CE.

Foster, Benjamin R. *Before the Muses: An Anthology of Akkadian Literature.* 2d ed. 2 vols. Bethesda, Md.: CDL, 1996. An extensive collection of prose and poetry, with a general introduction to the literary world of ancient Mesopotamia. An abridged edition, *From Distant Days: Myths, Tales, and Poetry of Ancient Mesopotamia*, was published in 1995.

Hallo, William W., and K. Lawson Younger, eds. *The Context of Scripture.* 3 vols. to date. Leiden, The Netherlands: E. J. Brill, 1997–. A new anthology of ancient New Eastern texts.

Matthews, Victor H., and Don C. Benjamin. *Old Testament Parallels: Laws and Stories from the Ancient Near East.* Rev. ed. New York: Paulist, 1997. Selections from ancient Near Eastern texts arranged according to the order of the biblical books.

Pritchard, James B., ed. *Ancient Near Eastern Texts Relating to the Old Testament.* 3d ed. Princeton, N.J.: Princeton University Press, 1969. The standard anthology. Its companion volume, *The Ancient Near East in Pictures Relating to the Old Testament*, 2d ed. (1969), is still useful, although much new material has come to light since its publication. There is an abridged edition of both, *The Ancient Near East: An Anthology of Texts and Pictures* (2 vols., 1958; 1975).

Vermes, Geza. *The Complete Dead Sea Scrolls in English.* New York: Allen Lane, 1997. Recently updated, this is the best translation available.

HISTORICAL SURVEYS

Ahlström, Gösta. *The History of Ancient Palestine.* Minneapolis: Fortress, 1993. An idiosyncratic yet stimulating survey from earliest times to the Hellenistic period.

Ben-Sasson, Haim H., ed. *A History of the Jewish People.* Cambridge, Mass.: Harvard University Press, 1976. Parts 1–4 give a compre-

hensive survey from the origins of biblical Israel through the compilation of the Mishnah and the Talmud, with emphasis on source analysis.

Grabbe, Lester L. *Judaism from Cyrus to Hadrian: Sources, History, Synthesis.* 2 vols. Minneapolis: Fortress, 1991, 1992. An extremely helpful survey, with judicious summaries of the primary sources, specific critiques of recent scholarly work, and extensive bibliographies.

Grant, Michael, and Rachel Kitzinger, eds. *Civilizations of the Ancient Mediterranean: Greece and Rome.* 3 vols. New York: Charles Scribner's Sons, 1988. Essays on all aspects of life in the Greco-Roman world.

Edwards, I. E. S., et al. *The Cambridge Ancient History.* 3d ed. Cambridge: Cambridge University Press, 1970–. Although earlier volumes are dated, the fullest account of ancient Mediterranean civilizations.

Hallo, William W., and William Kelly Simpson. *The Ancient Near East: A History.* 2d ed. Fort Worth, Tex.: Harcourt Brace College Publishers, 1998. Recently revised, this useful survey treats Mesopotamia and Egypt separately.

Kee, Howard C., et al. *The Cambridge Companion to the Bible.* New York: Cambridge University Press, 1997. A discursive treatment that sets the biblical traditions in their historical and social contexts.

Koester, Helmut. *Introduction to the New Testament.* 2d ed. Vol. 1, *History, Culture, and Religion of the Hellenistic Age*; vol. 2, *History and Literature of Early Christianity.* New York: de Gruyter, 1995; 2000. A comprehensive reconstruction of the development of the Jesus movement, and a detailed description of the broader world in which that development took place.

Kuhrt, Amélie. *The Ancient Near East, c. 3000–330 BC.* New York: Routledge, 1996. A detailed and masterful treatment.

Millar, Fergus. *The Roman Near East 31 BC–AD 337.* Cambridge, Mass.: Harvard University Press, 1993. A political and cultural history of the peoples and provinces of the Roman Near East through the reign of Constantine, based on a wide array of literary and archaeological sources.

Miller, J. Maxwell, and John H. Hayes. *A History of Ancient Israel and Judah*. Philadelphia: Westminster, 1986. An excellent history of Israel and Judah through the Persian period, with careful attention to historiographical issues.

Safrai, S., and M. Stern, eds. *The Jewish People in the First Century: Historical Geography, Political History, Social, Cultural and Religious Life and Institutions*. 2 vols. Assen, The Netherlands: Van Gorcum; Philadelphia: Fortress, 1974–76. A landmark anthology of essays concerning formative Judaism.

Sasson, Jack M., ed. *Civilizations of the Ancient East*. 4 vols. New York: Simon & Schuster/Macmillan, 1995. A compendium of essays on all aspects of life in the ancient Near East.

Schürer, Emil. *The History of the Jewish People in the Time of Jesus Christ (175 B.C.–A.D. 135)*. Rev. by Geza Vermes et al. 3 vols. Edinburgh: T. & T. Clark, 1973–87. Substantially updated version of a classic work.

Soggin, J. Alberto. *An Introduction to the History of Israel and Judah*. 2d ed. Valley Forge, Pa.: Trinity, 1993. A valuable survey, with special attention to historiography.

Vaux, Roland de. *The Early History of Israel*. Trans. David Smith. Philadelphia: Westminster, 1978. A detailed treatment of nonbiblical and biblical evidence for the history of Israel before the monarchy.

SOCIAL HISTORY AND INSTITUTIONS

Albertz, Rainer. *A History of Israelite Religion in the Old Testament Period*. Trans. John Bowden. 2 vols. Louisville, Ky.: Westminster John

Knox, 1994. A detailed survey with special focus on social history.

Dearman, J. Andrew. *Religion and Culture in Ancient Israel*. Peabody, Mass.: Hendrickson, 1992. A useful discussion of biblical and nonbiblical evidence.

Matthews, Victor H., and Don C. Benjamin. *Social World of Ancient Israel, 1250–587 BCE*. Peabody, Mass.: Hendrickson, 1993. An accessible survey, organized by social roles.

Vaux, Roland de. *Ancient Israel: Its Life and Institutions*. Trans. John McHugh. New York: McGraw-Hill, 1961. A valuable and detailed survey of the biblical data that also refers to archaeological evidence and nonbiblical sources.

ATLASES

Aharoni, Yohanan, et al. *The Macmillan Bible Atlas*. 3d ed. New York: Macmillan, 1993. The handiest historical atlas, with 271 maps covering from prehistoric times to the second century CE.

Bahat, Dan. *The Illustrated Atlas of Jerusalem*. Trans. Shlomo Ketko. New York: Simon & Schuster, 1990.

Baines, John, and Jaromír Malék. *Cultural Atlas of Ancient Egypt*. Rev. ed. New York: Facts on File, 2000.

Cornell, Tim. *Atlas of the Roman World*. New York: Facts on File, 1982.

Day, John. *The Oxford Bible Atlas*. 3d ed. Oxford: Oxford University Press, 1984.

Levi, Peter. *Atlas of the Greek World*. New York: Facts on File, 1980.

Roaf, Michael. *Cultural Atlas of Mesopotamia and the Ancient Near East*. New York: Facts on File, 1990.

Rogerson, John. *Atlas of the Bible*. Oxford: Phaidon, 1989.

Contributors

THE EDITOR

MICHAEL D. COOGAN is Professor of Religious Studies at Stonehill College and Director of Publications for the Semitic Museum at Harvard University. He has participated in and directed archaeological excavations in Israel, Jordan, Cyprus, and Egypt. A frequent contributor to scholarly journals, he is also the editor of *The Illustrated Guide to World Religions*, coeditor of *The Oxford Companion to the Bible* and *Scripture and Other Artifacts*, and editor and translator of *Stories from Ancient Canaan*.

THE AUTHORS

EDWARD F. CAMPBELL JR. is Professor Emeritus of Old Testament at McCormick Theological Seminary. He directed the Joint Archaeological Expedition to Tell Balatah/Shechem and serves as publication director of the final report series. The author of *The Chronology of the Amarna Letters*, *Ruth* (in the Anchor Bible), and *Shechem II: Portrait of a Hill Country Vale*, he is completing a volume on Shechem's architecture and stratigraphy.

MORDECHAI COGAN teaches the history of the biblical period at the Hebrew University of Jerusalem. In addition to numerous scholarly articles and book reviews, he has written commentaries on the biblical books of Joel and Obadiah (in Hebrew), is coauthor of *II Kings*, and is completing *I Kings* (both in the Anchor Bible).

BARBARA GELLER is Associate Professor and Chair of the Department of Religion at Wellesley College. Her publications have focused on Jewish women in the Roman Empire and the impact of the Christianization of the empire on the Jewish, Christian, and pagan communities of fourth- through sixth-century Palestine.

LEONARD J. GREENSPOON is Philip M. and Ethel Klutznick Chair in Jewish Civilization and Chair of the Department of Classical and Near Eastern Studies at Creighton University. He has written or edited a half dozen books and more than one hundred scholarly articles on topics ranging from ancient translations to the Bible in comic strips. In addition to working on a biography of Jewish scholar Harry M. Orlinsky and a popular history of Bible translating, he is editing the book of Joshua for Biblia Hebraica Quinta (the definitive edition of the Hebrew Bible) and translating the same book for the New English Translation of the Septuagint.

JO ANN HACKETT is Professor of the Practice of Biblical Hebrew and Northwest Semitic Epigraphy at Harvard University. She is the author of *The Balaam Text from Tell Deir 'Alla* and has also written extensively on epigraphy, child sacrifice, and women in the books of Judges and 1 and 2 Samuel. She is currently working on a book of translations of Phoenician and Punic inscriptions and on a project to develop a digital edition of Ugaritic texts.

MARY JOAN WINN LEITH is Associate Professor of Religious Studies at Stonehill College. She is the author of *Wadi Daliyeh I: The Wadi Daliyeh Seal Impressions* and a contributor to the *Macmillan Encyclopedia of Women in Religion* and to the forthcoming revised edition of the *New Oxford Annotated Bible*. She is currently at work on a reference text titled *People of the Bible*.

AMY-JILL LEVINE is E. Rhodes and Leona B. Carpenter Professor of New Testament Studies and Director of the Carpenter Program in Religion, Gender, and Sexuality at Vanderbilt Divinity School. She has published books on the Gospel of Matthew and Jewish women in antiquity. Forthcoming is her book *Threatened Bodies: Women, Culture, Apocrypha*; she is also editing a ten-volume series on feminist interpretations of early Christian texts.

CAROL MEYERS is Professor of Biblical Studies and Archaeology at Duke University and is currently codirector of the Sepphoris Regional Project. She has written, edited, and coedited twelve books, including *Discovering Eve: Ancient Israelite Women in Context; Families in Ancient Israel; Haggai, Zechariah 1–8* and *Zechariah 9–14* (both in the Anchor Bible); and *Women in Scripture*.

WAYNE T. PITARD is Professor of Religious Studies at the University of Illinois at Urbana-Champaign. He is the author of *Ancient Damascus: A Historical Study of the Syrian City-State from Earliest Times until Its Fall to the Assyrians in 732* and numerous articles on the history of Syria-Palestine, the Ugaritic tablets, and concepts of death and afterlife in ancient Syria.

CAROL A. REDMOUNT is Professor of Egyptian and Syro-Palestinian Archaeology at the University of California–Berkeley. She has excavated throughout the Near East since 1971 and in Egypt since 1978; since 1992 she has directed excavations at Tell el-Muqdam in the Egyptian delta. Her research and publications focus on the archaeology of the delta, interrelationships between Egypt and Syria-Palestine in the second millennium BCE, and ancient and ethnoarchaeological ceramic studies.

DANIEL N. SCHOWALTER is Professor of Religion at Carthage College. He is the author of *The Emperor and the Gods: Images from the Time of Trajan* and contributes to the Archaeological Resources for New Testament Studies series. He is writing a commentary on the Petrine Epistles.

LAWRENCE E. STAGER is Dorot Professor of the Archaeology of Israel and Director of the Semitic Museum at Harvard University. He has directed archaeological expeditions to Carthage (Tunisia), Idalion (Cyprus), and Ashkelon (Israel). His publications have focused on the archaeology and history of Canaanites, Phoenicians, Israelites, and Philistines. He is currently writing a book on the shared cosmology and symbolism of Jerusalem and the Garden of Eden.

Index